AF522393

Sufism in Punjab
Mystics, Literature and Shrines

Sufism in Punjab
Mystics, Literature and Shrines

edited by

Surinder Singh
Ishwar Dayal Gaur

AAKAR

Sufism in Punjab: Mystics, Literature and Shrines
edited by Surinder Singh & Ishwar Dayal Gaur

First Published 2009

ISBN 978-81-89833-93-0

Published by
AAKAR BOOKS
28 E Pocket IV, Mayur Vihar Phase I, Delhi-110 091
Phone : 011-2279 5505 Telefax : 011-2279 5641
aakarbooks@gmail.com; www.aakarbooks.com

Printed at
Arpit Printographers
E-mail: arpitprinto@yahoo.com

To

the memory of

Ustad Nusrat Fateh Ali Khan

13 October 1948 – 16 August 1997

Who rose to be the greatest exponent of Qawwali in the recent times. Who popularized the message of sufism, which embodies the principles of cosmic love and universal humanism, in all parts of the inhabited world. Whose art represents a convergence of several elements – a family tradition of music going back across six centuries, a perfect mastery over Hindustani classical music, a deep understanding of Punjabi sufiana kalaam and a natural sensitivity towards Punjabi folklore. Whose passionate and soulful renditions faithfully communicate the ideology of the great Punjabi sufi poets and translate the true meaning of each and every word contained therein. Who brought the sublime joy of spiritual experience to millions of human hearts. Who erased the boundaries of nation, race, class, religion and gender in a world torn by conflicts and violence. Who stood as a bridge between West (Pakistani) Punjab and East (Indian) Punjab. Who emerged as the greatest cultural icon of the Punjabi diaspora that is spread in all continents of the world.

Acknowledgements

It is our pleasant duty to express our gratitude to a number of institutions and individuals, who enabled us to undertake a project culminating in the present volume. First and foremost, we are grateful to our sponsor, the Iran Culture House, New Delhi, (the educational and cultural wing of the embassy of the Islamic Republic of Iran), for collaborating with the Department of History, Panjab University, Chandigarh, in organizing a national seminar on the theme of this book.

A number of our friends helped us in different ways. Hardeep Singh Dhillon of the Indian Police Service, who has documented the composite culture of undivided Punjab in the audio-visual mode, provided valuable assistance in organizing the above seminar. Harnesh Inder Singh (USA) and Balvinder Singh Jassar (Canada) met our requirements of literature that was not available here. We are indebted to them.

Our colleagues J.S. Dhanki, Sukhmani Bal Riar and Devi Sirohi have been consistent in providing moral support to our academic activities. The administrative staff of our department – Sudershan Singh, Tilak Raj, Rita Rani, Indra Rani, Navjot Kaur, Madan Lal and Pawan Kumar – helped us throughout the course of the present project. We are thankful to them.

We shall be failing in our duty if we do not acknowledge the invisible contribution of our families towards our professional pursuits. The unsaid blessings of our mothers, Agya Kaur and (late) Kaushalya Devi, have enabled us to overcome numerous hurdles in our path. Our wives, Paramjit and Asha, have provided unconditional support to us so that we could pursue our academic goals. Our daughters, Jasmine and Mrignaini, have not only taken pride in our humble achievements, but have also looked forward to the final outcome of our recent efforts.

Last but not least, we are grateful to Shri K.K. Saxena of the Aakar Books for undertaking the task of publishing this volume with exemplary diligence and enthusiasm.

Surinder Singh
Ishwar Dayal Gaur

Contents

Acknowledgements *vii*

Introduction
Surinder Singh and *Ishwar Dayal Gaur* 1

Part I : Sufi Mystics

1. Advent of Sufism in Medieval Punjab: A Narrative of its Historical Role
Iqtidar Husain Siddiqui 49
2. Sons of Bread and Sons of Soul : Lineal and Spiritual Descendants of Baba Farid and the Issue of Succession
Tanvir Anjum 63
3. Path of Shaikh Bahauddin Zakariya : A Contrastive Model of Mysticism
Humaira Arif Dasti 80
4. Suhrawardi Mysticism in South-Western Punjab : Contribution of Syed Jalaluddin Bukhari Makhdum-i-Jahaniyan
Aneesa Iqbal Sabir 97
5. A Panoramic Reconstruction of Sufism in the Jammu Hills
Jigar Mohammed 119
6. Development of Qadiri Mysticism at Lahore: Principles and Practices of Miyan Mir
Surinder Singh 135
7. Role of Sufis and Bhaktas in North-Western India during the Eighteenth Century
Zahir Uddin Malik 158

Part II : Sufi Literature

8. Theory and Practice of Islamic Mysticism : An Exposition by Ali bin Usman Hujwiri
Mohammad Tazeem 179
9. Baba Farid : The Pioneer of Punjabi Sufi Poetry
Saeed Ahmad 196

10. Authenticity of Malfuz Literature : A Case Study of the Rahat-ul-Qulub
S.M. Azizuddin Husain 214

11. Female Voice in Punjabi Sufi Poetry: Its Character and Concerns
Ishwar Dayal Gaur 233

12. Formation of Naqshbandi Mysticism : Studying the Major Writings of Shaikh Ahmad Sirhindi
Iqbal Sabir 257

13. Some Prominent Strands in the Poetry of Sultan Bahu
Tahir Kamran 278

Part III : Sufi Shrines

14. Early Sufi Tombs in South-Western Punjab : Understanding the Architectural Features
Subhash Parihar 303

15. Some Prominent Sufi Shrines of South-Eastern Punjab : A Study of their History and Form
Hitender Kumar 336

16. Shrine of Shaikh Sadruddin at Malerkotla : History, Politics and Culture
Salim Mohammed 356

17. Devotional Linkages of Punjab with the Chishti Shrine at Ajmer : Gleanings from the Vikalatnamas
Syed Liyaqat Hussain Moini 378

18. Historicity, Orality and the 'Lesser Shrines': Popular Culture and Change at the Dargah of Panj Pir at Abohar
Yogesh Snehi 402

Appendix
Shrine of Miyan Mir at Lahore : A Note from the Tahqiqat-i-Chishti
Surinder Singh 431

Contributors 437

Index 443

Introduction

Surinder Singh and *Ishwar Dayal Gaur*

The sufic experience of Punjab has been long, rich and varied. Owing to its frontier location and a long tradition of non-conformism, this region possessed a fertile cultural soil which readily accepted Islamic mysticism. The Ghaznavid annexation of Punjab, the establishment of the Delhi sultanate and the irruption of the Mongols from Central Asia broke the existing barriers and attracted a large number of migrants to settle in the garrison towns of Punjab.[1] In these circumstances, the Chishti and Suhrawardi orders were established in the region, both spreading to Delhi, Rajasthan and the Gangetic plain. During the heyday of the Mughal empire, the Qadiri and Naqshbandi orders rose to prominence and spread to the distant areas. The spiritual examplers belonging to different sufi orders established their hospices (*khanqahs*) in the urban centres of Punjab. With the passage of time, many of these hospices were transformed into shrines and, as centres of popular devotionalism, began to play a complex role in the processes of urbanization and acculturation. The sufis themselves came to be identified with the urban centres and vice versa e.g. Bahauddin Zakariya with Multan, Shaikh Farid with Pakpattan, Syed Jalaluddin Bukhari with Uch, Miyan Mir with Lahore, Shah Daula with Gujarat, Shaikh Haidar with Malerkotla, Shaikh Ahmad with Sirhind, Qutbuddin Munawwar with Hansi and Bu Ali Qalandar with Panipat. The growth of sufism generated a considerable literary activity, both in the elite and non-elite languages. While a few mystical discourses were associated with Shaikh Farid, half a dozen such collections were recorded on behalf of Syed Jalaluddin Bukhari. Ali bin Usman Hujwiri wrote the earliest Indian treatise on mysticism, while Shaikh Ahmad Sirhindi produced several works on religious themes in addition to 534 letters. Dara Shukoh wrote an account of Miyan Mir and his disciples, while Mufti Ghulam Sarwar Lahori compiled a comprehensive biographical dictionary (*tazkira*) of mystics that included several lesser known saints of Punjab. Equally important, a number of sufi poets – Shaikh Farid, Shah Husain, Sultan Bahu, Bulleh Shah, Fard Faqir and Khwaja Ghulam Farid – produced devotional poetry in Punjabi, which advocated a passionate love for God in the indigenous folk idiom. In spite of the migration of Muslims from east Punjab during partition, hundreds of small sufi shrines (which commemorate obscure Muslim saints and which are evenly scattered in the rural and urban areas) have not only survived in the new non-Muslim environment, but have also remained unharmed during the recent bouts of Hindu and Sikh fundamentalism. Thus, we see that during the last one thousand years, sufism has penetrated all aspects of human life in Punjab.

Inheritance and Beginnings

The scholarly interest in Islamic mysticism has to be traced to intellectual currents in western Europe. As the European powers established colonial rule in the Asian countries from the late eighteenth century onwards, the alien administrators felt constrained to learn the socio-cultural traits of the natives, in particular their religious customs and spiritual life. It was in these circumstances that the orientalists discovered sufism. Some officials of the British East India Company – William Jones, John Malcolm and James William Graham – began to take a scholarly interest in the historical phenomenon of sufism. They came to believe that sufis were freethinkers who were characterized by a fondness for music and dance; that they were averse to dogmatic rituals and material pursuits; that they had little to do with Islam; that they displayed a considerable similarity to Christianity, Greek philosophy and Indian Vedanta; that sufism was an abstract mystical philosophy which could be traced to Persian poetry.[2] In western Europe, interest in sufism was manifested in the writings of F.R.D. Tholuck, Alfred von Kremer, E.H. Palmer and John P. Brown. In the second half of the nineteenth century, a good number of sufi texts, both in Arabic and Persian, were published in a vast area extending from Cairo to Lucknow. In his masterpiece on the literary history of Persia, Edward G. Browne offered an intense account of the influence of sufi thought on Persian poetry. But the most significant advances in the subject were brought about by the Herculean efforts of Reynolds A. Nicholson, M. Louis Massignon[3] and Asin Palacios. Nicholson produced the standard texts of classical mystical treatises of Jalaluddin Rumi, Sarraj, Fariddudin Attar, Ibn-i-Arabi and Ali bin Usman Hujwiri. In his analytical writings, Nicholson traced sufism to ascetic tendencies within Islam during the Umayyad period, emphasized non-Islamic influences on sufism like neo-Platonism and recognized the distinctive contribution of Maruf

Karkhi, Zu ul-Nun Misri and Abu Yazid Bistami. Massignon produced a monumental biographical study of Mansur al-Hallaj, which was followed up by the publication of the poetry and texts associated with the martyr mystic. In another significant work, he mapped the origin and development of sufism, including a technical vocabulary of sufi terminology. In his voluminous writings, Asin Palacios highlighted the impact of Christianity on sufism, but he was chiefly recognized for his explorations on Ghazzali, Ibn Hazam and Ibn-i-Arabi. Arthur J. Arberry prepared the original texts of the works by such sufi ideologues as Kharraz, Niffari, Junaid and Tirmizi.[4] It may be suggested that this rich literary heritage must have shaped, to some extent, the understanding of the Indian scholars who entered the field of sufi studies in the first half of the twentieth century.

As the Indian historians began to study sufism, it was felt that the subject could not be studied in isolation from the formative phase of sufism in western and central Asia. Mohammad Habib (1935) traced the origin of sufism to concrete political and social conditions which were marked by the territorial expansion of Islam, powerful aristocracies, social inequalities, dominance of clerics and inadequacy of Islamic sciences. Alienated by these circumstances, the early mystics (designated as quietists by Nicholson) began their search for true religion. They adopted an attitude of withdrawal from the society and focused their attention on repentance (*tauba*) or spiritual rebirth, which was regarded by later specialists as merely the first of the several stages in the spiritual path.[5] With the emergence of mystic schools around 850 AD, mystic doctrines began to appear in a highly developed form. Mohammad Habib has categorized twelve mystic orders (which were identified by Ali bin Usman Hujwiri) into left, right and centre, on the basis of their distance from the orthodoxy and their insistence on individuality. Shaikh Junaid Baghdadi,[6] who stood between the left and right, adopted the path of sobriety (*sahv*), kept away from both rapture (*sukr*) and externalism (*zahiriat*) of the clerics. Ultimately the debate was manifested in two distinct viewpoints which could not be reconciled. On the one hand, Shaikh Shihabuddin Suhrawardi appeared as the flag bearer of the centrist schools and consolidated the essential ideas of Shaikh Junaid Baghdadi in *Awarif-ul-Maarif*,[7] which rejected the externalism of the clerics, but advocated a strict adherence to the prophetic practice (*sunnah*). On the other hand Muhiuddin Ibn-i-Arabi (1164-1240) assumed the leadership of the leftist schools and developed the controversial monistic doctrine (*wahdat-ul-wujud*) drawing,[8] to some extent, from the ideas of Mansur al-Hallaj, Abu Yazid Bistami and Zu ul-Nun Misri. These two thinkers spearheaded the culmination of Muslim mystic philosophy, to which little could be added later on.[9]

As the studies on Indian sufism took off, the historians encountered a wide variety of sources. These were entirely different from the familiar court-sponsored Persian chronicles, not only in their form and style, but also in the objectives sought to be achieved by the writers. What was more important, the historian was required to distinguish between the genuine and spurious works. Mohammad Habib, while working on the mystical beliefs and practices of Shaikh Nasiruddin Mahmud Chiragh-i-Delhi, realized that the task of reconstructing the history of Indian sufism had to be accompanied by a constant assessment of the authenticity of our sources. He undertook the onerous task of drawing a distinction between the genuine and spurious works, which was essential for reconstructing the history of sufism in north-western India, particularly the Chishti order. Habib's investigation led to the conclusion that very few works – *Fuwaid-ul-Fuad*, *Khair-ul-Majalis* and *Siyar-ul-Auliya* – were authentic and, therefore, indispensable for our researches. He examined the circumstances in which each of these works was produced. In spite of the avowed Chishti aversion to writing, Nizamuddin Auliya permitted the poet Amir Hasan Ala Sijzi to record his conversations, *Fuwaid-ul-Fuad*, extending from 1307 to 1322. The Shaikh took a keen interest in the enterprise, revising the text and filling the lacunae. Free from futile ornamentation, the work was simple, lucid and accurate. It laid the foundation of a new type of mystic literature known as *malfuzat*. It became a model for subsequent recorders who imitated it, but who failed to equal it. Thirty years later, when Hamid Qalandar began to record the conversations of Shaikh Nasiruddin Mahmud, the latter subjected the text to a close examination and prevented the intrusion of miracles and flattery. This compilation, entitled *Khair-ul-Majalis*, promised to fill up the gaps left in the *Fuwaid-ul-Fuad*.[10] Apart from the record of conversations (*malfuzat*), contemporary evidence on the growth of sufi orders is also found in another genre of sufi literature i.e. memoirs (*tazkiras*). Amir Khurd's *Siyar-ul-Auliya* stood at the top of this list. The author was eminently equipped to write a detailed history of the Chishti order in India. His family had a long association with such leading Chishti saints as Shaikh Farid, Nizamuddin Auliya and Nasiruddin Mahmud. He incorporated a large part of *Fuwaid-ul-Fuad* in his work. But his work was marred by a tendency to insert superfluous verses and description of miracles. A critical history of the Chishti order, opines Mohammad Habib, has to be based on three principal works – *Fuwaid-ul-Fuad*, *Khair-ul-Majalis* and *Siyar-ul-Auliya* – till the discovery of fresh genuine material. He attributes the value of these works to Nizamuddin Auliya who, during his years in Delhi from 1252 to 1325, collected information about mystics from foreign migrants and those from the provinces.[11]

While Mohammad Habib expresses a sense of satisfaction at the availability of three authentic sources on the history of Chishtis, he also sounds a note of caution regarding the existence of a large mass of fabricated sufi literature. These were claimed to have been the conversations of prominent Chishtis from Shaikh Usman Haruni to Shaikh Nasiruddin Mahmud. The compilation of these conversations has been attributed, in most cases, to their most prominent disciple. Mohammed Habib has identified three general characteristics that were largely common to them. Firstly, the fabricated literature inculcated principles which were at variance with what Nizamuddin Auliya and Nasiruddin Mahmud had expounded in *Fuwaid-ul-Fuad* and *Khair-ul-Majalis*. Secondly, the real authors of the fabricated works had committed blunders about well known facts and dates of Indian history, which have been wrongly attributed to the Chishti saints. Thirdly, the internal evidence was supplemented by conclusive external evidence to prove the fact of fabrication.[12] In an attempt to explain the profusion of fabricated conversations from the mid fourteenth century onwards, Mohammad Habib focuses on the convergence of the vested interests of several social groups – purchasers, calligraphists, compilers and booksellers. Small in size and journalistic in approach, these books were a mixture of mysticism, theology and fiction, the last element being larger than others. To these was added a new element, prayer formulae (*aurad*), which were believed to bring fantastic rewards. Mohammed Habib remarks that the forged mystic literature was purposely 'uttered' by the booksellers of Delhi and provincial capitals for the purpose of honest trade.[13]

Name of the saint	*Title of the work*	*Compilation attributed to*
Usman Haruni	Anis-ul-Arwah	Muinuddin Chishti
Muinuddin Chishti	Dalil-ul-Arifin	Qutbuddin Bakhtiyar Kaki
Qutbuddin Bakhtiyar Kaki	Fuwaid-ul-Salikin	Fariduddin Ganj-i-Shakar
Fariduddin Ganj-i-Shakar	Asrar-ul-Auliya	Badruddin Ishaq
Fariduddin Ganj-i-Shakar	Rahat-ul-Qulub	Nizamuddin Auliya
Nizamuddin Auliya	Afzal-ul-Fawaid	Amir Khusro
Nasiruddin Mahmud	Miftah-ul-Ashiqin	Muhibullah

Mohammad Habib's judgement on the spurious *malfuzat* exercised a powerful influence on the subsequent generations of historians,[14] even though efforts were made to examine some new aspects of the problem of authenticity of mystic literature. For instance, fresh attempts were made to account for the emergence of spurious compilations of mystical discourses. According to one view, the fabricated literature tried to fill a vacuum in the Chishti order, which was caused by the transfer of capital by Muhammad bin Tughluq from Delhi to Daulatabad. This hypothesis, however, fails to reconcile with the appearance of inauthentic sufi literature during the lifetime of Nizamuddin Auliya (1245-1325).[15] According to another view, the conscious decision on the part of early Indian Chishtis caused a dearth of information about them and, in the circumstances, the credulous followers were forced to resort to spurious works. Further, the Chishti forgeries exhibited two recurrent characteristics – (i) they came into existence at an early date and (ii) though spurious *diwans* and *aurad* collections appeared at random, the fraudulent *malfuzat* were sequential and 'complete' in their patterning.[16] These attempts at exploring the nature of spurious works have led, paradoxically, to recognition of their historical value. It has been realized that even if these writings did not represent an accurate image of the Chishti saints, they illustrated the popular response to the Chishti mysticism as well as the religious thought of the period.[17] A more recent study underlines the mass popularity and easy availability of the spurious *malfuzat*, as compared to the genuine ones. It also holds that the distinction between the two kinds of texts was not absolute and that the distinction was significant primarily from the academic point of view. Since a contemporary writer like Ruknuddin Dabir Kashani aimed at making an overall presentation of sufi teaching, he included excerpts from apocryphal Chishti works because he was not deterred by their anachronisms and contradictions. "In other words, the inauthentic *malfuzat* were popular manifestations of religious sentiment among Indian Muslims attached to the Chishti order."[18]

Chishtis and Suhrawardis

The above insights of Mohammad Habib find a strong presence in the studies of Khaliq Ahmad Nizami, who focused his attention on two mystic orders, Chishti and Suhrawardi, which were established in north western India during the thirteenth and fourteenth century. These studies were essentially based on three sources – *Fuwaid-ul-Fuad*, *Khair-ul-Majalis* and *Siyar-ul-Auliya*.[19] To some extent, they relied on Fazlullah Jamali's *Siyar-ul-Arifin* and Abdul Haq Muhaddis Dehalvi's *Akhbar-ul-Akhyar*. But the works which had been condemned as fabricated were generally avoided. Now it became possible to trace the contribution of five major Chishti saints – Muinuddin Chishti, Qutbuddin Bakhtiyar Kaki, Fariduddin Ganj-i-Shakar, Nizamuddin Auliya and Nasiruddin Mahmud – who constituted the links in an unbroken chain of spiritual genealogy. Though these exemplars were identified with one particular city or town, their influence extended over a much larger area, which was said to constitute their spiritual jurisdiction (*wilayat*). They kept aloof from contemporary rulers and refused to accept gifts in any form. They lived a life of extreme poverty and met their frugal needs from unasked charity (*futuh*).[20] Their mystic principles were best illustrated in the organization of their hospices (*khanqahs*) where each component – the Shaikh's family, disciples and visitors – contributed towards collective living.[21] The disciples were divided into two categories, those who had consecrated their lives to mysticism and those who merely sought spiritual betterment. The former were required to shun government service, while the latter were free to carry on worldly pursuits and earn a living. The novices underwent an elaborate training programme, which included the study of religious and mystical literature as well as spiritual exercises. On completion of the course, the trainee was granted (i) the certificate of succession (*khilafatnama*), which certified his academic accomplishments,[22] and (ii) permission to enroll disciples and gave instructions for future independent activities. Since the Chishtis were committed to the service of humanity, they permitted free access to the common people who sought amulets (*tawiz*) or verbal advice for mundane problems. The popularity of the Chishti saints has been attributed to their understanding of the Indian conditions and religious attitudes, besides the willingness to assimilate indigenous customs.[23] They used local dialects while conversing with the common people. Yet Nizami holds that the devotional verses (*shalokas*), which have been attributed to Shaikh Farid in the Sikh scripture, have not been composed by the Chishti saint of Pakpattan.[24]

The mystical beliefs and practices of the Suhrawardis, as reconstructed by Nizami, appear to be just the opposite of the Chishtis. Bahauddin Zakariya, the founder of the order in Multan, was one of the several disciples of Shihabuddin Suhrawardi of Baghdad, who had migrated to India in the wake of the Ghuzz and Mongol devastation of Ajam. The Suhrawardis exercised sway in Punjab and Sind, while operating from Multan and Uch. They believed in hereditary succession to spiritual headship of their convents. They emphasized external forms of religion and did not tolerate deviations from the prescribed code. Averse to starvation and self-mortification, they paid equal attention to the body and spirit. Their principal hospice at Multan was large in size and aristocratic in organization. Its granaries were stocked with cereals and treasuries were replete with gold and silver coins. Entry was restricted to the select few and inmates were provided separate rooms.[25] Acting in conformity with the traditions laid by the Suhrawardi masters of west Asia, they cultivated cordial relations with the Delhi rulers, participated in political developments and received land grants. On some occasions, they used their influence to save Multan from destruction by the Mongols. The accumulation of wealth by the Suhrawardis provoked persistent criticism from contemporaries, but they failed to develop a logical response to the issue. This brings us to the limited sway of the Suhrawardis. Nizami argues that unlike the

Chishtis, who believed in the control of emotional life as a prerequisite to the control of external behaviour, the Suhrawardis tackled the problem from the other end and emphasized the necessity of regulating actions prior to the control of emotions. "This dampened the prospects of Suhrawardi expansion in a non-Muslim environment. It worked well in Muslim surroundings and served the spiritual needs of the Muslim community but when it came to non-Muslim lands, its progress stopped."[26]

Sufism or Revivalism

The role of Shaikh Ahmad Sirhindi has been the subject of a contentious debate among historians, who have expressed diametrically opposite views on his attitude to the Mughal state, the Islamic revival and the mystic path. Ishtiaq Husain Qureshi (1962) places Sirhindi against the background of an ideological cum political struggle between heterodoxy and orthodoxy. He argues that during the reign of Akbar, heterodoxy was in the seat of power as the Iranis (Shias) and Rajputs (Hindus) occupied high positions in the Mughal state. In his opinion, Sirhindi was able to assume the role of the renewer of the second millennium (*mujaddid alf-i-sani*) on the basis of two mystical experiences, viz. rejection of monism (*wahdat-ul-wujud*) and conferment of a high position in the hierarchy of Muslim saints.[27] More than Sirhindi, it was Qureshi who treats monism as the biggest threat to Islamic orthodoxy. He asserts that monism had played a major role in the growth of heterodoxy; it tended to ignore the differences between religious philosophies and codes of behaviour; it was fatal for a community (Muslims) which believed in its uniqueness and must maintain its separate identity or perish.[28] In Qureshi's opinion, Sirhindi succeeded in exercising a profound influence on the society and state. It was owing to his efforts that Islamic mysticism began to align itself with the orthodoxy. It was owing to the influence of his ideas that Shahjahan and Aurangzeb introduced a series of spectacular administrative measures – restrictions on building new temples, removal of the name of the Persian ruler from the *khutba* and coinage of Golconda, the execution of Dara Shukoh, the reimposition of *jaziya*. Though they failed to arrest the decline of the Mughal empire, yet they demonstrated publicly that orthodoxy was in command.[29]

The above understanding of Sirhindi finds a complete reversal in a major study by Saiyid Athar Abbas Rizvi (1965), which endeavours to place Sirhindi in the broader context of the revival of theological studies in the fifteenth and sixteenth centuries as well as the parallel development of the Naqshbandi order. He views Sirhindi's mission as a reaction against the cultural integration promoted by Akbar, the prevalence of pantheistic mysticism in the cities of northern India and proximity of Sirhind to Hindu centres of pilgrimage.[30] Sirhindi wished to strengthen the *shariat* by purging it of innovation and replacing the doctrine of *wahdat-ul-wujud* by *wahdat-ul-shuhud*. He tried to realize these objectives by bringing, through a large number of letters, the Mughal ruling class to his point of view. He underlined the need for a renewer (*mujaddid*) and perfect man (*qayyum*) to rejuvenate Islam in the beginning of the second millennium. His claims of a high spiritual status, which were essentially based on revelations and miracles, earned the ire of his contemporaries. There was no evidence to suggest that Jahangir had given any pledge at his accession to uphold Islam. The emperor not only continued to follow the policy of religious toleration enunciated by Akbar, he also imprisoned Sirhindi for a short period. Sirhindi's mission had several negative aspects. He subjected the Shias to severe condemnation. Not only did he revile the Hindu gods, he wanted the Mughal state to pour humiliation on them.[31] He injected baseless fears regarding the Hindus in the minds of the Muslims. He saw the Mughal occupation of the Kangra fort and the execution of Guru Arjun Dev in a communal perspective. Though he deputed his disciples to propagate his ideas in the different parts of the Indian subcontinent, but they failed to make any headway. In the long run, the ongoing trend of cultural assimilation based on pantheism – as articulated by Muhibullah Allahabadi, Miyan Mir, Mulla Shah Badakhshi and Dara Shukoh – prevailed over sectarian revivalism as espoused by Sirhindi.[32]

Yohannan Friedmann's (1971) book constitutes a major departure in the writings on Sirhindi. He laments that the modern historians of the Indian subcontinent, owing to the influence of contemporary politics, had focused on Sirhindi's attitude to state and religion, which was peripheral to his thought. He argues that Sirhindi was essentially a sufi and therefore, had to be assessed within a sufi framework of reference. He shows that the image of Sirhindi, from the early seventeenth century to the present, had passed through the phase of rejection, defense and glorification.[33] Sirhindi claimed to be a disciple of God without mediation, implying a status equal to the Prophet. He did not travel from intoxication to sobriety, but both these states were always present in him. His attitude towards the *shariat* was deeply influenced by his sufi outlook. He was not interested in legal injunctions of the *shariat*, but strove to incorporate it, as a major Islamic concept, in his comprehensive sufi world view. He did not condemn Ibn-i-Arabi's opinions, but interpreted them in a manner that rendered them compatible with his own understanding of proper Islamic belief.[34] He believed that the Prophet had two individuations, bodily human and spiritual angelic. The former weakened to the point of disappearance at the end of the millennium, while the latter continued to gain strength. Since the community was deprived of the prophetic guidance, this task would be performed by a renewer (*mahdi*). Towards the end of his life, he entrusted to a common believer the task of providing prophetic guidance and enabling the Prophet to reach the spiritual stage of Ibrahim.[35]

Sharply disagreeing with Friedmann, who is said to have placed Sirhindi in an imaginary environment, Shuja Alhaq (1997) refuses to hold Sirhindi's views on state and religion as peripheral to his thought. Shuja Alhaq insists that it was not possible to examine Sirhindi's discourse on mysticism in isolation from his ideas on state, religion, Islam and non-Muslims.[36] On the one hand, he invalidates the mystical experiences of Sirhindi and, on the other, demolishes his contribution to the advancement of mystic thought. Sirhindi sought to synthesize *wilayat-i-Muhammadi* with *wilayat-i-Ibrahimi* and to provide a bodily form to the still surviving spiritual form of Muhammad and, in this manner, persistently fiddled with the idea of prophethood for himself.[37] Sirhindi struck at the finality of prophethood, suggested continuity of prophethood and shattered the myth of immutability of the *shariat*. Sirhindi failed to explain why prophethood went into oblivion for one thousand years, how could he discover this limitation in it during his own times and how could he claim the prerogative of sharing in the perfections of prophethood.[38] It was not possible for him to gain crucial insights and spiritual elevation during a tutelage of just two months under Khwaja Baqi Billah. Even if he did, it was not appropriate for him to derive general conclusions which were applicable to the entire humanity or to suggest his own path as a standard pattern for all others.[39] Sirhindi assumed the impossible task of building the edifice of sufism on his avowed orthodox dualism and bringing sufism within the fold of the *shariat* and under the jurisdiction of clerics. Owing to his theological background, Sirhindi failed to comprehend sufism as a life-long praxis in which an individual struggled against human finitude for the sake of the infinite. He wrongly separated mystical experience from its doctrine and failed to understand that unitary experience was only an experiential dimension of the doctrine of unity. He failed to comprehend the intellectual aspects of the doctrine of *wahdat-ul-wujud* and failed to appreciate its Islamic and non-Islamic sources. It is surprising that he should have attributed the idea of an illusory world to the unitarians. Instead of proposing an alternative monistic system, he coined the word phenomenological monism (*wahdat-ul-shuhud*) for what was orthodox dualism. In the final analysis, Sirhindi laid the foundation of a revivalist movement which identified Islam with political domination and advocated the sway of *shariat* in all walks of life. It checked the evolution of a pluralistic spiritual culture, leaving no room for sufism to survive.[40]

Regional Cultural Context

The study of Richard M. Eaton (1978) on the sufis of Bijapur constitutes a paradigm shift in the studies on sufism in South Asia. It differes widely from the classical approach, which treated the sufi as a practitioner and transmitter of esoteric Islam, not as an organic part of his society, but as standing above or beyond the social order.[41] Unlike the writings on north Indian sufism, Eaton does not confine himself to any one sufi order or any one sufi. Instead he examines the role of all sufis, irrespective of their ethnic identities and ideological affiliations, but places them squarely in their regional cultural context. As social types, they have been categorized as warrior, reformist, literati, landed and dervish, though they have not been seen as mutually exclusive. More significantly, the author has explored their social role in relation to the rulers, clerics, Islam and non-Muslims. The more significant period was marked by the establishment of the Adil Shahi dynasty, the adoption of Sunni Islam (1583) in place of the Shia creed at the level of the state, the emergence of Bijapur as a prominent centre of Islamic culture, the evolution of Hindu-Muslim syncretism and the migration of sufis from different parts of India and the Arab lands. The Chishtis, who were indigenous Deccanis and had settled outside the city of Bijapur on the Shahpur Hillock, devoted their energies in wielding the pen. Apart from Persian writings on mystical doctrines, they produced folk literature in Dakhani which was a blend of simple tenets of Islam, terminologies of the sufi tradition and local imagery of existing literary forms.[42] In contrast, the Qadiri and Shattari sufis, who were essentially foreigners, established their convents (*khanqahs*) within the city of Bijapur. They consorted with orthodox elements and sought to reform the Adil Shah court on strict Islamic lines. Since they received land grants from the state, their establishments came within the jurisdiction of the state and they felt obliged to participate in sectarian administrative measures. In these circumstances, the dervishes (*majzubs*) adopted an attitude of withdrawal from the society and offered ideological opposition to the landed sufis (*inamdars*). The Mughal annexation (1686) and natural calamities destroyed the socio-political structure. As the sufi networks disintegrated, the folk literature and sufi shrines survived the turmoil of the eighteenth century. Having acquired their own spiritual power and legends, the sufi shrines continued to function as 'dynamic catalysts' in deepening Islamic acculturation among several convert communities, in particular the weavers.[43]

Eaton's findings and insights, particularly regarding the relationship of sufi shrines with Islamic acculturation, turned out to be seminal and enabled him to explore the same relationship in the cultural context of medieval Punjab. We learn that during his life time, Shaikh Farid (1175-1265) had developed a tradition of Islamic devotionalism based on the *tawiz-futuh* system. A large number of devotees visited the Pakpattan convent to receive amulets (*tawiz*) which were supposed to answer their mundane needs. On their part, the devotees made offerings (*futuh*), generally in the form of kind, which were distributed among the visitors. After the demise of Shaikh Farid, a series of rituals – death anniversary of the saint (*urs*), community kitchen (*langar*), devotional singing (*qawwali*), succession to the spiritual seat (*dastar bandi*) and annual entry into the sanctum sanctorum (*bahishti darwaza*) – were institutionalized. The shrine began to play a new socio-political role when it received land grants from the Tughluq rulers.[44] These endowments were managed by the spiritual head (*sajjadah nishin*) and, in this role, he came to be known as the *diwan*. Since he was authorized to receive the state share from crops on which revenue was charged in kind, he began to promote the cultivation of foodgrains. A large number of Jat clans, taking advantage of the newly introduced Persian wheel, shifted to sedentary agriculture.[45] At the same time, they underwent a slow process of Islamization owing to their participation in the rituals of the shrine. The relationship of the clans with the shrine was further cemented, as the clan chiefs offered their daughters in marriage to the *diwan* or his immediate relatives. As an intermediary institution, the shrine played a dual role, political and religious. On the one hand, it stood as a link between the clans and the Delhi sultanate through the instrument of land grants and, on the other, between the clans and Islam through a series of rituals.[46]

As Eaton's gaze travelled across centuries and entered the twentieth century, he found that the Pakpattan shrine had continued to sustain and mediate Islam. He has attempted to map this long social process on the basis of documents related to a dispute over succession to the headship of the shrine, particularly the legal depositions of hundreds of devotees who were, in fact, peasants from the districts of Montgomery, Bahawalpur and Lyallpur. In the eyes of these people, Shaikh Farid was a friend both of God and his devotees; his spiritual charisma (*baraka*) was passed on to the *diwan* and the shrine; the latter served as intermediaries of an intermediary and were vehicles for the Shaikh's meditative powers; Shaikh Farid had been fused with the shrine, which linked heaven and earth as well as past and present. The shrine was a site for the exchange of religious goods. The devotees offered *nazrana* to the *diwan* or the shrine in return for concrete favours – good crops, female fertility and relief from illness. The goods were spent on a community kitchen where three or four *mans* of wheat was consumed every day with commensurate quantity of lentils. The core rituals, as mentioned above, were held with the same sanctity and pageantry. The Jat and Rajput clans expressed firm belief in traditions of their conversions to Islam at the hands of Shaikh Farid. His descendants had established 'daughter' shrines in different parts of Punjab, which were dedicated to him. The shrines, being in relation to each other and subordinate to the principal shrine at Pakpattan, constituted a large network of sacred space which represented the spiritual domain (*wilayat*) of Shaikh Farid. In these circumstances, the British court not only upheld the custom by which a *diwan* nominated his successor, but also decreed that the custom was in conformity with the Muslim law. "In the last analysis, The Court of God transcended the Court of Man in the eyes of the shrine's common devotees."[47]

Eaton's path-breaking studies have generated a considerable interest in the history of major sufi shrines. P.M. Currie (1989) has produced a full scale study on the shrine of Muinuddin Chishti at Ajmer. An effort has been made to disentangle history of the saint from the mass of legends. The evolution of the shrine as a sacred structure was marked by additions to the structure, royal visits and land grants. The office of the spiritual head (*sajjadah nishin*) was marred by succession disputes, while the community of attendants appeared more interested in material than spiritual matters.[48] The celebration of the death anniversary of the saint included an unedifying spectacle, when boiling rice pudding was looted in a scramble. Currie's alleged 'brazenly positivist view' provoked Syed Liyaqat Hussain Moini (2004) – who enjoyed the advantage of being the scion of one of the families of custodians (*khuddam*) – to put the record straight. His study on the Ajmer shrine includes a 87-page critique of Currie's book, which was supposed to abound in errors of fact and judgement, besides having a large dose of distortion and prejudice.[49] Moini describes the elaborate rituals – daily, weekly, monthly and annual – many of which have been derived from local customs. His examination of hundreds of Persian documents (Dargah Files, Rajasthan State Archives, Bikaner) has led to the advancement of a fresh perspective on the role of the custodians (*khuddam*) who maintained the sanctity of the shrine through elaborate procedures, provided services to the pilgrims as per the conditions laid in *vikalatnamas*, propagated the true Chishti ideals and promoted communal harmony.[50] The Mughal rulers conferred land grants for the maintenance of the shrine and the custodians, besides introducing reforms in the ceremonial practices.[51]

Sometimes scholars have tended to view the sufi shrines exclusively in terms of their political relationship with the dominant ruling class and their role in providing legitimacy to the medieval states in return for financial endowments.[52] When Akbar established a new capital at Fatehpur Sikri, he constructed a white marble mausoleum in the memory of the famous Chishti saint Shaikh Salim within the courtyard of the great public mosque. The tomb became a major pilgrimage site (*dargah*), giving rise to the formation of a cult in the name of the saint. 'By thus emplacing Shaikh Salim's tomb within the walls of the Fatehpur Sikri mosque, Akbar was able to draw upon that perceptible sanctity adhering to it, and to assimilate this to his own authority.' Significantly, Akbar did not permit Shaikh Salim's descendents to retain control and management of the shrine. Instead, many of them were enlisted as *mansabdars* who attained high ranks and provided meritorious services to the Mughal empire. In a parallel development, Akbar undertook fourteen pilgrimages, from 1568 to 1574, to the shrine of Muinuddin Chishti at Ajmer. But faced with quarrels among the descendents of the saint over the division of emeperor's gifts to the shrine, Akbar seized control over the establishment and, thus, opened the door to intrusion of Mughal courtly culture into that of the Chishti order.[53] John F. Richards suggests that, firstly, Akbar might have used his control over two major Chishti shrines and his growing influence over members of the Chishti order in an ongoing ideological struggle with the orthodox clerics and, secondly, that the association with Chishtis must have added to Akbar's political appeal and his own popular reputation as a mystic.[54] On a different note, Akbar's patronage of the Chishti shrines at Fatehpur Sikri and Ajmer has been perceived as a pragmatic move to anchor imperial legitimacy in the two major provinces of Punjab and Rajasthan. Later on, as Akbar assumed absolute political power with claims to spiritual authority, he abandoned Fatehpur Sikri as capital and lost interest in the Chishti connection.[55]

The shrine of Salar Masud Ghazi at Bahraich has passed through a historical experience which is entirely different from that undergone by some other prominent sufi centres of South Asia. Recent studies have focused on the historical role of Salar Masud Ghazi, the rich mosaic of rituals at his shrine and its complex interface with diverse religio-cultural traditions.[56] The attempt to discover the historicity of the saint presents two images, which were almost opposite to each other. According to Abdul Rahman Chishti, the author of a Persian hagiographical account entitled *Mirat-i-Masudi*, Salar Masud Ghazi was a nephew of Sultan Mahmud of Ghazni, who died fighting against the local Hindu rulers of Bahraich and who was venerated as a Muslim warrior saint. In the folk narratives (*jangnamas*), which were transmitted by balladeers called Dafalis, Salar Masud Ghazi appears as a saint who laid down his life in a valiant attempt to protect his innumerable followers (cowherds and cows) from the wrath of Raja Sohar Dev and, while doing so, he interrupted his marriage ceremony which was never completed. Whatever the truth, the shrine of the martyr had become an important centre of pilgrimage by the early fourteenth century. The shrine is a large conglomeration of buildings including several graves, a gateway, a mosque, a masonary well, a water reservoir and rest houses – all of which were raised at different times. The major festivities include the *urs*, *basant mela* and *jesht mela*. The last mentioned was a 12-day festival which was attended by nearly half a million pilgrims. Arriving in the form of marriage parties, the pilgrims participate in the annual symbolic marriage of Salar Masud Ghazi with Zahira Bibi. It is believed that lepers, who bathe in the water with which the saint's grave has been washed, are cured of their disease. It has been found that the rituals have been assimilated from the Shia traditions rooted in the battle of Karbala as well as the agricultural calendar of the local peasantry. Salar Masud Ghazi has been often associated with legendary Rajput warriors like Pabuji and Gugga Pir, besides the multi-faceted cult of Panch Pirs. In addition to the Muslims, a majority of devotees belonged to middle and low castes like Ahirs, Lal Begis, Julahas, Doms, Mirasis and Nats. Scholarly studies on the shrine enable us to understand the processes of cultural fusion and identity formation, besides the caste structure and Hindu-Muslim relations.

Primacy of the Text

Carl W. Ernst and Bruce B. Lawrence (2002) do not limit their study on the Chishti order to one set of sufis or one period or one region, as the Chishti experience was not limited to sufis or Muslims or Asians. They question Trimingham's three stage theory of the development of sufism, which perceives the triumph of institutionalized religion over personal religion as the decline of mysticism. Having rejected the circular argument about a privileged golden age, they have advanced a periodization of five divisions in the history of the Chishtis – two early periods outside India that were followed by three pertaining to India: (1) the formative period from seventh to tenth century culminating in Abu Ishaq Shami who was the first sufi master to reside at Chisht; (2) the foundational period at Chisht from tenth to twelfth century, extending from Abu Ishaq Shami to Usman Harwani; (3) the first cycle of the Indian Chishtis, from twelfth to fourteenth century, extending from Muinuddin Chishti to Nizamuddin Auliya; (4) the second cycle of Indian Chishtis, from fourteenth to eighteenth century, which marked the dispersal of the order from Delhi to different parts of the Indian subcontinent and the profusion of sublineages that extended to the Mughal period; (5) third cycle of the Indian Chishtis, from eighteenth to twenty first century, characterized by the decline of the Mughal empire, along with the British ascendancy in India and Wahabi control of Arabia, leading to tensions over internal reform in sufism.[57]

In their attempt to reconstruct the history of the Chishtis, Ernst and Lawrence have developed what may be called the text-centric approach. They have drawn our attention to little known hagiographical writings as well as sufi manuals, with reference to the dominant concerns and literary styles of the writers. While focusing on the various aspects of the life of Nizamuddin Auliya, they show the relative advantage of *Siyar-ul-Auliya* over *Fuwaid-ul-Fuad*. In case of Shah Mina (d.1465), they underline the divergent hagiographical perspectives of Abdul Haq Muhaddis Dehalvi and Irtida Ali Khan. While discussing the Chishti practice of *zikr*, they highlight the content of Nizamuddin Aurangabadi's (d.1730) *Nizam-ul-Qulub*; for *sama*,[58] they examine the tracts of five Chishti writers; for the practice of pilgrimage to sufi shrines, they uncover the conditions laid in a treatise on the subject entitled *Makhzan-ul-Aras* which was penned by Muhammad Najib Qadiri in 1742-43. These exercises, no doubt, have enabled us to discern the predilections of the hagiographers as well as the lines of argument adopted by them. But, in themselves, these exercises do not constitute history. In fact, the historian's craft obliges us to draw our facts from diverse sources (sufi and non-sufi) and, placing them in their cultural context, to develop a coherent and holistic account of the historical phenomena. Moreover, it appears that most of the above texts are normative and prescriptive in nature, having been produced to provide instructions to the seekers of the mystical path. The hagiographers also aimed at justifying the beliefs and practices of their discipline in order to meet the objections of the rival sufi ideologues and, in this manner, to establish their identity and legitimacy in the intensely competitive world of sufism. The sufi manuals offer an ideal picture, not the actual situation. These may be compared with the administrative manuals of the Mughal times (like *Siyaq Nama* and *Hidayat-ul-Qawanin*), which were meant for the instruction of revenue clerks and are an inadequate guide to the actual functioning of the Mughal polity.

Our authors do not accept that the Chishtis suffered a decline after an initial golden period and that it experienced a revival in the eighteenth century. They perceive several continuities in the Chishti mystical practices cutting across the three Indian cycles, with a perpetual tendency to respond to the changing circumstances. During the colonial period, fresh opportunities were offered by the new modes of communication – railways, printing press and postal and telegraph services. At the same time, fresh challenges were posed by the rise of an English-educated middle class, the emergence of communitarian consciousness and the Wahabi assault on the entire edifice of sufism. In these circumstances, the Chishti leadership of the colonial period, belonging both to the Nizami and Sabiri branch of the Chishtis, developed a pragmatic approach to propagate their ideas. Shaikh Sulaiman (d.1850) of Taunsa established religious schools in various parts of Punjab and linked them to instructions in the mystical insights of the Nizami Chishti branch. Other Chishti leaders – Khwaja Hasan Nizami, Haji Imdad Allah, Ashraf Ali Thanvi and Zauqi Shah – produced a large number of books and pamphlets, besides writing articles in newspapers and magazines. While reiterating their commitment to the mystical doctrines of early Chishti masters, they defended the Islamic credentials of sufism and reformulated it in conformity with the canonical injunctions of Islam. While they defended sufism against the Wahabi opposition, they did not hesitate to reform the customs practiced at the sufi shrines. What is equally important, they began to participate in active politics, both national and regional.[59]

In the post-colonial period, the Chishtis (like other sufi brotherhoods) faced severe opposition from diverse sources viz. orientalists, Islamic fundamentalists and secular modernists. The Chishti exemplars developed new strategies of survival and techniques of reformulation, so that their discipline could thrive in a new set of contexts. Captain Wahid Bakhsh Sial (d.1951), who belonged to the Sabiri branch of the Chishtis, elucidated the principal methods of recollection (*zikr*) on the basis of Haji Imdad Allah's *Ziya-ul-Qulub*. However, he assigned a central place to audition (*sama*) in the mystical experience and treated it as the culmination of the spiritual discipline which alone could lead to annihilation (*fana*) in God. Hazrat Inayat Khan (d.1927), who belonged to the Nizami branch of the Chishtis, propagated sufism in western Europe, USA and Canada. Conscious of the deep rooted western prejudice against Islam, he presented sufism as a universal spiritualistic path which was not tied to Islam.[60] The work of these two Chishti exemplars produced extraordinary results, because the printing press has been supplemented by new modes of communication – sound recordings, films, television and internet. Sufi teachings were popularized on a vast scale and became accessible to a widening audience which included non-sufis, non-Muslims and non-Asians. The worldwide availability of devotional music, as practiced by Sabri brothers and Nusrat Fateh Ali Khan, brought sufism into the fast emerging global hybrid culture. The proliferation of sufi websites has led to the formation of virtual sufi communities that cut across barriers of nation, language and race. Looking into the future, Ernst and Lawrence feel that the new modes of communication were likely to reassert the basic Chishti emphasis on *zikr* and *sama* and that the diasporic Chishtis could link with other sufi and Muslim groups. In spite of its global sweep, the Chishti spiritual discipline would retain its Indianness owing to the location of the Chishti sacred sites in the subcontinent.[61]

A major chunk of modern literature on Indian sufism revolves around the lives of prominent mystics and remains confined to the ideological boundaries of different mystic orders. Moving away from the conventional pattern, Riazul Islam (2002) seeks to discover the impact of sufism on South Asian society during the fourteenth century and, in the process, perceives this impact in such aspects as offerings (*futuh*), employment (*kasb*), institution of discipleship (*piri-muridi*), family life, political inclinations, ethical living and attitude towards knowledge and learning. Since the object was to develop a broad conceptual understanding of sufism, the exercise overlooks the geographical barriers between South Asia and West Asia as well as the ideological barriers between different mystic orders. In addition to the role of Nizamuddin Auliya and Nasiruddin Mahmud, we are persuaded to recognize the contribution of several sufi examplers – Sharafuddin Yahya Maneri, Ashraf Jahangir Simnani, Syed Muhammad Gesudaraz and Syed Jalaluddin Bukhari Makhdum-i-Jahaniyan Jahangasht – particularly through their discourses and letters. Since the early Chishtis were averse to both earning livelihood (*kasb*) and receiving land grants,[62] they were constrained to survive on unasked charity (*futuh*) which, to an extent, paved way for the redistribution of wealth. The later Chishtis – Nasiruddin, Gesudaraz and Simnani – expressed themselves in favour of earning livelihood, because they refused to see any contradiction between employment (*kasb*) and absolute faith in God (*tawakkul*). On these matters, we encounter a clear contrast between Baghdad-Khurasan-Bukhara region and South Asia. In the former,[63] the mystics did not hesitate to engage in various professions and, in the latter, the voluntary withdrawal of mystics from work generated penury and begging (*suwal*). The mystics controlled the lives of their disciples through securing the surrender of will and exercising imaginative power (*tasir-i-tasawwur*). Regarding matrimony, the attitudes ranged from strict celibacy to large family units. Departing from the hallowed Chishti tradition, Simnani built a strong case for cordial relations with the ruling elite,[64] while Gesudaraz received endowments from Bahmani rulers and played an active role in court politics. In the ultimate analysis, sufism promoted ethical conduct in the form of humanism, compassion, generosity, forgiveness, service and sacrifice. At the same time, it exercised a baneful influence in the society owing to credulousness regarding the power of mystics, slavish mentality among disciples, belief in miracles, devaluation of human effort, erosion of scientific attitude and corruption in the management of hospices and shrines.

Punjabi Sufi Poetry and its Vernacular Character

Medieval Punjab was characterized by currents of socio-communal harmony, anti-hierarchical/patriarchal struggles, counter hegemonic literature and non-conformist ethos. In the making of this culture, a historic role was played by sufis, bhaktas and gurus. They stand out as the avant-garde saints of medieval Punjab. A perusal of the Punjabi sufi poetry, from Shaikh Farid (1175-1165) to Khwaja Ghulam Farid (1841-1901), explicitly underscores their strong opposition to communitarian forms or spectacles. Since the Punjabi sufis did not subscribe to the idea and practice of cultural, religious and linguistic 'otherness,' they set forth traditions of syncretic culture at all levels. While studying the Punjabi sufi poetry, it needs to be appreciated that Islam constituted an important aspect of the history of Punjab. As a result, the historical experiences of the region – as manifested in culture, literature, language and politics – were vernacularized in the form of sufism. The two-pronged process of Islamization of Punjab and Punjabization of Islam was a peculiar phenomenon and, undoubtedly, it was initiated by the sufis who were sons of the soil. We can discern the vernacularization of Islam and the critique of socio-religious orthodoxy in the devotional verses of Shaikh Farid, Shah Husain, Sultan Bahu, Bulleh Shah and other sufi poets. It may be understood that vernacularization did not only mean communication of Islamic mysticism through the 'mother tongue.' It also meant combining the simplest tenets of Islam and terminology of the sufi tradition with the imagery of prevailing literary forms. Above all, vernacularization meant the dissemination of Islamic mysticism through the vernacular milieu. What is being suggested is that Islamic mysticism did not operate independently of local and particular forms of identity. It is also significant to remember that the Punjab sufis, who chose to versify Islamic mysticism in the Punjabi vernacular, were trained in the great socio-religious and linguistic traditions of Islam. They belonged to 'post-graduate creed' and were not 'illiterate mystics' who could 'fall a prey in the hands of the devil.'[65] It may be premised that the classical and aristocratic elements in Islam, who desired their revelation and ritual to be expressed exclusively in the sacred Arabic language, must have felt offended by the phenomenon of vernacular sufism. However, the vernacularity involved in the Punjabi sufi poetry remains unknown to those who mainly rely on translations, available in the languages of metropolitan countries.

The vernacular sufis across the Indian subcontinent had an exemplary understanding of the creative linkages between the grand Islamic religious *route* and local *roots*.[66] The Punjabi sufis projected their indigenous character in a number of ways. The land of the five rivers,

Punjab, was their motherland; 'vernacular' Islam was their way of life and the numerous dialects of Punjabi language were not only their mother tongues, but they were also a medium of expressing their sufic experience. Nothing better illustrates the historically evolved character of the medieval culture – which was both syncretic and vernacular – than the Punjabi sufi poetry. In other words, no other genre is so comprehensive in range and appeal to describe the medieval Punjabi life and Punjabi sufism, particularly when one understands that the geographical division of Punjab in 1947 (i) deprived the Punjabi people of their shared sacred space of shrines and *mazars* of sufi saints and poets (ii) segmented the Punjabi people into Shahmukhi-using 'Muslim' Punjabis and 'Gurmukhi' using 'Sikh' Punjabis. Let us discuss the salient features of Punjabi sufi poetry, which illumine the nature of Punjab sufism.

Locally rooted: The prominent feature that certifies the vernacular character of the Punjabi sufi poetry is that it is grounded in 'indigenous resources'[67] – in the ecology of Punjab (its birds, animals, rivers, deserts, mountains, pastures and seasons), in its poetic genres (*doha, geet, kafi, bani, baramah, qissa*), in its vernaculars (Khari Boli, Brajbhasa, Rajasthani, Punjabi, Siraiki, Sindi and Hindko), in its love legends (Hir-Ranjha, Sassi-Punnun and Sohni-Mahiwal), in its folk religions, traditions, beliefs and myths, and in its social folk landscapes like collective spinning (*trinjan*) and marriage scenes.

Islamicate character: The Punjabi sufi poetry originated in the Punjabi cultural milieu, when Islam made Punjab its abode. The Punjabi soil imbibed the Islamic mysticism and reproduced it in vernacular form and ethos. This reproduction was a socio-cultural and linguistic fusion, which is one of the chief characteristics of the Punjabi sufi poetry and affirms its Islamicate,[68] rather than Islamic character. Recent studies on sufism have recognized the historical and cultural significance of sufi poetry composed in Islamicate languages. For instance, Carl W. Ernst observes, "Since most of the scholarship on sufi poetry has focused on Arabic and particularly Persian materials, there are far fewer translations and studies available for sufi poetry in Turkic, Indic, African, and Southeast Asian languages. Although poetry in these languages plays an important role in sufi practice, it has been neglected as literature because of cultural hierarchies in premodern Islamicate societies, which are reflected even in modern Western Scholarship."[69]

Non-missionary: The Punjabi sufis did not introduce Islamic mysticism with the spirit of missionary-style proselytization or missionary propaganda. The Islamic flavour and fragrance created by them in their poetry need not to be tangled with the phenomenon of Islamization of territory, as the latter was the major concern of the orthodox Islamic ecclesiastical class. Thus, the Punjabi sufis never (as some scholars perceive),[70] tended to describe and sustain their communitarian group boundaries, with a view to project their Islamic religious background. Actually, the sufis, bhaktas and gurus began to be identified denominationally only in the colonial and post-colonial Punjab, when a vigorous attempt was made to situate the Punjabi mystic poetry in the straitjackets of Islamic mystic poetry (*sufi-kav*) and Sikh mystic poetry (*gurmat-kav*). In this attempt, attention was not paid to the socio-cultural and religious vernacularity of the Punjabi sufi poetry and the sufi poets.

The male imagery of the Beloved and non-conformism: Bridal symbolism and bridal mysticism underscores an another vernacular character of the Punjabi sufis. It is true that their male identity is present in their verses, but this is so only for the sake of their names. The first Punjabi poet, Shaikh Farid, initiated to pick up the bridal symbolism/ mysticism: 'The day a maid is engaged/her marriage day is fixed./... Death, the groom will come and take/life, his bride, away in marriage.' Originally an Indic tradition, bridal mysticism in sufi poetry describes the soul as a longing girl or a loving bride and God or Prophet Muhammad the longed-for bridegroom.[71] Bridal symbolism added the dimension of non-conformism to the Punjabi sufi poetry. From its very birth in the twelfth-thirteenth centuries, the Punjabi sufi poetry was non-conformist in the sense that it defied the dominant image of the social patriarchs. The sufi poets illumined the image of He-Beloved. Thus Punjabi sufi poetry at a single stroke, it may be argued, dismantled the social masculinity. The female voice of a he-sufi poet represents 'her' marginalized voice. For instance, Bulleh Shah sings:

> *Haji lok makke nun jandey /mera mahi Ranjha Mecca*
> The pilgrims go to Mecca, my Mecca is dear Ranjha.

Anti-formalist: That sufism posed a bold challenge to religious orthodoxy can be examplified with the help of their verses. For example, the parochial echo and ego of religious ritualism, advocated by the religious patriarchs, was critiqued intrepidly and loudly by Sultan Bahu:

> *Allah parhon hafiz hoyon, / na geyya hajabon parda hoo. / parh parh alam fazal hoyon, / te talab hoyon zar da hoo. / lakh hazar kitaban parhian, / par zalam nafs na marda hoo. / bajh fakir koi na mare, / eho chor andar da hoo.*
>
> Even after learning the Quran by heart you could not unveil the curtain. By gaining such knowledge you become even more greedy for wealth. Even by reading thousands of books you are unable to kill your inner-ego. O Bahu, none else kill the thief of their inner-selves, except the faqirs.

Fusion of love, beauty and martyrdom: love (*ishq*) and beauty (*husan*) constituted the aesthetic rationale of Punjabi sufi poetry. Both these constituents helped a sufi transcend the socio-religious boundaries, constructed from 'above'. The organic unity of love and beauty confronted with pedantic knowledge (*ilm*) of the priestly class. For constructing the image of *husan*, a sufi poet, who personified *ishq*, picked up metaphors / similes and poetic genres from the vernacular cultural repertoire. He knew that socio-cultural context was the best guarantee for artistic objectification of mystic experience. Therefore, he made subtle uses of folklore.[72] Often we find a Punjabi sufi poet assuming himself as Hir and yearning for 'her' Beloved / beloved Ranjha. He revealed his pains of separation in the indigenous poetic genre of *baramah*. He addressed his He-Beloved with numerous vernacular epithets as *sajjan*, *suhag*, *sohna*, *dilbar*, *kant* etc., and brought into use a number of images such as that of a jogi, Lord Krishna, marriage, dowry, veiled woman, spinning wheel etc. to reveal the organic unity of *ishq* and *husan* or his erotic love with his He-Beloved. In Punjabi sufi poetry, *ishq* plays a venturesome game of non-conformism against both the social and religious patriarchs. The game eventually culminated in the martyrdom of love and lover (*ishq* and *ashiq*). The Punjabi sufi poetry, particularly of Sultan Bahu, Bulleh Shah and Waris Shah, draws no distinction between a lover and a martyr. Waris Shah, for example, made Hir inform her 'patriarchal' brother: 'The fruit of love will ripen on a severed head' (*'sir ditiyan bajh na ishq pakkey, eh nahin sukhlian yarian vey'*). The cultural production of the meanings of *ishq* and *husan* or the entire Islamic mysticism points out the aesthetic vitality of Punjabi sufi poetry.

Dialogical: Another characteristic of the Punjabi sufi poetry is its dialogical nature. Bulleh Shah's *kafis* are best illustrations of it. His *kafi* "is a miniature drama in which diverse, contrasting tones converge to create the final meaning."[73] But the (sufi) *qissa-kars* in their narratives of love legends courageously dismantled the authoritarian monologue of patriarchs by introducing the element of conversation and dialogue of the rebel-lovers. For example, Hir entered into a debate with her mother, father and brother, and, on the day of her marriage (*nikah*), she polemically pleaded her case (of love with Ranjha) in front of the local judge. Thus in sufi poetry, particularly in its *qissa* genre, a certain relation between distinct 'voices' can be seen and understood. Each voice takes its stand as a conscious reaction to the ideological position of the other.

Synthesis of secular and devout worlds: The non-conformism of the Punjabi sufis against the orthodox religious patriarchy conspicuously and dramatically emerges in the genre of *qissa*-poetry in which an extra-religious (or social) theme such as the romantic love of Hir-Ranjha, Sohni-Mahiwal and Sassi-Punnun remains prominent. From the viewpoint of this theme, Punjabi sufi poetry displays its unique feature of a synthesis of secular and devout worlds, and of religious and secular languages. The poetry under reference boldly combines religious belief with human passion, not in order to contrast and evaluate one against the other, but to enrich the combination of both. It venerates the heroes of the love-romances, a characteristic recognized in the 'Sikh' mysticism or Sikh religious traditions. For example Bhai Gurdas 'cannonized these lovers as saints when he held out their examples as those of the love-divine.' Guru Gobind Singh also alluded to the romances of Hir-Ranjha.[74]

Though now Punjabi sufi poetry is no longer composed or created, it still survives as a cultural legacy among the Punjabis. Musicians and singers are keeping this legacy intact. The female myths in the Punjabi sufi poetry have endowed it with an aesthetic quality that has been claimed by musicians and singers. They sing the native legends of lovers like Sassi, Hir, Sohni, Marvi and Mira Bai.[75] With the emergence of Punjabi diaspora and the global appearance of audio-video and electronic media, the singing of Punjabi sufi poetry has crossed the boundaries of Indian subcontinent as is evident from the remarkable success of the present day practitioners of *qawwali* such as Nusrat Fateh Ali Khan and exponents of kaafi-singing like Pathaney Khan and Abida Parveen. In recent times, sufi music has also made an entry into the cyberspace.[76]

Approaches to the Study of Punjabi Sufi Poetry

The first book on the history of Punjabi literature, which was written by Mohan Singh (Diwana) in English, appeared in 1933. Dividing his entire narrative into 'The Pre-Nanak Age', 'The Age of Nanak', 'The Later Moghul Period', 'The Age of Ranjit Singh' and 'The British Period', Mohan Singh offers us only stray references to Punjabi sufi poets. After a gap of sixty years, a two-volume study emerged from the pen of Sant Singh Sekhon. In these two volumes, a sufficient space has been given to Punjabi sufism and sufi poets. The difference between Mohan Singh and Sant Singh Sekhon is worthy of note. For the former the 'Age of Nanak' is the 'golden age', whereas for the latter 'Shaikh Farid was a great cultural ancestor of the Punjabi people.' But Sekhon is quite paradoxical in his approach: on the one hand, he regards Shaikh Farid as cultural ancestor; on the other hand, he is of the opinion that sufism hardly exercised its influence on Punjabi life. Rather he presents an extremely negative and distorted picture of the popularity of sufism among the general masses of Punjab. Considering sufism in Punjab a *proletarian* phenomenon, Sekhon observes: "...the common peasant and labourer were attracted by these sufi fakirs' spiritual romanticism and the wayward life at their *khanqahs* where they could indulge in free drinking of hemp, some kind of a transcendental and substitute gratification of the instinct for freedom from all moral and social restraints."[77] In developing his understanding, Sekhon pays no heed to contemporary sources and modern writings on the development of sufism in north-western India.

The exclusive study of Punjabi sufism begins with the book of Lajwanti Rama Krishna. Her study, which is the first standard work of reference in English, appeared in 1938. She traces both the genesis and changing character of Punjabi sufi poetry in the perspective of *sacred route* of Arabia and *classical* Persian language, on the one hand, and the *Great Tradition* of Hinduism and Buddhism, on the other.[78] Obviously, these 'great' religious perspectives ten to dilute the vitality and legitimacy of vernacularity involved in Punjabi sufism.In other words, a small narrative of Punjab sufism gets lost in the maze of grand narratives. To Lajwanti Rama Krishna, fifteenth-sixteenth centuries are historically significant, as during this period Shaikh Ibrahim Fari (1450-1575) emerged s a precursor or trendsetter of Punjabi poetry and the sufis mtured into th 'nationalist' poets.[79] A student of history can fairly recall that this period, which is considered as a watershed in the history of Punjab, coincides with the period of Guru Nanak (1469-1539), who may be designated as a *nationalist* poet because he defied Babur in his *Babur Bani*, when the latter invaded Hindustan in the second decade of the sixteenth centur. Again the historical sense might enable one to appreciate the revival of the fifteenth-sixteenth centuries (i.e. the Age of Guru Nanak) by Lajwanti Rama Krishna in the second decade of the twentieth century when the communitarian middle class politics was a dominant feature of the India National Movement and the 'two nation' theory was about to take birth, just few yearsbefore the pulication of the work under reference

Thus it was in the wake of politically communitarian milieu of the forties of the twentieth century, Lajwanti Rama Krishna constructs the inferior-superior syndrome in Islam, Hinduism and Sikism. She makes her story empirically 'true' while excluding the Islamic theme of unitarianism (*wahdat-ul-wujud*) and inserting the selective hitorical data into its plot: the Mughal emperor Akbar laid the foundation of a new religion, *Din-i-Ilahi*, when his faith in the superiority of Islam got "shattered"; intolerance (fanaticism) of Aurangzeb obliged sufis to drive swiftly towards Hinduism; Hindu Vedantic thought "overpowered" the beliefs of sufis Miyan ir, Dara Shuoh, Abul Fazl and Fayzi were "devoted" scholars of different religious systems and philosophies o India. Lajwanti Rama Krishna confuses the Divine Messenger, Prophet Muhammad,with the DivineIncarnate, Krishna. She also traces the origns of sufi vegetarianism to the Indian (Hindu) philosophy of non-violence (*ahimsa*). It is interestig to read the homologous pairs which can be constructed from her trict but arbitrary categories of the Punjab sufis: i) orthodo sufism: convrsion (as reprsented by Baba Farid and Ali Haider); (ii) Vedantic/non-orthodox sufism: philosphy (as represented by Bulleh Shah); and (iii) popular sufim: superstitions (as represented by Fard Faqr).[80] These homologous pairs cease to be valid and historical from the viwpoint of the Quranic Unitarian thught. Moreover, the socio-cultural fusion, as represented by Akbar or by the Punjab sufis, has been decoded by Lajwanti Rama Krisna in the light of cross-cultural study with an objective to demostrate the supeiority of one culture and religion over the other. Further, in her opinion, th Punjabi sufi poetry is devoid of aesthetic and beauty of language. She oes not draw a distinction between the beauty of classical/elite language and that of vernacular lnguage. Hence, she premises: "Having been evolved in the villages, it (Punjabi sufi poetry) lacks that point of extreme elaboration to which sufi poets carried other languages, such as Persian and Urdu". In spite of the absence of 'dazzling brilliancy and poetic conceit', the Punjabi sufi poetry appeals to our athor because it "always maintained dignity, order, and sincerity."[81]

Lajwanti Rama Krishna's discourse, which understood sufism as an Islamized form of Vedanta philosophy, was followed after a gap of about forty years by S.R. Sharda (1975). So far as historical details are concerned, Sharda's work needs to be read as a canvas profusely dotted with the Vedantic colour, which was initially picked up by Lajwanti Rama Krishna. Sharda regards the work of his predecessor as the "so far only one scientific study of Punjabi sufism." To him trans-Indus sufism is orthodoxically Islamic, while cis-Indus sufism is overwhelmingly imbued with the Indian thought, esoterically as well exoterically. He considers Punjab as a rendezvous where Greek Neo-Platonic and Indian Vedantic forms of sufism merged into each other. He believes that the resultant fusion has been unknown and not experienced anywhere else in the Muslim world. He too is of the opinion that sufism attainted its heights in the Punjab under "the impact of Vaishnava Vedantic Bhakti." Like Lajwanti Rama Krishna, he also considered Farid Sani as the first representative of Vaishnava Vedantic sufism. For him, the permeation of Hindu thought in sufi practice is tremendous as well as amazing. It is tremendous because, Sharda remarks, a good number of notable sufis followed gradually all the ideas of the Hindu mystics; and it was amazing because the vanquished cast their impact over the victors who were bigoted people and regarded Hinduism as *kufar*."[82]

In 1975, when S.R. Sharda's work was published, we also find the opportunity to read an important book entitled, *Mystical Dimension of*

Islam, which was written by Annemarie Schimmel. This comprehensive attempt may be viewed as a synthesis of history, literature, philosophy, semiotics and anthropology. The kind of rigorous multi-disciplinary exercise, in which Schimmel gets engaged, is evident from her own view on a demanding subject like Islamic mysticism: "To write about Sufism, or Islamic mysticism, is an almost impossible task. At the first step, a wide mountain range appears before eye – and the longer the seeker pursues the path, the more difficult it seems to reach any goal at all."[83] In the last (eighth) chapter, 'Sufism in Indo-Pakistan', Schimmel deals with, in a separate section, 'Mystical Poetry in the Regional Languages – Sindi, Panjabi, Pashto.' Unlike Lajwanti Rama Krishna and S.R. Sharda, who broadly situate Punjab sufis in Vedantic philosophy of Hinduism, Schimmel narrates regional sufism from the viewpoint of vernacular cultures and languages (Sindi, Panjabi and Pashto). She appreciates the aesthetics of regional sufi poetry and, hence, aptly illumines the vernacularization of sufism in terms of indigenous poetic genres and folk tales. Schimmel appreciates the role of 'rustic, idiomatic and musical' nature of the vernaculars (Punjabi, Sindi and Pashto) to express mystical feelings, though not mystical theories. The mystical themes such as yearning of the soul, burning love and longing for pain, expressed through indigenous musical modes like *doha* and *kafi*, appeal to her as a mark of vernacular sufism. She understands the vernacularization of Persian and Turkish mystical poetry which, in its themes, critiqued the theologians. In this context, she cites the *siharfi* of Sultan Bahu who directs his sarcasm on the knowledge of the lawyer (*mufti*). In the vernacular poetry, what Schimmel seems to suggest, intuitive knowledge, as distinct from the sensory and cognitive knowledge (i.e. book learning, scholarship, religious specialization and teaching etc.), is more prominent. Schimmel appreciates the wisdom of vernacular sufis for having exploited the rural imagery, drawn from gardening and planting, besides the motifs of spinning and weaving, to spread the ideas of sufism. To illustrate her point, she again cites a popular *siharfi* of Sultan Bahu.

For Schimmel vernacular/regional sufism, first, stands for a more popular vehicle for religious feeling than the colder, formal discipline of the theologians (*ulama*), and, second, it communicates, so far as its vernacular character is concerned, an element of fervent anti-intellectualism. Schimmel discovers a shared or common tradition in the vernacular regions of Punjab and Sind – a tradition of "inserting the folk tales into the context of mystical thought."[84] Shah Husain and Bulleh Shah employed the theme of Hir Ranjha, while Shah Abul Latif of Sind relied on the folk tales like Sohni Mahiwal and Sassi Punnun. It may be premised that Schimmel constructs the vernacular discourse about vernacular sufis, instead of contextualizing them in 'Islamic' or 'Vedantic' grand-framework.

A decade back (1997), a seminal study on sufism was made by Shuja Alhaq in two volumes under the very meaningful and thought provoking title, *A Forgotten Vision: Study of Human Spirituality in the Light of the Islamic Tradition*. The title itself unequivocally suggests that the author plunges into the challenging task of deconstructing the narrow and sectarian discourse on spirituality. Shuja Alhaq, indeed, performs his venturesome exercise fastidiously,[85] so far as historical emplotment, argumentative acumen and methodological expertise are concerned. In the second volume, he studies sufism in Punjab with which we are presently concerned. But before we study it, let us briefly familiarize ourselves with his approach and methodology. When we read the author's *Prologue* along with its sub-title, *Unification and the End of Religion,* we are obliged to recall two statements made by Karl Marx nearly two centuries ago: first, 'religion is the opium of the people', and second, 'the starting point of all criticism is the criticism of religion.' Shuja Alhaq, right at the outset, apologizes: "...for those who are in love with their past, their bygone worlds, their mosques, churches, temples and synagogues, there may not be much in this work, except disappointment..."[86]

Throughout the two volumes, Shuja Alhaq remains constantly concerned with the issue of 'form' and 'content' of religion. To tackle this issue, he travels the lanes of history, once trodden by Mansur al-Hallaj, Bayazid Bistami, Abu Said and Ibn Arabi from the ninth to thirteenth centuries. For him, history of religion ought to deal essentially with 'content' or essence. He finds no difference between 'form' and a scholastic theologian because both tend to erode the 'essence' of religion. He approaches the issue of Islamic spirituality mainly from the viewpoint of its inner dimension. He categorically states that the Quran is "preeminently an exposition of the Unitarian doctrine", not "a book of Law." The said doctrine underscores the inward unity of man and God, though apparently the two are poles apart, separated by "the nothingness of the one and the mightiness of the other."

Shuja Alhaq arrays his study on Islamic spirituality into three phases. In its first phase, Islamic spirituality came into conflict with the Law/state, and the conflict culminated in the martyrdom of Mansur al-Hallaj (858-922). In the second phase sufism recognized the superficial schism between Muslim and non-Muslim or between belief and non-belief. It is in the second phase that the Unitarian doctrine was understood as 'supra-religious i.e. beyond the pale of 'forms.' In the final or the third phase, with the advent of Islam in India, sufism severed its connections with the state because the Law was not considered as "a potent code for the social existence," particularly when Islam arrived on a space which was culturally and religiously pluralistic. Shuja Alhaq does not intend to *revive* sufism but *reviews* it to "unveil and develop its kernel within the parameters of Islam." He studies the issue of human spirituality with help of two key concepts. First, that sufism does not mark the origin of Islamic spirituality, which is already enshrined in the Quran. Second, the inward dimension and outward dimension of sufism also need to be demarcated because sufism itself "was not free from a contention between the orthodox and Unitarian sufis."

While dilating upon the Indian spirituality, Shuja Alhaq narrows down his study to Punjab. He understands that it was on its historically evolved multi-layered socio-cultural and religious space that sufism flourished,[87] with its rebellious and non-conformist voice being directed against orthodoxy. The sufis neither believed in schism, nor in hierarchy. Their holistic worldview, rooted in the human spirituality of the Quran, never let them see everything as separate and differentiated. Since this shade of spirituality rooted in the Quran was identical with the Indian Unitary thought, which draws distinction between unitary knowledge (*vidya*) and ignorance (*avidya*), some scholars like Lajwanti Rama Krishna and S. R. Sharda have had a strong tendency to view Indian/Punjab sufism in the light of Hindu/Vedantic unitary thought, as we have discussed.

Unlike the Vedantic school of sufism, Shuja Alhaq explains that the Chishti sufis played a significant role in the non-antagonistic development of Islam when it arrived in India to govern the multi-religious and multi-cultural society. The Chishtis outrightly rejected the notion of a homogenous chosen Muslim community of God as advocated by the Islamic orthodoxy, which considered the non-Muslim majority population as infidels. The Chishtis looked upon sufism as a way of life, whose practice and ideal were different from the rulers and their allies, the *ulama*.[88] The transcendental culture of the sufis, as described by the author, does not endorse the discourse, which regards the Chishti sufis as 'missionaries' who created "religious fervour among the Muslims."[89] The writer traces the history of transcendental culture of the Indian Chishti sufis to the Persian sufi tradition vis-à-vis the Indian Suhrawardis "whose parent order originated in the Arab world." He also informs us that sufism acquired a good deal of autonomy vis-à-vis state and *shariat* as it penetrated into the Persian world. Initially, the Indian sufis inherited the Unitarian doctrine through the Persian sufis, Bayazid Bistami, (d.875) and Abu Said (978-1061), and also imbibed the influence of Mansur al-Hallaj. The Chishtis argued that since the state adhered to the Law, it is not obligatory on their part also to remain adhered to it. Conversely, they followed the path of syncretism, paving the way for "the development of supra or cross religious spirituality."[90] Thus, Shuja Alhaq's discourse of Islam/sufism deflates the community-centric historiographical discourse fabricated by historians – Ishtiaq Husain Qureshi, Aziz Ahmad and Jadunath Sarkar – who 'imagine' Muslims as a monolithic community.[91]

In Shuja Alhaq's narrative of the Punjabi sufis, we meet Shaikh Farid as a pioneer of cross religious spirituality. The open-ended and counter-hegemonic character of his *jamat khana* (situated at Ajodhan/Pakpattan) remained away from the status covetously hankered after by some mystics. Shaikh Farid was a paragon of voluntary poverty, autonomy of spiritual life vis-à-vis official Islam. He symbolized the synthesis of intellect (*aql*) and love (*ishq*). It may be argued that the Chishtis were aware of the fact that without the practice of these virtues, a spiritual 'state' could not be founded in the 'new' land of pluralistic faiths.[92] Thus implicitly, the sufis were equating state with 'form' and spirituality with 'essence.' That Punjab sufis never reposed their faith in religious formalism strengthens Shuja Alhaq's critique of 'form'. He quotes a few couplets of Shaikh Farid and narrates the life style of Mian Mir to underscore a distinction between pretension (form) and purity (content). Shuja Alhaq even eulogizes Shah Husain as *be-shara* sufi. From the viewpoint of religious ostentations, Shuja Alhaq traces similarities or what he calls 'invisible line of continuity' between the two prominent sufi masters, the Chishti, Shaikh Farid and the Qadiri, Miyan Mir.[93] While bringing the non-conformist character of the Punjab sufis to the fore in his narrative of the human spirituality, Shuja Alhaq does not seem to be much concerned with the denominational boundaries of the sufi order (*silsilahs*).

Shuja Alhaq aptly locates the streaks of transcendental culture in the language of the Punjab sufis. For instance, Shah Husain held the *sadhs* or *sadhus* in high esteem because he called himself a *faqir* and finds the *sadhus* sharing the same goal with him, the cultivation of *faqiri*, or perfect formlessness. Thus Shah Husain was able to evolve a spiritual language which was increasingly contemplative, informal and universal, that is, free from predominantly religious undertones.[94] Shuja Alhaq also finds similarities in the language of Sultan Bahu and Bulleh Shah.[95] Bulleh Shah, for instance, is "bitter, even contemptuous of the representatives of Islamic orthodoxy. He compares the *mullah* with the lamp-man (*mashalchi*). Both provide others light but are ever in darkness themselves."[96] Thus instead of legitimizing the religious 'forms', Shuja Alhaq appreciates the literary 'dress' of the sufi poetry – its words, metaphors, colours and notes. Only the *literary* dress can offset the effects of *religious* dress, he seems to suggest.

Relying on the Unitarian doctrine and locating non-conformism in

(i) the poetry of Shaikh Farid, (ii) the life style of Miyan Mir, (iii) the inebriated image of Shah Husain and (iv) the bold anti-orthodox poetic language of Sultan Bahu and Bulleh Shah, Shuja Alhaq constructs a new genealogy of the Punjab sufis, irrespective of their affiliations with the divergent *silsilahs*. He inaugurates the thematic study of sufism in Punjab starting from Shaikh Farid in the twelfth-thirteenth centuries to Bulleh Shah in the eighteenth century and, in the process, makes us familiar with its ideological credentials.

Three Conceptual Frameworks

In the preceding account we have broadly read three conceptual historiographical frameworks for studying the Punjab sufis. The first one, designed by Lajwanti Rama Krishna, projects the Vedantic character of the sufis. This framework accentuates the superiority of Hinduism or what its architect calls 'old Indian vigour' which "asserted itself and influenced the sufi beliefs who came to India with the object of leading the Indian to the Beloved by Muhammad's path..."[97] Written in the colonial milieu, her concern with the Punjabi sufis appears to be a tireless effort in constructing their image anew in her own perspective. Her discourse on the Punjabi sufis is not different from the colonial masters whose construction of the 'native society' was not substantially compatible with what the 'natives' knew about themselves.[98] Thus she remains reluctant or unwilling to study the historical roots of Islamic mysticism when she deals with the Punjabi sufis. The second framework of Annemarie Schimmel projects the regional identity of the sufis, focusing on vernacular languages and vernacular culture. Her way of perceiving the local genres of sufi poetry and its local cultural motifs reminds us of the concept of vernacular collective memory and cultural history of small rather than the 'imagined' large monolithic communities. Normally vernacular expressions convey what social reality feels like, rather than what it should be like.[99] German as she was, Schimmel seems to have appreciated the significance of *cultures* underlined by J.G. Herder (1744-1803). It is stated that as opposed to 'civilization', culture, by contrast, "chiefly a German acceptance, refers to a *particular* pattern of life, ultimately unimportable, with a focus on specific 'meaningful' historical *products* rather than on general capabilities."[100] The third conceptual framework is associated with Shuja Alhaq. He illumines the inherent tension between the religious 'form' and the 'content.' A reading of his discourse on sufism enables one to argue that 'form' is a kind of censorship imposed on the content of a religion. He assigns the term 'human spirituality' to 'content' so as to liberate sufism from the 'fabricated' orthodox form of Islam; and he situates it (human spirituality) in the Quranic Unitarian doctrine. He ventures into the enterprise of that historiographical discourse which critically compares the inside and outside aspects of religion and keeps alive the Unitarian doctrine, which is much needed in the present scenario of religious fundamentalism and communalism in the South Asian societies. He is 'progressive' in the sense that unlike orthodox Marxists who have a peculiar aversion to study the 'progressive' inner dimension of religion, he highlights it and lets his critical leash loose against the advocates of 'form', a distorted and fanatic picture of religion. Form breeds domination and parochialism, a study of Shuja Alhaq's writing on sufism suggests. He digs down and uncovers the concealed layers of human spirituality hidden in the 'form'.

Present State of Academic Interest

There can be no doubt that sufism constituted a major ingredient of Punjabi culture and appears before us as its most prominent defining feature. During the medieval times, it permeated all aspects of human life in the region. Its historical legacy is manifested in contemporary documentation, hagiographical works, polemical texts, mystical poetry and folk memory. What is equally important, innumerable sufi shrines have survived to our own times and continue to attract millions of people as their permanent devotees. It is a paradox that sufism, to a large extent, has been denied its rightful place in the academic life of contemporary Punjab and neighbouring states, particularly in terms of teaching and research in the discipline of History. This marginalization of sufism is a product of the partisan view of the history of Punjab which, in turn, is rooted in the socio-political developments in the region since the British annexation. In the late nineteenth century, the socio-religious reform movements generated a powerful wave of communitarian consciousness among the Punjabi middle classes. Fuelled by the forces let loose by colonialism, the communitarian consciousness assumed the form of full scale communalism in the first half of the twentieth century. The large scale violence, which occurred on both sides of the Radcliffe Line during partition, provided legitimacy to the communal ideology. In the post-1947 Indian Punjab, the struggle for a Punjabi speaking state culminated in the reorganization of three states – Punjab, Haryana and Himachal Pardesh. The new scenario might have brought major gains to the political elite, but it accentuated the existing religious/linguistic divides and raised the unsolvable majority-minority tangle.

It is in these ominous circumstances that the education system and intellectual life began to expand and flourish. The contribution of sufis (and for that matter, the bhaktas and gurus) to the Punjabi culture was confronted by the communal backlash, with the rise of middle classes among the Muslims, Hindus and Sikhs under the colonial dispensation.

The syncretic socio-cultural traditions of Punjab experienced the terrible ordeal of fission, as communitarian denominations were foisted on them under the colonial exercise of census. With the partition of Punjab into west (Pakistani) Punjab and east (Hindustani) Punjab, the rich legacy of medieval saints (sufis, bhaktas and gurus) was also subjected to partition and consequently relegated to the background vis-a-vis the newly born nationalisms. We should not be surprised that the middle classes began to identify sufism with Islam, *sirguna* bhakti with Hinduism and *nirguna* bhakti with Sikhism. They began to see the major religious traditions in terms of monolithic communities and, tracing their current differences back to the medieval times, denied the evolution of Punjabi cultural fusion which had been defined by the sublime ideal of non-conformism and which had been collectively developed by sufis, bhaktas and gurus. Not only this, the divisive attitude was also applied to language and script. Shahmukhi was identified with the Muslim Punjabis, Gurmukhi was identified with the Sikh Punjabis and Devnagari was identified with Hindu Punjabis. The politically-oriented linguistic postures and state-oriented nationalisms (which are essentially the legacies of colonialism and are rooted in the two-nation theory) perceived Shaikh Farid in narrow communitarian grooves as the earliest Urdu poet or the founder of Siraiki poetry or a Muslim sufi poet. In the history of Punjabi literature, which has been produced in the east Punjab, the poetry of Shaikh Farid is placed under the rubric of Pre-Nanak Period. That is why we do not see any Farid Period either in the history of Punjabi literature or in the history of Punjab (as taught in the universities and colleges), even though the verses of Shaikh Farid have been enshrined in the Sikh scripture, Adi Granth. It is interesting to note that Max Arthur Macaullife, who wrote *The Sikh Religion* in six volumes, does not enlist Shaikh Farid (1173-1265), but Shaikh Ibrahim/Farid Sani (1450-1575) as the real author of the said verses. This approach has been faithfully followed by Lajwanti Rama Krishna and Khaliq Ahmad Nizami. As an implication of this school of thought, the origin of Punjabi language and literature has been confined to the fifteenth and sixteenth centuries.

In due course, the present state of Punjab acquired three state funded universities – Panjab University at Chandigarh (partly under central control and funding since 1966), Punjabi University at Patiala and Guru Nanak Dev University at Amritsar. Each university has a Department of History, besides a few centres (or Chairs) which have been created to undertake research in specific fields of knowledge. Punjabi University, Patiala, has nurtured (in addition to its Department of History) a Department of Punjab Historical Studies, which brings out a bi-annual journal entitled *Panjab Past and Present*. It also organizes the annual sessions of the Punjab History Conference and publishes its proceedings. It may be added that these universities have separate departments – Religion, Philosophy, Literature and Languages – where historical studies are pursued, besides their own specialized areas. Last but not least, the subject of History is being taught both at the graduate and post graduate levels in hundreds of colleges which are affiliated to one or the other of the three universities. For a variety of reasons, which are too well known to be identified, History is an extremely popular subject among the students.

It is not the popularity of History as such, but it is the content of the syllabi of the subject, which calls for some discussion. Apart from several papers on Indian and non-Indian history, there are papers on the History of Punjab. At some levels, History of Punjab has been made a compulsory subject. This brings us to the content of the syllabi on the History of Punjab. The syllabi of all the universities, by and large, have reduced the history of Punjab to the history of the Sikhs. The two terminal dates are 1469 and 1849, the former indicating the birth of the first Sikh guru and the second marking the extinction of the Sikh kingdom. These dates, owing to repeated use over a long period of time, have acquired such an aura of sanctity that it has become impossible to suggest a more scientific chronological framework. Under this syllabus, the themes are – the contribution of the ten Sikh gurus to the development of the Sikhism, the revolt of Banda Bahadur, the persecuton of the Sikhs under the Mughal governors, the rise of Dal Khalsa and the Sikh misals, the emergence of the Sikh kingdom under Ranjit Singh, the Anglo-Sikh relations and the fall of the Sikh kingdom.

The above dispensation refuses to conceive Punjab as a region which experienced a specific socio-cultural evolution. It views the eighteenth century as a Sikh-Muslim (religious) conflict. It insists on seeing an essentially non-religious phenomenon like the agrarian system as 'Sikh.' Any historical development that cannot be specifically associated with the Sikhs (e.g. the pastoral tribes), is pushed into oblivion. It is not surprising that sufism has become a major casualty, as it does not figure in the current set of syllabi on the History of Punjab. As we underline the absence of sufism from the syllabi, we must hasten to note that three sufis do figure in the texts that are being currently used at the undergraduate and post graduate levels. But their presence is purely incidental to the dominant Sikh-centric discourse. Shaikh Farid is mentioned because his mystical verses (*salokas*) have been included, along with the devotional outpourings of several other saints, in the Sikh scripture Adi Granth. Miyan Mir makes a fleeting appearance because he was invited by Guru Arjun Dev to lay the foundation of the Harmandir Sahib and subsequently interceded with the Mughal government on behalf of the Sikh gurus. Shaikh Ahmad Sirhindi is seen in a negative role, because he is believed to have instigated the Mughal officers to execute Guru Arjun Dev and to have persuaded the Mughal ruling elite to adopt intolerance against the non-Muslims (including the Sikhs). If these incidental references had not been made, a student of the History of Punjab would remain absolutely ignorant about the role of sufis in the making of medieval Punjab. The absence of sufism from the syllabi is a matter of serious concern, because this very prejudice has made a strong intrusion in the research which has been undertaken in the universities of Punjab. If we scan the research output on the history of Punjab, as manifested in various forms – books, journals, proceedings of conferences and unpublished theses – our observation regarding the absence of sufism stands proved. This particular trend in historiography finds a close parallel in western Punjab (Pakistan), where teaching and research in History fails to recognize the role of bhakti and Sikh movements.

Essays in the present volume constitute a 'transgressive' text in the sense that they transcend the conventional boundaries and communitarian standards of writing the history of Punjab. These essays are organized in three segments that are defined by a broad unity of themes. The first part comprises studies on sufis and sufi orders that were established in medieval Punjab. Iqtidar Husain Siddiqui, in his attempt to assess the contribution of sufis to the making of a multi-cultural society, shows that Punjab was the primordial space where sufis from across the north-western frontier arrived and flourished, that the city of Lahore echoed the literary currents of sufism with the production of *Kashf-ul-Mahjub* in the eleventh century and that Punjab was the first region where the culture of inter-religious dialogue took root. While discussing these themes, the writer offers an alternative to the long-held views on the character of the major sufi orders, the Chishtis and Suhrawardis. Tanvir Anjum examines the issue of spiritual succession among the descendants of Shaikh Farid, keeping in view the early Chishti precedents. She draws a clear distinction between the disciples who inherited the spiritual domain (*khilafat*) and lineal descendants (*sajjadah nishins*) who acquired the guardianship of the shrine. Humaira Arif Dasti's paper constitutes a departure from the conventional understanding of the mystical path developed and propagated by Shaikh Bahauddin Zakariya. She explores the beliefs and practices of the saint in the context of the socio-political conditions prevailing in Multan during the thirteenth century and, having discovered a close link between the two, builds a case for the somewhat controversial methods of the Suhrawardi saint. Aneesa Iqbal Sabir traces the emergence of Syed Jalaluddin Bukhari Makhdum-i-Jahaniyan as a prominent Suhrawardi mystic, with reference to his ardent advocacy of the canonical law (*shariat*) and close relations with the ruling elite. She also delves into his mystical discourses (*malfuzat*) and highlights his work as the scholarly head of a seminary at Uch. Jigar Mohammed finds that sufism in the Jammu hills has been associated with the conditions prevailing in the neighbouring regions – Punjab, Kashmir and Central Asia – which encouraged migration of sufis to a more congenial environment of the Jammu hills. He probes such themes as the preservation of ecology and making of a charismatic image, besides the benevolent role of the sufi shrines and royal patronage. Surinder Singh undertakes a detailed study of Miyan Mir's contribution to the development of the Qadiri order, while focusing on the saint's mystical principles and meditational practices. He also explores the phenomenon of *piri-muridi* and relations with the contemporary rulers, hinting at the possibilities of an alliance between the Qadiris and the Mughal state, which had distanced itself from the Naqshbandis. Zahir Uddin Malik shows that the violent political upheavals of the eighteenth century did not dampen the enthusiasm of sufis and bhaktas, who continued their endeavours in their chosen fields of activity. He focuses his attention on the powerful Chishti revival in south-western Punjab by the spiritual descendants of Maulana Fakhruddin Dehalvi and juxtaposes this trend with the equally significant contribution of sufi poets and Hindu bhaktas and, thus, offers a complex analysis of the socio-cultural scenario.

In its second component, the present volume includes essays that are rooted in the various forms of sufi literature – Persian and vernacular, hagiographical and poetical. Mohammad Tazeem presents an analysis of *Kashf-ul-Mahjub*, the earliest treatise on Islamic mysticism which was produced in Lahore in the early eleventh century. It engages with the theoretical issues ranging from the nature of mystical knowledge and fundamental postulates of mysticism to the practical aspects like matrimony and audition. Saeed Ahmad dilates on the essential features of Shaikh Farid's devotional verses (*salokas*) in Lehandi dialect and underlines their ideological conformity with his life pattern and the social role of his shrine. He impresses upon the need to recognize twelfth-thirteenth centuries as the 'Age of Farid' in the history and literature of Punjab. S.M. Azizuddin Husain reopens the vexed issue of the early Chishti discourses (*malfuzat*), some of which had been repeatedly dubbed as spurious during the last six decades. Focusing his attention on the *Rahat-ul-Qulub*, a record of Shaikh Farid's conversations which were recorded by Shaikh Nizamuddin Auliya, the writer shows it to be a genuine compilation on the basis of various forms of evidence. Ishwar Dayal Gaur accounts for the preference of the Punjabi sufi poets for the female persona as the voice of their poetry. To him, the female voice was a revolutionary literary stance which was adopted by the Punjab sufis to critique and debunk the medieval patriarchal social system. The author brings in references to Rabia Basri, Ibn-i-Arabi and Jalaluddin Rumi in order to historically substantiate his argument and to show the vernacularization of the exotic sufi traditions in medieval Punjab. Iqbal Sabir chooses to examine the major writings of Shaikh Ahmad Sirhindi (other than his letters) and relates them to the socio-political conditions of the Mughal period. Though some of these works are quite polemical in nature, yet they are indispensable for reconstructing the growth of the Naqshbandi order and the contribution of Sirhindi himself to the development of the Islamic mystical thought. Tahir Kamran highlights the major strands in the mystical poetry of Sultan Bahu which have acquired immense popularity since the Mughal times. Keeping in view the nagging gulf between theology and mysticism, he focuses on the centrality of love (*ishq*), the futility of outward form and the role of the spiritual preceptor (*murshid*) as a guide to the novices.

The third segment of the present volume has been devoted to the emergence of sufi shrines, with reference to their structural forms and social networks. Subhash Parihar explores the architectural features of the sufi tombs of Multan and Uch, which had emerged as important centres of sufism, particularly of the Suhrawardi order, during the sultanate period. The extant structures, flat roofed and domed, were characterized by the use of bricks, slopping walls, glazed tiles, carved woodwork and cut-bricks and, in this sense, indicated the development of the Punjab provincial style of architecture which was distinct from that practiced at Delhi and other parts of northern India. Hitender Kumar describes the architectural characteristics of sufi tombs located in the medieval towns of south-eastern Punjab i.e. Hansi, Panipat and Thanesar. Covering a long span of time comprising the sultanate and Mughal period, the structures appear to have been built under the shadow of the Delhi-based imperial style. Complemented by the historical accounts of sufis, most of whom belonged to the Chishti tradition, the study underlines the need to preserve the monuments which are found in a state neglect. Salim Mohammad locates the shrine of Shaikh Sadruddin of Malerkotla in the socio-cultural milieu of the Malwa region of Punjab. By identifying subtle interface with a major Hindu seasonal festival as well as the Sikh tradition of martyrdom, the paper highlights the creation of a shared cultural space that has withstood the onslaught of sectarianism. It also traces the transmission of the lore of the saint through such diverse modes as the spiritual descendants, devotees, popular pamphlets and Qawwali recordings.

Syed Liaqat Hussain Moini brings to light the devotional links of the people of Punjab, both the elite and ordinary as well as Muslims and Hindus, with the shrine of Khwaja Muinuddin Chishti at Ajmer. The writer suggests that this important trend was associated with the revival of the Chishti order, which occurred in Punjab during the eighteenth century. This study is largely based on a unique form of evidence i.e. the letters of authorization (*vikalatnamas*), which were given by the devotees to the custodians (*khuddam*) of the shrine, who provided a variety of services during their pilgrimage to the sacred place. Yogesh Snehi maps the emergence and survival of the 'Lesser Shrines,' with reference to the Panj Pir *dargah* at Abohar, an important town in medieval Punjab. Drawing from a rich stock of textual records and oral traditions, the writer explores the complexities introduced in the historical role of the shrine by the influence of parallel devotional cults, diversity of legends and demographic changes in the wake of partition.

NOTES AND REFERENCES

1. The horse-troop garrison towns, which were established by the Turkish conquerors in the thirteenth century, performed multiple functions e.g. subjugation of the marches, iqta management, agrarian expansion, revenue collection, safeguarding trade routes, markets and monetization. Andre Wink, *Al-Hind: The Making of the Indo-Islamic World*, Vol. II, Oxford India Paperbacks, Delhi, 1999, p. 264.
2. Carl W. Ernst, *The Shambhala Guide to Sufism*, Shambhala South Asia Editions, Boston, Massachusetts, 1997, pp. 8-16.
3. Three articles on mysticism by Massignon, originally in French, are now available in English translation. M. Waseem, *On Becoming an Indian Muslim: French Essays on Aspects of Syncretism*, Oxford University Press, Delhi, 2003.
4. Arthur J. Arberry, *An Introduction to the History of Sufism*, Orient Longman, New Delhi, Reprint, 1992, pp. 40-57.
5. Mohammad Habib, *Politics and Society During the Early Medieval Period*, (Collected Works of Professor Mohammad Habib), Vol. I, Ed., K.A. Nizami, People's Publishing House, New Delhi, 1974, pp. 277-278.
6. Often regarded as the greatest of all sufis, Shaikh Junaid Baghdadi (d.910) was a subtle and sharp thinker, with an extremely obscure style and some daring ideas. His mystic doctrine was based on two pillars i.e. covenant which God made with men at creation and passing away (*fana*) from a impermanent temporal existence to real existence with God. He was also concerned with the idea of spiritual states, which were transient and succeeded one another. The ultimate stage of survival was equivalent to sobriety, which appeared after the overpowering drunkenness of ecstasy. It was on this doctrine of sobriety that his fame as a mystic rests. Julian Baldick, *Mystical Islam: An Introduction to Sufism*, Tauris Parke Paperbacks, London, Reprint, 1992, pp. 44-46.
7. In this classic work, the author has elucidated the concepts of knowledge

(*ilm*) and reason (*aql*), state (*hal*) and station (*maqam*), annihilation (*fana*) and subsistence (*baqa*). The work also discussed such mystical concepts as hospice (*khanqah*), assembly (*suhbat*) and audition (*sama*). It is interesting that Shaikh Farid treated it as a standard text on the discipline and had prepared its summary. Surinder Singh, 'The Study of an Early Treatise on Islamic Mysticism,' *Proceedings of the Punjab History Conference*, Twenty Fourth Session, 15-17 March, 1991, pp. 63-72.

8. Ibn-i-Arabi (1165-1240) was a celebrated mystic of the pantheistic doctrine. Born at Murcia in Spain, he went east in 1201 never to return. He travelled extensively and died at Baghdad. He belonged nominally to Zahiri school as to ritual, rejected authority (*taqlid*) in doctrinal matters and passed for a esoteric (*batini*) in matters of belief. His sole guide was inner light with which he believed himself illumined in a special way. He believed that all Being was essentially one, as it all was a manifestation of the divine substance. Thus different religions were equal. An extremely prolific writer, his principal works are *Fusus-ul-Hikam* and *Futuhat-i-Makkiya*. M.Th. Houtsma et al., (Ed.), *The Encyclopaedia of Islam*, Vol. II, E.J. Brill, Leyden, 1927, pp. 361-362.
9. Mohammad Habib, op. cit., pp. 288-290.
10. This work was marked by clarity of thought and expression. It does not have meaningless miracles, vague mystical lucubrations and anything ethereal. Besides evidence on the lives of early Chishti and non-Chishti saints, it offers a lucid exposition of ideals, aims and activities of the Chishti order. Khaliq Ahmad Nizami, Ed., *Khair-ul-Majalis*, Aligarh Muslim University, Aligarh, 1959, pp. 3, 27.
11. Mohammad Habib, op. cit., p. 393.
12. Ibid., p. 401.
13. Mohammad Habib, op. cit., pp. 429-433; following Habib, Rizvi also accepts that these very seven collections of mystical discourses were fabricated. Saiyid Athar Abbas Rizvi, *A History of Sufism in India*, Vol.I, Munshiram Manoharlal, New Delhi, 1978, p. 4.
14. Mohammad Habib's approach to the apocryphal discourses is criticized on the grounds that while it has been partly framed in terms of traditional standards, it draws primarily upon modern western categories of analysis that are foreign to the material under consideration. It has been argued that his distaste for miracle stories could even be said to reveal a positivistic bias. Carl W. Ernst, *Eternal Garden: Mysticism, History and Politics at a South Asian Sufi Center*, Oxford University Press, Delhi, Second Edition, 2004, p. 79.
15. Khaliq Ahmad Nizami, *Shaikh Nizamuddin Auliya*, Idarah-i-Adabiyat-i-Delli, Delhi, 1991, p. 195; Saiyid Athar Abbas Rizvi, *A History of Sufism in India*, Vol. I, p. 5.
16. Bruce B. Lawrence, *Notes From a Distant Flute: Sufi Literature in Pre-Mughal India*, Imperial Iranian Academy of Philosophy, Tehran, 1978, p. 35.
17. Khaliq Ahmad Nizami, *Supplement to Elliot and Dowson's History of India*, Vol.II, Idarah-i-Adabiyat-i-Delli, Delhi, 1981, p. 64; Khaliq Ahmad Nizami, *On History and Historians of Medieval India*, Munshiram Manoharlal, New

Delhi, 1983, p. 167.

18. Carl W. Ernst, op. cit., pp. 79-80.
19. In contrast to the limited literary activity of the Chishtis upto the middle of the fourteenth century, their next generation turned out to be the most prolific writers in the entire history of the order. This dramatic shift in the literary fortunes may be attributed to the establishment of regional kingdoms, the dispersal of the disciples of Nizamuddin Auliya to many parts of Hindustan and their efforts to disseminate teachings, besides the urge of the migrants from Iran and Central Asia to comment on the mystical doctrine of Ibn-i-Arabi. Bruce B. Lawrence, *Notes From A Distant Flute: Sufi Literature in Pre-Mughal India*, p. 46.
20. Khaliq Ahmad Nizami, *Religion and Politics in India During the Thirteenth Century*, (first published in 1961 by the Idarah-i-Adabiyat-i-Delli, Delhi), New Edition, Oxford University Press, Delhi, 2002, pp. 214-220.
21. Ibid., pp. 220-229.
22. The certificate of succession (*khilafatnama*) which was granted by Shaikh Farid to Nizamuddin Auliya, has been included in the *Siyar-ul-Auliya* by Amir Khurd. For a English translation of the same, see Khaliq Ahmad Nizami, *The Life and Times of Shaikh Farid Ganj-i-Shakar*, Idarah-i-Adabiyat-i-Delli, 1955, pp. 98-99.
23. The Chishti practice of bowing before the shaikh, presenting water to the visitor, circulating the begging bowl, shaving the head of a new entrant to the mystical circle, audition parties and the inverted penitence of forty days had close resemblance to Hindu and Buddhist practices. Khaliq Ahmad Nizami, *Religion and Politics in India During the Thirteenth Century*, p. 191.
24. Khaliq Ahmad Nizami, *The Life and Times of Shaikh Farid Ganj-i-Shakar*, pp. 121-122.
25. For a comparative picture of the Chishti and Suhrawardi convents (*khanqahs*), with reference to their structure and organization, besides their role in the midst of a caste-based Hindu society and a class-based Delhi sultanate, see Khaliq Ahmad Nizami, 'Some Aspects of Khanqah Life in Medieval India,' Khaliq Ahmad Nizami, *Studies in Medieval India: History and Culture*, Kitab Mahal, Allahabad, 1966, pp. 80-96.
26. Khaliq Ahmad Nizami, *Religion and Politics in India During the Thirteenth Century*, pp. 191-192.
27. Ishtiaq Husain Qureshi, *The Muslim Community of the Indo-Pakistan Subcontinent 610-1947*, Renaissance Publishing House, New Delhi, Reprint, 1985, pp. 166-174.
28. Like Sirhindi, Qureshi treats the Muslims of the Indian subcontinent as a monolithic and undifferentiated community, which was clearly demarcated from the non-Muslims in all respects. As a leading historian and intellectual of Pakistan, he felt constrained to invoke the idea of a unique Muslim identity, because it formed the ideological basis of the new state, which was facing difficulties in integrating diverse ethnic groups in the political structure.

29. Ishtiaq Husain Qureshi, op. cit., pp. 177-181.
30. Saiyid Athar Abbas Rizvi, *Muslim Revivalist Movements in Northern India in the Sixteenth and Seventeenth Centuries*, Agra University, Agra, 1965, pp. 212-214.
31. With some difference in detail, a majority of Indian scholars have concluded that Sirhindi's claim of spiritual excellence was unacceptable, that he had a fanatically communalist attitude towards the Shias and Hindus, that he failed to exercise any influence on Jahangir or any of his nobles, that he failed to move the Mughal state away from the policy of religious toleration and that the later trend of his glorification was merely a part of the modern separatist tradition. S. Nurul Hasan, 'Shaikh Ahmad Sirhindi and Mughal Politics,' *Proceedings of the Indian History Congress*, Eighth Session, Annamalainagar, 1945, pp. 248-257; Irfan Habib, 'The Political Role of Shaikh Ahmad Sirhindi and Shah Waliullah,' in Krishna Mohan Shrimali, Ed., *Essays in Indian Art, Religion and Society*, Munshiram Manoharlal, New Delhi, 1987, pp. 219-235; M. Mujeeb, *The Indian Muslims*, George Allen & Unwin, London, 1967, pp. 244-247; Mohammad Yasin, *A Social History of Islamic India 1605-1748*, Munshiram Manoharlal, Second Revised Edition, 1974, pp. 128-145. For a different interpretation, see Khaliq Ahmad Nizami, 'Naqshbandi Influence on Mughal Rulers and Politics,' in Khaliq Ahmad Nizami, Ed., *State and Culture in Medieval India*, Adam Publishers & Distributors, New Delhi, 1985, pp. 156-176.
32. Saiyid Athar Abbas Rizvi, op. cit., pp. 334-375.
33. In a significant contribution, the author traces the changing image of Sirhindi in the Indian Muslim literature from the seventeenth century to the present times. Yohanan Friedmann, *Shaykh Ahmad Sirhindi: An Outline of His Thought and a Study of His Image in the Eyes of the Posterity*, (first published in 1971 by Mcgill-Queens University Press), Oxford India Paperbacks, Delhi, 2000, pp. 87-111.
34. Ibid., pp. 62-68.
35. Ibid., pp. 15-19.
36. Shuja Alhaq, *A Forgotten Vision: A Study of Human Spirituality in the Light of the Islamic Tradition*, Vol.II, Vikas Publishing House, New Delhi, 1997, pp. 323-324.
37. Ibid., p. 328.
38. Ibid., pp. 343-344.
39. Ibid., pp. 346-347.
40. Ibid., p. 356.
41. Richard Maxwell Eaton, *Sufis of Bijapur 1300-1700: Social Roles of Sufis in Medieval India*, (first published in 1978 by the Princeton University Press, Princeton, New Jersey), Munshiram Manoharlal, New Delhi, 1996, p. xxvii.
42. An analysis of the content of the *chakki namas* and *charkha namas* shows three interwoven themes (1) an ontological link established between God, Prophet Muhammad, one's own pir and the reciter herself (2) the use of the grindstone or the spinning wheel or the mechanical parts thereof, to illustrate the above and (3) the use of the mystics' *zikr* to accompany and even to regulate the various phases of women's work. Ibid., p.161; also

see, the author's 'Sufi Folk Literature and the Expansion of Indian Islam,' in Richard M. Eaton, *Essays in Islam and Indian History*, Oxford University Press, Delhi, 2000, pp. 189-199.

43. Richard M. Eaton, *Sufis of Bijapur*, pp. 288-296.
44. Richard M. Eaton, 'The Political and Religious Authority of the Shrine of Baba Farid,' in Richard M. Eaton, *Essays in Islam and Indian History*, pp. 205-209.
45. The idea had already been advanced that the northward migration of the Jat clans from Sind to the fertile plains of Punjab was accompanied by their transformation from pastoralism to agriculture. This process was facilitated by the availability of the Persian wheel in this area. In keeping with their new status as cultivators and even *zamindars*, the Jats adopted the ideology of Sikhism. Irfan Habib, 'Jatts of Punjab and Sind' in Harbans Singh and N. Gerald Barrier, Eds., *Essays in Honour of Dr. Ganda Singh*, Punjabi University, Patiala, 1976, pp. 92-103.
46. Richard M. Eaton, 'The Political and Religious Authority of the Shrine of Baba Farid,' pp. 220-224.
47. Richard M. Eaton, 'Court of Man, Court of God: Local Perceptions of the Shrine of Baba Farid, Pakpattan, Punjab', in Richard M. Eaton, *Essays in Islam and Indian History*, pp. 225-246.
48. P.M. Currie, *The Shrine and Cult of Muinuddin Chishti of Ajmer*, Oxford University Press, Delhi, 1989, pp. 141-163.
49. S. Liyaqat H. Moini, *The Chishti Shrine of Ajmer: Pirs, Pilgrims and Practices*, Publication Scheme, Jaipur, 2004, pp. 127-214.
50. The *vikalatnamas* in the Murad-Masud Collection have enabled the author to map the process by which the position of custodians (*khuddam*) was institutionalized during the reign of Aurangzeb and followed in the subsequent centuries. The devotee, both Muslim and Hindu, signed a pledge or deed by which he attached himself (along with his family, relatives, clansmen and followers) to a particular custodian (*khadim*). The latter assisted the devotee in performing the pilgrimage and, in return, received remuneration (*nazar o niyaz*) for his services. In case the devotee was not able to visit personally, the *khadim* acted as his representative (*vakil*) during the pilgrimage, offered prayers on behalf of the devotee and sent the symbolic gifts (*tabarruk*) to him through a messenger. Moini, op. cit., pp. 114-115.
51. Ibid., pp. 102-113.
52. There has been a fairly long tradition of the Chishti sufis participating in the launching of new Indo-Muslim states that emerged after the disintegration of the Delhi sultanate. For details, see Richard M. Eaton, 'Temple Desecration and Indo-Muslim States,' in *Essays in Islam and Indian History*, pp. 101-104.
53. Ibid., p. 104.
54. John F. Richards, 'The Formulation of Imperial Authority under Akbar and Jahangir,' in Muzaffar Alam and Sanjay Subrahmanyam, Ed., *The Mughal State 1526-1750*, Oxford University Press, Delhi 1998, pp. 132-135.
55. Carl W. Ernst and Bruce B. Lawrence, *Sufi Martyrs of Love: The Chishti Order*

in South Asia and Beyond, Palgrave Macmillan, New York, 2002, pp. 98-101.

56. Tahir Mahmud, 'The Dargah of Saiyyid Salar Masud Ghazi in Bahraich: Legend, Tradition and Reality,' in Christian W. Troll, (Ed.), *Muslim Shrines in India*, Oxford University Press, Delhi, 1989, pp. 24-43; Shahid Amin, 'On Retelling the Muslim Conquest of North India,' in Partha Chatterjee and Anjan Ghosh, (Eds.), *History and the Present*, Permanent Black, New Delhi, pp. 24-43; Marc Gaborieu, 'The Ghazi Miyan Cult in Western Nepal and Northern India,' in M. Waseem, (Ed.), *On Being an Indian Muslim: French Essays on Aspects of Syncretism*, Oxford University Press, Delhi, 2003, pp. 238-263; Kerrin Grafin Schwerin, 'The Cow-Saving Muslim Saint: Elite and Folk Representations of a Tomb Cult in Oudh,' in Mushirul Hasan and Asim Roy, (Eds.), *Living Together Separately: Cultural India in History and Politics*, Oxford University Press, Delhi, 2005, pp. 172-193.
57. Ibid., pp. 11-14.
58. In a painstaking exploration, Lawrence has shown that the early Indian Chishti theorists Hamiduddin Nagauri, Fakhruddin Zarradi, Masud Bakk and Ashraf Jahangir Simnani were direct heirs of Ahmad Ghazzali on the issue of *sama*. All championed the experience of mystic music both for the adepts and beginners. Unlike Ghazzali, they did not demolish the arguments of their opponents. They delineated the benefits which, in their opinion, accrued to the sincere participants in the exercise. Bruce B. Lawrence, 'The Early Chishti Approach to Sama,' in Milton Israel and N.K. Wagle, *Islamic Society and Culture: Essays in Honour of Professor Aziz Ahmad*, Manohar, New Delhi, 1983, p. 89.
59. For example, Shaikh Sulaiman of Taunsa urged his followers to resist the expansion of Sikh power in Punjab. When Khwaja Hasan Nizami visited some Islamic countries under the auspices of Halqah-i-Mashaikh and met a variety of Muslim circles, he was placed under surveillance by the British government. Zauqi Shah, influenced by the confrontational politics, adopted a anti-Hindi polemic in line with the Jamaat-i-Islami and became an active member of the Muslim League.
60. Ernst and Lawrence, op. cit., pp. 134,142.
61. Ibid., pp. 143-145.
62. Riazul Islam, *Sufism in South Asia: Impact on Fourteenth Century Muslim Society*, Oxford University Press, Karachi, 2002, pp. 170-174.
63. In the Baghdad-Khurasan-Bukhara region, a large number of mystics emerged from the ranks of mercantile and artisanal classes. Therefore, we come across a ubiquity of professional surnames among them e.g. goldsmith, dealer in perfumes, banker, merchant, pedlar, copyist, goldsmith, jeweller, butcher, blacksmith, fuller, weaver, bleacher, dyer, tanner etc. In South Asia prominent mystics came from the social elite like the Saiyyids. Those who belonged to inferior social backgrounds could acquire some local fame, but could not enjoy widespread popularity. Owing to the stigma attached to lowly professions, they did not use the suffix indicating their professional occupation. Ibid., pp. 198-202.
64. Ibid., pp. 269-271.
65. It is Muhammad Habib who is of the opinion that "Muslim mysticism is a

post-graduate creed." Once Shaikh Qutbuddin Bakhtiyar Kaki told Shaikh Farid, "An illiterate mystic falls a prey in the hands of the devil." As quoted in Khaliq Ahmad Nizami, *The Life and Times of Shaikh Farid-ud-din Ganj-i-Shakar*, p. 82.

66. For detail see David Gilmartin and Bruce B. Lawrence, 'Introduction' in David Gilmartin and Bruce B. Lawrence, eds., *Beyond Turk and Hindu: Rethinking Religious Identities in Islamicate South Asia*, New Delhi, India Research Press, 2002; Richard M. Eaton, 'Introduction' in Richard M. Eaton, ed., *India's Islamic Traditions, 711-1750*, Oxford University Press, Delhi, 2003; Rafiuddin Ahmed, ed., *Understanding the Bengal Muslims: Interpretative Essays*, New Delhi, Oxford University Press, 2001; Asim Roy, *Islam in South Asia: A Regional Perspective*, South Asian Publishers, New Delhi, 1996; Mushirul Hasan and Asim Roy, eds., *Living Together Separately: Cultural India in History and Politics.*, New Delhi, Oxford University Press, 2005; M. Waseem, ed., *On Becoming an Indian Muslim: French Essays on Aspects of Syncretism*, Oxford University Press, Delhi, 2003 ; a link between the great Arabic and Persian traditions on the one hand and little vernacular traditions of the singing sufi poetry have been discussed by Shemeem Burney Abbas in her *The Female Voice in Sufi Ritual: Devotional Practices of Pakistan and India*, Oxford University Press, Karachi, 2003.
67. Shemeem Burney Abbas, op. cit., p. 10.
68. It was Marshall G.S. Hodgson who coined the term *Islamicate* that refers to the broad expanse of Africa and Asia that was influenced by Muslim rulers but not restricted to the practice of Islam as a religion. Marshall G.S. Hodgson, *The Venture of Islam: Conscience and History in a World Civilization*, Chicago University Press, Chicago, 1974, pp. 57-60 as quoted in David Gilmartin and Bruce B. Lawrence, eds., *Beyond Turk and Hindu: Rethinking Religious Identities in Islamicate South Asia*, p. 2.
69. Carl W. Ernst, *The Shambhala Guide to Sufism*, Shambhala South Asia Editions, Boston, 2000, pp. 173-74.
70. Attar Singh, *Secularization of Modern Punjabi Poetry*, Punjab Prakashan, Chandigarh, 1988, p. 23.
71. Annemarie Schimmel, *Mystical Dimension of Islam*, Sang-E- Meel Publications, Lahore, 2003, (first published in 1975), p. 434.
72. Najm Hosain Syed, *Recurrent Patterns in Punjabi Poetry*, City Press, Karachi, 2003, (first published in 1968), pp. 20, 21, and 32.
73. Ibid., p. 22.
74. Attar Singh, *Secularization of Modern Punjabi Poetry*, p. 33.
75. Shemeem Burney Abbas, *The Female Voice in Sufi Ritual: Devotional Practices of Pakistan and India*, p. 85.
76. Carl W. Ernst and Bruce B. Lawrence, *Sufi Martyrs of Love: The Chishti Order in South Asia and Beyond*, Palgrave Macmillan, New York, 2002, pp. 138-44.
77. Sant Singh Sekhon, *A History of Panjabi Literature*, Vol. II, Punjabi University, Patiala, 1996, p. 21.
78. Lajwanti Rama Krishna, *Panjabi Sufi Poets, A.D. 1460-1900*, Ashajanak Publications, New Delhi, 1973. p. 1.
79. Ibid., p. 8 and 20.

80. Ibid., pp. 5-10. It reminds us of Peter Brown's identification of the 'two-tier' theory of religion, critiqued by Barbara D. Metcalf. According to the theory 'rational monotheism is a higher form of religion and therefore maps onto the upper classes and the educated; superstition and syncretism represent more primitive religion and are presumed characteristic of the humble. By this reckoning, the upper classes are good Muslims; the rural and uneducated Muslims, more immersed in local cultures, are taken as deviant...' Barbara D. Metcalf, *Islamic Contestations: Essays on Muslims in India and Pakistan*, Oxford University Press, Delhi, 2004, p. 204.
81. Lajwanti Rama Krishna, *Panjabi Sufi Poets, A.D. 1460-1900*, p. 10.
82. S.R. Sharda, *Sufi Thought: Its Development in Punjab and its Impact on Panjabi Literature from Baba Farid to AD 1850*, Munshiram Manoharlal, New Delhi, 1998, (first published in 1975), pp. xxiv, 250 and 259.
83. Annemarie Schimmel, *Mystical Dimension of Islam*, p. xvii.
84. Ibid., p. 384-386.
85. The dedications cited in the beginning of the second volume of his book speak of Shuja Alhaq's exercise as venturesome. The first dedication reads: "This work was undertaken when one was living in the United Kingdom. One has this feeling that it could not have been written anywhere else in the world. It is therefore dedicated to the peoples and seasons of the United Kingdom." The second dedication reads: "And finally, this book is dedicated to each of those countless individuals whose soul yearns to relate and unite with all humankind but cannot do so due to the conditioning and confinement in the boundaries of the religion in which s/he is born." Shuja Alhaq, *A Forgotten Vision: Study of Human Spirituality in the Light of the Islamic Tradition*, Vol. I, Vikas Publishing House, New Delhi, 1997.
86. Ibid., p. 46.
87. Ibid., pp. 29-50.
88. Shuja Alhaq, *A Forgotten Vision: Study of Human Spirituality in the Light of the Islamic Tradition*, Vol. II, p. 368.
89. I.H. Qureshi, *The Muslim Community of the Indo-Pakistan Subcontinent (610-1947)*, Bureau of Composition, Compilation and Translation, University of Karachi, Karachi, Reprint, 2003, p. 66.
90. Shuja Alhaq, *A Forgotten Vision: Study of Human Spirituality in the Light of the Islamic Tradition*, Vol. II, p. 369.
91. I.H. Qureshi, *The Muslim Community of the Indo-Pakistan Subcontinent (610-1947)*; Aziz Ahmad, *Studies in Islamic Culture in the Indian Environment*, Oxford University Press, Delhi, 1999, (first published in 1964), p. 74.
92. Shuja Alhaq, *A Forgotten Vision: Study of Human Spirituality in the Light of the Islamic Tradition*, Vol. II, p. 178-192.
93. Ibid., pp. 213-219.
94. Ibid., p. 224.
95. Ibid., p. 236 and 377.
96. Ibid., p. 380.
97. Lajwanti Rama Krishna, *Panjab Sufi Poets, A.D. 1460-1900*, p. 154.
98. K.N. Panikkar, *Culture, Ideology, Hegemony: Intellectuals and Social Consciousness in Colonial India*, Tulika, New Delhi, Reprint 1998, (first published in 1995), p. 109.

99. John Bodnar, *Remaking America: Public Memory, Commemoration, and Patriotism in the Twentieth century*, Princeton, N.J., 1992, pp. 14, 247 as quoted in Alon Confino, 'Collective Memory and Cultural History: Problems of Method', *American Historical Review*, December 1997, p. 1401.
100. J.G. Merquior, *The Veil and the Mask: Essays on Culture and Ideology*, Routledge & Kegan Paul, London, 1979, p. 42.

PART I

Sufi Mystics

1

Advent of Sufism in Medieval Punjab

A Narrative of its Historical Role

Iqtidar Husain Siddiqui

In the present exercise, an effort is being made to examine the cultural role performed by the sufis and their fraternities (*silsilahs*) in Punjab during the medieval period. Since the subject is vast, I would confine my attempt to the contribution of sufis in the making of a pluralist society and a composite culture from the eleventh century to the first half of the sixteenth century A.D. The discussion is preceded by a brief reference to the rise of sufism in Islam and the development of two different traditions, called the 'Maghrabi' and 'Ajami' respectively, before it came to India. Like in other religious traditions, sufism in Islam is the outgrowth of mystic speculation, but rooted in the Quran and the Sunna (Prophetic tradition). By the tenth century AD the appeal of sufism grew, so that the sufi way of life and intellectual currents became equally essential elements in Islamic religious thought. All this happened in the face of increasing materialism and consumerism in the Muslim society. In an attempt to prevent the Muslims from turning wholly materialistic in their approach to life, sufism aimed at a state of piety and perfection. This was to be achieved by man through purification of his inner self of the greed for worldly pleasures and adoption of moderation in life. Selfless service rendered by the early sufis to people, irrespective of creed and social identity, increased their popularity.

As for the above mentioned two different traditions of sufism, the Maghrabi tradition was established by Shaikh Abdul Qasim bin Muhammad al-Junaid of Baghdad (d. 910 AD). Junaid was an orthodox exponent of the 'sober' type of sufism. But, like other sufis, he also believed in the possibility of achieving the mystical communication with God.[1] His followers followed orthodox sufism and opposed syncretism that had become a distinct feature of the Ajami tradition, which was represented by the Qalandars and also, to some extent, by the Chishtis. The Chishtis adopted some non-Islamic practices that were not found at variance with the Islamic canonical law (*shariat*), but helpful in heightening their cosmic consciousness. It is also worth stressing that their stay in the midst of people, their concern for the well being of mankind and their service to all those whom they found in distress, distinguished them from the mystics of other traditions. Their introduction of public kitchen (*langar*) to provide food to all and sundry was an important contribution to our cultural heritage. In Punjab, the followers of both the traditions settled and established their hospices. This fundamental fact goes a long way in developing our understanding on the nature of sufism in medieval Punjab.

Migration of Early Sufis to Punjab

Punjab appears to have had precedence over other regions of the Indian subcontinent in receiving the first sufi of eminence. It was sometime in the later half of the eleventh century that a scholarly sufi, Shaikh Husain Zinjani, was sent by his spiritual preceptor (*pir*), Shaikh Muhammad bin Hasan al-Khattali, from Ghazni to Lahore for catering to the spiritual needs of the people there. Jinjani followed the mystical school of Junaid. On his death, his mission was continued by Shaikh Ali bin Usman Hujwiri, another disciple of Khattali. Their presence not only popularized sufism but also gave rise to the cult of the shrine (*dargah*) in the region.[2] Later on, even the villages around Lahore attracted dervishes who lived in the midst of people and earned their livelihood by carrying on cultivation like their fellow inhabitants.[3] These early sufis promoted spiritual temper and accomplished a high degree of reconciliation between the spiritual and worldly life.

A word may be added here about *Kashf-ul-Mahjub*, the first treatise on sufism in Persian, which was authored by Hujwiri. Written in Lahore during the eleventh century, it gave the city an edge over the urban centres of Iran and Central Asia, as regards the Persian literature on sufism was concerned.[4] The writer describes the history of sufism and biographical details of the sufis who flourished from early times down to his own age. The popular traditions about the early sufis, as incorporated by the compiler, inspired the sufis in every age and moulded their personalities. As no mention is made of the sufi orders (*silsilahs*) and the eminent sufis are identified by their affiliation to a master who followed a particular tradition developed by some early sufi, the *silsilah* organization seems to have been a later development. For instance, Hujwiri calls his own mentor (*pir*) the follower of Junaid Baghdadi in his way of sobriety, in contrast to that of Shaikh Bayazid Bistami's way of intoxication.[5]

The first sufi order to be introduced in Punjab was the Gazrun *silsilah* of Iranian mystics. Shaikh Safiuddin Gazruni arrived in Uch and established his hospice (*khanqah*) there sometimes towards the close of the twelfth century AD. Though he appears to have gained popularity among the local people, as the legends about him suggest, yet none of his spiritual successors could leave any lasting influence. They continued to maintain his shrine (*dargah*) as it had become a place of visitation. It was one of the popular shrines in the fourteenth century.[6] Unlike Shaikh Safiuddin Gazruni, Shaikh Bahauddin Zakariya, a Punjab-born sufi, introduced the Suhrawardi *silsilah* that exercised a lasting influence on the region as well as the Indian subcontinent.

Rethinking on the Suhrawardi Order

Shaikh Bahauddin Zakariya (1182-1162) was born in Punjab in a family of scholars. Having completed his education at Kot Aror, he left for foreign lands in order to pursue higher education. He paid visits to the seats of learning and benefited from scholars of different countries. In Baghdad, he visited Shaikh Shihabuddin Suhrawardi[7] and became his disciple (*murid*). Found sincere in his love of God and piety, the great Suhrawardi Shaikh instructed him in esoteric sciences and conferred upon him the spiritual robe (*khirqa*) along with the permission to enroll disciples as a sufi master (*khilafat*) after just seventeen days. This caused envy among the senior disciples of the Shaikh. They submitted to him:

> We have been in service for several years, yet we have not gained such favours; the Hindi (Indian) came and got Shaikhi (the status of a shaikh) along with so many other favours within such a short time.

The Shaikh replied:

> You brought wet wood that does not easily catch fire, but Zakariya brought dry wood which burns into flames when a single breath is blown on it.[8]

Shaikh Bahauddin Zakariya was allowed to return to India the same day and asked to settle in Multan. In this town, his hospice (*khanqah*) soon become a popular sufi center both for the Indians and foreigners. An erudite scholar of religious sciences, he performed the combined role of an interpreter of canonical law (*mujtahid*), teacher and sufi Shaikh. The little relevant evidence available in miscellaneous sources shows that besides the elite, even the rustics like the Afghans[9] and toilers like the Kambos[10] could become his disciples and benefit from their association with him. His erudition, devotion to God and strict adherence to the canonical law (*shariat*) contributed to his fame and popularity even beyond the frontiers of India. The aspirants for truth arrived from Khurasan and Central Asia to seek spiritual guidance and joined the circle of his disciples.[11] Since the city of Multan had already emerged as an entrepot of long-distance commerce, it received foreign merchants who moved in caravans between different countries. They visited him and sought his blessings for safety and success in their enterprise. They offered unasked gifts in cash and kind (*futuh*) that constituted a permanent source of income for the hospice.

Some words are in order about Shaikh Bahauddin Zakariya's relations with the Delhi sultans and members of the ruling elite. As an ardent follower of the Prophet, the Shaikh could not keep himself away from the contemporary rulers. In Punjab and Sind, people had suffered miserably first at the hands of Jalaluddin Khwarizm Shah and then at the hands of the Mongol invaders, who entered the region in the former's pursuit from 1221 and 1224. Nasiruddin Qubacha, the ruler of Multan, failed to defend them against the foreign invaders. As a result, the Shaikh lost confidence in Qubacha and, along with the judge (*qazi*) of Multan, wrote a letter to Sultan Shamsuddin Iltutmish of Delhi, inviting him to occupy Multan and Sind territories. The letter was intercepted and presented to Qubacha. The Shaikh admitted that he had written it under divine inspiration. He was not harmed but the *qazi* was put to death.[12] Having conquered Punjab and Sind in 1228, Iltutmish seems to have made a large land grant to Shaikh Bahauddin Zakariya and appointed him the Shaikh-ul-Islam. His function was to manage the *khanqah*, which was maintained by the state for providing comfort and facilities to the travellers. The fortress-like *khanqah* of Multan, built on the crest of one of the two hills, seems to have been constructed under the order of Iltutmish about this time. The state charity houses, which were established along the highways at different places for the benefit of travellers and other needy people, were known as *khanqah* in these parts, whereas in the Arab lands they were called *ribats*.[13]

Doubtless, Shaikh Bahauddin Zakariya was the richest sufi of India, yet he strictly followed the traditions of piety and righteousness, believing that services rendered to human beings meant the service of God. He not only looked after the travellers who arrived in Multan, but also showed concern for the security and well being of the people in Multan and the area around his spiritual domain.[14] On the Mongol irruption in Central Asia, there was an exodus of Muslims to north-western India and all of them travelled to different places via Multan. Being a far sighted man, the Shaikh kept a store of food grains and money ready to meet any emergency situation. At times, even the governor (*wali*) was compelled by the scarcity of food grains to seek help from the Shaikh. The Shaikh did not hesitate to provide food grains to him also.[15] In short, the Shaikh showed great farsightedness by accumulating wealth and maintaining granaries, because the circumstances were critical and conservation of resources was the need of the hour. In 1241, when the Mongols laid siege to Multan and the city was found vulnerable, the Shaikh negotiated with the Mongols through Shamsuddin Kurt, the Mongol ally from Herat, paid a huge amount of money and saved Multan from destruction. The Mongols left Multan and sacked Lahore before they returned to their base in Ghazni.[16]

Shaikh Bahauddin Zakariya also built a college (*madrasah*) where students were admitted for higher education. Some highly accomplished teachers were employed to impart instructions in Islamic sciences. The Shaikh himself delivered lectures and rewarded the teachers with money if he was impressed with their work.[17] He was also not niggardly in assisting people with cash, but he was certainly opposed to sycophancy and parasitic tendency. Some contemporary sufis are reported to have been critical of the possession of wealth by the Shaikh. Shaikh Nizamuddin Auliya made a brief mention of the letter written by Shaikh Jalaluddin Tabrezi to the Shaikh expressing his disapproval of the possession of wealth by a sufi. But the latter Chishti sources exaggerate the controversy between Shaikh Bahauddin Zakariya and Shaikh Hamiduddin Sufi Nagauri over it. In an attempt to glorify the saintly qualities possessed by the early Chishti sufis, they contend that the Suhrawardi Shaikh had greater love for wealth than for spirituality.[18] Their views also find echo in several modern works. Writing with a pro-Chishti bias, Khaliq Ahmad Nizami maintains:

> Contemporary mystic thought could not reconcile itself to the idea of accumulating wealth and at the same time claiming to be the guardian of the spiritual welfare of the people ... Shaikh Bahauddin Zakariya made every possible effort to convince his critics that it was not so much the wealth as its improper use that was detrimental to spiritual progress, but they stuck to their views and repeatedly told him, two opposites cannot meet at one place.[19]

In short, a correct understanding of the role of a great man in history is not possible without the knowledge of the circumstances in which he lived and worked. With improvement in political conditions under Sultan Ghiasuddin Balban (1266-1287), Shaikh Bahauddin Zakariya's son and spiritual successor, Shaikh Sadruddin Arif, was relieved of all worries caused by frequent Mongol invasions. Balban was successful in defending the north-western frontier against the Mongols. Therefore, the Shaikh did not feel the need to accumulate wealth for meeting emergency situations. It is said that he had spent on the needy seven lakh *tankas* that he had received as his share in the wealth bequeathed by his father.[20] Shaikh Sadruddin Arif's son and spiritual successor, Shaikh Ruknuddin Abul Fateh, maintained his grandfather's and father's traditions. Ziauddin Barani who belonged to the Chishti *silsilah* pays him a rich tribute in these words:

> Shaikh Ruknuddin (Suhrawardi of Multan) performed well the function of *mashaikh* (sufi saints). The entire population of the Indus valley from Multan (region) and Uchh and below became attached to his sanctified place. They paid allegiance to him; many ulama of the city (Multan) as well as the region of India had turned his devout disciples (*murids*).[21]

Besides Multan, another center of the Suhrawardi *silsilah* was Uch. Shaikh Bahauddin Zakariya sent one of his disciples, Shaikh Jalaluddin Surkh Bukhari, an immigrant from Bukhara, to work there as his spiritual representative (*khalifa*). Shaikh Jalaluddin Surkh Bukhari popularized the Suhrawardi *silsilah* in southern Punjab and the region of Sind. His son and grandson, Shaikh Kabiruddin Bukhari and Syed Jalaluddin Bukhari, the latter popularly known as Makhdum-i-Jahanian Jahangasht were the *khalifas* of Shaikh Bahauddin Zakariya's son and grandson, Shaikh Sadruddin Arif and Shaikh Ruknuddin Abul Fateh respectively. The statement made by Makhdum-i-Jahanian Jahangasht about the Suhrawardi hospice in Uch shows that a fairly large number of eminent scholars were included in the circles of the Suhrawardi sufis and they considerably added to the popularity of the *silsilah*.[22] Like the Shaikhs of Multan, the Suhrawardis of Uch maintained close relations with the Delhi sultans and received villages in land grant for the maintenance of their hospices.[23] The most famous Suhrawardi sufi of Uch was Makhdum-i-Jahanian Jahangasht (1308-1384), who had acquired widespread fame as a world-trotter. He was a *khalifa* of Shaikh Ruknuddin Abul Fateh. The latter instructed him in the popular sciences, besides esoteric subjects. He was particularly inspired to cultivate the noble qualities of modesty, humility and compassion to purify himself of worldly desires. Once Makhdum-i-Jahanian Jahangasht told his disciples how his mentor's counseling saved him from being attached to the world:

> Sultan Muhammad (bin Tughlaq) appointed this helpless one (i.e., the Shaikh himself) Shaikh-ul-Islam in Siwistan (modern Sehwan} and entrusted the charges of forty *khanqahs* (royal charity houses) to me (in Sind province). Shaikh Qutb Alam Rukn al-Haque wad-din asked me: Relinquish (the office) and go for *haj* (pilgrimage to Mecca). He thus brought me out of the mirth. I relinquished the office. No body knows what arrogance I might have otherwise had.[24]

As ordered by his Shaikh, Makhdum-i-Jahanian performed *haj* and also visited the famous centres of learning and culture in the western and Central Asia. On his return to India during the reign of Sultan Firuz Shah Tughluq (1351-1388), he acquired wide popularity. The sultan went out of his way to cultivate friendly relations with him. The sultan received him with respect whenever he visited Delhi. On the Shaikh's recommendation, the sultan granted stipends, fixed maintenance allowances and land grants to deserving Muslims and Hindus.[25] After his demise (1384) the cities of Multan and Uch became famous for the shrines (*dargahs*) of the Suhrawardi sufis.

Chishti Merger of Austerity and Vernacularity

Punjab also has the privilege of having been the birth place of the first great Chishti saint, Shaikh Fariduddin Ganj-i-Shakar (1175-1265), who was popularly known as Baba Farid. A word may be added here about the early Chishti sufis who arrived in India from abroad before we discuss Shaikh Farid's role in enriching the cultural heritage of the Indian subcontinent in general and Punjab in particular. Of Shaikh Farid's spiritual predecessors, Khwaja Muinuddin Chishti, who lies buried in Ajmer, was the founder of the Chishti *silsilah* in India. His disciple and spiritual successor (*khalifa*), Khwaja Qutbuddin Bakhtiyar Kaki, also a foreign immigrant to Delhi, was the spiritual preceptor (*pir*) of Shaikh Farid. Biographical details in the contemporary and other standard sources about them are scanty. Later writers have incorporated popular legends about both of them which were current in their times. Even the account furnished by Amir Khurd in the *Siyar-ul-Auliya,* a late fourteenth century work, is not free from hagiographic embroidery. His statement about the date of Khwaja Muinuddin Chishti's arrival in India has been accepted by modern scholars uncritically. According to Amir Khurd, the Shaikh having come to India, settled down in Ajmer under the rule of Rai Pithora when there was no Muslim population and that he lived in an uncongenial atmosphere.[26] Many popular legends about the miraculous power displayed by the Shaikh have been fabricated on the basis of Amir Khurd's account. This has, however, contributed to the popularity of his *dargah* in Ajmer. The supernatural aura that has surrounded the saint and his *dargah* needs to be looked at dispassionately. The modern scholars have portrayed him either by exaggerating the facts or belittling the importance of his historical role.[27] The relevant evidence contained in the mystical discourses (*malfuzat*) of Shaikh Hamiduddin Nagauri, one of his spiritual successors, reveals that like other emigrant sufi saints, Khwaja Muinuddin Chishti arrived in Delhi and thence proceeded to Ajmer during the reign of Sultan Shamsuddin Iltutmish, after the Rajput resistance in the region had been subdued.[28] Another standard source is the *Tarikh-i-Muhammadi,* compiled by Muhammad Bihamad Khani in 1446 A.D. The compiler appears to have carefully sifted historical material from miscellaneous sources about the early sultans, poets and sufis who flourished in India. In the section related to the sufi saints, he states:

> During the turmoil caused by Chingiz Khan's invasion of Central Asia, Muinuddin Sijzi migrated from Khurasan to India and settled in Ajmer, one of the fortified places in the country. He had already distinguished himself in piety and devotion (to God). He arrived in India during the early years of Sultan Shamsuddin Iltutmish's reign.[29]

The relevant evidence contained in the *Fawaid-ul-Fuad* tends to suggest that Khwaja Muinuddin Chishti was a man of wide sympathies and compassion. His teaching had a transforming effect on his disciples.[30] But it is also worth recalling that he was a foreigner and, as such, not conversant with Indian dialects. Since there was a communication gap between him and the local people, his popularity and influence must have remained confined to the foreign immigrants in the provincial army and government officials posted in Ajmer. As a matter of fact, the greatness of Shaikh Farid and his *khalifa* Shaikh Nizamuddin Auliya turned his and Khwaja Qutbuddin Bakhtiyar Kaki's shrines into popular *dargahs* in the Indian subcontinent. As they happened to be the spiritual predecessors of Shaikh Farid and Shaikh Nizamuddin Auliya, the later Chishtis and their devotees also had to cherish their memories and pay homage at their *dargahs* in Ajmer and Delhi. It is noteworthy that Shaikh Farid and Shaikh Nizamuddin Auliya were Indian-born sufis and their mother tongue was either Punjabi or Hindi, which were spoken in Punjab and Delhi. Like the Suhrawardis of Multan, they had a tremendous appeal among the local Indians.

Shaikh Farid (1175-1265) was born in the town of Kahtwal, a dependency of the territorial unit of Multan. His parents, being religious minded persons, influenced him deeply. Moreover, he seems to have had a mystic bent of mind since his childhood.[31] Fond of learning, he acquired authoritative knowledge of the popular sciences and then became the disciple of Khwaja Qutbuddin Bakhtiyar Kaki. Impressed by his sincerity, his mentor (*pir*) conferred upon him the authorization to enroll disciples (*khilafat*) in a short time. After his initiation into the Chishti *silsilah*, he resided first in Hansi (Haryana) and then moved to Ajodhan which was a small town, but situated along the highway linking Multan with Delhi. Being a man of religion and love, Shaikh Farid performed severe spiritual exercises, including those of Hindu yogis, such as breath control.[32] He lived a life of extreme austerity, although at times he received unasked offerings (*futuh*) that he distributed among people on the same day. Nothing was saved for the morrow, because he believed that saving money clashed with his concept of trust in God's mercy (*tawakkul*). He had become an exemplar in this regard. Likewise, he was known for his humanism and concern for general good. Praising his mentor's trust in God, Shaikh Nizamuddin Auliya told his visitors:

> When Sultan Nasiruddin Mahmud led the expedition towards Multan, he passed via Ajodhan. Ghiasuddin (Balban), who was known as Ulugh Khan at that time, came from the royal army camp to pay visit to the Shaikh. He brought cash and four documents. Each document contained the grant of one village for the Shaikh. As he placed the cash and the documents before the Shaikh, the latter asked: "What are these?" Ulugh Khan said in reply, "This is the cash and four documents, each regarding the grant of one village; the cash is for the dervishes and the four villages for the Shaikh." Thereupon, the Shaikh smiled and said, "Leave the cash with me, it will be spent on the dervishes but take back the documents because many other people need them."[33]

Some words are in order about the Shaikh Farid's humanism. As service of mankind had become a life mission with him, he was opposed to slavery. Some other sufis appear to have sympathized with the slaves and a few of them nominated the slaves as their successors in preference to their sons.[34] But Shaikh Farid seems to have been the first sufi to show his opposition to the institution of slavery. He did not own any slave and encouraged his rich disciples to manumit their slaves. The following incident sheds light on the Shaikh's attitude towards slavery. Once, Qazi Sharafuddin, the grandson of Qazi Hamiduddin Nagauri, decided to travel from Nagaur to Ajodhan for paying a visit to his mentor, Shaikh Farid. He had purchased a youthful slave girl for one hundred *tankahs*. The slave girl cooked victuals and handed them wrapped in a piece of cloth to her master. This packet was meant as a gift for Shaikh Farid. In Ajodhan, Nagauri presented her gift to Shaikh Farid and mentioned her name. At once Shaikh Farid prayed for her freedom from slavery. Nagauri thought that his mentor's prayers were always answered by God and that she would gain freedom. He also thought that it was better for him to sell her without delay and save himself from monetary loss. Soon after he realized that if he granted her freedom himself he would be able to please his *pir*. He went to the *pir* and told him that he had decided to grant her freedom. Shaikh Farid was besides himself with joy.[35] Shaikh Nizamuddin Auliya, his spiritual successor, followed him strictly in this regard.[36] It may be added that Shaikh Farid considered woman as equal to man in terms of human rights. He held that men and women were equal in the eyes of God and that only the personal piety of a person was the sole criterion to judge his or her worth and superiority.[37]

Lastly, we may briefly describe Shaikh Farid's attitude towards education and learning. Unlike the sufis of the past, he encouraged his disciples in their pursuit of knowledge. He considered it necessary for a sufi to acquire knowledge of different religious sciences. He himself possessed a collection of books and sometimes read portions from them, while imparting instructions to the disciples. Also interesting is his association with scholars and leading poets.[38] He was himself a poet and composed verses both in Persian language and Punjabi dialect. His extant Punjabi verses, which underline the importance of divine love, enabled the Punjabi language to develop into a vehicle for expressing spiritual philosophy. His Punjabi verses appear to have gained popularity among the Hindus and Muslims even beyond the boundaries of Punjab. The sufis of different regions recited his verses during the course of delivering sermons in order to illustrate some subtle points. We may quote two couplets found in the Persian works composed in Gujarat and Delhi. The fifteenth century sufi of Ahmadabad, Shah Alam Suhrawardi, is reported to have recited the following couplet.[39]

Topi laindi bawli de dey kharhi nilaj
Chooha billi na ma nahin poonjhal pandhey chhaj

Emphasizing the insignificance and transitory nature of wealth and other worldly possessions, Shaikh Rizqullah Mushtaqi quotes the following lines, which had been composed by Shaikh Farid:[40]

Jatt ghar zamin na payi mubiya mubandi tatt
Chito pardesi pahna hi oah nihayi jatt

Of the spiritual successors of Shaikh Farid, only two appear to have outlived their mentor. His son-in-law, Shaikh Badruddin Ishaq, died a few years after his *pir's* death (A.D. 1265). As regards Shaikh Burhanuddin, son of Shaikh Jamaluddin of Hansi, he resided in Hansi but did not enroll disciples out of respect for Shaikh Nizamuddin Auliya, the successor of his master. Shaikh Nizamuddin Auliya, who resided in Delhi, was able to turn the Chishti *silsilah* into a popular spiritual discipline. Unlike the Chishti *silsilah*, the Suhrawardi *silsilah* remained elitist in the sense that only select educated people, who were found capable of having inquisitive perception of religion, were accepted as disciples and trained to act as spiritual guides. It may also be added that the spiritual successors of Shaikh Alauddin Ali Sabir, who was buried in Kaliyar in the life time of his *pir*, seems to have gained much popularity in Punjab. The *khalifa* of Shaikh Alauddin Ali Sabir was Shaikh Shamsuddin Turk who took abode in Panipat and founded the Sabri branch of the Chishti *silsilah*. With the passage of time, the devotees of the shrine of Shaikh Alauddin Ali Sabir at Kaliyar increased in Punjab and the whole of north-western India. His shrine is the second most popular shrine after that of Ajmer in northern India.

Role of Wandering Dervishes

A brief mention may be made of the wandering dervishes, called Qalandars and Juwaliqs, because the way of life adopted by them went a long way in the making of a pluralist society in medieval India. They entered Punjab during the thirteenth century. They discarded rituals and followed an eclectic faith. They belonged to two groups. One was formed by the followers of Shaikh Muhammad Yunus Jamaluddin of Sava (d. 1232), while the other belonged to that of Haidari Qalandars. The Juwaliqs put on leather garments and, in contrast to them, the Haidari Qalandars put on coarse clothes with iron chains.[41] They differed from the sufis with regard to the establishment of a hospice or making a family. They practiced celibacy and depended for their survival on God's mercy. They also shaved their head, beard, moustache and even eye brows. With the exception of a few Qalandars – such as Lal Shahbaz Qalandar of Sehwan in Sind, Abu Bakr Tusi, Ramzan Qalandar and Bu Ali Qalandar of Panipat[42] — the Qalandars and Juvaliqs were uneducated people belonging to the lower strata of society. They were hostile to the sufis who maintained *khanqahs* and, at times, entered into violent conflict with them.[43] It may, however, be pointed out that by the beginning of the thirteenth century, the Qalandari *silsilah* had lost its importance among the social elite of the Muslim community because its followers, with the exception of a few, had walked out on their legacy of renunciation, abstention and discipline. Generally they wandered like vagabonds, consuming Indian hemp or other intoxicants. Influenced by the Nath Panthi Yogis, they wore ear rings, or even passed a thick iron wire (*seekh*) through their male organ and had its ends sealed. They were called sealed with iron wire (*seekh muhr*). As regards the ordinary Muslims and Hindus, they looked upon Qalandars as special recipients of divine grace. The following couplet ascribed to Nam Dev and contained in the Guru Granth Sahib shows how popular they were:

Come God, the Qalandar
Wearing the dress of an Abdal.[44]

In spite of their strange beliefs and practices, it should be conceded that the Qalandars also contributed to the popularity of sufism in India. Their life style had appeal among the masses and it went a long way in bringing Hindus and Muslims closer to each other culturally.

In the fifteenth century the place of the Chishti and Suhrawardi sufis was taken by the followers of the Qadiri *silsalah*. Though the *silsilah* was founded after the death of Shaikh Abdul Qadir Gilani in Baghdad in 1166 AD, it took more than two centuries to be introduced in India. The sack of Baghdad by Hulegu in 1258 was the reason for this delay. Its representatives in Baghdad were either killed or had fled to Egypt and other parts of Africa. However, the first emigrant Qadiri sufi who arrived in India from abroad was Shaikh Muhammad al-Hussaini.[45] He settled in Uch in the beginning of the fifteen century. He and his son, Shaikh Abdul Qadir Sani, succeeded in popularizing the Qadiri *silsilah* in Punjab. Their disciples spread even out side Punjab. The grandson of Abdul Qadir Sani, Shaikh Hamid Qadiri, and the latter's *khalifa* Shaikh Daud Qadiri of Jheni expanded the activities of the *silsilah* and raised its prestige. Before Miyan Mir and Mulla Shah Badakhshi, Shaikh Daud emerged as the most charismatic Qadiri saint who flourished in Punjab since the reign of Sher Shah Sur. He established his *khanqah* near the fort of Shergarh, (Jheni town), brought an extensive tract of land under cultivation and ran a large community kitchen (*langar*) with its income. Twice a year, he distributed all that he had in his *khanqah*. On the death anniversary of Shaikh Abdul Qadir Gilani, money and cooked food was distributed. Thousands of people received money and food in charity. During his stay in this *khanqah*, Abdul Qadir Badauni saw that Akbar's nobles and their soldiers were served food when they were on expedition to the north-western frontier region. Even fodder was supplied from the Shaikh's farm for their animals.[46]

To conclude, the sufis who lived with their disciples in their respective hospices performed an important social role. Their magnanimity and tolerant attitude toward the people, irrespective of birth or creed, paved the way for interaction between the followers of different religious traditions. In fact, they were the pioneers in starting inter-religious dialogues for communal harmony and peace among the followers of different religions, particularly Islam and Hinduism. All this served to illuminate the relevance of sufism to the speculative and intellectual traditions of theosophical learning, giving rise to the Bhakti cult. No history of the development of composite culture and languages – Punjabi, Hindi and Urdu – and making of a pluralist society in Punjab would be complete without reference to the role of the sufis, *khanqahs* and *dargahs*.

NOTES AND REFERENCES

1. Cf. A.J. Arberry, 'Al-Djunaid,' in *Encyclopaedia of Islam* (New Edition), E.J. Brill, Leiden, 1965, Vol. II, p. 6000.
2. Amir Hasan Sijzi was told by Shaikh Nizamuddin Auliya that many saints lay buried in Lahore. The former told the Shaikh that during his stay in Lahore, he visited the graves of several sufi saints including that of Shaikh Husain Zinjani. Thereupon the Shaikh related that Shaikh Husain Zinjani and Ali bin Usman Hujwiri were the disciples of the same *pir* who was the Qutb (celestial pole of sainthood) of the age. Zinjani lived in Lahore for many years. Before his death, his *pir* asked Hujwiri to leave for Lahore and take abode there. The latter submitted that Zinjani was already there. Again the *pir* said to him, "You go to Lahore." Hujwiri travelled to Lahore and reached its vicinity when it was dark and the gates of the city had been closed. When the gates were reopened the following morning, Hujwiri

found people coming out with the bier of Zinjani. Hujwiri took his place in Lahore. Amir Hasan Sijzi, *Fawaid-ul-Fuad,* Malik Sirajuddin and Sons, Lahore, 1966, p. 57.

3. Ibid., pp. 93, 233.
4. Shaikh Ali bin Usman Hujwiri is believed to have arrived in Lahore during the reign of Sultan Ibrahim of Ghazni (r.1058-1099 AD).
5. Amir Hasan Sijzi, *Fawaid-ul-Fuad*, p. 84.
6. Syed Alauddin Asad, *Jami-ul-Ulum* (Malfuzat of Syed Jalaluddin Bukhari Makhdum-i-Jahanian Jahangasht), ed. Qazi Sajjad Hussain, Indian Council of Historical Research, New Delhi, 1987, p. 306.
7. Shaikh Shihabuddin Suhrawardi (1145-1234 AD) gained popularity in the Islamic world on account of his important treatise on practical aspects of sufism. His work, entitled *Awarif-ul-Maarif,* enjoyed wide popularity among the sufis of different orders.
8. Amir Hasan Sijzi, *Fawaid-ul-Fuad*, pp. 71-72.
9. Ibid., p. 15.
10. The Kambos belonged to one of the Hindu castes of Punjab and were either peasants or daily wage earners. They emerged as a new social formation owing to their association with the Suhrawardis of Multan. Their children were educated in the seminary (*madarsa*) founded by Shaikh Bahauddin Zakariya. Cf. Iqtidar Husain Siddiqui, *Mughal Relations with the Indian Ruling Elite*, Munshiram Manoharlal, New Delhi, 1983, pp. 91-94.
11. Syed Alauddin Asad, *Jami-ul-Ulum*, p.409; Abdur Rehman Jami, *Nafhat-ul Uns*, pp.542-45; Shaikh Fazlullah Jamali, *Siyar-ul-Arifin*, Matba Rizvi, Delhi, 1893, p. 110.
12. Amir Hasan, *Fawaid-ul-Fuad*, pp. 206-07.
13. Ibn Battuta, *Ajaib-ul-Asfar*, Urdu tr., Mohammad Husain, Islamabad reprint, 1983, Vol.II, p. 237; Shoaib Firdausi, *Manaqib-ul-Asfiya*, Calcutta, 1895, pp. 134-35; Syed Alauddin Asad,*Jami-ul-Ulum*, pp. 83-84, 257, 454, 455; Abdul Kareem, *Corpus of Bengal Inscriptions*, Dhaka.
14. Amir Hasan Sijzi, *Fawaid-ul-Fuad*, pp. 181-182, 185, 235.
15. Ibid., p. 380.
16. Minhajus Siraj Jurjani, *Tabaqat-i-Nasiri*, English Translation, H.G. Raverty, Oriental Books Corporation, New Delhi, Reprint, 1970, Vol. II, p. 6.
17. Amir Hasan Sijzi, *Fawaid-ul-Fuad*, pp. 378-79.
18. Cf. Amir Khurd, *Siyar-ul Auliya*, (Delhi, 1302 H.), p. 158; Shaikh Muhammad Husaini Gesudaraz is said to have remarked, "The shaikhs of Multan were inclined to accumulate wealth, the sufis of Khurasan were engaged in trade and commerce, whereas our khwajgan (masters) had nothing to do with mundane things, *Jawami-ul-Kilam*,Kanpur, 1356 AH/1937 AD, p. 213.
19. Khaliq Ahmad Nizami, *Some Aspects of Religion and Politics in India during the Thirteenth Century*, Idarah-i-Adabiyat-i-Delli, Second Edition, Delhi, 1974, p. 228.
20. Shaikh Fazlullah Jamali, *Siyar-ul-Arifin*, p. 129.
21. Syed Alauddin Asad, *Jami-ul-Ulum*, p. 306.
22. Ibid., p. 253.
23. Ibid., p. 257.

24. Ibid., pp. 640-649.
25. Amir Khurd, *Siyar-ul-Auliya*, pp. 46-47.
26. Yusuf Husain, *Glimpses of Medieval Indian Culture*, Asia Publishing House, Bombay, 1959, p. 37; Khaliq Ahmad Nizami, *Some Aspects of Religion and Politics in India during the Thirteenth Century*, p. 184; Saiyid Athar Abbas Rizvi, *A History of Sufism in India*, Vol. 1, Munshiram Manoharlal, New Delhi, 1978, pp. 116-18, 122-23.
27. Anonymous, *Surur-us-Sudur*, Ms. No.1361, Habib Ganj Collection, Maulana Azad Library, Aligarh Muslim University, Aligarh, pp. 227-28.
28. Muhammad Bihamad Khani, *Tarikh-i-Muhammadi*, Ms. No.137, British Library, London, p. 140.
29. Amir Hasan Sijzi, *Fawaid-ul-Fuad*, pp. 346, 405.
30. Ibid, p. 209.
31. Cf. Khaliq Ahmad Nizami, *The Life and Times of Shaikh Fariduddin Ganj-i-Shakar*, Idarah-i-Adabiyat-i-Delli, Delhi, Reprint, 1987, p. 26.
32. Amir Hasan Sijzi, *Fawaid-ul-Fuad*, pp. 6-7.
33. Ibid., pp. 125-126.
34. Ibid., p. 171.
35. Ibid., pp. 316-17.
36. Cf. Iqtidar Husain Siddiqui, 'The Attitude of the Chishti Saints Towards Women During the Thirteenth and Fourteenth Centuries' in A.J. Qaisar and S.P. Verma, Ed., *Art and Culture: Nurul Hasan Felicitation Volume*, Publication Scheme, Jaipur, 1995, pp. 92-93.
37. Ibid., pp., 218-219.
38. Cf. *Jumat-i-Shahiya*, Ms. Aftab Collection, No.134, Maulana Azad Library, Aligarh Muslim University, Aligarh, f.101a.
39. Shaikh Rizqullah Mushtaqui, *Waqiat-i-Mushtaqui*, Ed., Iqtidar Husain Siddiqui, Raza Library, Rampur, 2002, p. 216.
40. Cf. Simon Digby, 'Qalandars and Related Groups', *Islam in Asia*, Vol. 1, Ed., Yohanan Friedmann, Jerusalem, 1984, pp. 60-108.
41. They maintained their *khanqahs* and *langar* to feed people. During the month of Ramzan, the *langar* of the Qalandars fed large number of people daily. cf. Hamid Qalandar, *Khair-ul-Majalis*, Ed., K.A. Nizami, Aligarh Muslim University, Aligarh, 1959, p. 85.
42. Amir Hasan Sijzi, *Fawaid-ul-Fuad*, pp. 7,81.
43. Cf. Shaikh Fazlullah Jamali, *Siyar-ul-Arfin*, p. 67.
44. Cf. Max Arthur Macauliffe, *The Sikh Religion*, Vol. VI, S. Chand & Co., New Delhi, (Reprint), 1966, p. 69.
45. Shaikh Abdul Haq Muhaddis Dehlavi, *Akhbar-ul-Akhyar*, Matba Hashimi, AH1280, 1863, p. 202.
46. Abdul Qadir Badauni, *Muntakhab-ut-Tawarikh*, Vol. III, Eng. Tr. Wolseley Haig and B.P. Ambashthya, Academica Asiatica, Patna, 1973, pp. 47-55.

2

'Sons of Bread and Sons of Soul'

Lineal and Spiritual Descendants of Baba Farid and the Issue of Succession

Tanvir Anjum

> Shaikh Nizamuddin Auliya narrates that once he was sitting with Baba Farid and his son, Shaikh Nizamuddin, who was his namesake and served in the army. Pointing towards them, Baba Farid said: "You both are my sons. You [Nizamuddin, the warrior] are my 'son of the bread' (*farzand-i nani*) and you [Shaikh Nizamuddin Auliya] are my 'son of the soul' (*farzand-i jani* or *ruhi*). The statement of Baba Farid, the Chishti sufi Shaikh of the thirteenth century, implied that Nizamuddin was his successor, but by lineage, whereas Shaikh Nizamuddin Auliya was his spiritual successor.

In recent times, scholarly attempts have been made to explore the manner in which the spiritual legacy of a Shaikh was transmitted after his demise to the next generation. It has been observed that there were two claimants to his spiritual legacy, disciples and descendants. The most accomplished disciple (*khalifa*) inherited the spiritual authority (*wilayat*) and this transmission was symbolized by the transference of the Shaikh's insignia (*amanat* or *tabarrukat*) to the successor. The spiritual charisma of the Shaikh was also transmitted both to his burial site and his lineal descendants. The latter not only tended the grave, but also fostered a lasting cult of the Shaikh. In fact, the most closely and most directly related descendant of the Shaikh was recognized as the head of the community which lived at the shrine. This man, who was known as the *sajjadah nishin*, was believed to represent the saint on earth and to symbolize the saint's continued activity and interest in the lives of his devotees. He did not perform any administrative duties at the shrine. But, acting as a figurehead, he presided over several rituals which were periodically held at the shrine. He was the recipient of a considerable reverence from the devotees as well as substantial land grants from the contemporary rulers. He claimed a share, along with the custodians (*khuddam*) in the offerings which were made at the shrine by the large number of pilgrims. As the titular head of the shrine, he was often called the Diwan, but the office itself did not carry overtones of the spiritual legacy of the Shaikh. On the death of prominent Chishti Shaikhs, we encounter conflicts between the descendants and disciples, because both tried to secure the entire spiritual legacy of the Shaikh for themselves. In actual practice, the descendants failed to inherit the spiritual domain (*wilayat*) for themselves, while the disciples failed to gain the control of the shrine. In modern times, the descendants themselves have been involved in protracted litigation with a view to acquire the office of the *sajjadah nishin*, which carried enormous political clout, social prestige and economic privileges.

The issue of spiritual succession is quite crucial in sufism. Generally, the sufi Shaikhs used to grant spiritual succession (*khilafat*) to a few or more of their disciples and, thus, authorized them to enroll further disciples, and hence, disseminate the teachings of their order (*silsilah*) But the criterion of granting *khilafat* to a disciple was his spiritual excellence. Then, from among the *khulafa* (spiritual successors or the disciples who were authorized by their preceptors to enroll disciples and impart spiritual training and instruction to the people), spiritually the most accomplished one was designated as the principal spiritual successor, or the next head of his *silsilah* (spiritual lineage or initiatic genealogy). However, the disciples of a sufi Shaikh at times included their own sons, grandsons or sons-in-law, but their spiritual succession was based on their spiritual excellence, and not on the grounds of their blood, lineage or matrimonial/familial relationship.

During the thirteenth century India, the institution of *sajjadah nishin* (hereditary succession for the custodianship of a sufi shrine) emerged. Its centre of gravity was the living *sajjadah nishin*, who was generally the hereditary successor or lineal descendant of a sufi Shaikh and also a custodian of his ancestor's shrine. Though Baba Farid had appointed Shaikh Nizamuddin Auliya as his spiritual successor during his life-time, his lineal descendants assumed the guardianship of his shrine in Ajodhan after his demise, and over time, came to represent the religious/spiritual authority, accompanied by political influence and economic power. The present paper examines the origin of the institution of *sajjadah nishin* in Ajodhan, which started in the wake of Baba Farid's death in 1265. It also explores the patterns of spiritual succession among the early Chishtis in Persia, and later in India during the thirteenth and fourteenth centuries, the origin of the practice of *sajjadah nishin* among the descendants of Baba Farid and the issue of maintenance and upkeep of Baba Farid's *jamaat khana* (a sufi dwelling having a spacious hall where the sufi Shaikh and his disciples lived together, received visitors and held discussions) after his demise.

Coming back to the issue of spiritual succession, among the early Chishtis of Persia, one comes across both types of succession patterns, that is, when a disciple having no blood relationship with his preceptor spiritually succeeded him and when a disciple-son was designated as a spiritual successor. However, in both the cases, merit had prevailed. Khwaja Abu Ishaq Shami, the first Chishti, who was a disciple of Khwaja Abu Dinawari, was succeeded by his most accomplished disciple, Khwaja Abu Ahmad ibn Farasnafah Chishti. Khwaja Abu Ahmad was, however, succeeded by his son Khwaja Abu Muhammad Chishti,[1] who was in turn succeeded by his son Khwaja Abu Yusuf Chishti.[2] Khwaja Abu Yusuf was succeeded by his son Khwaja Maudud Chishti.[3] Nonetheless, Khwaja Maudud's spiritual successor, Haji Sharif Zandani, was not his son or relative. Similarly, Haji Sharif's successor, Khwaja Usman Harwani, was also not related to his preceptor through lineage.

Early Chishti Precedents

After the introduction of Chishti *silsilah* in India by Khwaja Usman Harwani's spiritual successor (*khalifah*), Khwaja Muinuddin Chishti of Ajmer, there is no instance of a son or a grandson or a close relative becoming a principal spiritual successor of a Chishti Shaikh during the thirteenth and fourteenth centuries. The Shaikhs in the main line of the Chishti leadership, that is, Khwaja Muinuddin Chishti, Shaikh Qutbuddin Bakhtiyar Kaki, Baba Farid, Shaikh Nizamuddin Auliya and Shaikh Nasiruddin Mahmud, were not related to each other through lineage. In fact, two of them, Shaikh Nizamuddin Auliya and his principal spiritual successor, Shaikh Nasiruddin Mahmud, never married, and thus remained celibate throughout their lives. On the contrary, Khwaja Muinuddin Chishti, Shaikh Qutbuddin Bakhtiyar Kaki and Baba Farid were married, and had off-springs as well. These Chishti Shaikhs did not appoint any of their descendants (son or grandson) as their spiritual successors (*khulafa*). Contrary to the Chishti practice, hereditary succession in spiritual affairs was prevalent among the Suhrawardis in India during the two centuries. Shaikh Bahauddin Zakariya of Multan was succeeded by his son, Shaikh Sadruddin Arif, who was in turn succeeded by his son, Shaikh Ruknuddin Abul Fateh.[4]

Our involvement with the issue of succession obliges us to understand the role of the Shaikh in the pusuit of the spiritual discipline and his position in the hierarchy of his particular order. The north Indian society of the sultanate period cultivated a fair idea about the attributes of a Shaikh. Though some of the attributes appeared to be contradictory, a Shaikh generally possessed several of them in varying combinations and, in this manner, acquired acceptability among the common masses. First and foremost, a Shaikh was believed to be a recipient of divine grace. His descent was traced to the Prophet or his companions or a prestigious sufi order. He had a reputation for strict orthodoxy, besides the frequent practice of austerities. He had acquired a mastery over Islamic sciences and classical sufi literature. In many cases, he produced his own writings on aspects of the mystic discipline. He acquired popularity for performing a variety of miracles, ranging from intervention in the natural phenomena to political developments, though he disfavoured a vulgar display of these powers. Besides a long life, he possessed a refined taste for mystical poetry and musical sessions. Though he was kind towards disciples and visitors, yet he maintained a certain aloofness from the ordinary people. Despite the profession of humility in the claims to spiritual authority, he was capable of uncompromising arrogance which could assume the form of wrath against opponents. The Shaikh's degree of conformity to (or deviation from) the Muslim law came to resemble the division between pure and impure castes among the Hindus as well as noble (*ashraf*) and base (*ajlaf*) social groups among the Muslims. The attributes of a Shaikh, as identified by Simon Digby in an important contribution, enable us to understand the relative position of various claimants to the legacy of sufi masters.[5]

The Chishti Shaikhs in India seemed to be extremely mindful of the critical issues pertaining to spiritual succession. They explicitly rejected the notion of hereditary succession in spiritual affairs. According to an incident narrated by Shaikh Nizamuddin Auliya to his disciples and devotees in his *jamaat khana*, there was a certain sufi Shaikh in Ghazni, who appointed his slave named Zirak as his spiritual successor before his death. Shaikh Nizamuddin Auliya further added that the Shaikh had four sons, who wanted to be selected as successors, but the Shaikh did not appoint any one of them as his *khalifa*.[6] On another occasion, Shaikh Nizamuddin Auliya stated that Shaikh Qutbuddin Bakhtiyar Kaki had two sons, but his 'real son' was Shaikh Fariduddin,[7] who was his principal spiritual successor. A similar statement by Khwaja Muinuddin Chishti has been recorded in *Saba Sanabil*, when the Khwaja talked about his *sons*, and clarified that by his sons, he meant his *khulafa* or his *farzandan-i ma'anwi* (spiritual successors).[8] These statements clearly show that according to the Chishti Shaikhs, lineage by birth was insignificant as compared to the spiritual succession and the *khulafa* were considered the real successors of their preceptors. It is worthy of mention that all the Chishti Shaikhs from Shaikh Muinuddin Chishti to Syed Muhammad Gesudiraz, who assumed the leadership of the *silsilah* as principal spiritual successors of their preceptors, were Syeds, that is, descendants of the Prophet Muhammad (Peace be upon Him). However, they never used the title of Syeds with their names, and instead preferred to be addressed as Shaikh, which emphasized their spiritual status as sufi masters rather than their illustrious ancestry.[9]

It is important to note that often the sons of the Chishti Shaikhs were not worthy of receiving spiritual succession. Khwaja Muinuddin Chishti's sons had accepted a land grant from the state.[10] They lacked the qualities and characteristics of their father and, therefore, none of them could spiritually succeed the Khwaja. *Fawaid-ul-Fuad*, a fourteenth century *malfuz* (conversations or table talks or informal discourses of the sufi Shaikhs recorded by their disciples), informs us that Shaikh Qutbuddin Bakhtiyar Kaki had two sons. One of them died in infancy, whereas the other was unworthy of his father.[11] In the same way, Baba Farid's sons were also not much inclined towards sufism. However, among the descendants of these Chishti Shaikhs, only the descendants of Baba Farid received prominence in the Delhi sultanate, as they were approached by the sultans of Delhi and also enjoyed popular respect and devotion. As for the family of Shaikh Qutbuddin Bakhtiyar Kaki, it remained in obscurity, whereas the family of Khwaja Muinuddin Chishti received popular attention later on. However, the practice of appointing *sajjadah nishins* was and is still prevalent among the descendants of Khwaja Muinuddin Chishti and Baba Farid.

Before analyzing the phenomenon of *sajjadah nishini* among the descendants of Baba Farid, it is necessary to explore its meaning and trace the historical roots of the concept of *sajjadah*. Moreover, it seems pertinent to briefly discuss *sajjadah nishini* in the family of Khwaja Muinuddin Chishti as well. Literally, the Persian and Urdu word *sajjadah*[12] is used to refer to a prayer-mat, throne, or a seat, whereas the Arabic word *sujjada* is used in similar meaning, though pronounced differently.[13] The term *sajjadah* has often been used in a symbolic sense to denote authority as well. Thus, the term is used both in its literal sense as well as in its symbolic connotation. Nonetheless, the translation of the term *sajjadah* into English as 'the spiritual seat' is far from satisfactory. Such a translation confuses the concept of *sajjadah nishini* with the *khilafat*, i.e. spiritual succession, and that of *sajjadah nishin* with the *khalifa*, i.e. the spiritual successor. While using the semantic construct of 'spiritual seat', one is likely to assume that all the *sajjadah nishins* were necessarily the spiritual successors of the sufi Shaikhs whereas, as a matter of fact, it was not a prerequisite for *sajjadah nishin*. So a *sajjadah nishin* is a hereditary custodian of a sufi Shaikh, and thus, the former is related to the latter through ties of lineal descent.

As far as the historical roots of the concept of *sajjadah* are concerned, the term *sajjadah* is commonly found in the fourteenth century historical and hagiographical texts. For instance, in his *Tarikh-i-Firuz Shahi*, Ziauddin Barani refers to *sajjadah* in the context of Shaikh Alauddin, the grandson of Baba Farid, and Shaikh Ruknuddin Abul Fateh, the grandson of Shaikh Bahauddin Zakariya.[14] Similarly, Shams Siraj Afif also refers to *sajjadah-i tariqat* in his *Tarikh-i-Firuz Shahi* in the sense of spiritual succession.[15] In a likewise manner, the concept of *sajjadah* finds frequent mention in Amir Khurd's *Siyar-ul-Auliya*, particularly in the context of the family and descendants of Baba Farid.[16] It can be inferred from these three historical and hagiographical texts that, in the fourteenth century India, the term *sajjadah* was being used in two meanings: first, for spiritual succession among the sufis, and secondly, for the practice of hereditary succession among them. Though the concepts of *sajjadah* and *khilafat*, or *sajjadah nishin* and *khalifa* have been used interchangeably in various texts, the identification of these two concepts is mistaken, and hence, these need to be differentiated. As opposed to the concept of *sajjadah*, the concept of *khilafat* and the related practice of granting *khilafat* to a disciple by his preceptor entail that a disciple is authorized by his preceptor to enroll further disciples in his *silsilah*, and thus, disseminate the teachings and traditions of his preceptors and his *silsilah*.

It is useful here to briefly discuss the Chishti practice of granting the relics (*tabarrukat*) of the Chishti Shaikhs to one of the *khulafa* after the demise of a Shaikh.[17] The selection of the recipient of the relics was made by the Shaikh himself. It symbolized that one of the *khulafa* was designated as the principal successor of the Shaikh, and the recipient assumed leadership of the *silsilah*. Generally, these relics included the *khirqah* (a patched cloak or robe), *musalla* (a prayer-mat), *kullah* (a turban or cap), *asa* (a staff) and wooden sandals of the Shaikh.[18] It is important to note that the regalia that were passed on to the principal successor of a Chishti Shaikh included a prayer-mat. Thus, a *sajjadah nishin* cannot be an inheritor of the Shaikh's prayer-mat, as far as the Indian Chishtis were concerned. Nevertheless, if a *sajjadah* is taken as a seat or cot of the Shaikh, the Chishti Shaikhs in India did not include it in the list of the relics. Hagiographical accounts reveal that Baba Farid's relics including his patched robe, prayer mat, staff and turban were received by Shaikh Nizamuddin Auliya.[19] These relics did not include anything such as a seat or a cot. If *sajjadah* had been of any symbolic value, Baba Farid would have granted it to Shaikh Nizamuddin Auliya.

Sajjadah-nashini in the family of Khwaja Muinuddin Chishti

In the family of Khwaja Muinuddin Chishti one comes across the recurrent practice of appointing *sajjadah nishin*,[20] whereby the descendants of the Khwaja were designated one after another as the guardian of their ancestor's shrine in Ajmer. Hagiographical sources inform that Khwaja Muinuddin Chishti of Ajmer had three sons: one of them, Shaikh Hussamuddin, had disappeared, while the other two were Shaikh Fakhruddin and Shaikh Ziauddin Abu Sa'id. The eldest son, Shaikh Fakhruddin,[21] assumed the *sajjadah* after his father's demise. After the demise of Shaikh Fakhruddin, his brother, Shaikh Ziauddin Abu Sa'id, succeeded him. After Shaikh Ziauddin, two grandsons of Khwaja Muinuddin Chishti named Shaikh Rafiuddin Bayazid and Shaikh Nuruddin Muhammad became *sajjadah nishin*s one after another.[22] Nevertheless, these *sajjadah nishin*s were never approached by the Sultans of Delhi, especially the Tughluqs, but they enjoyed the patronage of the rulers of other independent kingdoms in the fifteenth century. Later, they enjoyed the patronage of the Mughal rulers as well.[23] It is important to mention that there existed jealousy and competitiveness among the descendants of Khwaja Muinuddin Chishti for getting political favours.[24]

Here it is important to note that these descendants of Khwaja Muinuddin Chishti do not find any mention in important hagiographical texts of the fourteenth century such as *Fawaid-ul-Fuad* or *Siyar-ul-Auliya*. According to Currie, the descendants of Khwaja Muinuddin Chishti are mentioned in a seventeenth century hagiographical work, *Siyar-ul-Aqtab*, written by Allah Diya Chishti in 1647, but even then there is no mention of their being appointed as *sajjadah nishin*s. The information that Khwaja Muinuddin Chishti's son, Shaikh Fakhruddin, was made the *sajjadah nishin* of Ajmer after his father's demise finds mention in *Hasht Bahisht*, which is an apocryphal collection of the *malfuzat* of the early Chishti Shaikhs of India. Currie further observes that it is unlikely that the first *sajjadah nishin* was buried in the town of Sarwar and not within the premises of the *dargah* of Ajmer.[25] Similarly, *Gulzar-i-Abrar* and *Akhbar-ul-Akhyar* are also seventeenth and eighteenth century accounts respectively. So the practice of appointing the son and grandson of Khwaja Muinuddin Chishti as *sajjadah nishin*s seems to be a latter-day fabrication, as its historical authenticity is dubious.

Sajjadah-nashini among the Descendants of Baba Farid

As for the descendants of Baba Farid, Amir Khurd informs that he had five sons and three daughters.[26] After his demise, his son, Shaikh Badruddin Sulaiman (d. 1281), sat on the *sajjadah* of his father with the consent of his brothers and other disciples of his father.[27] He remained the *sajjadah nishin* for almost sixteen years, i.e. from 1265 to 1281. The major rituals at the shrine had become instituted during these years.

These included the ritual of *dastar bandi* or 'tying on of the turban', which corresponded to the succession ceremony at the royal court in Delhi.[28] Shaikh Badruddin Sulaiman was succeeded by his son. Thus began the practice of perpetual succession to the *sajjadah* in Ajodhan, which became a tradition continuing to date.[29] Amir Khurd further informs about Shaikh Badruddin Sulaiman that he was not a disciple of his father, as he had entered the fold of discipleship of two Shaikhs of Chisht, Khwaja Zoar and Khwaja Ghaur, at the behest of his father. Shaikh Badruddin Sulaiman had also received *khilafat* from them.[30] After the demise of Shaikh Badruddin Sulaiman, his sixteen-year old son, Shaikh Alauddin, succeeded the *sajjadah* of his father. He remained the *sajjadah nishin* for the next fifty-four years till his death.[31] Amir Khurd records that he was known for his piety, godliness and austerity, but *Siyar-ul-Auliya* fails to mention whose disciple or *khalifa* he was. However, the account does mention that when someone used to approach him for becoming his disciple, he used to ask his attendants to take him to the tomb of Baba Farid and grant him a turban (*kullah*) symbolizing discipleship.[32] Shaikh Alauddin might have been spiritually associated with his grandfather, Baba Farid, and might have received spiritual guidance from him as well, but he succeeded his father as a *sajjadah nishin*. It is important to bear in mind that Shaikh Alauddin's father and grandfather were the successors and representatives of two different branches of Chishti *silsilah*. Amir Khurd further informs that after Shaikh Alauddin's demise, his son, Shaikh Muizzuddin, succeeded the *sajjadah* of Baba Farid.[33] Again the account fails to mention whose disciple he was. After the demise of Shaikh Muizzuddin, his son Shaikhzada Muazzam Afzaluddin Fuzail was designated as the next *sajjadah nishin*.[34] The practice of appointing *sajjadah nishin*s continued further and still continues. The later *sajjadah nishin*s came to be known as *diwan*s like the *sajjadah nishin*s of Ajmer.

A few important inferences can be drawn from Amir Khurd's account. The first *sajjadah nishin*, who was Baba Farid's own son, was not a disciple of Baba Farid. Though Baba Farid's son must have gained spiritual benefit from his father, he was the spiritual successor or the *khalifa* of the Khwajas of Chisht. He must have enrolled disciples in his own branch of the Chishti *silsilah*, rather than in his father's branch. Nizami observes that no contemporary or semi-contemporary authority refers to his having received *khilafat* from his father.[35] The account of Amir Khurd implies that over the generations, it had become less important whose disciple was the *sajjadah nishin*, or whether the *sajjadah nishin* was a *khalifa* of a sufi Shaikh or not, and the blood relationship with Baba Farid seems to have become more important than any other consideration. Amir Khurd's account suggests that his contemporary *sajjadah nishin*, Muazzam Afzaluddin Fuzail, was the first among the *sajjadah nishins* to assume the title of *Shaikhzadah* (literally meaning the son of a Shaikh), which implies a greater emphasis on lineage or ancestry instead of spirituality, piety or godliness.

Hagiographical sources suggest that Baba Farid was not satisfied with the spirituality of his sons. That was why, on one occasion, he expressed his wish to appoint his daughter Bibi Sharifa as his spiritual successor.[36] However, Baba Farid did not actually do so. Amir Khurd informs us that when Baba Farid was on his death-bed, the issue of his spiritual succession was raised by his disciples and sons. Amir Khurd's grandfather, Syed Muhammad Kirmani (d. 1311), came to Ajodhan from Delhi in order to see Baba Farid, but the latter's sons tried to prevent him from meeting their father. However, the Saiyyid went inside the cell and met Baba Farid. Amir Khurd records that his grandfather feared that the sons of Baba Farid would not like him (Syed Muhammad Kirmani) talking about Shaikh Nizamuddin Auliya at that time. However, during the conversation, the Syed conveyed the regards of Shaikh Nizamuddin Auliya to Baba Farid. At that moment, Baba Farid entrusted all his relics to Syed Muhammad Kirmani and instructed him to deliver them to Shaikh Nizamuddin Auliya, which indicated that Baba Farid had appointed Shaikh Nizamuddin Auliya as his principal spiritual successor. Amir Khurd further states that it was a great disappointment to the sons of Baba Farid, who were hoping to be designated as their father's spiritual successor. Therefore, they furiously quarrelled with Syed Muhammad Kirmani for having deprived them of something precious.[37]

The account of Baba Farid's burial is also relevant here. It appears that Baba Farid had not specifically instructed his descendants about the place of his burial. After his demise, his family-members decided to bury him in the graveyard outside the boundary wall of the town of Ajodhan, where Baba Farid used to pray and meditate during his lifetime. However, Baba Farid's favourite son, Khwaja Nizamuddin, who was endowed with worldly wisdom by virtue of being in the military service of Ullugh Khan (Ghiasuddin Balban), argued that if they buried the Shaikh outside the town, nobody would pay any attention to the family of Baba Farid. The devotees visiting the tomb of Baba Farid would return without visiting them. Therefore, they decided to bury the Shaikh inside the town near his *jamaat khana*.[38] It shows that the descendants of Baba Farid were desirous of getting the same respect and devotion from the people which their illustrious ancestor received in his lifetime. Moreover, the possibility that the family of Baba Farid feared a reduction in the amount of unasked charity (*futuh*) in the *jamaat khana* after his demise, cannot be ruled out. If the descendants of Baba Farid had buried him outside the city, it would have deprived them of enormous amount of *futuh* pouring into the *jamaat khana*.

Another critical but relatively ignored and understudied issue, pertaining to spiritual succession among the Chishtis in India, is that the principal spiritual successor did not assume the directorship of a *khanqah* or *jamaat khana* after the demise of their preceptor. In fact, the principal spiritual successors of the Chishti Shaikhs did not live in the same place where their preceptors resided. In many cases, these spiritual successors were directed by their own preceptors to take residence at a specific place. Baba Farid lived in Ajodhan in the Punjab, but his successor, Shaikh Nizamuddin Auliya, lived in Ghiyaspur in the vicinity of Delhi. It appears that the issues of directorship of a *jamaat khana* and guardianship of a shrine after a Shaikh's demise had nothing to do with the question of spiritual succession. For this reason, the hagiographical sources are silent as to who would supervise and manage the *jamaat khana* after a Shaikh's demise, as this question seems not to bother the hagiographers much.

As far as the upkeep and maintenance of Baba Farid's *jamaat khana* at Ajodhan, including the running of community kitchen (*langar*) was concerned, Baba Farid had assigned various duties to his disciples during his lifetime.[39] Shaikh Badruddin Ishaq was responsible for the management of the *jamaat khana*. After Baba Farid's demise, he continued his responsibilities, but some differences developed between him and Shaikh Badruddin Sulaiman, the son of Baba Farid and the incumbent *sajjadah-nashin*. Disheartened, Shaikh Badruddin Ishaq left the *jamaat khana* and took residence elsewhere.[40] After Shaikh Badruddin Ishaq's departure, the issue of supervision and management of the *jamaat khana* might have been raised. At this critical juncture, the family of Baba Farid or the incumbent *sajjadah-nashin* must have directly assumed this responsibility, in addition to the self-assumed duty of guardianship of Baba Farid's shrine. The newly added responsibility of managing the *jamaat khana* must have increased the influence of the family among the people. Moreover, it must have placed the *futuh* and other resources of the *jamaat khana* at the disposal of the descendants of Baba Farid.

With regard to the legacy of Baba Farid, the continuation of the institution of *jamaat khana*, including the community kitchen (*langar*), was considered necessary and this, in turn, created the need for additional financial resources. A little less than a century after the demise of Baba Farid (d. 1265), Sultan Firuz Shah Tughluq (r.1351-1388) awarded land grants and cash stipends to the descendants of the Chishti saint. The endowments were meant for the maintenance and upkeep of the *jamaat khana*, which was under the supervision of Baba Farid's descendants. After the Delhi sultans, the Mughul emperors also offered land grants to the *sajjadah nishins*. Over centuries, the prestige and authority of a *sajjadah nishin* came to depend on the extent of *langar* and the splendour of the *urs* festivals.[41] Moreover, the shrine of Baba Farid got precedence over his *jamaat khana*, which became less significant as an institution. The practice of appointing *sajjadah nishins* as hereditary successors to a Shaikh was motivated as much on pragmatic grounds arising out of the need to continue the institution of *jamaat khanah*, as by the desire of the descendants to become heir to the respect, devotion and reverence of the people, which their ancestor commanded. That Baba Farid himself favoured hereditary succession to the seat of spiritual authority (*sajjadah nishini*) is indicated by the following episode. At the demise of Shaikh Jamaluddin Hansavi, who headed the Chishti hospice at Hansi, Baba Farid accepted the minor son of the deceased, Maulana Burhanuddin Sufi, as his own spiritual successor (*khalifa*). On this occasion, Baba Farid gave him two relics – a prayer mat and a staff – which he had earlier conferred upon his father. By doing so, Baba Farid also appointed Maulana Burhanuddin Sufi as the head of the Chishti hospice at Hansi. The choice of Baba Farid was not hindered by two handicaps – the incumbent was a minor and had not acquired any spiritual training. To be the *sajjadah nishin* of the Chishti *khanqah* at Hansi, it was enough that Maulana Burhanuddin Sufi was the son of Shaikh Jamaluddin Hansavi. No other qualification was required. It is significant that Baba Farid directed Maulana Burhanuddin Sufi to receive formal spiritual training from Shaikh Nizamuddin Auliya, because it was only after this tutelage that he could enroll disciples of his own. It is equally significant that, in due course, Maulana Burhanuddin Sufi was succeeded as *sajjadah nishin* of the Chishti hospice at Hansi by his son and grandson, Shaikh Qutbuddin Munawwar and Shaikh Nuruddin.

The practice of hereditary succession in spiritual affairs prevalent among the Suhrawardis might have also influenced Baba Farid and his descendants, since Ajodhan was not very far from Multan which was the spiritual centre of the Suhrawardi order. In this context, we may also consider the practice followed at the Uch branch of the Suhrawardi order. This branch was originally founded by Syed Jalaluddin Surkh Bukhari (d. 1291), a disciple of Shaikh Bahauddin Zakariya. He had three sons – Syed Ahmad Kabir, Syed Bahauddin and Syed Muhammad. Syed Ahmad Kabir received spiritual training first from his father and then from Shaikh Sadruddin Arif (the son of Shaikh Bahauddin Zakariya). He was blessed with two sons, Syed Jalaluddin Bukhari (who became popular as Makhdum-i-Jahaniyan Jahangasht) and Raju Qattal. The former, having refused to accept the patronage of Sultan Muhammad bin

Tughluq (r. 1325-1351), left for his extensive travels in the Islamic lands. During his long absence from Uch, the Suhrawardi hospice was administered by Raju Qattal. On returning to Uch during the reign of Sultan Firuz Shah Tughluq (r. 1351-1388), he assumed the headship of the Uch hospice. The lineal descendants of the two brothers are reputed to have expanded the activities of the Suhrawardi order in different parts of western India. The progeny of Jahangasht – son Syed Mahmud Nasiruddin, grandson Syed Hamid Kabir and great grandson Syed Raknuddin Abul Fateh – carried on the mystical traditions of the Suhrawardi order during the fourteenth and fifteenth centuries from their seat in Uch. Thus there is no doubt that the principle of hereditary succession had become firmly established in the *khanqahs* of the two major sufi orders of Punjab, Chishtis and Suhrawardis.

Initially, at least, two conditions were considered prerequisite to qualify for the *sajjadah nishini* in Ajodhan: first, the *sajjadah nishin* must possess some degree of godliness and piety; and second, he must be a direct descendant of the deceased Shaikh. With the passage of time, the second precondition emphasizing the lineage of a *sajjadah nishin* seems to have taken precedence over the first one. Consequently, the issue of *sajjadah nishini* became a bone of contention among the rival contenders to the *sajjadah* and resulted in power politics in the ensuing centuries. Meanwhile, the lands which the descendants of Baba Farid possessed in the region kept on increasing, turning the family of the Chishti Shaikh, who preferred *faqr* or voluntary poverty to *ghina* or wealth, into landed magnates. Thus, departing from the teachings of their ancestor as well as the traditions of the Chishti order, the descendants of Baba Farid acquired endowments from the rulers as well as from the nobles (*umara*), high state officials, local landlords and wealthy merchants. Consequently, these descendants enjoyed social prestige and economic prosperity along with religious/spiritual and political authority in the ensuing centuries.

APPENDIX

Spiritual Successors of Baba Farid

1. Shaikh Najibuddin Mutawakkil
2. Shaikh Badruddin Ishaq
3. Shaikh Jamaluddin Hansavi
4. Shaikh Nizamuddin Auliya
5. Shaikh Arif
6. Shaikh Ali Sabir
7. Maulana Fakhruddin Safahani[42]

Sajjadah Nashins of Baba Farid's Khanqah

1. Shaikh Badruddin Sulaiman
2. Shaikh Alauddin
3. Shaikh Muizzuddin
4. Shaikh Fazl
5. Shaikh Munawwar
6. Shaikh Nuruddin
7. Shaikh Bahauddin
8. Shaikh Muhammad
9. Shaikh Ahmad
10. Shaikh Ataullah
11. Shaikh Muhammad
12. Shaikh Ibrahim
13. Shaikh Tajuddin Mahmud
14. Shaikh Faizullah
15. Shaikh Ibrahim
16. Shaikh Muhammad
17. Shaikh Muhammad Ashraf
18. Shaikh Muhammad Saeed
19. Shaikh Muhammad Yusuf
20. Shaikh Abdus Subhan
21. Shaikh Ghulam Rasul
22. Shaikh Muhammad Yar
23. Shaikh Sharfuddin
24. Shaikh Allah Jawaya
25. Shaikh Sharfuddin[43]

NOTES AND REFERENCES

1. Saiyyid Muhammad Mubarak Alawi Kirmani alias Amir Khurd, *Siyar-ul-Auliya*, (compiled in 1351-82 A.D.), ed. Chiranji Lal, Muhibb-i Hind Press, Delhi, 1302 A.H./1885 A.D., p. 213. Henceforth, referred to as Amir Khurd. See also Idarah-i Tasnif-o Talif, *Anwar-i Asfiya*, Shaikh Ghulam Ali and Sons, Lahore, n.d. pp. 72-73.
2. Amir Khurd, *Siyar-ul-Auliya*, p. 213. However, according to *Safinat-ul-Auliya* and *Anwar-i Asfiya*, Khwaja Abu Yusuf Chishti was the nephew of Khwaja Abu Muhammad Chishti. Dara Shikoh, *Safinat-ul-Auliya*, Urdu Translation, Muhammad Ali Lutfi, Nafis Academy, Karachi, 1959, p. 125, and *Anwar-i Asfiya*, pp. 96.
3. Amir Khurd, *Siyar-ul-Auliya*, p. 213, Dara Shikoh, *Safinat-ul-Auliya*, p. 125, and *Anwar-i Asfiya*, pp. 96, 112.
4. S. Moinul Haq, 'The Suhrawardis,' *Journal of the Pakistan Historical Society*, (Karachi), Vol. XXIII, Part II (April 1975), pp. 78, 87.
5. Simon Digby, 'The Sufi Shaikh as A Source of Authority in Medieval India,'

in *India's Islamic Traditions 711-1750*, Ed., Richard M. Eaton, Oxford University Press, Delhi, 2003, pp. 237-41.

6. For details, see Amir Hasan Ala Sijzi Dehlavi, *Fawaid-ul-Fuad*, (Mystical discourses (*malfuz*) of Shaikh Nizamuddin Auliya), ed. Khwaja Hasan Sani Nizami Dehlavi, Urdu Academy, Delhi, 1992, (Reprint), pp. 5-6. Henceforth, referred to as Sijzi. For a similar incident narrated by Shaikh Nizamuddin Auliya in his *majlis*, see Jandar, *Durr-i Nizami*, MS, as cited in Muhammad Aslam, *Malfuzati Adab ki Tarikhi Ahammiyyat*, Research Society of Pakistan, University of the Punjab, Lahore, 1995, p. 67.
7. Amir Hasan Ala Sijzi, *Fawaid-ul-Fuad*, p. 105.
8. Mir Abdul Wahid Bilgrami, *Saba Sanabil*, (compiled in 969 AH/1561 AD), Urdu Translation, Mufti Muhammad Khalil Khan Barakati, Hamid and Co., Lahore, n.d., p. 436.
9. Carl W. Ernst and Bruce B. Lawrence, *Sufi Martyrs of Love: The Chishti Order in South Asia and Beyond*, Palgrave Macmillan, New York, 2002, p. 66.
10. Amir Khurd, *Siyar-ul-Auliya*, p. 53.
11. Muhammad Ghausi Shattari Mandavi, *Gulzar-i Abrar*, (The Garden of the Pious), (compiled in 1014 AH/1605 AD), Urdu Translation. Fazl Ahmad Juri, *Adhkar-i-Abrar*, Islamic Book Foundation, Lahore, 1395 AH/1975 AD, p. 42. It was on this occasion that Shaikh Nizamuddin Auliya had said that Shaikh Qutbuddin Bakhtiyar Kaki's real son was Shaikh Fariduddin. Amir Hasan Ala Sijzi, *Fawaid al-Fuad*, pp. 104-5.
12. *Sajjadah* is also referred to as *gaddi* (literally meaning a throne or seat of authority), and thus, *sajjadah-nashin* are also referred to as *gaddi-nashin*. However, the terms *gaddi* and *gaddi-nashin* seemed to have been coined at a later stage.
13. Maulavi Abdul Aziz, Maulana Muhammad Sa'id and Maulavi Muhammad Munir, *Lughat-i Sa'idi*, 3rd ed. H.M. Sa'id Co.,Karachi, 1957, p. 402. Sarah F. D. Ansari has understood *sajjadah* as 'carpet', as she has translated *sajjadah-nashin* in a literal sense as the 'one who sits on the carpet', and the 'head of *pir* family' in general sense. Idem, *Sufi Saints and State Power: The Pirs of Sind, 1843-1947*, Cambridge University Press, Cambridge, 1992, see glossary, p. xviii.
14. Ziauddin Barani, *Tarikh-i Firuz Shahi*, (completed in 1359), ed. Saiyyid Ahmad Khan, Bibliotheca Indica, The Asiatic Society of Bengal, Calcutta, 1862, p. 347. It is important to bear in mind that Shaikh Alauddin was not a spiritual successor or *khalifah* of Baba Farid, whereas Shaikh Ruknuddin was the grandson as well as the spiritual successor of his father and grandfather.
15. For instance, see Shams Siraj Afif, *Tarikh-i Firuz Shahi*, (*Manaqib-i Firuz Shahi*), Urdu Translation, Maulavi Muhammad Fida Ali Talib, Darul Taba Jamiah Usmaniya, 1938, pp. 37, 98.
16. See, for instance, Amir Khurd, *Siyar-ul-Auliya*, pp. 188-89, 191, 193-94, 197. In addition to the discussion on Baba Farid's family and descendants, Amir Khurd also uses the concept of *sajjadah* for explaining the spiritual succession among the pre-Indian Chishtis. However, here the usage of the concept of *sajjadah* suggests that it has been used in the sense of *khilafat*.

See pp. 212-13.

17. See a detailed discussion in Simon Digby, "*Tabarrukat* and Succession among the Great Chishti Shaikhs of the Delhi Sultanate", in *Delhi Through the Ages: Essays in Urban History, Culture and Society*, ed. R. E. Frykenberg, Oxford University Press, Delhi, 1986, pp. 63-103.
18. For instance, Shaikh Qutbuddin Bakhtiyar Kaki was granted a turban and a cap (*kullah wa dastar*), wooden staff (*asa*), robe (*khirqah*), Quran, prayer mat (*janamaz*), and wooden sandals (*n'alayn*) by his preceptor, Khwaja Muinuddin Chishti. Abdul Haqq Muhaddis Dehalvi, *Akhbar-al-Akhyar*, p. 32. Similarly, after Shaikh Qutbuddin Bakhtiyar Kaki's demise, his *khalifa*, Baba Farid, was granted his preceptor's *khirqah* along with other regalia such as prayer mat, staff and wooden sandals by Shaikh Hamiduddin Nagauri. In a similar manner, before his demise, Baba Farid asked his disciple and son-in-law, Shaikh Badruddin Ishaq, to deliver the *khirqah* he (Baba Farid) had received from his preceptor to Shaikh Nizamuddin Auliya. As for other relics such as his prayer mat and cap, Baba Farid had granted these to Shaikh Nizamuddin Auliya during his life-time. Hamid bin Fazl Allah Jamali, *Siyar-ul-Arifin*, (compiled between 1531-35 A.D.) Rizwi Press, Delhi, 1311 AH/1893 AD, pp. 29, 58, 67.
19. Amir Khurd, *Siyar-ul-Auliya*, p. 123, and Jamali, *Siyar-ul-Arifin*, pp. 58, 67.
20. Abdul Rahman Chishti, *Mirat-ul-Asrar*, Vol. II, pp. 44-45, and W. D. Begg, *The Holy Biography of Hazrat Khwaja Muinuddin Chishti—A Symbol of Love and Peace in India*, The Chishti Sufi Mission of America, Tuscon, Arizona, 1977), pp. 161-63. The genealogical list of the *sajjadah-nashins* of Ajmer in Begg informs that Syed Alauddin, the fifteenth *sajjadah-nashin*, assumed the title of *diwan* for the first time. p. 162.
21. Shaikh Fakhruddin used to cultivate land in Mandan near Ajmer and it was on his insistence that his father had visited Delhi in order to get the relevant documents. Abdul Rahman Chishti, *Mirat-ul-Asrar*, Vol. II, pp. 44, 46, 130. However, the account seems apocryphal. See a detailed discussion in Tanvir Anjum, "Chishti Silsilah and the Delhi Sultanate: A Study of their Relationship during the 13th and 14th Centuries", Unpublished Ph.D. Dissertation, Department of History, Quaid-i-Azam University, Islamabad, 2005, Chapter 3, pp. 228-32.
22. Shaikh Fakhruddin's son, Shaikh Hussamuddin *Sokhtah* (literally meaning the burnt one, burnt in the love of God), who was named by his father after the name of his disappeared brother, was known for his piety and austerity. He was a disciple of Shaikh Nizamuddin Auliya. His son, Khwaja Muinuddin, the Younger, named after his great grandfather, was a *khalifah* of Shaikh Nasiruddin Mahmud. See details in Mandavi, *Gulzar-i-Abrar*, pp. 32-33, and Shaikh Abdul Haqq Muhaddis Dehlavi, *Akhbar-ul-Akhyar fi Asrar-ul-Abrar*, (Reports of the Righteous on the Secrets of the Pious), (compiled in 1590), Kutub Khanah-i Rahimiyyah, Deoband, n.d., pp. 119-22.
23. Owing to the weakening of the central authority in 1400, Ajmer was annexed by Hindu rulers and the descendants of the Khwaja were forced to migrate from Ajmer. They took shelter under the independent Muslim

sultans of Gujrat and Malwa (Mandu), who held them in high esteem. Later, Ajmer was captured by Sultan Mahmud Khalji of Mandu. Abdul Rahman Chishti, *Mirat-ul-Asrar*, Vol. II, pp. 52-53. See further details of *sajjadah-nashins* of Ajmer to the present day in Begg, *The Holy Biography of Hazrat Khwaja Muinuddin Chishti*, pp. 163-80, and P. M. Currie, *The Shrine and Cult of Mu'in al-din Chishti of Ajmer,* Oxford University Press, Delhi, 1989, pp. 150-163; also see the details of endowments, offerings, income of the *sajjadah-nashins*, remuneration of other officials and expenditure of the *dargah*, pp. 174-84.

24. See details in Mandavi, *Gulzar-i-Abrar*, p. 34.
25. Currie, *The Shrine and Cult of Mu'in al-din Chishti of Ajmer*, p. 150.
26. For their biographical sketches, see Amir Khurd, *Siyar-ul-Auliya*, pp. 186-93.
27. Ibid., p. 188.
28. Richard M. Eaton, "The Political and Religious Authority of the Shrine of Baba Farid" in *Moral Conduct and Authority: The Place of Adab in South Asian Islam*, ed. Barbara Daly Metcalf, University of California Press, Berkley, 1984, pp. 337, 339.
29. See the list of *sajjadah-nashins* of Baba Farid's shrine in Khaliq Ahmad Nizami, *The Life and Times of Shaikh Farid-ud-Din Ganj-i-Shakar*, Appendix D, "Sajjadah Nashins of Baba Farid's Khanqah," Muslim University, Aligarh, 1955, p. 123.
30. Amir Khurd, *Siyar-ul-Auliya*, p. 189. Amir Khurd also informs that contrary to the practice of the Chishti Shaikhs of India, Shaikh Badruddin Sulaiman did not shave his head and grew long locks. Ibid., p. 188. See also Abdul Rahman Chishti, *Mirat-ul-Asrar*, Vol. II, pp. 213-14.
31. Amir Khurd, *Siyar-ul-Auliya*, p. 193.
32. Ibid., p. 194.
33. Ibid., p. 196.
34. Ibid., p. 197.
35. Nonetheless, Nizami considers it a historiographical omission. Idem, *The Life and Times of Shaikh Farid-ud-Din Ganj-i-Shakar*, p. 60, n. 8.
36. Baba Farid stated, "Had the succession of spiritual affairs been allowed to be granted to women, I would have appointed my daughter Bibi Sharifa as my successor. Had there been some more women like her, women would have been granted a superior status than men." Amir Khurd, *Siyar-ul-Auliya*, p. 191. The inference of Nizami from the statement of Shaikh Nasiruddin Mahmud that Baba Farid once desired to make his son Shaikh Nizamuddin as his spiritual successor appears to be incorrect. Nizami seems to have misinterpreted an incident narrated in *Khair-ul-Majalis*. Khaliq Ahmad Nizami, *The Life and Times of Shaikh Farid-ud-Din Ganj-i-Shakar*, p. 63. See details of an incident narrated by Shaikh Nasiruddin in this regard. Hamid Qalandar, *Khair-ul-Majalis*, (The Best of Assemblies), (*Malfuz* of Shaikh Nasiruddin Mahmud Chiragh-i Dehli), ed. Khaliq Ahmad Nizami, Aligarh Muslim University, Aligarh,1959, p. 224.
37. Amir Khurd, *Siyar-ul-Auliya*, pp. 121-22.
38. Ibid., p. 90.

39. Khaliq Ahmad Nizami, *The Life and Times of Shaikh Farid-ud-Din Ganj-i-Shakar*, pp. 48-49, 52.
40. Amir Khurd, *Siyar-ul-Auliya*, pp. 171-72.
41. David Gilmartin, *Empire and Islam: Punjab and the Making of Pakistan*, I. B. Tauris, London, 1988, pp. 43, 45.
42. Khaliq Ahmad Nizami, *The Life and Times of Shaikh Farid-ud-Din Ganj-i-Shakar*, Idarah-i-Adabiyat-i-Delli, Delhi, Reprint, 1973, p.67.
43. Ibid., p. 123.

3

Path of Shaikh Bahauddin Zakariya

A Contrastive Model of Mysticism

Humaira Arif Dasti

Shaikh Bahauddin Zakariya (1182-1262) laid the foundation of the Suhrawardi order in Multan, which played a significant role in the socio-cultural history of north-western India. His ancestors had migrated from Mecca and settled in Multan. His father Shaikh Wajihuddin was married to the daughter of Maulana Husamuddin Tirmizi, who had migrated to Punjab in the wake of Mongol invasions. Bahauddin Zakariya was born at Kot Karor, a village near Multan. While still a young boy, he memorized the Quran and learnt to recite it in seven styles of recitation. During a long stay in the famous centres of education – Khurasan, Bukhara, Madina and Palestine – he studied the traditional subjects. For several years, he performed religious devotions at the mausoleum of Prophet Muhammad in Madina and learnt the prophetic traditions (*hadis*) from a distinguished scholar of the discipline. During a visit to Baghdad, he was initiated into the Suhrawardi order by Shaikh Shihabuddin Suhrawardi.[1] According to one account, he was made a spiritual successor (*khalifa*) after a tutelage of just seventeen days. His mentor declared that senior aspirants could not achieve their aims as they brought green wood which would not catch fire, while Bahauddin Zakariya brought dry wood which began to burn at a single breath.[2] On returning to Multan, Bahauddin Zakariya planted the seeds of the Suhrawardi order in spite of the opposition of some religious men of the city. The Shaikh's multifarious activities – mystical, educational and literary – were undertaken precisely at the time when Shaikh Farid Ganj-i-Shakar was engaged in organizing the Chishti order from the neighbouring town of Pakpattan. Bahauddin Zakariya has been criticized by several contemporaries and modern writers for his involvement in politics and accumulation of wealth. However, we can make an objective assessment of his life and work by placing them in their socio-political context and the legacy of his mission.

Conditions in the Multan Region

During the late twelfth and early thirteenth century, the political condition in Punjab was characterized by the decline of the Ghaznavid rule, establishment of the Delhi sultanate, internal conflict in the new ruling class and recurrent Mongol invasions. The emergence and expansion of the Saljuq empire threatened the existence of the Ghaznavids, whose sway was reduced to parts of the southern and eastern Afghanistan and Punjab. As the Saljuqs began to loose ground to the Ghuzz Turks, the Ghurid princes (who had been the vassals of the Saljuqs) availed themselves of the opportunity to build their own political power. In this rise of the Ghurids, a notable role was played by Izzuddin Husain, Bahauddin Sam and Alauddin Jahansoz. A tripartite division of the Ghurid empire placed Ghazni in the hands of Sultan Muizzuddin (r. 1173-1206) who went on to lay the foundation of the Delhi sultanate. The series of his military expeditions, which were spread over three decades, brought about a fundamental change in the history of Punjab. On the one hand, he wiped out the Ghaznavid power and, on the other, he established his sway over western and central Punjab by occupying the strongholds of Peshawar, Sialkot, Lahore, Multan, Uch and Bathinda. In the post-Tarain phase, he annexed south eastern Punjab up to Delhi and extended the frontiers of the new kingdom to Ajmer, Gwalior and Benares, paving the way for quick success in Bihar and Bengal.[3] The sudden and unexpected death of Sultan Muizzuddin in 1206 marked the beginning of a power struggle in Punjab among his Turkish slave officers – Qutbuddin Aibak in Delhi and Lahore, Nasiruddin Qubacha in Multan and Uch and Tajuddin Yalduz in Ghazni. The place of Aibak was taken after his death (1210) by Shamsuddin Iltutmish. But the power struggle continued as before. After a series of military operations, Iltutmish defeated his rivals (Yalduz and Qubacha) and, by 1220, established a firm control over Punjab and placed his son Nasiruddin Mahmud in charge of Lahore.[4]

During the period under study, Multan became the focus of attention owing to the rebellious activities of the successive officers associated with it – Kabir Khan Ayaz, Izzuddin Balban Kishlu Khan and Sher Khan. During the reigns of Iltutmish and his successor Ruknuddin Firuz Shah, Ayaz had served as the governor of Multan and Sunam respectively. He joined the revolt raised by the governors of Lahore and Hansi. He managed to extract the administration of Multan from Sultan Raziya, but began to rule independently over Multan, Uch and Sind.[5] Ayaz and his son Tajuddin Abu Bakr Ayaz defended Multan against the

Qarlugh expansion. During the reign of Nasiruddin Mahmud (r. 1246-1266), Kishlu Khan was given the charge of Multan and Uch. When Saifuddin Hasan Qarlugh besieged Multan (1249), Kishlu Khan surrendered the fort and retreated to Uch. Sher Khan, who was holding the charge of Lahore and Bathinda, ousted the Qarlugh agent from Multan. Not only did he assume control of Multan, but also established his sway over Uch. Thus began a conflict between the two officers, Kishlu Khan and Sher Khan, for the possession of Multan. The Delhi sultan marched into Punjab, expelled Sher Khan and restored to Kishlu Khan the charge of Multan and Uch. Alienated from Delhi sultanate, Sher Khan went to Turkistan and sought asylum at the court of the Mongol chief Mangu Khan. Kishlu Khan, feeling uneasy at the rise of Ulugh Khan at Delhi, sent his son to the court of the Mongol ruler Halaku. He also joined hands with the rebel Qutlugh Khan and participated in an abortive attempt to dislodge the sultan. Subsequently, he fled to Khurasan and appeared at the court of Halaku. He secured the promise of support in return for accepting a Mongol resident (*shahna*) in his territories. From now onwards (1259), he began to rule independently in Multan and Uch, which came under the protection of the Mongols.[6]

The city and hinterland of Multan commanded immense strategic and economic importance. The region formed an irregular triangle, being enclosed by the Chenab and Satluj. The streams of the Ravi and Beas separately traversed through the area before merging with the Chenab and Satluj just above Uch. The land near the confluence of the rivers was regularly flooded during the summer months. The soil was entirely alluvial. Wheat and cotton were the major crops, while the date palm was also cultivated. The climate was generally dry, with heat and dust being proverbial. The rainfall was extremely scanty, the average varying from 4 to 7 inches.[7] From the point of view human settlement, Multan appears to have been better placed than the Sind Sagar Doab on its northwest and the Thar Desert on its south. The city of Multan emerged as a significant entrepot, because it was situated at the crossroads of the overland and riverine routes that connected India with the lands on the west, Iran and Arabian Sea. It was suitably connected with several urban centres in the region viz. Lahore, Dipalpur, Pakpattan, Tulamba, Uch and Bhakkar. It appears that the transcontinental route connecting Delhi with Qandhar, which passed through Multan, overtook others in significance.[8] Multanis, who played a prominent role in long distance trade, dealt in horses, slaves and indigo.[9] Since Ziauddin Barani, refers to Multanis in conjunction with Sahs, it indicates that Multanis were Hindus who were engaged in usury and commerce. We must hasten to point out that some Multanis were

Muslims also.[10] We are aware that Hamiduddin, who was appointed as the chief judge by Alauddin Khalji, was known as a great merchant (*malikut tujjar*) and had been engaged in taking interest since the time of his grandfather and father.[11] This Sultan had assigned a special role to the Multanis in his scheme of price regulation. He appointed them as officers in the market of non-agricultural goods (*sarai adl*) in Delhi and gave them an advance of 20 lac tankas, so that they were able to bring superior quality textiles to the capital for sale.[12] The prosperity of the Multanis was also based on the interest which they earned from loans advanced to the nobles of the Delhi sultanate.[13] It may be suggested that the Multanis had not risen to sudden prominence towards the end of the thirteenth century and that they had been playing a multifarious role in the internal and external trade as well as the polity of the Delhi sultanate for a long time.

Mystical Beliefs and Practices

In his mystical ideology, Shaikh Bahauddin Zakariya faithfully adhered to the path of his spiritual preceptor Shaikh Shihabuddin Suhrawardi who, in turn, had imbibed the teachings of Shaikh Junaid Baghdadi. The last named stood against free-thinking and deviations from the canonical law and, therefore, advocated that the mystical path (*tariqat*) was subordinate to the religious law (*shariat*) under all circumstances. This position was opposed to the extremely rebellious mystics who treated *shariat* and *tariqat* as mutually exclusive and believed that the former acted as a guide in the everyday life of the individual and could not provide guidance in the higher spiritual matters.[14] Shaikh Bahauddin Zakariya laid utmost emphasis on performing obligatory religious duties, because it served as the basis of all spiritual progress. He attached secondary importance to recollection of God (*zikr*), supererogatory prayers and sufi discipline.[15] For him, mysticism (*tariqat*) was more than a method to learn spiritual purity. It meant that every thought and action was related to the larger purpose of returning to the Divine. It also meant that the seekers were responsible for controlling themselves at every moment and every place. The Shaikh's emphasis on the internal and external make-up of the seeker required a strict observance of the Quran, *hadis*, *shariat* and mystical practices, besides subordination to political authority and social etiquette.

According to the Shaikh's advice, as recorded in the *Majma-ul-Akhbar*, a seeker was required to remember God with love and sincerity. The latter achieved this state when, during prayer and recollection of God (*zikr*), every thought other than God was expelled from the heart. His behaviour was guided by only those thoughts and actions which were essential. Only then God gave him the wisdom to undertake good actions. In his advice to a disciple Rehman, the Shaikh required him to engage in recollection of God (*zikr*) at all times, because by doing so he could reach his ultimate destination. Love was like a fire that destroyed every kind of dirt and filth. When his love became steadfast, then he became attached to *zikr-i-mushahida*. It was on the basis of this particular kind of *zikr* that God promised success and prosperity, in accordance with the Quranic verse, "Undertake excessive *zikr*, so that you become successful."[16]

It appears that Shaikh Bahauddin Zakariya provided instructions to his disciples by writing letters to them. He had high expectations from his disciples, particularly regarding a single minded commitment to God. In a letter to one of his disciples, he narrated an anecdote which must have been learnt from his spiritual teacher Shaikh Shihabuddin Suhrawardi. We are told that Shaikh Shihabuddin Suhrawardi and his mentor Abu Najib Abdul Qahir went on a pilgrimage to Mecca. When they entered the Kaaba, Abu Najib Abdul Qahir reached a higher plane of spiritual consciousness (*alam-i-asrar*) and became so immersed in this state that he did not pay any attention to the arrival of Hazrat Khizar, who ultimately left the place. When he regained his worldly consciousness, his disciple gathered courage and asked the reason for not paying attention to a prophet who had come to see him. Abu Najib Abdul Qahir became red with anger and said, "Alas, you do not know the reason. If Hazrat Khizar had come, he will do so again. But this moment is more precious as we were engaged in a communion with God. If this moment had been wasted, it would not have come again and we would have felt ashamed till the day of judgement." While this conversation was in progress, Hazrat Khizar arrived and was met by Abu Najib Abdul Qahir with all marks of respect. The moral of the story is that the seeker was required to defend his time as something exceedingly precious. He should cleanse his heart of all thoughts, so that only God resided in it. He should avoid meeting people and make this action impermissible for himself. He should realize that social intercourse resulted in wastage of time. He should acquire loving intimacy from remembering God (*zikr*). If he failed to do this, he would not feel the sweet fragrance of God's love. The Shaikh wrote to another disciple that eating less led to good health, discarding sinful actions led to protection of the soul and offering greetings to the Prophet led to the consolidation of religion.[17] Approving the mystical method of the Shaikh, Nizamuddin Auliya stated that he modelled his life on the Quranic injunction, "Eat of what is pure and act righteously."

Miracles have been attributed to most sufis. The hagiographical literature was so replete with the accounts of miracles that they had become an indispensable part of such writings. The sufis themselves had a different attitude to the performance of miracles.[18] In the case Shaikh Bahauddin Zakariya, we have at least one reference which shows his aversion to the act. According to an incident recorded in the mystical discourses of Syed Jalaluddin Bukhari Makhdum-i-Jahaniyan, *Jami-ul-Ulum*, one day Shaikh Bahauddin Zakariya was taking rest, while his disciple Ali Khokhar Darvesh was pulling the fan to freshen the air of the room. When the disciple left for offering his supererogatory prayer, he beckoned the fan to keep moving. When the Shaikh woke up, he was surprised to find that the disciple was missing, while the fan was moving. The Shaikh was outraged at this display of miraculous power by his disciple. Giving vent to his anger, the Shaikh cursed the disciple with perpetual hunger, so that the more he ate the hungrier he felt. It was only the kind intervention of Shaikh Jalal Tabrezi which miraculously cured the poor disciple of his misery. Offering a different version of the episode, Syed Muhammad Gesudaraz narrates that Shaikh Bahauddin Zakariya kicked Ali Khokhar Darvesh (reason not mentioned) as a result of which the latter's hunger and libido were so activated that he ate and indulged himself endlessly and went about scolding his own mentor.[19]

It is true that Shaikh Bahauddin Zakariya did not show interest in the philosophical aspects of mysticism, but confined himself to the practical aspects and spiritual purity. This view is confirmed by a book in Arabic *al-Aurad*, the authorship of which has been attributed to the Shaikh. A commentary of this work was prepared by Maulana Ali bin Ahmad Ghuri, who was a disciple of Ruknuddin Abul Fateh, the grandson of the Shaikh. This work elucidates some basic religious doctrines and lays down instructions for the seeker in simple and direct manner.[20] It also comprises prayers and *zikr* formulae, which have been compiled in the style of early traditionists (*muhadissin*), who provided legal solutions that were applicable to social phenomena.

Owing to the inspiration and encouragement of the Shaikh, a number of people belonging to his mystical circle devoted their energies to literary production. The first person in this category was Fakhruddin Iraqi. He was a nephew of Shaikh Shihabuddin Suhrawardi and had studied *Fasus-ul-Hikam* under the tutelage of Sadruddin Qunvi, who was a disciple of Ibn-i-Arabi. Iraqi is said to have fallen in love with a certain youth and followed him and a group of dervishes to India. On reaching Multan, he was so impressed by the magnetic personality of Shaikh Bahauddin Zakariya that he stayed in the city for the next twenty five years and composed laudatory verses (*qasidahs*) in his praise. According to one account, Iraqi locked himself in a cell (acting on the directions of the Shaikh) for ten days and did not permit anyone to enter. On the eleventh day, he was overcome by emotion and sang aloud while weeping:

The wine wherewith the cup they first filled high
Was borrowed from the saqi's langorous eye.

Since such an act of singing was not permitted within the precincts of the Suhrawardi hospice, the inmates lodged a complaint with Shaikh Bahauddin Zakariya who, instead of issuing any reprimand, exclaimed that the recitation of poetry was forbidden for the complainants, but not for Iraqi. After a few days, it was learnt that the poems of Iraqi were being sung in the bazaar and taverns to the accompaniment of musical instruments. When the matter was reported to the Shaikh, he went to Iraqi's cell and sought an explanation. Iraqi emerged out of his cell, placed his head at the Shaikh's feet and started weeping. The Shaikh raised his head from the ground, conferred his own robe on him and brought an end to his stay in the cell. The author of *Siyar-ul-Arifin* would have us believe that Iraqi wrote his book entitled *Flashes* (*Lamaat*) at the inspiration of Shaikh Bahauddin Zakariya. Written in the traditional form of poetry mixed with prose, it deals with several problems of mystic life in general and his own life in particular i.e. love revealed through the medium of human beauty. He believed that love was the only thing that existed in the world; the lover, beloved and love are one and, therefore, the question of union and separation was irrelevant; the separation wished by the beloved was a thousand times better and more beautiful than the union desired by the lover; God was the eternally beautiful beloved, while the lover loved every order and action of the beloved; heart and love were one; love sometimes grew out of the heart like flowers; the whole world was nothing but an echo of love's eternal song. In view of these ideas, it may be suggested that Iraqi transformed the mystical thoughts of Ibn-i-Arabi into a poetic form. We learn that Shaikh Bahauddin Zakariya had married his daughter to Iraqi. However, immediately after the death of the Shaikh (1262), Iraqi left Multan and reached Konya, where he met Sadruddin Qunvi and perhaps Jalaluddin Rumi. Following his death in 1289, Iraqi was buried in Damascus near the grave of Ibn-i-Arabi. Annemarie Schimmel opines that Shaikh Bahauddin Zakariya would not have been so well known if the noted poet Iraqi had not lived in his entourage for nearly twenty five years.[21]

Another creative intellectual associated with the mystical circle of Shaikh Bahauddin Zakariya was Sadruddin Ahmad bin Najmuddin Saiyyid Husaini, who was the reputed author of such works as *Kanz-ul-Rumuz*, *Zad-ul-Musafirin*, *Tarb-i-Majalis* and *Nuzhat-ul-Arwah*. It was in response to the questions raised by Husaini that Mahmud Shabistari composed his *masnavi* entitled *Gulshan-i-Raz*. It is believed that Husaini completed his collection of poetry (*diwan*) *Kanz-ul-Rumuz* during his stay at the convent of Shaikh Bahauddin Zakariya. In this work, we come across poetic verses in the praise of Shaikh Bahauddin Zakariya and his son Shaikh Sadruddin Arif.[22]

Sometimes the contemporary writings refer to ascetics called Qalandars and Jawaliqs who were known for their extremely unorthodox conduct. Though they were engaged in spiritual pursuits, yet they differed widely from the conventional sufis. They were opposed to the settled life of convents (*khanqahs*) and remained always on the move. They could be easily recognized owing to their outlandish appearance, particularly clothes and hair.[23] But it was their impudent behaviour which gave maximum offence to the mystics. Shaikh Bahauddin Zakariya, as a rule, did not permit the Qalandars to enter his hospice. But sometimes he felt constrained to recognize their spiritual attainments. Once during the course of his travels, the Shaikh happened to be present at a congregation of the Jawaliqs. When he fixed his gaze on them, he saw light emanating from one of them. He went close to that person and asked, "What are you doing here in the company of these people." He replied, "Zakariya, so that you are informed that in each group of the commoners, there is one of distinction and excellence."[24] However, this encounter did not reduce the Shaikh's aversion to them. Interestingly, this attitude was mutual. The Jawaliqs had doubts regarding the spiritual credentials of the Shaikh, probably because of his possession of wealth and the aristocratic character of his *khanqah*. Once a group of Jawaliqs came to the *khanqah* of Shaikh Bahauddin Zakariya and demanded something. Since the Shaikh had a bad opinion about them, he refused to meet their demand. The Jawaliqs went out of the *khanqah*, created an uproar and even threw brickbats at the door. The Shaikh had the door closed and declared that he had not settled there on his own and that the place had been selected as his abode by a man of God (Shaikh Shihabuddin Suhrawardi). This statement had the desired effect. When the door was opened, the Jawaliqs prostrated themselves before the Shaikh and went away.[25]

Involvement in Politics

Following in the footsteps of their masters in west Asia, the Indian Suhrawardis maintained close relations with the ruling class and did not hesitate to take part in contemporary politics. The following incident, as related by Shaikh Nizamuddin Auliya, assumes relevance in this context. We are aware of the conflict between Sultan Shamsuddin Iltutmish (r. 1210-1236) and Nasiruddin Qubacha, who held the territories of Multan and Uch. In these circumstances, two eminent citizens of Multan – Shaikh Bahauddin Zakariya and the judge (*qazi*) of the city – sent letters to Iltutmish, probably assuring their support. The letters fell into the hands of Qubacha, who was so incensed that he had the *qazi* killed and summoned the Shaikh to his court. The Shaikh went to the court and fearlessly sat on the right side of Qubacha as he used to do in the past. Qubacha handed over the Shaikh's letter. The Shaikh read the letter, confirmed that it was written by him and that it was in his own handwriting. Qubacha sought his explanation for having written such a letter. The Shaikh declared that what he had written was true, that he himself was free to do what he liked and that Qubacha could do nothing as he was powerless. Qubacha still thought of punishing the Shaikh. He invited the Shaikh to join him for meals. He anticipated that the Shaikh would refuse, as he was very particular about not eating at any one's house and, in case of his refusal, he would get an excuse to do him some harm. However, the Shaikh joined others in eating the food. Qubacha's anger subsided and the Shaikh left for his lodge.[26]

We can expect that the final defeat of Qubacha at the hands of Iltutmish must have eased the situation for Shaikh Bahauddin Zakariya. Subsequently, the Shaikh developed cordial relations with the Sultan of Delhi. The remaining part of the Shaikh's life coincided with the reigns of the successors of Iltutmish. However, we do not know the Shaikh's attitude towards them or towards the powerful governors of Multan – Kabir Khan Ayaz and Izzuddin Balban Kishlu Khan – who administered the region as virtually independent rulers. The Shaikh appears to have kept aloof from the internal conflict within the ruling class, which often spilled over from Delhi to Multan. However, the Shaikh did intervene when Multan was threatened by the Mongols and the very life of its inhabitants was at stake.

During the early thirteenth century, the rise of the Mongols caused widespread devastation in central and western Asia. After the occupation of China and Transoxiana, Chengiz Khan overran the kingdom of Khwarizm and turned towards Afghanistan. Jalaluddin Mangbarni, the Khwarizmian prince, offered some resistance from Ghur and Ghazni before fleeing to India. When Jalaluddin Mangbarni entered Punjab in 1221, Nasiruddin Qubacha was ruling over Multan and Uch, with the strong intention of occupying Lahore also. However, Qubacha's position became vulnerable as he had to bear the brunt of Mangbarni's hostile presence in central Punjab. In 1224, an army of 20,000 Mongols (two *tumans*) under Tarbai Toqshin arrived in pursuit of Mangbarni. They invaded Multan and besieged the city. The people of Multan offered a stiff resistance to the invaders, who were forced to raise the siege and retreat. The compiler of the *Fuwaid-ul-Fuad* would have us believe that three sufis came to the rescue of Multan and employed their miraculous powers to save the city. It is related that once these three saints – Shaikh Bahauddin Zakariya, Shaikh Jalaluddin Tabrezi and Shaikh Qutbuddin Bakhtiyar Kaki – were together at Multan, which was then under the rule of Qubacha. An army of infidels (Mongols) attacked Multan and laid siege to the walled city. On one night, Shaikh Qutbuddin Bakhtiyar Kaki gave an arrow to Qubacha and asked him to shoot it in the dark. This was done. Next morning, it was found that all the invaders had disappeared. The episode does hint at the unspecified role played by the three saints in ensuring the safety of the city from destruction at the hands of the Mongols.[27]

In 1246 a Mongol army led by Malik Shamsuddin and Sali Nuyin marched to Hindustan and laid siege to the city of Multan. At this time Chengiz Khan, a slave of Sultan Iltutmish was the governor of Multan. After resisting the invaders for fourteen days, Chengiz Khan sent Shaikh Bahauddin Zakariya to the Mongol general Malik Shamsuddin, so as to persuade him to accept money and raise the siege. The Shaikh met Malik Shamsuddin who, in turn, carried the proposal to Sali Nuyin. It was agreed that Chengiz Khan would pay a ransom of one lakh *dinars* and the invaders would retreat. Next day, the Shaikh delivered the said amount to Sali Nuyin and Chengiz Khan's presents for Malik Shamsuddin. In this manner, the active intervention of Shaikh Bahauddin Zakariya saved the inhabitants of Multan from death and destruction.[28]

Emphasis on Form

Shaikh Bahauddin Zakariya was extremely punctilious regarding the outward form of devotion. He did not tolerate even a minor deviation from what he regarded as the correct religious practice. He appears to have offended a number of people by his somewhat self-righteous attitude, which was considerably similar to that of the orthodox theologians. Let us consider the following examples that were quoted by Shaikh Nizamuddin Auliya during the course of his mystical discourses. According to one of these incidents, Shaikh Bahauddin Zakariya believed that a disciple must complete his ablutions or prayers before getting up to pay respects to his spiritual mentor. Once the Shaikh reached the bank of a river, where he found that a group of his disciples was engaged in performing the ablutions. As soon as they saw the Shaikh, they left their ablutions unfinished and paid their respects. However, one of them continued to perform the task till he had completed it and only then rose to pay his respects to his mentor. On observing the difference between the respective conducts of his disciples, the Shaikh declared that only one of them was a mystic (*darvesh*).[29] This remark shows that in the eyes of the Shaikh the performance of a prescribed ritual was essential as well as meritorious. Even if a person dreamt that he had missed one of his regular prayers, he should feel penitent and take a vow of repentance for and abstinence from sins, because this opportunity could be denied owing to his death which could come any time.[30]

There was a man called Sulaiman who was known among the people of Multan for his devotional exercises. One day, Shaikh Bahauddin Zakariya went to meet him, apparently to check what he had heard from others. He asked Sulaiman to stand up and offer prayer of two *rakaat*. Contrary to the prescribed rule, Sulaiman did not keep the required space between his feet. The Shaikh advised him on the space between the feet, which could be neither more nor less than what was prescribed. However, Sulaiman failed to observe the rule of space between his feet, even though he tried a number of times. Thereupon, the Shaikh asked Sulaiman to leave Multan and to settle in Uch, which the man actually did.[31]

We learn that Shaikh Bahauddin Zakariya walked everyday to the mosque attached to the seminary (*madrasah*) of Qazi Qutbuddin Kashani, who was known for his erudition and piety. Kashani asked the Shaikh the reason for his walking all the way to the place and offering his morning prayer behind someone else. The Shaikh replied that his conduct conformed to a Prophetic tradition (*hadis*) according to which "One's praying behind a pious and learned man was as if one had prayed behind a prophet." One morning, the Shaikh arrived when the first *rakaat* had been completed and he joined the congregation in the second *rakaat*. When Kashani was still in the midst of *tashahhud*, the Shaikh stood up and completed his prayer before Kashani could turn to the right to say *salam*, denoting the completion of *tashahhud*. Kashani asked, "Why did you stand up before the *salam*. The *imam* may have made a mistake which needed correction by performing the *sajdah-i-sahw*. Since you stood up before *salam*, you may have missed it." The Shaikh replied that if one learnt through inner light that the *imam* had not made any mistake by observing the obligatory details of prayer, one was allowed to rise. In response, Kashani observed that the light, which was not in harmony with the *shariat*, was nothing but darkness. Since the Shaikh was not prepared for this outcome of the encounter, he never came again to the place for prayer.[32]

Shaikh Bahauddin Zakariya was strict not only about religious obligations and the manner of their observance, but he also paid equal attention to one's dress and hair. In case, he found anyone in improper dress or wearing his hair in an unacceptable manner, he did not hesitate to issue a sharp reprimand. Once a learned scholar (*danishmand*) arrived from Bukhara to Multan and came to pay his respects to Shaikh Bahauddin Zakariya. The Shaikh was angered on seeing the visitor, as he had curled hair (*mujaad*) and the end of his turban was hanging loose. The Shaikh asked the visitor the purpose of arriving with two snakes i.e. curled hair and loose end of the turban. The visitor was so upset by the remark that he immediately got his head shaved in the very presence of the Shaikh.[33] It appears that people belonging to the mystic circle of the Shaikh had also adopted the same attitude. A group of the Shaikh's companions, while on a visit to the *khanqah* of Shaikh Nizamuddin Auliya at Delhi, walked out of meals on seeing a guest supporting curled hair (*mujaad*).[34]

Assessment and Legacy

Shaikh Bahauddin Zakariya and his successors have been criticized on several grounds – accumulation of wealth, elitist character of the Suhrawardi *khanqah*, participation in politics and limited expansion in non-Muslim environment – which were connected with one another. Most often, a small incident is quoted on the authority of *Fuwaid-ul-Fuad* and which has been repeated in *Siyar-ul-Auliya*. It is related that the governor of Multan, on one occasion, borrowed some grain from Shaikh Bahauddin Zakariya. When this grain was being removed from his granaries, pitchers of silver *tankahs* were found concealed therein.[35] The abundance of wealth excited the cupidity of robbers, who resorted to blackmail in order to extract money from the Shaikh's sons. It is also alleged that the Shaikh paid huge sums of money to the tutors of his sons. Our attention is drawn to the lavish and aristocratic organization of the Suhrawardi *khanqah* at Multan. It was not open to the common people and it was run on the principles of social hierarchy which appeared incompatible with the substance of mysticism. In fact, Suhrawardi accumulation of wealth had generated an acrimonious debate within the larger mystic circle of north-western India. Jalaluddin Tabrezi (a Suhrawardi) and Hamiduddin Nagauri Suwali (a Chishti) carried out a lengthy correspondence with Shaikh Bahauddin Zakariya on this subject. We also come across a verbal duel between Shaikh Bahauddin Zakariya and Hamiduddin Nagauri Suwali on this issue. In the words of Nizami, "The replies given by the Suhrawardi saints were more rhetorical than logical and the quick witted questioners refused to be confused by rhetoric and platitudes."[36] In an attempt to explain the limited appeal of the Suhrawardis, it has been argued that they (in contrast to the Chishtis) emphasized the necessity of regulating actions prior to the control of emotions. This dampened the prospects of Suhrawardi expansion in a non-Muslim environment. It worked well in Muslim surroundings and served the spiritual needs of the Muslim community, but when it came to non-Muslim lands its progress stopped. On the question of religious conversion, the Suhrawardi attitude of sectarianism is highlighted along with the Chishti stance of communal harmony.[37]

Qazi Javed is strongly critical of the association of Suhrawardis with the contemporary rulers. In his eyes, the support of Shaikh Bahauddin Zakariya for Iltutmish was decisive in shaping the future development of the Suhrawardi order. Having come under the regional influence, it lost its independence and became a puppet in the hands of the rulers.[38] The outlook of the Suhrawardis gradually became similar to that of the courtly theologians and nobles, so that Ruknuddin Abul Fateh and Syed Jalaluddin Bukhari began to advocate unconditional subordination to the rulers. In justification of their stance, they argued that it helped in creating an Islamic atmosphere in the royal court. The merger of mysticism and politics of mutual accommodation caused great harm to the former. In fact, this trend had surfaced in the times of Shaikh Bahauddin Zakariya.[39]

It is not possible for us to agree with the above understanding on account of several factors. It is not only harsh and one-sided, but also fails to pay adequate attention to the socio-political context in which Shaikh Bahauddin Zakariya lived. Firstly, we are bound to keep in mind the mystical inheritance of the Indian Suhrawardis. They had imbibed the teachings of the famous Suhrawardi masters of West Asia, particularly Abu Najib Abdul Qahir and Shaikh Shihabuddin Suhrawardi. These saints, having been inspired by the mystical ideology of Shaikh Junaid Baghdadi, had clearly rejected the ideas of intoxication (*sukr*) and stressed the Islamic law (*shariat*) as the foundation of spiritual development. On the one hand, they recognized the significance of the outward form of devotion and, on the other, they cultivated intimate relations with the caliphate.[40] When the Indian Suhrawardis laid the foundation of the order in Multan, they brought with them a fully developed system of thought and planted it successfully in the new environment. They could not be blamed for this, because this is what they were expected to do. In all situations, they displayed their loyalty and commitment to the mystical principles of their order, though they might have been required to make some minor compromises.

Secondly, the Multan region was passing through a critical phase during the first half of the thirteenth century. The Delhi sultanate had not consolidated as a systematic political structure, because there were perpetual factional conflicts within the ruling class. The political condition was further complicated by the intrusion of foreign invaders – Mongols, Khwarizmians and Qarlughs – who succeeded in establishing their sway in different parts of Punjab and threatened to annex Multan also. The successive governors of Multan, Kabir Khan Ayaz and Izzuddin Balban Kishlu Khan, thought it prudent to rule independently of Delhi, formally or informally. The Mongols had extended their influence up to the Beas, while the Delhi sultanate displayed its inability to recover the lost territories. The Mongols, who were notorious for their destruction and cruelty, had struck terror in all directions. The common people were the worst sufferers of internal instability and foreign invasions. Since their socio-economic life was frequently disrupted, they found it difficult to protect their homes and hearths.

Nobody was more conscious of the gravity of the situation than Shaikh Bahauddin Zakariya. Since he was born and brought up in Multan, he was aware of the socio-economic conditions of the people as well as their religious beliefs and practices. During his long stay in West Asia, he must have observed the emergence of mystic orders and political disintegration of the caliphate, besides the challenge posed by the Mongol irruption. When he established the Suhrawardi order in Multan during the first quarter of the thirteenth century, he found this region in the midst of political instability and economic disruption. The crisis, in fact, continued till the very end of his life (1265). This extraordinary situation could be mitigated only by extraordinary measures. This provides a clue to the Shaikh's political involvement and accumulation of wealth. He sought to achieve these aims by forging an intimate alliance with the ruling class, which brought in exalted titles, valuable gifts and land grants. His initiative appears to have led to the promotion of trade which, despite the constant threat of foreign invasions, was the only source of survival and prosperity of the people of Multan. Besides being a centre of mystic discipline, his *khanqah* also served as a centre of education, as the seminary (*madrasah*) attached to it provided instructions in exegesis (*tafsir*), Prophetic traditions (*hadis*) and Muslim jurisprudence (*fiqh*). The *khanqah* became a meeting ground of mystics, scholars, nobles, merchants, musicians and commoners. The presence of such eminent poets as Fakhruddin Iraqi and Sadruddin Ahmad bin Najmuddin Saiyyid Husaini indicates that the literary atmosphere of the *khanqah* attracted creative minds from distant lands. As a rule, discussion on theological matters was avoided. Emphasis was laid on the discipline of inner life and emotional integration in the light of religious teachings, rather than intellectual advancement through casuistry.

In contrast to the Chishtis who stood for starvation and self-mortification, Shaikh Bahauddin Zakariya advocated a normal and balanced life which accorded equal care to the body and spirit. By negating the ascetic and passive tendencies in Islamic mysticism, he introduced a contrastive model of human development which was designed to resolve political, social and spiritual problems of the society. This dispensation was based on a judicious merger between the Islamic law (*shariat*) and Islamic spirituality (*tariqat*). He believed in the continuity of the religious structure of Islam and maintaining the purity of its outward form. But he did not hesitate to mould the mystical dimension of Islam to suit the dire socio-political needs of the locality. He performed this difficult task by weaving the different threads of spiritual thought into a holistic pattern which, though contrastive in relation to parallel systems, manifested itself in an aesthetic image. It was on account of these factors that the Shaikh's mystical approach was adopted by a large number of people of Multan. The success of the Shaikh's mission was reflected in his rich legacy as well as the consolidation and expansion of the Suhrawardi order under his able successors. It is true that his immediate successor Shaikh Sadruddin Arif (d.1285) discarded a few fundamental principles of his predecessor. However, the subsequent Suhrawardi examplers reverted to the mystical school of Shaikh Bahauddin Zakariya. Shaikh Ruknuddin Abul Fateh who served for nearly half a century (1285-1335) as the spiritual head of the Suhrawardi order in Multan, carried the discipline to the greatest heights of popularity. Syed Jalaluddin Surkh Bukhari, a disciple of Shaikh Bahauddin Zakariya, founded a branch of the order in the neighbouring town of Uch. It was under the stewardship of his charismatic grandson, Syed Jalaluddin Bukhari Makhdum-i-Jahaniyan, that the Uch branch played a significant role in the socio-political life of north-western India. Thus we see that the mystical doctrines and practices of Shaikh Bahauddin Zakariya can be better appreciated if they are viewed in their specific context and assessed in terms of their long term consequences.

NOTES AND REFERENCES

1. Khaliq Ahmad Nizami, *Religion and Politics in India during the Thirteenth Century*, Oxford University Press, Delhi, New Edition, 2002, p. 238.
2. Amir Hasan Ala Sijzi, *Fawaid-ul-Fuad*, (Spiritual and Literary Discourses of Nizamuddin Auliya), English Translation, Ziyaul Hasan Faruqi, D.K. Printworld, New Delhi, 1995, p. 135.
3. For a detailed account of the military expeditions of Sultan Muizzuddin, see A.B.M. Habibullah, *The Foundation of Muslim Rule in India*, Central Book Depot, Allahabad, Third Revised Edition, 1976, pp. 46-64.
4. Mohammad Habib and Khaliq Ahmad Nizami, (Ed.), *A Comprehensive History of India, Vol.V*, (*The Delhi Sultanate A.D. 1206-1526*), People's Publishing House, New Delhi, Reprint, 1982, pp. 214-215.
5. Minhaj-us-Siraj Jurjani, *Tabqat-i-Nasiri*, Persian Text, Ed., Nassau Lees, Khadim Husain and Abdul Hayy, Bibliotheca Indica, Calcutta, 1864, pp. 233-235.
6. Ibid., pp. 269-273.
7. *Imperial Gazetteer of India, Provincial Series*: *Punjab*, Vol. II. Superintendent of Printing, Calcutta, 1908, p. 224.

8. H.C. Verma, *A Study of Trade and Military Routes*, Naya Prokash, Calcutta, 1978, pp. 123-129.
9. Andre Wink, *Al-Hind: The Making of the Indo-Islamic World*, Vol. II, Oxford University Press, Delhi, 1999, pp. 243-244.
10. Tapan Raychaudhury and Irfan Habib, (Ed.), *The Cambridge Economic History of India*, Vol. I, c.1200-c.1750, Orient Longman, New Delhi, Reprint, 2004, p. 85.
11. Barani would have us believe that a foreign scholar of Prophetic traditions (*hadis*), Maulana Shamsuddin Turk, reprimanded Sultan Alauddin Khalji for appointing as the chief judge of the kingdom a man called Hamid Multani Bachha, who apparently did not possess the learning required for the high post. The Maulana warned that the Sultan would be severely punished on the day of judgement for assigning the implementation of the *shariat* to the worldly minded and greedy persons. Ziauddin Barani, *Tarikh-i-Firuz Shahi*, Persian Text, Ed., Saiyyid Ahmad Khan, W.N. Lees and Kabiruddin, Bibliotheca Indica, Calcutta, 1860, p. 298.
12. Ibid., p. 311.
13. Ibid., p. 120.
14. It has been argued that Ali bin Usman Hujwiri and Shaikh Farid followed the middle course and believed that the *shariat* and *tariqat* were complementary. Qazi Javed, *Punjab Key Sufi Danishwar*, Fiction House, Lahore, 2005, p. 73.
15. Saiyid Athar Abbas Rizvi, *A History of Sufism in India*, Vol. I, Munshiram Manoharlal, New Delhi, 1978, p. 193.
16. Abdul Haq Muhaddis Dehalvi, *Akhbar-ul-Akhyar*, Urdu Translation, Maulana Subhan Mahmud and Maulana Muhammad Fazil, Nur Publishing House, New Delhi, 1990, p. 64.
17. Ibid., p. 65.
18. In an attempt to explain the widespread belief in miracles, a modern writer argues that sufism had to seek the support of the miraculous in order to make up for the defects in its theological foundations. The orthodoxy, which was based on the Quran and *sunnah*, enjoyed the support of the state. On the other hand, miracles made the sufi superior to the representative of the orthodoxy and, by inference, to orthodoxy itself. M. Mujeeb, *The Indian Muslims*, George Allen & Unwin, London, 1967, 120.
19. Riazul Islam, *Sufism in South Asia: Impact on Fourteenth Century Muslim Society*, Oxford University Press, Karachi, 2002, p. 44.
20. Qazi Javed, op. cit., p. 74.
21. Annemarie Schimmel, *Mystical Dimensions of Islam*, Sang-e-Meel Publications, Lahore, Reprint, 2003, pp. 352-354.
22. Qazi Javed, op. cit., pp. 74-75; Shaikh Muhammad Ikram, *Ab-i-Kausar*, Taj Company, Delhi, Reprint, 1987, pp. 260-261.
23. The antinomian groups among the broad category of sufis figure frequently in the hagiographical traditions of the Delhi sultanate. Certain groups in these sources can be distinguished by the peculiarities of their appearance, costume and insignia, failure to perform prescribed Muslim duties and other supererogatory pious acts, occasional violent attacks on the sufis

and episodes of immoral conduct. These groups are denominated Qalandari, Haydaris, Jawaliqs and Muwallihs. Kumkum Srivastava, 'The Qalandars and the Qalandriyya Path (Tariqa)' in Anup Taneja, Ed., *Sufi Cults and the Evolution of Medieval Indian Culture*, Indian Council of Historical Research & Northern Book Centre, New Delhi, 2003, p. 253.

24. Amir Hasan Ala Sijzi Dehalvi, *Fawaid-ul-Fuad*, pp. 75-76.
25. Ibid., pp. 143-144.
26. Ibid., pp. 253-254.
27. Ibid., p. 234.
28. It is not clear why Minhaj has failed to record the episode. Our information is entirely based on *Tarikh Nama-i-Herat* by Saif bin Muhammad Haravi. Khaliq Ahmad Nizami, *Religion and Politics in India During the Thirteenth Century*, p. 272.
29. Amir Hasan Ala Sijzi Dehalvi, *Fawaid-ul-Fuad*, p.414; responding to a question, Nizamuddin Auliya stated that one should complete one's supererogatory prayers without break and only then rise to meet a saintly visitor. During the same discourse, he argued that the command of a Shaikh must be carried out irrespective of what one was doing, as the command of a Shaikh was equal to that of the Prophet.
30. Amir Hasan Ala Sijzi Dehalvi, *Fawaid-ul-Fuad*, pp. 404-405.
31. Ibid., pp. 399-400.
32. Ibid., pp. 420-421.
33. Ibid., p. 399.
34. Ibid., pp. 374-375.
35. Ibid., p. 403.
36. Khaliq Ahmad Nizami, *Religion and Politics in India during the Thirteenth Century*, p. 245.
37. Ibid., pp. 191-192.
38. Qazi Javed, *Punjab Key Sufi Danishwar*, p. 71-72.
39. Ibid., pp. 76-77.
40. Shaikh Najibuddin Abdul Qahir, the founder of the Suhrawardi order, attended coronation ceremonies. His lectures were attended by a large number of people including caliphs, sultans, nobles, clerics and commoners. He served as the principal of Nizamiyah Madrasah. During his visit to Syria, he stayed with the ruler as the state guest. He delivered sermons to the army which was mobilized to fight the Christian powers. Not surprisingly, he rode on a camel in great style. Following his example, Shaikh Shihabuddin Suhrawardi gave religious instructions under court patronage. He served as the royal ambassador to the court of Irbal. He came out in support of the caliph when Baghdad was attacked by the Khwarizm Shah. He dedicated his books on mysticism to the caliph. Nizami, op cit., pp. 267-268.

4

Suhrawardi Mysticism in South-Western Punjab

Contribution of Syed Jalaluddin Bukhari Makhdum-i-Jahaniyan

Aneesa Iqbal Sabir

Since the times of Ghaznavid occupation, Punjab has provided a fertile ground for the development of sufism. The impact of several sufi masters – Ali bin Usman Hujwiri of Lahore, Shaikh Fariduddin Ganj-i-Shakar of Pakpattan, Shaikh Bahauddin Zakariya of Multan, Bu Ali Qalandar of Panipat, Shaikh Ahmad of Sirhind and Hazrat Miyan Mir of Lahore – can be felt even today. During the medieval period, the adherents of different sufi orders – Chishti, Suhrawardi, Qadiri and Naqshbandi – worked zealously to preach their teachings. Our sources are rich in evidence regarding the members of these orders, who developed spiritual norms while living in various cities and towns of the region. Shaikh Bahauddin Zakariya (1182-1262) of Multan, who laid the foundation of the Suhrawardi order in the Indian subcontinent, enjoyed a tremendous reputation for his piety, scholarship and spirituality. Being the chief successor (*khalifa*) of Shaikh Shihabuddin Suhrawardi of Baghdad, Shaikh Bahauddin Zakariya earned great fame and popularity throughout the Islamic world.[1] He was one of the most influential mystic teachers of his age and held independent views on issues of religion and politics. According to Shaikh Nizamuddin Auliya of Delhi, Shaikh Bahauddin Zakariya possessed not only great organizing capacity, but also a very remarkable understanding of human nature.[2] Endowed with immense intuitive intelligence, he established a hospice (*khanqah*) at Multan, a place of considerable strategic importance in the thirteenth century. He lived and worked in this city for more than halfa century, s that his hospice emerged as a prominent centre of mystic discipline in medieval India. During this long period of spiritual activities, he attracted a large number of talented disciples. His son Shaikh Sadruddin Arif (d. 1285) succeeded him as his chief successor and *sajjadah nishin* at Multan, while Syed Jalaluddin Surkh Bukhari (d.1291) established another Suhrawardi centre at Uch, an ancient town of south western Punjab which was situated near the meeting place of the five rivers, the Panjnad.[3] The history of the Suhrawardi order in the Indian subcontinent revolves mainly around these two branches – Multan and Uch.[4] Syed Jalaluddin Bukhari, popularly known as Makhdum-i-Jahaniyan Jahan Gasht, was the grandson of Syed Jalaluddin Surkh Bukhari and the son of Syed Ahmad Kabir. It was under the stewardship of Bukhari that the Uch branch of the Suhrawardi order became an important factor in the religious and political life of north-western India, including Punjab, Sind and Gujarat.

Born on 14 Shaban 707 AH/ 19 January 1308 in Uch,[5] Syed Jalaluddin Bukhari was brought up in an environment which was permeated with scholarship and spiritualism. He received his elementary education in Uch under the guidance of Shaikh Jamal Khandan Ru and Shaikh Bahauddin (the *qazi* of Uch). Thereafter, he went to Multan and joined the seminary at the shrine of the late Shaikh Bahauddin Zakariya. The then *sajjadah nishin* Shaikh Ruknuddin Abul Fateh took special care of Bukhari's education and assigned this responsibility to Shaikh Musa and Maulana Majduddin, both of whom were renowned teachers. Bukhari stayed at Multan for a year and studied the Hidaya and Bazdawi under them. Later he proceeded to Hejaz and studied under the eminent scholars of Mecca and Madina, the two holy cities. In particular, he benefited from the erudition and spiritual excellence of Shaikh Abdullah Yafai and Shaikh Abdullah Matri.[6] On his return to Uch, Bukhari plunged into mysticism. It may be mentioned that during his childhood, he was under the spiritual influence of his grandfather Syed Jalaluddin Surkh Bukhari and received preliminary mystical training under his father Syed Ahmad Kabir. This early experience had motivated Bukhari to join the discipline of the Suhrawardi order at Multan. Shaikh Ruknuddin Abul Fateh had initially provided formal mystical education to Bukhari. Yet finding the pupil competent to tread the mystical path and, bearing in mind the spiritual background of his family, he authorized him to act as his spiritual successor (*khalifa*).[7] Within a short time of his return to Uch, Bukhari earned a high reputation both as a scholar of Islamic sciences and an exponent of the Suhrawardi order.

Bukhari was a widely travelled man. He is said to have visited several places in the Indian subcontinent and the Islamic world, with the object of preaching Islamic spirituality and benefiting from meetings with eminent mystic-scholars. In the words of Abdul Haq Muhaddis Dehalvi, "He travelled widely and received the blessings and benedictions from saints." (*siyahat bisyar kard wa bisyari az auliya niamat wa barkat yaft*).[8] According to the author of *Khazinat-ul-Asfiya*, Bukhari journeyed through several countries – Egypt, Syria, Iraq, Iran, Balkh, Bukhara and Khurasan – and obtained spiritual benefit from renowned sufis and performed the Haj several times, six of which were Haj-i-Akbar. Shaikh Jamali Kambo (the famous mystic scholar of Delhi in the sixteenth century), during the course of his journey to various places in the Islamic world, came across several houses and rooms where Bukhari had stayed during his sojourns in those parts during the fourteenth century.[9] It was on account of these journeys that Bukhari came to be known as Jahan Gasht (world traveller).

We are informed that Bukhari stayed for seven years at Mecca. He spent more than two years at Madina where, on one occasion, he led the prayers as *imam* in the Prophet's mosque (Masjid-i-Nabwi). In Yemen, he met an ascetic (*darvesh*) who lived in a cave on a mountain and held discussions with him on the gnosis of God (*maarifat*). In Aden, he called on Basal Qutb who was ailing during those days. Bukhari lived in Damascus for several months and has described the quality of blankets woven in this beautiful city. He also availed of the opportunity to visit Koh-i-Labnan (perhaps the Golan Heights). He was deeply impressed by the principal mosque in the city of Madain. In Shokarah, a famous town in Iraq, Bukhari met Shaikh Sharafuddin Mahmud Tustari (a renowned *khalifa* of Shaikh Shihabuddin Suhrawardi), who was said to have been 120 years of age. Bukhari studied the *Awarif-ul-Maarif* under him and received the authority of succession (*khilafatnama*) from him in 748 AH/1347 AD. In Shiraz, he taught the *Mishkat-ul-Masabih* to a group of students who were desirous of studying it. The *qazi* of Shiraz, having listened to one of the sermons of Bukhari, presented two beautiful trays full of gold and silver coins. Bukhari accepted the lavish gift, but distributed it among the poor and needy. He visited Tabrez as well. It has been mentioned in his *malfuzat* that the mosques of this famous city were surrounded by beautiful trees and plants.[10]

During Bukhari's sojourn in Samarqand, the ruler (Badshah-i-Samarqand) sought his judgement on the legality of eating prawns, as the local theologians had issued a legal opinion (*fatwa*) against the practice. Bukhari gave an opinion in favour of its consumption as food. In Gazrun, a famous town near Shiraz, he paid homage at the graves of Shaikh Abu Ishaq Gazruni and Shaikh Aminuddin Gazruni. He provided the benefit of his erudition to the scholars and novices at the former's convent. He met Shaikh Imamuddin (the brother and *sajjadah nishin* of Shaikh Aminuddin Gazruni's shrine) and received the gift of personal belongings – carpet, shirt and staff – of the deceased.[11] Bukhari also travelled to a number of places in the regions now known as Arab Emirates and northern part of modern Saudi Arabia. It appears from Bukhari's *malfuzat* that the inhabitants of Ahsa, Qatif and Bahrain were Shia, while the local ruler was Sunni. Bukhari is believed to have visited to China, Mongolia and even Ceylon. In spite of these journeys to different parts of the globe, Bukhari had great love for India. He believed that the blessing, which God had bestowed on India, could not be claimed by any other country in the world.[12] It may be mentioned that he visited Jaunpur, a city in the eastern part of modern Uttar Pradesh, on two occasions.[13] He also used to visit Delhi after every two or three years, as will be described below.

At this juncture, it is interesting to mention that when Bukhari was staying at Mecca, his teacher Shaikh Abdullah Yafai praised the Chishti sufis of Delhi and, in particular, described the virtuous qualities of Shaikh Nasiruddin Mahmud Chiragh-i-Delhi. Since then Bukhari developed a keen desire to benefit from this saint. When he got an opportunity to visit Delhi, he joined the mystic circle of Shaikh Nasiruddin Mahmud and, thus acquired an affiliation with the Chishti order in addition to his existing association with the Suhrawardi discipline. Shaikh Nasiruddin Mahmud was so impressed by the new entrant that he conferred the authority of succession (*khilafat*) and bestowed his own cloak (*khirqa*) and turban (*dastar*).[14] From then onwards, Bukhari came to be recognized by the followers of both the Suhrawardi and Chishti orders. He enrolled disciples in both the orders and trained them in accordance with their choice. He deputed his disciples (*khalifas*) to different parts of the Indian subcontinent and abroad to propagate the teachings of two sufi orders. His popularity began to spread in all directions.[15] Throughout the centuries, he was regarded as one of the most distinguished mystic-scholars of the pre-Mughal period. In his *Akhbar-ul-Akhyar*, Shaikh Abdul Haq Muhaddis Dehalvi has accepted Bukhari's excellence in learning and sainthood (*jami ast miyan-i ilm wa wilayat*).[16]

Relations with Rulers

We are aware of Muhammad bin Tughluq's (r.1325-1351) vigorous attempt to utilize the services of sufis (particularly belonging to the Chishti order) in running the affairs of the state. But these efforts did not bear fruit in the case of Bukhari. To be fair to the sultan, he was keen to win over the saint. He conferred the title of Shaikh-ul-Islam on Bukhari,[17] the charge of forty convents (*khanqahs*) and a corresponding land grant in Sehwan. In spite of these favours, Bukhari did not stay at his new post and left for travels in the Islamic lands. He seems to have returned to Punjab only during the reign of Firuz Shah Tughluq (r.1351-1388). He revived the Suhrawardi centre at Uch in a manner that his reputation spread to Delhi as well as Sind. On the one hand, he developed friendly relations with the sultan and, on the other, extended his influence to the local potentates of Sind. Shaikh Nasiruddin Mahmud Chiragh-i-Delhi appears to have been instrumental in bringing a rapprochement between the Delhi sultanate and Bukhari. The latter assisted the sultan in settling the political turmoil in Sind. The two Samma chiefs, Banbhina and Juna, had established their sway in Sind and, with the support of the Mongols, posed a serious challenge to the Delhi sultanate. Since Delhi's first military expedition to Sind had ended in a disaster, a second campaign was initiated against the Samma chiefs. The arrival of the Delhi army forced the inhabitants to flee, leaving their crops to be captured. The local resistance was weakened by a severe famine and scarcity of foodgrains. In these circumstances, the Samma chiefs sent an emissary to Bukhari and sought his mediation in securing peace from Delhi. Bukhari arrived on the scene of war and met the sultan. He declared that Sind could not be annexed earlier owing to the prayers of a holy woman; since she had died, the occupation of Sind by Delhi could no longer be delayed. In the wake of Bukhari's intervention, the sultan stopped the military operations and accepted the surrender by the Samma chiefs.[18] Peace was restored in Sind and a new administration was put in place.

Bukhari had the best of relations with Firuz Shah Tughluq. There was immense affection between them. They trusted each other like intimate friends. Bukhari followed a particular attitude towards the sultan for several years. After every one or two years, he travelled from Uch to Delhi. On these occasions, he stayed at the Firuzabad palace or the hospital (Dar-ul-Shafa) or the residence of Prince Fateh Khan. When Bukhari went to meet the sultan, the latter got up from the throne and showed deep reverence for the visitor. The two sat together on a carpet that was spread on the floor and engaged in a dialogue. When Bukhari took leave to return, the sultan remained standing till he had gone out of sight. During these days, the sultan also visited Bukhari after every two or three days. Showing great affection for each other, they remained engaged in long conversations. Bukhari availed himself of the opportunity to present the petitions, which the people of Uch and Delhi had prepared. The sultan passed instant orders for the redressal of grievances. When Bukhari left Delhi for Uch, the sultan saw him off up to one stage of the journey. The saint followed this schedule for several years, each visit being longer than the previous one. While parting on the occasion of the last visit, Bukhari declared that this probably could be their last meeting, as both of them had become old. He also advised the sultan to refrain from the royal pastime of hunting and pleasure trips.[19]

Though Firuz Shah Tughluq regarded himself as a humble follower of Bukhari, the sultan's *wazir* Khan-i-Jahan nurtured a hostile attitude towards the saint and even used uncomplimentary language for him. Circumstances leading to the change of *wazir's* heart have been recorded in the *Siyar-ul-Arifin*. Once the *wazir* imprisoned the son of a petty government functionary (*muharrir*) and subjected him to torture. The officer failed to see any possibility of the release of his son. Since he happened to be a follower of Bukhari, he requested the saint to make a recommendation to the *wazir* for the release of his son. Bukhari went to the *wazir's* bungalow for this purpose. However, the *wazir* sent an angry message through a servant, refusing to accept the recommendation. The *wazir* even refused to meet the visitor and asked him not to come again. Bukhari was not disheartened. It is said that he came to the *wazir's* door as many as nineteen times, but every time he was met with the same curt refusal. When Bukhari went for the twentieth time, the *wazir* sent a message from inside the house, "Oh Syed! Are you not ashamed? You have been given a negative answer so many times. But still you come to my door and insist on making the recommendation. Bukhari replied, "My dear! Every time I come here, I get the just reward for a virtuous act. But this oppressed person does not achieve his aim. I wish that I am able to get him released by your own hands and, thus, I am able to ensure that the reward for this meritorious act is credited to you." Hearing this, the *wazir* felt immensely ashamed of his previous conduct. He bared his head, put a rope around his neck and fell at the feet of Bukhari. He became a devoted follower and offered a large amount of money as gift. The saint gave the entire amount to the oppressed person and returned to his house.[20] The author of *Mirat-i-Sikandari* would have us believe that the blessings of Bukhari enabled a devotee, Muzaffar Khan, to lay the foundation of the kingdom of Gujarat in the post-Timur period.[21]

Major Collection of Discourses

Let us begin by tracing the genesis of the *Jami-ul-Ulum*. We learn that Bukhari visited Delhi in 1379 to meet Firuz Shah Tughluq. But he could not meet the sultan as he was away from the capital. Bukhari stayed in the capital for several months, so that he could achieve his object. During this period he appears to have delivered mystical discourses to an audience of followers and admirers. Syed Alauddin Ali bin Syed Husaini, who remained present on these occasions for nearly nine months (28 Rabi-us-Sani 781 AH to 17 Muharram 782 AH), recorded the conversations, which have come to be known as the *Jami-ul-Ulum*.[22]

The exercise was undertaken at the direction of the saint, so that his views could be communicated to his disciples, particularly those who could not be present in person. Commenting on the nature of the recordings, a modern writer has stated that the opinions appear to have been expressed by a scholar who is deeply rooted in both the Prophetic traditions (*hadis*) and Muslim jurisprudence (*fiqh*). A comparison with some other sufi discourses – *Fuwaid-ul-Fuad*, *Khair-ul-Majalis*, *Jawami-ul-Kilam* and *Tuhfat-ul-Majalis* – indicates that the *Jami-ul-Ulum* contains a much larger number of revelations and miracles.[23]

A perusal of *Jami-ul-Ulum* enables us to comprehend the mystical beliefs and practices of Bukhari. He laid considerable emphasis on a strict adherence to the Muslim law (*shariat*) and led the others by his own example. He believed that seekers of the spiritual path (*rah-i-suluk*) were bound to follow the path shown by the Prophet, because there was no other way to achieve sainthood (*wilayat*) and the highest station in mysticism. Reverence for the Prophet extended to his companions (*ashab*), among whom the pious caliphs occupied an exalted position. Since the companions had been groomed by the Prophet himself, they were perfect in their virtues. It was therefore imperative not only to show utmost consideration for the companions, but also to follow their example in practice. The path of the companions was the most appropriate way, because they had adopted it directly from the Prophet. The companions, like the stars in the sky, showed the correct path to the seekers. Denial of the companions was tantamount to denial of Islam as well as the Prophet.[24] It was understood that the Muslim canon (*shariat*) and the mystical path (*tariqat*) could not be placed in separate compartments. *Tariqat* was nothing but *shariat* itself, so that the former could not be achieved without following the latter. *Tariqat* was like a straight path which had been derived from the *shariat*. It was like extracting the essential essence from something, just as refined flour (*maida*) was extracted from wheat, but the cause of refined flour continued to be wheat. Though clarified butter (*ghee*) was extracted from milk, yet the origin of the former was traced to the latter. The *shariat* aimed at stating the oneness of God, while *tariqat* sought to gain this experience through intense research. Furthermore, *tariqat* stood for cleanliness of the inner being, purity of conscience and adornment of the outward conduct through refined manners. It follows that pride in one's lineage was futile, because a person was identified by his conduct. It was worth recalling that Noah's lineage failed to save his ark from shipwreck in the stormy sea.

A perusal of *Jami-ul-Ulum* indicates that Bukhari was a strict adherent of the *shariat* and did not tolerate any deviation from it. Whenever he learnt about any deviation from it, particularly at the hands of any saintly person, he did not hesitate to intervene and stop what was seen as an objectionable practice. Once a person, who claimed to be God's friend (*wali allah*), arrived in Uch and settled there. A large number of people began to visit him, so that he acquired a lot of popularity. Bukhari also went to see him. Finding the eminent Suhrawardi sufi by his side, the man was filled with arrogance and exclaimed, "O Syed! God Almighty has just left me." Bukhari was outaraged and said, "O unfortunate one! You have turned an infidel (*kafir*). Recite the confession of faith and become a Muslim once again." Thereafter he went to the local judge (*qazi*) and complained against the impostor, saying, "If the person repents, he should be pardoned. If he does not, then he should be punished in accordance with the *shariat* and put to death." The *qazi* hesitated to take any action, as the man counted several influential persons among his followers. Bukhari was disappointed and reported the matter to the local administrator (*hakim-i-shahr*). He declared that the person was preaching infidelity (*kufr*) in the city and that if he was not punished, he would be constrained to approach the sultan of Delhi. Bukhari's demand was accepted and the man was expelled from the city.[25]

We encounter another similar anecdote in the *Jami-ul-Ulum*. An ascetic (*darvesh*) named Usman lived in a mountainous cave at Rohri, near Uch. A majority of his followers were said to have been Khurasanis. This man often proclaimed that God had exempted him from offering the obligatory prayers (*namaz*). Bukhari went up to him and, quoting a tradition of the Prophet, asked, "Why don't you offer the prayers." Usman replied, "My Syed! Jibreel brings the food of paradise for me. He conveys the salutations of God for me and, confirming my proximity in the court of the Supreme Being, has informed me that I have been exempted from offering the prayers." Taken aback, Bukhari argued, "Do not utter nonsense. If the exalted Prophet has not been exempted from prayers, how could an insignificant fool like you be exempted from the obligation. It is the devil (*shaitan*) not the angel, who has been misguiding you."[26] In short, Bukhari persuaded Usman to repent for his unorthodox conduct and return to the righteous path.

During the fourteenth century, the seekers were afflicted by doubts regarding several mystical practices. Bukhari assumed the task of clarifying the doubts during his discourses. For instance, the Suhrawardis permitted a seeker to undertake the forty day spiritual penance (*chilla*); this position stood in sharp contrast to that of the Chishtis who did not favour the practice. Muslim devotees, who participated in the congregational Friday prayers, were advised to occupy their minds in such a manner that they did not hear the names of oppressive rulers. In contrast to the Chishtis, the Suhrawardis accepted gifts from contemporary rulers. On one occasion, Bukhari received a gift of thirty seven sets of clothing from Firuz Shah Tughluq, which were delivered by the *wazir* Khan-i-Jahan. What is somewhat surprising, Bukhari did not take the food which was sent from the royal kitchen, on the grounds that the wealth of the rulers came from legally doubtful sources. However, Bukhari agreed to consume this food if the sultan purchased it with borrowed money. Suhrawardi sufis consumed food in extremely limited quantities. Bukhari's spiritual mentor, Shaikh Ruknuddin Abul Fateh, took some dried fruit boiled in milk and this too only once a day. He did not eat anything other than this during the whole day. His relatives summoned a physician named Farid and complained about the negligible quantity of food consumed by the saint. Farid partook a specimen of the diet and declared that it was sufficient not only for a day, but for the entire week. Bukhari recommended that a person could get his head shaved; but such a person was expected to seek the permission of his wife if he was married and that of his mother if he was unmarried. The permission was desirable lest the action should give offence to his wife or mother, as the case might be. Bukhari permitted the contentious mystical practice of audition (*sama*) only under strict conditions. He allowed the group of singers (*qawwals*) to sing, but forbade them from clapping with their hands or using musical instruments, on the grounds that it had been forbidden by all the four schools of Muslim jurisprudence. It was not permissible to play the drums (*daf* and *tabl*) except on the occasions of marriage and battle, besides the commencement of the journey of a caravan.[27]

The structure of Islamic mysticism was built on the foundation of discipleship (*piri-muridi*). The mystic circles felt deeply concerned about the functioning of this institution. Therefore, the sufis prescribed tough qualifications for those who aspired to act as spiritual preceptors (*shaikhs*, *pirs* or *murshids*) and seekers (*saliks* or *murids*). During the course of his mystical discourses, Bukhari has expressed his opinions on the subject and these have been recorded in the *Jami-ul-Ulum*. He has laid three basic qualifications for the Shaikh, who was expected to possess the knowledge of *shariat*, *tariqat* and *haqiqat*; his opinion should be sought by the other contemporary scholars; he should acquire a virtuous disposition by suppressing his physical needs and worldly desires. Without these qualities, a person could not be called a saint (*wali*), even if he was otherwise righteous and pious. His command over the *shariat* had to be perfect. Only then he could acquire the knowledge of *tariqat* and *haqiqat* which were higher stages on the spiritual path. In fact, he was also required to master such Islamic sciences as *fiqh* (jurisprudence), *usul* (principles of law) and *kalam* (scholasticism).[28] The three types of knowledge – *ilm-i-aqwal*, *ilm-i-afaal* and *ilm-i-hal* – were respectively associated with *shariat, haqiqat* and *tariqat*. This relation has been expounded by the Prophet himself. Every learned person could not claim to be a Shaikh. He should have treaded the long and arduous path of mysticism, drawing his authority from the Prophet. Finally Bukhari feels that the Shaikh must fulfill ten conditions which included keeping the obligatory fasts, remembering death at all times, accompanying the dead to the graveyard for burial, helping the orphans, spending on charity and enquiring after the sick.[29] In addition, the Shaikh was required to be generous towards the novice and to guide him with honesty. In case the Shaikh did not acquire perfection in the above qualities, he could not do justice to his role in the propagation of mysticism.

The qualities prescribed for the Shaikh were matched by those laid for the seeker. In fact, they were even more strict and demanding. First and foremost, the seeker had to be a learned person, because an illiterate person was totally unfit for initiation into the mystical path. Bukhari approves the practice followed by the sufis of Ajam (Persia). If the newly arrived novice was a scholar, he was immediately allotted a cell (*hujra*) in the convent (*khanqah*) and permitted to engage in spiritual exercises. In case, the novice was not educated, he was sent to a seminary (*madrasah*) and, after he had acquired a certain amount of learning, he was enrolled for spiritual training.[30] A seeker was also required to possess several qualities of head and heart. He had to discard greed for wealth, hypocrisy, jealousy, anger, animosity, arrogance, litigation, pomp and grandeur. Bukhari has recommended ten different ideals, which a seeker was expected to follow – to control his senses, to improve his character, to engage in contemplation, to recite the Quran, to fear God, to abide by the commands of God, to feel ashamed before God as He watched every action at all times, to remain contented with whatever came his way, to spend whatever he received and to strive for a union with the Supreme Being. While using the different parts of his body – eyes, hands, nose and mouth – the seeker should ensure that they were used only for those actions – seeing, receiving, smelling and eating – which were permissible under the religious law. However, he should reserve his heart only for the entry of God and none else.[31] He was expected to eat only the permissible (*halal*) food and this had to be eaten quickly, but in small morsels. He should take such a diet that only a small quantity produced a sense of satisfaction. He should drink little water and this too slowly. He should eat little meat, not more than once or twice a week and its quantity should not be more than 50 *dirhams*.[32] Since one of his basic aims was to control the evil desires, this could be done by spiritual exercises (*riyazat*), which implied a drastic reduction in food, sleep and speech.

While choosing a Shaikh for himself, opines Bukhari, the seeker should look for a person who was compassionate in disposition and familiar with the difficulties encountered on the mystical path. Since there was one Prophet in the eyes of the seeker, he should have only one Shaikh. In case, he decided to have another one, he should reserve his prime commitment to the first one and should place absolute trust in him. As a second step, the seeker should strike a judicious balance between retirement (*khilwat*) and assembly (*suhbat*), as both contributed in their own unique ways, to spiritual progress. A beginner should devote adequate time to retirement (*khilwat*) following in the footsteps of the Prophet, who practiced frequent solitude in the Ghar-i-Hira. During such occasions, the seeker should engage in repeating God's name (*zikr*) as well as the confession of faith (*kalima*), remembering to do this exercise to the optimum limit.[33] He should pay due attention to the assembly (*suhbat*) of the Shaikh, following in the footsteps of the companions (*ashab*) who derived immense spiritual benefit from their association with the Prophet. The seeker should avail of every opportunity of staying in the company of the Shaikh, though this was not an easy task. In earlier times, a Shaikh would have a maximum of eighty or a hundred disciples, so that there was adequate scope of providing companionship. In later times, this number went up to thousands but, as Bukhari complains, none of them availed the opportunity of *suhbat*. If the time for *suhbat* was little, its value was equal to that of a forty-day penance (*chilla*). But if the duration of *suhbat* was prolonged, there was no limit to its value in terms of the forty-day penance.[34] The seeker should stay in the company of his Shaikh at least for a few days. During this rare opportunity, he should sincerely follow the conduct of his Shaikh and should have absolute faith in him, which has the same significance in mysticism as intention had in the obligatory prayers (*namaz*). By doing so, the seeker slowly graduated from one stage to the other i.e. *shariat* to *tariqat* and *tariqat* to *haqiqat*. During these experiences, the seeker should show firm determination to move ahead continuously on the spiritual path. He should avoid making an open display of his spiritual accomplishments. He should discard arrogance which was likely to be caused by the special attention shown by the Shaikh. His real aim was to achieve nearness to God and this could happen only if his heart was purged of all worldly pollutants. He had to understand that the heart of a devout Muslim (*momin*) was the sacred abode (*haram*) of God.

The controversial utterances and the cruel execution of Mansur al-Hallaj have been a perpetual theme of discussion in the mystic circles.[35] Bukhari has felt constrained to participate in the hallowed debate and express his views, which have been preserved in the *Jami-ul-Ulum*. While discussing the subject, Bukhari relates that when Mansur was teaching, a voice said, "Is there anyone who can annihilate his soul for my sake." Mansur replied that he was the truth and that he was firm on sacrificing his soul. Bukhari has argued that Mansur did not make this statement in a state of intoxication (*sukr*); if Mansur was in such a state, he would have made different and incoherent statements in the manner of people affected by madness; in fact, when Qazi Abu Yusuf asked Mansur to clarify his position, Mansur repeated his original statement; this provoked the jurists to hold Mansur guilty of infidelity and pronounce the death sentence for him. On being questioned, Bukhari held that the opinion of both the externalist clerics and great mystics on Mansur's punishment was just; the former held that Mansur's statement amounted to infidelity, while the latter held that Mansur had asserted his claim of divinity. Bukhari again quoted the precedent of Mansur when he was elucidating his views on love. He argued that when the lover was overcome with love of the beloved, his own being was annihilated and he survived only in the being of the beloved. When Majnun was asked his name, he replied that it was Laila. This meant that he himself had been conquered and subjugated, while the beloved continued to exist. Similarly Mansur had annihilated and assimilated himself into the beloved, while his beloved continued to exist. Mansur had made his utterance when he had been engulfed by the passion of love. This may be understood in the context of the statement that love could not achieve perfection till one did not end one's life with the sword of self-mortification. In this sense, Mansur's self-annihilation was nothing but an attempt to ensure the perfection of his love for the Supreme Being.[36]

A modern writer has sought to understand Bukhari's liberal stance on Mansur, with reference to his (Bukhari's) association with Sharfuddin Yahya Maneri and his affiliation with the Chishti order. In his understanding, Bukhari kept away from philosophic discussions on mysticism, but focused on the practical aspects of mysticism and questions of religious interest. This was attributed to Bukhari's primary adherence to the Suhrawardi traditions. But he was also under the influence of Sharfuddin Yahya Maneri and often studied his letters. The two shared a common opposition to free-thinking (*azad khiali*) and deviation from the fundamentals of Islam (*inhraf pasandi*). Bukhari had adopted at the level of senses the mystical ideas propounded by Maneri at the level of philosophy. To understand the mystical beliefs of Bukhari, it is imperative to recall that he was associated with both the Suhrawardi and Chishti mystic disciplines, owing to his discipleship under masters of the two orders viz. Shaikh Ruknuddin Abul Fateh and Shaikh Nasiruddin Mahmud Chiragh-i-Delhi. As a result, he assimilated the mystic ideologies of both the orders and went on to develop a moderate and equitable understanding of mysticism. That is why we encounter his close contact with the ruling elite and adherence to the *shariat* along with a clear inclination towards renunciation and reason. This particular mystical position explains Bukhari's soft attitude towards Mansur. It becomes evident that Bukhari did not adopt a narrow and rigid stance on mystical matters and therefore showed a remarkable capacity to see more than one side of the picture.[37]

Minor Collections of Discourses

Besides the *Jami-ul-Ulum*, there is another collection of Bukhari's mystical discourses which was entitled *Khazana-i-Jawahar-i-Jalaliya*. Its compiler Fazlullah bin Ziaul Abbasi was one of the disciples of Bukhari. He received permission to reside in the old mosque of Uch as well as the authority (*khirqa-i-khilafat*) to enroll disciples in 1376. During a conversation, Bukhari claimed that he had received inner knowledge from the mystics of several Islamic lands – Mecca, Madina, Syria, Iraq, Yemen, Aden, Shiraz and Baghdad – and was looking for a seeker who could record it for the benefit of posterity. The compiler volunteered to handle the task and, after receiving Bukhari's permission, recorded the *malfuzat* pertaining to the last six years (1378-1384) of his mentor's life.[38] Internal evidence of this work indicates that it was completed during the lifetime of Bukhari. The compiler was a man of vast knowledge, as he has referred to a large number of books on mysticism and has inserted his own verses, while elaborating the teachings of his mentor. In the opinion of Bukhari, repentance (*tauba*) was the first stage in the path of mysticism, when the seeker sought forgiveness for past sins and promised to shun such acts in the future. Since early times, the mystics were firm on keeping away from the members of the ruling class. There were doubts about the legality of the income of the state and, on this ground, a certain sufi did not even drink the water from a canal excavated by the state. The mystic practice of audition was always under discussion. Bukhari asserted that no jurist (*faqih*) had ever given a decision in favour of audition (*sama*) and dance (*raqs*), but the practice had been perpetuated by the greed of musicians. When sufis permitted audition, they invariably prescribed strict conditions under which the practice could be held. In fact, there could be no audition without conditions, just as there could be no prayers without ablutions, fast without abstinence, cultivation without seed, tree without fruit, house without door and bird without feathers. In case a mystic felt the need for audition, it could be held after long intervals. The singer should not be a stranger, the mind should be immersed in God and the listening should be followed by fasting and contemplation.[39]

It appears that Bukhari was often required to give his advice on the practical aspects of mysticism. A mystic was required to wear simple clothes and to discard his moustache, but he could shave (*malhuq*) the hair of his head. Ordinarily he did not require a house, as he could live in the corner of a mosque. If he built a cell (*hujra*) for himself, it was to be done only for facilitating prayers and protection against extreme weather. A person could construct a house in the locality of the learned and righteous, but it should not be raised with illegal wealth. Marriage was essential, but it should be ensured that the woman was chaste, religious minded and belonging to a good family. Every effort should be made to ensure that she offered her prayers and, if she did not do so, she could be chastised or even divorced. Bukhari has expressed his anguish at the marriage customs of his times. These occasions were marked by wasteful expenditure, superfluous ostentation and status consciousness. The elite class was invited to the feast, while the poor neighbours were ignored. Musical instruments were played for celebrations and costly clothes were worn in order to meet the demands of fashion. What was even worse, people gave their daughters in marriage to such worthless men as fornicators (*fasiq*).[40]

Another collection of Bukhari's conversations was the *Siraj-ul-Hidaya*. It was compiled in 1371 by Ahmad Barani, who was also known as Ahmad Muin Siyahposh Iraji. Manuscripts of the work were found in the Maulana Azad Library of the Aligarh Muslim University, besides the personal collection of Khaliq Ahmad Nizami of Aligarh and Muhammad Iqbal Mujaddidi of Lahore. It pertains to the period when the Delhi army was engaged in a military expedition against the Samma chiefs of Thatta and Firuz Shah Tughluq as well as eminent nobles like Khan-i-Azam Zafar Khan used to meet Bukhari. The *Siraj-ul-Hidaya* is divided into nine chapters which focused on such issues as injunctions of the Muslim law (*ahkam-i-shara*), the Prophetic traditions (*hadis*), Muslim jurisprudence (*fiqh*) and the opening chapter of the Quran (*surah-i-fatiha*). The work also highlights the existence of seventy three sects among the Muslims, several moralistic stories and verses in Arabic and Persian.[41] Apart from the elucidation of religious and mystical themes, the work often brings in matters of political and social significance. For example, India was treated as a country which had been specially blessed by God. The Suhrawardi mystics accepted government positions as well as landed endowments. The people were exhorted to be loyal towards their rulers in accordance with an oft-quoted Prophetic tradition. The socially inferior groups were regarded unfit for education, while the Chishti attitude to the distribution of food without discrimination was applauded. The practice of hoarding was condemned, while imposition of several taxes was regarded as irreligious. A number of popular practices were disapproved e.g. display of fireworks on the *Shab-i-Barat*, sacrificing animals to mark the return of the sultan and nobles, use of musical instruments during audition, kissing of graves and appearance of women without veils.[42]

We may briefly refer to a few other collections of Bukhari's discourses. One of them was the *Mazhar-i-Jalali*, the only manuscript of which was in the possession of the *sajjadah nishin* of the Suhrawardi shrine at Uch. While nothing is known about the compiler and the circumstances of its compilation, the content pertains to prescriptions regarding the unity of God, faith, prayer, religious duties and jurisprudence. Another collection, *Manaqib-i-Makhdum-i-Jahaniyan*, was compiled after the death of Firuz Shah Tughluq. An incomplete manuscript of the work, which has been bound with a tract called *Wazaif-i-Shahi*, was preserved in the library of the Asiatic Society of Bengal, Calcutta. Nothing was known about the compiler except that he settled the village of Nizampura situated to the south of Samana in Punjab. The work refers to the Thatta campaign and the Gujarat rebellion, besides the names of several nobles and officers of the Tughluq period.[43] There is another record of Bukhari's meetings, entitled *Fuwaid-ul-Mukhlisin*. Compiled by Muhammad Jafar Tumasi, it provides biographical details regarding the saint. A manuscript of the work was in the possession of Mahmud Sherani of Lahore.

Among the works associated with Bukhari, we come across a collection of letters entitled *Muqarrir Nama*. Numbering forty two in all and compiled in 776 AH/1374 AD, these letters were addressed to one Tajuddin bin Muin Siyahposh. These epistles were written in response to the questions posed by the above mentioned seeker.[44] They constitute a store of knowledge on a variety of religious, mystical and moral issues. The reader finds valuable information about aspects of Quranic and Prophetic teachings. For example, the first letter discusses the benefits of keeping the company of the good and pious people, besides the harm of participating in the gatherings of bad people. The second letter examines the significance of exhortation (*nasihat*). The third letter sheds light on the benefits of knowledge and, in this connection, Bukhari states that one should first acquire knowledge (*ilm*) and only then move to action (*amal*), because the former was like a tree and the latter was like fruit. The fifth and sixth letters underline the significance of action (*amal*). The seventh letter highlights the results of making efforts and, in this context, Bukhari feels that unless work was done, the reward could not be achieved. In the eighth letter, the saint argues that the object of acquiring knowledge should be the revival of the Muslim law (*ihya-i-shariat*). The ninth letter focuses on self-accountabilty, while the tenth one warns that interest in poetry was a sheer wastage of time and that it did not promise any reward on the day of resurrection (*akhirat*). The eleventh letter shows that the knowledge of a Muslim had always to be in conformity with the Muslim law (*shariat*), while the twelfth one seeks to link the benefits of knowledge to the day of resurrection. In the fifteenth letter, Bukhari argues that the foundation of Islam lay in lawful eating and, in support of this argument, he quotes a verse in which Allah exhorts people to eat lawful food and to be clean. In the eighteenth letter, it is stated that the saint (*darvesh*) who was engaged in selfishness and evil desires, could not achieve the ultimate truth. The twenty first letter contains a few instructions for the seeker. To achieve his goals, he was advised to adopt the way of God, which was done through two things – first by keeping patience and second by being hopeful with regard to God. When he reached this point, he attained gnosis (*maarifat*) of the highest stage, which was the basis of religion. For the purpose of a seeker, gnosis lay in four principles – he should not tell lies, he should avoid back biting, he should be kind to God's creatures and he should be trustworthy.[45]

Prescribing a code of conduct for the mystic, Bukhari states that he should offer prayers neither with the fear of hell, nor with the hope of paradise and its boons. Rather he should try to please God and attain His nearness. If he achieved some spiritual success, he should not reveal it among the people of this world. On the other hand, if he acquired something worldly like money, he should spend it on the needy and himself maintain poverty (*faqr*) and patience (*tahammul*). He should remain engaged in prayer and meditation and, at all times, he should be grateful to God as it was the distinct quality of God's friends (*auliya*) i.e. sufis. In the twenty fourth letter, it has been suggested that a sufi should spend his night in reading the Quran. In the twenty seventh letter, Bukhari writes that the spiritual mentor (*pir*) should always be affectionate towards the disciple and that he should always exhort the disciple to follow the *shariat*. The twenty third letter has prescribed some conditions for the spiritual heads (*sajjadah nishins*) of sufi shrines. The person desirous of occupying the seat was required to renounce love of the world, self praise etc. Secondly, he was required to follow the instructions of his spiritual mentor. Thirdly, he was expected to remain engaged in prayer. In the twenty ninth letter, the disciple was asked to assimilate his mentor's spiritual method into his own being. In the last and forty second epistle, Bukhari has asked the sufi not to waste his time and to spend every moment of his life in God's remembrance. Thus, we find that the *Muqarrir Nama* is a significant source to reconstruct mysticism as understood and practiced in the fourteenth century. On the one hand, it explores a number of mystical doctrines and concepts. On the other hand, it provides details regarding a variety of spiritual practices, prayers and meditations.[46]

Education and Learning

Syed Jalaluddin Bukhari believed that education was essential for those who wished to tread the path of mysticism. He established a seminary at his hospice (*khanqah*) at Uch. Religious education was provided to students who arrived from far and near. Renowned teachers and learned theologians were employed to teach. Their classes were attended by disciples, followers and even visitors. They taught the Holy Quran, the Prophetic traditions (*hadis*) and Islamic mysticism (*tasawwuf*). Bukhari himself delivered lectures on different Islamic sciences to selected students, either before or after the morning prayer. According to the compiler of the *Jami-ul-Ulum*, Bukhari preferred to teach *Tafsir-i-Madark* instead of the *Tafsir-i-Kashshaf* owing to two reasons – the author of the latter was a Mutazilite and the former was prescribed in the syllabus of the seminary.[47] Bukhari was an expert (*qari*) at the recitation of the Quran. He had mastered the seven methods of reciting the Holy Book, having learnt the art during his sojourn at Mecca and Medina. Bukhari himself taught this discipline to his students, who included his own grandson Hamid bin Mahmud and some women of Uch. Bukhari laid a considerable emphasis on the teaching of *hadis* and, in this regard, a distinct pattern was followed. First a *hadis* was read and its words were explained in accordance with the principles of grammar. Then Bukhari described the meanings of difficult words on the basis of lexico-graphy. This was followed by a complete elucidation of the tradition.[48] For the study of traditions, the well known collections were referred viz. *Sahih-ul-Bukhari, Sahih Muslim, Tirmizi, Sunan-i-Abu Daud, Mishkat-ul-Masabih* and *Jami-ul-Saghir*. Another important subject taught at the seminary was Muslim jurisprudence (*fiqh*). Bukhari, who possessed a remarkable understanding of the subject, highlighted the differences among the four schools and, in the end, emphasized the universality of the Hanifite interpretation. The teaching of this subject was based on the famous book entitled *Hidaya*, which was taught by Bukhari to his grandson Hamid bin Mahmud.[49]

The students at the Uch seminary were also taught the principles of grammar (*sarf o nahv*) and lexicography (*lughat*), so that they could learn Arabic and acquire proficiency in the language. The syllabi also required the study of *Sharh Kabir Chahl Ism, Asrar-ul-Dawat, Mashariq-ul-Anwar, Qasida-i-Lamiya, Kitab-i-Muttafiq, Aqaid-i-Nafsi, Awarif-ul-Maarif* and *Aurad-i-Shaikh Shihabuddin Suhrawardi*. Bukhari taught the *Sharh Kabir Chahl Ism* to Shaikhzada Fakhruddin Gazruni. He taught *Asrar-i-Dawat* to Abdul Rehman Zaffari. Since the latter was an Arab, Bukhari conversed with him in Arabic. It appears that the Uch seminary was overcrowded and there was a dearth of teachers. Students, who studied at the preliminary and middle levels, were taught by the senior students who had studied advanced literature. Students, who had missed some lessons, were asked to take the help of their batch-mates. Syed Alauddin Ali bin Syed Husaini, the compiler of *Jami-ul-Ulum*, received some lessons from Muhammad Zaffari. One of the salient features of education at the Uch seminary was the emphasis on etiquettes and manners. The students were exhorted to be respectful towards their teachers and elders. In the classrooms, they were required not to ask any question during the course of the lecture. They could seek the answers to their queries only at the end of the lecture.[50] The teachers were expected to be kind and generous to the students. Besides the classroom teaching, open discussions were also held on important topics when both the teachers and students participated. Bukhari was often requested to perform the ceremony of *Tasmiya Khwani* for children,[51] when he recited the Bismillah and wrote the alphabet on the wooden slate.

Syed Jalaluddin Bukhari had a rich collection of books, which was an integral part of the Uch seminary. He employed a variety of means to acquire books on different subjects which were required for teaching purposes. He had himself brought a copy of *Sharh Kabir Chahl Ism* from Madina, which was in Arabic. A manuscript of the *Awarif-ul-Maarif*, which was a personal copy of the eminent mystic Shaikh Shihabuddin Suhrawardi, was also found here. It had been received by Bukhari from his distinguished teacher Shaikh Abdullah Matri. He arranged the transcription of the *Asrar-i-Dawat* for his library. A copy of this book was in the possession of Abdul Rahman Zaffari, who agreed to its transcription only after some initial reluctance.[52] Once an eminent scholar of Islamic sciences – traditions and jurisprudence – arrived in Uch and stayed in the Suhrawardi hospice. He had written a book on the Quranic exegesis (*tafsir*) in seven volumes. On his return, he presented this multi-volume treatise which became a part of the library.[53] When Shaikh Qutbuddin Damishqi completed his famous Arabic work *Risala-i-Makkiya*, he sent a copy to Bukhari. The latter was an expert in the art of calligraphy and had transcribed a copy of the Quran in his own hand. It was believed that he had transcribed this copy during the course of his sittings at the mausoleum of Prophet Muhammad at Madina. Presently this copy was in the possession of the spiritual head (*sajjadah nishin*) at Uch. A copy of this manuscript was displayed on the occasion of the pilgrimage to the shrine.[54]

Towards the close of the present study, we may consider the contribution of Syed Jalaluddin Bukhari as an author and translator. He wrote a few brochures on various aspects of Islamic mysticism, which were apparently prepared to meet the needs of students and seekers. During his sojourn at Mecca, he compiled the *Arbain Sufiya* which comprised an account of forty mystics. Since the work has become extinct, it is not possible to identify the mystics whose lives have been the subject of study. Another work attributed to Bukhari was *Amal wa Asghal*, which contained the sayings of saints, litanies and sacred phrases (*wazaif*) which were recited daily at different moments of the spiritual journey. Compiled by Jafar Badr Alam bin Jalaluddin Maqsud Alam, a manuscript of this work was preserved in the library of the Department of Justice at Bharuch in Gujarat. Bukhari has also displayed his scholarship in the domain of translation. He translated into Persian the *Risala-i-Makkiya*, an Arabic treatise on mysticism written by Shaikh Qutbuddin Damishqi. Owing to the nature of its content, this work has been ranked with such classics as *Kashf-ul-Mahjub*, *Risala-i-Qushairiya* and *Awarif-ul-Maarif*. The author Damishqi sent a copy of this book to Bukhari, who translated it from Arabic to Persian and included it in the syllabus of the seminary. Manuscripts of this translation were preserved in the libraries of the Cambridge University, United Kingdom, and Princeton University, USA.[55] Bukhari was believed to have translated the Quran into Persian. Shaikh Ehsanul Haq of Muradabad, who was a descendant of the seventeenth century Chishti sufi Shaikh Ibrahim Muradabadi, possessed a copy of this translation. It has been claimed that the manuscript was transcribed by Bukhari himself. Muhammad Ayub Qadri, who has examined the style of writing and the quality of paper, believes that the manuscript belonged to the fourteenth century. If this judgement was correct, the work was undoubtedly the first ever Persian translation of the Quran in the Indian subcontinent. The manuscript did not have some sections of the Quran, but the translated portions were provided in red ink. A specimen of the translation, pertaining to the *Surat-ul-Nisa* which has been provided by Qadri, indicates that the language was simple and understandable.[56]

NOTES AND REFERENCES

1. Khaliq Ahmad Nizami, *Some Aspects of Religion and Politics in India during the Thirteenth Century*, Second Revised Edition, Idarah-i-Adabiyat-i-Delli, Delhi, 1974, p. 178.
2. Amir Hasan Ala Sijzi, *Fuwaid-ul-Fuwad*, Nawal Kishore Press, Lucknow, 1302 AH, p. 221.
3. Shaikh Muhammad Ikram, *Aab-i-Kausar*, Reprint, Taj Company, Delhi, 1987, p. 276.
4. Khaliq Ahmad Nizami, *Some Aspects of Religion and Politics in India during the Thirteenth Century*, p. 224.
5. Nizam Yamani, *Lataif-i-Ashrafi*, Vol. I, Nusrat-ul-Matabi, Delhi, 1299 AH, p.232; Abdul Haq Muhaddis Dehalvi, *Akhbar-ul-Akhyar*, Matba-i-Mujtaba, Delhi, 1332 AH, p.143; Saiyid Athar Abbas Rizvi, *A History of Sufism in India*, Vol. I, Munshiram Manoharlal, New Delhi, 1978, p. 277.

6. Muhammad Ayub Qadiri, *Makhdum-i-Jahaniyan Jahan Gasht*, Idarah-i-Tahqiq o Tasneef, Karachi, 1963, pp. 88-96.
7. Sujan Rai Bhandari, *Khulasat-ut-Tawarikh*, Ed., M. Zafar Hasan, Delhi, 1918, p. 62; Ghulam Sarwar Lahori, *Khazinat-ul-Asfiya*, Vol. I, Nawal Kishore Press, Lucknow, n.d., p. 58.
8. Abdul Haq Muhaddis Dehalvi, *Akhbar-ul-Akhyar*, p. 142.
9. Hamid bin Fazlullah Jamali, *Siyar-ul-Arifin*, Matba-i-Rizvi, Delhi, 1311 AH, p. 152.
10. Muhammad Ayub Qadiri, op. cit., pp. 118-120.
11. Ibid., pp. 121-123.
12. Khaliq Ahmad Nizami, *On History and Historians of Medieval India*, Munshiram Manoharlal, New Delhi, 1983, p. 189.
13. Iqbal Ahmad, *Tarikh-i-Shiraz-i-Hind Jaunpur*, Jaunpur, 1963, pp. 78-81.
14. Muhammad Ayub Qadiri, op. cit., p. 105.
15. Muhammad Qasim Hindu Shah Farishta, *Tarikh-i-Farishta*, Vol. II, Urdu Translation, Nawal Kishore Press, Lucknow, 1933, p. 685; Ali Hasan Khan, *Maasir-i-Siddiqi*, Vol. I, Nawal Kishore Press, Lucknow, 1924, p. 37; Abdul Hai Husaini, *Nuzhat-ul-Khwatir*, Idarah-i-Dairatul Maarif, Hyderabad, 1947, p. 52.
16. Abdul Haq Muhaddis Dehalvi, *Akhbar-ul-Akhyar*, p. 142.
17. Shaikh-ul-Islam was both an office and an honorific title. Some eminent saints were given this title, though they were not required to perform any specific duties or functions. Sometimes the title was loosely used for distinguished saints, though it was not conferred by the sultan. When appointed by the state, he could be put in charge of the ecclesiastical affairs, including the patronage of saints. Khaliq Ahmad Nizami, *Some Aspects of Religion and Poilitics in India during the Thirteenth Century*, p. 159.
18. Shams Siraj Afif, *Tarikh-i-Firuz Shahi*, Ed., Maulavi Wilayat Husain, Bibliotheca Indica, Calcutta, 1890, pp. 239-244.
19. Ibid., pp. 514-516.
20. Hamid bin Fazlullah Jamali, *Siyar-ul-Arifin*, pp. 227-228, quoted in Qazi Javed, *Punjab Key Sufi Danishwar*, Fiction House Lahore, 2005, pp. 115-116.
21. Shaikh Sikandar bin Muhammad urf Manjhu bin Akbar, *Mirat-i-Sikandari*, M.S. University of Baroda, 1961, p. 8, quoted in Surinder Singh, 'The Making of Medieval Punjab: Politics, Society and Economy c.1200-c.1400,' Presidential Address, Medieval Section, Punjab History Conference, 40th Session, 14-16 March 2008 (separately printed text), p. 31.
22. A manuscript of the work transcribed in 1786 was in the possession of the *sajjadah nishin* of the shrine at Uch. Two manuscripts of the work were preserved in the Raza Library, Rampur, while one each was available in the Central Library, Hyderabad, and Asiatic Society of Bengal, Calcutta.
23. Muhammad Aslam, *Malfuzati Adab ki Tarikhi Ahmiyat*, Idarah-i-Tahqiqat-i-Pakistan, University of Punjab, Lahore, 1995, p. 208.
24. Syed Alauddin Ali bin Syed Husain, *Jami-ul-Ulum*, Urdu Translation, Maulavi Zulfiqar Ahmad, entitled *Al-Durrul-Manzum*, Matba Ansari, Delhi, 1309 AH/1891 AD, pp. 594-595.
25. Maulavi Zulfiqar Ahmad, *Al-Durrul-Manzum*, p. 413.

26. Ibid., p. 275.
27. Muhammad Aslam, *Malfuzati Adab Ki Tarikhi Ahmiyat*, pp. 209-217.
28. Maulavi Zulfiqar Ahmad, *Al-Durrul-Manzum*, p. 703.
29. Muhammad Ayub Qadiri, *Makhdum-i-Jahaniyan Jahan Gasht*, p. 171.
30. Maulavi Zulfiqar Ahmad, *Al-Durrul-Manzum*, p. 541.
31. Ibid., p. 520.
32. Ibid., pp. 518-519.
33. Ibid., p. 598.
34. Ibid., p. 328.
35. Mansur al-Hallaj (858-922 AD) was a Persian mystic and theologian who wrote in Arabic. From 873 to 897 he lived in retirement with sufi teachers Tustari, Amr Makki and Junaid. Then he broke with them and went out into the world to preach asceticism and mysticism in Khurasan, Ahwaz, Fars, Turkistan and India (Gujarat). On his return from Mecca to Baghdad in 908 AD, disciples gathered around him. He was accused of being a charlatan by the Mutazilites, excommunicated by a *tawki* of the Imamiya and a *fatwa* of the Zahiriya, and twice arrested by the Abbasid police. He was put on the pillory in 913 AD and spent eight years in a prison in Baghdad. He was executed at the orders of *wazir* Hamid after a seven month trial on a *fatwa* approved by a Maliki *qazi* Abu Umar. On 26 March 922 AD, he was flogged, mutilated, exposed on a gibbet (*maslub*), decapitated and burnt. H.A.R. Gibb and J.H. Kramers, *Shorter Encyclopaedia of Islam*, E.J. Brill, Leiden, 1953, p. 128.
36. Qazi Javed, *Punjab Key Sufi Danishwar*, pp. 109-110.
37. Ibid., p. 107.
38. Manuscripts of this work were available in a few public libraries and private collections. One of these was found in the library of Makhdum Shamsuddin Thamin of Uch. Transcribed in 1244 AH/1829 AD, it was written in a clean hand but was incomplete. A manuscript, which was in the possession of the *sajjadah nishin* of the Uch shrine, was transcribed in 1265 AH/1849 AD and ran into 424 pages. Another manuscript, which was preserved in the Central Library, Hyderabad, consisted of 213 folios. Manuscripts of the work were also found the Kutubkhana-i-Dan Miyana Sharif, district Sargodha, Pakistan, and the personal collection of Maulana Muhammad Ali Mukhdi in district Attock, Pakistan.
39. Muhammad Aslam, *Malfuzati Adab ki Tarikhi Ahmiyat*, pp. 229-330.
40. Ibid., pp. 231-235.
41. Muhammad Ayub Qadiri, *Makhdum-i-Jahaniyan Jahan Gasht*, pp. 240-241.
42. Khaliq Ahmad Nizami, *On History and Historians of Medieval India*, Munshiram Manoharlal, New Delhi, 1983, pp. 189-192.
43. Muhammad Ayub Qadiri, *Makhdum-i-Jahaniyan Jahan Gasht*, pp. 256-259.
44. A manuscript of this work was a part of the Subhanullah Collection of the Maulana Azad Library, Aligarh Muslim University, Aligarh. It was not possible to know the date of its transcription, though the month was Ramzan. Another manuscript was available in the Central Library, Hyderabad. Still another one, transcribed in the eleventh century Hijri, was in the private possession of Maulavi Taslimuddin Salim Narnauli,

Jaipur, Rajasthan.
45. Muhammad Ayub Qadiri, *Makhdum-i-Jahaniyan Jahan Gasht*, pp. 243-245.
46. Ibid., pp. 246-248.
47. Mutazalites represented a school of thought which was born out of, or inserted itself into, the controversies of civil war between Ali bin Abi Talib and the companions of Zubair and Talhah, and the absolute condemnatory views of the Kharijites. It applied reason to the solution of philosophic problems, leading to the birth of *kalam*, the Islamic theology. Owing to its historical position between the point of view of the Umayyads and Shias, it lent itself easily for a time to being the dominant philosophy of the Abbasids. As rationalists and materialists, the Mutazilites held that the Quran is created. This was proclaimed as the official doctrine by caliph al-Mamun in 827 AD. Under caliph al-Mutawwakil, this doctrine was suppressed. It reappeared as the theology of the Twelve Imam Shiaism. It established the widespread use of rational arguments in the subsequent development of theology and many of its conclusions were adopted by the mainstream, although the school as a whole was attacked as heretical. Cyril Glasse, *The Concise Encyclopaedia of Islam*, Stacey International, London, Reprint, 2004, p. 334.
48. Maulavi Zulfiqar Ahmad, *Al-Durrul-Manzum*, pp. 465-466.
49. Muhammad Ayub Qadiri, *Makhdum-i-Jahaniyan Jahan Gasht*, p. 192.
50. Ibid., pp. 193-194.
51. By *tasmiya* is meant the title given to Bismillah or intitial sentence 'In the name of God, the compassionate and merciful.' It occurs at the commencement of each chapter of the Quran, with the exception of Surah IX. It is also used at the commencement of any religious act, except sacrifice, such as prayer and ablution. Thomas Patrick Hughes, *Dictionary of Islam*, Cosmo Publications, New Delhi, Reprint, 1977, p. 629.
52. Maulavi Zulfiqar Ahmad, *Al-Durrul-Manzum*, 478-479.
53. Ibid., pp. 567-569.
54. Muhammad Ayub Qadiri, *Makhdum-i-Jahaniyan Jahan Gasht*, p. 195.
55. Ibid., pp. 259-260.
56. Ibid., pp. 262-263.

5

A Panoramic Reconstruction of Sufism in the Jammu Hills

Jigar Mohammed

Notwithstanding the fact that several modern historians have studied Indian sufism, most of them have confined their studies to the teachings and practices of sufis, as prescribed by their orders (*silsilahs*). Historians like Khaliq Ahmad Nizami and Saiyid Athar Abbas Rizvi have produced monumental works on Indian sufism. It is true that Richard Maxwell Eaton[1] and Abdul Qaiyum Rafiqi[2] have undertaken detailed studies on the development of sufism in the regional contexts of Bijapur and Kashmir. Though these studies are just a few exceptions, yet these have been possible owing to the availability of considerable hagiographical literature, particularly the biographical memoirs and mystical discourses. Hardly any attempt has been made to explore the development of sufism in the hills, where the socio-economic life has been somewhat slower than in the plains and where the hagiographical literature is virtually non-existent. As such, vernacular sufism has received scant attention from the historians. In the hilly areas, the sufis were obliged to put in a much greater effort in their activities, so as to overcome the difficulties posed by the topographic and economic factors. In a partial attempt to fill this gap, the present paper seeks to explore the historical aspects of sufism in the Jammu hills.[3]

Vernacular and Vernacularity

Sufism entered the Indian subcontinent in the twelfth century as a new socio-religious force.[4] Within a short period, it mushroomed to different parts of India. From Punjab to Rajputana, from Jammu and Kashmir to Kerala, sufism influenced the life and thought of the people. Though on the eve of its advent, Muslim population in most parts of India was virtually negligible, yet the sufis hardly faced any local resistance to their activities. Sufism received enthusiastic social response. It adjusted itself with the indigenous cultural modes in a smooth manner. As a result, it became a catalyst in shaping and consolidating the Indian regional identities from the thirteenth century onwards. In this context, sufi shrines of the different regions – Ajodhan, Sirhind, Delhi, Ajmer and Gulbarga – played a significant role. A study of Indian literatures and languages reveals that several sufis contributed to enriching vernacular language(s) as medium of inter-faith dialogue and communication with the common people. For example, Richard Maxwell Eaton has shown that the sufis of Bijapur contributed tremendously to the promotion of vernacular idiom and Dakhani language. Underlining the importance of folk poetry of the Bijapur sufis, Eaton states, "The bulk of the folk poetry written by the sufis was sung by village women as they did various household chores. The most common types included the *chakki-nama*, so called because it was sung while grinding food grains at the grindstone or *chakki* and the *charkha-nama*, sung while spinning thread at the spinning wheel or *charkha*. Other types of such folk poetry included the *lori-nama*, or lullaby, the *shadi-nama* or wedding song, the *suhagan-nama* or married woman's song, and the *suhaila* or eulogistic song."[5] Observing the continuous popularity of the sufi folk literature, Eaton further observes, "Sufi folk literature can be found today in both written and oral traditions. Despite the intrusion of modern media in the villages, folk poetry relating to household chores is still sung."[6]

The lullabies and riddles (*loris* and *pahelis*) composed by Amir Khusro (1253-1325 AD) inspired the use of vernacular language for literary purposes.[7] Khaliq Ahmad Nizami finds sufi hospices (*khanqahs*) as fertile grounds for the growth of common medium of communication among people of different linguistic backgrounds. The desire of the Muslim mystics to develop social proximity with the Hindus, so as to appreciate their religious life and thought, facilitated the evolution of a common medium of communication for the exchange of ideas. The earliest known sentences of the Hindvi language are found in the mystic records. That the birth place of the Urdu language was the *khanqah* of the medieval sufis can hardly be questioned.[8] In Kashmir, Shaikh Nuruddin or Nand Rishi, one of the most popular sufis of Kashmir, composed his mystical poetry in the Kashmiri dialect, which could be easily comprehended by the common people of the region. In this manner, he strengthened the concept of Kashmiri vernacular identity. It is rightly observed that Nuruddin Rishi, through the use of Kashmiri dialect, was able to create a framework for a regional culture and "to propagate a devotional religion, which was significantly outside the purview of the state."[9]

Apart from vernacular language, one may discern the 'vernacularity' involved in the life pattern of the Indian sufis. They respectfully followed the regional cultural values pertaining to food, clothes, housing and means of livelihood. Most of the sufis lived in very simple houses, ate simple food, wore simple dress and propagated non-violence. Sufis like Shaikh Hamiduddin Nagauri advocated vegetarianism in deference to the local customs. Similarly, in Kashmir, Nuruddin Rishi was a protagonist of non-violence. Social groups like that of the peasants and artisans, observing that the sufis respected their sentiments and life styles, found no hesitation in entering their circle of influence and in seeking guidance from them. The sufis adopted the life style of the common people and, thus, identified themselves with te local cltures. In this sense, the sufis contributed to the development of regional identities. Though essentially Islamic in its origin, the mystic movement spread to various regions of the Indian subcontinent, because it assimilated and imbibed elements from the cultures and religions that were different from its own.[10]

The holistic vision of sufis and their mission of diffusing the message of divine love and social harmony led them to settle in all those areas where they could perform their activities and spread their teachings. They were love (*ishq*)oriented nomadic saints who believed in travelling with a specific purpose. Murray T. Titus has aptly described them, "Usually they have been individuals endowed with piety and religious zeal, frequently men of learning, who, through their own personal interest in the spread of Islam, and inspired with a divine call, have been content to wander from place to pace and gather disciples."[11] What is being suggested is that the sufis never belived in geographical boundaries, just as they did not believe in caste and sectarian barricades. They made no distinction between hills and plains, between desert and fertile land and between urban and rural areas in order to spread sufism. For them, each place and social group had potentialities of spiritual betterment. Therefore, the topography of the Jammu region could not dampen their zeal for settling and propagating sufism. The different areas of the Jammu hills witnessed the arrival of sufis during the medieval period and this process continued till the nineteenth century.

The task of reconstructing the history of sufism in the Jammu hills poses several challenges. The most formidable among them is the pauciy of suitable contemporary sources. Most sufi shrines do not possess any historical records pertaining tothe sufis associated with them. Some information may be acquired from either the present spiritual heads (*sajjadah nishin*) or the oral traditions/folklore, preserved in the dialects such as Dogri, Kishtwari, Bhadrawahi, Gojri and Pahari. Local cultures and collective memory have incorporated the stories of the spectacular deeds of the sufis and the miraculous powers of their shrines. A large number of legends are associated with the arrival, settlement and activities f the sufis. These are narrated both by the caretakers and followers of the shrine. Some ineteenth cntury source such as te *Gulabnama* of Diwan Kirpa Ram, *Rajdarshani* of Ganeshdas Badehra and some travel accounts also contain some information regarding the role of sufis and their shrines in the socio-cultural scenario of the Jammu hills.

Arrival of the Sufis

Almost all the leading sufi orders (*silsilahs*), coming to India, made the Punjab region as their first abode. For instance, theChishti, Surawardi, Qadiri nd Naqshbandi rders appeared first in Punjab and only afterwards spread to other parts of India. From Ali bin Usman Hujwiri to Khwaja Baqi Billah, all the sufis, irrespetive of their spiritual disciplines, found favourable social environmet in Punjab for the prsuit of their sfic activities. Geographically and culturally, the Jamu regionwas closely ssociated wth Punjab. Besides, during the medieval period twenty-two principalities, which existed in the moder Jammu region, were treatd under the Punjab hill states.[12] The Mughal sources such as the *Ain-i-Akbari* and *Khulasat-ut-Tawarikh* also reveal that most of the states of the Jammu hills were either parts of the province (*suba*) f Lahore or that of Multan.[13] Different routes from Punjab to Kashmir passed through the Jammu region. Also in the nineteenth century, every part of the modern Jammu and Kasmir state was included in he political jurisdiction o the kingdom of ahore under Maharaja Ranjit Singh (r. 1799-1839). Geographical proximity and socio-economic links of the Jammuregion wih Punjab facilitatd cultural exchange between these two regios. Most parts of the Jammu region were hilly in character and its population was largely Hindu. Fredrick Drew, who came to Jammu and Kashmir in the nineteenth century durng the reign of Maharaj Ranbir Singh (1857-1885) and travelled to different parts of the region, found that most of the hill principalities were feudatories of Jammu, the most powerful state.[14] Thus the Jammu region was quite close to Punjab which had emerged as the first hub of sufsm in te Indian subcontinent.

Since the Jammu hill states were situated on the border of Kashmir,sufism of Kashmir also seems to have influenced the social life of the Jammu region.[15] Sufism appeared in Kashmir during the fourteenth century. Syed Sharfuddin, popularly known as Bulbul Shah, arrived in Kashmir during the early fourteenth century. Suhadeva (r. 1301-1320), a scion of the Damra dynasty, ruled over Kashmir at that time. Syed Sharfuddin was a Suhrawardi sufi and came to Kashmir from Turkistan. During the second half of the fourteenth century, the

Kubrawi order was introduced in Kashmir by Mir yed Ali Hamadani, popularly known asShah-i-Hamadan. In the beginning of the fifteenth century Syed Hilal, a Naqshbandi sufi, came to Kashmir and settled there. Similarly, Shaikh Niamatullah Qadiri also visited Kashmir for a short period. His disciple Shaikh Mirak Mir settled in Kashmir and introduced the Qadiri order there. More importantly, in Kashmir an indigenous sufi brotherhood, known as the Rishi order, emerged during the fifteenth century.

Thus two border regions of Jammu i.e. Punjab and Kashmir had nurtured various centers of sufism and, Jammu being situated between these two regions, attracted the attention of sufis from both the directions. Pir Roshan Wali Shah is believed to be the earliest sufi who came to Jammu from Mecca in the first half of the thirteenth century (1242). But, the hagiographical traditions inform us that the majority of sufis arrived in Jammu from the fifteenth to the nineteenth century. Pir Lakhdata, Pir Buddhan Ali Shah, Hazrat Zainuddin Rishi, Baba Latifuddin Rishi, Pir Mitha, Pir Zahir Wali Shah, Sanjha Pir or Sher Khan Shah Pathan and Baba Karam Shah belonged to the fifteenth century. But a large number of sufis came from Punjab during the late eighteenth and nineteenth centuries. Mention may be made of Baba Jiwan Shah, Baba Rah, Qutub Zaman Hazrat Jiwan Shah, Mustafa or Nau Gaza Baba. During this period, Punjab was in the grip of the political anarchy, particularly due to the repeated invasions of Ahmad Shah Abdali. But the Jammu region under the rule of Ranjit Dev (1733-1783) was a peaceful region, i.e. an abode of peace (*Dar-ul-Aman*).[16] It seems, therefore, that sufis found a congenial atmosphere in the Jammu region for the propagation of their philosophy among the people. A number of sufis, who migrated to Jammu from Punjab in the mid nineteenth century, did so owing to the political chaos and internecine struggle for throne among the successors of Maharaja Ranjit Singh.[17] But in Jammu hills Maharaja Gulab Singh (r. 1846-1857) established peace and security in an effective manner. Consequently, several sufis of Punjab looked upon the Jammu hills as more suitable than Punjab for their mystic activities. They, therefore, migrated and settled here. Thus the growth of sufism in the Jammu hills was associated with the political stability afforded by the region. It is important to mention that the sufis of Punjab were the followers of the creed of non-violence. It is known that when Mongol leader Amir Timur's expansionist policies created widespread dislocation in Central Asia and Persia, it became difficult for the sufis and scholars to carry on their mystic and scholarly activities. Therefore, many sufis migrated from these areas to India. It was in these circumstances that Syed Ali Hamadani migrated to Kashmir for the propagation of the teachings of the Kubrawi order.[18]

The migration of sufis was not a one-way traffic. The sufis, by their very vocation, were obliged to travel to foreign lands for acquiring mystical knowledge and learning from the experience of renowned masters. It is not surprising that the natives of the Jammu hills should travel and settle in other parts of the Indian subcontinent. Let us consider the case of Miskin Shah Sahib (d. 1859). A native of Kishtwar, he became a disciple of Shah Niyaz Ahmad (d.1834) who, in turn, was a spiritual successor (*khalifa*) of the famous Chishti sufi of Punjab, Khwaja Nur Muhammad Muharvi. Miskin Shah Sahib, who had received initial initiation in the Qadiri and Naqshbandi order, established a hospice (*khanqah*) at Jaipur at the advice of his mentor.[19]

The sufis of the Jammu hills were addressed with the different honorific titles, which varied from period to period. The most popular appellation used for them was the 'pir,'[20] which was/is used mostly for the sufis of the period from thirteenth to the seventeenth century. Pir Roshan Ali Shah, Pir Mitha, Pir Lakhdata, Pir Zahir Wali Shah and Pir Shahan Shah Wali were the famous sufis of the Jammu hills for whom the term pir has been used since the medieval period. The expression of 'Shah' was also frequently used for the sufis as a suffix to their names. Bargad Ali Shah, Pir Ali Shah, Fazal Shah, Mangal Shah, Pir Bukhar Shah, Pir Sufi Shah, Qasim Shah, Khaki Shah and Sayyid Shah Ghulam Badshah were the prominent sufis whose names carried this term. The appellation of 'Sayeen' was used for some famous sufis. Similarly, the expressions of 'Shaikh', 'Syed', 'Baba' and 'Qalandar' were also in vogue.[21] It has already been mentioned that some of the sufis of Kishtwar used the term 'Rishi' as a symbol of their identity in terms of their order. However, the terms Pir, Shah, Sayeen, Shaikh, Syed, Baba and Qalandar were not used to mark the identity of a particular sufi order. These appellations were used merely as a mark of respect.

Prominent sufis

The modern Jammu region comprises of districts such as Jammu, Kathua, Udhampur, Doda, Punch, Rajouri, Samba, Riasi, Kishtwar and Ramban. They are profusely dotted with sufi shrines. Like other parts of Punjab and Kashmir, the sufis of different orders settled in the Jammu hills. The sufis such as Pir Roshan Shah Wali, Pir Lakhdatta, Baba Budhan Shah, Pir Mitha, Pir Zahiri Wali Shah, Pir Shahan Shah Wali, Pir Muhabbat Ali Shah, Baba Sher Khan Pathan (also known as Sanjha Pir), Faqir Baba Faiz Bakhsh Shah Bukhari, Qutub Zaman Hazrat Baba Jiwan Shah, Panch Pir, Rah Baba and Baba Barkat Ali Shah came to Jammu and settled in the different areas such as Jammu proper, Satwari, Akhnur, Kunjwani and Rihari.[22] Shaikh Fariduddin Qadiri, Hazrat Muhammad Asraruddin, Hazrat Muahmmad Akhyaruddin,[23] Shaikh Zain Alla Din, Baba Latifuddin Rishi and Zainuddin Rishi settled in

Kishtwar.[24] Baba Pir Tode Shah settled in the modern Kathua district. Mustafa or Nua Baba, Pir Baba Karam Shah, Hazrat Nadir Ali Shah Baghdadi and Pir Wali Shah settled in the different parts of modern Udhampur district. Pir Sayyid Ghulam Shah Badshah settled at Shahdara Sharif in the modern Rajouri district.[25] Similarly, Baba Sain Lal Din settled in Rajouri. Hazrat Nadir Ali Shah Baghdadi settled at Ram Nagar in Udhampur district. Pir Lakhdatta established his residence at Banni in tahsil Basoli of Kathua district. Alla Pir settled at Punch. Hazrat Kasim Shah settled at Dera Mehta in Doda district and Hazrat Haji Muhammad Akram did so at Doda proper. Panch Pir settled at Jammu, Basoli, Rajouri, Purmandal and Ramnagar. Hazrat Shaikh Abdul Qadir Jilani settled in Punch.[26] Several shrines of the sufi saints exist in Punch, Rajouri, Doda, Udhampur and Jammu districts.

From the viewpoint of their regional background, the sufis of Jammu hills can be situated into four categories: sufis from (i) Punjab, (ii) Kashmir, (iii) foreign lands and (iv) the indigenous sufis of Jammu hills. The hagiographical traditions reveal that majority of sufis of Jammu hills came from Punjab. Pir Lakhdatta, Baba Buddhan Ali Shah, Baba Jiwan Shah of Akhnur, Baba Rah, Baba Jiwan Shah of Jiwan Shah Muhallah, Pir Baba Tode Shah, Pir Wali Shah, Mustafa Baba or Nau Baba, Sain Lal Din and Pir Ghulam Badshah came to Jammu from the different parts of Punjab. Some of the sufis either came from Kashmir or were initiated into sufism by the sufis of Kashmir in Jammu hills, particularly in Kishtwar, Doda, Badhrawah, Punch and Rajouri. According to the oral tradition, such types of sufis were initated into the sufism either by Mir Syed Ali Hamadani or Shaikh Nuruddin Rishi.[27] However, arrival of the Qadiri sufi Fariduddin along with his companion intensified the processes of Kishtwar's association with sufism in a systematic way.[28] Hazrat Miskin Shah Kishtwari, Hazrat Sayyid Abu Sikandar Ali, Zainuddin Rishi, Latifuddin and others were the products of Kashmir sufism and shifted to different areas of the modern Doda district. The arrival of some sufis in the Jammu hills is associated with some foreign countries also. Pir Roshan Ali or Nau Gaza Pir, Hazrat Shah Muhammad Ghazi, Pir Mitha, Faqir Baba Faiz Bukhari, Baba Barkat Ali and Hazarat Nazar Ali Shah came from Mecca, Baghdad, Iran, Arabia and Kazakistan. Hazrat Shawan Sarkoti, Pir Muhabbat Ali, Pir Wali Shah and Baba Sain Lal Din belonged to the Jammu hills. There were some indigenous sufis who first accepted Islam and then got initiation into sufism. Majority of such sufis belonged to the Rishi order of Kishtwar. The geographical background of the sufis shows that the Jammu hill states were well connected with different parts of India and foreign countries, so far as propagation of sufism is concerned. It becomes evident that the Jammu hills not only welcomed the arrival of sufism, but also became a common meeting ground for the diverse mystical ideologies. We can discern the possibilities of the emergence of a continuous social discourse among the sufis and inhabitants of the Jammu hills.

The philosophical background, in terms of affiliation to a specific mystical order (*silsilah*), is not known in the case of most sufis of the Jammu hills. Since the information regarding the life and works of these sufis is based on hagiographical traditions, the present spiritual heads (*sajjadah nishins*) and caretakers of the sufi shrines narrate miracles, social activities and social support of the sufis. But there were sufis whose order-based identity is well established. In Kishtwar, a majority of sufis belonged either to the Qadiri or Rishi order. Hazrat Shaikh Zainuddin and Hazrat Baba Latifuddin belonged to the Rishi order. Sayyid Fariduddin, Israruddin, Shah Abdal, Sayyid Bahauddin Samani, Darwesh Muhammad and Yar Muhammad of Kishtwar belonged to the Qadiri order.[15] It is important to mention that the genealogical history, philosophy, activities and social contacts of the Qadiri sufis are recorded in a manuscript, entitled *Rauzat-ul-Arifin*, written by Hafiz Ziauddin of Kishtwar. Baba Jiwan Shah of Jiwan Shah Muhalla, Jammu district, belonged to the Chishti order. He is known to belong to the family of Shaikh Fariduddin Ganj-i-Shakar of Ajodhan.

Charisma of the Sufis

Most sufis have been remembered as charismatic figures. This awe-inspiring image has been constructed, over a period of time spanning centuries, primarily with the help of miracles which have been attributed to the sufis by their devout followers. Though the stories of miracles appear incredible and impossible, yet they provide interesting insights into the personality of the individual sufi as well as the larger phenomenon of sufism. Most sufis of the Jammu hills were reputed to perform miracles (*kashf wa karamat*). Some miracles of Pir Roshan Shah Wali are described in the *Rajdarshani*. It is said that the miracles of Pir Roshan Shah Wali obliged the king of Jammu, Raja Sarab-li-Dhar, to see the sufi in person. The king also requested the Pir to settle in Jammu. The Pir accepted the offer of the king, who provided all facilities to the Pir. A miracle narrated in *Rajdarshani* is associated with the death of Pir Roshan Shah Wali. Ganeshdas Badehra, the author of *Rajdharshani*, found the shrine and hospice (*khanqah*) of Pir Roshan Wali to be very popular during the nineteenth century. Narrating the meeting of the Pir with the Raja Sarab-li-Dhar and his death, Ganeshdas Badehra writes, "...a long man of towering body named Roshan Shah Wali, one of the close associates of the Prophet, of an Arab-like gait, came to the *chakla* of Jammu like a *faqir* and met Raja Sarab-li-Dhar and gave him the tidings of safety, that the army of Islam would not endanger his life and faith, nor would it harm Jammu. But the countries of the Punjab and Hindustan would be trampled under hoofs of the steeds of the Musalman. 'So I a feeble ant, has been deputed by the Holy and popular Rasul to guard Jammu.' He uttered such words, took off his skull from his head like a turban, walked headless for some steps and going near the Gumat gate, sat in side and gave up the ghost. They buried him there as per his will. His *khanqah* exists to this day and enjoys the same reverence."[29]

Similarly, Pir Mitha is acknowledged for his miracles. It is said that once he roped his horse near his hut and went away. After some time, the horse felt thirsty. There was nobody to provide water to the horse. But suddenly a fountain and two trees sprang up. The horse quenched his thirst and gratified his hunger with the leaves of the trees. It was believed that Pir Mitha could also cure a patient by his miraculous faculty. A hagiographical story says that once the queen of Jammu fell ill. All efforts failed to restore her good health. Pir Mitha came to know about the indisposition of the queen through some royal water carriers (*bhishtis*) who supplied water of rivers and wells to the royal palace, situated at modern Dalpatian Mohallah. Generally the water carriers fetched water from Pir Koh to the palace, and the house of Pir Mitha was situated on the way to Pir Koh. Once Pir Mitha, who was aware of the Queen's nagging illness, touched the container of the water carrier. The latter did not approve the action of Pir Mitha. He spilled all the water, declaring it to have become impure. But whenever the water carrier passed by the house of the Pir, the latter would touch the water pot. Ultimately, the water carrier brought the water, touched by the Pir, to the palace. When the queen drank it, she recovered from her ailment. It was a matter of surprise for all. When the king learnt that it was the miracle of the Pir, which had cured the queen, he became his devotee. After the death of the Pir, his shrine received royal patronage in perpetuity.[30] Several such miracles are associated with almost all the sufis of the Jammu hills. These stories had great significance so far as the popularity of the sufis is concerned. A large number of people are said to have become their followers after hearing the wondrous tales. The sufis still 'survive' in/through the stories revealing their miraculous deeds.

Social Concerns

The sufis performed a variety of roles while living in the midst of the common people. On the one hand, they propagated their mystical ideas by delivering sermons and holding discussions. On the other hand, they showed an equal concern for the material welfare of their followers and disciples. A significant social activity of the Jammu sufis was their organization of the community kitchen (*langar*).[31] It was not a simple act of charity to provide food to the needy. Rather it was intended to discourage the social practice of exclusion. Segregation and untouchability were the worst social evils, prevalent in the different parts of the country. In the Jammu hills, the topographical features also obstructed social intercourse among the inhabitants of different localities and pockets. The organization of *langar* by the sufis thus intended to associate people with the concept and practice of inclusiveness. The extent of the popularity of *langar* can be estimated from the fact that most sufi shrines of Jammu hills organize *langar* till date on various occasions. At the time of *langar*, people cast off their respective social identities and consider their participation in *langar* as a sacred duty. It is also interesting to mention that people's donations (*futuh*) to the organization of *langar* has been a salient feature of popular devotion since the medieval times.[32] The managers of the sufi shrine were expected to conceal the name of the donor who, in turn, was expected to refrain from seeking undue socio-political mileage from the act.

The sufic tradition of *langar*, which was inaugurated by Shaikh Farid in the twelfth-thirteenth centuries, seems to have been consolidated in the Jammu hills by the association of the sufis of this region with Guru Nanak. Secondly, a number of sufis of Jammu, who originally came from Punjab, must have been acquainted with the 'Sikh' tradition of *langar*. For example, Pir Mitha, who had arrived from Multan, met Guru Nanak, the founder of the Sikh institution of *langar*. He was much impressed by the personality of the Guru. He presented some grains to the Guru so that he could cook and eat it. Guru Nanak accepted the offering of the Pir and passed it on to his companion-disciple, Mardana. Assuming that the Guru did not eat grains, the Pir offered some milk to him. Again the Guru handed it over to Mardana. The Pir was much perplexed and presumed that since the Guru was a non-Muslim, he did not accept anything offered by a Muslim. Guru Nanak understood the apprehension of the Pir. He called him and delivered a sermon on spirituality. Afterwards, the Pir committed himself to social services. A similar association between Baba Buddhan Shah and Guru Nanak is attested both by the sufi and Sikh traditions of Punjab and Jammu regions. According to one such tradition, both Baba Buddhan Shah and Guru Nanak enjoyed the company of each other. They used to hold meetings to exchange their views on social and spiritual issues. Baba Buddhan Shah also went to Anand Sahib and met Guru Nanak and stayed there for some time.[33] Thus, what is being suggested is that the sufis of Jammu hills respected the sentiment of the 'others'. They became a bridge among the people of different religions and social backgrounds. Their convents (*khanqahs*) and shrines acted as meeting places for people belonging to different religions and regions. They became instrumental in establishing the concept that "regions pray together and stay together."[34]

Apart from maintaining and promoting social harmony, the sufis of the Jammu hills also made earnest efforts to maintain ecological balance. For instance, they participated in the plantation of trees and founded water resources, particularly the *baolis* (wells with steps). It was believed that the leaves and fruits of these trees and water of these resources were helpful in curing certain diseases. Pir Lakhdata is remembered for the plantation of such trees and creation of such water resources. Shah Ghulam Badshah of Rajouri is said to have planted a tree, which became everlasting one, known as Sadabahar. It still survives. It yields fruit throughout the year, but their plucking is forbidden. Only those fruits can be used which naturally fall to the ground. It is believed that whosoever gets the fruit and eats it, his or her prayer is granted. The uniqueness of this fruit is that it never gets perished. It is also believed that whosoever wishes to be blessed with a child should eat the leaves of this tree.[35] The concern of the Jammu sufis with ecology led to the evolution of the culture of preserving trees and clean water. The protection and the maintenance of water resources such as *baolis*, tanks, wells and lakes are understood to be a social duty in the Jammu hills. A large number of rites in the area are associated with the water resources and trees. Even in the present times, it is customary to organize festivals, fairs and other religious functions near the water resources and to treat the water of these places as antidote to several common miseries. It is important to mention that both in Islam and Hinduism tree plantation is regarded as a pious practice.

Sufi Shrines

The multifarious services of the sufis were appreciated and supported by the people of the Jammu hills. The extent of the people's attachment to the sufis can be estimated from the fact that the sufi shrines have been protected by the people for generations. Even today a large number of people visit these shrines on every Thursday. The spiritual heads (*sajjadah nishins* or *gaddi nishins*) continue to organize annual death anniversaries (*urs*) in the memory of the 'departed' sufis. Apart from the common people, the rulers of Jammu, since the time of Maharaja Gulab Singh, have looked after the preservation of these shrines.[36] Gulab Singh, as a feudatory (*jagirdar*) of Maharaja Ranjit Singh, requested the latter for the grant of land to the shrine of Shah Ghulam Badshah, situated in Rajouri district. Maharaja Ranjit Singh accepted the request and granted land for meeting the expenses of the shrine.[37] Similarly, Maharaja Gulab Singh granted an endowment of fifty *kanals* to the shrine of Pir Wali Shah at Katra in Udhampur district.[38] Both Maharaja Ranbir Singh (1857-1885) and Maharaja Pratap Singh (1885-1925) extended financial support and renovated a number of sufi shrines in the Jammu hills. More importantly, Jai Singh, the king of Kishtwar, accepted Islam under the influence of Sayyid Fariduddin Qadiri during the seventeenth century and received the title of Bakhtiyar Khan.[39] Baba Jiwan Shah was much respected by Maharaja Pratap Singh and his brother Amar Singh. It is known that Maharaja Pratap Singh extended financial support to Baba Jiwan Shah both in cash (*wazifa*) and kind to meet the expenses of his mystic activities. The Maharaja always looked forward to the opportunity to meet the Baba. Therefore, he frequently invited Baba Jiwan Shah to his palace. The Maharaja is said to have presented a *hukka* and a *dhoosa* to the Baba during his visit to the palace.[40]

The location of the sufi shrines conferred a specific identity to the area concerned. Some localities of the Jammu hills are even known after the name of the prominent sufi of the place. The localities such as Pir Mitha, Lakhdata Bazar and Jiwan Shah may be cited in this connection. It may be mentioned that the nomenclature of these localities was dedicated to the sufis who had migrated to the Jammu hills. It is known that Pir Mitha came to Jammu from Persia via Lahore during the reign of Raja Biram Dev (1454-1489) of Jammu. Since Raja Biram Dev was a liberal ruler,[41] Pir Mitha's arrival was welcomed. The real name of Pir Mitha was Syed Qutub Alam. He belonged to Sabzwar in Persia. He liked sweets and milk very much. Generally, his followers in Jammu offered him sweets when ever they came to meet him. Therefore, they started calling him Pir Mitha and he became popular with this name. The followers of Syed Qutub Alam gave him a new name (Pir Mitha) in accordance with their own perception, thus providing social legitimacy to the activities of the sufi. Regarding the arrival, settlement and following of Pir Mitha in Jammu, *Rajdarshani* records a very interesting account. According to it, benevolence and generosity of Raja Biram Dev inspired a number of enlightened saints (*darveshes*) to visit Jammu and settle here. In 867 AH/1462 AD a Syed named Qutub Alam came to Jammu from the country of Sabazwar. A large number of Hindus and Muslims became his followers. As sugar and sweets were his favourites, most of the visitors offered him gifts of milk, sugar, sweets and sugar cane. He also spoke sweet words to the people. Hence, he came to be known popularly as Pir Mitha. His tomb still blesses the people of Jammu. The people of Jahud tribe, Musalmans and Gujjars celebrate a fair at his *khanqah* in the month of *katik* on the full moon day."[42]

The sufi establishments became instrumental in promoting commercial activities and led to the foundation of towns and villages. Most of the sufi shrines of Jammu hills are situated on the trade routes. It may be mentioned that in the hills it was very difficult to discover a route connecting one area to the other. When the sufis settled at different places of the Jammu hills, they began to be inhabited by people of different social backgrounds. Pir Roshan Wali Shah (also known as Nau Gaza Pir) settled at Gummat, which is known to have emerged as an important commercial centre of Jammu city from medieval period onwards. *Rajdarshani* mentions that the *khanqah* of Pir Roshan Wali Shah had been a hub of social gatherings and remained in a flourishing condition.[43] Similarly, Pir Mitha is an important part of the old city of Jammu and is a very old market. Lakhdata Bazar, named after Pir Lakhdata, is situated in the heart of the old city of Jammu. One of the sufis of Jammu hills is known as Rah Baba i.e. a discoverer of a route. His real name was Mian Muhammad Ibrahim. Maharaja Pratap Singh has constructed a road leading up to his shrine. Therefore, people started addressing him as Rah Baba.[44] In the popular perception, it was Mian Muhammad Ibrahim, not the king, who was the real power behind the construction of the road. The tradition of annual commemoration of the death anniversary (*urs*) and people's visits to the sufi shrines on every Thursday were instrumental in the organization of the commercial activities around the sufi shrines. Thus these sufis and their shrines served the purpose of connecting the people of one area with that of the other. The route followed by the devotees and travellers facilitated the socio-economic development of the area. The sense of isolation, which generally prevailed in the hills, was broken and replaced by a new binding force for the scattered communities. It is important to mention that nowadays some sufi shrines are attracting devotees on a wide scale and are receiving large unasked charity in the form of money. The endowment is utilized for public welfare activities. A huge university at Rajouri has been established in the name of Baba Shah Ghulam Badshah. The university is imparting technical education to the students. Similarly, the endowment of the shrine of Fariduddin Qadiri is being utilized for the promotion of education in the Kishtwar district of Jammu region. Thus, the sufis and their shrines are working for the retention of the glorious legacy of these places, which are alive even in the present age. They are promoting dialogues between past and present in a continuous process.

The sufis of the Jammu hills brought about social harmony during the medieval period, while their shrines have continued to promote the same social ideals in more recent times. It is not surprising that some shrines are being maintained by non-Muslims. The sufis migrated from distant places and made a permanent home in the Jammu hills. Having received a tremendous social support, they propagated pluralism and inclusiveness. They initiated a continuous dialogue between indigenous and non-indigenous cultures, besides building bridges between different regions. As a result, the inter-regional contact between Punjab and Jammu, became a dominant socio-economic trend. The resilient survival of the sufi shrines in almost all the localities upto our own times, irrespective of the topography and nature of the population, speaks volumes of the everlasting influence of sufism on the social life of the region. These structures, though old and silent, stand as a living symbol of a historically evolved cultural heritage. The life and work of the sufis, including their piety and charisma, continues to remind the present generation of the harmony and prosperity that prevailed in the Jammu hills under the guidance of the 'departed' sufis.

NOTES AND REFERENCES

1. Richard Maxwell Eaton, *Sufis of Bijapur, 1300-1700*, Princeton University Press, Princeton, New Jersey, 1978.
2. Abdul Qaiyum Rafiqi, *Sufism in Kashmir*, Crown Publishers, Srinagar, 2003.
3. According to *Tarikh-i-Azmi* of Kashmir (1417), Jammu came into existence around 900AD. However, the first contemporary and authentic reference to Jammu is available in the memoirs of Timur who sacked this town in the course of his Indian invasion (1398-99). Timur's account shows that Jammu then was the focal point of local power. See *Malfuzat-i-Timur* in Elliot and Dowson, *History of India*, III, pp. 467-72 as quoted in M.L. Kapur, *History of Jammu and Kashmir State: The Making of the State*, Vol. I, Jammu Kashmir History Publications, 1980, pp. 9-10.
4. For detail see Annemarie Schimmel, *Islam in the Indian Subcontinent*, Sang-E-Meel Publications, Lahore, 2003.
5. Richard Maxwell Eaton, *Sufis of Bijapur, 1300-1700*, p. 157.
6. Ibid, p.158.
7. Mohan Singh, *An Introduction to Panjabi Literature*, Nanak Singh Pustak Mala, Amritsar, nd. p. 43. Also see Mohammad Wahid Mirza, *The Life and Works of Amir Khusrau*, Idarahi-i Adabiyat-i, Delli, Delhi, 1974.
8. Khaliq Ahmad Nizami, *Some Aspects of Religion and Politics in India during the Thirteenth Century*, Idarah-i-Adabiyat-i-Delli, Delhi, 1974, p. 264.
9. Chitralekha Zutshi, *Language of Belonging: Islam, Regional Identity and the Making of Kashmir*, Permanent Black, Delhi, 2003, p. 23.
10. Khaliq Ahmad Nizami, *Some Aspects of Religion and Politics in India during the Thirteenth Century*, Oxford University Press, Delhi, 2002, p. 53.
11. Murray T. Titus, *Indian Islam: A Religious History of Islam in India*, Oriental Books Reprint Corporation, New Delhi, 1979, p. 42.
12. J. Hutchison and J.P. Vogel, *History of Punjab Hill States*, Low Price Publications, Delhi 1993, pp. 514-729.
13. Abul Fazl, *Ain-i-Akbari, Vol.II*, Eng. Tr. by H.S. Jarret, corrected and further annotated by Sir J.N.Sarkar, Low Price Publications, Delhi, 1994, pp. 324-25.
14. Frederick Drew, *The Jammu and Kashmir Territories: A Geographical Account*, Jay Kay Book House, Jammu, 1999, pp. 9-10.
15. A.Q. Rafiqi, *Sufism in Kashmir*, pp. 19, 35-154.
16. Ganeshdas Badehra, *Rajdarshani* (Persian), Eng Tr. by S.D.S. Charak, Annotated by Anita K. Billawaria, Jay Kay Book House, Jammu, 1991, 163. According to the *Rajdarshani*, "...from among the Muslim Mian Sufi Shah

and Khairi Shah were renowned and popular there (Jammu). The tombs of both these are situated near large domed mausoleum of Pir Mitha." *Ibid.*, p. 163. It is important to mention here that the *Rajdarshani* was written during the reign of Maharaja Gulab Singh(1846-57), the founder of the Jammu and Kashmir state. It is written in Persian. Ganeshdas Badehra, its author, belonged to Punjab. He was brought to Jammu by Maharaja Gulab Singh. However, the space given to the sufis and their shrines in the *Rajdarshani* shows that in both the 18th and early 19th century sufism continued to be a popular social trend of Jammu hills and both the state and society treated it as a source of cultural developments in the hills. The *Rajdarshani* also shows that inclusiveness was very much appreciated in Jammu hills during medieval and early modern period.

17. For detail see Sita Ram Kohli, *Sunset of the Sikh Empire*, ed., Khushwant Singh, Orient Longmans, Bombay, 1967.
18. Ever since the emergence of sufism, the sufis have been travelling in different parts of the world to acquire education in religion and mysticism, besides interacting with eminent scholars and mystics. Khwaja Muinuddin Chishti, the founder of the Chishti order in India, visited Samarqand, Bukhara, Harvan (Nishapur), Baghdad, Tabrez, Aush, Isfahan, Sabzwar, Mihan, Khirqan, Astrabad, Balkh and Ghazni before his arrival in Lahore, which was followed by his jouney to Ajmer. The famous Suhrawardi masters, Shaikh Bahauddin Zakariya and Syed Jalaluddin Bukhari Makhdum-i-Jahaniyan Jahangasht, acquired great fame on account of their extensive travels in the Islamic lands.
19. Saiyid Athar Abbas Rizvi, *A History of Sufism in India*, Vol. II, Munshiram Manoharlal, New Delhi, 1983, p. 316.
20. *Pir*, a Persian word, and etymologically 'elder', is a term denoting a spiritual director or guide among the sufis. For detail see Asim Roy, *Islam in South Asia: A Regional Perspective*, South Asian Publishers, New Delhi, 1996, pp. 100-120.
21. Shiv Nirmohi, *Duggar ke Darvesh*, Shivalik Prakashan, Udhampur, 2005, pp. 44-163.
22. Ibid., pp. 44-146.
23. Shivji Dhar, *Tarikh-i-Kishtwar*(Persian), Jammu, 1962, pp. 36-37.
24. Abdul Qaiyum Rafiqi, *Sufism in Kashmir*, p. 191.
25. Mirza Zafarullah Khan, *Tazkirah-i-Bemisal: Rajgan-i-Rajour* (Urdu), Jalandhar, p. 137.
26. Shiv Nirmohi, *Duggar ke Darvesh*, p. 154.
27. Both Sayyid Ali Hamadani and Nuruddin Rishi enjoyed huge social support in Kashmir. Sayyid Ali Hamadani belonged to Hamadan in Persia and came to Kashmir during second half of the 14th century. He introduced Kubraviya *silsilah* in Kashmir. But Nuruddin Rishi was an indigenous sufi of Kashmir. He introduced the Rishi order in Kashmir. Nuruddin Rishi was very popular among both the Muslims and Hindus. The latter called him Nand Rishi.
28. Molvi Hashmatullah Lakhnavi, *Mukhtasar Tarikh-i-Jammu wa Kashmir* (Urdu), Jay and Kay Book House, Jammu, 1992, p. 166. G.M.D.

Sufi, *Kashir, Vol.I,* Life and Light Publishers, Delhi, 1974, pp. 66, 115-16.

29. Ganeshdas Badehra, *Rajdarshani*, p. 74.
30. Zohra Khatoon, *Muslim Saints and Their Shrines*, Jay Kay Book House, Jammu, 1990, pp. 17-18.
31. It is understood that Fariduddin Ganj-i-Shakar, popularly known as Baba Farid, was the first to introduce the tradition of *langar* in Ajodhan (Punjab). After that *langar* became an integral component of the concept of social welfare in Punjab. Later on Guru Nanak institutionalized the *langar* system.
32. In the context of the historical importance and genesis of sufi *langar*, one may read two essays of Richard Eaton (i) 'The Political and Religious Authority of the Shrine of Baba Farid' and (ii) 'Court of Man, Court of God: Local Perceptions of the Shrine of Baba Farid, Pakpattan, Punjab' in Richard M. Eaton, *Essays on Islam and Indian History*, Oxford University Press, New Delhi, 2000, pp. 203-248.
33. Zohra Khatoon, *Muslim Saints and Their Shrines*, p. 29.
34. Mridu Rai, *Islam, Rights and History of Kashmir, Muslim Subjects*, Delhi, 2004, pp. 76-77. Also see Khwaja Hasan Sani Nizami, 'Sufi Tradition and its Impact on Religious Thought' in Asghar Ali Engineer, *Islam in India: The Impact of Civilizations*, Shipra, New Delhi, 2002, p. 69.
35. Khush Dil Maini, *Ziarat-i-Sayyid Baba Ghulam Shah Badshah*, Shahdara Sharif (Urdu), Jammu, 2000, pp. 3-4.
36. The reverence of the ruling elite for sufis has been an old tradition, which was formed with the establishment of the Delhi sultanate. Qutbuddin Aibak and Shamsuddin Iltutmish had much regard for Khwaja Qutbuddin Bakhtiyar Kaki, while Ghiasuddin Balban had the same attitude towards Shaikh Fariduddin Ganj-i-Shakar. Muhammad bin Tughluq expressed deep devotion towards Shaikh Alauddin Mauj Darya, the grandson of Shaikh Farid. Firuz Shah Tughluq had intimate friendship with Syed Jalaluddin Bukhari Makhdum-i-Jahaniyan Jahangasht. Akbar was devoted to Shaikh Salim Chishti of Fatehpur Sikri and the shrine of Muinuddin Chishti at Ajmer.
37. Shiv Nirmohi, *Duggar ke Darvesh*, p. 119.
38. Ibid., p. 107.
39. Sadullah Sad Faridabadi, *Shah Farid-ud-din Baghdadi* (Urdu), Doda, 2000, pp. 94-96. Molvi Hashmatullah, *Mukhtasar Tarikh-i-Jammu wa Kashmir*, p. 167.
40. Zohra Khatoon, *Muslim Saints and their Shrines*, pp. 42-43. The tradition of the royal respect to the sufis and their shrines in India can be traced from thirteenth century onwards. Since the sufis and their had huge social support, the kings tried to associate with them to establish them that they respected the sentiments of the people.
41. S.D.S. Charak, *A Short History of Jammu Raj*, Ajay Publisher, Jammu, 1985, p. 79.
42. Ganesh Das Badehra, *Rajdarshani*, pp. 122-23.
43. Ibid., p. 74.
44. Zohra Khatoon, *Muslim Saints and their Shrines*, pp. 50-51.

6

Development of Qadiri Mysticism at Lahore

Principles and Practices of Miyan Mir

Surinder Singh

Miyan Mir is known to the people of Punjab as a Muslim saint who laid the foundation of Harmandir Sahib (Amritsar), the most sacred place of the Sikhs. The Sikh tradition preserves the accounts of intimate friendship between Miyan Mir and the Sikh gurus. It is believed that the Qadiri sufi offered to intercede with Jahangir on behalf of Guru Arjun Dev,[1] who was ultimately put to death. It is claimed that he was instrumental in securing the release of Guru Hargobind who had been imprisoned in the fort of Gwalior at the orders of Jahangir.[2] Till today, the Sikh preachers have continued to narrate the stories of sufi-guru understanding to the Sikh congregations during the course of religious services. We must hasten to point out that Miyan Mir did not figure only in the Sikh tradition. Brief references regarding him are found in the Persian chronicles of the seventeenth century viz. Jahangir's *Tuzuk-i-Jahangiri*, Dara Shukoh's *Safinat-ul-Auliya*, Abdul Hamid Lahori's *Badshah Nama* and Muhammad Saleh Kambo's *Amal-i-Saleh*. But it is Dara Shukoh's *Sakinat-ul-Auliya* which offers the most detailed biography of Miyan Mir. The prince found a large number of stories about the saint, which were circulating in the contemporary socio-cultural milieu. Even when these were narrated by reliable persons (*mardum motmid*), the inevitable differences appeared among the several versions. In these circumstances, Dara Shukoh prepared an authentic biography after diligent research (*tahqiq*) and corroboration of facts from the companions of the saint (*ashab Hazrat Miyan Jio*). The work basically aims at describing the early career, mystical beliefs and meditational techniques of Miyan Mir.[3] It also pays adequate attention to the saint's miracles and identifies the spots where he sat for contemplation. The work devotes a considerable space to his disciples, both living and dead.

It is significant that Dara Shukoh reserves one-fifth of the work exclusively to his own mentor Mulla Shah Badakhshi and, while doing so, includes his writings – 11 letters, 10 sonnets (*ghazals*) and 18 quatrains (*rubais*) – which promise to strengthen our understanding of the development of the Qadiri order in north-western India.[4] It is on Dara Shukoh's *Sakinat-ul-Auliya* that the present paper is largely based.

Before we explore the contribution of Miyan Mir to the growth of the Qadiri order, it would be appropriate to understand the conditions prevailing in Punjab during his life time. The region became an arena of protracted conflict between the emerging Mughal power and the second Afghan empire. The restoration of Humayun and enthronement of Akbar marked the beginning of a new phase in history, when several administrative-cum-military measures were initiated for the consolidation of the Mughal state in north-western India. To begin with, the incursions of Mirza Hakim (the foster brother of Akbar) into Punjab were beaten back and remnants of Afghan power in the region were wiped out. A centralized polity was erected on the foundation of the twin institutions of military ranks (*mansabs*) and revenue assignments (*jagirs*). Land revenue began to be collected on the basis of statistics regarding cultivated area and agricultural prices. The growing power of the Mughal state undermined the position of the rural intermediaries, as reflected in the execution of Dulla Bhatti, his father and grandfather (*zamindars* of a fertile pocket in the Rachna Doab).[5] During the period 1585-1598, when Lahore served as the imperial headquarters, the neighbouring regions – Kashmir, Sind and Baluchistan – were integrated into the Mughal empire. At the same time, the chiefs of the Punjab hill states were reduced to vassalage, while the north-western frontier was pacified by suppressing the Afghan tribes. The transcontinental trade route, which connected the Gangetic plain with Central Asia and which passed through Punjab, began to attract a considerable traffic. The expansion of economic activities – agriculture, industry and commerce – gave a fresh impetus to the process of urbanization in Lahore, Batala, Samana, Sialkot, Gujarat and Wazirabad. The metropolis of Lahore, assisted by a variety of factors, emerged as a premier centre of education and learning.[6] The Sikh gurus offered the vision of an egalitarian society, which had a special appeal for the underprivileged groups inhabiting the area between the Ravi and Satluj. Shah Husain Lahori (1539-1599) advocated, through his Punjabi verses (*qafis*), a passionate love for God, often alluding to the lover-rebels Hir and Ranjha. From the mid fifteenth century onwards, a number of mystics – Shaikh Muhammad Husaini, Shaikh Daud, Shaikh Abu Ishaq and Shah Abul Maali – became instrumental in planting the seeds of the Qadiri order in central Punjab.[7] It was in this socio-cultural milieu that Miyan Mir expounded the Qadiri mysticism.

Emergence of Miyan Mir as a Mystic

The real name of Miyan Mir was Mir Muhammad, but he was addressed by his companions and disciples as Miyan Jio. He was born in AD 1531 at Siwistan, a town situated between Thatta and Bhakkar. Since he grew to adulthood in this region, he often conversed in the Sindi language. His father, Qazi Sayin Ditta bin Qazi Qalandar Faruqi, was a mystic of high stature. His mother, Bibi Fatima, was the daughter of Qazi Qadin, a distinguished scholar who had adopted the path of renunciation. It was believed that Miyan Mir was twenty eighth descendant of Umar Faruq, the second pious caliph. He lost his father at the age of seven. It was the ardent desire of his mother that the child should be groomed as a mystic.[8] From the age of twelve onwards, he started acquiring mystical knowledge (*ilm-i-batin*) from his mother, who was verily the Rabia of the age. After a short time, he was permitted to engage in independent travelling and spiritual pursuits. During the course of his wanderings in the hills of Siwistan, he met Khwaja Khizar (who was affiliated to the Qadiri order)[9] and enrolled himself as a disciple.[10] During this phase, his training consisted of spiritual discipline (*riyazat*) and self-mortification (*mujahida*). In spite of the tutelage of a living spiritual preceptor, Miyan Mir – being an Uwaisi – is said to have received spiritual instructions from the soul (*ruhaniyat*) of Abdul Qadir Gilani, just as the latter did so from Prophet Muhammad. An Uwaisi was one who did not need a spiritual guide in human form, but was instructed by the Prophet without the role of any mediator.[11] There were sufis who followed the prophetic example and instructed their disciples through their soul (*ruhaniyat*), and not through their actual presence. Viewed in this perspective, Miyan Mir was an Uwaisi of the Prophet. It may be pointed out that the rank of Uwaisi was possessed in extremely rare cases.[12]

Since Shaikh Khizar allowed Miyan Mir to go to any place of his choice, the latter travelled northwards and arrived at Lahore. At this juncture, he was twenty five years of age. The Mughal rule had just been reestablished and the new emperor Akbar had initiated several measures to consolidate the nascent empire. In these circumstances, Miyan Mir started taking lessons from an outstanding scholar Maulana Saadullah, who specialized in exoteric knowledge (*ilm-i-zahir*) and mystical knowledge (*ilm-i-batin*). He also studied for a number of years under Maulana Niamatullah (a pupil of Maulana Saadullah and teacher of Dara Shukoh's tutor, Shaikh Mirak) who, however, failed to discern the spiritual qualities possessed by his student. It was probably during this period that Miyan Mir acquired a considerable proficiency in traditional (*manqulat*) and rational sciences (*maaqulat*).[13] He acquired such mastery over Ibn-i-Arabi's *Futuhat-i-Makkiya* (Meccan Revelations) that he quoted it extensively in his discussions. He had also memorized Jami's commentary on Ibn-i-Arabi's *Fasus-ul-Hikam* (Bezels of Wisdom). The contemporary scholars began to seek his opinion on intricate questions related to different aspects of mysticism (*tasawwuf*).[14]

Having completed his formal education, Miyan Mir began to undertake spiritual exercises. For this purpose, he selected appropriate places which provided freedom from disturbances and peace of mind. He began his day by paying homage at the tombs of holy men. Then, accompanied by a few companions, he went to the gardens and jungles that were not frequented by people. Each one of them sat separately under the shade of some tree and plunged into contemplation. However, they collected at one place at the time of obligatory prayers (*namaz*) and thus followed a practice which had been sanctified by Prophet Muhammad and communicated as a tradition by Abu Huraira. In the second half of the sixteenth century, the city of Lahore was experiencing a vigorous urban growth, owing to political and economic factors. It became increasingly difficult for the sufis to locate a place which could guarantee an environment suitable for their needs.[15] For this reason, Miyan Mir appears to have shifted to Sirhind where he stayed for a year or so. He was afflicted by a number of physical ailments, including a pain in his knees. He was nursed with utmost devotion by a native of Sirhind, Haji Niamatullah Sirhindi, who was enrolled as a disciple. On his return to Lahore, Miyan Mir settled in Muhalla Baghbanan, also known as Khafipura,[16] and lived here till the end of his life (21 August 1635). It was during this period that the city of Lahore emerged as a leading centre of the Qadiri order in the Indian subcontinent. Dara Shukoh provides the following list of places, located in Lahore and its neighbourhood, where Miyan Mir and his disciples sat for contemplation.[17]

1. Under the trees at the cell of Shaikh Hud, village Mirdad near the tomb of Shaikh Bilawal.
2. A sandy hillock on the eastern side of the city, near village Bhogiwal.
3. A building in the Bagh Swami Jal near the Bagh Sultan Parvez.
4. Under a Saras tree in Baghicha Naulakha which was reputed to have conversed with Mulla Khwaja Kalan regarding medicinal uses of its parts and advice on wearing its rosary.
5. A building in a tank, then under water, in the Bagh of Mirza Kamran.
6. A dilapidated structure in the Bagh Qaleech Khan, located in a corner of Bagh Mirza Kamran.
7. In the environs of Bagh Anarkali on the southern side of the city.

8. A domed structure, without any door, at the southern corner of the above garden.
9. A building at the corner of Talab Ananta, near Sarai Khushal Khan.
10. A dome on the road leading from Lahore to Ferozepur, located on the south of Lahore.
11. A small verandah under a huge tree at the tomb of Peshrau Khan, near the tomb of Miyan Mir.
12. Under a *ber* tree (*jahau*) in the graveyard if Bibi Haj Taj.
13. Under trees in Bagh Baddu, near Bhogiwal, located on the south of the city.
14. Under a *shisham* tree along the boundary wall of Bagh Qasim Khan.
15. A dome at the gate of the tomb of Ahmad Beg Khan, near the old Idgah and Bauli Daulat Khan.
16. At a well in Bagh Faizi, where the tomb of Dai Dilaram stood.
17. At the tomb of Ruknuddin Ruhela, near old Alam Ganj, famous as Alam Ganj Qaleech Khan.
18. In the garden and tomb of Shaikh Chuhar, adjoining Bagh Khan Azam.
19. In Bagh Khan Azam at the palace of Shah Murad and the tomb of his son.
20. In Bagh Raju near Daulatabad and Ichhra.
21. In Changi, then submerged under water, near Bagh Jawahar Khan.
22. Under a tree, located in the environs of Ichhra, which fell in the year of Miyan Mir's death.
23. In a wheat field on the eastern side of Bagh Hoshiar Khan.
24. The tomb of Shaikh Abdul Rahman on the western side of Bagh Hoshiar Khan.
25. In Bagh Murtaza Khan, then known as Bagh Wazir Khan.
26. In the garden of Muhammad Taqi, who was the *diwan-i-buyutat* of emperor Jahangir.
27. In the Bagh Mulk Ali Kotwal.
28. In the Bagh Abdul Rahim Khan-i-Khanan.
29. In Bagh Khatun.
30. At Bela on the river Ravi, near Shahdara.
31. In Bagh Mirza Momin.

Mystical Beliefs and Practices

Miyan Mir's mystical doctrine was constructed on the foundation of a strict adherence to canonical law (*shariat*) and, on this issue, he followed the precedents established by such eminent sufi masters like Shaikh

Junaid Baghdadi and Abdul Qadir Gilani. In his opinion, adherence to the canonical law constituted the first of the three stages in the path of mysticism (*suluk*), when the seeker (*salik*) faithfully fulfilled the obligations prescribed by Islam. In consequence, the second stage representing the mystical path leading to God (*tariqat*) was reflected on the mirror of his heart. This condition involved purification of the inner self from evil intentions, comprehending the transitory nature of human existence and obliterating everything from the heart except God. A successful fulfilment of these conditions led to the removal of veil of human nature from his heart and ensured the revelation of the final stage, the ultimate reality (*haqiqat*), on him. Miyan Mir believed that the human being was constituted of three elements – body (*nafs*), heart (*dil*) and soul (*ruh*).[18] Each one of these could be reformed by observing the rules of the *shariat, tariqat* and *haqiqat*.[19]

During the course of a conversation with Mulla Abdul Hakim Sialkoti,[20] who was a renowned scholar and teacher, Miyan Mir underlined the implications of prayer (*namaz*) for the mystical journey. He explained, "There are two ways of achieving union with God. The first is passion (*jazbah*) by virtue of which God pulls the novice towards Himself in one spontaneous moment and absorbs him in His own being. The second is the path of mysticism (*suluk*) in which the novice undergoes discipline (*riyazat*) and self-mortification (*mujahida*) under the guidance of a wise mentor (*buzurg*) and, by doing so, experiences the revelation of the first stage of his journey called *alam-i-malkut*.[21] Thereafter, his spiritual guide (*pir*) directs him to leave for a jungle or garden and engage himself in solitary meditation, so that he avoids any association with other people and secures nearness to God." Mulla Abdul Hakim Sialkoti objected to this method on the grounds that it demolished the purpose of congregational prayer (*namaz-i-jamaat*). Miyan Mir argued, on the basis of a prophetic tradition (*hadis*), that it was obligatory for a Muslim to understand the true nature of prayer (*namaz*) and endeavour to achieve concentration of the mind (*huzur-i-qalb*), for these two conditions were more important than the congregational prayer as such. It was true that he and his companions went to the jungles and meditated while sitting separately under trees at different spots. But they assembled at one place at the appropriate time and offered the congregational prayer (*namaz-i-jamaat*) which was never allowed to lapse.[22]

Miyan Mir believed that a person who had chosen the path of mysticism (*suluk*) should remain in constant communion with God. In theory and practice, he followed the spirit of the following couplet:

Kas-i ku ghafil az haq yak zamanast
Aan dam kafir ast amma nihan ast

> A person who is forgetful of God even for a moment becomes an infidel for that moment, even though a hidden one.

His faith in God (*tawakkul*) was so strong that he would throw away the drinking water, which was placed in an earthen cup (*kuza*) by his side at night. He did not allow any idle thought (*khatra*) to dilute his faith at any time.[23] He knew several ways of driving away distracting thoughts and often gave advice on this matter to his companions, none of whom was troubled by this problem.[24] It was believed that idle thoughts (*khatra*) were generated by personal desires (*khatir*). Once the latter was suppressed, the former also disappeared. Possession of these characteristics enabled Miyan Mir to remain in a perpetual state of self-annihilation (*istaghraq*), entirely oblivious of his physical environment. Indeed, it was difficult to appreciate the depth of his absorption in contemplation (*mushahida*). He often felt constrained to enquire about the day of the week and even the month of the year. He remained so strongly entrenched in self-annihilation that he was often found unconscious of the piece of bread held his hand while eating.[25]

Miyan Mir had severed all worldly connections, as there was no need for a gnostic to cultivate social relations. He believed that one who possessed the knowledge of God did not require the knowledge of the world.[26] Therefore, he nurtured a strong aversion to the company of people and preferred to close his doors on them. So long as he was young, he spent the whole day in the gardens and jungles. When he returned to his cell (*hujra*) after the evening prayers (*namaz-i-maghrib*), he locked the door from inside with a chain. During old age, when his movements were restricted due to pain in the knees, he confined himself to the cell even during the day. In ordinary circumstances, he did not entertain any visitor. Any person, who insisted on seeing him, was however allowed to enter. Miyan Mir offered a prayer for the well being of the visitor, who was then expected to leave. He explained, "Friends! You have your work and commitments to attend to. So do I. Kindly go. Involve yourself in your work, so that I may also do the same."[27] It may be pointed out that he remained a celibate and thus absolved himself of the multifarious obligations that were associated with married life. Rationale of this attitude was illustrated by the following episode. The wife of Mulla Hamid Gujar (who was one of the scholars of Lahore, but had adopted the path of mysticism in later life), sent a complaint to Miyan Mir through Shaikh Daud Bhervi. She prayed that her husband took no interest in his household which was in a state of ruin and that she had virtually become a widow. Miyan Mir expressed his helplessness in the matter, saying, "It is a characteristic feature of our method that a sufi (*sahib-i-shughal*) pays no attention to strangers."[28]

Miyan Mir's personal conduct did not conform to the standard sufi practices. Unlike most sufis, he did not wear a patched coat (*khirqa-i-muraqqa*). Instead, he wore a shirt (*jama*) of coarse cloth and wrapped a low priced turban (*dastar*) on his head. He washed this set of clothing with his own hands on the river bank. His disciples adopted the same apparel. He believed that one's garments should not disclose one's identity as a recluse (*faqir*). He knew that there were several people who dressed in patched coats with the sole purpose of self-promotion (*khud numai*), while their interior did not conform to their exterior.[29] Miyan Mir, as a rule, did not accept offerings from the members of the ruling elite, because he regarded himself as a rich man (*ghani*) and not a needy mendicant. He made an exception in the case of traders and artisans (*ahl-i-hirfat*) from whom he accepted offerings in small quantities. He spent a part of it on himself and gave away the rest to the needy. If a devoted follower made an offering from his legitimate income (*wajh-i-halal*), he did not refuse it. He also accepted cooked food from wherever it was received. But he did not permit anyone to bring food regularly, as the practice generated the habit of hoping for food and thus threatened to undermine one's faith in God.[30] He and his disciples did not keep the rosary (*tasbih*) in their hands. Whenever he saw a rosary in anyone's hand, he recited a verse in Hindi whose meaning was reflected in the following quatrain (*rubai*):[31]

Tasbih ba-man ajab dar amad ba zuban
Gufta keh mara chira kuni sar gardan
Gar dil ba-iwaz hamin ba-girdani tu
Dani keh barai cheest khalq al-insan

The rosary spoke to me in a strange tongue.It asked me why I was rolling it. If you had rolled your heart instead, you would have learnt the object of the creation of human being.

Miyan Mir had reduced his physical needs to a minimum. He had attuned his physique in such a manner that he could fast continuously for one or two weeks, without letting his condition be known. According to Mulla Shah Badakhshi, the souls of this fraternity (*sufis*) received nourishment from the invisible world (*alam-i-ghaib*) and their food consisted of God's name (*yaad-i-haq*). Miyan Mir claimed that nothing was cooked in his house for thirty years. In the later stages of his life, he employed a servant (*khadim*) to cook his food which was always of the same kind. He took his meals in the company of his disciples. If any one of them was not present, his share was kept aside. Shaikh Muhammad Lahori received special attention in this regard, as he was required to maintain a large household.[32] Miyan Mir, it was claimed, slept neither during the day nor at night. Shaikh Qutb has stated that Miyan Mir did not feel like sleeping at all. Miyan Muhammad would have us believe that, for many years, Miyan Mir spent the whole night in just one breath, while he did so in four breaths when he had crossed the age of eighty and had become weak due to old age.[33] The floor of his house, or rather cell, was furnished with a mat of split reeds (*buriya*). Since his life was organized on the principle of self-effacement, he wished to be buried after his death in nitrous earth (*shora zamin*), so that no trace was left of his bones. He forbade his companions from setting up a shop (*tomb*) over his grave, as it had been done in the case of other sufis.[34] In this light, his strong disapproval of Shaikh Bahauddin Zakariya's way becomes understandable.[35] He said, "I am surprised. What kind of recluse (*faqir*) is this Shaikh Bahauddin Zakariya Multani. Let him appear again in this world and learn asceticism (*faqiri*) from me. Then he would understand the true meaning of saintliness (*darveshi*) and asceticism (*faqiri*)."[36]

Miyan Mir was fond of listening to devotional singing (*sama*). He possessed a good understanding of the classical Hindustani music (*naghma-i-Hindi*). Whenever any singer (*qawwal*) turned up, he organized a musical session. Such occasions were rare, as he did not keep any singer (*qawwal*) in his service, nor did he invite any one to visit him. During the course of these meetings, his face glowed with happiness and hair of his beard stood out one after the other. But he conducted himself with utmost dignity (*tamkeen o waqar*) and did not make any movement whatsoever. His adherence to the canonical law (*shariat*) and self control were so steadfast that he never fell in a state of ecstasy (*wajd*) or dance (*raqs*). He could clearly distinguish between an audition which enabled the bird of one's imagination to fly to the greatest heights of reality (*haqiqat*) and an audition which was marked by a deceitful enjoyment and awakened the (sleeping) devil of one's brain. Though the disciples of Miyan Mir followed this practice, Mulla Shah Badakhshi was an exception to the rule. Whenever he encountered a singing party (*qawwals*) during his walks in the gardens and jungles, he brought it back and organized an audition (*sama*). During the performance, he was filled with immense joy and would start singing his own mystical quatrains (*rubais*) on the tunes of his native Mawra-ul-Nahr. Falling in a state of intoxication, he (sometimes) behaved in a strange manner. Interestingly, some mystics (shaikhs) of Delhi visited Lahore merely to participate in the ecstasy and dance that were generated in the wake of audition.[37]

Given the nature of sufi tradition and the state of sufi literature, it is impossible to encounter a sufi who is not credited with miracles. This is equally true of Miyan Mir who is said to have exhibited numerous miracles, though in an involuntary manner. It is another matter that he exercised utmost caution in concealing them. He strongly disapproved the act of performing miracles. He reprimanded a dearly loved disciple, Miyan Natha, who sought to stop rain, wind and thunder of clouds through his miraculous powers. The master emphatically declared that such an attempt was nothing but self-promotion (*khud faroshi*) and amounted to undue interference in matters that fell under the divine jurisdiction (*karkhana haq subhana o taala*).[38] In his opinion, miracles were of two kinds – *akhtiari* and *iztrari*. The former were exhibited by those *ahl-i-daawat* who, in order to fulfill a desire, repeated one of the numerous names of God and, by doing so, achieved their aim. The latter were those which could not be performed by any voluntary effort, but were entirely willed by God. It may be pointed out that Miyan Mir did not relish any discussion on the subject of miracles and, if anyone tried to involve him in such a dialogue, he recited the following verse:[39]

> *Har keh u az kashf khud goyed sukhan*
> *Kashf u ra kafsh kun bar sar bazan*
>
> If any one talks about his revelations (miracles), knock his revelation on the head with your shoe.

Dara Shukoh has recorded, on the basis of information provided by Miyan Mir's senior disciples and reliable persons, more than forty miracles said to have been performed by the Qadiri sufi.[40] A brief description of some of these miracles would enable us to form a better understanding of the role of Miyan Mir in the society of his times. For example, he revived a bird which had been killed by a hunter. He rightly predicted the retreat of the Uzbegs from Kabul. He transformed himself into a fruit-laden tree and, on another occasion, into a shop. He appeared near Khurasan and saved the goods of a merchant from being desroyed in a storm. He was instrumental in the violent death of an impudent messenger who demanded the former's turban on behalf of a Mughal prince He disappeaed from his cell at midnight, prayed at the Ghar-i-Hira near Mecca and returned to Lahore the next morning.He foretold the miserable end of an arrogant mystic and his servants, owing to their greed for money. He correctly predicted the recovery from illness of a lady who lived in Bukhara. He cured a boy of plague and another of dumbness. He predicted that Abdul Ha Muhaddis Dehalviand his son would escae the wrath of Jahangir. He transformed the saline water of a newly dug well into sweet water. He foretold that a government official of Lahore would not be transferred to Kabul, as the original oder had been withdrawn. He prophesied the Mughal conquest of the fort of Kanra. His prayer was instrumental in the payment of stipend to Suf Nasir which had been sanctioned by emperor Akbar. He correctly predicted that the news of Mulla Saeed Khan's death, whohad travelled from Lahore to Agra was wrong. He foretold that the money stolen by the maid of Fazil's grandfather, would be returne. He saved the marriage of Mulla Sangin Sufi by advising him to eturn to his native place in Badakhshan.

Training of Disciples

Miyan Mir enrolled few discipls, because it was rare to find one who was truly nclined toards God (*khuda talb*). But when he did take a novice under his tutelage, he saw to it that he was guided to his destination on the piritual path. His attitude in this regard stood in sharp contrast o the spiritual preceptors (shaikhs of the day, who enrolled a large number of disciples only to acquire cheap popularity and undeserved attention but who, in fact, led them to the path of infidelity. Miyan Mir prescribed such a tough regimen for the novices that very few aspirants were found to possess the required aptitude and commitment. Therefore, whenever a person expressed his desire to enroll himself as a disciple, Miyan Mir turned his face away, did not allow him to sit and asked him to leave forthwith, saying that the path of mysticism was full of hazards.[41] On such occasions, he recited the following couplet:

> *Shart awwal dar tareeq maarifat dani keh chest*
> *Tark kardan har do alam ra wa pusht pa zadan*
>
> Do you know the first requirement on the path of mysticism. It is to renounce both the worlds and to kick them with the back of the foot.

It appears that Miyan Mir's course for the novices was divided into a few distinct stages. At each stage, the novice was required to fulfill certain conditions so that he was able to move to the next stage. His physical burden and mental rigour increased progressively as he graduated from one stage to the other. To begin with, a novice was required to demonstrate a strong commitment to adopt the path of renunciation and solitude (*tark o tajrid*) by severing all worldly attachments. Miyan Mir argued, "A person who has taken his bath cannot be called clean even if a single hair of his head remains unclean, while all parts of his body have been washed properly. Similarly a person who has snapped all worldly bonds cannot claim to be solitary (*mujarrad*) if he is troubled even by a single worldly thought (*khatra*)." In the next stage of his training, the novice was directed to effect a drastic reduction in the amount of his food, sleep and speech. Miyan Mir advised his disciples to take packed food along with them, while going out in the jungle for meditation – a practice said to have been followed by Prophet Muhammad – for he believed that the biggest distraction for the novice was posed by hunger. Miyan Mir, acting in line with the method of Sahl bin Tustari, gave instructions to the novice in accordance with the latter's preparedness and sincerity, so that he reached an exalted spiritual status in a short time and his inner self was cleansed of everything except God.[42]

In the early phase of their mutual relationship, Miyan Mir projected himself as the beloved (*maashuq*) and expected the novice (*talib*) to assume the role of the lover (*ashiq*). After a certain period of time, when the novice was found steadfast in his love (*ishq*), the roles were reversed – Miyan Mir became the lover and treated the novice as his beloved. This practice was followed merely to test the sincerity and commitment of the novice and to distinguish him from the ambitious and self-indulgent (*ahl-i-hawas*), whose devotion to the spiritual path faded away in a short time. Therefore, the novice was required to display perfection in his desire (*talb*) to adopt the spiritual path, to the extent of erasing his own self. The more a Shaikh (mentor) overlooked a novice, the more should be the attraction of the novice for the Shaikh.[43] Miyan Mir often recited the following couplet:

> *Kas-i ra imtihan na karda sad baar*
> *Na girdani tu u ra sahib-i-asrar*
>
> A person, who has not been tested a hundred times, could not be recognized as a knower of secrets.

Dara Shukoh observes that a novice should not be discouraged by the outward attitude of the Shaikh, because inwardly it was characterized by wisdom (*hikmat*). His role might be compared with parents who had the betterment of their son in mind, when they chastised him. To a novice, the Shaikh was a greater benefactor than his own parents. The role of the Shaikh has been compared to that of a duck who provided warmth (training and instructions) of her wings to the eggs on the sea shore and when the ducklings (novices) emerged out of the shells and began to swim in the sea, the Shaikh watched their spiritual activities from the sea shore.[44] It is not surprising that Miyan Mir nurtured a high opinion of the role of the Shaikh vis-à-vis the training of the novice. It was true that the novices served their Shaikh with a high degree of devotion and some of them displayed such humility as to even pick the excrement (*fuzla*) of the Shaikh. But this service was a simple task, because anyone could perform it. But the Shaikh, who cleansed the novice's inner self of every ingredient except God, performed a much greater task.[45] We must hasten to point out that Miyan Mir's high opinion regarding the role of the Shaikh, did not prevent him from treating his disciples as friends. In fact, the word disciple (*murid*) never escaped from his lips, for in his own words, "The institution of mentor-disciple (*piri-muridi*) did not exist in the days of the Prophet. It was substituted by companionship (*suhbat*). Whoever sits in my company (*suhbat*) is one of my friends."[46]

In his *Sakinat-ul-Auliya*, Dara Shukoh has provided brief

biographical sketches of as many as twenty three disciples of Miyan Mir. On analyzing these notices, we find that these disciples not only hailed from different regions of the Indian subcontinent, but they also came from different social strata. Besides the city of Lahore, they came from Bhera, Sialkot, Kashmir, Sirhind, Sunam, Delhi, Mewat, Bihar and even Badakhshan. Abdul Rahman Mirza Madari was a Syed, Mulla Hamid a Gujjar, Haji Mustapha a Kalal and Miyan Natha a son of oil-makers (*assar*). Haji Muhammad Banyani had held an official rank (*mansab*) of 100 and Miyan Muhammad Murad had relinquished his post as the *mufti* of Lahore before engaging themselves in spiritual pursuits. Mulla Hamid Gujjar, Mulla Abdul Ghafur and Shaikh Muhammad Lahori were reputed scholars, who had given up the profession of teaching in favour of mysticism.[47] Let us take a close look at two of the disciples, Miyan Natha and Miyan Abul Maali, who were exceptional in many ways.

Miyan Natha was the most dearly loved disciple of Miyan Mir. A native of Sirhind, he belonged to a family of oil-makers (*assar*) and was totally illiterate. It was Miyan Mir's standard practice to permit a novice to stay only during the period of his training and, after putting him on the path of mysticism, to expect him to leave. However, an exception was made in the case of Miyan Natha, who enrolled himself during Miyan Mir's youth and stayed on till his (Miyan Natha's) death. The spiritual mentor paid a considerable attention to the spiritual progress of the novice. When the latter achieved the stage of intoxication (*sukr*) and self-annihilation (*istaghraq*), he discontinued the obligatory religious observances. He spent several days and nights at a stretch in such deserted places as deserts, jungles, graveyards and tombs. He often sat cross-legged on the top of walls, unmindful of the risk to his life. The fame of his spiritual accomplishments spread far and wide, so that a person travelled all the way from Jaunpur to confirm what he had heard. Miyan Natha had acquired an enviable reputation for possessing miraculous powers. It was believed that he could interact with supernatural beings (*jins*) and inanimate objects like trees. Dara Shukoh argues that sufis exhibit such powers when they enter the *alam-i-malkut*, that these were bestowed merely to test the steadfastness to spiritual life and that any deviation from the same reduces a sufi to the level of an alchemist. Nevertheless, the circle of Miyan Mir attributed several miracles to Miyan Natha, for example, reviving a dead rat and seeking safety from a storm on the verbal advice of a dome (*gunbad*). Though he did not possess any formal knowledge of medicine, he cured Miyan Mir of a boil on the eye lid by applying a paste of cucumber seeds (*tukhm-i-khiyar*) and thus pre-empted a surgery. Miyan Mir felt that this disciple, who had not been educated in the science of medicine, had learnt the treatment when he went into the *alam-i-malkut* during contemplation (*muraqaba*). On such occasions, Miyan Mir expressed his amazement at the spiritual eminence achieved by this son of an oil maker. Miyan Natha breathed his last in the presence of Miyan Mir who expressed his desire of being buried alongside the deceased. The tombs of the mentor and disciple are located side by side.[48]

Miyan Abul Maali was the son of the local judge (*qazi*) of Bhera, a town on the bank of the Jehlam. He acquired his education in this town but, leaving his wife and children, came to Lahore and enrolled himself as a disciple of Miyan Mir. Owing to the kind attention of the mentor, the novice achieved genuine serenity. But so much heat was generated in his body that he was given coriander (*gashniz*) to eat and the same was rubbed on his body. He displayed an awareness of the secrets of human existence. Since he did not wear any garb, there was no contradiction between his interior and exterior. Once during the sickness of Dara Shukoh, he was sent by Miyan Mir to the jungle and directed to read some passages and, as a result, the prince was cured. Miyan Abul Maali undertook spiritual penance and contemplation (*riyazat o mujahidat*) so that he was overtaken by passion and intoxication (*sahib-i-sukr*). He began to exhibit the traits of the *malamatis*, discarded the obligatory religious observances and his outward conduct began to contravene the Islamic law (*shariat*). A large number of miracles were attributed to him and illiterate people (*ghair ulama*) became his followers. Dara Shukoh expressed deep concern at his deviation from the principles of the Qadiri order. However, Mulla Shah Badakhshi argued that the man's inner self was pure, that he was a gnostic (*arif*), that he had temporarily lost his consciousness and that he could be brought back to consciousness if he were to come to him. Despite these angularities, Miyan Abul Maali was recognized as an erudite scholar. He could explain the meaning of oneness of God (*tauhid*) and mysticism (*maarifat*) in an eloquent manner. Full of compassion and kindness, his eyes often welled up with tears and he wept. He composed couplets that were imbued with pain and pathos. He wrote a commentary on the selected verses from Jalaluddin Rumi's famous *masnavi*. He gave this piece of writing to Dara Shukoh, who included it in the *Sakinat-ul-Auliya*.[49]

Contact with Rulers

Miyan Mir's practice of mysticism did not permit any formal association with the ruling class and, therefore, he scrupulously avoided any contact with the high and mighty. It is not surprising that he refused to remember a nobleman in the pleasant moments, in spite of the fact that a specific request had been made.[50] However, if the contemporary rulers took the initiative for a meeting, he did not refuse. Circumstances had been created for such meetings because, by the early decades of the seventeenth century, Miyan Mir's fame as a mystic par excellence had penetrated the exclusiveness of the corridors of power. Let us recall Jahangir's account of his meeting with the saint. "As it was reported to me that in Lahore one Miyan Shaikh Muhammad Mir by name, who was a dervish, a Sindi by origin, very eloquent, virtuous, austere, of auspicious temperament, a lord of ecstasy, had seated himself in the corner of reliance upon God and retirement, and was rich in poverty and independent of the world, my truth seeking mind was not at rest without meeting him, and my desire to see him increased. As it was impossible to go to Lahore, I wrote a note to him, and explained to him the desire of my heart, and that saint, notwithstanding his great age and weakness, took the trouble to come. I sat with him for a long time alone, and enjoyed a thorough interview with him. Truly he is noble personage, and in this age he is a great gain and a delightful existence. This suppliant for grace was taken out of himself by companionship with him, and heard from him sublime words of truth and religious knowledge. Although I desired to make him some gift, I found that his spirit was too high for this, and so did not express my wish. I left him the skin of a white antelope to pray upon, and he immediately bade me farewell and went back to Lahore."[51]

The above description of the meeting has been largely corroborated by Dara Shukoh. The prince would have us believe that Jahangir had little faith in saints (*auliya o darveshan*) and alleges that the emperor was even guilty of ill-treating them. But contrary to his prejudices,[52] the emperor invited the Qadiri sufi for a meeting.[53] The two remained together for some time and conversed on several subjects. Miyan Mir's words of advice had a spontaneous impact on the mind of the emperor, who expressed a desire to be enrolled as a disciple, saying, "All my possessions – kingdom, treasure, retainers, pomp and splendour – are like stone and rubbish (*sang o khas*) in my eyes. If you turn your kind attention towards me, I would severe all connections with this world." Since Miyan Mir could not acccept the proposal, he reasoned, "A perfect mystic (*sufi kamil*) is one who does not distinguish between stone and jewel. Since, as you say, you possess such an attitude, you are already a mystic." When the emperor could not be put off, Miyan Mir argued, "Your existence is necessary for the care of humankind (*pasbani-i-khalqallah*). The bounty of your justice will enable the ascetics (*fuqra*) to engage in their spiritual pursuits with peace of mind." However, he added that if the emperor could entrust his imperial duties to a substitute, he could be initiated into the spiritual path. The argument satisfied the emperor, who expressed a desire to fulfill any desire of the saint. Miyan Mir, thereupon, said, "Allow me to go." Jahangir allowed the visitor to depart with suitable expressions of reverence.[54]

Since Jahangir derived immense benefit from this meeting with Miyan Mir, he wished to avail of another similar opportunity. He had written two letters (*niyaz namas*) to the saint, one before the above meeting and the other after that. In the first letter, Jahangir had merely expressed a desire to meet Miyan Mir. The second letter was written when the Shah of Iran had attacked Qandhar, which was a cause of deep concern for the Mughals. In these circumstances, he requested Miyan Mir to remember him, of and on, in his prayers. He also hoped that the saint (through his spiritual charisma) would protect the people of God from the high-handedness of the oppressors and desired that those who had violated their promise would suffer from divine retribution (*ghazb-i-izadi*).[55]

Shahjahan (r.1628-1656), the son and successor of Jahangir, paid two visits to the humble abode of Miyan Mir at Baghbanpura, a locality in the city of Lahore. On both these occasions, he was accompanied by his eldest son, Dara Shukoh, and three other persons. The first meeting was characterized by a pleasant and fruitful conversation, in which Miyan Mir offered advice on several matters, including the administration of the realm. He stated, "It is imperative for just rulers (*padshahan adil*) to attend to the welfare of the peasantry (*raiyat*) and empire (*mamlikat*). The king should remain constantly engaged in working for the prosperity of the kingdom. For if the peasantry (*raiyat*) is contented and the country is flourishing, the army remains peaceful and treasury abundant (*sipah asudah wa khazana maamur ast*)." This counsel was followed by a discussion on Islam and Muslim community (*din o millat*). The emperor was so overwhelmed and touched that he declared, "I have not seen any saint who is so perfect in his renunciation (*tark o tajrid*) and independent in his beliefs (*be-niyazi o be-taaluqi*).[56]

During the second meeting, Shahjahan was accompanied by the same four persons who were present earlier. On this occasion too, a cordial and illuminating dialogue took place. The emperor requested Miyan Mir to turn his (Shahjahan's) mind away from the world. Miyan Mir responded, "Whenever you perform a good deed which brings happiness to the heart of Muslims, pray to God at that moment for yourself and do not demand anything from God except He Himself." He underlined the basic contradiction between two objectives – achieving worldly success and nearness to God. He elucidated his views by reciting the following couplet:

Ham khuda khwahi o ham duniya-i-dun
Een khyal ast muhal ast o junoon

> You crave for God as well as this despicable world. This is a mere passing idea, an impossible proposition or rather insanity.

During the course of this meeting, which took place on 28 December 1634, Miyan Mir articulated his views on spiritual and mundane matters, while the emperor and his companions felt greatly enriched. At the end of the meeting, the emperor made an offering (*niyaz*) of a turban and rosary to Miyan Mir, as the latter did not accept worldly gifts. The saint returned the turban and accepted the rosary which, however, was given to Dara Shukoh. Miyan Mir admitted that the kings occupied a unique position (*mazhar khas*) in the society and also possessed special qualities. But his own interaction with the kings did not affect his beliefs and practices in any manner. He continued to be engaged in his usual spiritual pursuits in accordance with his well-established schedule. A mystic was sovereign in his spiritual domain and, therefore, he was in no way subordinate to the worldly rulers.[57] According to the Persian chronicles of the reign, Shahjahan found only two mystics in the whole empire who were worthy of reverence – Shah Fazlullah of Burhanpur and Miyan Mir of Lahore.[58]

Dara Shukoh was a keen student of comparative religion and a mystic in his own right. He possessed unbounded veneration for Miyan Mir who also happened to be the spiritual preceptor of the former's mentor, Mulla Shah Badakhshi. On his part Miyan Mir showered immense love and affection on the prince. The intimate relation between the two was illustrated in several ways. Once Dara Shukoh fell ill. The physicians were unable to cure the disease which continued for as long as four months. During the course of his first visit to Miyan Mir, Shahjahan requested the saint to pray for the recovery of his ailing son. Miyan Mir took Dara Shukoh's hand in his own, recited a prayer over his own earthen cup of water and asked the prince to drink it. After one week, the prince began to show signs of recovery. He sent an emissary to Miyan Mir, with a request to pray for the complete restoration of his health. In response, Miyan Mir declared that the prince would be fully cured at a particular hour after four days. The prophecy turned out to be true.[59]

By the time of the second meeting between Shahjahan and Miyan Mir, Dara Shukoh had become intimately attached to the saint. When the emperor and his companions were coming towards Miyan Mir's abode, Dara Shukoh (out of devotion and humility) took off his shoes and walked bare-foot to the destination. During the meeting, Miyan Mir chewed cloves (*qaranfal*) and spat them out – an act which was not relished by those who were present. But Dara Shukoh collected them from the floor with utmost devotion (*kamal iradat o ikhlas*) and ate them. From that moment onwards, Dara Shukoh began to experience a transformation of his inner self. He began to develop revulsion towards the worldly affairs, to draw closer to Miyan Mir's circle of companions and to reach a stage of inner equilibrium. He began to hope that he would be counted among the beggars (*zimra gadaiyan*) of the saint on the day of judgement (*roz mehshar*). When Shahjahan and his companions left the place, Dara Shukoh went upto Miyan Mir all alone, placed his head on the master's feet and rubbed it for a long time. Miyan Mir reciprocated this gesture of devotion and humility by caressing the prince's head with a cheerful countenance. Besides, he was pleased to learn that the prince had walked bare-foot to his quarters.[60]

Miyan Mir nurtured a high opinion about Dara Shukoh's spiritual inclinations. He took a keen interest in the prince's physical well-being as well as spiritual progress. Once he told his disciples – Mulla Saleh, Shaikh Ahmad and Miyan Haji Muhammad Banyani – that he always prayed for the spiritual progress of the prince and asked them to follow the suit. On another occasion, Miyan Mir was found reciting something while holding a rosary in his hand – something he had never done before. On being questioned, he explained that he was doing so for Dara Shukoh who was not keeping well. Similarly, replying to another question posed by a disciple (Miyan Haji Muhammad Banyani) he declared that Dara Shukoh was as valuable to him as his own life and eyes (*u khud jan-i-ma o chashm-i-ma ast*). Sometimes, Miyan Mir directed his companions to hold Dara Shukoh's face in their imagination while they were engaged in contemplation. It was on account of this reason that all the companions of Miyan Mir bore great kindness (*inayat*) towards the prince even after the demise of the master. So long as Miyan Mir was alive, Dara Shukoh received spiritual inspiration from him and, after his death, the process continued through the exalted soul (*ruh pur futuh*) of the deceased. Therefore, Dara Shukoh regarded himself as an Uwaisi of Miyan Mir. He has also described two esoteric experiences wherein he received spiritual instructions from Miyan Mir, who had appeared to him in his dreams.[61] Dara Shukoh has characterized the second vision, which occurred on 20 December 1641, as *Lailat-ul-Qadr* when he was elevated to the status of Sultan-ul-Azkar owing to the blessings of Miyan Mir.[62]

Miyan Mir made a multifarious contribution to the social, political and cultural developments of the Mughal period. He was a product of the traditional system of education, which was largely based on theological and mystical texts in Arabic and Persian. As such, he came to represent an elite tradition of mysticism, which was quite distinct from the vernacular tradition which was represented by Shah Husain and Bulleh Shah. He gave a final shape to the mystical ideology of the Qadiri order by assimilating the doctrines of Ibn-i-Arabi. He introduced new methods of individual contemplation and spiritual exercises, focusing on inner sincerity and not on outward devotion. These attitudes were reflected in his approach to the training of disciples. The fame of his intellectual acumen and spiritual eminence spread to all parts of the Indian subcontinent and to all segments of the society. In spite of the above mentioned elite orientation, he maintained friendly relation with the Sikh leadership which represented the underprivileged sections – peasants and artisans – of central Punjab. At the same time, he enjoyed cordial relations with the Mughal rulers, Jahangir and Shahjahan. He was on most intimate terms with Dara Shukoh who swore allegiance to the Qadiri order and believed in the common ground between Islam and Hinduism. It appears that during the late sixteenth and early seventeenth century, there was a contest between the Qadiri and Naqshbandis to bring the Mughal ruling elite under their influence. It was not possible for the Mughal rulers to restructure their polity on the principles of Sunni orthodoxy, as advocated by Shaikh Ahmad Sirhindi. Therefore, it began to show a definite tilt towards the Qadiri order, particularly when it had acquired a considerable popularity and prestige under the stewardship of Miyan Mir. It is possible to imagine the possibilities of Dara Shukoh's intimacy with the Lahore-based Qadiri network. The tragic death (1659) of the prince, as a consequence of the war of succession among the sons of Shahjahan, did not permit these possibilities to develop into a mutually beneficial relationship between the Mughal state and the Qadiri order, similar to Akbar's absorption of the Ajmer-based Chishti discipline into the Mughal imperial ideology.

NOTES AND REFERENCES

1. M.A. Macauliffe, *The Sikh Religion*, Vol. III, Munshiram Manoharlal, New Delhi, Reprint, 1963, pp. 94-95; Khushwant Singh, *A History of the Sikhs*, Vol. I, Oxford University Press, Delhi, 1978, p. 63.
2. Giani Gian Singh, *Tawarikh Guru Khalsa*, Vol. I, Language Department, Punjab, Patiala, 1970, pp. 425-426; Giani Gian Singh, *Panth Prakash*, Language Department, Punjab, Patiala, 1970, pp. 127-128; Indubhushan Banerjee, *Evolution of the Khalsa*, Vol. II, A. Mukherjee & Co., Calcutta, 3rd. Edition, 1972, p. 165.
3. Dara Shukoh, *Sakinat-ul-Auliya*, Ed., Tara Chand and Syed Raza Jalali Naini, ELMI, Tehran, 1963, p. 248.
4. An early attempt at analyzing the work focuses on the characteristics of the Qadiri order, the life of Miyan Mir, his mystical beliefs and practices, his miracles, brief notices of his disciples, a biographical sketch of his sister Jamal Khatun, Mulla Shah Badakhshi's conception of mysticism, his association with Dara Shukoh and Jahanara. Bikrama Jit Hasrat, *Dara Shikuh: Life and Works*, Munshiram Manoharlal, New Delhi, Second Revised Edition, 1982, pp. 64-95.

5. Surinder Singh, "Mughal Centralization and Local Resistance: An Exploration in the Ballad of Dulla Bhatti," in Surinder Singh and Ishwar Dayal Gaur, (Ed.), *Popular Literature and Pre-modern Societies in South Asia*, Pearson-Longman, New Delhi, 2008, pp. 89-112.
6. Surinder Singh, "Darul Sultanat Lahore: The Socio-Cultural Profile of an Urban Centre," *Proceedings of the Indian History Congress*, 54th. Session, Mysore, 1993, pp. 289-290.
7. Surinder Singh, "Muslim Saints in the Mughal Province of Punjab," *Islamic Culture*, Vol. LX, No. 1, January 1986, pp. 90-92.
8. Dara Shukoh, *Sakinat-ul-Auliya*, p. 26; Miyan Mir himself related that his mother, who could discern secrets (*sahib-i-kashf*), realized at the birth of his elder brother that he would not acquire any spiritual qualities. Therefore she prayed to God for the boon of another son who should be a gnostic and ascetic (*arif o tarik*) and who should be completely immersed in His thoughts. A supernatural voice told her that God would grant her a son and daughter possessing these qualities and this actually happened.
9. Dara Shukoh, *Safinat-ul-Auliya*, Urdu Translation, Muhammad Waris Kamil, Sabri Book Depot, Deoband, (undated), p. 90; Mufti Muhammad Ghulam Sarwar, *Khazinat-ul-Asfiya*, Vol. I, Kanpur, 1894, pp. 136-137.
10. Shaikh Khizar lived an abstemious life. He did not accept anything in charity, not even the offerings from *zakat*. Every winter, he shifted to the hills of Siwistan and lived a solitary existence. He satisfied his hunger with wild fruit and wore a small piece of cloth, covering his body from the waist to the knees. He had dug an oven (*tanur*) in which he burnt the wood collected from the jungle. He spent the winter nights in the oven. He kept away from people and visited the town only twice a year. Dara Shukoh, *Sakinat-ul-Auliya*, pp. 27-28.
11. The word is traced to Uwais al-Qarani, a legendary figure, who had never met the Prophet, but communicated with him in dreams and visions. Uwais is the prototype of *fard*, the exceptional person in whom spiritual realization is spontaneous. The term Uwaisian transmission means to lay claim to a link with some spiritual figure with whom contact would have been clearly impossible. A form of pious or impious deceit, according to the case, some sufis have asserted an Uwaisian transmission of authority, that is, across time and space without the two persons actually meeting. Cyril Glasse, *The Concise Encyclopaedia of Islam*, Revised Edition, Stacey International, London, Reprint, 2004, p. 467.
12. Dara Shukoh, *Sakinat-ul-Auliya*, pp. 29-30.
13. Ibid., pp. 30-31.
14. Muhammad Saleh Kambo, *Amal-i-Saleh*, Vol. III, Bibliotheca Indica, Calcutta, 1939, p. 363.
15. In this context, Miyan Mir has related a personal experience, indicating that even a deserted house outside the city could not ensure peace, which could be disturbed by the merry-making of a marriage party. Dara Shukoh, *Sakinat-ul-Auliya*, 31-32.
16. Ibid., pp. 33-34.
17. Ibid., pp. 126-128.

18. Ibid., pp. 67, 83.
19. In a letter to princess Jahanara, Mulla Shah Badakhshi conceives an organic relationship between the three stages and maintains that eminent sufis of the past – Husain bin Mansur, Bayazid Bistami, Junaid Baghdadi and Abdul Qadir Jilani – had made ecstatic utterances on achieving the final stage and when they merged with the infinite reality. Dara Shukoh, *Sakinat-ul-Auliya*, p. 188.
20. Abdul Hamid Lahori, *Badshah Nama*, Vol. I, Part II, p. 340; Muhammad Saleh Kambo, *Amal-i-Saleh*, Vol. III, pp. 382-383.
21. It signified the celestial and angelic kingdom, which stood midway between *alam-i-nasut* (the world of humanity) and *alam-i-jabrut* (the world of divine omnipotence). Saiyid Athar Abbas Rizvi, *A History of Sufism in India*, Vol. I, Munshiram Manoharlal, New Delhi, 1978, p. 234.
22. Dara Shukoh, *Sakinat-ul-Auliya*, pp. 50-51.
23. When a government official requested Miyan Mir to remember him at his leisure, the latter promptly remarked, "Curse that moment when your thought intrudes into my heart." Dara Shukoh, *Sakinat-ul-Auliya*, p. 46.
24. Ibid., pp. 32-33.
25. Ibid., pp. 42.
26. Abdul Hamid Lahori, *Badshah Nama*, Vol. I, Part II, p. 30; Muhammad Saleh Kambo, *Amal-i-Saleh*, Vol. III, p. 364.
27. Dara Shukoh, *Sakinat-ul-Auliya*, p. 44.
28. Ibid., p. 92.
29. Ibid., p. 60; Haji Muhammad Banyani, a senior disciple of Miyan Mir, used to wear badly torn clothes, as he found them agreeable to his solitary (*tajrid*) state. When he passed through the market, a large crowd gathered around him. Some people fell at his feet, while others kissed his hands. Miyan Mir strongly disapproved of his style and directed him to wear proper clothes, so that no one would know that he belonged to the fraternity of sufis. Ibid., p. 61.
30. Dara Shukoh, *Sakinat-ul-Auliya*, p. 43-44; Dara Shukoh, *Safinat-ul-Auliya*, p. 91; Muhammad Saleh Kambo, *Amal-i-Saleh*, Vol. III, p. 364.
31. Dara Shukoh, *Sakinat-ul-Auliya*, p. 66.
32. Ibid., p. 41-42; Miyan Mir has related that there was no food in his house when his brother paid a visit and, as a result of his prayer, food was brought for the occasion by an angel (*farishta*).
33. Ibid., *Sakinat-ul-Auliya*, p. 33.
34. Ibid., p. 63.
35. Shaikh Bahauddin Zakariya, the famous Suhrawardi sufi of Multan, associated freely with the ruling elite, accepted financial assistance from the state and amassed wealth. His convent possessed huge granaries of cereals, while his treasuries were replete with gold and silver. Khaliq Ahmad Nizami, *Religion and Politics in India during the Thirteenth Century*, Oxford University Press, Delhi, 2002, p. 243.
36. Dara Shukoh, *Sakinat-ul-Auliya*, p. 62.
37. Ibid., pp. 69-73.
38. Ibid., p. 140.

39. Ibid., pp. 100-101.
40. Ibid., pp. 100-125.
41. Ibid., pp. 37-38.
42. Ibid., pp. 38-39.
43. Mulla Shah Badakhshi repeatedly approached Miyan Mir for an unbelievably long period of three years, before he was allowed to pursue mysticism under his guidance; Ibid., p. 39.
44. Ibid., p. 40.
45. Miyan Mir gave this response when, during the course of a discussion, Mulla Saeed Khan related an anecdote from the *Nafhat-ul-Uns*, according to which a disciple of Shaikh Junaid Baghdadi claimed to have picked the excrement of his preceptor for thirty years. Ibid., p. 38.
46. Ibid., pp. 73-74.
47. Surinder Singh, "Darul Sultanate Lahore: The Socio-Cultural Profile of an Urban Centre," *Proceedings of the Indian History Congress*, 54th Session, Mysore, 1993, p. 292.
48. Dara Shukoh, *Sakinat-ul-Auliya*, pp. 134-140.
49. Ibid., pp. 220-222.
50. On occasions like this, he quoted a statement of his mentor Shaikh Khizar, "May that moment be cursed when your thought enters my heart." (*Khak-i-bar aan waqt baad keh tu dar khatir guzri*). Ibid., p. 46.
51. Nuruddin Jahangir, *Tuzuk-i-Jahangiri*, Vol. II, English Translation, Alexander Rogers and Henry Beveridge, Low Price Publicaions, New Delhi, Reprint, 1989, p. 219.
52. In a recent reexamination of the religious attitudes of Jahangir, it has been concluded that he did not deviate from Akbar's religious tolerance, that he did not base the state policy on Islamic orthodoxy, that Guru Arjun Dev was executed due to political despotism and not religious persecution, that the order regarding the banishment of Jain monks was never implemented, that Jahangir bestowed land grants on the temples of the Chaitanya sect at Vrindavan, that Jahangir had high regard for the ascetic Gosain Jadrup and that the few sectarian statements in the emperor's memoirs were designed for a particular audience. M. Athar Ali, "The Religious World of Jahangir," in M. Athar Ali, *Mughal India: Studies in Polity, Ideas, Society and Culture*, Oxford University Press, Delhi, 2006, pp. 183-199.
53. Since Jahangir had not heard of Miyan Mir at Lahore, he could not meet him in the city itself. It was only after having left Lahore that he learnt about Miyan Mir's spiritual accomplishments and, owing to the impossibility of turning back with the royal cavalcade, he requested Miyan Mir to travel out of the city and meet him.
54. Dara Shukoh, *Sakinat-ul-Auliya*, pp. 46-47.
55. Ibid., pp. 47-48.
56. Ibid., p. 48.
57. Ibid., p. 48.
58. Abdul Hamid Lahori, *Badshah Nama*, Vol. I, Part II, p. 331; Muhammad Saleh Kambo, *Amal-i-Saleh*, Vol. III, p. 366.

59. Dara Shukoh, *Sakinat-ul-Auliya*, p. 65.
60. Ibid., pp. 51-52.
61. Ibid., pp. 54-55.
62. The literal meaning of *Lailat-ul-Qadr* was the night of power. It has been characterized as a mysterious night in the month of Ramzan, the precise date of which was said to have been known only to the Prophet and a few of his companions. It has been alluded to in the *Surat-ul-Qadr* (XCVII) of the Holy Quran. The excellences of the night were said to be innumerable. It was believed that during the solemn hours the entire animal and vegetable creation bowed down in humble adoration to the Almighty. T.P. Hughes, *Dictionary of Islam*, Munshiram Manoharlal, New Delhi, Reprint, 1976, pp. 282-283.

7

Role of Sufis and Bhaktas in North-Western India during the Eighteenth Century

Zahir Uddin Malik

The eighteenth century in Indian history is characterized as an epoch of political anarchy and social chaos that spread unchecked in the wake of the collapse of the Mughal empire. But disintegration of the imperial center and its administrative institutions did not produce any profound effect on the pre-existing pluralistic socio-cultural structure, which was distinguished by widespread Hindu-Muslim symbiosis and cultural syncretism in northern India. Religious ideologies did not play any role in the relentless struggles for political hegemony between prominent regional powers as represented by the Marathas, Jats, Sikhs and Afghans. Even the foreign invasions launched by the rulers of Afghanistan from Ahmad Shah to Zaman Shah (1748-1800) on the Punjab were inspired more by motives of territorial expansion and plunder of wealth than religious considerations. The armed forces ranged on opposite sides in numerous battles comprised of combatants who belonged to diverse creeds and clans. In the midst of political convulsions and general lawlessness, some seminal sufi movements, like the revival of the Chishti order, took place in Delhi and Punjab. These were matched by the Hindu bhakti or pantheistic movement which epitomized the concepts of the unity of God, devotion to God, spiritual discipline, religious tolerance and social harmony. These ideas had been propounded by the early Muslim mystics and Hindu bhakti saints, sannyasis and jogis. Many strands of sufic thought, including the concept of Unity of Being (*wahdat ul wujud*), were found compatible with Upanishadic pantheism. In fact, the radiation of sufi-bhakti movements is the finest flower of medieval civilization that preserved the social fabric in a religion-dominated society. The syndrome of mystic modes of life and thinking continued to influence the outlook of people at different societal levels throughout the eighteenth century. These trends were, however, subdued by the perceptible rise of religious nationalism, Hindu and Muslim, in the nineteenth century.

It is against this background that this essay seeks explore the salient aspects of socio-religious reformation which was undertaken by the sufi saints (*mashaikh*), chiefly of the Chishti order, in Punjab during the eighteenth century. Their commitment to peaceful religious and moral rejuvenation was a response to many challenges put up by the political decline for the Muslim community and the Indian society at large. It also takes into account facets of the Hindu bhakti movement generated independently by the Hindu ascetics and their religious philosophy, mystic thought, rites and practices as well as their impact on people with whom they interacted. Their gospel of devotion to God, self-realization and improvement provided the basis for catholic outlook and generous tolerance, which contributed to slowing contemporary squalor and reducing social tensions. The inclusion of their teachings and activities within the framework of the essay is dictated by the reason that these devout bhaktas and pious mendicants had begun to share space with Muslim sufis in the contemporary chronicles, besides a large number of treatises on Hindu religion, philosophy and doctrines. This constituted a distinct trend in the eighteenth century historiographies. The present study is divided into two sections. The introductory part makes a preview of the specific characteristics of Islamic mysticism in an unavoidable compression, since these have direct relevance to the understanding of the subject under discussion. The second part offers narrative analysis of the objectives of mystic movements as set forth by their major exponents and the paradigm adopted by them for expansion of the avowed religious mission. It also attempts to reevaluate their social roles in providing spiritual guidance and humanitarian services through building the institutions of *khanqahs*, *langars* and *madrasahs*. Needless to state, the study is based on evidence drawn from the original biographical literature (hagiographies) of seminal importance as well as modern works.

Mystic Thought and Practice

In this era of post-modernism, materialism and consumerism many people have adopted a hedonistic outlook of life. They find no reason to trouble with the concerns of mysticism, an anti-body philosophy underlining the concepts of desirelessness in and detachment from material objects. Even religion, from which mysticism has stemmed, is generally viewed as a fundamental source of civil discord and an easily available instrument for political mobilization. Parallel to this approach to the ideology of mysticism, there is a growing recognition of the omnipresence of the Supreme Being, the wise designer of the universe, the most Gracious and Merciful. The darkening scenario of violence, ethic conflicts and natural calamities as well as trials and tribulation in practical life reveal the truth of Divine Will, which asserts its omnipotence at frequent intervals by unmaking what human beings have made to control nature and environment. "The whole 'Universal Reason' is nothing in the presence of a single divine order." Though surrounded by unprecedented wealth and comforts of life, they suffer from depression and want of vision, besides yearning for real inner tranquility with secure and serene environments. In sequel to such a plight, an inward process of self-realization and self-introspection begins, rekindling man's latent faith in Almighty God. It is hoped that this would lead him right onward to adopt submission to the Divine Will on which depends the success of human efforts. For, "to do is thy duty, the result is not thy concern," is the common message articulated both in Gita and Quran. In effect, it seeks to prove the futility of age-long debate between fate and free will among seekers of true knowledge, about theoretical construct of cause and effect and laws of nature for governance of the universe. Further, the mystic thought and praxis stress the significance of motiveless devotion to God, which leads to lasting peace and enables a person to overcome inertia. This will alone project the path to a virtuous and harmonious social life in the mundane society that is full of distractions and temptations. "Verily, man is in loss, except those who believe and do righteous good deeds." Therefore, "Turn in prayers to your Lord and sacrifice to Him alone," because there is no peace but in remembering God in a humble spirit and contrite heart (Quran).

The firm belief in the doctrine of unity of God (*tauhid*), continuous devotion to Him alone and selfless service to his creatures constitute the foundation of mysticism, which is common to every religion.[1] The only differentiation is found in the modes and manners of worshiping God, which have been religiously prescribed by prophets and messengers sent by Him for the spiritual and moral upliftment of mankind. Thus Islamic mysticism (*tasawwuf*) has come to rest on what Prophet Muhammad defined monotheism, its precepts and attributes as revealed to him and enshrined in the Quran, besides the manner in which he preached and practiced them day and night at home and in public, now categorized *shariat*. The believers had implicit confidence in his truthfulness and moral soundness as well as in his wisdom and rationality.[2] "The whole of Islam is founded on the love of God and the love of the Prophet,"[3] writes Khalifa Abdul Hakim. But diversity in matters of prayers to God should not be a cause of friction among followers of different religious faiths. The holy Quran explicitly states,

"There is no compulsion in religion, to you be your religion and to me my religion." It further explains the issue of plurality and co-existence of religions in the world in the following words:

> We (God) have set for each (group) of you a particular code and path. Had God willed, He could have made you one people (of only one religion), but He tests you by the separate regulations He has made for you.... So, (do not lose yourself in these differences but) endeavour to surpass each other through your good deeds.[4]

Thus Islamic mysticism (*tasawwuf*) is essentially based on the Quran and the traditions of the Prophet, though it absorbed in the course of its movement some influences of local cultures in lands where Islam had spread. It was to adjust with the milieu in which it had come to stay, both in terms of life style and socio-religious ceremonies. Quran defines a Muslim, "Those who believe in the unseen establish daily prayers and spend out of what we have given them. The essential nature of unseen is pure light. "God is the light of the heavens and earth." Prophet Muhammad himself used to retire to the cave of Hira to meditate for a certain period of time every year. He also performed prayers at night and before dawn, besides five prayers in congregation. The Muslim sufi strove hard to tread the similar esoteric path by patterning his conduct and activities on that of the Prophet. Taha Husain, a leading Arab scholar, has traced beginnings of sufism to asceticism and found it unobjectionable. He says:

> *Din* is knowledge from God, which knows no limits while modern knowledge, like ancient knowledge, is limited by limitation of human reason.[5]

In quest of inspired knowledge and spiritual perfection, the sufi performs mystic and ascetic exercises. On mountains, hollow caves, desolation and forests, he prays and keeps fast, besides spending days and nights in repetition of God's name (*zikr*), meditation and contemplation. In this manner, he suffers all kinds of physical pains in hostile surroundings for years. Having succeeded in achieving spiritual enlightenment or gnosis (*marifat*) he does not remain within the limits of his purified soul and does not consider it the end of journey, but feels himself related to all human beings as he is and addresses to humanity in general and in an élan of love. In the supreme moment of the mystical experience, the mystic finds the essence of the creative act of transforming the social order on religious and moral lines. Keeping himself away from contemporary politics, the privileged space for lying and deception, the sufi quietly worked for betterment of the common people at the grass-root level, without politically organizing them or setting up public platforms for his image building. Belief in the Unity of Being (*wahdat ul wujud*)[6] broadened his outlook and shaped his behavior to treat all human beings with tolerance and sympathy. Khwaja Muinuddin Chishti (1141-1236) of Ajmer, the founder of the Chishti order in India, interpreted religion in terms of social service and exhorted his disciples to develop river-like generosity, sun-like affection and earth-like hospitality. "The highest form of devotion (*ta'at*) was to address the misery of those in distress, to fulfill the needs of the helpless and to feed the hungry."[7]

These cardinal teachings of the most celebrated and distinguished sufi saints (*auliya*) of India formed the kernel of the entire philosophy of mystic thought and life, which was its very Weltanschauung. In specificity, the thrust was on cultivating qualities of humanism and selfless social service to the disadvantaged segments of population, who came into their contact for spiritual blessings. The theoretical concepts of mysticism could make a meaningful impact on the thinking and character of people only if these were backed by practical application and the propounders lived up to the lofty norms. In this context, numerous examples may be illustrated from the lives of saints, which were required to draw inspiration for facing challenging perceptions about spirituality and morality in the modern age.

It is learnt that once Maulana Fakhruddin Dehalvi (1714-1785), son of Shaikh Nizamuddin Aurangabadi (d. 1730), planned to embark on the Haj pilgrimage. When he was about to board the ship a women approached him and stated that she had no money to marry her young daughter or even to feed the family. Hearing her miserable condition, the sufi-scholar gave her the whole amount of money which was meant to cover his expenses for the pilgrimage. Sympathetic to every one, good or bad, soft in speech and cultured in manners, the Shaikh could not see any one in distress and, therefore, always tried to help him with whatever means he had at his disposal. He went to see persons suffering from illness. He also went to express condolence to the bereaved family on the demise of some of its members known to him. Once an Afghan came to his hospice (*khanqah*) and assaulted him without any provocation. The Shaikh offered his head saying, 'Do whatever you intend to do with it.' The Afghan did not strike again and returned. But after sometime he came back, accompanied by a few companions, to do his foul deed. Composed and unperturbed, the Shaikh stood up to welcome and ask their well being. His courteous and peaceful disposition in response to their evil designs made them ashamed. They repented, wept and sought his forgiveness.[8]

The tendency towards ecstasy is not essentially the marked characteristic of a true sufi. The role of a sufi comes to rest on his being an instrument in strengthening the bonds of submission to God through prayers, recitation of God's attributes and doing noble deeds for his fellow beings. The sufi is not a wielder of magic wand by which he could cure the psychological and bodily ills of people, for God is the true healer and solvent of His creatures' problems. In the words of Maulana Fazal Rehman Ganj Muradabadi (1793-1885), "Sufi is not who flies in air or crosses ocean on foot, or walks on fire, but one who lives and acts in accordance with rules of *shariah* spontaneously." He himself helped a large number of people financially and socially, by distributing money among the needy, feeding the hungry in his *langar* and recommending applications of jobless person to officers of the district (Kanpur, U.P.) which were generally accepted. He himself lived a very simple life, a strict vegetarian, prayed and slept on the same wooden cot.[9] The portrait of the sufi as healer, magician, physician or psycheist drawn by some writers is based on erroneous assumptions, which betrays their lack of understanding of the basic principles and practices of Islamic mysticism.

Development of Sufism in Punjab

In the medieval times, the region of Panjab was a great centre of long mystical movements. Diverse schools of religious thought were founded by illustrious sufi saints (*mashaikh*) for wide diffusion of principles and practices of their respective systems. The prominent mystical orders (*silsilahs*) which won popularity were: Suhrawardi order, established by Shaikh Bahauddin Zakariya (d.1262); Chishti order, established by Fariduddin Masud Ganj-i-Shakar (d.1262); and Qadiri order, introduced by Shah Niamatullah Qadiri (d.1413). These mystical orders generated spiritual and intellectual ferment throughout the province. They exerted transformational effect on various social classes and professional groups, who were imbued with religious outlook towards life. Compared with other orders, the Qadiri order could not draw to its fold a huge following or strike deep roots anywhere, owing to its puritanical ideas, austere ways of life and simple mode of worship shorn of rituals. It was in the seventeenth century that the order gained fame and recognition in the larger circles of high and low in the regions of Panjab and Kashmir. The two distinguished saints of the order, Miyan Mir (1550-1635) and his disciple Mulla Shah Badakhshi (1585-1661) made strenuous efforts for its expansion and development and, in the process, profoundly influenced people by their cosmopolitan ideas, altruistic attitude and deep humanism.[10]

Miyan Mir was a symbol of piety, learning and humanism. He espoused the lofty ideals of humanity, forbearance, sincerity and truthfulness. By the example of his pious life, he helped and guided ignorant people in moral rectitude. He led a most frugal and temperate life and subsisted on simple diet. He exhorted his disciples to pursue the three golden principles, viz. little food, little speech and little sleep. When he was absorbed in prayers he felt no desire for food and remained without it for days and nights. He defined an ideal mystic as one who lived in society and inspired, consoled, infused faith and confidence in the deprived and destitute.[11] Miyan Mir's relations with contemporary Sikh Gurus were cordial and he cultivated friendly contacts with Guru Arjun Dev and Guru Hargobind. Along with other religious leaders of the place, he visited Guru Arjun Dev in prison where he had been put by the orders of Jahangir and publicly praised his piety and noble acts of service for the downtrodden. According to the Sikh tradition, Mian Mir had been requested by Guru Arjun Dev to lay the foundation of the Golden Temple at Amritsar.[12] Mulla Shah Badakhshi also preached the gospel of brotherhood, tolerance and austerity. He is reported to have given the following sermon to all those who came to seek his spiritual blessings for materialization of their worldly objects.

> Without doing any good deeds you want to solve your difficulties through sufi's (derweshs). It is not right. Feed the hungry, give clothes to the naked and fulfill the needs of the needy, and God will certainly fulfill all your desires.[13]

Revival of the Chishti Order

Khwaja Nur Muhammad Maharvi (1730-1790), the most favoured disciple of Maulana Fakhruddin Dehalvi (d. 1780), revived the traditions of the Chishti order that had fallen into shade in Punjab after the demise of Baba Farid (d. 1262). In the intervening period strong centres of the Suhrawardi and Naqshbandi orders had emerged at Multan and Sirhind. The credit for the regeneration and re-establishment of the Chishti order, therefore, goes to Khwaja Nur Muhammad, a renowned saint and scholar, who was immensely popular with the people. During his times momentous changes in politics and socio-economic structure were taking place, causing strife and disorders in the society. He belonged to a poor family of cultivators in the village of Chotala, where he was born on 2 April 1730. He received his early education in a school at the neighbouring village of Mahar. For higher education he went to several places like Dera Ghazi Khan and Lahore. Ultimately he went to Delhi and joined the *madrasah* of Ghaziuddin Khan, where he studied under Maulana Fakhruddin Dehalvi and acquired esoteric and exoteric knowledge. Through hard and painful struggle, he acquired education and became an accomplished scholar who was acknowledged by the learned divines (*ulema*) of this famous seminary. Highly impressed by his erudition and pious character, Maulana Fakhruddin Dehalvi initiated him as his disciple and instructed him to settle at Mahar (a village four *kos* in the west of Pak Pattan) and to establish a Chishti hospice (*khanqah*) there.[14] In compliance with the wishes of his teacher, he took up his abode at Mahar and, in the right earnest, set out to propagate the ideals of mysticism in resonance with the Chishti order. He explained in clear and unequivocal terms the spiritual aspects of religion and portrayed its true and authentic image. He unreservedly addressed the spiritual and worldly concerns of the people who thronged round him. His high spiritual status, profound learning and deep sympathy for the poor appealed to the people, who joined his mystic circle for spiritual guidance. In a short time, he gained enormous influence among the people and his *khanqah* emerged as a strong centre of sufism in Punjab. The accent of his message was on raising the moral standards to higher levels, cultivating self-restraint and tolerance, which he deemed essential for a peaceful and harmonious social life. He advised that one should take initiative in appeasing and reconciling the person who had quarreled with him. He stressed that reforming and serving the fellow beings was the highest form of worship to God. He never acted against the commands of his spiritual mentor (*pir*) whom he held in great reverence. The relationship between them was not of a master and slave, but it was based purely on mutual love and affection.[15] He kept himself out of the vortex of current politics and endeavoured vigorously for expansion and progress of the Chishti order. On account of his exertions, a number of new centres were established at such places as Taunsa, Ahmadpur, Chachran, Sakhad, Jalalpur, Siyal and Golarah.

The spiritual and moral mission of the Chishti order, thus inaugurated by Khwaja Nur Muhammad in Panjab, was further carried to great heights by his disciple and successor (*khalifa*) Khwaja Sulaiman Taunsavi, an eminent saint and scholar.[16] Having educated and trained him on the mystic path for six years, Khwaja Nur Muhammad awarded him with his succession (*khilafat*) at the age of 22 and asked him to settle at Taunsa, which would be the future centre of his religious reforms and social work. With his arrival, the desolated land of Sangar and Taunsa turned into a populous and prosperous settlement full of mosques, seminaries (*madrasahs*) and markets. Dedicated to learning and teaching, he established several schools (*madrasahs*) for the dissemination of spiritual and scholastic knowledge among the common folks of towns and villages in the area of his influence. In the main school of the new town, at least fifty teachers were engaged in imparting religious education with an emphasis on jurisprudence in which the saint had attained distinction. He himself gave regular discourses on different subjects of theology and spirituality, which were attended by a large number of students and theologians.[17] At this time, the province of the Panjab had passed under the sway of the Sikhs, which created feelings of insecurity and alienation among the local Muslims. He dispelled their fears and infused confidence by enlightening them with absolute faith in the mercy of Almighty God, the sole Protector and Preserver of mankind. He cautioned the Muslims against embarking on armed revolt because they seemed to him militarily weak, politically disintegrated and socially stratified. He thought that political power, even if regained, would not last for long unless its holders were animated with virtues of personal piety, social justice and benevolence for all.[18] He argued that the solution of current problems facing the Muslims lay in the invigoration of true faith and firmly following the norms and laws prescribed by the *shariat*. Cruel rulers were imposed by God on people as punishment for the grave sins repeatedly committed by them.[19]

Unruffled by repercussions of political events, Khwaja Sulaiman Taunsavi remained steadfast in the pursuit of his agenda of socio-religious reform through preaching and teaching. He succeeded in reversing the entrenched mindset and transforming the character of thousands of ignorant and egoistic people of Punjab and Afghanistan, who belonged to different social strata. He urged them to eschew violence, to avoid the company of wicked persons and hypocritical clerics, to forsake drinking wine, to give up taking bribes and to shun the bad habits of backbiting, fault-finding and jealousy. They should develop noble virtues of hospitality, honesty and humility. They should treat their neighbours and fellow beings with sympathy and affection.[20] He believed that indiscipline, disobedience to parents and distorted customs prevailing in families would have adverse effects on the moral fibre of the entire society. Thus, orderly functioning of family as an institution would reinforce bonds of mutual relationship between classes and groups in the society. A sufi of cosmopolitan outlook, he had a deep regard for the holy men of other religious faiths. In his lectures, he urged his followers to keep peaceful and brotherly relations with Hindus even under trying circumstances.[21] He maintained a large free kitchen (*langar*) which provided not only food, but also other necessities of life – clothes, medicines, blankets and shoes – to all those residing in the convent (*khanqah*). They comprised students, disciples, travellers and mendicants, numbering nearly five hundred persons. Uncalled charity (*futuh*) offered by believers, poor and opulent, was the only source of income to meet the expenditure of the establishment, for he never accepted land-endowments or any amount of money from the Nawab of Bahawalpur and other *zamindars* of the region. When the flow of offerings stopped, all those dependent on it, including the saint and his family, were on the verge of starvation. He lived very simple and contented life. Whatever reached him in the form of unsolicited offerings (*futuh*) was distributed without delay among the poor and needy. He propounded that renunciation of material objects did not include food, water, clothes and shelter, which were essential to keep the body alive as well as to worship God. Nor withdrawal from worldly affairs was construed to mean non-performance of family responsibilities. Maintaining and supporting families was a noble virtue recognized by mystics.[22]

Khwaja Muhammad Aqil (d.1814) was the grandson of Khwaja Nur Muhammad and son of Makhdum Sharif. He assumed the leadership of the Chishti order in his capacity as a distinguished successor (*khalifa*) of Khwaja Nur Muhammad. Following the example of his grandfather, Khwaja Muhammad Aqil worked consistently and vigorously for the expansion and consolidation of the order to which he swore allegiance. He had set up *khanqahs* at Chachran, Kotmattan and Ahmadpur which became centres of learning, culture, solace and guidance for aspirants on the path of spirituality. He kindled in them deep love and devotion towards God as well as belief in the validity of the canonical laws (*shariat*), the source of religious faith and moral values. For exposition and clear understanding of mystical thought and philosophy, the classical works of Ibn-i-Arabi, Ghazzali and Jami were systematically taught in the schools established and administered by this devout sufi. Besides theoretical discourses about the nature of sufism, the nature of God and world, special attention was paid to the teaching of scholastic theology, jurisprudence and Hadis. This was done to equip a future mystic for giving legal opinions in social matters and resolve theological disputations. Conforming to the traditions of his spiritual preceptors, he maintained a community kitchen (*langar*) for the supply of free food to the residents of the hospice (*khanqah*) and other poor and hungry persons. He explained in detail the methods and paths which could be followed by a novice to attain divine grace in many unique ways. He insisted on the importance of self-control and self-discipline. He asked the disciples never to give vent to anger, nor bear malice towards any one. They were advised to be friendly and compassionate, besides working for the welfare of all creatures.[23]

Saints and Bhaktas

Amongst the many contemporary saints and bhaktas, the most celebrated seem to be those who sprang from the lowest rung in the socio-economic scale, felt concerned for the woes of the common folks, worked for their spiritual uplift and liberated them from shackles of superstition, priesthood and caste restraints. In a period when the political horizon was overcast with clouds of civil wars, social chaos and moral debasement, the mystics inspired the urban poor and toiling peasants with faith in Almighty God and in higher moral values of simplicity, honesty and contentment that sustained them through vicissitudes of life and saved them from the general effects of prevailing strife and tension. These monotheists stood like a bride between the two apparently mutually antagonistic religious creeds and sought to effect reconciliation on both spiritual and social planes. From the commencement of eighteenth century, the contemporary scholars and historians, affected by their ideas of enlightenment and eclecticism, invariably devoted a section in their historical accounts to beliefs and custom of the Hindus, besides the distinct practices of the Sannyasis, Jogis and Bairagis. The number of books on Hinduism, either originally written or transcribed from old translation, seems to be quite large. Ancient Indian literature, which was written in Persian, touched the highest watermark and lent splendour to the prodigious cultural heritage of India. It was made accessible to the Persian knowing persons not only in Persia and Central Turkistan, but also western Europe, long before its masterpieces were rendered into English, German and French.

At the turn of eighteenth century Mirza Fakhruddin, at the suggestion of Kokaltash Khan (foster brother of the Mughal Emperor Jahandar Shah) complied an encyclopaedia entitled *Tuhfat-ul-Hind* in 1708-10. It was devoted o the themes of Indian philosophy, languages, music and arts.[24] Ali Muhammad Khan, the author of *Mirat-i-hmadi*, has briefly narrated innumrable Hindu castes, sub-castes, temples and shrines including Somnath. His account is authentic and unbised, reflecting his clear and sympathetic comprehension of these subjects.[25] Another valuable work containing a detailed narrative of Hindu religious philosophy, creeds, traditions, customs, sects and festivals is *Haft Tamasha*,[26] written by Mirza Hasan Qtil in 1793. Other Persian wrks dealing with the beliefs and practices of Sannyasis, Jogis and Bairagis are *Chaha Gulshan* ofRai Chatuman,[27] *Mira-i-Aftab Numa* of bdur Rehman, *Tarih-i- Farrukhabad* of Mr Waliullah. I the following pages, a bief sketch of a few saints and bhaktas, representing bhakti, sufistic and theosophical religious trends prevalent in eighteenth century, is presented.

Shaikh Muhammad Inayatullah was born at Qsur in the district of Lahore in the seond half of seventeenth cntury and died in 1735. His parents were Arains or petty cultivators, who were orignally Hindus but had converted to Islam. After ompleting his education, he igrated to Lahore where he established a college for igher studies in the religious philosophy and spiritual practices of the Qadiri and other mystic orders. He was a Qadiri-Shattari sufi, a scholar and writer. He was well versed in different methods prescribed by Hindu thinkers of ancient times for the attainment of salvation. A prolific writer, some of his works are *Dastur-ul-Amal, Islah-ul-Amal, Lataif Ghibia, Irshad-ulTalibin,* notes n

Jawahir Khams of Muhammad of Gwalior and commentary on the Holy Quran. Shaikh Muhammad Inayatullah was th spirital guide (*hadi*) of Bulleh Shah (1680-1757), the foremost sufipoet of Punjab and the most distinguished pantheisic saint of the region, who left an indelible mark of his mystic vision on the minds of the Punjabis. His relatives induced him to giv up the company his mentor on account of his low social origin and heterodoxy, but Bulleh Shah remained firm and continued to receive spiritual guidance from him.[28]

The real name of Bulleh Shah (1680-1757) was Abdullah and h was born at Pandoke in Qasur, near Lahore. The name f his teachr was Maulv Ghulam Murtaza, a native of Qasur.It was he who chose Shah Inayat Qairi Shattari of Lahore as is spiritual guide who, in turn appointed him his spiritual successor (*khalifa*). He was deeply influenced by the aishnava Vedantic Bhakti and the yogi practices like *trikuti* and *anahat shabd*. Lajwanti Rama Krishna and Mohan Singh hold that this influence is vividly reflected in his religious thought under the following categories: (a)The adoration of Prophet Muhammad on the pattern on which Vaishanavas adore Lord Krishna, (b) the identification of the spiritual guide with God, (c) wifely devotion, (d) the practice of concentrating on controlling of breath (*trikuti*) and hearing of unstruck sound (*anahat shabd*), (e) monism and (f) transmigration of soul. S.R. Sharda writes, "In some of the verses the Vaishnava colour is so dominant that one hesitates to admit him as the compositions of a Mohammadan. The vocabulary, the metaphors, atmosphere and the thought all are Vaishnava." For instance, Bulleh Shah said:

> When Lord Krishna sounded the flute and I heard its voice, sayeth Bulleh Shah, I cried in agony and since then I am wailing in pain of separation. Bulleh, the Gopi, turned mad and ran towards Lord Krishna. The Gopi asks where else she should go.[29]

In his verses, Bulleh Shah has expressed profound sentiments of reverence and love for Prophet Muhammad as incarnation of God, a position not assigned to him in Islamic religion. The Prophet declared himself only a messenger to convey and preach the Divine message to the mankind. But Bulleh Shah thought that God himself disguised as Prophet and appeared on the earth. With regard to the efficacy of Yogic practices as means to achieve communion with God, Bulleh Shah says,

> To attain Thee I have controlled breath, I have shut all the nine gates and have reached the tenth one. I pray Thee, accept my love.[30]

His concept of Karma or the theory that success, material or spiritual, is a direct consequence of one's noble acts in any field of enterprise is based on the Hindu Law, according to which the good conduct relates to the previous life of the individual and not to the present condition. Says he:

> Vision of God is denied to him because of his bad action in his previous lives, i.e. before his birth.

He believed in the unity of God, the Supreme Reality, to whose will he made absolute surrender.[31] "I verily dance at Thy will and the idea of oneness has been removed from myself." But the realization of God could not be dawned on a person without his prior grace. "If justice is done, I am doomed. I therefore pray Thee for Thy grace, so that I may be saved." About the creation of universe and interpretation of the idea of Prophethood of Muhammad, he says:

> When the one was single and alone, there was no light manifest. There was neither God nor the Tyrant. The Beloved one wearing the costumes came and Adam got his name fixed. From the one, Ahmad was made. He said Kun and Faikun was. So out of likeness, He created likeness. In Ahad, He inserted MIM (i.e. produced Ahmad) and then made the universe."[32]

A Rajput of Nerivana caste, Sivanarayan was born in Chandavan village in Ghazipur district where the sect of Siva Narayan, founded by him, flourished during the first half of eighteenth century. He was a prolific writer with eleven works in Hindi to his credit. He was a vigorous preacher and carried his mission to Delhi and Calcutta. He professed the adaptation of one Creator, the Lord of the world, opposed caste system, superstitious attachment to the holy relics of Hindus and Muslims, besides polygamy. He laid stress on the cultivation of such cardinal virtues of puritan life (*sadh*) as truth, temperance and mercy. He taught that to attain total illumination, one should act religiously in relationships involved in social behaviour under all circumstances. His popularity and influence spread far and wide. This ultimately gave him access to the Mughal court at Delhi. The reigning monarch Muhammad Shah (1719-1748), impressed by his Unitarian philosophy, piety and knowledge, became his disciple. Sivanarayan admitted into his fold members of diverse creeds and communities, granting latitude in observing some customary practices in which they were steeped prior to conversion. A simple ceremony took place for admitting a person into the sect. The Siva Narayanis assembled at the residence of some senior member on a fixed date, placed the sacred book in the center of the gathering, along with betel and sweetmeats. After the recitation of selected passages from the sacred text, these things were distributed among those who were present there. The novice was declared a legitimate member of the sect.[33]

A disciple of Udhaya Das, Birbhan was a inhabitant of Brijhasir, near Narnaul, in the province of Delhi. He composed couplets (*dohas*) in Hindi in the style of Kabir. These were recited in the religious congregations of his followers known as Sadhs or the pure. This sect of

Sadhs, though founded in the year 1658, was fully developed in the eighteenth century and enjoyed esteem and influence in the country. They had no temples but assembled at stated periods in houses on every full moon. Men and women brought their food and ate together, besides listening to the recitation of verses composed by Birbhan as well the poems of Kabir, Nanak and Dadu. Some idea of his pantheistic views may be obtained from the following verses.[34]

> Acknowledge but one God who made and can destroy you, to whom there is none superior, and to whom alone therefore is worship due, not to earth, nor stone, nor metal, nor wood, nor trees, nor any created things.
>
> Be modest and humble, set no affection on the world.
>
> Never lie nor speak ill to, or of any thing. Listen not to evil discourse, nor to any thing but the praises of the Creator, nor to tales, nor gossip, nor calumny, nor music, nor singing, except hymns.
>
> Never covet any thing, either of body or wealth, take not of another, God is the giver of all things, as your trust is in Him so shall you receive.
>
> Use of intoxicating substances, chewing pan, smoking tobacco are forbidden. Bow not down your head in the presence of idols or men.

Dedhraj was born (1771) in a poor Brahman family at village Dharsu in the Narnaul district. He held the doctrine of monotheism, regarding God as one, the Supreme Reality, all beautiful, incomparable and all-pervading. He opposed image worship, disapproved caste restrictions and raised his voice against Purdah. He tried to show the similarity and identity between Hinduism and Islam, pointing out the common features in the two streams of religious thought. He also sought to prove that all religions, though apparently dissimilar, are essentially the same and, therefore, underscore the idea of unity in plurality. Every thing emanated from the fountain of Godhead. The stage of spiritual illumination could be reached by self-negation, denial of one's own self, knowledge of his own essence, ceaseless and intense devotion. His monotheistic teachings attracted a large number of people in Jhajpur, Narnaul and Gurgaon areas.[35] Monotheism was the common features of the religious thought of these saints and preachers in the eighteenth century. A note of monotheism may be found in the devotional songs of Ram Prasad Sen, a devout worshipper of Goddess Kali, who lived in Bengal in this period. He says:

> What is the need of making idols of metal, stone or clay;
> You make an image and place it on the throne of your heart.[36]

Pran Nath was the most outstanding saint (*bhakta*) among the Hindu pantheists of the period who projected esoteric mysticism as a living moral force. Such thinkers sought to demonstrate, by their mystic vision and devotional fervour, that direct contact or the union of human spirit with the Divine Being and the transformation of duality into unity were possible to achieve, if the seekers after truth adopted their religious ways and practices. Pran Nath was a disciple of Deva Chandra, the founder of Pranami Sampradaya, a liberal and reformist movement in north India during the eighteenth century. He wrote *Kulzum Sarup* in the Gujarati language in which he attempted to show that the ideals of the Indian cosmogony and certain other esoteric aspects of Vedantic philosophy, as contained in the Upanishads, are similar to those embodied in the holy Quran and, in this manner, tried to prove the essential harmony between the two great religious systems. He believed in one God, denounced the formalities and superstitions among the Hindu as well as Muslims, condemned the caste system and laid stress on the nobility of Karma. Due to his catholicity and egalitarian outlook, he had to face stiff opposition from the highborn Hindus and Brahmins. He had acquired a great influence over Chhatrasal Bundela, by affecting the discovery of a diamond mine. The contemporary Muslim historians call him by the name of Ruhulla and hold that he was a popular saint of Bundelkhand. Through his contact with the saint, Raja Chhatrasal developed great regard for Islam and its Prophet in whose praise he recited two couplets every morning after taking bath. According to Murtaza Husain, the Quran and the Puranas were placed on high tables on opposite sides in the private chamber of the Raja's palace. On each side there sat Muslim *ulema* and Hindu priests who, in the presence of the Raja, discussed the subject of unity of God (*tauhid*). He lived in Panna till the end of his life and, on his death, he was buried and not cremated. At the ceremony of initiation, the followers of his sect, including Hindus and Muslims of different social rank, assembled and ate food together.[37]

NOTES AND REFERENCES

1. For example, Al-Biruni has testified the fact that Indians in ancient times believed in the unity of God, in his Arabic translation of *Yoga Sutra* written by the Indian sage Patanjali around 1300. He writes: The faith of the Hindus is that He is One, Eternal, without beginning and end; Acting as He wills, Almighty, wise, living, Giver of life, Ruling, Preserving, Unique in His Sovereignty, and He resembles nothing nor does any thing resembles Him." "In the name of One who hath no name; with whatever name though callest Him, He up lifteth His head."
2. Taha Husayn, *Mirat-ul-Islam*, Cairo, 1959, cited in Mazheruddin Siddiqi, *Modern Reformist Thought in the Muslim World*, Islamabad, 1982, p. 30.
3. Khalifa Abdul Hakim, *Fikr-i-Iqbal*, Lahore, 1964, pp. 320-21.
4. *Quran*, 5-48. This idea of religious tolerance has been expressed by a number of poets and thinkers. For instance, Dara Shikoh (1615-59) writes in the

Introduction to *Majma-ul-Bahrain* (1654), "Islam and infidelity are both galloping on the way towards exclaiming, He is one and none shares His sovereignty." Bikram Jit Hasrat, *Dara Shikoh: Life and Works*, Calcutta, 1955, p. 216. Also, "In the name of One who hath no name; with whatever name though callest Him, He uplifteth His Head," says Sanai.

5. Taha Husayn, *Mirat-ul-Islam*, pp. 285-86, cited in Mazheruddin Siddiqi, op. cit., p. 30.
6. Maulana Ubaidullah Sindi (1872-1944) has offered the following hermeneutical exposition on the doctrine of *wahdat-ul-wajud*, "That the real love of God soon passes away into the love of one's fellow-beings. The Quran teaches just this kind of love of God. I have learned this very truth from Quran that you should consider all human beings as one and tell the people any thing that you think contribute to the good of all." Kenneth Cragg and Ishaq Masad, *Theology of Unity* London, 1966, pp. 149-50. "That different religions constitute different interpretations of the same truth. The core of the religion is one and the same. Islam is the standard of truth on which all other religions can be judged. Every thing which conflicts with shariat is erroneous." Muhammad Sarwar, *Mawlana Ubaidullah Sindhi:Halat-i-Zindagi, Talimat aur Siyasi Afqar*, Lahore, 1967, pp. 239-249.
7. Shaikh Abdul Haqq Muhaddis Dihlawi (1551-1642), *Akhbar-ul-Akhyarfi Asrar-ul-Abrar*, Urdu Translation, Maulana Subhan Mahmud and Maulana Muhammad Fazil, Nur Publishing House, Delhi, 1990, pp. 56-59; Shaikh Fariduddin Mahmud, *Surur-us-Sudur*, Aligarh Ms., pp. 46, 47, 51-52; K.A. Nizami, *The Encyclopaedia of Islam*, New Edition, Vol. II, C-G, London, 1965, pp. 50-56.
8. Ghaziuddin Khan Nizam, *Manaqib-i-Fakhriya*, Aligarh Ms. p. 27; Khaliq Ahmad Nizami, *Tarikh-i-Mashaikh i-Chisht*, Delhi, 1984, Vol. V. p. 203. "Verily, the friends of God (*Auliya Allah*), No fear is upon them, nor are they sad." *Quran*, (Sura, 10-63).
9. *Malfuzat Maulana Fazal Rehman*, Patna, 1315 AH, Vol. I, pp. 8-10.
10. For details, see Dara Shikoh, *Sakinat ul-Auliya*, Ed., Tara Chand and Syed Muhammad Raza Jalali Naini, Iran, 1965.
11. Dara Shikoh, *Sakinat ul-Auliya*, pp. 46-49.
12. Max Arthur Macaulliffe, *The Sikh Religion*, Vol. III, Munshiram Manoharlal, New Delhi, Reprint, 1963, pp. 94-97.
13. Dara Shikoh, *Sakinat ul Auliya*, p. 44.
14. For details, Haji Najmuddin Nagauri, *Manaqib-ul-Mahbhubin*, Rampur, 1289 AH, pp. 54-55.
15. Ibid., pp. 90-92.
16. Khwaja Sulaiman Taunsawi was born in the village Gurgoji, His father, Zakariya, died when he was only an infant and he was brought up by his mother. He learnt Arabic from Maulvi Muhammad Aqil in the *madrasah* of Kotmattan and acquired mastery of classical works in logic, jurisprudence, exegesis and traditions. The works which he studied at this early age are mentioned as: *Qutbi* by Qutbuddin Razi, *Kafiyah* by Ibnul Hajib and *Mishkat* by Waliuddin Abu Abdullah. By the age of 16 years, he completed his studies in that school. Afterwards he proceeded from Kotmattan to Uch to

meet Khwaja Nur Muhammad and discuss with him the contentious issue of *sama* or mystic songs. But he was so overwhelmed by the spiritual personality and erudition of the saint that, instead of interacting, he requested him for initiation and guidance in his mystical discipline. He developed deep and sincere love for his spiritual mentor and spent most of his time in his service, except for visiting his mother at Kotmattan. Khaliq Ahmad Nizami, *Tarikh-i-Mashaikh-i-Chisht*, Vol. V, Delhi, 1984, pp. 321-329.

17. Khwaja Sulaiman Taunsawi assiduously applied himself to address spiritual and religious problems of students and disciples living in the *khanqah*. His knowledge of mystic thought and philosophy was profound. He expatiated clearly and elaborately complex ideas and categories contained in such works of seminal importance such as *Fasus-ul-Hikim* and *Futuhat-i-Makkiyya* (Shaikh Muhiuddin Ibn-i-Arabi), *Ihya-ulum-uddin* and *Kimiya-i-Saadat* (Abu Hamid Ghazali), *Awarif-ul-Maarif* (Shaikh Shihabuddin Suhrawardi) and *Kashf-ul-Mahjub* (Shaikh Ali Hujwiri). For details, Maulvi Allah Bakhsh Bilochi, *Khatim-i-Sulaimani:Halat wa Malfuzat Khwaja Sulaiman Taunsawi*, Lahore, 1325 AH, pp. 9-30.
18. Maulana Imamuddin, *Nafi-ul-Salikin*, Lahore, 1285 AH, pp. 25, 52. "Those who, if we give them power in the land, establish worship and pay the poor-due, and enjoin kindness and forbid inequity." Quran, XXII-41.
19. Maulana Imamuddin, *Nafi-ul-Salikin*, op.cit., pp. 22, 32, 40, 19, 5.
20. "The (faithful) slaves of the Baneficent are they who walk upon the earth modestly, and when the foolish ones address them answer peace." "Lo, we purified them with a pure thought, rememberance of the Home (of the Hereafter).' Quran, XXXVIII-47; Maulana Imamuddin, *Nafi-ul-Salikin*, pp. 112, 117, 152, 165.
21. Maulana Imamuddin, *Nafi-ul-Salikin*,p. 155.
22. Maulana Imamuddin, *Nafi-ul-Salikin*, p. 29, 175; Maulvi Allah Bakhsh Bilochi, *Khatim-i-Sulaimani*, pp. 66, 67, 71.
23. For details, see Haji Najmuddin Nagauri, *Manaqib-ul-Mahbubin*, pp. 123, 124; Khawja Gul Muhammad Ahmadpuri (d. 1828) *Takmila Siyar-ul-Auliya*, pp. 151-158. After the death of Khwaja Muhammad Aqil in 1814, his son Mian Ahmed Ali became the *sajjadah nishin* at the *khanqah* in Kotmattan. He enjoyed enormous influence and reputation as a great mystic and learned doctor (*alim*). Tribal chiefs and *zamindars* of the region held him in reverence. But he did not accept any land-endowments offered by any of them. He died in 1815 and was buried in the shrine of his father at Kotmattan. He was succeeded by Mian Khuda Bakhsh (d. 1852). Another notable *khalifa* of Shah Nur Muhammad was Hafiz Muhammad Jamal who established his *khanqah* and *madrasah* in Multan. He pursued similar goals of religious, educational and social reforms which his preceptors had set. He died in 1811. Haji Najmuddin Nagauri, *Manaqib-i- Mahbubin*, pp. 140-146. Khaliq Ahmad Nizami, *Tarikh-i-Mashaikh-i-Chisht*, Vol V, pp. 318-325.
24. Ms., Seminar Library, Department of History, Aligarh Muslim University, Aligarh.
25. Ali Muhammad Khan, *Mirat-i-Ahmadi*, Ed., Nawab Ali, Vol. III, (*Khatima*), Calcutta, 1930, pp. 132-142.

26. Muhammad Mushin Qatil, *Haft Tamasha Mirza Qateel*, Nawal Kishore, Lucknow, 1878.
27. Rai Chaturman's *Chahar Gulshan* is a general history of India from the earliest times to 1173 AH/1759 AD. The author was a Kayasth of Saksena tribe, who wrote it at the desire of Wazir Ghaziuddin Khan at the time of the second invasion of Ahmad Shah Abdali. It was divided into four sections as follows: (i) Subahs of Hindustan, (2) Subahs of the Deccan, (3) Itineraries from Delhi to various parts of India and (4) Orders of Muslim and Hindu faqirs. Topographical and statistical portions, largely pertaining to the first three parts, have been translated into English in Jadunath Sarkar, *India of Aurangzeb*, Calcutta, 1901. Vicaji D.B. Taraporewala and D.N. Marshall, *Mughal Bibliography: Select Persian Sources for the Study of Mughals in India*, The New Book Company, Bombay, 1962, pp. 48,126.
28. For details, see Lajwanti Rama Krishna, *Punjabi Sufi Poets*, New Delhi, 1973, pp. 63-69.
29. S.R. Sharda, *Sufi Thought: Its Development in Panjab and Its Impact on Panjabi Literature (From Baba Farid to 1850 AD)*, Munshiram Manoharlal, New Delhi, 1974.
30. Ibid., p. 151.
31. Ibid.
32. Ibid., p. 153.
33. H.H. Wilson, *The Religious Sects of the Hindus*, p. 200.
34. Ibid., pp. 197-99.
35. Kalikinkar Datta, *Survey of India's Social Life and Economic Condition in the Eighteenth Century*, Munshiram Manoharlal, New Delhi, Second Revised Edition, 1978, pp. 5-6.
36. Ibid., p. 8.
37. For detail see, Tara Chand, *Influence of Islam on Indian Culture*, The Indian Press, Allahabad, Reprint, 1976, pp. 160-161; Murtaza Husain, *Hadiqat-ul-Aqalim*, Munshi Nawal Kishore, Lucknow, p. 669; Maulvi Waliullah, *Tarikh-i-Farrukhbad*, Ms f.54; H.H. Wilson, *The Religious Sects of the Hindus*, p. 196; Bhagwan Das Gupta, *Maharaja Chhatrasal Bundela* Agra, 1958, Hindi, pp. 104, 107, 108, 111.

PART II

SUFI LITERATURE

8

Theory and Practice of Islamic Mysticism

An Exposition by Ali bin Usman Hujwiri

Mohammad Tazeem

Abul Hasan Ali bin Usman Hujwiri (d.1073 AD), the famous author of *Kashf-ul-Mahjub*, was born in Ghazni sometime in the first decade of the eleventh century. Motivated by a overpowering desire to acquire mystical knowledge, he undertook long journeys across Turkistan, Persia, Syria, Iraq and Azarbaijan beyond the Caspian Sea and visited such places as Samarqand, Uzkand, Maihana, Merv, Tus, Nishapur, Kish, Ramla, Bistam, Damascus and Baghdad. He received a major part his education under Abul Fazl Muhammad bin Hasan Khattali, but also acquired the knowledge of diverse subjects from Abul Qasim Gurgani, Khwaja Muzaffar and Abul Abbas Ahmad bin Muhammad Ashqani. Ultimately, at the advice of his spiritual teacher Khattali, he travelled eastwards and settled at Lahore. He is believed to have organized the construction of a mosque in the city.[1] At this time, Punjab was a part of the Ghaznavid empire. However, the imperial control remained weak owing to a combination of factors – internal conflict in the ruling family, rise of the Seljuqs in Central Asia, bifurcation of administrative functions in Punjab and the recalcitrance of the north Indian chieftains. It was only during the long reign of Sultan Ibrahim (r.1059-1099) that vigorous attempts were made to consolidate the Ghaznavid rule in Multan, Ajodhan, Jalandhar and Sirhind, besides sending plundering expeditions into the Gangetic plain.[2] Hujwiri, who must have been a witness to these developments, died around 1073 AD and earned the popular title of Data Ganj Bakhsh (Distributor of Unlimited Treasure). Soon after, his mausoleum began to attract pilgrims from far and wide. According to a local tradition, Rai Raju (deputy governor of Punjab on behalf of the Ghaznavids) became a disciple of Hujwiri and, after embracing Islam, became known as Shaikh Hindi. His descendants have continued to serve as managers and attendants (*mujawir o khadim*) of the tomb till the end of the nineteenth century. Maharaja Ranjit Singh (r.1799-1839) confirmed the revenue free status of land grants (*muafi*), including several wells, which had been enjoyed by the shrine since a long time.[3]

Hujwiri was a prolific writer. He claims to have written as many as nine books, pertaining to such themes as faith, method of mysticism, divine unity, union with God, annihilation and subsistence, life and sayings of Husain bin Mansur al-Hallaj, wearing of patched frocks and a collection of poetry.[4] Unfortunately none of these works has survived. Hujwiri's fame rests on his only surviving work, *Kashf-ul-Mahjub*. A modern writer, placing the work in the larger context of the ongoing discourse on religion and mysticism, has argued that emphasis on inner sincerity (*dakhli sadaqat*), as emphasized by Bistami and Mansur, had led to the erosion of religious law, apostasy from Islam and degeneration of sufism.[5] However, a group of moderate sufis advanced the middle path and advocated that there was no contradiction between religious truth (*mazhabi sachai*) and inner sincerity (*dakhli sadaqat*) and the two were complementary. Hujwiri, along with Ghazzali, were the outstanding ideologues of this trend.

Hujwiri wrote the book at the instance of one Abu Saeed al-Hujwiri, who had asked a set of questions on the meaning of the path of sufism, mystical doctrines and allegories, manifestation of divine love in human hearts and inability of intellect to comprehend its essence, besides the practical aspects of sufism which were connected with these theories.[6] Interestingly, the author mentions his own name frequently in the book as a precaution, because two of his earlier works had been projected by some clever impostors as their, by just erasing the name of the original author.[7]

From the point of view of its structure, *Kashf-ul-Mahjub* may be divided into four parts, suitable to the needs of the person for whom it was written. The first part, which forms the background, seeks to define the phenomenon of sufism and examines the significance of poverty, blame and distinctive sufi apparel. The second part, which forms a fourth of the work, contains the biographical sketches of a large number of historical figures – from pious caliphs to his own contemporaries – who practiced sufism in a variety of ways. The third part, which also forms a fourth of the work, elaborates the mystical principles of several sufi orders viz. Muhasibis, Qassaris, Taifuris, Junaidis, Nuris, Sahlis, Hakimis, Kharrazis, Khalifis, Sayyaris and Hululis. The last part, which is divided into eleven chapters, seeks to uncover the eleven veils i.e. theoretical and practical aspects of sufism. Of these, the tenth chapter is exceptional in the sense that it defines a large number of technical terms that were commonly employed in any discourse on sufism. It is possible to discern a clear thematic unity between the first and fourth parts. Taken together, they represent Hujwiri's exposition of the theory and practice of sufism as developed by him at Lahore during the middle of the eleventh century.

The meaning of the word sufi has always been a contentious issue, so that many books have been written the subject. The etymological roots have been traced to the woollen garment (*jama-i-suf*), the first in rank (*saff-i-awwal*), the quality of purity (*safa*) and the companions of the verandah (*ashab-i-suffa*). The word has no derivation responding to etymological requirements, as sufism was too exalted to have any genus from which it could be derived. Yet a sufi might be defined as a person who has been purified by love, who is absorbed in the Beloved and who has abandoned all else.[8] Hujwiri also analyses the definitions of classical savants – from Zu-ul Nun Misri to Abul Hasan Fushanja – that focus on one aspect of sufism or the other e.g. identity between words and state, essence of sufism as attribute of God, freedom from pollution of humanity, sufism as essence without form, turning away from the phenomenal world, purity of heart from discord, goodness of disposition, vision of nothing except God, regarding his exterior and interior as belonging to God, maintenance of right states with God, propriety of behaviour, good morals and freedom of bondage from desire.[9]

Postulates of Mysticism

It was incumbent on Muslims to acquire knowledge, particularly of subjects that had a bearing on the religious law, but this knowledge ought to be complemented with action. According to Muhammad bin Fazlul Balkhi, knowledge was of three types – from God, with God and of God – that were identical with the sacred law (*shariat*), spiritual stations and path (*tariqat*) and science of gnosis (*maarifat*). The path of sufism opened with the acquisition of gnosis (*maarifat*) of God, which is of two types – cognitional (*ilmi*) and emotional (*hali*). The theologians gave the name of gnosis to the right cognition of God, while the sufis used this term for the right feeling towards God.[10] Different ways of acquiring gnosis have been advocated viz. reason, demonstration, inspiration and intuition. Rejecting the efficacy of any of these methods, Hujwiri argued that knowledge of God could be acquired through His will and favour. "God causes man to know Him through Himself with a knowledge that is not linked to any faculty, a knowledge in which the existence of man is merely metaphorical." He also agreed with the view that when a seeker recognized the perfection of God's attributes, he was overwhelmed by a huge sense of amazement regarding divine reality and his own being.[11]

The seekers were required to assert the unification (*tauhid*) of God and having a perfect knowledge of this unification. They believed that God is one, without any sharer in His essence and attributes, without any substitute or partner in His actions. God has no space or substance, no constitution or body, no likes or children. God is free from all imperfections and exalted above all defects. God is living, knowing, forgiving, merciful, willing, powerful, hearing, seeing, speaking and subsistent. God exists from eternity and all objects of cognition are in His knowledge. He does what He wills, His decree being an absolute fact and His judgement being wisdom.[12] Having thus explained the implications of God's unification, Hujwiri argues that the Sunni view of the subject was based on true comprehension, as they perceived a single artificer who brought the entire universe into being. Junaid rightly held that since God is eternal and creation was phenomenal, there was no connection or homogeneity between the two. This amounts to annihilation of human attributes and perfect resignation to God. Sahl bin Abdullah rightly stated that human hearts knew God, but their intellects could not reach Him; that believers could behold him with their (spiritual) eyes by comprehending His infinity. In this context, caliph Abu Bakr declared that unification was the act of God in the heart of His creatures. Hujwiri opines that unification was a mystery revealed by God to His servants and it could not be expressed in language at all, much less in high sounding phrases.[13]

The seekers regarded faith (*iman*) as an important ingredient of sufism, but there were wide differences on its meanings among Mutazilites, Kharijites, lawyers and sufis. One set of sufis maintained that faith was verbal profession, verification and practice. But another set of sufis believed that faith was verbal profession and verification. Hujwiri, who claims to have written a book on the subject, insists that the difference between them was entirely one of expression and was devoid of substance. Faith had a principle and a derivative, the principle being verification in the heart, while derivative was observance of divine commands. The orthodox Muslims applied the name of faith to obedience, while the sufis believed that obedience was of no avail without gnosis. Those who saw evidence of gnosis in the beauty of God developed a longing for vision, which was an effect of love. Therefore faith and gnosis were love, and obedience was a sign of love. Whoever denied this neglected the command of God and knew nothing of gnosis. Again, some people believed that faith came entirely from God, while others maintained that it sprang entirely from man. In Hujwiri's final analysis, faith was really the absorption of all human attributes in the search of God. The establishment of gnosis in the heart of the gnostic led to the expulsion of agnosticism and his placement in the circle of its authority.[14]

Sufis regarded poverty as their pride, so that they lamented its departure and rejoiced at its arrival. In form it appeared as destitution, but in essence it meant averting gaze from all created things and in complete annihilation and seeing only God. It preserved a poor man's body from sin and his heart from evil thoughts, because his outward parts were absorbed in blessings of God, while his inward parts were protected by invisible grace.[15] Regarding the superiority of poverty as wealth, Hujwiri believed that poverty applied only to man and wealth only to God, so that these two attributes were not transferable from one to the other. Both wealth and poverty were divine gifts; the former was corrupted by forgetfulness and the latter by covetousness. Poverty was the separation of heart from everything but God, while wealth was the preoccupation of the heart with that which did not admit of being qualified. When the seeker's heart was cleared of all except God, the difference between wealth and poverty disappeared as both terms were transcended.[16] This position was followed by a debate on the relative merits of poverty (*faqr*) and purity (*safwat*). Some regarded poverty as superior because the word was associated with renunciation and humility, while others held purity as more honourable as the word came nearer to the notion of discarding all that contaminated and annihilated all that had a taint of the world. Hujwiri believed that both these words were symbols for the same idea. If the heart of the seeker was fixed on the idea, he did not bother whether he was called poor (*faqir*) or pure (*sufi*). However, the sufis were also divided on the superiority of poverty (*faqr*) and lowliness (*abasement*).[17]

A seeker, after consolidating his faith (*iman*), was required to undertake continuous and perpetual purification which was of two kinds, outward and inward. "Thus prayer requires purification of the body, and gnosis requires purification of the heart." Outward and inward purification were required to go together. The former was achieved by washing one's face, hands and feet with clean water, but the latter was achieved through repentance (*taubat*). Repentance was defined as turning back from what God had forbidden through fear of what he had commanded. Repentance comprised, according to the implication of a saying of the Prophet, three things – remorse for disobedience, immediate abandonment of sin and determination not to sin again. Repentance operated in three different ways – through fear of divine punishment, through desire for divine reward and for the sake of keeping the divine command. In repentance, man considered his evil conduct and sought deliverance from them, so that God made it easy for him to repent and led him back to obedience. However, there was difference of opinion as to whether or not the sins should be remembered.[18]

It was a common experience among the sufis that those who followed the path of truth were targets of vulgar blame. In accordance with His design, God caused the people, who were in communion with Him, to be blamed by the whole world, but preserved their hearts from being preoccupied by the world's blame. God guarded His lovers from paying any heed to the others, lest the eye of a stranger should behold the beauty of their spiritual state.[19] God also guarded them from seeing themselves, lest they should regard their own beauty and fall into self conceit and arrogance. Hujwiri holds, "Hence the blame of mankind is the food of the friends of God, because it is a token of divine approval; it is the delight of the saints of God, because it is a sign of nearness to Him." In order to avoid being distracted by public acclaim for spiritual merit, a Malamati was required to commit some act which was legally neither a great sin nor a trivial offence, so that the people rejected him. Hujwiri rejected the whole idea of blame as mere ostentation and nothing but hypocrisy. An ostentatious man deliberately acted in a manner to win popularity, but a Malamati purposely acted in a manner to incur public rejection. It was essential to have gained popularity before deliberately acting in a way to earn reprobation. Otherwise, making oneself unpopular was merely a pretext for winning popularity.[20]

A distinctive mark of sufis was the wearing of a patched frock (*muraqqa-i-khiraq*) – a practice sanctified by Prophet Muhammad, pious caliphs and eminent sufi masters. There were innumerable examples of sufis wearing the garment only to conceal their spiritual inadequacy and to gain cheap popularity. Though the sufis knew that the practice often reflected hypocrisy and ostentation, yet they insisted on it so that they were easily identified and, in case of any transgression, the people could rebuke them to shame.[21] The mantle was woven of wool to give a feeling of comfort and lightness. When the original was torn, it was repaired by inserting a patch. Some believed that the patch could be fixed at random, while others believed it should be neat and accurate and the stitches should be straight and regular, for a round patch indicated round principles. A spiritual director permitted a novice to wear a patched frock at the end of three years of spiritual discipline, each of which was respectively devoted to the service of people, the service of God and watching over his own heart. On acquiring the garment, the wearer purged his mind of sensual delights, as each part – collar, sleeve, gussets, hem and fringe – denoted one of the various spiritual qualities. A novice was permitted to tear the garment if forced to do so by the temporal authority. But if he tore it deliberately, he was not allowed by his peers to wear it again. Sufis generally changed their dress when graduating from one spiritual stage to the other. While other dresses pertained to a single stage, a patched frock comprised all stages of the spiritual path and to discard it was regarded equivalent to renouncing the whole path. Since travelling (*siyahat*) was the basis of their path, the sufis did not wear white garment during the course of their journey, as it did not retain its original appearance and could not be easily washed. Instead they wore a blue dress which was a badge of mourning. World being an abode of sorrow, the sufi found that his heart's desire could not be gained here. Therefore he clad himself in blue and sat down to mourn the union. Hujwiri wrote a separate book on the subject entitled 'The Mysteries of Patched Frocks and Means of Livelihood' (*Asrar al-khiraq wa'l maunat*) and recommended that it be acquired by a novice.[22]

Marriage was permitted to all, but it was obligatory for those who could not abstain from unlawful actions and an Apostolic custom (*sunna*) for those who could support a family. Some sufis held marriage to be a desirable means of quelling lust and freeing the mind from anxiety. It was possible to identify boons and evils both in marriage and celibacy, but the basic point lay in companionship and retirement. "Marriage is proper for those who prefer to associate with mankind, and celibacy is an ornament to those who seek retirement from mankind." If a sufi chose to marry, he was bound to provide his wife with lawful food and pay for her dowry out of lawful property, and not indulge in sensual pleasure so long any obligation towards God remained unfulfilled. Hujwiri puts his weight behind celibacy because, "In our time it is impossible for anyone to have a suitable wife, whose wants are not excessive and whose demands are not unreasonable." Hujwiri argued that Apostolic custom (*sunna*) regarding marriage had been wrongly understood and followed. He adopted a misogynist tone to highlight the conflicts – mythical and historical – caused by women. Justifying his own experience of celibacy, he maintained that sexual desire could be suppressed by applying two remedies – hunger and true love – which was collected by the dispersion of sensual thoughts, a love which established its control over different parts of the body and divested all the senses of their sensual quality. In the final analysis, a man was not ruined by marriage or celibacy, but the mischief lay in asserting one's will and yielding to one's desires.[23]

Fundamental Obligations

It was incumbent on Muslims to offer prayer (*namaz*) five times a day, in accordance prescribed conditions regarding cleanliness, garments, place, direction, recitation of the Quran, bowing and prostration with humility etc.[24] But sufis perceived a spiritual meaning in these steps, so that "purification takes the place of repentance, and dependence on a spiritual director takes the place of ascertaining the *qibla*, and standing in prayer takes the place of self-mortification, and reciting the Quran takes the place of inward meditation (*zikr*), and bowing the head takes the place of humility, and prostration takes the place of self-knowledge, and profession of faith takes the place of intimacy, and salutation takes the place of detachment from the world and escape from the bondage of stations." Those sufis, who were engaged in self-mortification or had attained steadfastness, ordered their disciples to perform four hundred bowings in prayer during a day and night, so that their bodies became habituated to devotion. Sufis, who had acquired states (*arbab-i-ahwal*) and achieved the station of union in their prayers, added supererogatory prayers to the obligatory ones. Some sufis performed obligatory acts of worship openly, but concealed those which were supererogatory so as to escape from the allegation of ostentation. Other sufis exhibited both kinds of acts of devotion on the ground that ostentation was unreal and piety was real.[25] Hujwiri perceived the impact of prayer in the various stations of love, which was mutual sentiment between man and God. Man's love for God manifested in his heart in the form of veneration and magnification, so that he abjured worldly associations in a desire for divine vision. God's love for man was manifested in His mercy and favour to him, who was kept safe from sin and bestowed with lofty spiritual stations. However, some sufis maintained that man could have excessive love (*ishq*) for God, but this could not be reciprocated. Whatever be the degree of man's love for God, the former was not relieved of his religious duties. A true lover delighted in the affliction that God made him suffer and, therefore, regarded kindness and unkindness with the same indifference.[26]

It was obligatory for Muslims to pay alms (*zakat*) as soon as they acquired a benefit. A benefit consisted of 200 *dirhams*, while alms due on this amounted to 5 *dirhams*. If he possessed 20 *dinars*, he was supposed to pay half a *dinar*. If he possessed five camels, he was required to pay a sheep. Hujwiri argued that even the sufis, who apparently did not possess worldly riches, were bound to pay alms in proportion to their blessings – material and spiritual. "Thus health is a great blessing for which every limb owes alms. Therefore healthy persons ought to occupy all their limbs with devotion and not yield them to pleasure and pastime, in order that the alms due for the blessing of health may be fully paid." Since the sufi knew that he had received spiritual blessings from God, he offered inward and outward acknowledgement for them in proportion to their worth. Generally the sufis themselves did not accept alms, as they were wedded to voluntary poverty. But they did accept alms under divine compulsion, not for their own needs but for enabling a brother Muslim to fulfill his religious obligation. In such a case the sufi, though a receiver of alms, had the upper hand. Hujwiri explains,

"Therefore God afflicts the dervish with a slight want in order that worldlings may be able to perform what is incumbent upon them." It was also believed that a sufi could dispose off the wealth and belongings of a disciple.[27]

Fasting was a religious practice which brought a person in communion with God. His entry in paradise depended on God's mercy, his rank therein depended on his religious devotion and his residence for ever was a recompense for fasting. Those who fasted without intermission sought the above compensation, while those who fasted during Ramzan sought renunciation of self-will and ostentation. Devout Muslims, who had attained manhood, fasted continuously for a month from the onset of Ramzan and fasted till the appearance of the moon of Shawwal. During this period, they not only abstained from food and drink, but also guarded the eye from lustful looks, the ear from listening to evil speech, the tongue from foul words and the body from following worldly pursuits and disobedience to God. While fasting, a person was required to imprison the five senses – sight, hearing, taste, smell and touch – which were not only open to knowledge and reason, but also to passion. Continual fasting was forbidden by Prophet Muhammad. The sufis undertook forty days' fast (*chilla*), originally derived from Moses, but motivated by the desire to hear the word of God spiritually. "The last degree in fasting is hunger, which is God's food on earth and is universally commanded in the eyes of law and reason." Hunger was an affliction of the body; it illumined the heart and purified the soul and led the spirit to the presence of God. A body nourished with food merely fuelled physical passions and lower soul, while hunger sharpened the intelligence and improved the mind and health. Merit of hunger belonged to one who abstained from eating, not to one who was debarred from eating. Hujwiri concludes, "Repletion combined with contemplation is better than hunger combined with mortification, because contemplation is battlefield of men whereas mortification is the playground of children."[28]

The seekers were required to follow certain rules regarding their food, sleep and speech. Though nourishment was essential for survival, a sufi was supposed to eat and drink in moderation.[29] It was expected that he ate slowly using his right hand and chewed the food properly and, while doing so, took only as much water as was required to moisten the liver. After finishing the meals, he was expected to praise God and wash his hands. He was required to avoid eating alone, but advised to share his food with others, particularly his companions in the company of dervishes. He was expected not to refuse the invitation of a dervish for meals, but to decline the same from a rich man.[30] About sleep, there was difference of opinion. One view held that the novice was not permitted to sleep unless overpowered by slumber, because it made him heedless of God. Others regarded sleep as a gift of God to those who showed their devotion through wakefulness. It was a matter of debate if sleep was related to sobriety or intoxication and if apostles received the revelations during sleep or wakefulness. A novice was permitted to sleep after he had met his religious obligations and settled worldly affairs. The sufis were equally conscious of the relative merits of speech and silence. The former was regarded essential for human beings to express their gratitude to God for His bounties. Those who were grounded in eloquence did not need the tongue to communicate with God who, in any case, was aware of our circumstances. Hujwiri believed that there were two kinds of speech and two kinds of silence – speech was either real or unreal, while silence was either fruition or forgetfulness. If one spoke the truth, his speech was better than his silence. But if one spoke falsehood, his silence was better than his speech.[31]

Companionship, Travels and Pilgrimage

The sufis regarded companionship as an essential requirement in the path of mysticism, as solitude was fatal to the seeker.[32] But companionship was meant for God, not for gratifying the lower soul or any selfish motive. The seekers derived religious benefit from companionship with one another. They were advised to associate either with a superior or with an inferior because, in the former case, they derived benefit from him and, in the latter case, the benefit was mutual. They were advised to discard a friend who required to be flattered or who needed to be offered apologies for a fault. It was incumbent on them to follow the rules of companionship like a religious obligation. They were expected to treat everyone according to his degree i.e. to treat the old men with respect like fathers, their own sort with agreeable familiarity like brothers and young men with affection like sons. They were also expected to renounce hate, envy and malice but not to withhold sincere admonition from anyone. They were bound not to speak evil of the absent, nor behave dishonestly. Since companionship was begun for God's sake, it could not be terminated by human acts or words. Companionship needed continuous nourishment by looking after the interests of others and neglecting one's own. The biggest enemy of companionship was selfishness.[33]

By the middle of the eleventh century, the sufis could be seen as divided into two categories – residents (*muqiman*) and travellers (*musafiran*) – each regarding the other as superior. The travelling ones regarded the resident ones as superior to themselves, because they went here and there in their own interest, while the resident ones were settled down in the service of God. The former represented search, while the latter exemplified attainment. Hence, those who had attained and settled were superior to those who were still seeking. In the same manner, the resident sufis regarded the travelling ones as superior to themselves, because they themselves were burdened with worldly encumbrances, while the travelling ones were detached from the world. Resident sufis had certain duties towards the travelling sufis. They were required to treat the visitor as an honoured guest, receiving him with joy and respect. They were expected to offer whatever food they had. They could not make enquiries about his name, the place from where he had arrived and his next destination. They had to presume that his name was servant of God, he had come from God and he was going to God. However, they could ascertain whether the visitor preferred to be alone or in company. In the former case, they needed to provide him with a room and, in the latter case, they had to converse with him in a friendly and sociable manner. When he prepared to sleep, they had to offer to wash his feet. During the morning bath, they had to offer to rub his back, knees and soles of the feet, besides offering a fresh set of clothes. They could not persuade him, against his inclination, to visit the unknown local holy men or to attend entertainments, hospitals and funerals. They could not make him an instrument of mendicancy (begging), conducting him from house to house. They were not required to meet any unreasonable demand of the visitor. They were also not obliged to pay attention to the visitor, unless the latter's attention was entirely focused on God.[34]

Since travelling constituted an important part of the spiritual pursuit, Hujwiri enumerates the rules required to be followed by the travelling sufis. The sufi could travel only for the sake of God, not for pleasure. His object had to be pilgrimage or war (against the infidels) or to seek knowledge or desire instructions or visit a venerable Shaikh or pay homage at a holy site or tomb of a saint. He could carry with him a patched frock, a prayer rug, a bucket rope, staff, shoes or clogs. Following the Apostolic custom (*sunna*), he could also carry comb, nail scissors, needle and a little box of antimony.[35] An adept sufi was permitted to carry more articles, but these were a shackle for the novice. When the sufis travelled in companionship, one of them was chosen as the commander and obeyed by the others. They were required to have trust in one another and not speak ill of their comrades in presence or behind backs. At a halting place, their attitude towards the host was expected to be courteous and moderate. They were free to decline the invitation to visit the people of the town along with their hosts. While sufis travelled outwardly, they were obliged to flee inwardly from their sensual affections.[36]

The Muslims regarded pilgrimage (*haj*) to Mecca as one of the five religious obligations. It was an elaborate ritual which consisted of several steps – putting on the pilgrim's garb, standing on the Arafat, going to Muzdalifa and Mashar-ul-Haram, circumambulating the Kaaba, running between Safa and Marwa, three days stay at Mina and throwing stones, offering the sacrifice and wearing ordinary garments. However, the sufis were apt to treat these actions as metaphors in an ongoing spiritual pursuit. For them, it might be possible to visit Mecca once in a year, but it was possible to see God in his heart three hundred and sixty times in a single day and night. The object of sufis in travelling through wilderness and desert was not the sanctuary itself, for to a lover of God it was unlawful to look upon His sanctuary. Rather their object was mortification in a longing that left them no rest and eager dissolution in a love that had no end. Hujwiri is emphatic that pilgrimage was of two types – in the absence of God and in the presence of God. He elaborates, "Anyone who is absent from God at Mecca is in the same position as if he were absent from God in his own house, and anyone who is present with God in his own house is in the same position as if he were present with God at Mecca. Pilgrimage is an act of mortification (*mujahadat*) for the sake of obtaining contemplation (*mushahadat*), and mortification does not become the direct cause of contemplation, but is only a means to it."[37]

Poetry, Audition and Ecstasy

Since audition (*sama*) was inseparably associated with the practice of sufism, Hujwiri examines the conflicting views regarding its legality and utility. While developing his own understanding on the subject, he examines the position of Prophet Muhammad, his companions and eminent sufis who had lived in the different parts of the Islamic world. He traces the origin of audition to the faculty of hearing, which was one of the five natural senses possessed by human beings. It was through hearing that the knowledge of God and belief in the Prophet became a basic obligation. It was hearing that made religion obligatory and, for this reason, the Sunnis regarded hearing as superior to sight in the domain of religious obligation. The prophets delivered sermons and formulated religious ordinances, but these were communicated to the believers through hearing. Thereafter, the prophets supplemented these actions by showing miracles which were corroborated by hearing. It was argued that listening to the recitation of the Quran constituted the most beneficial audition for the mind and most delightful to the ear. Though the Quran was revealed to the Prophet, yet he was fond of hearing it being recited. The listener was more perfect in state than the reader, for the latter might recite with or without true feeling, whereas the former felt truly. This was so because speech denoted pride, while hearing reflected a sort of humility.[38] There were opposite views regarding the propriety of listening to non-religious poetry. Prophet Muhammad and his companions enjoyed listening to such poetry, as more important than the form of expression was the theme which had to be lawful.

From a discussion of audition and poetry, Hujwiri moves on to underline the impact of music and singing. He declares, "Anyone who says that he finds no pleasure in sounds and melodies and music is either a liar or hypocrite or he is not in his right senses, and is outside the category of men and beasts." Traditions of Prophet Muhammad listening to singing of songs have been related by his companions and these have been collected by Abu Abdul Rahman al-Sulami in his *Kitab-i-Sama*. Even the theologians agreed that it was permissible to hear musical instruments, if they were used not for diversion and the mind was not led to wicked actions. The lawfulness of audition depended on the circumstances and could not be asserted in absolute terms. An audition was lawful if its effect on the mind was lawful, but it was unlawful if its effect was unlawful. Impact of audition varied with the temperament of the listeners, who were divided into two categories – those who heard the spiritual meaning and those who heard the material sound.[39] According to Zu ul-Nun Misri, those who listened spiritually attained God, whereas those who listened sensually fell into heresy. Audition was not required by the spiritual adepts who had reached the end of their journeys, but it was employed by beginners to obtain concentration when distracted by forgetfulness. In the opinion of acute observers, sufis were placed in different grades in the hierarchy of audition and the spiritual benefit which they derived from audition was proportionate to their rank.[40] By listening to devotional verses, penitents added to their contrition and remorse, lovers increased their longing for vision, novices verified the elucidation of spiritual matters and spiritually poor formed a foundation of hopelessness. "Audition is like the sun which shines on things but affects them differently; it burns or illumines or dissolves or nurtures."[41] We learn that in the hospitals of Rum, patients were made to listen twice a week to a stringed musical instrument for a length of time proportionate to their malady. Despite the spiritual benefits of audition, there was a long tradition of opposition to the practice on different grounds, particularly the risk of falling from penitence to sin, due to violent arousal of passions and corruption of virtues.

Hujwiri examines the various emotional states – *wajd*, *wujud*, *tawajud*, dance and tearing clothes – that flowed directly out of the emotion generated by audition. As verbal nouns, the meaning of *wajd* was grief and *wujud* was finding, but it was not easy to comprehend their significance in mysticism. The real sense of *wajd* was pain experienced at the loss of the beloved and failure to gain the object of desire. It was a mystery between the seeker and sought, which could be expounded only by revelation. The real sense of *wujud* was removal of grief from the heart and attainment of the desired object. It was the thrill of emotion in contemplation of God, which could not be reached by investigation as it was a grace bestowed by the Beloved on the lover. *Wujud* was characteristic of novices (*muridan*) and *wajd* that of gnostics (*arifan*). Since the spiritual status of gnostics was higher than the novices, *wajd* was higher and more perfect than *wujud*. A seeker overcome by *wajd* was in a dangerous position and deprived of his sense of discrimination, provided he possessed adequate knowledge and followed the religious law. If knowledge (*ilm*) preponderated over feeling (*hal*), the concerned person remained in the jurisdiction of divine commands and was recipient of divine rewards. *Tawajjud* was defined as taking pains to produce *wajd*, by focusing on evidence of God and thinking of union. It was permissible if done in a spiritual manner, but unlawful if done with outward motions and methodical dancing. Dancing (*raqs*) had no foundation in the religious law of Islam or the path of sufism. Some confusion had been caused because ecstatic movements of those who induced ecstasy (*ahl-i-tawajjud*) resembled dancing. A number of common people had adopted sufism in the belief that it was just this dancing and nothing more. When the heart throbbed with exhilaration, raptures became intense and ecstasy was manifested in physical movement. But that agitation (*iztirab*) was not dancing or bodily indulgence, but a disolution of the soul. So far as the practice of rending garments was concerned, Hujwiri argued, it had no foundation in sufism and could not be permitted in audition to anyone whose senses were controlled. But it could be allowed if a listener became so overpowered that he lost his sense of discrimination and became unconscious. The torn or discarded garment could be disposed off in a variety of ways – from gifting to the singer to distributing torn pieces among the fellow listeners, subject to the command of the spiritual director.[42]

Hujwiri concludes his discourse on audition by laying down rules that were required to be observed during the course of such a meeting. In the first instance, the audition parties had to be held seldom, but not made a habit. The venue ought to be cleared of the common (uninitiated) people, a spiritual director had to be present during the performance and the singer was expected to be a respectable person. The disposition of the listener could not be inclined towards amusement and his heart had to be purged of worldly thoughts. Once the power of audition manifested itself, the listener was obliged to merely follow it in accordance with the impact. If it agitated, he had to be agitated. If it calmed, he had to be calm. He was required to distinguish a strong natural impulse from the ardour of ecstasy. He was expected to have enough perception which was capable of receiving divine influence and doing justice to it. While in a state of emotion, he could neither expect any help from others, nor could refuse it if offered by anyone. He was forbidden from interfering with the singer or the other listeners. In case he was not participating in the audition, he was required not to observe or assess the state of intoxication being enjoyed by the listeners, but had to remain quiet hoping to receive the emerging spiritual blessings. It was desirable that the beginners were not allowed to attend musical concerts, lest their natures should become depraved. "These concerts are extremely dangerous and corrupting, because women on the roofs or elsewhere look at the dervishes who are engaged in audition, and in consequence of this the auditors have great obstacles to encounter." There were some ignorant sufis who treated audition as a religion in itself and had flung truth to the winds.[43]

NOTES AND REFERENCES

1. Despite the dearth of authentic evidence, some attempts have been made to reconstruct the life and career of Hujwiri. Saiyid Athar Abbas Rizvi, *A History of Sufism in India*, Vol.I, Munshiram Manoharlal, New Delhi, 1978, p. 112; Shaikh Muhammad Ikram, *Ab-i-Kausar*, Taj Company, New Delhi, Reprint, 1987, pp. 76-77; Muhammad Baqir, *Ahwal-o-Taalimat: Shaikh Abul Hasan Hujwiri Data Ganj Bakhsh*, Idarah-i-Tahqiqat-i-Pakistan, Punjab University, Lahore, 1989, pp. 6-7; Shaikh Parvaiz Amin Naqshbandy, *The Saints of Punjab*, Umar Publications, Lahore, 1998, pp. 1-14.
2. Gurbax Singh, "Punjab Under the Ghaznavid Occupation," in Fauja Singh, (Ed.), *History of the Punjab*, Vol.III, Punjabi University, Patiala, 1972, p. 87.
3. Nur Ahmad Chishti, *Tahqiqat-i-Chishti*, Al-Faisal, Nashiran wa Tajiran Kutb, Urdu Bazar, Lahore, 2001, pp. 168-172.
4. The author has complained that these works did not receive proper recognition, because the people either picked passages from some and used them for quoting in discussions; some read them but did not comprehend the meaning; other works were destroyed or mutilated or left unread. He felt anguished at the thought that the works of eminent sufis, having fallen into wrong hands, had been used to make lining for caps or binding for the poems of Abu Nuwas and the pleasantries of Jahiz. Ali bin Usman Hujwiri, *Kashf-ul-Mahjub*, English Translation, Reynold A. Nicholson, Taj Company, Delhi, Reprint, 1982, pp.xix-xx. (hereafter cited as Hujwiri).
5. Qazi Javed, *Punjab Key Sufi Danishwar*, Fiction House, Lahore, 2005, pp. 9-11. It is a far fetched proposition to attribute this approach to Hindu Vedantism and Ismailism. Moreover, there is no evidence to prove that the early Turkish invaders were opposed to this approach.
6. Hujwiri, p. 7.

7. Ibid., p. 2.
8. Ibid., pp. 30-34.
9. Ibid., pp. 36-44.
10. The Prophet regarded a learned man as superior to the (unlearned) worshipper. A majority of sufi masters considered knowledge (*ilm*) superior to both gnosis (*maarifat*) and reason (*aql*), because God possessed the attribute of *ilm* and because *ilm* had dominance over reason and not vice versa. Abu al-Najib al-Suhrawardi, *Kitab Adab-i-Muridin*, Abridged Translation and Introduction, Menahem Milson, Harvard University Press, Cambridge, 1975, p. 39.
11. Hujwiri, pp. 267-277.
12. This elucidation of the concept of unification of God may be compared with the exposition of the subject, which was offered a hundred years later. Shaikh Shihabuddin Suhrawardi, *Awarif-ul-Maarif*, English Translation, Wilberforce Clarke, Taj Company, Delhi, Reprint, 1984, pp. 105-112.
13. Hujwiri, pp. 278-285.
14. Ibid., pp. 286-290.
15. In the convent of Shaikh Farid at Ajodhan, the disciples were required to go to the jungle for collecting food and fuel. When sufficient materials could not be procured, Shaikh Farid permitted his disciples to circulate the begging bowl (*zanbil*) among the neighbours. But he was strongly opposed to borrowing money during times of distress. Khaliq Ahmad Nizami, *The Life and Times of Shaikh Fariduddin Ganj-i-Shakar*, Idarah-i-Adabiyat-i-Delli, Delhi, Reprint, 1973, pp. 48-49.
16. Hujwiri, pp. 16-24.
17. Ibid., pp. 58-61.
18. Ibid., pp. 291-297.
19. According to Abu al-Najib al-Suhrawardi (1097-1168), a sufi was different from the Malamati, for the latter was one who would not demonstrate a good work nor conceal a bad one, whereas the former did not concern himself at all with the opinion that the other people have of him. Abu al-Najib al-Suhrawardi, *Kitab Adab-i-Muridin*, p. 30.
20. Hujwiri, pp. 62-67.
21. The Prophet's practice (*sunnah*) was to wear the white garment. Since washing such an apparel consumed time, the sufis wore a blue apparel, even as a black one was better against defilement. The spiritual preceptor decided the kind of garment (material, colour and form) which his disciple ought to wear, the aim being to withdraw the latter from natural habits and sensual affections. Shaikh Shihabuddin Suhrawardi, *Awarif-ul-Maarif*, pp. 67-68.
22. Hujwiri, pp. 45-57.
23. Ibid., pp. 360-365.
24. For details regarding the time and content of prayers as well as the corresponding bodily movements, compare with the exposition of another sufi text. Shihabuddin Suhrawardi, *Awarif-i-Maarif*, pp. 199-211.
25. Hujwiri, pp. 301-304.
26. Ibid., pp. 300-313.

27. Ibid., pp. 314-318.
28. Ibid., pp. 320-325.
29. The sufis did not believe in gathering and storing food. They avoided gluttony. They did not find fault with food, nor praised it. They did not have fixed time for eating and did not make much ado about it. They ate only that food whose source was known to them. They avoided the food of the unjust and sinful people. They preferred to eat in company. Abu al-Najib al-Suhrawardi, *Kitab Adab-i-Muridin*, pp. 57-58.
30. Hujwiri, pp. 347-349.
31. Ibid., pp. 351-356.
32. The sufi was required to associate with people of his kind and those from whom he could benefit. He was dissuaded from associating with people who were opposed to his religious affiliation, even if they were related to him. He was expected to help his companions in obtaining their sustenance. He was asked to recognize the value of every man. There were rules for associating with various categories of people viz. elders, youngers, equals, masters, servants, visitors, rulers, wife and children. Abu al-Najib al-Suhrawardi, *Kitab Adab-i-Muridin*, pp. 45-48.
33. Hujwiri, pp. 337-339.
34. Ibid., pp. 340-344.
35. On the utility and mode of travelling, there was a considerable similarity between the views of Hujwiri and Suhrawardi, except that the latter added a leather container or jug for carrying water required for ablutions and washing. Abu al-Najib al-Suhrawardi, *Kitab Adab-i-Muridin*, pp. 52-55.
36. Hujwiri, pp. 345-347.
37. Ibid., pp. 326-329.
38. Ibid., pp. 393-396.
39. Ibid., pp. 401-402.
40. According to Shaikh Shihabuddin Suhrawardi, the participants in audition derived three benefits from it. Firstly, the seekers fought fatigue and despair which consisted of sweet sounds and harmonious melodies. Secondly, it knocked down the obstacles in the path of the seeker which often appeared owing to *nafs*. Thirdly, it converted the seeker's slow travelling into a swift flight, his laborious journey into an irresistible attraction and his status of a lover into that of a beloved of God. Surinder Singh, "The Study of an Early Treatise on Islamic Mysticism," *Proceedings of the Punjab History Conference*, Patiala, 24th Session, 15-17 March 1991, p. 72.
41. Hujwiri, pp. 406-407.
42. Ibid., pp. 416-417; since audition was one of the most contentious issues among the sufis, they have evolved several principles governing the various aspects of the exercise, including the rending of garments and subsequent distribution of its portions. For example, Abu al-Najib al-Suhrawardi, *Kitab Adab-i-Muridin*, pp. 61-66.
43. Hujwiri, pp. 419-420.

9

Baba Farid: The Pioneer of Punjabi Sufi Poetry

Saeed Ahmad

In the political, social and literary history of medieval Punjab, a number of elements associated with sufism – sufi saints, sufi poetry and sufi shrines – occupied an important as well as revered position. The non-sectarian and dynamic character of Punjabi literature is unequivocally revealed in the devotional poetry of the sufis, from Shaikh Farid to Ghulam Farid i.e. from the last quarter of the twelfth century to the end of the nineteenth century. The sufi saints and poets – like Baba Farid, Shah Husain, Sultan Bahu, Bulleh Shah, Waris Shah and others – composed their spiritually intoxicated and socially relevant verses in the Punjabi vernacular and in the variegated flavour and fragrance of its dialectics. Not only the vernaculars, but also the poetic genres like *doha* (or *dohra* or *saloka*) and *kafi*, which Punjabi sufi poets adopted, speak of their organic linkages with the indigenous space and soil. Thus the study of Punjab sufis calls into question the historiographical discourse which emplots them as Islamic missionaries who aimed at converting the non-Muslims to Islam. As a matter of fact, the Punjab sufis were strongly opposed to the social, religious and political domination of a single community/class. They added a new dimension to the devotional literature represented by Punjab bhaktas and Sikh Gurus of *sirguna* and *nirguna* traditions. A reading of the *dohas* and *kafis*, composed by them, makes one familiar with the historic Punjabi mystic traditions.

A Vernacular Sufi and Poet

The first celebrated sufi of the Punjabi soil was Shaikh Fariduddin Shakarganj, popularly known as Baba Farid or simply as Farid. During the last days of the Ghaznavid ruler Khusrau Malik, the Guzz invasion drove a large number of people from Afghanistan to Punjab. In these circumstances, Qazi Shuaib (the grandfather of Baba Farid) migrated from Kabul to Punjab. He was appointed as the local judge (*qazi*) of

Kahtwal, a town in Multan, situated between Maharan and Ajodhan. One of Qazi Shuaib's three sons was named Jamaluddin who was married to a Punjabi girl, Qarsum Bibi, of whom Farid was born in 1175.[1] At the age of eighteen Farid completed his early education in his native town, Kahtwal. Thereafter he left for Multan, which was then a renowned centre of Islamic learning. He joined the seminar (*madrasah*) located in the mosque of Maulana Minhajuddin Tirmizi. At this place, Farid first met Khwaja Qutbuddin Bakhtiyar Kaki (d. 1232 AD) who had come from Aush to Multan and was staying in the local mosque. When the latter left for Delhi, Farid also accompanied him and was admitted into his discipleship.[2] Under the guidance of his master, Farid went through the austere phases of the journey of mysticism. By virtue of his devotion and commitment, he was blessed at the same time both by his master, Khwaja Qutbuddin Bakhtiyar Kaki, and the latter's master Khwaja Muinuddin Chishti. "No saint before him, or even after him, was thus blessed by the master and the master of his master".[3] The name of Farid seems to have been recommended by his preceptor Khwaja Qutbuddin Bakhtiyar Kaki, as an acknowledgement of his cardinal place in the Chishti order in India.[4] At the time of his final departure, Khwaja Qutbuddin Bakhtiyar Kaki said to Farid, "My place is yours". With this utterance, the great Chishti saint of Delhi forever parted with his eminent disciple from Punjab.[5] Farid initially settled at Hansi, a town in Hissar district (present state of Haryana in India) where "a steady stream of followers and admirers continued to disturb him. He therefore decided to settle in Ajodhan, an obscure town in Punjab" (now in Pakistan).[6] In 1236 he moved to Ajodhan (Pak Pattan) where he stayed till he breathed his last in 1265.

The eriod of the twefth-thirteenth centuries, which is yet to be recognized as the 'Age of Baba Farid' in the history of culture, literature and language f Punjab, winessed the cosolidation ofTurkish rule nd also the spread of early Islamic mysticism that radiated mainly from Multan, Lahore and Delhi. Baba Farid was more or less the contemporary of Shams Tabrez, Khwaja Muinuddin Chishti, Shaikh Bahauddin Zakariya, Khwaja Qutbuddin BakhtiyarKaki and Shaikh Nizamuddin Aulya. He composed poetry in vernacular, preached sufism in all its variations of *sama*, *tasawwuf*, *zikr* and *pas-i-anfas* (*habs-i-dam*) – the four schools of 'ears', 'eye', 'tongue' and 'breath.'[7] He is said to be the pioneer of Punjabi poetry. His is the first recorded poetry in th Punjabi vernacular. Farid composed his verses in the genre of *doha*, a rhymed couplet. Each of the lines generally has a caesura, the significance of which varies according to the meaning. Usually one of the lines of the *dora* bears thename of Farid.The use of hs name "is not an egotistical intrusin nor has t the decorative virtue of personal seal commonly employed by poets. The personal name is an identification of the poet's self with every man and a placing of the lisener through this dentification into a position o omniscience and objectiity."[8] Baba Farid's one hundred thrty devotional vrses, under the heaing of *salok*, are enshrined in the Guru Granth Sahib, which was compiled by Guru Arjun Dev in 160. Out of these *salokas*, 112 are f Baba Farid and 18 are the interventions made by the four Sikh gurus viz. Guru Nanak, Guru Amar Das, Guru Ram Das and Guru Arjan Dev. About the discovery of the *salokas* of Baba Farid, it is said that Guru Nanak collected them from Shaikh Ibrahim, a direct descendant of Baba Farid and an apostolic successor who sang in the preceptor's name. Guru Nanak realized "the intrinsic value of these *salokas* as moments of ineffable intuition clamouring for expression. And since his ministry was to seek the eternal paradigms of truth wherever he could find them – amidst saints and scholars, amidst peasants and householders – he must have at once seen the need to recapture this poetry of vision which drew him like a flame."[9] In the context of the two historically prominent 'Babas' (Baba Farid and Baba Nanak) in the entire history of Punjab, it is significant to learn that both these saints have contributed tremendously to and have left an enduring influence on the social and cultural history of Punjab.[10] Both lived in turbulent and transitional periods of Indian history. Baba Farid witnessed the end of the Ghaznavid rule in Punjab and later on the Mongol deluge. Similarly, during the fifteenth-sixteenth centuries, Guru Nanak watched the socio-political crisis, the overthrow of the Afghan rule and the establishment of the Mughal Empire in northern India. Both Baba Farid and Baba Nanak "represented regeneration and spiritual elevation of man at times when worldly ambitions and political vicissitudes had victimized the common man in the caste ridden social order."[11]

In view of the impact of Baba Farid and Baba Nanak on the socio-political history and cultural ethos of Punjab, it is pertinent to identify the reason, which obliged Guru Arjun Dev to incorporate the *salokas* of Baba Farid in the Adi Granth, the sacred book of the Sikhs. For that matter, one needs to appreciate the traditions of Chishti order, which had been imbibed by Baba Farid. First, the spiritual leaders of the Chishti order believed in and led a family life; they did not recommend renunciation and retirement to jungles. In one of his *salokas* Baba Farid questions: "Farid, why wander from forest to forest, /trampling on thorns? / God lives in the heart. / Why look for Him in the forest?"[12] Second, the Chishti order recognized the supreme importance of the spiritual preceptor (guru/ murshid). Third, the principle of spiritual succession (*guru-gaddi*) was the cardinal feature of the Chishti order. The spiritual preceptor (*murshid*, *pir* or Shaikh) had the sole right to choose his successor and this succession was not (biologically) hereditary. We may say that in the Chishti order there were two kinds of family trees: one referred to biological genealogy and the other to a spiritual genealogy.[13] Fourth, one of the distinguishing features of the Chishti order in Punjab was the use of music for singing devotional verses. Khwaja Muinuddin Chishti, the founder of the order, found that music was a significant component of worship.[14] Fifth, service to humanity through common kitchen (*langar*) was another prominent attribute of the order under reference. Sixth, the Chishti sufis cultivated amicable relations with non-Muslims. All these characteristics of the Chishti order were identical with the socio-religious mission launched by Guru Nanak in the fifteenth century. [15]

Baba Farid used his mother tongue Lehandi to versify his mystic experience. He elevated the status of the vernacular as the vehicle of divine message. Lehandi became as much of an Islamic language as Arabic, Turkish or Persian. It became an instrument of literary expression of the highest order. Baba Farid endowed the Punjabi poetry with new form, vigour and vitality, which was unknown till then. In his poetry, he kept the sense of melody. To filter down an essentially esoteric mystical tradition in some sort of comprehensible and appealing form to the grass-roots level of the Punjab society, Baba Farid consciously exploited the rich repository of folk motifs and adapted the Persian and Arabic words in the vernacular accent. For example, Farid writes *nimaz* (prayer) as *nivaj*, *waqt* (time) as *wakhat* and *vuzu* (ablution) as *uju*. Baba Farid thus made a significant contribution to the building up of a particular flavour and identity of Punjabi language and, at the same time, facilitated Islam to spread in (rather fuse into) the Punjabi cultural complex and the amicable ambience of its popular culture and religious ethos. In Baba Farid's verses, we do not find the name of Prophet Muhammad nor the titles such as *nabi*, *rasul* and *paighambar*. Even the word *murshid*, an important term in sufi tradition, is not found.[16] Rather he addressed Allah (God) in one of the verses with non-Islamic words like *pritam* and *prabhu*.[17] Baba Farid portrayed God as benign, loving, forgiving and immensely powerful. To describe man's relation with the Almighty, Baba Farid employed the imagery of the love of man and woman. Every aspect of love, its passions, and its longing, and the agony of separation, the consummation of love, the eternal endeavour to win the favour of the beloved were utilized by Baba Farid to reveal his inexhaustible passion for God. He sang the devotional song of humility, forgiveness, love of mankind, renunciation and meditation. Gurbachan Singh Talib identifies some prominent themes in the verses of Baba Farid:

> There is the keen consciousness of inevitable death and the evanescence of life and of its pleasure, which lure man away from God. Thoughtless man

> is called back to the higher path of piety and spiritual enlightenment with humane compassion. There is then the expression of true religion, as that God dwells in the heart of the seeker and not in solitary and waste places. Hypocrisy and the false show of religion are castigated. Man is called upon to still the noise of senses to listen to the Voice of God. Some pieces are expressive of deep spiritual experience, such as can be expressed in symbols, as in these pieces. Thus, those spiritually weak are like timid females, trembling at the sight of swollen stream. They, however, pick up courage from the sight of 'heroes' (that is, men of God) crossing fearlessly over. Through this symbol is expressed the spiritual state of man, afraid to leave the pleasures of the world and to enter on the unknown and hard quest after God. In another great symbol the joy in God is likened to the fragrance of musk, wafted along the midnight breeze. This joy, however, comes to those keeping vigils in by prayer and not to those with eyelids slumber-oppressed. Men of God are like Swans, just alighted on the Pool of the World, not dipping their beaks in its water, but preparing ever to fly away. Life is like the Indian bride, loath to leave the parents' home, but carried away in wedlock by Death.[18]

Since Baba Farid was non-idolatrous, non-formalistic and disbeliever in the monopolized worship as represented by the orthodox priestly class, he may be said to be a forerunner of *nirguna* bhakti cult in Punjab, though 'historically' the cult originated in a period later than him. Let it be understood that religious poetry and devotional poetry are two different entities. The former is associated with and recognized by a particular religion as its central axis, whereas the latter does not entertain such denominational compulsions. Moreover, devotional poetry does not have communitarian and sectarian potentials, which can be exploited for vested religious interests. The poetry of Punjabi sufis, gurus and bhaktas retains its sanctity because of its universal appeal that transcends the limitations of time and space. For example, in the east Punjab, though sufi cult is almost extinct, yet sufi-poetry has not yet lost its appeal and sanctity.[19] Similarly, in the west Punjab, despite the negligible presence of Hindus and Sikhs, Guru Nanak is revered as a Baba and *pir*. Baba Farid's verses echo with the tones of devotional surrender and annihilation of *nirguna*-oriented tradition:

> I do not fear my youth going, / if love for Husband does not, / Farid, how many youths without love / have dried and withered away![20]
>
> O crows! you have searched the skeleton, / eaten up all flesh. / Please do not touch the two eyes; / I still hope to see my love.[21]

In the context of non-conformism of the devotional literary movement of Punjab, comprising Muslim, Hindu and Sikh saints, Baba Farid is looked upon as a cultural ancestor of Punjab. His poetry is a rich heritage of the Punjabis across the world. It is significant to observe that Baba

Farid did not smack of the superior attitude of his co-religionist ruling class. His verses did not offend the sentiments of the non-Muslims. They did not contain any disparaging reference to the caste system, to idolatry or to other peculiar features of the Brahmanical creed or creeds.[22] He strips off the evils disguised in the black-cloaked saintly appearance. He pronounces:

> Farid, my clothes are coloured black / and black my guise is too./ I wander about, burdened with sin, / and people called me dervish.[23]

Carl W. Ernst cites an incident from the Khuldabad *malfuzat* texts, which may further enrich the message, which Baba Farid intends to convey through the above-cited *saloka*. Once Baba Farid 'was visited by a group of black-cloaked dervishes (*siyah-push*). Although they appeared outwardly unremarkable, the Shaykh perceived something wrong about them, and he locked their leader into a room for three days, but supplied the others with bread and water. On the third day, the Shaykh told the leader that if he became a Muslim, he would be released. The leader agreed, and when he came out it was revealed that beneath his dervish cloak there was an idolater's belt [the term idolater's belt (*zunnar*) in Persian is indifferently applied to a Christian monk's belt, a Zoroastrian belt, or a Brahman's sacred thread]. The leader admitted that for thirty years he had been visiting the hospices of Khurasan and India, but that no one had seen through his disguise before.' Ernst argues that the purpose of the story is to show the ability of the sufi master to see through appearances and read one's inner thoughts.[24] The above cited *saloka* and the incident remind us of Bayazid Bistami (d.875) who once said: "Beneath this cloak of mine there is nothing but God."

It is premised, in the context of the following *saloka*, that Baba Farid is not agonized for his personal sins. Rather he "is taking upon himself the sins of the ruling class to which he belonged. Being invaders and conquerors on India, the people of this class were also oppressors. As a person Shaikh Farid had opted out of it, by becoming a dervish, but he was, all the same, a member of this class. And in this condition the collective consciousness of sin is not only natural to him, it is a proof of his sincerity"[25]

> Farid, why did you go to the city gate/ to see the beating of the gong? / It is beaten for no fault, / what shall happen to us full of guilt.[26]

Baba Farid was a socially aware dervish. He shared the sorrows and pains of the ordinary masses, while singing:

> Farid, I thought I alone suffered, /but there's suffering in the whole world. / Rising higher, I saw / the same fire in every house.[27]

> Farid, thought is my bedstead, / sorrow, the strings, / suffering separation, the mattress and cover. / This is my life, you see True Master.[28]

In an atmosphere of political subjugation, theological intellectualism and military violence, when the common people were undergoing suffering and loosing their confidence, Baba Farid conveyed the message of self-sacrifice, self-respect and dignity of the downtrodden. In Baba Farid, there seems to have been a strong streak of independence, which was almost rebellious in spirit. He anticipated the victory of the subalterns. He warned the hegemonic forces of his times:

> Farid, to sit at another's door! / Lord give me not that ! / If you keep me so, / take life from the body.[29]

> Farid, if your understanding is sharp / do not blacken the deeds of the others. / Bow your head and see / inside your own self.[30]

> Farid, do not abuse the earth [*khak*], / nothing is as great. / It is under the feet of the living,/ above the dead.[31]

In Islam there are by traditional account ninety-nine names of God.[32] Of these the most important are the two names in the invocation that prefaces nearly every *sura* of the Quran: "In the name of God, the merciful and the compassionate" (*bismillahal-rahmanal-rahim*). It is these attributes of God, which human beings are expected to follow and practice. For those who did not observe and practice them, Baba Farid suggested harsh punishment:

> Farid, get up, do ablutions, / say the morning prayer. / The head that does not bow to God / should be cut and brought down.[33]

> The head that does not bow to God, / what to do with it? / Burn it under the cooking pot in place of the firewood.[34]

Baba Farid sowed the seeds of revolutionary transformation, which was communicated more pronouncedly by Guru Nanak in the fifteenth-sixteenth centuries ("If you want to play the game of love, approach me with your head on the palm of your hand."). It was practiced initially by Guru Arjun Dev and later by Guru Teg Bahadur and many followers of the Sikh gurus, Banda Bahadur being the prominent one in the eighteenth century. It needs to be appreciated, if one is interested in the conflict-resolution-discourse of medieval Punjabi poetry, that the entire poetic discourse of Baba Farid is not like that of a 'missionary' who propagated Islam, Christianity, Hinduism and Sikhism among the people in the colonial Punjab. Rather Baba Farid condemned falseness and formalism and, by doing so, he built a critique that was repeated after two hundred years by Guru Nanak[35] and after five hundred years by Bulleh Shah.[36] Baba Farid said:

> Farid, a prayer mat on the shoulder, / a woolen shirt around the neck, / a dagger in the heart, / jaggery in the mouth, / outside appears light,/ in the heart is dark night.[37]

For Baba Farid outward ritualistic purification is less important than the inner one. That is why he said:

> Washed and bathed and dressed, / she slept without a thought, / Farid, soiled with asafoetida. / The smell of musk was gone.[38]

In the realm of Punjabi literary tradition, Baba Farid was the first poet who showed his utmost concern with humanity. He recognized and communicated in his mother tongue the sufferings of the rank and file, violence perpetrated by the ruling elite and invaders, and the difference between the privileged and non-privileged. He virtually ushered in a renaissance in medieval Punjab. We can discern the salient features of the said renaissance – such as moral fervour, spirit of freedom, rejection of sectarian tendencies and opposition to socio-religious and political patriarchy – in the teachings and sayings of Shaikh Farid. When Waris Shah (1767) versified his anti-patriarchal discourse in his *qissa Hir*, he paid a rich tribute to Baba Farid:

> Maudud's beloved son, Masaud, / the sweet-tongued, of all sweets the store: / Most perfect of the house of Chisht, / whose shrine, Pakpattan, is well-renowned; / The highest of the twenty-poles, / whose penance is famous all around; / His grace dispels all Punjab's sorrows; / and makes it peaceful evermore.[39]

In the *qissa Hir*, Baba Farid is ranked among the Panj Pir, who after having been pleased with the devotional singing and dance of Ranjha, blessed him with the love of Hir. By their blessings, the *pirs* helped the lovers in their struggle against the patriarchs of the Siyal community. In the domain of folk religion, Baba Farid has carved his own niche. In the Punjabi folk literature, we find charms and amulets read and written in the name of Baba Farid. These were employed as remedies to cure persons who were afflicted with tooth-pain or bitten by a snake, bee or scorpion. Many verses of Baba Farid are used as proverbs and sayings in the Punjabi society even in the present times.

Life Pattern

The life pattern of Baba Farid was compatible with what he uttered and suggested in his verses. The different facets of his life – his constant contemplation and devotion, his tattered garments, his concern for the poor and the needy, his simple blanket (*galim*) and rug (*shuqqah*), his habit of using the staff of his master as a pillow, his constant observance of fast, his daily small and simple intake of a one third bowl of *sherbet*, a few dried grapes and half a piece of bread, his choice of graveyards as a place for prayer[40] - collectively constituted the image of a sufi saint, named Baba Farid of the Chishti order. By perpetual fasting Baba Farid's body is said to have become so pure that "whatever he put into his mouth to allay the cravings of hunger, even earth and stones, was immediately turned into sugar, whence his name of Shakarganj or Sugar-store". Cunningham cites a Persian couplet that recorded his miraculous power: *Sang dar dast o guhar gardad, / Zaher dark am o shaker gardad* (Stones in his hand are changed to many [jewels], / And poison in his mouth to honey [sugar]).[41] By virtue of his aforesaid life pattern, Baba Farid inspired many scholars, merchants, government officials, artisans, sufis, qalandars and ordinary people to visit his *jamat-khana*. Some of them even de-classed themselves and became permanent inmates of his *jamat-khana*. For instance, Maulana Badruddin, a great scholar of Delhi, Syed Mahmud Kirmani, a flourishing businessman of Kirman, Nizamuddin Auliya, an excellent product of the academic institutions of Badaun and Delhi, Maulana Jamal Hanswi, a prosperous *khatib*, and many others became the humble servants of Baba Farid.[42]

Since power symbolism in Islam is primarily based on words i.e. the virtues and properties of the names of Allah, of phrases like the *Bismillah*, or Quranic verses (*Ayat al-Kursi)*, Baba Farid blessed the common masses with amulet (*tawiz*), a scrap of paper on which were written the names of God or some Quranic verses. His *tawiz* promised a protection against evil and illness, and boon for good fortune.[43] Maulana Badruddin Ishaq, the son-in-law of Baba Farid, used to write thousands of amulets every day to cope with the unending demand and, in his absence, Nizamuddin Auliya was assigned this task. Many of Baba Farid's practices, which were not approved by the orthodox priestly class of Islam, brought him closer to the non-Muslims. Mention may be made of his acceptance of Hindus among his disciples, his *salat-i-makoos* (saying prayers while hanging upside down from the branches of a tree into a well), *zanbil gardani* (sending around a begging bowl to collect alms) and *sama* (spiritual music).[44] Baba Farid was the first Indian sufi who showed his interest in the teachings of the yogis. His *khanqah* "was subjected to fertilization and cross-fertilization by their philosophy and practices."[45] Situated at one of the main routes from Multan to Delhi, Ajodhan became a melting pot of cultures and ideas. It is from Baba Farid that Ajodhan derives its modern name of Pak Pattan, or the "Ferry of the Pure One", that is, of Baba Farid.[46] Here at Ajodhan on a hillock 50 feet high, Baba Farid built up his monastery, which was just a thatched hall. His followers and travellers treated the place as a sanctuary, an oasis in a desert. Here he trained his disciples and sent them to different parts of India to spread the message of the Chishti order. Nizami draws the democratic face and features of a Chishti *jamaat khana*:

> [It] consisted of a big hall where all the inmates lived communally. The roof of this *jamat khanqah* was supported by a number of pillars and at the foot of each of these pillars a mystic could be seen with all his belongings

– bedding, books and rosary. They all slept, prayed, and studied on the ground and no discrimination, not even on the basis of seniority or piety, was permitted to prevail in the *jamat khanqah*. If food was available, all would partake of it; if not, all would suffer jointly the pangs of hunger. In the *jamat khanqah* of Shaikh Farid, the inmates had to pluck *pelu* and *delah* from the *kareel* trees, fetch water, collect wood from the jungle, and then a salt less dish could be prepared from them. The entire household rejoiced when the efforts of these people succeeded in providing a square meal for the inmates of the *jamat khanqah*...If any single place in medieval India could help us study the reactions of sensitive souls to the social and economic conditions then prevailing in the country, it was the *jamat khanqah* of the Chishti saints. Here came people disgusted, morose, and frustrated; with their personalities torn by inner conflicts and their hearts bleeding at the atrocities of the external world...The Chishti *jamat khanqah* remained open till midnight. All types of people – scholars, politicians, soldiers, Hindu *jogis*, *qalandars* – visited them...when Shaikh Mu'in-u'd-din Chishti was asked about the highest form of devotion he replied that it was nothing but helping the poor, the distressed, and the downtrodden.[47]

In Indian sufism, Baba Farid is the founder of the *khanqah* as the 'microcosm of transcendental culture', which refers to the space of communal life without being circumscribed by any boundary of worldly social relations based on caste, class or sect.[48]

Baba Farid was an intellectual saint but, as opposed to the elite scholars, he was organically linked with society, in particular the ordinary people. Fully imbued with spirituality, he appreciated the basic needs of a common human being. He understood, what can be put in Antonio Gramsci's conceptualization of an intellectual, that 'the error of the intellectual consists in believing that it is possible to know without understanding and especially without feeling and passion...that the intellectual can be an intellectual...if he is distinct and detached from the people-nation... In the absence of such a bond the relations between intellectuals and the people nation are reduced to contacts of a purely bureaucratic, formal kind; the intellectuals become a caste or a priesthood..."[49] Let us understand this facet of Baba Farid's personality with an anecdote from Muslim Nizami Dahlavi's *Tarikh-i-Faridi* as cited by Shuja Alhaq.

A certain conceited scholar of Islam used to visit Baba Farid. During his conversation with the sufi, the scholar (*maulana*) flaunted his religious erudition. Once he tried to humble Baba Farid when the latter argued that bread (*roti*) is the sixth pillar of Islam, the five pillars being the creed (*shahadah*), prayer (*salat*), alms-giving (*zakat*), fasting (*swam*) and pilgrimage (*hajj*).[50] The scholar got annoyed and, in anger, he parted with the company of Baba Farid, commenting disparagingly that the sufi was ignorant and tried to be wise and, hence, talked illogically.

After some time the scholar undertook a pilgrimage to Mecca. There he spent seven years in worship and in the performance of *hajjs*. When he was returning to Hindustan, his ship wrecked, but he succeeded in escaping on a wooden plank to an island. But there the scholar could catch sight neither of any human being nor of anything to eat. However, on the third day of his starvation he came across a man who was selling bread. The scholar revealed to him his great achievements at Mecca, and told him that if he fed him he would earn a great reward after death. But the vendor refused to provide him bread free of cost. Since the scholar had nothing to pay, the vendor eventually agreed to sell him bread in exchange for his seven *hajjs*. The scholar agreed to his proposal. Next time, the vendor sold bread to the scholar for all the prayers of his lifetime. But now the scholar had nothing to offer to the vendor so as to buy bread and to gratify his hunger. Then the vendor suggested that if the scholar could give him in writing all the rewards of his good works of the whole of his life, he would provide him with bread. The scholar agreed and got bread. In the meantime he found a ship sailing to Hindustan and he reached home. After some time, he visited Baba Farid. The sufi received him affectionately. The scholar narrated the experiences of his pilgrimage to Mecca. But during his conversation, he also said that he was still annoyed with the sufi for making bread the sixth element of Islam. Baba Farid submitted that in fact he had recently seen this written in a book. The scholar again got annoyed and demanded that the book be shown to him. Baba Farid gave him the said book. While turning its pages, the scholar suddenly found the same page on which he had signed the deed with the vendor of bread. He now fell at the feet of Baba Farid.[51]

Attitude towards State

Chishti sufis, who entered India during the middle ages, brought with them the tradition of keeping aloof from temporal authority. They completely cut themselves off from sultans, politics, government services and wealth. They shunned the idea of private property. Living in a small *kuchcha* house, a Chishti saint subsisted mostly on unsolicited charity (*futuh*). He considered fasting to be a means for expelling those desires from his self that get multiplied and lead to disillusionment. A Chishti and his *jamaat khana* were not a protégé of the ruling class. Though the Chishti *silsilah* was introduced simultaneously with the foundation of Delhi sultanate, Baba Farid and Nizamuddin Auliya were opposed to any contact with government and its allies.[52] Baba Farid was not bound by law to perform the duties concerning prayers, hospitality and alms. He maintained a large distance from the rulers and politics in the belief that (a) an association would distract him from a single-minded pursuit of his ideal which was living for the Lord alone, and (b) the whole of the income of the sultans was derived from prohibited sources.[53] Thus one of the most rebellious tendencies of the sufis of Punjab, especially the Chishtis, which made them popular among the masses, was their deliberate effort to keep aloof from the political power. Baba Farid abstained from Delhi and placed himself out of the easy access of the ruling elite, which was based in the capital of the Delhi sultanate. His disciple Nizamuddin Auliya turned the offer of the gift and land from Sultan Alauddin Khalji (r.1296-1316).[54] Seeking to establish their legitimacy both as Muslims and as Indians, Indo-Muslim rulers therefore turned to prominent sufis of this order for support and blessings.[55]

Posthumous Status

Baba Farid passed away in 1265, but his *dargah* continued to inspire devotees and others. His austere life, his charismatic power and the spiritual eminence of his immediate successors were among the important factors, which conferred popularity on his shrine.[56] It is stated that it was "really his popularity that led his sons to bury him in his khanqah against his will,[57] votaries being anticipated from Ajodhan (modern Pak Pattan) to offer prayers, invoke his blessings for the fulfillment of their desires and thereby to financially help his survivors. Since Ajodhan was situated on the merchant caravan route linking Multan with Delhi and other parts of the Delhi sultanate, the merchants, nobles and soldiers travelling from and to Delhi paid visits to the *dargah* and invoked the saint's help and blessing for success as well as safety from dacoits, illness and wild animals."[58]

After the demise of Baba Farid, the construction of the vast shrine (i.e. the sacred geographical space that was based on the Shaikh's tomb) began.[59] It had a mosque, welfare kitchen (*langar khana*) and a number of related buildings, which were raised during different times. Various places in the *dargah* complex became specific spots because they were blessed with spiritual powers. For instance, *bahishti darwaza* (door of paradise), which leads to the grave of Baba Farid, is believed to save the devotees from the fires of hell if they visit the grave while passing through it. About this charismatic 'door of paradise', C.M. Wades writes:

> There are two doors to this apartment, one to the north and one to the east. The one to the east, called the 'door of Paradise', is never opened except on the fifth day of the sacred Muharram, when numbers of pilgrims, both Hindus and Muslims, come to visit the shrine, believing that all who pass through this doorway are saved from the fire of perdition. The doorway is about two feet wide and cannot be entered without stooping, and the apartment itself is not capable of containing thirty people crowded together.

> Yet such is the care, which the saint takes of his votaries on the occasions, that no accident or loss of life has ever been known to occur. A superlative heaven is open to those who are first to enter the tomb on the day mentioned. The rush for precedence may, therefore, be better imagined than described. The crowd of pilgrims is said to be immense, and as they egress from the sacred doorway, after having rubbed their foreheads on the foot of the saint's grave, the air resounds with the shouts of Farid! Farid ![60]

The charismatic character of the *dargah* leads Richard M. Eaton to consider the shrine of Baba Farid (not the saint himself) as a significant catalyst in the conversion of the agrarian and pastoral population of the Punjab to Islam.[61] By the thirteenth century the lineal descendants of Baba Farid and his burial place became organically linked with his spiritual power (*baraka*). Eaton, therefore, identifies the institutionalization of the shrine from the view point of, first, patronage given by the Delhi court and, second, the extension of mass devotionalism into the countryside. During the late Khalji times, the governor of Dipalpur, Ghiasuddin Tughluq, who later on became the sultan, was one of the local nobles who got attracted to the spiritual power and piety of Shaikh Alauddin Mauj Darya, the grandson of Baba Farid. Ghiasuddin Tughluq would frequently visit the Shaikh at Ajodhan. On one such occasion, the Shaikh prophesied that Ghiasuddin Tughluq, his son Muhammad bin Tughluq and nephew Firuz Shah Tughluq were destined to be the rulers of Hindustan; and the prophecy proved to be true. Later on, Sultans Muhammad bin Tughluq (r. 1325-1351) conferred the city of Ajodhan on the shrine i.e. alienation of local revenues in favour of the shrine's support. Sultan Firuz Shah Tughluq (r. 1351-1388) got the tomb of Baba Farid repaired and "granted the robes of honour to his descendants and confirmed them in possession of their villages and lands."[62] Later on, the entire Mughal dynasty, believing that the blessings of Chishti Shaikhs underpinned their worldly success, vigorously patronized the order.

On entering India in 1526, Babur prayed at the shrine of the Chishti saint Shaikh Qutbuddin Bakhtiyar Kaki. In 1571 Akbar built a tomb for his father Humayun near the shrine of Shaikh Nizamuddin Auliya.[63] In the same year he began building his new capital of Fatehpur Sikri at the hospice site of Shaikh Salim Chishti. Jahangir built gates and other buildings at or near the Chishti shrine at Ajmer. That the spiritual power of the shrine had spread far and wide is evident from the fact that in the early fourteenth century the small memorial or cenotaph shrines of Baba Farid, built by the common masses, "began appearing, scattered throughout the countryside of central Punjab, and that the *baraka* and authority of Baba Farid became physically established over the land in much the same way that political/administrative authority was."[64] H.A. Rose provides us with the list of known Chishtis and their shrines situated in the Punjab at the towns such as Delhi, Karnal, Panipat, Ambala, Thanesar, Pak Pattan, Lahore, Jalandhar and other places.[65]

NOTES AND REFERENCES

1. Ganda Singh, 'Baba Farid – A Real Saint' in Attar Singh, ed., *Socio-Cultural Impact of Islam on India*, Publication Bureau Panjab University, Chandigarh, 1976, p. 16. For detail see Khaliq Ahmad Nizami, *The Life and Times of Shaikh Farid-ud-Din Ganj-i-Shakar*, Idarah-i-Adabiyat-i-Delli, Delhi, Reprint 1973, (first published in 1955), pp. 10-18.
2. Ibid., pp. 16-17.
3. Ibid., p. 22.
4. Sant Singh Sekhon, *A History of Panjabi Literature*, Punjabi University, Patiala, 1993, Vol. I, p. 16.
5. Khaliq Ahmad Nizami, *The Life and Times of Shaikh Farid-ud-Din Ganj-i-Shakar*, p. 33. 'The *majzub* or ecstatic element predominated in Qutbuddin Bakhtiyar Kaki to such an extent that he expired at an early age while listening to a verse sung in *sama*. In the sufi tradition, he became a martyr to love since he had offered his life as selflessly on behalf of his faith as had the early warriors of Islam.' Bruce B. Lawrence, *Notes from a Distant Flute: The Extant Literature of Pre-Mughal Indian Sufism*, Imperial Iranian Academy of Philosophy, Tehran, 1978, p. 22.
6. N.R. Farooqi, 'The Early Chishti Sufis of India: An Outline of Their Thought and an Account of the Popular Appeal of Their Shrines, ' *Islamic Culture*, Vol. LXXVII, No. I, January, 2003.
7. Mohan Singh, *A History of Panjabi Literature*, Kasturi Lal & Sons, Amritsar, Second Edition, 1956, p. 21.
8. Najm Hosain Syed, *Recurrent Patterns in Punjabi Poetry*, City Press, Karachi, Revised Edition 2003, (first published in 1968), pp. 35-39.
9. Darshan Singh Maini, *Studies in Punjabi Poetry*, Vikas Publishing House, New Delhi, 1979, p. 12.
10. Fot the socio-cultural contribution of the Chishti sufis, see Khaliq Ahmad Nizami, *Religion and Politics in India During the Thirteenth Century*, Oxford University Press, New Delhi, 2002, pp. 246-280. Professor Gibb is of the view that from the thirteenth century "sufism increasingly attracted the creative social and intellectual energies within the community to become the bearer or instrument of a social and cultural revolution." 'An Interpretation of Islamic History', *Journal of World History*, Vol. 1, No. 1, p. 59 as cited in Khaliq Ahmad Nizami, *Religion and Politics in India during the Thirteenth Century*, p. 276.
11. B.R. Grover, 'Baba Farid – a Man of the Masses' in Gurbachan Singh Talib, ed., *Baba Sheikh Farid: Life and Teachings*, Baba Farid Memorial Society, Patiala 1973, p. 79.
12. Brij Mohan Sagar, *Hymns of Sheikh Farid*, Guru Nanak Dev University, Amritsar, 1999, *saloka*, 19, p. 90.

13. Bruce B. Lawrence, 'Islam in India: The Functions of Institutional Sufism in the Islamization of Rajasthan, Gujrat and Kashmir', in Richard C. Martin, ed., *Contributions to Asian Studies: Islam in Local Context*, Leiden, Vol. 17, 1982, p. 31.
14. Shemeem Burney Abbas, *The Female Voice in Sufi Ritual: Devotional Practices of Pakistan and India*, Oxford University Press, Karachi, 2003, p. 14.
15. See Pritam Singh, *Sri Guru Granth Sahib Waaley 'Sekh Phareed' Di Bhaal* (Gurmukhi), Singh Brothers, Amritsar, 2008, p. 87.
16. Sant Singh Sekhon, *A History of Panjabi Literature*, Vol. I, p. 6.
17. For the Gurmukhi text see Sutinder Singh Noor, Ed., *Punjabi Sufi Kav*, Sahitya Akademi, New Delhi, 1997, pp. 1-28. Shuja Alhaq has rightly remarked: "It goes to the credit of the early Chishtis in India that they recreated sufi experience of divine reality in the indigenous languages. Between these Farid and Amir Khusrau...are pre-eminent. Thus they began the process of indigenization, and consequently, of universalization of the sufi legacy in a new socio-historical setting." Shuja Alhaq, *A Forgotten Vision: A Study of Human Spirituality in the Light of the Islamic Tradition*, Vikas Publishing House, New Delhi, 1997, p. 192.
18. Gurbachan Singh Talib, 'Brief Life-Sketch of Baba Sheikh Farid' in Gurbachan Singh Talib, Ed., *Baba Sheikh Farid: Life and Teachings*, pp. 10-11.
19. Harbhajan Singh, 'Punjabi Nirguna Kaav', *Punjabi Duniya* (A Punjabi Literary Journal), June 1969, No. 6, Language Department, Patiala, pp. 90-105.
20. Brij Mohan Sagar, *Hymns of Sheikh Farid, saloka*, 34, p. 93.
21. Ibid., *saloka*, 91, p. 102.
22. Sant Singh Sekhon, *A History of Panjabi Literature*, Vol. I, pp. 24-25.
23. Brij Mohan Sagar, *Hymns of Sheikh Farid, saloka*, 61, p. 29.
24. Carl W. Ernst, *Eternal Garden: Mysticism. History, and Politics at a South Asian Sufi Center*, Oxford University Press, Delhi, 2004, (first published in 1992), p. 163.
25. Sant Singh Sekhon, *A History of Panjabi Literature*, Vol. I, p. 31.
26. Brij Mohan Sagar, *Hymns of Sheikh Farid, saloka*, 39, p. 27.
27. Ibid., *saloka*, 81, pp. 100-101.
28. Ibid., *saloka*, 35, p. 93.
29. Ibid., *saloka*, 42, p. 94.
30. Ibid., *saloka*, 6, p. 88.
31. Ibid., *saloka*, 17, p. 90.
32. The English translation of these names is given in Carl W. Ernst, *The Shambhala Guide to Sufism*, Rupa & Co., New Delhi, 2000, pp. 82-84.
33. Brij Mohan Sagar, *Hymns of Sheikh Farid, saloka*, 71, p. 99.
34. Ibid., *saloka*, 72, p. 99.
35. The age of darkness was dark both for the Hindus and the Muslims. About the Hindus, Guru Nanak says: "Though men commit countless thefts, countless adulteries, utter countless falsehoods and countless words of abuse;/ Though they commit countless robberies and villainies night and day against their fellow creature; / yet the cotton thread is spun, and the Brahman cometh to twist it. / For the ceremony they kill a goat and cook

and eat it and everybody then saith, 'Put on the janeu.' The corrosive process was at work in the Muslim society as well, and Guru Nanak invited its attention to the essentials of the faith, which it professed. To be a Musalman, says Nanak, is not easy: "Make your mosque the abode of kindness / in it spread the prayer-mat of faith, / and as you read the Koran, think of what is just and what is lawful. / Let modesty be your circumcision – your pledge to God. / Thus will you be a good Musalman. / Let righteous conduct be your Kaba, / And truth your spiritual guide. / Let deeds of piety and prayer be your creed / and what is pleasing to the Lord your rosary of beads." As quoted in Anil Chandra Banerjee, *Guru Nanak and His Times*, Punjabi University, Patiala, 1971, pp. 80-81.

36. Bulleh Shah says: "In the fold of my cloak hides the beloved Thief, / To whom shall I complain? / Stealthily He escaped, / And a tumult arose in the world. / The Muslims are averse to being cremated; / The Hindus are loath to be buried. / Both die quarreling over this wrangle. / Such is the cause of enmity between them! / Somewhere He is Ram Das, somewhere Fateh Mohammed, / This indeed is the ancient uproar! / This quarrel came to an end, / When someone else made His appearance." J.R. Puri and T.R. Shangari, *Bulleh Shah: The Love-intoxicated Iconoclast*, Radha Soami Satsang, Beas, 1986, p. 402-403.
37. Brij Mohan Sagar, *Hymns of Sheikh Farid, saloka*, 50, p. 95.
38. Ibid., *saloka*, 33, p. 26.
39. Sant Singh Sekhon, *The Love of Hir and Ranjha*, Punjab Agriculture University, Ludhiana, 1978, p. 15.
40. For detail see K.A. Nizami, *The Life and Times of Shaikh Farid-ud-Din Ganj-i-Shakar*, pp. 36-45.
41. Alexander Cunningham, *The Ancient Geography of India*, Indological Book House, Varanasi, 1963, p. 184.
42. Khaliq Ahmad Nizami, *The Life and Times of Shaikh Farid-ud-Din Ganj-i-Shakar*, pp. 46-48.
43. Ibid. Also see Nisar Ahmed Faruqui, 'Baba Farid and the Depressed Class' in Gurbachan Singh Talib, Ed., *Baba Sheikh Farid: Life and Teachings*, pp. 52-57.
44. A.A.K. Soze, 'Sheikh Farid, the Missionary of Islam' in Gurbachan Singh Talib, op. cit., p. 32.
45. Qamar-ud-Din, 'Baba Farid: The Harbinger of Hindu-Muslim Unity' in Gurbachan Singh Talib, op. cit., p. 29.
46. Cunningham states, "the ancient town of Ajudhan [Ajodhan] is situated on the high bank of the old Satluj, 28 miles to the south-west of Dipalpur (Dipalpur)...Its foundation is assigned to a Hindu saint or raja, of the same name, of whom nothing else is recorded...For many centuries Ajudhan was the principal ferry on the Satluj. Here met the two great western roads from Dera Ghazi Khan and Dera Ismail Khan; the first via Mankera, Shorkot, and Harapa; the second via Multan. At this point the great conquerors Mahmud and Timur, and the great traveller Ibn Battuta, crossed the Satluj. The fort is said to have been captured by Sabuktugin in A.D. 977-78, during his plundering expeditions in Punjab; and again by Ibrahim

Ghaznavi in A.D. 1079-80...But as the old name of Ajudhan is the only one noted by Ibn Battuta in A.D.1334, and by Timur's historian in A.D. 1397, it seems probable that the present name of Pak Pattan is of comparatively recent date. It is, perhaps, not older than the reign of Akbar, when the saint's descendant, Nur-ud-din, revived the former reputation of the family by the success of his prayers for an heir to the throne". Alexander Cunningham, *Ancient Geography of India*, pp. 180-184.

47. Khaliq Ahmad, *Religion and Politics in India During the Thirteenth Century*, pp. 221, 225, 228 and 252.
48. Shuja Alhaq, *A Forgotten Vision: A Study of Human Spirituality in the Light of the Islamic Tradition*, Vol. II, p. 178.
49. As quoted in James Joll, *Gramsci*, Fontana, Glasgow, 1977, p. 101.
50. These five pillars of Islam have been explained in John Baldock, *The Essence of Sufism*, Arcturus, London, 2006, pp. 50-57.
51. Shuja Alhaq, *A Forgotten Vision: A Study of Human Spirituality in the Light of the Islamic Tradition* Vol. 2, pp. 180-182.
52. For the critique of the relation of sufis with the state, see Kunwar Mohammed Ashraf, *Indian Historiography and other Related Essays*, Eng. Tr., Jaweed Ashraf, Sunrise Publications, New Delhi, 2006, pp. 88-92.
53. Khaliq Ahmad Nizami, *Religion and Politics in India during the Thirteenth Century*, pp. 214, 216, 255-57.
54. A similar tendency of 'dissent' was prevalent among the 'Sikh' Gurus. When the Emperor Akbar wished to see Guru Amar Das at Goindwal, he was asked to dine in *Guru ka langar* in congregation (*pangat*) before seeing the Guru. The Emperor willingly agreed. After having taken meal and seen the Guru, Akbar offered a few villages revenue free for the support of the *langar*. The Guru declined the offer, saying that *langar* depended solely on the offerings of the Sikhs.
55. Richard M. Eaton, *The Rise of Islam and the Bengal Frontier, 1204-1760*, University of California Press, Berkeley, 1996, p. 84.
56. For detail see Iqtidar Husain Siddiqui, 'The Early Chishti Dargahs' in Christian W. Troll, Ed., *Muslim Shrines in India: Their Character, History and Significance*, Oxford University Press, Delhi, 2003, pp. 1-23.
57. Amir Khurd narrates a story about the saint burial. At the time of Farid's demise, one of his sons, Nizamuddin, was living at Patiali. He saw his father in a dream and rushed to Ajodhan. When he reached the gate of the town, it was sunset and the gate had already been closed. Nizamuddin, therefore, spent the night in an inn outside the town gate. Next morning when he entered the town, he saw the funeral of his father being brought out of the house for burial in a graveyard outside Ajodhan. Nizamuddin with a worldly wisdom shrewdly disagreed with his brothers, and dissuaded them from burying the departed Farid in the graveyard. He argued that if the Shaikh (Farid) was buried outside the town in the graveyard, people would go there, pray at the tomb and depart. In such a situation, he further asked that who would take care of Farid's family. The advice of Nizamuddin was readily accepted and the funeral was brought back to the house and the body of Baba Farid was buried at the place where

his tomb stands now. There was nothing in the house to purchase the shroud. Amir Khurd's grandmother gave a white sheet to cover his coffin and the door of his house was pulled down to provide unbaked bricks for the grave. Ahmad Nabi Khan, 'The Tomb of Baba Farid Ganj-i-Shakar at Pakpatan', *Journal of the Pakistan Historical Society*, Vol. XXVII, April 1979, Part II, pp, 143-144.

58. Iqtidar Husain Siddiqui, 'The Early Chishti Dargahs', p. 14.
59. Baba Farid passed away as he had lived without worldly means. "The man whose offer of constructing a *pucca* house for the Shaikh was refused by Baba Farid, built a dome over his grave. This tomb was later repaired by Firuz Shah Tughluq". Khaliq Ahmad Nizami, *The Life and Times of Shaikh Farid-ud-Din Ganj-i-Shakar*, p. 58.
60. *Journal of the Asiatic Society of Bengal*, March 1837, p. 192 as quoted in Iqtidar Husain Siddiqui, 'The Early Chishti Dargahs', p. 16.
61. Despite his popularity, Baba Farid did not *convert* the non-Muslims to Islam, though various sources like *Jawahir-I Faridi*, Rose's *Glossary* and oral tradition speak of the fourteen clans such as Bhan, Chhina, Dhudhi, Dogar, Gondal, Gondaal, Hans, Joiya, Khokhar, Siyal, Tiwana, Wattu, Kharral and Arain as converted by Baba Farid. It is also premised that conversion of non-Muslims to Islam was not a function of early sufis of Chishti order, including Baba Farid. (See, Mohammad Habib, 'Shaikh Nasirudin Mahmud Chiragh-i-Delhi as a Great Historical Personality', *Islamic Culture*, April 1946.). Eaton argues that Shaikh Farid was not personally instrumental in the conversion of pastoral clans, owing to a short stay of sixteen or twenty four years at Ajudhan. But his shrine, which was believed to have assimilated Shaikh Farid's spiritual power (*baraka*) through the line of successive *diwans*, had a much longer life spread across centuries. While reconstructing the story of their conversion to Islam, the clans recalled the name of Shaikh Farid and not any of his successors. Richard M. Eaton, *Essays on Islam and Indian History*, Oxford University Press, Delhi, 2000, p. 216.
62. Ibid., pp. 207-209. Also see Ahmad Nabi Khan, 'The Tomb of Baba Farid Ganj-i-Shakar at Pakpatan', *Journal of the Pakistan Historical Society*, April 1979, Vol. XXVII, Part II.
63. Richard M. Eaton, *Essays on Islam and Indian History*, pp. 101-103.
64. Ibid., p. 210.
65. H.A. Rose, *A Glossary of the Tribes and Castes of the Punjab and North-West Frontier Province*, Vol. I, Language Department, Patiala, Reprint, 1970, p. 580-81.

10

Authenticity of Malfuz Literature

A Case Study of the Rahat-ul-Qulub

S.M. Azizuddin Husain

The establishment and consolidation of the Delhi sultanate, which occurred during the thirteenth and fourteenth centuries, brought fundamental changes in the history of north-western India. These changes were visible in all aspects of human life – political, social and cultural. On the one hand, the process of military expansion was accompanied by the efforts to systematize the collection of land revenue. On the other hand, two principal mystic orders, Chishtis and Suhrawardis, carved out their spiritual domains (*vilayats*) in the region. The prominent sufi saints, who belonged to these orders, established themselves in the cities of Multan, Delhi and Ajmer. With the passage of time, their successors (*khalifas*) began to settle in the smaller towns of Ajodhan, Hansi, Panipat, Narnaul, Nagaur, Kol, Jalali and Amroha. At all these places, the sufis established their convents (*khanqahs*) in order to propagate Islamic mysticism (*tasawwuf*) and to guide young aspirants on the spiritual path. Day after day, the spiritually accomplished masters expounded their ideas in the presence of small congregations, which comprised both the formally enrolled disciples (*murids*) and the uninitiated commoners. The disciples, who had decided to emulate their preceptors (*pirs* or *murshids*) in dedicating their lives to mysticism, realized the crucial importance of these discourses or conversations. They began to record the spoken word in a manner that the compilations (*malfuzat*) assumed the form of books. The practice gave rise to a new genre in Persian literature, which stood in sharp contrast to the court-centric political chronicles. Here, we may mention some of them, particularly those pertaining to north-western India. It is generally held that Amir Hasan Ala Sijzi's *Fuwaid-ul-Fuad* (a compilation of the mystical discourses of Shaikh Nizamuddin Auliya) initiated the trend, though its pioneer status has often been contested. Hamid Qalandar's *Khair-ul-Majalis* recorded the conversations of Shaikh Nasiruddin Mahmud Chiragh-i-Dehli. The sayings of Syed Jalaluddin Bukhari, who was popular as Makhdum-i-Jahaniyan Jahangasht, are available in such works as *Jami-ul-Ulum*, *Khazana-i-Jalali* and *Siraj-ul-Hidaya*.

We come across considerable variations in the nature of the *malfuzat*, with reference to their form, content and style. In a few cases, the meetings are recorded in a strict chronological order and provide the exact dates on which these were held. In other cases, the meetings are numbered but the dates are ignored. In still others, the discussions are arranged in accordance with the religious and mystical themes. The descriptions of the meetings are vivid and interesting in some, while they tend to be verbose and dull in others. Some contain a large dose of miraculous stories, while others are interspersed with poetic verses. Whatever be the character of the *malfuzat*, it is certain that they were successfully employed in the sufi circles for the purpose of teaching and learning. For the modern researcher, they are more useful than the biographical dictionaries (*tazkiras*) and normative texts in reconstructing the history of different sufi orders. Besides the phenomenon of sufism, they enable us to uncover the socio-cultural aspects of the medieval Indian society.[1] Underlining their immense significance, Nizami writes, "In fact, through these records of conversations we can have a glimpse of the medieval society in all its fullness, if not in all its perfection – the moods and tensions of the common man, the inner yearnings of his soul, the religious thought at its higher and lower levels, the popular customs and manners and above all the problems of the people. If our history is to be something more than a mere record of political events and governmental changes, the *malfuz* literature of medieval India will have to be utilized both as a corrective of the impressions created by the court chronicles and as a source of information for the religious, cultural and literary movements of the period."[2]

Shaikh Farid (1175-1265) played a major role in the consolidation and expansion of the Chishti order in Punjab. Having established himself at Ajodhan (Pakpattan), he began to propagate the theory and practice of mysticism in accordance with the Chishti mystic ideals as well the fundamentals prescribed in *Awarif-ul-Maarif*. He also chalked the principles on which his convent (*jamaat khana*) was run, particularly with reference to the intake of unasked charity (*futuh*) and its distribution among the needy. He developed the methods and curriculum for the training of disciples and earned the credit for producing such a distinguished disciple as Nizamuddin Auliya. Having distanced himself from the contemporary rulers, he refused to accept land grants or financial assistance from the state sources.[3] But he made a conscious attempt to reach out to the people of west Punjab by composing devotional verses in the local language i.e. western Punjabi. What is equally important, his mystical discourses are available in the form of two Persian works, *Rahat-ul-Qulub* and *Asrar-ul-Auliya*, which were compiled by Nizamuddin Auliya and Badruddin Ishaq respectively. These works are a valuable source for reconstructing the early history of the Chishti order in north-western India. In this paper, an attempt is being made to re-examine the question of the authenticity of *Rahat-ul-Qulub*.

The Issue of Fabrication

In an article published in 1950, Mohammad Habib dismissed as many as ten mystic works as fabrications, which have been popularly attributed to prominent Chishti masters. He puts forward three arguments for this judgement, which are applicable to all the works in a general sense. Habib follows it up by analyzing the content of each work, with the aim of substantiating his judgement. First, we would take a look at the three arguments that go to show that several Chishti works were not genuine. Firstly, the fabricated literature of the Chishti order inculcates mystic principles that are at variance with what Nizamuddin Auliya and Nasiruddin Mahmud had expounded in their discourses recorded in the *Fuwaid-ul-Fuad* and *Khair-ul-Majalis*. Secondly, the real authors of the fabricated works commit blunders about the well known facts of Indian history, which could not have been committed by the Chishti saints to whom they are attributed. Thirdly, in addition to the internal evidence of these works, there is conclusive evidence about the fact of fabrication. Mohammad Habib argues, on the basis of specific statements in *Fuwaid-ul-Fuad* and *Khair-ul-Majalis*, that Nizamuddin Auliya had not written any book and this position was in conformity with the attitude of his Chishti predecessors. The author goes on to show that Nasiruddin Mahmud, the principal successor of Nizamuddin Auliya, expressed his surprise at the existence of manuscripts containing the conversations of the early Chishti saints (Shaikh Usman Haruni and Shaikh Qutbuddin Bakhtiyar Kaki), because these compilations did not exist in the time of his own spiritual preceptor Nizamuddin Auliya.[4] Thus, as early as the middle of the fourteenth century, the Chishti saints found themselves face to face with mystical discourses which were definitely forgeries.

Now, we would consider the factors that have enabled Mohammad Habib to dismiss *Rahat-ul-Qulub* as a spurious work. He rules out the possibility of Nizamuddin Auliya having written any book. But he admits that the saint had compiled, during the course of his stay at Ajodhan, a memoranda for purely personal use and that its manuscript was in his possession when *Fuwaid-ul-Fuad* was being compiled. But *Rahat-ul-Qulub* cannot be identified with any one of them. Also, it could not have been completed before *Fuwaid-ul-Fuad*, because it contains matter taken from the latter. The author of *Rahat-ul-Qulub* does not borrow directly from *Fuwaid-ul-Fuad*, which seems to have been out of his reach. But he borrows indirectly from it through other fabricated discourses. It also refers to works which could not have existed in the times of Nizamuddin Auliya. It contains several howlers which could not have been committed by Nizamuddin Auliya. It puts all the twenty four conversations of Shaikh Farid in the course of a single visit (1247-48) of his disciple Nizamuddin Auliya, whereas the latter paid three visits to Ajodhan during the life time of his master.[5] Having noted the above difficulties, Mohammad Habib undertakes a minute analysis of the content of *Rahat-ul-Qulub* and, after identifying several flaws, concludes that the work is a fabrication. These flaws are being mentioned below.

(i) According to *Rahat-ul-Qulub*, Shaikh Farid at the very first meeting promised Nizamuddin Auliya not only the certificate of succession (*khilafatnama*), but also the spiritual domination of Hindustan (*wilayat-i-Hindustan*). This is in sharp contrast to *Fuwaid-ul-Fuad* and *Khair-ul-Majalis* which show that Nizamuudin Auliya got this certificate during his third visit to Ajodhan and this too after proper instruction and training. (ii) The author of *Rahat-ul-Qulub* would have us believe that Nizamuddin Auliya sent a letter to Shaikh Farid, along with a quatrain paying rich tributes to his master, during the course of a visit to Hansi. But *Fuwaid-ul-Fuad* indicates that the letter and quatrain were sent by Nizamuddin Auliya from Delhi probably after his second visit to Ajodhan. (iii) The *Rahat-ul-Qulub* mentions specific dates when Nizamuddin Auliya visited the *khanqah* of Shaikh Farid, while the former was living all the time at the *khanqah*, receiving instructions from Shaikh Farid and meeting him several times in the course of the day. (iv) Shaikh Badruddin Ghaznavi and Qazi Hamiduddin Nagauri were declared to be present in 1247, whereas they had died several years before Nizamuddin Auliya reached Ajodhan. (v) The facts regarding the travels of Shaikh Farid to foreign lands, in particular his meeting with a pupil of Zu ul-Nun Misri at Badakhshan and Shaikh Shihabuddin Suhrawardi at Baghdad, were impossible. (vi) Though *Rahat-ul-Qulub* pertains to Shaikh Farid's conversations of the period 1247-48, yet it refers to the deaths of three persons – Sher Khan, Shaikh Bahauddin Zakariya and Shaikh Saifuddin Bakharzi – who died many years later. (vii) In view of the time of conversations of Shaikh Farid, he could not have been informed of the desolation of Baghdad at the hands of the Mongols. (viii) The references to the disciples of some early mystics like Khwaja Hasan Basri, Shaikh Junaid Baghdadi and Shaikh Zu ul-Nun Misri were wrong from the point of view of chronology. (ix) The retirement of four persons – Qazi Hamiduddin Nagauri, Qutbuddin Bakhtiyar Kaki, Jalaluddin Tabrezi and Badruddin Ghaznavi – for their devotion to a mosque is an invention. (xi) Owing to the predominance of miraculous element and prayer formulae in *Rahat-ul-Qulub* the image of Shaikh Farid i much different from that which emerges from *Fuwaid-ul-Fuad, Khair-ul-Majals* and *Siyar-ul-Auliy*. (xii) A number of spurious works have been mentioned in the *Rahat-ul-Qulub*.[6]

The judgement of Mohammad Habibon *Rahat-ul-Qulub* turned out to be so authoritative that the compilation was accepted as fabricated by a number of scholars, who did not undertake any independent reappraisal of its content. Khaliq Ahmad Nzami, in his influential biographical study on Shaikh Farid, as devoted an appendix to apocryphal *malfuz* literatre attributed to the saint. He rejects *Rahat-ul-Qulub*as a fabrication while essentially depending on the same set of arguments as put forward by Mohammad Habib[7] Saiyid Athar Abas Rizvi, while writing an introduction to his voluminous book on the history of Indian sufism, included *Rahat-ul-Qulub* in a list of seven fabricated works. He observes, "To cater for the spiritual curiosity of gullible admirers, the spurious *malfuzat* of the great Indian Chishtis were embroidered by anonymous authors who were bereft of either a feeling for history or a first hand knowledge of the lives of their heroes."[8] Regarding it safe to toe the same line, J.S. Grewal sttes, "These form of indigenous Indian literature were so popular that a whole range of literature was fabricated in the name of well known sufis."[9] Bruce B. Lawrece, while treating *Rahat-ul-Qulub*as one of the fabricated works, explores the circumstances in which such writings emerged. He writes, "The conscious decision on the part of Indian Chishtis not t write had a predictable consequence. The dearth of writings by or about these saints stood in such glaring contrast to their spiritual achievements and the legends which soon developed about them that credulous followers, seeking 'more' information to bolster their lively faith, found it in spurious works. Pious forgeries are hardly unique to the early Chishti silsilah; wherever saints have flourished bogus works have sprung up in the fertile soil of saint-worship. But the Chishti forgeries exhibit two recurrent characteristics: (1) They came into existence at an early date, probably in response to *Fawaid-ul-Fuad*, which they awkwardly imitate, and (2) though spurious *diwans* and *awrad* collections appear at random, the fraudulent *malfuzat* are sequential and 'complete' in their patterning."[10]

In a more recent study, Carl W. Ernst treats *Rahat-ul-Qulub* as one of the six spurious *malfuzat* along with *Anis-ul-Arwah, Dalil-ul-Arifin,*

Fawaid-ul-Salikin, Asrar-ul-Auliya and *Afzal-ul-Fawaid*. He puts forth the major characteristics of these works, while comparing them with the genuine discourses of Nizamuddin Auliya entitled *Fawaid-ul-Fuad*. In his understanding the spurious works lack the personal touch that made *Fawaid-ul-Fuad* such an effective presentation of the teachings of Nizamuddin Auliya. The false *malfuzat* focus on establishing the authority of the Chishti masters at all costs, even by making assertions that are factually impossible. The genuine *malfuzat* contain lively conversations, while the audiences in fabricated works are silent witnesses to monologues of saints. The spurious *malfuzat* are characterized by a profusion of exaggerated miracles designed to enhance the saint's prestige as well as an extreme fascination with chants (*aurad*). They occupy a secondary status in mystic literature, having plagiarized at length from *Fawaid-ul-Fuad*. They offer a simplistic reconstruction of the early history of the Chishti order. "The stress on presenting the unbroken initiatic line of the early Chishtis may have been due to anxiety about the dispersal of the Chishti order after the death of Nizamuddin in 1325. The primary concern of these texts is to establish the mere fact of spiritual authority rather than to convey the teachings upon which that authority rested."[11]

Authenticity of the Text

So far, we have examined the views of scholars who have treated *Rahat-ul-Qulub* as one of the spurious works that have emanated from the Chishti order. Now we would consider the evidence which leads us to accept *Rahat-ul-Qulub* as a genuine text i.e. a collection of the mystical discourses of Shaikh Farid which were compiled by his most distinguished disciple Nizamuddin Auliya. The latter has categorically stated and this has been duly recorded in *Fawaid-ul-Fuad* by Amir Hasan Ala Sijzi:[12]

> *Kalmat-i keh az shaikh istimah dashtam ba-*
> *nawishtam ta een ghayat aan majmua bar man ast*

> I have recorded whatever I heard from my Shaikh and this collection is in my possession.

On another occasion, Nizamuddin Auliya stated:[13]

> *Ham dar aan ayyam marde ra kaghazha-i-safed dad yak ja karda man aan ra bastam fawaid shaikh ham dar aan sibat kardam*

> During those days one person gave me white papers which were bound in the form of a book. I accepted these and recorded the discourses of the shaikh (Fariduddin Ganj-i-Shakar) in it.

The above two statements, when read in conjunction with each other, clearly establish the fact that Nizamuddin Auliya had already compiled the discourses of his mentor Shaikh Farid and that this volume was in his possession when the compilation of *Fawaid-ul-Fuad* was underway. It is true that Nizamuddin Auliya did not mention the title of the manuscript. It is quite possible that he had not decided, at that particular point of time, to bring the work to the notice of his contemporaries and, therefore, did not feel the need to frame a title for the same. Mohammad Habib recognizes the existence of this volume, but he refers to it as "a memoranda for personal use, which Nizamuddin Auliya said that he had compiled at Ajodhan and the manuscript of which was with him when the *Fawaid-ul-Fuad* was being written." Mohammad Habib is not willing to accept "a memoranda for personal use" as the complete manuscript of *Rahat-ul-Qulub*. Of course, he wonders at the fate of this volume and speculates that Amir Khurd did not find it among the papers of Nizamuddin Auliya and, therefore, could not quote from it while writing his history of the Chishti order entitled *Siyar-ul-Auliya*.[14] It is quite intriguing that Mohammad Habib, who was thoroughly familiar with *Fawaid-ul-Fuad*, should have ignored the above mentioned statements which prove that Nizamuddin Auliya had compiled the conversations of Shaikh Farid and that the volume was also in the possession of the Chishti saint of Delhi. In order to deny the authenticity of *Rahat-ul-Qulub*, Mohammad Habib relies on another statement of Nizamuddin Auliya which has been recorded in *Fawaid-ul-Fuad*. According to this statement, he is reported to have said, "A friend was present. He said, 'A man showed me a book in Awadh and said it was written by you.' Nizamuddin Auliya replied, "He spoke wrongly. I have not written any book."[15]

Tafawat gufta ast man hech kitabe na nawishta am

The above statement does not mean that Nizamuddin Auliya had not written any book. Our argument rests on the distinction between two words – author (*musannif*) and editor (*murattib*). Nizamuddin Auliya must be referred to as the compiler, and not the author, of the discourses of Shaikh Farid. In the same manner, Amir Hasan Ala Sijzi cannot be designated as the author of *Fawaid-ul-Fuad*, because he was merely its compiler. It is possible to offer several such examples. Inayatullah Khan and Hamiduddin Khan compiled the orders of Aurangzeb in a volume which was given the title of *Ahkam-i-Alamgiri*. They have continued to be treated as compilers of this work and, therefore, have not been recognized as its authors. Reverting to our own subject, it is perfectly understandable for Nizamuddin Auliya to admit that he had not written any book. While making this admission, the Chishti saint did not deny that he had compiled the discourses of his mentor Shaikh Farid. Therefore, we do not see any contradiction in the various statements of Nizamuddin Auliya which pertain to his compilation of Shaikh Farid's conversations and which have been recorded in *Fawaid-ul-Fuad*.

Mohammad Habib recognizes two works (other than *Fawaid-ul-Fuad*) which were associated with Nizamuddin Auliya viz. (i) a treatise falsely attributed to him which a visitor had seen at Awadh and (ii) a memoranda for purely personal use which he had compiled at Ajodhan and which was in his possession when *Fawaid-ul-Fuad* was being compiled. Mohammad Habib is emphatic that *Rahat-ul-Qulub* cannot be identified with any one of these two works. That his stance suffers from a contradiction is indicated by his own observation, "It (*Rahat-ul-Qulub*) could not have been completed before the *Fawaid-ul-Fuad*, for it contains matter taken from the *Fawaid-ul-Fuad*; the author (of *Rahat-ul-Qulub*) however does not borrow directly from the *Fawaid-ul-Fuad*, which seems to have been out of his reach, but indirectly through the other fabricated *malfuzat*."[16] As is clear from this statement, Mohammad Habib accepts the existence of the discourses of Shaikh Farid which had been compiled by his principal disciple Nizamuddin Auliya during his sojourn at Ajodhan. The problem is that Mohammad Habib insists on designating this work as 'a memoranda for personal use' and not as *Rahat-ul-Qulub* which, according to him, was completed only after the compilation of *Fawaid-ul-Fuad* and which assimilated the content of *Fawaid-ul-Fuad* from other fabricated *malfuzat*. Having assumed this stance, Mohammad Habib is still conscious of the existence of Nizamuddin Auliya's personal memoranda, but fails to make any guess regarding its ultimate fate. In these circumstances, we feel that Mohammad Habib should have investigated the journey of this so-called personal memoranda, before declaring *Rahat-ul-Qulub* as a fabrication.

There is another flaw in Mohammad Habib's verdict on *Rahat-ul-Qulub*. He bases himself on the plea that Amir Khurd, the author of *Siyar-ul-Auliya*, did not find Nizamuddin Auliya's personal memoranda from the Shaikh's papers and, therefore, he does not quote from it on any occasion. In response to this, our argument is: Do we have the means to know if Amir Khurd made any attempt whatsoever to search or retrieve the work in question. Further, if Amir Khurd fails to quote from *Rahat-ul-Qulub* in his history of the Chishti order, it does not lead us to the conclusion that *Rahat-ul-Qulub* did not exist at that juncture. We have several cases from medieval times, where historians have either failed to mention the existing sources or have failed to quote from them. Let us take the example of Kewal Ram, who compiled *Tazkira-ul-Umara* which contains biographical notes on the Mughal nobles. In his bibliography, Kewal Ram names several Persian sources, but he does not mention two major works – Shaikh Farid Bhakkari's *Zakhirat-ul-Khwanin* and Shah Nawaz Khan's *Maasir-ul-Umara* – which are encyclopaedic dictionaries of the Mughal nobility. Are we entitled to treat these two works as spurious, just because Kewal Ram fails to include them in his bibliography. Even today, we come across instances where scholars do not quote the opinions of other writers just to avoid them. Reverting to our main argument, it is crucial to note that Amir Khurd has himself stated, "Some of the *malfuzat* of Shaikh Shaikh-ul-Alam Farid-ul-Haq wa al-Din were compiled by Shaikh-ul-Mashaikh (Nizamuddin Auliya) with his own pen."[17] This statement conclusively proves that the mystical discourses of Shaikh Farid had been compiled by Nizamuddin Auliya and that too with his own hands. It is surprising that Mohammad Habib has overlooked this evidence, which is crucial to the theme under discussion. It is equally surprising that a number of scholars, who have encountered the so-called spurious Chishti works, have failed to identify this glaring flaw in Mohammad Habib's position.

Presence of the Text in Other Sources

It is interesting to note that *Rahat-ul-Qulub* has been mentioned in a number of works, which have appeared from the first half of the fourteenth century onwards. We may start with *Shamail-ul-Atqiya*, which was written by Ruknuddin Dabir Kashani who was a disciple of Burhanuddin Gharib (d.1337). According to a major history of the Chishti order *Siyar-ul-Auliya*, Burhanuddin Gharib was one of the most intimate disciples of Nizamuddin Auliya, who captivated others by his mystical pursuits and who was devoted to devotional singing (*sama*) as well as a distinctive style of dance.[18] Even after shifting to the Deccan, he appears to have maintained contact with the Chishti leadership at Delhi. He was held in such high esteem by Nasiruddin Mahmud Chiragh-i-Dehli that the latter observed his death anniversary (*urs*) every year. It was under Burhanuddin Gharib's close supervision that a promising and learned disciple Ruknuddin Dabir Kashani wrote *Shamail-ul-Atqiya*. The *Rahat-ul-Qulub* figures in the bibliography of this treatise, which is a proof of its being a genuine work. It has already been argued that the author would not have made it a part of the bibliography if it were a fabricated text.[19] It may be suggested that Kashani had acquired familiarity with the early north Indian Chishti traditions, owing to his close association with Burhanuddin Gharib.

Having said that, it would be appropriate to examine the content of *Shamail-ul-Atqiya*, as brought to the fore by Carl W. Ernst. The text under reference is one of the four major *malfuzat* that emanated from the circle of Burhanuddin Gharib in the Deccan. This monumental treatise is encyclopaedic in its scope. It is an enormous collection of excerpts from sufi writings and oral traditions, including a full range of topics on theory and practice of mysticism. The first section, consisting of fifty two chapters, is devoted to Islamic rituals. The second section focuses on theology and anthropology. The work develops the Chishti *malfuzat* tradition by incorporating many of Burhanuddin Gharib's oral teachings. More important for our purpose is the preface, which comprises a bibliography of over 250 classical authorities on sufism and religion. This bibliography enumerates 75 works on Islamic religious sciences, 125 books on sufism and 50 sources of oral traditions. A number of these works are no longer extant, though quotations from them are available in the treatise. The bibliography, which can be called an ordered catalogue of texts rather than a closed canon, becomes essentially open ended owing to the inclusion of oral sources. "The Chishti *malfuzat*, which straddle the boundary between text and speech, are prominently featured in the catalogue."[20] We are indebted to Carl W. Ernst for providing this catalogue as Appendix A - A Sufi Bookshelf: The Bibliography of Ruknuddin Dabir Kashani. Under its Section VIII entitled 'Great Books of the Science of the Path and Reality from the Writings and Works of the Masters Possessing Saintship and the Saints Possessing Saintship,' it lists *Rahat-ul-Qulub* at serial number 105 as the *malfuzat* of Fariduddin Ajodhani (d.664/1265), but does not give the name of its compiler.[21]

Maulana Muhammad Mujeer Wajih, who was a scholarly disciple of Nasiruddin Mahmud Chiragh-i-Dehli, wrote a book entitled *Mifati-ul-Jinan* around 756 AH/1355 AD. This book was vetted by another scholar named Khwaja Kamaluddin. It contains several discourses which are available in *Rahat-ul-Qulub*, but are not found in any other work. Shaikh Abdul Haq Muhaddis Dehalvi, one of the most eminent scholars of the reign of Akbar, writes in his famous treatise on mystics *Akhbar-ul-Akhyar*, "Some of the *malfuzat* of Ganj-i-Shakar were compiled by Nizamuddin Auliya." Shah Muhammad Bulaq, who was associated with the shrine of Nizamuddin Auliya, wrote (1619) a biography of the famous Chishti saint which was entitled *Matlub-ul-Talibeen*. In this work, he has made frequent references to *Rahat-ul-Qulub*. He categorically states, "In his book *Rahat-ul-Qulub*, the Sultan-ul-Mashaikh (Nizamuddin Auliya) has compiled, meeting after meeting, the discourses of Shaikh Fariduddin Ganj-i-Shakar." Khwaja Ghulam Farid (d.1901), a prominent Chishti mystic and a famous poet, has referred to *Rahat-ul-Qulub* in his own conversations which are available in a compilation entitled *Maqabis-i-Majalis*. Thus, we see that from the early fourteenth century onwards, scholars have frequently and repeatedly referred to *Rahat-ul-Qulub*. But none of them has ever raised any doubt regarding its authenticity.[22] This fact is extremely significant in the context of the present argument.

It is interesting to note that scholars, who regard several *malfuzat* as spurious and as replete with cheap mystic ideas, have come to realize that even these possess some historical value and, therefore, need not be rejected outright. For example, Nizami observes that during the last six hundred years both historians and religious biographers, with the solitary example of Abdul Haq Muhaddis Dehalvi, have based their accounts on apocryphal literature. They illustrate the manner in which mystic ideas of the early Chishti saints were understood and interpreted by the succeeding generations. "If they do not contain the ideology of the saints, they at least contain the popular reactions to this ideology and reveal the religious thought of the period at its lower level." Nizami advises us not to construct the mystic ideology of the age on the basis of fabricated *malfuzat*. At the same time, he admits, "If carefully and critically studied in the light of the genuine mystic literature of the period, these works will show the mentality, capacity, learning and outlook of the credulous people of medieval India."[23]

The above sentiment echoes in the understanding of Ernst, who observes that the traditional Chishti circles from an early date accepted the spurious *malfuzat* as genuine and, even in the present times, the followers of the Chishti order rely primarily on these inauthentic *malfuzat* for their understanding of the early history of the Chishti order. The author argues that the inauthentic texts have retained their popularity in Urdu translation and that their authenticity has been defended by traditionally-minded scholars. What is surprising, they are more easily available than the genuine texts, like the discourses of Nasiruddin Mahmud and Burhanuddin Gharib. The most common book, which is available in Urdu translation at the shrine of Shaikh Farid in Pakpattan, contains seven inauthentic texts and only one original one. Ernst argues that the theoretical distinction between genuine and spurious *malfuzat* has been undermined by the inclusion of both categories – inauthentic and authentic – in Ruknuddin Dabir Kashani's *Shamail-ul-Atqiya*. This enables Ernst to suggest that the distinction between the genuine and false *malfuzat* is not absolute and that the distinction is significant primarily from the academic point of view. "Both kinds of texts contain extracts from sufi teaching, and both illustrate the charisma of the sufi teacher; the difference is primarily in emphasis. Ruknuddin, too, was attempting to represent the breadth of the sufi tradition in the widest possible way. His concern was not to establish rigid standards of textual authenticity but to summarize the range and depth of sufi teaching available to the Chishti masters in his day, and in his experience the literary tradition was closely tied to the oral one."[24] Since Kashani aimed at making an overall presentation of sufi teaching, he made reference to the spurious Chishti *malfuzat*, without being deterred by their anachronisms and contradictions. Kashani's inclusion of excerpts from apocryphal works goes to show that hagiographic interest in the early Chishti order had reached a fairly high level even at an early date. "In other words, concludes Ernst, "the inauthentic *malfuzat* were popular manifestations of religious sentiment among Indian Muslims attached to the Chishti order."[25]

Traditions of Shaikh Farid

One of the issues relating to *Rahat-ul-Qulub* is the chronological frame of the conversations which are recorded in it. The problem has been compounded by the fact that we encounter marked differences between the printed Persian text and its Urdu translation. According to the former, the first meeting occurred on 15 Rajab 655 AH/ 1256 AD and the last one has been placed on 2 Rabi-ul-Awwal 656 AH/1257 AD. These dates are absolutely unacceptable. It is true that Shaikh Farid was at the height of his popularity at this point of time. But this time span does not match with the stay of Nizamuddin Auliya at Ajodhan. It would be possible to solve the problem if we consider the important phases in the life of Nizamuddin Auliya. This is not an easy task, because Amir Khurd assigns to him an age of 80 years and Syed Muhammad Gesudaraz offers a figure of 75 years. If we consider the following table, which identifies some important landmarks in the life of Nizamuddin Auliya, we may be able to find an answer to this question. We find that his tutelage under Shaikh Farid extended for four years from 1266 to 1270, culminating in the grant of the certificate of succession (*khilafatnama*). It would be safe to suggest that the mystical discourses of Shaikh Farid were recorded by Nizamuddin Auliya during this period i.e. 1266 to 1270.

1. Birth 645 AH/1247 AD
2. Arrival in Delhi 661 AH/1262 AD
3. Enrolment under Shaikh Farid 665 AH/1266 AD
4. Grant of succession certificate 669 AH/1270 AD
5. Completing study of *Mashariq-ul-Anwar* 679 AH/1280 AD
6. Stay at Ghiyaspur between 680 AH/1281 AD and 686 AH/1287 AD
7. Facing the *mahzar-i-sama* 723-24 AH/ 1323-24 AD
8. Death 725 AH/1324-1325 AD

Now we would focus on some important traditions of Shaikh Farid that are recorded in *Rahat-ul-Qulub*. On Friday, second of the above said month (the year is not mentioned), Nizamuddin (Auliya) visited Shaikh Farid. Shaikh Jamaluddin Hansavi, Shaikh Badruddin Ghaznavi and some other friends were also present in the lodge (*khanqah*). Shaikh Farid discussed the importance of Roz-i-Ashura (tenth day of Muharram, the first month of the Hijri calendar). He said that on this day even the animals did not feed their cubs. On this day, Imam Husain, son of Ali and Fatima and the grandson of Prophet Muhammad, was martyred at Karbala by the army of Yazid in 680 AH. From that day, the Muslims observed first ten days of Muharram as the period of mourning. Shaikh Fariduddin said that the day Imam Husain was killed, a pious person saw Bibi Fatima, the daughter of Prophet Muhammad, in a dream. He saw that she was cleaning a piece of land and asked her why she was doing that. She replied that her son Husain would be killed on this spot. Thereafter, the Shaikh explained the meaning of prayers which were offered on Shab-i-Ashura (night of the tenth of Muharram) and Roz-i-Ashura (tenth day of Muharram).[26]

On Saturday, 4th Safar of the aforementioned year, Nizamuddin (Auliya) paid a visit to the *khanqah* of Shaikh Farid. The Shaikh asked him to sit down and he obeyed. Shaikh Burhanuddin had given him a letter, which was addressed to Shaikh Farid. The letter was handed over to Shaikh Farid who read it. Some travellers arrived from Multan and visited the *khanqah* of Shaikh Farid. They were asked to sit. Later food was served to them.[27]

Shaikh Farid related the tradition regarding the grant of patched coat (*khirqa*) to Prophet Muhammad from the court of God on the night of heavenly ascent (*shab-i-mairaj*). On returning to earth after the ascent, the Prophet informed his senior companions that he had received a patched coat from the divine source and that he would confer it on one of them, who would give a correct answer to his question. In the first instance, the Prophet called Hazrat Abu Bakr Siddiq and said, "If I give this patched coat to you, what will you do with it?" Hazrat Abu Bakr replied that he would adopt the path of truth, that he would worship the Almighty God and that he would spend all material wealth in the path of God. When the Prophet posed the same question to Hazrat Umar Faruq, he promised to dispense justice to the people and to defend the oppressed. Hazrat Usman declared that he would promote social harmony, that he would pursue the ideal of truth and that he would engage in the works of charity. Hazrat Ali declared that in case the patched coat was bestowed on him, he would assume the task of concealing the sins of God's creatures with a veil. On hearing these words, the Prophet announced, "I grant this patched coat (*khirqa*) on you, because God had directed me to grant it to my companion who gave this particular answer to my question." After relating this tradition, Shaikh Farid was so overpowered by emotion that he began to weep and then became unconscious. When he regained his consciousness, he explained the meaning of sainthood (*darveshi*). He said that sainthood was nothing but assumption of the veil, that the habit of wearing a veil was the very basis of morality and that its loss pushed a person into calamities. He also declared that a person, who adopted the veil as a part of his conduct, lived in peace and security. Therefore, a mystic was bound to understand the true principles of sainthood (*darveshi*) which could not be expressed in speech and writing. The patched coat of the mystics was associated with that apparel (*khirqa-i-mairaj*) which was acquired by the Prophet during his heavenly ascent.[28]

More often than not, mystic literature narrates encounters between sufis and Hindu ascetics, who were designated as Jogis. The *Rahat-ul-Qulub* is no exception. This is shown by the following instance which involved Shaikh Farid. We are told that an old Jogi, who was reputed for having performed hard penace (*mujahida*), visited the hospice of Shaikh Farid. The visitor placed his head at the feet of Shaikh Farid and remained in that posture for a long time. Shaikh Farid directed the Jogi to get up and asked a number of simple questions by way of courtesy – How do you do? Where have you come from? The Jogi confessed that he was unable to reply owing to fear (of the presence of the Shaikh). Shaikh Farid told Nizamuddin Auliya that the Jogi had come with the intention of making tall claims, that the Jogi unsuccessfully tried to raise his head from the ground and that he would have remained in the same posture till the day of judgement, had he not repented. Thereafter, Shaikh Farid enquired about the excellence that he had acquired. The Jogi replied that he, like others belonging to his order, possessed the power to fly in the air. In response to Shaikh Farid's request, the Jogi demonstrated his skill of flying in the air. Shaikh Farid brought the Jogi down on earth by using his spiritual power. As a consequence, the Jogi abandoned his own creed and embraced Islam.[29]

According to another episode, in which Shaikh Farid was present along with Nizamuddin Auliya, a Jogi visited the convent (*khanqah*) at Pakpattan. He was asked to expound the ideology and method of his creed. He replied that the human being was composed of two characteristics – *Alam-i-Alavi* from head to the navel and *Alam-i-Safli* from navel to the feet. Intervening in the conversation, Shaikh Farid explained, "Yes. It is just like the manner it has been defined. We may add that the former is associated with truthful living and ethical conduct, while the latter was associated with purity and abstinence." Shaikh Farid made clear that he was impressed with the Jogi's explanation.[30]

One day Badruddin Ishaq posed a question to Shaikh Farid, "What do we mean by extravagance? What is the limit of extravagance?" The Shaikh replied that whatever was spent without any sense of direction and whatever was not spent for the sake of God was extravagance. He added that whatever was spent for the sake of God was not extravagance.[31] On Saturday, 8th of the said month (the year is not mentioned), Nizamuddin (Auliya) availed the opportunity of kissing the feet of Shaikh Fariduddin Ganj-i-Shakar. In his sermon, the Shaikh laid emphasis on avoiding illegal food and keeping distance from people who were involved in worldly affairs.[32]

In a meeting (*majlis*) dated 11th Shawwal of the above mentioned year, Shaikh Farid related that Sultan Nasiruddin was present in Multan on one occasion. One day, the Sultan along with Ghiasuddin (Balban) paid a visit to the hospice (*khanqah*) and requested the Shaikh to pray for him. The Sultan submitted, "I wish to offer some villages for you and some cash for the saints (*darvesh*) of the *khanqah*. The Shaikh smiled and asked the Sultan to take back the offer because there were so many people who were eager to acquire these villages and suggested that these be assigned to them. He also declared that none of the saints (*khwajgan*) and mystics (*mashaikh*) of their order had ever accepted such offers. Thereafter tears appeared in the eyes of the Shaikh-ul-Islam (Shaikh Farid). After a pause, he explained that if he accepted the villages and cash from the Sultan, the saints would say that he (Shaikh Farid) had villages in his possession and that he was very rich.[33]

A Parallel Case

Besides *Rahat-ul-Qulub*, there is another compilation of the discourses of Shaikh Farid. Entitled *Asrar-ul-Auliya*, its compilation has been attributed to Badruddin Ishaq, the son-in-law of Shaikh Farid. Mohammad Habib's demonstrates that *Asrar-ul-Auliya* is a spurious work and, while doing so, he employs the methodology that he applied in the case of *Rahat-ul-Qulub*. We are obliged to consider his objections regarding *Asrar-ul-Auliya* and offer our own response, so that we are able conclude our discussion on *Rahat-ul-Qulub*. With regard to *Asrar-ul-Auliya*, Mohammad Habib argues that Nizamuddin Auliya and Amir Khurd do not refer to it in the *Fawaid-ul-Fuad* and *Siyar-ul-Auliya*. The given dates of the conversations (1223-24 to 1245-46) cannot be reconciled with the life spans of people who are mentioned in them. The conversations appear in the form of monologues by Shaikh Farid, while the persons present are seen as passive listeners. The work lifts sentences verbatim from *Fawaid-ul-Fuad* and repeats the errors contained in *Anis-ul-Arwah* and *Dalil-ul-Arifin*. It wrongly refers to the visits of Shaikh Farid to foreign lands viz. Baghdad, Syria, Damascus, Siwistan and Ghazni. Its description of the meetings of Shaikh Farid at Baghdad with eminent mystics – Shihabuddin Suhrawardi, Bahauddin Zakariya and Jalaluddin Tabrezi – was not based on facts. It is equally wrong to include the accounts of the meetings between Nizamuddin Auliya and

Badruddin Ghaznavi. The compiler was ignorant of contemporary political history, including the Mongol conquest of Central Asia. Its depiction of Shaikh Farid as frequently falling into fits of unconsciousness was far from evidence of sober history.[34]

There are several grounds on which it is possible to show that *Asrar-ul-Auliya* was not a spurious work as alleged by Mohammad Habib. It is true that Syed Muhammad Gesudaraz (d.1422) hints at a dispute regarding the identity of the compiler of *Asrar-ul-Auliya*. But there is no doubt that the collection of these discourses of Shaikh Farid did exist and this was available in Ajodhan. Efforts were made to deny the contribution of Badruddin Ishaq, because of the jealousy of the natural descendants of Shaikh Farid and this feeling was generated by the typical small town (*qasbati*) mentality. *Asrar-ul-Auliya* cannot be designated as fake owing to the presence of miraculous elements, because this phenomenon was common to almost all mystic works including the *Siyar-ul-Auliya*, which Mohammad Habib accepts as authentic. It was not possible for Badruddin Ishaq to consult *Fawaid-ul-Fuad*, because the former died in 1268 and the latter was compiled in 1322. If Amir Khurd was ignorant of the travels of Shaikh Farid, it does not mean that he did not travel out of Ajodhan to foreign lands. Shaikh Farid might not have met Jalaluddin Tabrezi at Kahtwal (as alleged by Mohammad Habib), but there can be no difficulty in the meeting taking place at Badaun, where Shaikh Farid went every year to meet his brother Najibuddin Mutawakkil. Mohammad Habib has wrongly quoted *Asrar-ul-Auliya* on the issue of Shaikh Farid and Shaikh Bahauddin Zakariya attending the funeral of Shaikh Saaduddin Hamviya at Baghdad, as the incident occurred long before Shaikh Farid had settled permanently at Ajodhan. Further, Badruddin Ishaq cannot be blamed for inadequate knowledge of contemporary history, because he was essentially a mystic and not a historian. It is possible that Ajodhan, being a small town as compared to Delhi, did not possess relevant books on the subject. Moreover, the education in mystic circles revolved around traditional subjects (*manqulat*) and not rational subjects (*maaqulat*).[35]

Before concluding this discussion, we would quote from *Fawaid-ul-Fuad* an episode, which has been regarded as authentic by all historians. We learn that, on a certain occasion, Shaikh Farid was teaching *Awarif-ul-Maarif* to a group of selected disciples including Nizamuddin (Auliya). It so happened that the copy of this book had not been transcribed properly and there were several errors. Shaikh Farid proceeded slowly with the lesson, because he stopped frequently to correct the errors. Nizamuddin intervened to say that Shaikh Najibuddin Mutawakkil possessed a better copy of the book. Shaikh Farid was annoyed at the remark and asked if he (Shaikh Farid) was not capable of correcting a defective manuscript. When Nizamuddin realized that he had offended his mentor, he fell at his feet and sought forgiveness for his insolent remark. Shaikh Farid did not relent and, as a result, Nizamuddin sank into a state of depression and even toyed with the idea of committing suicide. Shihabuddin (a son of Shaikh Farid who was a friend of Nizamuddin) interceded on behalf of Nizamuddin. Shaikh Farid pardoned Nizamuddin and, bestowing a special dress on him, said that his actions were aimed at the perfection of his disciple. The episode not only reflects the nature of discipleship (*piri-muridi*), but it also speaks volumes about the prevailing state of books and the quality of their transcription. It may be suggested that *Rahat-ul-Qulub* too contained errors, particularly regarding the dates, which might have crept owing to the negligence of the scribes. Even in our own times, the literary productions in Urdu and Persian suffer from inaccuracies relating to dates.

In view of the above discussion, we are entitled to conclude that the authenticity of the so-called spurious *malfuzat* is an open question. It is no longer possible to accept Mohammad Habib's verdict on the genuineness of the *malfuz* literature that emanated from the early history of the Chishti order. If we refuse to accord due attention to this body of literature, we would deprive ourselves of important sources of information and, thus, our task of reconstructing the history of the Chishtis order would be marred by imperfections. If the *malfuz* literature shows presence of inaccuracies, we do have the means to remedy the situation. The need of the time is to undertake a critical re-examination of these works and, after a suitable collation of several manuscripts, extract the factual information which can be utilized for historical reconstruction by modern scholars. What we are suggesting, in fact, is a revival of the art of preparing fresh texts of contemporary works after appropriate editing and annotation. Such a project was pursued by the Asiatic Society of Bengal under the banner of Bibliotheca Indica during the late nineteenth and early twentieth centuries. An exercise of this nature, if applied to the mystic literature, would go a long way in promoting fresh studies on sufism in South Asia.

NOTES AND REFERENCES

1. It has been suggested that even for interpreting political issues, we need to explore the mentality of men of the period as seen in religion and culture. In order to investigate this culture, it would be appropriate to place the well known Persian chronicles of the sultanate period alongside the Hindu and Muslim religious literature, which reveals a variety of ideas – religious, ethical and aesthetic – of the authors. Peter Hardy, *Historians of Medieval India: Studies in Indo-Muslim Historical Writing*, Munshiram Manoharlal, New Delhi, Reprint, 1997, p. 131.

2. Khaliq Ahmad Nizami, *On History and Historians of Medieval India*, Munshiram Manoharlal, New Delhi, 1983, p. 167.
3. For details on the life of Shaikh Farid and his contribution to the development of the Chishti order, see Khaliq Ahmad Nizami, *The Life and Times of Shaikh Fariduddin Ganj-i-Shakar*, Idarah-i-Adabiyat-i-Delli, Delhi, Reprint, 1973; Saiyid Athar Abbas Rizvi, *A History of Sufism in India*, Vol.I, Munshiram Manoharlal, New Delhi, 1978, pp.138-148; Muneera Haeri, *The Chishtis: A Living Light*, Oxford University Press, Karachi, 2000, pp. 70-108.
4. Mohammad Habib, 'Chishti Mystic Records of the Sultanate Period,' in Khaliq Ahmad Nizami, (Ed.), *Politics and Society during the Early Medieval Period: Collected Works of Professor Mohammad Habib*, Vol.I, People's Publishing House, New Delhi, 1974, pp. 401-402.
5. Ibid., pp. 417-418.
6. Ibid., 418-420.
7. Khaliq Ahmad Nizami, *The Life and Times of Shaikh Fariduddin Ganj-i-Shakar*, pp. 118-120.
8. This author does not agree with Nizami's hypothesis that the fabricated works tried to fill a vacuum in the Chishti order, which was caused by the transfer of capital by Muhammad bin Tughluq from Delhi to Daultabad. Rizvi argues that the inauthentic sufi literature had begun to appear by the time of Shaikh Nizamuddin Auliya, as the reference to his alleged work would tend to indicate. Rizvi, op. cit., p. 5.
9. J.S. Grewal, 'The Sufi Beliefs and Attitudes in India,' *Islamic Perspective*, (Special issue on Sufism and Communal Harmony), Institute of Islamic Studies, Bombay, Vol.VII, January 1991, p. 26. Surprisingly, this is the only article in the journal which is without any footnotes, references and bibliography.
10. Bruce B. Lawrence, *Notes From A Distant Flute: Sufi Literature in Pre-Mughal India*, Imperial Iranian Academy of Philosophy, Tehran, 1978, p. 35.
11. Carl W. Ernst, *Eternal Garden: Mysticism, History and Politics in A South Asian Sufi Center*, Oxford University Press, Delhi, Second Edition, 2004, p. 78.
12. Amir Hasan Ala Sijzi, *Fawaid-ul-Fuad*, Persian Text, p. 31.
13. Ibid., p. 31.
14. Mohammad Habib, op. cit., p. 417.
15. Amir Hasan Ala Sijzi, *Fawaid-ul-Fuad*, p. 45.
16. Mohammad Habib, op. cit., p. 417.
17. Amir Khurd (Syed Muhammad bin Mubarak Kirmani), *Siyar-ul-Auliya*, Persian Text, Matba Muhib-i-Hind, Delhi, 1302 AH/1885 AD, p. 47.
18. Ibid., pp. 288-289.
19. Allama Akhlaq Husain Dehalvi, *Ainah-i-Malfuzat*, Kutb Khana Anjuman Taraqqi-i-Urdu, Delhi, 1983, p. 218.
20. Carl W.Ernst, *Eternal Garden: Mysticism, History and Politics at A South Asian Sufi Center*, pp. 75-76.
21. Ibid., p. 258.
22. Allama Akhlaq Husain Dehalvi, *Ainah-i-Malfuzat*, pp. 219-222.
23. Khaliq Ahmad Nizami, *Supplement to Elliot and Dowson's Hstory of India*, Vol. II, Idarah-i-Adabiyat-i-Delli, 1981, pp. 63-64.

24. Carl W. Ernst, *Eternal Garden: Mysticism, History and Politics at A South Asian Sufi Center*, p. 79.
25. Ibid., p. 80.
26. Nizamuddin Auliya, *Rahat-ul-Qulub*, Ms, Khuda Bakhsh Oriental Public Library, Patna, ff.3b-4b.
27. Ibid., f.6b.
28. Ibid., f.15b.
29. This tradition points to the characteristics of such an eminent mystic like Shaikh Farid. On the one hand, he possessed the power to know the innermost thoughts in the minds of his visitors and, on the other hand, he possessed the ability to reform the people who were found to be misguided. Allama Akhlaq Hasan Dehalvi, *Ainah-i-Malfuzat*, pp. 265-268.
30. Ibid., pp. 269-271.
31. Nizamuddin Auliya, *Rahat-ul-Qulub*, ff.16a-b.
32. Ibid., f.21a.
33. Ibid., f.50a.
34. Mohammad Habib, op. cit., pp. 414-417.
35. S.M. Azizuddin Husain, 'Malfuzat of the Sufis of Punjab,' Presidential Address, Medieval Section, *Proceedings of the Punjab History Conference*, 38th Session, March 18-20 March 2006, Punjabi University, Patiala, pp. 116-130.

11

Female Voice in Punjabi Sufi Poetry

Its Character and Concerns

Ishwar Dayal Gaur

> "Whether or not the Sufi poets were 'feminists' cannot be claimed... as the term 'feminist' is a fairly recent one. However, the female myths in Sufi poetry certainly represent the voices of marginalized groups and continue to be used as *representative* frames even today."
>
> —*Shemeem Burney Abbas*[1]

The female voice, which resounds in the Punjabi sufi poetry and has crossed the frontiers of Indo-Pak subcontinent with the aid of audio-video technology, reveals two significant but entwined traits of a sufi: first his spiritual chivalry (*jawanmardi*) and second, his 'infidelity.' Devoid of the former, a sufi cannot be an infidel and, hence, cannot be capable of becoming a lover (*ashiq*). A sufi is infidel because he is bold enough to discard the hegemonic socio-religious norms and forms. He cannot afford to be canonical and normative in the strict theological or scholastic sense of these terms. A sufi's spiritual chivalry alludes to his non-conformist character in the sense that he breaks stagnancy and its logic/principle that helps it persist and prevail. Thus an infidel sufi belongs to the category of those mystics who remain intoxicated with the love of God (*sahiban-i-sukr*). In the state of intoxication (*sukr*), love prevails upon intellect and reason. This condition of mind erases a distinction between faith and the sense of observance of the norms of behaviour. This state of mind is "*kufr-i-tariqat* (apparent infidelity brought about by the mystic search for God), which is yet much higher stage than the externals of Islam."[2] Though 'infidelity' had been active in sufism since Mansur al-Hallaj (858-921), but it was presented as a paradigm of sufic life style by Abu Said bin Abi al-Khair (967-1049), a Khurasanian sufi, who stated:

> *Ta dar nazar-i khalq nagardi kafir*
> *Dar mazhab-i ashiqan Musalman nashawi*
>
> As long as you do not become an infidel in the eyes of the people / You won't be reckoned a believer in the sight of lovers.[3]

Similarly, Bulleh Shah (1680-1758), a prominent and popular Punjabi sufi recited:

> *Bullia aashq hoyon rabb da, hoi mulamat lakh / log kafir kafir aakhdey, / tunu aakho aakho aakh*
>
> Bullia [Bulleh Shah], you have become the lover of God, / and reaped a thousand reproaches. / They go on calling you infidel, / you keep on saying, 'Yes, I am.[4]

Introducing the theme of Female Voice

The medieval Indian *patriarchal* poets and theologians, like Amir Khusro (d. 1325), Isami (b. 1311) and Shah Waliullah (d. 1763), in their writings legitimatised the male superiority and ascendancy over all other creations, while looking down upon woman as essentially deficient in intellect.[5] Their only advice to her was to keep herself confined to domestic work, particularly the spinning wheel and needle, and to remain confined to space between the wall in front of her and the door behind her.[6] This kind of narrow space, which was allotted to a woman, enabled the patriarchs to have an excellent all-around 'visibility' so as to watch her closely. Visibility was *a trap*, which prevented her from coming into contact with others. She was 'seen', but she could not 'see'. This space under reference constituted a compact model of the patriarchal disciplinary mechanism.[7] The patriarchal discourse of 'spinning wheel', unlike that of the non-conformist sufis, tended to create passivity in woman and further fortified the boundaries of her imprisonment in the name of privacy and modesty. In other words, the spinning wheel of the 'elders' was such an instrument of the patriarchal home-prison and punishment that it would not systematically permit women to 'speak', rather made them 'silent' physically and mentally. Silence meant docility. It transformed a woman into a raw material that could be given the form desired by a patriarch. Once he had silenced her, he could do whatever he desired: turn her into maid, goddess, plaything and mother hen so on and so forth.[8] Thus when we read the Punjabi love legends of Hir-Ranjha, Sassi-Punnun and Sohni-Mahiwal, we find out in them an inherent tension between 'ought to be silent' and 'not to be silent', or between 'to domesticate' and 'not to be domesticated.' Domestication and silence are interchangeable terms in a patriarchal set up. Rachel Bowlby informs us: "in one French usage, *domestiquer* means quite simply the subjugation of a tribe to a colonizing power. To 'domesticate' is to bring the foreign or primitive or alien into line with the 'domestic' civilization and power, just as a 'domesticated' animal is one that has been tamed into home life."[9] The historic and popular example of this silence as 'required' by the patriarchs in the medieval Punjabi literature is that of Hir Siyal of Jhang (west Punjab) who is said to have lived from AD 1425 to 1452. Because of her audacious and argumentative vocality, she faced oppression and eventually met a fatal end. In the domain of Punjabi narrative poetry (*qissa*), Hir was portrayed as a proto-martyr. She ceased to be a mere 'historical' character; rather she emerged as a motif of love, non-conformism and martyrdom in the Punjabi sufi poetry. Hir haunted the literary memory of the Punjabi sufis.

Female Persona in Sufi Poetry

The present paper attempts to study the Punjabi sufi poets' preference for the female persona as the voice (mask) of their verses and, in the process, to illumine the female voice assumed by Shaikh Farid (1173-1266), Shah Husain (1539-1599) and Bulleh Shah (1680-1758).[10] Songs and poems composed in vernaculars by sufis illustrate the regional shades and varieties of Indian sufism. In their verses, the vernacular sufis did not subscribe to the patriarchal symbolic order, which *immortalized* woman as physically and mentally inferior to a masculine brain and brawn.

The female voice of the sufis of Punjab was a 'new', nay a 'revolutionary' way of conceiving or imagining themselves as female-lover of the He-Beloved. They parted with the Persian mystic tradition of perceiving God as female Beloved / Bride. To Jalaluddin Rumi (d.1273), a famous Persian mystic, the creative activity of God reveals itself best in a woman and she is not created but the creator. Similarly, Ibn-i-Arabi (1165-1240), whose life span coincides with that of Shaikh Farid, was of the view that God cannot be seen apart from matter, and He is seen more perfectly in the human *materia* than in any other, and more perfectly in woman than in man.[11] Ibn-i-Arabi transformed "the unity in erotic love between man and woman into a replica of union between God and human being."[12] For him it was the highest spiritual experience. This feminine dimension of the Reality was indeed of a revolutionary nature, as Islam has been traditionally a patriarchal religion and and as such part of the greater patriarchal religious tradion i.e. the Abrahamic tradition which has been perennially suspicious of woman, often associating her with 'the Devil itself'.[13]

However, the Punjabi sufi poets followed the Indic tradition of longing for God in the image of a bridegroom. According to the Indic ideals of marriage, a husband is the representative of divine power.

The Indic mystic tradition describes the soul as the longing maiden, a loving bride or a faithful wife. Sociologically and culturally, in India the man-woman relationship is perceived in two forms, classical and romantic. The former projects man and woman in the relationship of husband and wife, while the latter situates this relationship in the cultural domain of love. This kind of erotic relationship finds it difficult to adjust itself in the social frame of the husband-wife relationship.[14] This is the reason that in the themes of Indian poetry and literature, the classical form (i.e. man and woman as husband and wife) has been more universally accepted; and in accordance "with the make-up of the Indian mind the lover in Indian folklore and literature has been the woman."[15]

Thus the medieval Punjabi sufi poetry was an avant-garde literary movement that brought about the marginalized female voice to the forefront. Apart from these sufis who directly impersonated the role of a female, the Punjabi poet narrators (*qissa-kars*) like Waris Shah, Ahmad Gujjar, Mukbal, Hashim and others made her speak against the patriarchal socio-religious customs and conventions. The female, as portrayed in the love-legends, directly confronts the advocates of patriarchy. These legends are fully soaked in the sufic ambience of love, beauty and boldness. The Punjabi sufi poets and *qissa-kars* also amplified the female voice by introducing the *jogi* (or *yogi*), *bhakti* and *pir* traditions, which together constitute the theme of non-conformism in the history of medieval Punjabi culture and literature. In the verses of the sufi poets and the *qissa-kars*, we meet, for example, Balnath jogi, Panj Pirs[16] and Lord Krishna or Sham (the Black Krishna)[17] as the signifiers of non-conformism and eroticism. These non-conformist 'icons' enabled the sufi poets to legitimatize the rebellious female voice and transfigure the image of a female-lover into a lover-martyr.[18] What I wish to suggest is, particularly, in the context of martyrology, that the sufi poets and *qissa-kars* in their own times deconstructed the longstanding and fossilized masculine image of a martyr and created a new image of the martyr and martyrdom – an image, which has its own narrative and aesthetics. For example, the poetry of Sultan Bahu (1629-1691) may be said to have rich aesthetic exposition of a martyr and a lover. In this connection, we may read the following couplet:

> Someone who is chaste but does not love the Lord / is polluted in both mind and spirit. / Some achieve union in the idol-house of their hearts, / while others continue to be isolated in the mosque. / Only those who readily offer their heads / at the altar of God win the game of love. Those who have not sacrificed their all for the Friend / will never meet him, O Bahu.[19]

Generally, the Punjabi sufi poets portray a female receiving martyrdom in the social field while fighting against patriarchs for her right to 'speak' and 'live' according to her own terms.

The sufis under reference (Shaikh Farid, Shah Husain and Bulleh Shah) assumed the persona of a female - the persona of love, eroticism, non-conformism and rebellion i.e. the counter-hegemonic voice of the marginalized and the suppressed - during the times when masculinity and martialty were dominant politically as well as socially, and when women in general were excluded from the domain of knowledge and writing skills. Speaking and writing during the medieval times were monopolized only by the 'powerful' i.e. patriarchs. Sultan Bahu indirectly attacks on this patriarchal monopoly,[20] which was crucial in silencing women and denying them the opportunities for creative expressions i.e. production of written literature. The domination was activated and practiced through divergent subtle means. The heads of families and the priestly class of *qazis* played a decisive role in consolidating the established social norms and traditions set by the institution of patriarchy. For instance, the celebrated Punjabi *qissa-kar* of the eighteenth century, Waris Shah, in his *Hir* (composed in 1767) exposes the role of Shamsuddin, the *qazi* of Jhang (a village in west Punjab), who acts as a catalyst of the patriarchs of the Siyal family to indoctrinate the mind of a rebellious daughter, Hir. She continues her love affair with Dhido Ranjha, the herdsman, despite the warning and advice of the elders of the family. The *qazi* reminds her of the social position and class status of her father, Chuchak Siyal. He prescribes the code of 'good' conduct that is expected from Hir, who is the daughter of a chief (*sardar*) of five villages. For that purpose, the council of the elders assembles in the house of Chuchak Siyal, where Hir is instructed to remain confined to the house and spin in the company of her maiden friends.[21] The code of conduct imposed by the patriarchs tends to manoeuvre Hir. She is treated as an object/instrument of utility in the feudal socio-economic dispensation. A patriarch (in his/her position as husband or father or mother) is the direct oppressor and beneficiary of the subordination of women.[22]

A notable attribute of the female persona of the Punjab sufis is that they did not emulate the conventional masculine linguistic style or behaviour to project themselves as female. At the level of language, poetic genre and physical appearance, they (particularly Shah Husain and Bulleh Shah), adopted such practices that strengthened their 'female' persona. Shah Husain was enamoured of dancing and singing. He freely mingled in the company of dancers and musicians. To shed his 'masculine' identity, he shaved clean his moustaches and beard. He even "refused to accept those persons as disciples who were unwilling to shave their faces" [masculinity].[23] Bulleh Shah followed the poetic genre of *baramah* to express his *feminist* physical pangs and pains, precipitated by his ardent desire to meet the Beloved. To appease his mentor (Inayat Shah), he learnt the art of dancing from a dancing girl, as the mentor had love for music and dancing. Dressed as a woman, Bulleh Shah began to sing and dance outside the mosque where Inayat Shah was resting. On this occasion, he sang the following *kafi*:

> *Terey ishq nachaya kar thaiya thaiya / ishq dera merey andar keeta / bhar key zehir* [*da*] *piala peeta / jhbdey aavin vey tabiba nahin tey main mar gainiyan / terey ishq nachaya kar thaiya thaiya.* [24]

> Your love has made me dance to a fast beat! / Your love has taken abode within my heart! / This cup of poison I drank all by myself. / Come, come, O physician, or else I breathe my last! / Your love has made me dance to a fast beat![25]

Such an effeminate sufi style was a form of the symbolic cry against the patriarchs and their allies. The sufis discovered and illumined the 'lost' female community and its identity through such stylization. Both Shah Husain and Bulleh Shah resuscitate the image of a 'drunken' sufi, named Jalaluddin Rumi (1207-73), who sought ecstasy in dancing, singing, poetry and music. Sufi poets, particularly the *qissa-kars*, could discern how a female, the marginalized one, was intensely desirous of an aesthetic revelation of her bodily pleasures. Such a desire, unlike that of the modern and post-modern one, could not be realized in the medieval patriarchal society. Nevertheless, her desire was carried out on her part by the sufi *qissa-kar* like Waris Shah. He portrays the soma of Hir: 'In her brows, which are like arches of Lahore, a full moon shines. Her cheeks pulsate like petals of rose and they are red like the colour of wine. Her lips red like rubies are brilliant. Her chin resembles with the pear-fruit of Iran. Her teeth form a chord of lilies and look like the seeds of a pomegranate. She is tall like a cypress brought from the paradise. Her neck is like that of a swan. Her arms are rolls of kneaded butter; and thighs round and slender and camphor- white. On her bosom, which heaves like a wave, two silken spheroids rise and fall and her navel like a musk-pod floats on the crystal of a heavenly pool. Her loins are velvet-soft, and her white shins are slim like the shafts of a minaret.' The winsome make-up of Hir's face reminds Waris Shah of the beautiful calligraphy of a book, most probably of the Quran, because he further writes that to behold Hir is like a pilgrimage to Prophet's cenotaph. Hir outshines the beauty of the loveliest queens. Waris Shah not only enhances the physical appearance of Hir but also alludes to the depth of her determination that is reflected in her gait: 'Hir shines like a sword that is just unsheathed to fall upon the fatal block, she sways in the air, and she marches like a victor as hosts have marched ever from Punjab to Hindustan on conquering raids.'[26]

The metaphorical description of the glamour and beauty of Hir's body image by Waris Shah is not only a sensual narrative of the female soma. Rather the portrayal embodies profound signification to be appreciated by a reader. Hir, who is an embodiment of a sound body and a sound mind, is supposed to confront the patriarchs who are physically, socially and theologically strong. Such a female image is strong enough to confront the reason, ego and physical power of the patriarchs. It is Waris Shah, a sufi (or for that matter Shah Husain and Bulleh Shah who time and again in their verses refer to Hir), who spoke and wrote on behalf of Hir and immortalized her struggle as well as her marginalized voice. Was it not a revolution, so far as the issue of making the suppressed female voice echo is concerned! In their verses, the Punjabi sufi poets transform the female resentment into a rebellion. The former is defined as 'auto-intoxication, the evil secretion in a sealed vessel, whereas the latter i.e. a rebellion removes the seal and allows the whole being to come into play. It liberates the stagnant waters and turns them into a raging torrent.[27] Thus the female voice of the Punjabi sufis needs to be appreciated as a bold literary stride, when many women writers in the nineteenth century Europe "adopted male pen-names, both to ensure that their work would receive serious critical attention untainted by stereotypes of women's inferior skill, and also to escape the charge of 'coarseness' or indecency which fell on women dealing with the literary themes of sexuality and passion."[28]

Since sufism is basically transcendental, holistic and unitarian, the Punjabi sufi poetry counters the communitarian and sectarian ideology, which materializes communal beliefs as practices. The verses composed by Shaikh Farid, Shah Husain, Bulleh Shah and Sultan Bahu testify the statement. What is being suggested is that the Punjabi sufi poetry is essentially anti-patriarchal and anti-sectarian, and speaks on behalf of the subaltern or marginalized strata of the society and classes such as women. Bulleh Shah *stooped down* to *elevate* the voice of those females who were looked down upon as 'polluted' by those who believed in caste taboos:

> *Main choretri aan sachey sahib di sarkaron / dhian ki chhajli gian ka jharu kam krodh nit jharun / main choretri aan sachey sahib di sarkaron / kazi janey hakim janey pharag khati begaron / din raat main eho mangdi dur na kar darbaron / main choretri aan sachey sahib di sarkaron / tud bajhon mera hor na koi main val karun pukaron / Bullha Shah Inayat karkey bakhra miley didaron / main choretri aan sachey sahib di sarkaron.*[29]

> I am sweeperess in the service of the true Lord. / With the *chhajli*[30] of contemplation and the broom of knowledge, / I sweep of the chaff of lust and anger. / I am sweeperess in the service of the true Lord. / Let the *qazi* know! Let the judge mark! / I am free from all forced labour. / Day and night I beg: "Send me not away from Your Court." / I am sweeperess in the service of the true Lord. / Besides You there is none who is mine; / To whom should I cry for help? / "For the sake of my spouse Inayat, pray

> give me a share of Your sight," entreats Bullah. / I am sweeperess in the service of the true Lord.[31]

With reference to the sufis' concern with the marginalized female voice, it would not be incongruous to make a mention of Fard Faqir (1720-1790) who is said to have lived in Gujarat, a town in west Punjab. His *Kasabnama Bafindgan*, a treatise on the profession of weavers, sheds light on the ill treatment meted out to the artisans by the ruling elite. Fard Faqir revealed their sufferings:

> Being rulers they sit on carpets and practice tyranny; / artisans they call menials and drink their blood. / By force they take them to work without fearing God, / Fard, the sufferer's sighs will fall on them one day. / The artisans have to pay the first tax and they have to suffer this loss. / Carrying the load of the poor on their heads they (rulers) themselves go to hell.[32]

It may be recalled that in the Punjabi sufi poetry, particularly in the love-legends (*qissas*), Dhido Ranjha, a son of the chief of Takht Hazara, and Izzat Beg Mirza, a rich merchant from Bokhara, are remembered and eulogized, when they become 'marginalized' and victims of the patriarchal social set up. In their respective times, both had become the buffalo-herdsmen (*mahinwals*). Najm Hosain Syed comments: "A rich merchant [Izzat Beg] from Bokhara, he had given up his wealth, his trade and disbanded his caravan. He could have, as an affluent merchant, asked for the hand of Sohni, and Tulla the potter would have thought it his good fortune to have him as a son-in-law. But Izzat Beg spends all his wealth in buying pots made by Tulla – heaps and heaps of them – for he knows that is what money can do. He knows that to get Sohni he has to transform his consciousness, to be reborn as Mahinwal [buffalo-herdsman]."[33]

The Punjabi sufis may be said to have opened up a whole new array of Punjabi cultural texts for a legitimate discussion on the female voice and have thus facilitated the conflation of history and literature. In their own historical times, from the middle of the twelfth century to the middle of the eighteenth century, they constructed their respective texts on female voice, though in their own divergent mystic literary locutions. It would not be an exaggeration to say that the Punjabi literature was born with a female persona and her voice echoed first during the twelfth century in the sufi-self of Shaikh Farid. This voice was not merely creative and imaginative. With the passage of time, it became ideologically more critical and pungent, as is evident from the verses of Shah Husain in the sixteenth century and of Bulleh Shah in the eighteenth century. The sufi poetry did not merely mean a technical mode of writing. Rather it had deep social, political and philosophical implications. The Punjab sufis were socially literary activists who could perceive connections between social commitments and literature. They never let their mystic verses flourish on the assumption that there was an isolable experience called beauty or aesthetic. They never alienated their mysticism from social life and social relations. Their literature was not a solitary fetish or fad. Certainly, their texts call for an attention to what is called new historicism's dialogic relationship between history and literature.[34]

God of Beauty and Belief

Since the sufis made a female voice speak against patriarchs, it would be interesting to pay attention to the semantic of the masculine denominations – like *pritam, prabhu, kant, sain, shah, sahib, suhag, sajan* and *mitter* – which Shaikh Farid, Shah Husain and Bulleh Shah picked up to address their He-Beloved in order to communicate their erotic relationship with Him. These names are the essence, qualified by attributes. A woman also seeks these attributes or ideals in her social spouse. A sufi's Beloved is the Sweetest, Greatest, Protector, Erotic, Worth-remembering, Graceful, Most Loved, Vital, Friend, Companion, Helper, Dear One, Owner of Wealth and Boundless. God is also Bridegroom (*suhag*) without whom a sufi ever remains incomplete and insatiate. The said devotional vernacular names/virtues of God are not different from the Quranic names of Allah i.e. Merciful (*al-Rahman*), Preserver (*al-Muhayman*), Gracious (*al-Latif*), Gentle (*al-Halim*), Preserver (*al-Hafiz*), Loving (*al-Wadud*), Protector (*al-Wakil*), Preventer (*al-Mani*). Also the eternal beauty and majesty i.e. *Jamal* and *Jalal*, which Zu ul-Nun, the Egyptian mystic (c. 796- 861), underlines to illumine the divine qualities, are present in the Punjabi vernacular denominations used for God like *Sajan* and *Sahib*. The concept of love relationship between the Divine and a devotee is shared by all the sufis. Zu ul-Nun Misri says: "O God! Publicly I call Thee, 'My Lord', but in solitude I call Thee 'O My Beloved'!" This Egyptian mystic is said to have formulated for the first time a theory of intuitive knowledge of God (*marifa*), or gnosis, as opposed to discursive learning and knowledge (*ilm*). He is also said to have given to the earlier asceticism the definitely pantheistic bent and quasi-erotic expression, which is recognized as the chief characteristic of sufism.[35] In the Punjabi sufi poetry, a sufi's soul wails at times, then cries and yearns for union with his Beloved.

One may trace the history of the motif of 'bridal' mysticism to the Punjabi sufi poetry since Shaikh Farid (1175-1265). He was the first Punjabi sufi in whose verses we discover the pains and pangs of a woman. The female self of Shaikh Farid expressed his love for his *divine* Husband as well as his resentment against a *social* patriarch. In this connection his allegorical language helps us understand and construct the picture of a patriarch. In his very first *doha*, he invokes the feminine metaphors of a bride, a maid, her engagement, her marriage, her helpless life, her destiny and her stranger bridegroom who would take her away from her parents to a place, which is not known to her.

> *Jit diharey dhan vari sahey leye likhaey / malak jo kani sunida muh dekhaley aeye/ jind nimani kadhiey hada ku karkaey/ sahey likhey na chalani jind ku samjhaey / jind vauhti maran var lai jasi parnaiey.*[36]
>
> The day a maid is engaged / her marriage day is fixed. / The Angel of Death, / the ears had heard, / comes and shows his face. / He takes the helpless life, / cracking the bones. / Make life understand: / the fixed time cannot go away. / Death, the groom, will come and take life, his bride, away in marriage.[37]

The above *doha* of Shaikh Farid may be decoded on two planes, historically and sociologically, so as to contextualize his female voice. Let us first understand its historical implications. Shaikh Farid's own preoccupation with death and sins may be comprehended in the perspective of the time he was living in. His life span coincided with the spell of the Turkish invasions on the Punjab. It was a time when the Turks, under the leadership of Muizzuddin Muhammad bin Sam (Muhammad Ghori), were laying the foundation of the Delhi Sultanate; and places like Multan, Uch, Nahrwala, Lahore and Peshawar were being attacked. Also during this period, Chengiz Khan started his famous march for the conquest of Muslim Asia and within forty years (1228-1260) the Mongols had brought all lands up to the frontiers of Poland and Syria under their sway and had conquered India up to Lahore.It is observed that the Mongolsmust have killed at least eigt million Muslim men and women in cold blood for th establishment of their politicalauthorit. In uch circumtances Inda was the only country where refugees could find both scurity and livelihood.[38] Such a massive destruction and te resultant deplorable social milieu must have stired the sensitive self of a sufi, Shaikh Farid. He looed upon theoppressing political patriarchs as personification ofdeath-grooms and identified himself (and the subjugated) with a bride who was feeble and helpless in the patriarchal setup.[39]

Sociologically speaking, the image of a woman, which Shaikh Fard constructs to convey the mystic union of life (as a bride) with death (as a bridegroom), enables us to perceive the oppressed position of women in the society. The above-cited couplet of Shaikh Farid underscores that during his times maidens were married off to grooms unknown to them and who took them to places unknown to them. This must have been a traumatic experience for them and kept them in a state of uncertainty, fear and subordination. In the patriarchal setup, the road that leads to her love is formidable. She cannot tread on it, as it is mazy, marshy and complex. Shaikh Farid characterizes the road metaphorically: "Farid, the street is muddy, / His house is far, / and I in love with Him."[40] A rebelling female surviving in the sufi-self of Shaikh Farid condemns the patriarchal slavery. She seeks liberation and salvation: "Farid, to sit at another's door! / Lord, give me not that! / If you keep me so, / take life from the body."[41] Many other verses of Shaikh Farid can be cited so as to listen to the agonies of his 'female' self. He was the first Punjabi sufi poet who introduced a female narrator in the Punjabi poetry. Later after a gap of two hundred years, we encounter a feminine voice in the *bani* of Guru Nanak,[42] and more prominently in the *kafis* of Shah Husain and Bulleh Shah, and in the qissa of *Hir* versified by Waris Shah.

But one significant point that distinguishes Shaikh Farid from the other prominent Punjabi sufis like Shah Husain and Bulleh Shah is that he defines his relationship with God in the Indic classical context of wife-husband relationship (the hierarchy that prevails in the social patriarchy), whereas the later Punjabi sufis lay equal stress upon the non-hierarchical relationship between the she-lover and the He-Beloved. Shaikh Farid is *married* to the He-Beloved, and Shah Husain and Bulleh Shah are *betrothed* to Him. They are *maiden* sufis and Shaikh Farid is a *married* sufi. In their (Shah Husain and Bulleh Shah) verses one finds a prominent reference to dowry, which a betrothed girl after marriage takes to her in-laws. Shah Husain sings:

> *Tunu aho katt valali, / ni kuriey, tunu aho katt valali. / sari umar gavaee ainvey, / pachhi na ghati aa chhchhi . / galiana vich phirey latkandi, / aeh gal nahio bhuli. / Kahey husain fakir sain da/ daj vihuni chali.*[43]
>
> Spin, O simple one / Spin, O girl, simple one. / You have wasted your life in vain, / There is no bobbin in your basket. / You are just loitering in the streets, / It is not a good thing. / Says Husain, fakir of the Lord, / You will go without dowry.[44]

With reference to the above-cited *kafi*, it is important to observe that the sufis did not look upon the spinning wheel with a male gaze i.e. dismissive attitude towards the female artistic and productive activities (and achievements) such as spinning, quilting, embroidery etc. Conversely, the sufis created 'feminist' aesthetic, while elevating female artistic activities to the level of spirituality. Annemarie Schimmel states: "...in the Punjab the poets knew that the spinning of fine threads which 'God will buy from the cotton of one's self' (allusion to Sura 9/112) can serve as a perfect image of the careful work that is required to reach one's goal. For: would God buy coarse yarn? Besides, the sound of the spinning wheel resembles the sound of the *dhikr* [*zikr*], in which the pious with low voice repeat thousands of time the names of God."[45] Besides the spinning wheel, the sufis elevated the status of so many marginalized activities such as related to agricultural labour. In their verses, they employed the names of things in everyday use in the agricultural arena, as: (i) *Goil* (a small hut of mud and grass, built on pasture land for the cowherd, or made in fields for the person who keeps watch). It stands for the temporary stay of a sufi; (ii) *Chhaj* (a tray of thin reeds, used for winnowing agricultural products); (iii) *Chhajli* (a tray larger than *chhaj* and used to winnow the threshing floor). It symbolizes a sufi's humility. He calls himself a sweeper. He calls the beliefs of divergent people the threshing floor, which he winnows to separate the right from the wrong; (iv) *Jharu* or *baukar* (a broom used to for sweeping the floor or to gather the grain spread in the sun). It stands for a sufi's wisdom; (v) *Angithi* (a small object made of iron or earth to hold fire). The sufi's heart is an eternal *angithi* full of fire i.e. separation's pangs; (vi) *Bhambar* (a flame or big fire). In sufi language it is also love's flame, which consumes the body; and (vii) *Ghund* (that part of a woman's veil which she throws over her face to conceal it from men). Ignorance is a sufi's *ghund*.[46]

Since Shah Husain and Bulleh Shah, unlike Shaikh Farid, are *virgins*[47], their relationship with their He-Beloved is more of romantic or of erotic nature than of Indian classical type, wherein the wife is exhorted to win husband's love and acceptance by *subjecting* herself absolutely to him. Both the prominent sufi poets under reference obliterate the difference between their *female*-self and the *male*-self of the Beloved. Invoking the motif of Hir and Ranjha, Shah Husain sings:

> *Ranjha Ranjha kardi main aapey Ranjha hoi / saddo ni mainu Dhido Ranjha, Hir na aakho koi.*[48]
>
> Ever calling upon Ranjha, / I have become Ranjha myself. / Call me Ranjha, everybody, / Nobody call me Hir./[49]

The female self of Bulleh Shah sings the similar romantic relationship of equality with his Lord.[50] What needs to be appreciated in these verses is that the *sufic* female-self and the *social* female-self merge together in a sufi to the extent that a *patriarchal* kind of distinction between a male and a female gets blurred, or, one can safely say, obliterated.[51] Hence in this sense, the sufi poetry is *transgressive* in its nature. It celebrates 'love' in a way, which is not permitted by theological definition of religion. The absolute unity of Hir and Ranjha or of the female self of a sufi and the He-Beloved, as in the *kafis* of Shah Husain and Bulleh Shah, alludes to the concept of absolute unity (*fana*) that was first employed by Bayazid Bistami of Iran (d. 875). He attains this state by constant mortification, by "emptying himself of himself, until he had reached, at least for a moment, the world of absolute unity, where, as he said, lover, beloved, and love are one, and where he himself is the wine, the wine-drinker, and the cupbearer."[52] The purpose of citing Bayazid Bistami is simply to understand the manner in which the Punjabi sufis, with the help of the indigenous motifs of Hir and Ranjha, vernacularized Islamic mysticism.

A sufic image of the He-beloved is aesthetically different from the one that perceives a husband or a lover in *patriarchal* terms i.e. he is masculine and martial. For example, Bulleh Shah's Beloved holds a staff in his hand (not sword) and a blanket on his shoulders (not a royal robe). He is benign (not domineering). He is a cowherd (not a chief). He is the lord of flute (not of weapons). His village-home, from where he sets out to meet his lover, is not less than a throne. He wears a *mukat* (a crown which a bridegroom wears on the occasion of his marriage) and his forehead is decorated with *tilak* (a ceremonial mark, different from the one that symbolizes the royal lunar or solar lineage of a monarch).[53] In the entire range of Punjabi sufi poetry as well as *qissa* poetry, a non-patriarchal aesthetic image of the Beloved / beloved is a historic and ideological literary progressive step in many respects. The significant one is that a sufi constructs a *physical image* of the Beloved. Thus a sufi synthesizes the *nirguna* and *sirguna* bhakti traditions. He-Beloved is anthropomorphized in the form of Dhido Ranjha of Takht Hazara. The only exception in the Punjabi *qissa* wherein a feminist aesthetic narrative of a lover is missing is that of the *qissa* of Mirza-Sahiban, which was composed in the seventeenth century by the *qissa-kar* Pilu.

That Bulleh Shah is a virgin and, hence, is inordinately excited to catch a glimpse of the face of the He-Beloved obliges us to make a mention of the motif of veil (*ghungat*) in the Punjabi sufi poetry. Let us understand this motif historically. It was Rabia Basri (d. 801), one of the most famous women saints of Islam and a prominent figure in the sufi tradition, who replaced the fear of God with that of love. She provided the theme of Divine Love with an ecstatic voice:

> I love Thee in two ways: one selfishly, / the other a love that is worthy of Thee. / It is selfish love when I spend all my time/ thinking exclusively of Thee and no other. / The other kind of love is when the veil / is raised by Thee, thus revealing Thyself to me. /Neither way am I praiseworthy. / In both the praise all Thine.[54]

The 'veil' Rabia talks about in the eighth century reappears after a gap of one thousand years in the vernacular Punjabi sufi verses of Bulleh Shah and Waris Shah. The discourse of 'veil', which is involved in this motif, signifies that social and religious patriarchs (without their mediation or intervention) do not permit the formation of a direct linkage between a social lover (or the Supreme Lover) and a social beloved (or the Supreme Beloved). The female-self of Bulleh Shah sings and demands:

Ghungat chuk o sajna hun sharman kahnu rakhian vey / zulf kundal ney ghera paiya, bisiyar ho key dang chalaiya / vekh asan vall taras na aaiya, karkey khuni akhian vey / ghungat chuk o sajna hun sharman kahnu rakhian vey / do nainan da tir chalaiya, main aajiz dey seney laiya / ghail karkey mukh chhupaiya, chorian aeh kin dasiyan vey / ghungat chuk o sajna hun sharman kahnu rakhian vey / birhon katari tunu kass mari, / tad main hoi beydil bhari / mur na lai sar hamari, pattian terian kachian vey / ghungat chuk o sajna hun sharman kahnu rakhian vey / nehun laga key man har lita, pher na aapna darshan dita / zehar piala aapey pita, aklon san main kachian vey / ghungat chuk o sajna hun sharman kahnu rakhian vey.'[55]

Lift your veil, my Beloved ! / Why do you feel bashful now? / Your curly locks entwine my heart, / They bite me like the serpents. / You do not pity my sad plight, / You look at me with blood-shot eyes. / Lift your veil, my Beloved ! / You flung your arrow of two eyes, / Aimed at the breast of poor me ! / Inflicting a wound, you hid your face: / Who taught you such tricks, my love ! / Lift your veil, my Beloved ! / The dirk of separation / You aimed with such perfection, / I got disheartened, disillusioned. / You never cared to call on me, / Your promises proved so brittle ! / Lift your veil, my Beloved ! / With your love, O dear, / You captured my heart. / Never later you showed your face. / This cup of poison I drank myself, / I was indeed an unripe innocent. / Lift your veil, my Beloved ![56]

In this verse, Bulleh Shah addresses his mentor Inayat Shah. The 'locks' (*zulf*) he talks about are that of Inayat Shah who kept long hair. These locks conceal the beautiful face of the mentor as well as of the Supreme He-Beloved. Nevertheless, the 'locks' also signify the patriarchal barricades, which do not allow a female-Bulleh Shah to have a sight of the Beloved. Bulleh Shah's contemporary, Waris Shah, critiqued the socio-religious patriarchal norms of the veil under our discussion. In his *qissa Hir*, Dhido Ranjha, having assumed the guise of a jogi narrates the demerits of a veil to Hir:

The veil deserves to be put in fire; /it is the cause of many ills. / It hides the splendour of a beautiful face, / and in the open ruin invites. / It drowns the lover's heart in sorrow, / or stifles it like a bird in a cage. / Come, see the world in all its glory, / let not the veil keep you in siege. / The veil blinds even those who have eyes, / take off the evil, discover your lights. / Pearls ought not to be buried in earth, / nor flowers, Waris, scorched on coals.[57]

In the Punjabi sufi poetry, the motif of veil is interlocked with the motif of painful separation (*virah*). When a sufi listens to the divine call, he becomes aware of his *virah* from the source of all being. Thus *virah* refers to "certain psychological state, which comprises suffering, waiting, and ardent desire... It is almost always to the woman that this sentiment is attributed; it is she who is described as a *virahini*, moaning and awaiting the return of the husband, who is far away. Kabir is the first to attempt a mystical interpretation of this popular theme by making the *virahini* a (feminine) symbol of the bride-soul, who languishes in anguished waiting for her divine husband."[58] The prominent Indic motif of *virah,* which has a long history in the lyrical and romantic poetry of ancient and medieval India, amplifies the female voice in the Punjabi sufi poetry. In a typical mystic idiom, Shaikh Farid refers to the longing of the bridal soul for nocturnal raptures of the anticipated embrace. The archetypal imagery of wedlock, bedchamber, musk and flower underscores that Shaikh Farid was not indifferent to the ecstasy emanating from the appeasement of the body's hungers. No hermit or sufi, who abandoned corporeal delights and scoffed at the pleasures of existence, could have created the poetry of warm, sensuous imagery and symbols.[59] Shaikh Farid speaks of erotic languor and smouldering:

> I burn and writhe in agony, / I wring my hands in despair, / I am crazed with a longing for the Sahib [Husband]. / You forsook and you had a cause, / For I was in error, not Thou, O Lord, / For such a Sire as thee little did I care / When my youth faded, I fell into despair.[60]

> I slept not with my husband last night, / my body is pining away; Go ask the wife whom her husband has put away, / how she passeth the night.[61]

The Quran and *hadis* strongly enjoin marriage on the believers. Junaid Baghdadi (d. 910), a leading sufi of Iraqian school of mysticism, is said to have admitted: 'I need sex the way I need food.'[62] In sufism, whether of Islamic or Indic variety, sensuousness, which is an inalienable dimension of human being, is inseparably connected with the contemplation of the Divine. Shaikh Farid provokes the reader to interact with a woman and realize her mental agonies and physical discomforts.[63] He introduces a nightingale[64] in one of his verses to highlight the theme of *virah*:

> O black koel, what makes you black? / Separation from my love has burnt me. / Separated from my love, what joy can I have? / When He shows grace, then God unites.[65]

Representing himself both as a nightingale and a female, a sufi longs for eternal beauty. Longing in mysticism is the highest state that a sufi can reach because it results in creativity, whereas union brings about silence and annihilation.[66] The theme of *virah,* which was introduced by Shaikh Farid, also pervades Shah Husain's *kafis* and Bulleh Shah's *baramah,*[67] a poem that deals with the peculiarities of twelve months and the feelings of the she-lover in each of these months. Shah Husain's female self is inflicted with pains of separation. He cries:

> Without the Beloved, the nights are long. / Ranjha is the yogi, I am his spouse, / Maddened and deserted, I am addressed as mad. / I am immature, do not know what devotion means, / But I am stretched on the frame of separation.[68]

Thus the Punjab sufis in their *virah* reveal the multiple celebrations of woman's body. They explicitly glorify her emotions and realize the experience of her body. They represent and articulate her luxuriant pleasure, her pangs of separation and her longings. They break her silence – a silence, which is highly desired by a patriarch. The female-self of the Punjabi sufis with reference to *virah*, as narrated in the poetic genre of *baramah*, critiques a male's linear perception of time. Annie Leclerc defines this perception of time: "From their [male] birth to their death, the segment of time they occupy is straight. Nothing in their flesh is aware of time's curves. Their eyes, their pulse, neglect the seasons. They can only see History, they fight only for History"; whereas a female speaks about another sense of time, another adventure. Thirteen times a year, she experiences the cyclical changes of her body.[69]

The mystic or sufic female voice of Shah Husain and Bulleh Shah speaks in cultural diction. They were spiritually intoxicated sufis who lived in a perpetual state of ecstasy. Their verses exposed the heartlessness and hollowness, madness and mockery of cruel, unintelligent orthodoxy and superstition. In one of his verses, Shah Husain visualizes himself as a happy woman who joyfully dances and defies the established religious as well as social patriarchal parameters. Since Shah Husain indulges in dancing, he is devoid of the attributes defined by the patriarchs. In fact, the female in Shah Husain refuses to conform to the patriarchal norms of modesty.

> *Shak gia beshaki hoi tan maiṇ augun nachi han / je shah naal main jhumar pavan sada suhagan sachi han / jhuthey da muh kala hoia ashak di gall sachi hai / Shak gia beshaki hoi tan main augun nachi han.*[70]
>
> The doubt [about God] has vanished / and doubtlessness is established / therefore I, devoid of qualities, dance. / If I play (thus) with the Beloved / I am ever a happy woman. / The liar's face (he who accused) has been blackened / and the lover's statement has been proved true; / because the doubt has vanished / and doubtlessness is established, / therefore I, devoid of qualities, dance.[71]

Unlike the monologue-*doha* of Shaikh Farid, the *kafis* of Shah Husain and Bulleh Shah are dialogical; they underline the inter-gender relationship between mother and daughter. For instance, in one of the *kafis* of Shah Husain, Hir addresses her mother:

> *Ni maey, mainu kherian di, / gall na aakh / ranjhan mainhda main ranjhan di, / kherian nu kuri jhaak / lok janey hir kamli hoi, / hirey da var chak / kahey husain fakir sain da.*[72]
>
> Mother, do not speak to me of the Kheras. / Ranjha is mine, I Ranjha's,/ The Kheras entertain false hopes. / People think Hir is gone mad, / And Hir is pledged to the cowherd. / Says Husain, fakir of the Lord, / The Creator Himself knows.

The female self of Bulleh Shah apprises 'her' mother of 'her' love-stricken state of mind; she has become a rebel and non-conformist. In true love, false shame and fear of reproach disappear. She has burnt her bodice and veil. She reveals to her mother that she has laid her bed in the garden. She sleeps with her Beloved and presses against his breast. Her heart and body are joined to his.[73]

To make the female voice more clear and conspicuous, loud and bold, Shah Husain and Bulleh Shah transform the Punjabi love legend of Hir-Ranjha into metaphors. They combine folklore, folk society, its sensibility and their mysticism together. Though apparently Hir and Ranjha are 'worldly' metaphors, nevertheless the sufi poets, on the one hand, endeavour to make the 'other-world' appear real and, on the other hand, try to emphasize the unity between the material and spiritual worlds. Such a mixture tends to cause uneasiness to a dualist who perceives a desacralization of the celestial when it is combined with the terrestrial. This unique synthesis created by Shah Husain and Bulleh Shah needs exploration at the hands of a historian, who is interested in exploring the traditions of non-conformism in the history, culture and society of Punjab. The motifs of spinning wheel (*charkha*) and Hir occur and reoccur in the Punjabi sufi poetry and underscore its utmost concern with the female's dreams and aspirations. Shah Husain and Bulleh Shah voluntarily remain no longer masculine gender in their verses. To be one with their Beloved, they encourage their female-counterpart to transcend the patriarchal barricades. For that purpose, they suggest the non-conformist traditions of devotional bhakti/sufism as an alternative ideology to be practiced.

Representation of a sufi's soul as a longing woman induced an Indian sufi to use feminine diction in his verses. For this reason, household occupations could easily be used as symbols for spiritual pursuits. As Gujarat and Bijapur are particularly rich in *chakki-nama* (milstone poems), *charkha-nama* (spinning poems), *lori-nama* (lullaby), *shadi-nama* (wedding song) and *suhagan-nama* (married woman's song), similarly, Punjabi sufi poetry is connected with spinning and weaving.[74] The *kafis* of Shah Husain and Bulleh Shah are replete with the vocabulary drawn from spinning, such as handloom, spinning wheel, yarn, web, weft, spool etc:

> Spin, O simple one, / Spin, O girl, simple one. / You have wasted your life in vain, / There is no bobbin in your basket. / You are just loitering in the streets, / It is not a good thing. / Says Husain, fakir of he Lord, / You will go without a dowry.[75]

> Put your mind in spinning, O girl! / Your mother ever counsels you, / Why do you roam thus aimlessly? / Do not forsake of your modesty. / Heed the counsel, O ignorant girl! / Put your mind in spinning, O girl.[76]

The imagery used by the Shah Husain and Bulleh Shah is a part and parcel of their environment and experience. They dramatize their mystic experience in terms of the experience of a female, whether she is a lover who aspires for a beloved of her own choice or a domestic worker who spins. Their *kafis* are 'miniature drama in which diverse, contrasting tones converge to create the mystic as well social meanings.'[77] The task of spinning is highly exacting. Concentration, will, patience and skill, which are involved in spinning/meditation, are the characteristics of both a woman and a sufi as observed and versified by Shah Husain and Bulleh Shah. In this regard, the difference between a sufi and a woman gets obliterated; spinning and *zikr* (rememberence of God) coalesce together. The virgin female voice of a sufi echoes more boldly when Shah Husain uses the metaphors of shawl, bridal palanquin, husband's embrace, embroidery, broom, dowry, in-laws and maternal parents.

Towards a Conclusion

The orthodox might maintain that it is profane to speak of the love of God. To them love implies kinship, but God is unlike His creation in every respect. But the sufis countered this proposition. They made love and eroticism the rationale of their relationship with God.[78] The concept of the unity of being (*wahdat-ul-wujud*) is that God and the world constitute a single unity. Therefore, neither can be known in isolation from each other. The theme of love and kinship relation, which is articulated in a female voice, is present in the verses of the Punjabi sufis. It so much permeates the Punjabi sufi and *qissa* poetry that, it may be argued, the physical and the spiritual, the ephemeral and the eternal are woven into a pattern of fascinating consistency and symmetry. It also underlines the strong tendencies of love and revolt or non-conformism in the social life of medieval Punjab. As a result Punjabi sufi poets and *qissa-kars* and their works transcended the barricades of established traditions.

A study of the female voice in the verses of Shaikh Farid, Shah Husain and Bulleh Shah reveals that the Punjabi sufi poets were socially, spiritually and politically aware at the same time. They did not seek poetic articulation simply for their pure mystical vision; they were also concerned with human concerns of more mundane character. They exhibited a keen awareness of social injustice prevalent in the socio-political situation of their times. Their poetry is about the right of the suppressed to speak and write. The Punjabi sufi poetry, so far as it is a career of female voice, is ecstatic; and eroticism occupies a significant space in it. The aim of all mystical eroticism is to create unity from duality. The female voice of the Punjab sufis excludes an intermediary both from the spiritual as well as social domains of life. It is the intermediary or 'law' or patriarchy that separates a human being from his/her Beloved/beloved.

In the context of the female voice, it seems necessary to mention that in their practical life Punjabi sufis had displayed their concern with the helpless and poor women. They allowed many a women in the circle of their disciples (*murids*). Shaikh Nizamuddin Auliya, who was intimately associated with the socio-cultural life of medieval Punjab, is said to have financially supported prostitutes and widows.[79]

The success of the Punjab sufis in making eroticism serve the overall aesthetic mood of their verses depends on their poetic skill of having brought eroticism into harmony with the 'other' theme i.e. the longing for Supreme Being. In their verses, we find an ideal fusion of mysticism and eroticism. The sufis of Punjab spiritualized and legitimized the Punjab lovers and their legends. They referred to their name and their geographical habitation as a metaphor for communicating their mystic love. On the other hand, the Punjabi *qissa-kars* historicized these legends and narrated them in the sufi ambience. In the spiritualization and the emplotment of these love legends (for example, Hir-Ranjha), a sufi poet like Shah Husain and a *qissa-kar* like Waris Shah presented sufi mysticism against the Islamic orthodoxy, which was defended by the social and religious patriarchs. In the verses of the Punjabi sufi poets and *qissa-kars*, the mystic love and mundane love are inextricably joined.

From the viewpoint of contemporary 'patriarchal' institution, which maintains its hegemony through various forms and images, and transforms women into commodities, her desire into sexuality and her eroticism into pornography, the female voice of the sufis of medieval Punjab needs to be reread by those who claim to be the protagonists of gender issue.

NOTES AND REFERENCES

1. Shemeem Burney Abbas, *The Female Voice in Sufi Ritual: Devotional Practices of Pakistan and India*, Oxford University Press, Karachi, 2003, p. 85.
2. Muhammad Umar, *Islam in Northern India during the Eighteenth Century*, Munshiram Manoharlal, New Delhi, p. 96.
3. Shuja Alhaq, *A Forgotten Vision: A Study of Human Spirituality in the Light of the Islamic Tradition*, Vol. I, Vikas Publishing House, New Delhi, 1997, p. 174.
4. J.R. Puri and T.R. Shangari, *Bulleh Shah: The Love-Intoxicated Iconoclast*, Radha Soami Satsang, Beas, 1986, p. 460; for the Gurmukhi text see Jit Singh Sital, *Bulleh Shah: Jivan Te Rachna*, Punjabi University, Patiala, Fourth Reprint 1996, p. 91.
5. Riffat Hassan talks about the three theological assumptions, while tracing the roots of the Islamic belief that men are superior to women. The three theological assumption are: (i) that God's primary creation is man, not

woman, since woman is believed to have been created from man's rib and is, therefore, derivative and secondary ontologically; (ii) that woman, not man, was the primary agent of what is customarily described as 'man's fall' or expulsion from the Garden of Eden, and hence 'all daughters of Eve' are to be regarded with hatred, suspicion and contempt; and (iii) that woman was created not only *from* man but also *for* man, which makes her existence merely instrumental and not of fundamental importance. Riffat Hassan also explains and critiques these three theological assumptions. For detail see Riffat Hassan, 'Feminism in Islam' in Arvind Sharma and Katherine K. Young, eds., *Feminism and World Religions,* State University of New York Press, Albany, 1999, pp. 254-278.

6. For detail see Mohammad Wahid Mirza, *The Life and Works of Amir Khusrau,* Idarah-i-Adabiyat Delli, Delhi, reprint 1974, first published in 1935, p.193-195; S.H. Aksari, *Khusrau's Works as Sources of Social History,* Publication Division, Amir Khusrau Memorial Volume, New Delhi, 1975, pp. 160-161; I.H. Siddiqui, 'Socio-political Role of Women in the Sultanate of Delhi' in Kiran Pawar, ed., *Women in Indian History,* Vision & Venture, Patiala, and New Delhi, 1996, pp.87-101; and Gulfishan Khan, 'Shah Waliullah Dihlawi: A Traditional Perspective of Feminism', Type-script of the paper presented at a seminar on 'Sufi and Bhakti Movements in Medieval India', Department of History, Aligarh Muslim University, Aligarh 13-15 January, 2004.
7. I have borrowed this linguistic expression from Michel Foucault when he describes 'Panopticism' in his *Discipline and Punish: The Birth of the Prison,* Penguin Books Ltd., Harmondsworth, Middlesex, England, pp. 165-228.
8. Annie Leclerc, 'Woman's Word' in Deborah Cameron, ed., *The Feminist Critique of Language: Reader,* Routledge, London, Reprint 1992, p. 76.
9. Rachel Bowlby, 'Domestication' in Victor E. Taylor and Charles E. Winquist, eds., *Postmodernism: Critical Concepts, Vol. III, Disciplinary Texts: Humanities and Social Sciences,* Routledge, London, 1998, p. 789.
10. Let it be added as a passing reference that in the medieval Punjabi literature the female voice was also prominent in the *bani* of Sikh gurus i.e. in the *nirguna* bhakti tradition.
11. Shuja Alhaq, *A Forgotten Vision: A Study of Human Spirituality in the Light of the Islamic Tradition,* Vol. I, p. 224; Annemarie Schimmel, *Mystical Dimensions of Islam,* Sang-e-Meel Publications, Lahore, 2003, first published in 1975, p. 431.
12. Shuja Alhaq, *A Forgotten Vision: A Study of Human Spirituality in the Light of the Islamic Tradition,* Vol. I, p. 225.
13. Ibid., p. 225.
14. According to the (Hindu) *Laws of Manu,* a husband must be constantly worshipped as a god by a faithful wife, though he is devoid of virtue, or seeks pleasure elsewhere. It is further stated that 'no sacrifice, no vow, no fast must be performed by women apart from their husbands; if a wife obeys her husband, she will, for that reason alone, be exalted in heaven.' As quoted in Richard Lannoy, *The Speaking Tree: A Study of Indian Culture and Society,* Oxford University Press, London, Reprint, 1975, p. 103.
15. Sant Singh Sekhon, *A History of Panjabi Literature,* Punjabi University,

Patiala, 1993, vol. I, p. 20.

16. Khwaja Khizar, Farid Shakarganj, Lal Shahbaz Qalandar, Bahauddin Zakariya and Syed Jalaluddin Bukhari.
17. See the *kafis* of Bulleh Shah in Sutinder Singh Noor, ed., *Punjabi Sufi Kaav* (in Gurmukhi), Sahitya Akademi, New Delhi, 1997, pp. 196, 201, 226, 264.
18. For detail see Ishwar Dayal Gaur, *Martyr As Bridegroom: A Folk Representation of Bhagat Singh*, Anthem Press, Delhi, 2008, pp. 38-42.
19. J.R. Puri and Kirpal Singh Khak, *Abyat of Hazrat Sultan Bahu*, ed., Maqsood Saqib, Suchet Kitab Ghar, Lahore, 2004, p. 56.
20. *"Parh parh ilm hazaar kitaban, / aalam hoyey bharey hoo. / harf ik ishq da parh na jaanan, / bhulley phiran vicharey hoo . / ishq aakal vich manzil bhari, / saiayan kohan dey parey hoo."* "They have become great scholars after reading thousand of books. They are incompetent to decipher the word of love, and knock around helplessly under an illusion. There is a distance of hundreds of miles between love (*ishq*) and reason (*aqal*)." Sutinder Singh Noor, ed., *Punjabi Sufi Kaav*, Siharfi No. 35, p. 128.
21. See Jit Singh Sital, ed., *Hir Waris*, Navyug Publishers, Delhi, 1973, p. 51, Stanza No. 107.
22. Sylvia Walby, *Theorizing Patriarchy*, Blackwell, Cambridge, 1994, p. 178.
23. Lajwanti Rama Krishna, *Panjabi Sufi-Poets A.D. 1460-1900*, Ashajanak Publications, New Delhi, 1973, p. 33.
24. Jagtar, *Bulleh Shah- Jeevan Ate Rachna* (Gurmukhi), Lokgeet Prakashan, 2008, p. 26 and 80.
25. J.R. Puri and T.R. Shangari, *Bulleh Shah: The Love-Intoxicated Iconoclast*, p. 191.
26. Sant Singh Sekhon, *The Love of Hir and Ranjha*, Punjab Agricultural University, Ludhiana, 1978, pp. 29-31. For the Gurmukhi text see Jit Singh Sital, ed., *Hir Waris*, Stanza No. 53-55.
27. Albert Camus, *The Rebel*, Penguin Books Ltd., Harmondsworth, Middlesex, England, Reprint, 1954, p. 23.
28. 'Introduction: Why is Language a feminist issue?' in Deborah Cameron, ed., *The Feminist Critique of Language: Reader*, p. 6.
29. Jagtar, *Bulleh Shah- Jeevan Ate Rachna*, p. 158.
30. A winnowing implement for separating grain from chaff.
31. J.R. Puri and T.R. Shangari, *Bulleh Shah: The Love-Intoxicated Iconoclast*, p. 340.
32. Lajwanti Rama Krishna, *Panjabi Sufi-Poets A.D. 1460-1900*, p. 106.
33. Najm Hosain Syed, *Recurrent Patterns in Punjabi Poetry*, City Press, Karachi, 2003, first published in 1968, p. 139.
34. Prafulla Kar, 'New Historicism and the Interpretation of the Text', *Studies in Humanities and Social Sciences*, Journal of the Inter-University Centre of Humanities and Social Sciences, Vol. II No. I, Simla, 1995, pp. 75-83.
35. Annemarie Schimmel, *Mystical Dimensions of Islam*, p. 43.
36. For the Gurmukhi text see Brij Mohan Sagar, *Hymns of Sheikh Farid*, Guru Nanak Dev University, Amritsar, 1999, p. 23.
37. Ibid., p. 87.
38. Mohammad Habib, 'Introduction' in Khaliq Ahmad Nizami, *Religion and Politics in India During the Thirteenth Century*, Oxford University Press, New

Delhi, 2002, first published in 1961, pp. xix-xxi.

39. Let me add here that the devastation caused by Babur in the sixteenth century also moved Guru Nanak who narrated it in *Rag Tilang*. Nanak characterized the invader, Babur, as 'bridegroom' and his army as 'a crowd of sins' whom he identified with his 'bridal procession.' The pillage brought about by the invader-bridegroom, Babur, obliged Nanak to immediately think of the pitiable condition of a bride or the subjugated. His depiction of the captive women is both literal and symbolic. *Guru Granth Sahib*, pp. 722 and 417.
40. Brij Mohan Sagar, *Hymns of Sheikh Farid*, p. 91; for the Gurmukhi text see p. 25.
41. Ibid., p. 94; for the Gurmukhi text see p. 27.
42. Guru Nanak (1469-1539) gave a fresh orientation to the patriarchal words like *khasam* (husband) and *sahib* (feudal lord), and employed them to address the Supreme Being. Nanak's three couplets are sufficient to illustrate the point under reference: (a) "They have come to be liked in his heart by the *khasam*, / who have mediated on Him alone." (b) "My heart, the *khasam's* will is true. / In the *darbar* of the *khasam*, the music-player goes to dwell" (c) "She is low-caste who forgets the *khasam* / If the beggar gives a cry at the door, / the *khasam* in the *mahal* hears." As quoted in Sant Singh Sekhon, *A History of Panjabi Literature*, Vol. I, p. 67.
43. For the Gurmukhi text see Sutinder Singh Noor, ed., *Punjabi Sufi Kaav*, p. 46.
44. English translation by Sant Singh Sekhon, *A History of Panjabi Literature*, vol. II., Punjabi University, Patiala, 1996, p. 164.
45. Annemarie Schimmel, *Islam in the Indian Subcontinent*, Sang-e- Meel Publications, Lahore, 2003, p. 140.
46. Lajwanti Rama Krishna, *Panjabi Sufi-Poets A.D. 1460-1900*, p. 16-18.
47. In their actual life both the sufis remained unmarried.
48. For the Gurmukhi version see Mohan Singh Diwana, *Shah Husain, 165 Kafian*, Kasturi Lal and Sons, Amritsar, n.d. p. 51.
49. English translation by Sant Singh Sekhon, *A History of Panjabi Literature*, Vol. II, pp. 180-81.
50. English translation by J.R. Puri and T.R. Shangari, *Bulleh Shah: The Love-Intoxicated Iconoclast*, pp. 276-77. For the Gurmukhi text see Jagtar, *Bulleh Shah –Jeevan Ate Rachna*, pp. 105-106.
51. Writing about emotions and the Indian awakening, Rajat Kanta Ray observes, "Divine and earthly love, when they reach a certain pitch, have a psychical tendency to shade into each other. In Indian culture this became a doctrine; an ingrained attitude of mind." Rajat Kanta Ray, *Exploring Emotional History: Gender, Mentality and Literature in the Indian Awakening*, Oxford University Press, New Delhi, 2003, first published in 2001, p. 58.
52. Annemarie Schimmel, *Mystical Dimensions of Islam*, p. 49
53. Sutinder Singh Noor, ed., *Punjabi Sufi Kaav*, *kafi* no, 7, 8, 18 and 35.
54. John Baldock, *The Essence of Sufism*, Arcturus Publishing Limited, London, 2006, p. 91.
55. For the Gurmukhi version see Jagtar, *Bulleh Shah –Jeevan Ate Rachna*, pp. 138-139.

56. English translation by J.R. Puri and T.R. Shangari, *Bulleh Shah: The Love Intoxicated Iconoclast*, pp. 258-259.
57. English translation by Sant Singh Sekhon, *The Love of Hir and Ranjha*, p. 163.
58. Charlotte Vaudeville, 'The Concept of Divine Love in Jayasi' *Padmavat: Virah and Ishq'* in M. Waseem, Tr. and Ed., *On Becoming an Indian Muslims: French Essays on Aspects of Syncretism*, Oxford University Press, New Delhi, 2003, P. 168.
59. Darshan Singh Maini, *Studies in Punjabi Poetry*, New Delhi, Vikas Publishing House, 1979, p. 16.
60. English translation by Darshan Singh Maini, ibid., p.16; for Gurmukhi version see Brij Sagar, *Hymns of Sheikh Farid*, p. 37.
61. English translation ibid., p. 92; for the Gurmukhi text see p. 30.
62. As quoted in Asim Roy, *Islam in South Asia: A Regional Perspective*, South Asian Publishers, New Delhi, 1996, p. 77.
63. The following tragic event that occurred in the life of Shaikh Farid also demands attention of the reader: One of Shaikh Farid's daughters became "a widow in her early youth and did not marry again. She rather devoted herself to religion in such a way that the saint remarked, 'Had it been permitted to give *khilafatnama* (grant of authority by a master sufi to his disciple to enroll *murids* in the *silsilah*) of the Shaikh and his *sajjadah* (prayer carpet) to a woman, I would have given them to Bibi Sharifa.'" Iqtidar Husain Siddiqui, 'The Attitude of the Chishti Saints towards Women during the Thirteenth and Fourteenth Centuries' in Ahsan Jan Qaisar and Som Prakash Verma, eds., *Art and Culture*, Felicitation Volume in Honour of Professor S. Nurul Hasan, Publication Scheme, Jaipur, 1993, pp. 91-92.
64. We observe that the motif of rose and nightingale in the Persian and Turkish mystic poetry are said to have appeared very prominently. Ruzbihan Baqli, an Iranian mystic of the twelfth century, illumined the prophetic tradition according to which Muhammad declared the red rose to be the manifestation of God's glory. Since this flower reveals divine beauty and glory most perfectly, the nightingale, a symbol of the longing soul, loves it passionately.
65. English translation by Brij Sagar, *Hymns of Sheikh Farid*, pp. 112-113; for the Gurmukhi text see p. 37.
66. Annemarie Schimmel, *Mystical Dimensions of Islam*, p. 307
67. Jagtar, *Bulleh Shah- Jeevan Ate Rachna*, pp.183-189.
68. Sant Singh Sekhon, *A History of Panjabi Literature*, vol. II, p. 175.
69. Annie Leclerc, 'Woman's Word' in Deborah Cameron, ed., *The Feminist Critique of Language: A Reader*, p. 77.
70. Lajwanti Rama Krishna, *Panjabi Sufi Poets*, p. 43.
71. Lajwanti Rama Krishna, *Panjabi Sufi Poets*, p. 43. Similarly, Shah Husain's contemporary Shah Abul Karim (1536-1624), a Sindi sufi poet justifies his mystical dancing: "Some people engaged themselves in reading books and some in other occupation. I learnt the sama only and did not care for any other occupation." To this Sindi sufi there was no difference between the *zikr* and the *sama*. Motilal Jotwani, *Sindi Literature and Society*, New Delhi, 1979, p. 26.

72. For the Gurmukhi version see Mohan Singh Diwana, *Shah Husain, 165 Kafian*, pp. 63-65.
73. J.R. Puri and T.R. Shangari, *Bulleh Shah: The Love-Intoxicated Iconoclast*, p. 283.
74. Richard Maxwell Eaton, *Sufis of Bijapur 1300-1700:Social Roles of Sufis in Medieval India*, Princeton, Princeton University Press, 1978, pp. 155-173; Annemarie Schimmel, *Islam in the Indian Subcontinent*, pp. 139-140.
75. Sant Singh Sekhon, *A History of Panjabi Literature*, Vol. II, p. 164.
76. J.R. Puri and T.R. Shangari, *Bulleh Shah: The Love-Intoxicated Iconoclast*, p. 384.
77. Najm Hosain Syed, *Recurrent Patterns in Punjabi Poetry*, p. 22.
78. R.C. Zaehner, *Mysticism Sacred and Profane*, London, 1971, p. 205.
79. For detail see Iqtidar Husain Siddiqui, 'The Attitude of the Chishti Saints towards Women during the Thirteenth and Fourteenth Centuries' in Ahsan Jan Qaisar and Som Prakash Verma, eds., *Art and Culture*, pp. 91-94.

12

Formation of Naqshbandi Mysticism

Studying the Major Writings of Shaikh Ahmad Sirhindi

Iqbal Sabir

Shaikh Ahmad Sirhindi (1563-1624) emerged as the most important mystic of the Indian subcontinent during the Mughal period. He played a multifarious role in the religious, social and political domains.[1] It was owing to his strenuous efforts that the Naqshbandi order became the principal mystical discipline for nearly two hundred years and exercised a deep influence on the religious life of the Muslims. He devoted his energies to revive the Muslim law (*shariat*) in its pristine purity and, in the process, sought to weed out the innovations which had crept into it during the previous centuries. He distanced himself from the time-serving theologians and free-thinking mystics. He developed the concept of unity of appearance (*wahdat-ul-shuhud*) in order to counter the principle of unity of existence (*wahdat-ul-wujud*), which had gained strong currency among the people inclined towards mysticism. He took a keen interest in contemporary politics and unleashed a campaign to change the policies of the Mughal state. In particular, he expressed a strong dissatisfaction against the intervention of Akbar in religious affairs, which had caused a grave concern in the orthodox circles. Jahangir, who noted the presence of Sirhindi's disciples in every city of the Mughal empire,[2] saw him as a potential threat to his power and even imprisoned him for a short period. Notwithstanding this punitive measure, the influence of Sirhindi spread to every corner of the Indian subcontinent. He was hailed as the renewer of the second millennium (*mujaddid alf-i-sani*) by his contemporaries. Not only this, his fame spread to lands beyond the Indian frontier like Afghanistan, Central Asia, Persia, Arabia, Turkey, China and Indonesia.[3] Sirhindi's tremendous reputation as a towering Muslim ideologue must be attributed, to a large extent, to his literary productions in the form of letters and brochures.

It would be appropriate to appreciate the ideas and activities of Sirhindi in the context of his times. He was born at Sirhind which was an important town on the Agra-Lahore highway.[4] His descent was traced to the second pious caliph Umar al-Faruq al-Azam. One of his ancestors was Imam Rafiuddin (a disciple of Syed Jalaluddin Bukhari of Uch) who is said to have established the town of Sirhind at the instance of Firuz Shah Tughluq.[5] He received his early education from the scholars of Sirhind, including his own father Shaikh Abdul Ahad Faruqi who was a reputed interpreter of the concept of unity of existence (*wahdat-ul-wujud*).[6] He acquired higher education at Sialkot, where he studied under Maulana Kamal Kashmiri and Shaikh Yaqub Sarafi Kashmiri.[7] He also benefited from the scholarship of Qazi Bahlul Badakhshani under whom he studied such works as *Tafsir-i-Wahidi, Tafsir-i-Baizawi, Sahih-ul-Bukhari, Mishkat-i-Tabrizi, Shamail-i-Tirmizi, Jami Saghir-i-Suyuti, Qasidah-i-Burdah* and *Mishkat-ul-Masabih.*[8] He received preliminary mystical training as well as initiation in several sufi orders under the guidance of his father. At a relatively young age, he started teaching in his ancestral seminary at Sirhind. He stayed at Agra, the capital of the Mughal empire, for a period of nine years (1583-1592).[9] He came in contact with the leading nobles and prominent intellectuals, including Abul Fazl and Faizi. He felt deeply distressed at the prevailing scenario. Akbar was engaged in experiments in the religious domain.[10] He assumed the position of a just ruler (*imam-i-adil*) and interpreter of the Muslim law (*mujtahid*) through a royal decree (*mahzar*). He developed an attitude of distrust towards the conservative theologians, deprived them of their land grants and humiliated them in several ways. In the court circles, the fundamental principles of Islam were undermined. Doubts were expressed regarding the prophethood of Muhammad, including his divine revelation (*wahi*) and prophetic miracles (*mojizat*). The growing influence of Shias was manifested in their condemnation of the Prophet's wife Aisha and his companions. What was worse, some attempts were made to treat Akbar as a prophet and invest him with divine attributes.[11] It is in these circumstances that Sirhindi wrote two brochures, Proofs of Prophecy (*Isbat-un-Nubuwwah*) and Refutation of the Shias (*Risala Radd-i-Rawafiz*). Returning to his native place in 1592, Sirhindi devoted himself to teaching. In 1600, he was initiated into the Naqshbandi order under the tutelage of Khwaja Baqi Billah.[12] This was a turning point in his life.

Sirhindi was not only an erudite scholar and profound thinker. He was also a prolific writer. He expounded and communicated his ideas in as many as 534 letters which have come to be known as *Maktubat-i-*

Imam Rabbani. These letters were brought out in the form of three volumes during the later part of his life. These letters were characterized by certain distinct features. Sirhindi himself supervised the task of their compilation. He chose the editor for each volume from amongst his disciples. He decided the sequence of letters which were arranged in a chronological order. The first volume, which contained 313 letters, was compiled by Shaikh Yar Muhammad Jadid Badakhshi in 1616 under the title of *Durr-ul-Maarifat*. The second volume, which contained 99 letters, was compiled by Khwaja Abdul Haiy in 1619 under the title of *Nur-ul-Khalaiq*. The third volume, which contained 114 letters, was compiled by Khwaja Muhammad Ḥashim Kishmi in 1623 under the title of *Maarifat-i-Haqaiq*. Each letter is preceded by the editor's brief introduction, which provides the name of the addressee as well as the nature of the subject. The letters have been written to nearly 200 persons, most of whom had adopted the path of mysticism. In most cases, the letters were written in response to the questions posed by Sirhindi's disciples. However, he also wrote many letters on his own initiative.[13] He wrote about 70 letters to the Mughal nobles including Shaikh Farid Bukhari, Abdur Rahim Khan-i-Khanan, Khan-i-Jahan, Qulich Khan, Sadr-i-Jahan, Khan-i-Azam and Mirza Darab. The entire corpus of letters throws valuable light on the political and social conditions during the heyday of the Mughal empire. They are indispensable for understanding Sirhindi's ideas on religion and mysticism.[14] In addition to his letters, Sirhindi produced half a dozen works on a variety of subjects. In the following pages, an attempt is being made to analyse the content of these works as they have not received adequate scholarly attention.

Isbat-un-Nubuwwah

The first work of Sirhindi is a brochure in Arabic entitled *Isbat-un-Nubuwwah* i.e. Proofs of Prophecy.[15] It was written during the course of his stay (1582-83) at Agra. It comprises a preface, an introduction (*muqaddemah*) and two chapters (*maqalas*).[16] The preface opens with the praise of God and His last messenger Prophet Muhammad.[17] Thereafter, Sirhindi describes the circumstances in which the brochure was written. He observed deviations in the religious beliefs of the people regarding the prophecy. There was enough evidence to show that a particular person (apparently emperor Akbar) was shrewdly claiming himself as the prophet,[18] but there were serious defects in such claims. Several un-Islamic ideas had penetrated the Muslim community. Tyrannical rulers inflicted sufferings on the righteous theologians (*ulama*), who had firm belief in the Prophet and Muslim law. Several *ulama* of Islam had been put to death. The situation had reached such a pass that even the clarification (*tashrih*) of the name of the Prophet had been discarded.

Those, who bore the sacred word Muhammad as a part of their names, were forced to change their names. Cow slaughter, which was a common practice among the Muslims, was prohibited. Mosques and tombs were in a state of ruin. The religious practices and places of worship, which belonged to non-believers, were held in respect. Religious customs of Islam were declared false, while those of non-believers were introduced. The religious injunctions (*ahkam*) of non-believers were translated into Persian, so that all traces of Islam could be erased. The malady of doubt had become so widespread that even the physicians (rulers) themselves had come into the grip of the disease. Efforts were made to detect the cause of the weakness in individual beliefs. There was no reason other than the remoteness (*bud al ahd*) from the days of the Prophet, the influence of the science of philosophy and the books of Indian philosophers (*kutub-i hukama al-Hindi*).

In these circumstances, Sirhindi held polemical discussions (*munazirahs*) with those who had studied philosophy and who claimed to have benefited from the works of infidels, but who have gone astray in supporting the prophecy for a particular person (Akbar). These people openly proclaim that prophecy is just wisdom (*hikmat*) and convenience (*maslahat*), that it is merely concerned with reforming the external conditions of people and that its main purpose is to protect the people from sexual freedom and mutual differences. They also believe that prophecy has nothing to do with salvation on the day of resurrection (*najat-i-ukhrawiyah*), but it is concerned with obtaining excellence in civilized morals (*tahzib-i-akhlaq*) and spiritual actions (*al-amal il-qalbiyah*), as described by philosophers in their works. They have sought support from the monumental work of Imam Ghazzali, who is said to have given precedence to moral actions over prayers and fasting. The sciences of philosophers are superfluous, because they do not contribute to spiritual advancement and have been plagiarized from the holy scriptures of ancient prophets.[19] Sirhindi's attitude to philosophers was inspired by the writings of Imam Ghazzali. But unlike Ghazzali, Sirhindi lumps together all philosophers and their sciences and rejects them in totality.[20]

In response to the issues raised by Akbar and his supporters, Sirhindi argues that eternal wisdom (*hikmat-i-azaliyah*) and divine favour (*inayat-i-ilahiyah*) enabled the advent of the prophets, so that they could complete the human souls and cure spiritual diseases. This becomes possible only when prophets frighten the recalcitrants, communicate good news to the believers and inform them of the ultimate reward and punishment. This task is essential because human beings, overpowered by their desires, fall a prey to sin. It is the prophet's mission that leads to ultimate salvation and eternal prosperity. The role of prophecy cannot be undermined by our remoteness from the age of

Prophet Muhammad. If we can recognize the contribution of Galen (the physician) and Sobayah (the Arab grammarian) by studying their writings, we can also understand the mission of the Prophet by considering the Quranic injunctions and prophetic traditions (*ahadis*). If we do so, we will reach the conclusion that Prophet Muhammad is the most superior of all the prophets and that the remoteness of time is not an obstacle to this conviction, as in the case of Galen and Sobayah.[21]

In the introduction (*muqaddemah*) to the work, Sirhindi examines the views expressed by scholasticism and philosophy on prophecy, which is followed by a discussion on the miracles (*mojizah*) of prophets. Thereafter, in two chapters, Sirhindi explores the reality of prophecy and its necessity for the people. He argues that natural faculties of human beings are incapable of knowing the existence of the numerous worlds which constitute the universe. Right from his birth, human being is provided with a few senses viz. touch, sight, hearing, taste and discrimination. It is the sense of reason (*aql*) which enables him to discriminate between the legality and desirability of things. There is a stage beyond reason where human being is able to visualize things which cannot be seen with ordinary eyes. Those who rely on reason have failed to reach this stage and, therefore, are unable to appreciate the reality of prophecy. An outstanding characteristic of prophecy is the ability to comprehend what cannot be understood through reason.[22] It is God who convinces the Prophet through signs and miracles, his unique role as His messenger. It is God who is empowered to ensure the invisibility of the angel during revelation of the Quran.[23] The proof of prophecy lies in Muhammad's own claim on the subject and the miracles of his life, including the revelation of the Quran. In this manner,[24] Sirhindi rejects the objections against prophecy that were raised by philosophers and reasonists.

Risalah Radd-i-Rawafiz

Written in 1593 in the Persian language, this epistle is profusely punctuated with Quranic verses, prophetic traditions and Arabic quotations. It is written in refutation of a brochure which was brought out by the Shia clerics of Mashhad on the occasion of its siege by Abdullah Khan Uzbek. The latter work itself was produced in reaction to a book compiled by the Sunni theologians of Transoxiana, which attacked the Shia doctrines and Shia opposition to the first three caliphs. Apart from an introduction, Sirhindi's epistle is divided into three parts – the first describes the various Shia sects, the second contains a trenchant criticism of Shia beliefs and the third is devoted to the praise of the Prophet's family. The work begins with the praise of God and pays rich tributes to the Prophet, the pious caliphs, their companions and descendants. Thereafter, Sirhindi highlights the glory of Islam during the early centuries of its history in the Indian subcontinent. Though the arrival of Islam was relatively late, yet due to the strenuous efforts of several people – rulers, sufis and saints – Islamic traditions began to develop. In fact, the Muslim community of the country required a prominent position, because its members strictly followed the path of the righteous (*ahl-i-sunnat wa al-jamaat*). Generally they followed the Hanafite religious path. The Shafite and Hanabalite schools are equally true, but they have hardly any followers in this country. In order to strengthen his argument, Sirhindi quotes the following poetical verses of Amir Khusro,[25] the famous Persian poet of the early sultanate period:

1. What a fine country is India where is found the brightness of religion (Islam) and the *shariat* receives the highest form of respect and dignity.
2. Strong and powerful Hindus have been destroyed and lower classes among them are paying wealth (i.e. taxes like *kharaj* and *jaziya*).
3. Here Islam has received great respect and protection, while the supporters of infidelity (*kufr*) are oppressed.
4. If the *shariat* had not permitted the treatment of non-Muslims as *zimmis*, the very name of Hindus would have disappeared from the country.
5. From Ghazni to the banks of the river (perhaps the Ganges) you will observe the glory of Islam.
6. Neither is there any trace of Christians, who due to lack of fear of God, regard Jesus Christ, the slave of God, to be God.
7. Nor is there any battle and resistance from the side of the Jews, who according to the Quran, turn to the Torah.
8. There is not to be found any fire worshipper who expresses happiness over fire worship and the fire complains to them again and again.
9. All the Muslims follow the Hanafite way in sincerity like all the four schools (Hanafite, Shafite, Hanbalite and Malikite).
10. Neither is there any enmity with Shafite, nor any sort of (without reason) association with Zaid. All are wholehearted lovers of the faith of *ahl-i sunnat wa jamaat*.
11. There is no Mutazilite who, on account of their ill-kept beliefs, were themselves deprived of the sight of God.
12. There is no Shia (Rafzi), because of whose wrong religion, the loyal companions of the Prophet of Islam could feel distressed.
13. There is no Kharji with dog's habit, who because of his enmity, could pass any bad remark against the lion of God (*sher-i-khuda*) i.e. Ali, the fourth pious caliph.

14. What a nice country is India where Muslims are always born as seekers of religion and even the fish that comes out of the river is Sunni.

Sirhindi suggests that the Indian subcontinent remained free from the Shias during a period of five hundred years since the advent of Islam. During the reign of Abdullah Khan Uzbek, the Shias became engaged in seditious activities. Many of them were killed, but many migrated to India and became associated with the rulers and nobles. Through outwardly attractive arguments, they misled innocent people and weaned them away from the path of the righteous (*ahl-i-sunnat wa jamaat*). While the Muslims of Khurasan were saved from the religious malpractices of the Shias, the arrival of these people of evil faith (*bad aqidah*) created serious problems for the Indian Muslims, who were faced with a new sedition.[26] For, Shia scholars and students were engaged in propagating their religious beliefs all over the place, including the courts of rulers and nobles. Sirhindi claims to have refuted them with rational and traditional arguments (*dalail-i-aqli wa naqli*) and enlightened the ruling elite regarding the mistaken beliefs of the Shias.[27] Being a descendant of the second pious caliph Umar al-Faruq al-Azam and acting in accordance with a prophetic tradition, Sirhindi channelized his literary and religious efforts into a written form, so that people could benefit from it.[28] After assessing the attitude of Shias towards Hazrat Ali, he examines the characteristics of several Shia sects, each of which accuses the other of infidelity. Some of these sects (*taifas*) are Sabaiyah, Kamiliyah, Bayaniyah, Mughiriyah, Jinahiyah, Mansuriyah, Khitabiyah, Ghurabiyah, Zammiyah, Yunusiyah, Mafuziyah, Ismailiyah, Zaidiyah, Imamiyah etc.[29]

As for the method followed by Sirhindi, he considers the respective arguments of the two sides – Sunni clerics of Transoxiana and Shia theologians of Mashhad – on five controversial points and concludes each one with his own judgement in favour of the former. Firstly, he accepts the exalted status of the first three caliphs in the spiritual hierarchy of Islam, as the prophetic traditions prove that Prophet Muhammad held them in great affection and high esteem. The issue under discussion is whether the sayings and acts of the Prophet are based on revelation (*wahi*) or his own interpretation (*ijtihad*). Again traditions (*hadis*) prove that the Prophet often decided matters through his own intellect and duly considered the different views expressed by his companions.[30] Doubts are expressed regarding the authenticity of the religious works of Shias, who are also accused of transposing words (*tahrif*) in some verses of the Quran,[31] so that their meaning was altered. Secondly, Sirhindi rejects the Shia contention that Ali's right to caliphate was usurped by the first three caliphs. Basing himself on a Quranic verse,[32] he argues that the allegiance (*baiat*) of the three caliphs to the Prophet was such an excellent act that they earned God's pleasure for it. There is no definite statement of the Prophet (*nass*) in favour of Ali's succession.[33] Reliable traditionists, who hold Ali in high esteem for his excellence in worldly and religious matters, have failed to refer to such a tradition. Even Ali himself failed to bring forward any such tradition while delaying his allegiance to Abu Bakr or when caliph Umar formed a six member panel or when Ali himself was securing the allegiance of Amir Muawiya's men.[34] Finally Abu Bakr's withdrawal of the garden of Fidak was not motivated by any ill will against the Prophet's daughter Fatima.[35]

Thirdly, Abu Bakr enjoyed superiority (*afzaliyat*) over all other companions of the Prophet. Having remained in the Prophet's company for twenty three years, he had assimilated several Prophetic virtues.[36] Owing to his immense love for his master, Abu Bakr had annihilated himself into (the love of) the Prophet (*fana fi-rasul*). A person, who had acquired such an exalted position, cannot be condemned. The words of Shias against him are harsh, troublesome and painful.[37] Fourthly, Ali not only extended his own allegiance to the first three caliphs, but also did not prevent other Muslims from doing so. His support cannot be attributed to force (*jabr*) or subterfuge (*taqaiyya*). Being one of the greatest of companions (*sahaba*) who was reputed for his bravery, Ali cannot be guilty of such impious an act as subterfuge. Attributing such a conduct amounted to committing a sin and those who committed the sin were infidels.[38] Fifthly, Sirhindi brings to light several prophetic traditions which prove that any kind of opposition to the first three caliphs was treated as infidelity. In this connection, Sirhindi mobilizes the opinion of several experts of Islamic religious sciences – traditionists, theologians, jurists and mystics – and thus tries to show that there was a consensus in the Muslim community (*ijma-i-ummat*) on the issue. He quotes several traditions in favour of Aisha, the Prophet's wife, who was also the daughter of caliph Abu Bakr.[39] He undertakes a similar exercise with regard to the Prophet's family (*ahl-i-bait*).[40]

Mabda o Maad

The title of the above work may be translated as *Beginning and Return*. It was written over a period of ten years from 1008 AH/1599 AD to 1019 AH/1610 AD. The final version was prepared by one of Sirhind's disciples, Muhammad Siddiq Kishmi.[41] Sirhindi refers to it many times in the first volume of his letters, *Maktubat-i-Imam Rabbani*. It has been quoted extensively in Muhammad Hashim Kishmi's *Zubdat-ul-Maqamat* and Badruddin Sirhindi's *Hazrat-ul-Quds*, both of which deal with the life and thought of Sirhindi. Differing in form and content from the earlier two works, *Mabda o Maad* reflects the tremendous change which Sirhindi underwent owing to his association with Khwaja Baqi Billah. It was intended to be an esoteric work and contains mystical insights which (as claimed by Sirhindi) had not been offered by any one so far. In the words of Friedmann, "In view of the extensive quotations in the contemporary material, *Mabda o Maad* seems to have been very popular in the seventeenth century, although modern research has virtually ignored it."[42] Introducing the book, its compiler Muhammad Siddiq Kishmi states that it comprises several minute and pleasing discussions as well as numerous deep and sublime secrets. The author of the brochure is a distinguished person owing to his association with the second pious caliph, the Hanafite school of jurisprudence and the Naqshbandi sufi order. Not only this, the author is a renowned religious leader (*imam*), a proof of God for human beings, an object of veneration for saints,[43] discloser of the secrets of the opening chapter of the Quran (*surah-i-fatiha*), renovator of the second millennium (*mujaddid alf-i-sani*), one who had benefited (*uwaisi*) from the spirit of elderly mystics, one who is gifted with divine gnosis (*arif-i-rabbani*) and one who is the leader of all Muslims (*Shaikh-ul-Islam*).[44] It may be noted that *Mabda o Maad* consists of 61 short chapters on a variety of mystical subjects, each of which is designated as Minha.

In this work, Sirhindi describes his own spiritual progress, with reference to the significance of various stages and the figures who provided the required benediction. He began his spiritual journey under the tutelage of Khwaja Baqi Billah. Owing to the attention of his mentor, he reached the spiritual goal (*jazbah*) of the saints of the Naqshbandi order, which is attained by annihilating oneself into the quality of Qaiyyumiat.[45] After acquiring the perfections of this stage, he received the guidance of the fourth caliph Ali and moved to the stage of the divine name. He was assisted by the spirituality of Khwaja Bahauddin Naqshband to reach the stageof Qabliyat-i-Ula or Haqiqat-i-Muhammadiyyah. He received guidancefrom the second caliph Umar al-Faruq and reached the stage of Aqtabi-Muhammadiyyah. At this stage, he receved guidance from Prophet Muhammad and Khwaja Alauddin Attar, ho was a senior discile of Khwaja Bahauddin Naqshband.[46] This stage, whee Dairah-i-Zilliyat and Asl-i-Khalis meet, is nown as Maqam-i-Aqtab On being installed at this stae, Sirhindi received the robe of Qutb-i-Irshad rom Prophet Muhammad. After tavelling through seeral other stages, he reached the highest stage of Asl-ul-Asl and received assistance from the sirituality of Ghaus-i-Azam Shaikh Abdul Qadir Gilani. Thereafter, he wassent back to the world, just as at the conclusion of the previous spiritual journeys.[47] He received spiritual wealth (*nisbat-i-fardiyat*) from his father Shaikh Abul Ahad

Faruqi, who had received th same from Shah Kamal Qadiri.[48] He learnt the habit of vluntary prayers (*ibadat-i-nafilah*) from his father, who had acuired this blessing from Chishti saints Shaikh Abdul Quddus Gangohi and his son Shaih Ruknuddin. He learnt to acquire the inpired knowledge (*ilm-i-ladunni*) from the spirituality of Khwaja Khizar.[49] He was also benefited by thespirituality of Shaikh Shihabuddin Suhrawardi, Shaikh Qutbudin Bakhtiyar Kaki and the Kubrai saints.[50]

Sirhindi pays considerable attention to the mthod adopted by a spiritual preceptor (*pir*) to train his disciples. Before initiatin a person in the spiritual discipline, the mentor should ask him to seek divine favour (*istikharah*) and, ruling out any uncertainty, egin the task of training. At the outset, he should direct the seeker to undertake repentance (*taubah*) without which it is futile to embark n the spiritual path. Thereafter, he should give lessons in accordance with the seeker's capacity of acquiring spirituality and cultivating patience. He should pay full attention to the seeker and familiarize him with the conditions of the spiritual path. He should strictly inculcate the teachings of Quran and Ahadis, besides the traditions of minent mysics. He must ask the seeker to discard those inspirations which are even slightly opposed to the Quran and Ahadis. He should exhort the discile to nurtre correct beliefs (*aqaid*) in accordance with the righteous (*ahl-i-sunnat wa jamaat*) of the Sunni sect. Hemust ensure that the disciple learns the principles of jurisprudence (*ahkam-i-fiqh*).[51] He must clarify that befiefs (*itiqad*) and practice (*amal*) are two wings, without which it is not possible to fly along the spiritual path. A seeker acquires the authority to enroll his own disciples not through his spiritual excellence, but through the mentor's pleasure. Khwaja Muhammad Naqshband granted his succeson (*khilafat*) to Maulana Yaqub Charkhi even befoe the completon of the latter's spiritual training.[52]

In the eyes of Sirhindi, the spiritual preceptor plays a crucial role in the training of his disciples. The disciple was expected to acquire perfection in following (*taqlid*) and compliance (*ittiba*), just as Abu Bakr emerged as a perfect follower of the Prophet. He clearly states, "Whatever excellence is achieved by a disciple, it is achieved by following (*taqlid*) his mentor." Even the mistake of the mentor is better than the disciple's right course.[53] But Sirhindi hastens to sound a note of caution. He warns the disciple not to exaggerate his love for the mentor. The faith of a disciple in his mentor's excellence is merely the outcome of his love, which has brought benefit (*ifadah*) and gain (*istifadah*). It is necessary that the disciple does not prefer his mentor to those pious personalities whose excellence has been recognized in the canonical law (*shariat*). The excessive love of Shias for the Prophet's family and descendants (*ahl-i-bait*) deserves condemnation, just like the excessive love of Christians for Jesus Christ. However, the disciple is permitted to prefer his own mentor to spiritual figures other than those whose excellence has been recognized by the *shariat*. This form of conduct on the part of the disciple is correct and necessary in spiritualdom (*tariqat*). Speaking for himself, Sirhindi takes pride in receiving spiritual training from Khwaja Baqi Billah and expresses his gratitude to God for providing him with this glorious opportunity.[54]

Sirhindi gives credit to Khwaja Bahauddin Naqshband for introducing the concept of six sides or directions (*shash jihat*) in the seeker's heart which was like a mirror. These six sides are soul (*nafs*), heart (*qalb*), spirit (*ruh*), secret (*sirr*), hidden (*khafi*) and hiding (*ikhfa*). Whatever is held by individuals from these six sides is possessed only by the heart. Contrary to the other sufi orders where spiritual journey remains confined to inside of the heart (*batin-i-qalb*), the Naqshbandis reach the deepest point in the depth of the heart (*abtan-i-batin*). Due to this reason, the science (*ulum*) and gnosis (*maarif*) of above six sides are inspired in the heart (*maqam-i-qalb*). It is on account of the blessings of the Naqshbandi saints that Sirhindi learnt the condition of the heart at various stages.[55] Regarding the nature of God, Sirhindi holds that He exists with His essence and, for His existence, He does not depend on His being.[56] He also feels that if knowledge of things, which disappear during the stage of annihilation, come back during the stage of union (*baqa*), they are beneficial to the spirituality of the seeker (*arif*).[57] Sirhindi is convinced about the superiority of Imam Abu Hanifa in his role as interpreter (*mujtahid*) of the Muslim law (*shariat*) as compared to the other three founders of legal schools. Therefore, discarding his initial wavering between Hanafite and Shafite schools, Sirhindi comes round to accept the former and accordingly decides that there was no need to repeat the opening chapter of the Quran (*surah-i-fatiha*) behind the prayer leader (*imam*).[58] Finally, Sirhindi discusses the superiority of spiritual knowledge (*ilm-i-batin*) over outward knowledge (*ilm-i-zahir*) and that of prophecy (*nubuwwah*) over sainthood (*wilayat*).[59]

Mukashifat-i-Ainiyah

Another work of Sirhindi, which is entitled *Mukashifat-i-Ainiyah*, comprises several drafts (*musawwadat*) on different themes. These drafts were originally preserved by some disciples of Sirhindi. Though the themes were discussed in the collections of Sirhindi's letters, yet his followers felt that the drafts ought to be given the shape of a treatise. The task was taken up by Muhammad Hashim Kishmi, the compiler of the third volume of *Maktubat-i-Imam Rabbani* and the author of *Zubdat-ul-Maqamat*. During a period of two years (1641-1643), he collected the drafts from the disciples (*khalifas*) of Sirhindi and completed the task.

The final title of the work *Mukashifat-i-Ainiyah Mujaddidiyah* offers a chronogram, which indicates the year of its compilation as 1053 AH/ 1643 AD.[60] Muhammad Hashim Kishmi, the compiler, has contributed a preface in which the characteristics of the volume have been brought to light. He writes, "An inspiration was put into the heart of this mendicant (*faqir*), who is devoted to the shrine of his mentor, that these drafts must be copied, arranged and compiled because the gnosis of these pages belongs to the Shaikh. Though the subjects, which are discussed in these pages, are available in the other brochures and letters of the Shaikh, yet the style of description is different. Accordingly, these drafts (*musawwadat*) have been compiled in the form of a brochure (*risala*) with the title of *Mukashifat*."[61] The preface is followed by the genealogical trees (*shajras*) of three major sufi orders – Qadiri, Naqshbandi and Chishti. While opening with the Qadiri order, Sirhindi quotes a prophetic tradition (*hadis*), "My descendants are like the boat of Noah. Whoever rode on it acquired salvation. Those who lagged behind were destroyed." Therefore, Sirhindi admitted that he bore the robe of the Qadiris (*khirqah-i-Qadiriyah*) from a pious brother, who had received it from his spiritual preceptor Shaikh Kamal. The last mentioned, in turn, received it from his mentor Shah Fuzail. Mentioning the name of every saint of the order, Sirhindi traces the Qadiri spiritual genealogy to Shaikh Abdul Qadir Gilani and carries it to Prophet Muhammad through Ali. Similarly, he traces the spiritual genealogy of the Naqshbandis to the Prophet through the first caliph Abu Bakr Siddique. The line of the Chishtis is also traced to the Prophet through Ali. The brochure also contains the text of letters of authority (*ijazatnamas*) that were granted by Sirhindi to his spiritual successors – Shaikh Hamid Bengali, Mir Muhammad Numan, Shaikh Muhammad bin Tahir and the compiler himself, Muhammad Hashim Kishmi.[62]

Sirhindi highlights the spiritual excellence of the mystical path of the Naqshbandi saints, who are referred to as Hazrat-i-Khwajgan. He asserts that their method of spiritual training is unique. The acceptance of destruction and depression is called the spirit (*jazbah*). Owing to the high spiritual stages of the Naqshbandi saints, this spirit did not have any equivalent in other sufi orders. Its face bears complete resemblance with the circle of the unseen (*dairah-i-ghaib*). This, in turn, resembles the extreme of extremes (*nihayat-ul-nihayat*), the object of deputation (*mansha-i-taiyyun*) and capability of the community (*qabliyat-i-jamiah*), which means the deputation of Muhammad (*taiyyun-i-Muhammadi*). On this basis, it may be stated that in the Naqshbandi method of spiritual training, the end (*nihayat*) is inserted in the beginning (*bidayat*). That is why the elders (*akabir*) of the Naqshbandi path made excellent progress after attaining the journey inside God (*sair-i fi-Allah*). In this context,

Sirhindi describes the spiritual eminence of the four pious caliphs (*khulafa-i-rashidin*), but makes special reference to the first and fourth viz. Abu Bakr Siddique and Ali al-Murtaza. He also mentions the distinctive qualities of the Naqshbandi saints like Khwaja Abdul Khaliq Ghujdawani, Khwaja Muhammad Parsa, Khwaja Alauddin Attar,[63] Maulana Yaqub Charkhi and Khwaja Ubaidullah Ahrar.

Sirhindi traces the spiritual growth of some prominent Naqshbandi saints. Khwaja Muhammad Naqshband, after attaining the spirit (*jazbah*) of the early Naqshbandi saints (*khwajgan*), turned to the higher spiritual path (*suluk-i-fauqani*) and, rising to the peak, achieved the honour of *fana fi-Allah* and *baqi Allah*. He also covered, one by one, the successive stages of *wilayat*, *shahadat* and *siddiqiat*.[64] Khwaja Baqi Billah was not only a perfect mystic (*arif*), he was (for Sirhindi) a mentor (*shaikhana*), master (*maulana*) and refuge (*malazana*). He was honoured with the exalted company of Naqshbandi saints (*khwajgan*), even though he had not received any formal spiritual training. When he reached the stage of spirit (*jazbah*), he attained the experience of ruining (*istihlak*) and vanishing (*izmihlal*), besides the appearance of oneness in abundance. His inner self was filled and illumined by divine light of the extreme of extreme (*nihayat-ul-nihayat*), with which the stage of *qutbiyat-i-irshad* is concerned. After being authorized by his spiritual preceptor, Khwaja Baqi Billah was conferred with mediated light (*mauquf alaih nur*) and began to train seekers with the appearance of oneness in abundance and achieved a high rank in the stage of *qutbiyat-i-irshad*. The seekers acquired more spiritual benefit by keeping his company than by undertaking hard spiritual exercises. He also received share from the stages of twelve *aqtab* and climbed to the highest point (*fauq*) in the particular way of Faruq-i-Azam. He also completed the journey in heavens (*suluk-i-afaqi*) upto the stage of divine names (*ayan-i-sabilah*). In the meantime, the divine mercy (*inayat-i-khudawandi*) turned towards him and the path of journey in heavens (*suluk-i-afaqi*) was opened to him. While undertaking this journey, he moved towards the name which was his guardian and patron. Having reached this station, he attained the three stages of *wilayat*, *shahadat* and *siddiqiyat*. At this juncture, he disappeared into the point of extreme of extreme (*nihayat-ul-nihayat*) and, in this manner, he was honoured with that great martyrdom (*shahadat-i-uzma*), which was commended by Ali in favour of his son Hasan, "This son of mine is the leader."[65]

In the work under review, Sirhindi expresses his opinion on a large variety of themes viz. the names and attributes of God, the excellences of the words and verses of the Quran,[66] besides the contribution of the Naqshbandi saints of Central Asia. He also discusses the significance of classical mystical texts viz. Abdul Qadir Gilani's *Futuh-ul-Ghaib*,[67]

Shihabuddin Suhrawardi's *Awarif-ul-Maarif* and Abdullah Ansari Harawi's *Manazil-i-Sairin*. He examines the nature of the spiritual journey and the states experienced by a seeker at various stages. We are told that when a seeker desires to go beyond the physical world, he looks towards its origin i.e. the world of spirits (*alam-i-arwah*). Due to its resemblance with adumbration (*zilliyat*), he experiences the spirits – particularly griefs (*shewanat*) or names (*asma*) – that are appropriate to the physical world. He wrongly realizes this experience as the appearance of truth (God), though its manifest (*mashhud*) is the physical world and its origin is the world of spirits (*alam-i-arwah*).[68] Elaborating his understanding on the oneness of God (*tauhid*), Sirhindi proposes two categories – unity of appearance (*tauhid-i-shuhudi*) and unity of existence (*tauhid-i-wujudi*).[69] The former type is indispensable to the Naqshbandi spiritual discipline. It means that until the manifest (*mashhud*) of the seeker becomes one and acquires abundance (*kasrat*) and entirely disappears from his eyes, he does not get any share from the stage of annihilation (*maqam-i-fana*), which is the initial stage of sainthood (*wilayat*). To see oneness (*wahdat*) does not mean to see all as one, but it is to see *kasrat* itself. At this juncture, the seeker experiences *kasrat* as *wahdat* which is not favourable for achieving the truth. Similarly, *kasrat* means the same particular or imagined shapes and faces of possibility and, owing to their elevation, the seeker finds himself in a position to see oneness (*wahdat*). It is only with the disappearance of *kasrat* that the seeker sees *wahdat*.[70]

Hazar nukta-i barik tar zi mu injast
Na har ki sar batrashad qalandari danad

In this way there are a thousand points that are thinner than hair. Every one who shaves his head does not become a qalandar.

As for the second type of oneness (*tauhid-i-wujudi*), Sirhindi does not regard it as an essential ingredient of the Naqshbandi way. During the spiritual journey, it is experienced only by some seekers and not by others. This kind of oneness is realized only by those who receive an increasing share from the absorption of heart (*injizab-i-qalbi*), which they achieve by passing over more stages of the path (*suluk*). However, there is another group of saints who do not experience this type of oneness, as this very absorption of the heart becomes an obstacle for them. This type of oneness is caused by momentary spiritual intoxication (*sukr-i-waqt*), domination of spiritual ecstasy (*ghalba-i-hal*) and supremacy of heart's love. It must be understood that *tauhid-i-shuhudi* is attained only after realizing the *tauhid-i-wujudi*. Those, who realize both types of *tauhid*, continue to experience abundance (*kasrat*) of its vision (*ruyat-i-kasrat*) till they are capable of *tauhid-i-wujudi*. They do not realize *tauhid-i-*

shuhudi unless *kasrat* disappears from their vision. Also, they do not proceed beyond the stage of *tauhid-i-wujudi*. Sirhindi claims the honour of having attained the benefits of both types of *tauhid*. In the beginning, the *tauhid-i-wujudi* was revealed to him. He remained at this stage for several years and acquired its subtleties and realities. When he passed across this stage, he was honoured with the realization of *tauhid-i-shuhudi*, so that the gnosis of both the stages was conferred on him.[71]

Maarif-i-Ladunniyah

The title of this work may be translated as *Inspired Gnosis*. A mystical work written in Persian,[72] it is similar in structure to *Mabda o Maad*. Sirhindi appears to have written it at the beginning of his mystical career i.e. some time after joining the Naqshbandi order under the tutelage of Khwaja Baqi Billah.[73] It comprises of nearly forty sections, which are devoted to different religious and mystical subjects. It opens with a discussion on the significance of the word Allah, which is composed of three alphabets – *alif, laam* and *hey*. It argues that each alphabet signifies a specific form of praise, so that their convergence in a single word shows that it is the greatest name of God (*ism-i-azam*).[74] It uncovers the secrets of divine attributes (*sifat-i-ilahiya*) and sheds light on the hidden meaning of some Quranic verses.[75] It identifies the various stages in the spiritual journey of the seeker, while drawing attention to the stage of completion and assemblage between allegory and purity. It discusses the concept of oneness in three categories i.e. unity of essence, attributes and actions (*wahdat-i-zati, sifati* and *afali*). In his own words:

> *Chun zat-i u taala yaganah ast ki asla gunjaish-i kasrat na darad ...Chun zat-i u taqaddus ba umur kasrat mutamaizah taluq paida kard, fel wa sifat-i u niz taluq paida kardand. Chih inha dar kharij ain zat and pas hamchunanki zat bawastah-i taluq ba ashiya-i mutaddidah zawat-i mutaddidah mi numayad, fel-o sifat-i u niz bawastah hamin taluq mutaddid wa mutakasir mi numayand. Maslan fel-i haq subhqnahu wa taala az azal ta abad yak fel ast.*
>
> Since the essence of God is single, it has no capacity for abundance or plurality.... As His essence is connected with many extraordinary things, His actions and attributes too make similar connections. Therefore essence, owing to its connection with several things, appears in several numbers. His actions and attributes due to this connection, seem to be numerous and abundant.[76]

The work reiterates Sirhindi's stance regarding the reality of Muhammad's prophecy (*haqiqat-i-Muhammadiyyah*). The author highlights the difference between the mystics and experts in scholasticism (*ilm-i-kalam*) regarding the most effective spiritual way. He also underlines the relation of *shariat* with *tariqat* and *haqiqat*. In this context, he explains, "*Haqiqat* means the reality of *shariat*. It is not true that *haqiqat* is separate from the *shariat*. By *tariqat* is meant the method to comply with the reality of the *shariat*. It is not aimed at differentiating between *shariat* and *haqiqat*."[77] While dealing with the mystical concept of annihilation, Sirhindi proposes several types – bodily annihilation (*fana-i-jasadi*), spiritual annihilation (*fana-i-ruhi*), annihilation of the heart (*fana-i-qalbi*), annihilation of soul (*fana-i-nafs*), annihilation of secret (*fana-i-sirr*), annihilation of hidden (*fana-i-khafi*) and annihilation of most hidden (*fana-i-ikhfa*).[78] Sirhindi brings out the special features of the different stages – *wilayat*, *shahadat* and *siddiqiyat* – which were attained by eminent mystics in the past. Besides the excellence of Prophet Muhammad, Sirhindi dwells on the superiority of the Naqshbandi order as well as his own spiritual progress. The work ends by exposing the activities of the opponents of Islam.[79]

Towards the end of the present exercise, we would briefly refer to Sirhindi's minor works. One of them is *Risala-i-Tahliliyah* which was written in Arabic around 1007-08 AH/1598-99 AD.[80] Its basic object is to highlight the significance of the Muslim confession of faith (*kalima-i-taiyyibah*). This is indicated by its very name *Tahliliyah* which means, "Praising God by proclaiming, There is no god but God (*la illah illallah*)." Sirhindi wrote this brochure at a time when Akbar and his supporters had removed the second part of the *kalima* i.e. Muhammad is the Prophet of God (*Muhammad ur rasul allah*), by introducing a new confession, "There is no god but God and Akbar is God's *khalifa*."[81] In this work, Sirhindi discusses such subjects as the virtues of the confession of faith, stages of monotheism (*tauhid*) in the light of Islamic beliefs and philosophic understanding, besides arguments regarding the prophecy and its excellences. Sirhindi also explores the meanings of some words that are frequently used in the mystical discourse e.g. Allah, *kalima*, *jalalat* and *tauhid*. He also draws a distinction between *tauhid* of the common men and *tauhid* of the spiritual elite.[82] In yet another work, entitled *Taliqat bar Sharh-i-Rubaiyat*, Sirhindi offers his critical explanation regarding two quatrains (*rubaiyat*) of his mentor Khwaja Baqi Billah.[83] These verses are focused on the theme of the existence of God. Sirhindi discusses the diverse aspects of the theme and, in the process, removes the doubts from the mind of the readers. The author also examines the theme of oneness of God (*tauhid*), as elucidated by the elder saints of the Naqshbandi order i.e. unity in abundance (*wahdat dar kasrat*).[84]

NOTES AND REFERENCES

1. Saiyyid Muhiyuddin Abul Kalam Azad, *Tazkira*, Sahitya Academy, New Delhi, 1968, pp. 263-264.
2. Jahangir, *Tuzuk-i-Jahangiri*, Persian Text, Ed., Saiyyid Ahmad, Aligarh, 1864, p. 272.
3. Khaliq Ahmad Nizami, 'The Naqshbandiyya Order,' in *Islamic Spirituality*,

Ed., Sayyid Hussain Nasr, Vol. II, New York, 1991, pp. 162, 183-84, 187-88; also see Khaliq Ahmad Nizami, 'Naqshbandi Influence on Mughal Rulers and Politics,' in Khaliq Ahmad Nizami, *State and Culture in Mughal India*, Adam Publishers and Distributors, Delhi, 1985, p. 160.

4. For historical background of the town, see Fauja Singh, Ed., *Sirhind Through the Ages*, Punjabi University, Patiala, 1972.
5. Khwaja Muhammad Hashim Kishmi, *Zubdat-ul-Maqamat*, Munshi Nawal Kishore, Kanpur, 1890, p. 90; Badruddin Sirhindi, *Hazrat-ul-Quds*, Vol. II, Punjab Waqf Board, Lahore, 1971, p. 31.
6. For details regarding Abdul Ahad Faruqi, see Iqbal Sabir, 'Shaikh Abdul Ahad Faruqi Sirhindi: A Renowned Sixteenth Century Sufi of South Asia,, ' in *Dr. K.N. Chitnis Felicitation Volume: Some Aspects of Medieval India*, Samant Publications, Mumbai, 2006, pp. 47-60.
7. Shaikh Yaqub Sarafi Kashmiri (1502-1595) was a famous scholar and spiritual successor of Shaikh Husain Khwarizmi, an eminent Kubrawi saint. He had travelled extensively in Arabia and Persia. He was authorized by Allama Ibn Hajjar Asqalani to give instructions in Hadis. He had many disciples in different parts of India, particularly Kashmir. He had produced several sublime works including a commentary on the Quran. Abdul Qadir Badauni, *Muntakhab-ut-Tawarikh*, Persian Text, Bibliotheca Indica, Calcutta, 1869, pp. 142-49; Abdul Qayyum Rafiqi, *Sufism in Kashmir: From the Fourteenth to the Sixteenth Century*, Bhartiya Publishing House, Varanasi, 1976, pp. 116-124.
8. Contemporary and later works do not provide any information about Qazi Bahlul Badakhshani. But we do learn that he had studied under Shaikh Abdul Rahman bin Fahd of Hejaz, a renowned scholar of Hadis and himself emerged as an expert in this subject. Khwaja Muhammad Hashim Kishmi, *Zubdat-ul-Maqamat*, p. 128.
9. It is not possible to agree with Friedmann that Sirhindi was invited to the Mughal court. In fact Sirhindi went to Agra on his own accord, his object being to interact with scholars and theologians of the capital. Yohanan Friedmann, *Shaykh Ahmad Sirhindi: An Outline of His Thought and a Study of His Image in the Eyes of Posterity*, Oxford University Press, Reprint, Delhi, 2000, p.xiii; Kamaluddin Muhammad Ehsan, *Rauzat-i-Qaiyyumiyah*, Urdu Translation, Vol. I, Allah Walon Ki Dukan, Lahore, 1335 AH/1916 AD, p. 62.
10. Iqbal Sabir, 'Hazrat Mujaddid Alf-i-Sani Ahad-i-Akbari Mein,' in *Ziyah-ul-Wajih*, Vol. 9, No. 6, June 1998, Ed., Wajahatullah Khan, Jamia Furqania, Rampur, pp. 19-24.
11. Abdul Qadir Badauni, *Muntakhab-ut-Tawarikh*, Vol. II, 272-74, 277-79; Abul Fazl, *Ain-i-Akbari*, Vol. II, Persian Text, Munshi Nawal Kishore, Lucknow, 1822, p.224; Khaliq Ahmad Nizami, *Akbar and Religion*, Idarah-i-Adabiyat-i-Delli, Delhi, 1989, pp. 131-32, 187-89.
12. Shaikh Ahmad Sirhindi, *Maktubat-i-Imam Rabbani*, Vol. I, Letter 290; for details regarding Sirhindi's mentor, see Iqbal Sabir, 'Khwaja Baqi Billah: The Founder of the Naqshbandi Silsilah in India,' in *Islamic Heritage in South Asian Subcontinent*, Ed., I.H. Siddiqui and Nazir Ahmad, Publication Scheme, Jaipur, 2000, pp. 137-156.

13. Yohanan Friedmann, op. cit., pp. 2-3.
14. Hasan Murtaza, 'Letters of Shaikh Ahmad: A New Source for Historical Study (1563-1624),' *Proceedings of the Indian History Congress*, Patna, 1946, p. 274; Zawwar Husain, *Hazrat Mujaddid Alf-i-Sani*, Karachi, 1995, p. 683.
15. This brochure was first published from Amritsar in the beginning of the twentieth century along with an edition of *Maktubat-i-Imam Rabbani*. This book is not available any more. The present writer has relied on the Karachi edition of 1963 which has an edited text, Urdu translation and a scholarly introduction by Ghulam Mustafa Khan, formerly Head of the Department of Urdu, Sind University, Hyderabad. The text is based on two manuscripts belonging to (i) Maulavi Jamiluddin Ahmad of Khanqah-i-Sirajia, Kundiyan, District Mianwali, Pakistan and (ii) Maulana Zaid Abul Hasan Faruqi, formerly incharge of Khanqah-i-Mazhariya, Delhi.
16. The second chapter, which was devoted to the refutation of philosophers and the adverse impact of their sciences, is not included in the present edition of *Isbat-un-Nubuwwah*. A copy of this portion was in the possession of Shah Aziz Miyan of Khanqah-i-Niyaziyah, Bareilly, Uttar Pradesh, who died nearly fifty years ago. This copy is no longer available. The present writer received this information from his teacher and supervisor Khaliq Ahmad Nizami.
17. Shaikh Ahmad Sirhindi, *Isbat-un-Nubuwwah*, Ed., Ghulam Mustafa Khan, Aala Kutub Khana, Karachi, 1383 AH/1963 AD, p. 5.
18. This particular person was none other than Akbar. Abdul Qadir Badauni, *Muntakhab-ut-Tawarikh*, Vol. II, p.273; V.A. Smith, *Akbar: The Great Mogul*, S. Chand & Co, New Delhi, Reprint, 1966, pp. 154-59; Muhammad Aslam, *Din-i-Ilahi Aur Us Ka Pasmanzar*, Nudwat-ul-Musannifin, Delhi, 1969, pp. 182-84.
19. Shaikh Ahmad Sirhindi, *Isbat-un-Nubuwwah*, pp. 5-7.
20. Yohanan Friedmann, op. cit., p. 55.
21. Shaikh Ahmad Sirhindi, *Isbat-un-Nubuwwah*, pp. 8-9.
22. Ibid., pp. 18-19.
23. Ibid., pp. 20-31.
24. Ibid., pp. 34-48.
25. Shaikh Ahmad Sirhindi, *Radd-i-Rawafiz*, Ed., Mahbub Ilahi, Idarah-i-Saidiyah Mujaddidiyah, Lahore, 1964, p. 6.
26. Ibid., p. 7.
27. This statement of Sirhindi is clear evidence of his association with Mughal nobles. It also reveals that, during his sojourn at Agra, he sometimes visited the court of Akbar.
28. Shaikh Ahmad Sirhindi, *Radd-i-Rawafiz*, pp. 7-8.
29. Ibid., pp. 9-15.
30. Ibid., pp. 30-33.
31. Quran, Surah 75, Verse 17.
32. Undoubtedly, Allah Almighty has been pleased by faithfuls when they took (O, Prophet) oath of allegiance to you under this tree. Quran, Surah 48, Verse 18.
33. Shaikh Ahmad Sirhindi, *Radd-i-Rawafiz*, pp. 34-36.

34. Ibid., pp. 36-38.
35. Ibid., pp. 38-39; Sirhindi argues that the action of Abu Bakr was based on a tradition which runs as, "There is no trend of leaving heritage (*warsah*) amongst Prophets. Whatever we leave is charity." For details, see Jarullah Zamakhshari, *Al-Muwaffiqah Bain Ahl al-Bait wa as-Sahabah*, Urdu Translation, Ahtashamul Hasan Kandhalvi, Maktabah-i-Burhan, Delhi, 1956, pp. 34-35.
36. Abu Bakr's sincere devotion to the Prophet has inspired Allama Iqbal to compose the following verse:
    Parwaney ko chiragh hai, bulbul ko phul bus / Siddiq key liye hai khuda ka rasul bus
    (Moth needs nothing but the lamp and nightingale desires just the flower / But to Siddique, nothing but God's Prophet)
37. Shaikh Ahmad Sirhindi, *Radd-i-Rawafiz*, pp. 40-41. In support of his argument Sirhindi quotes two traditions. (i) "Allah has not inserted anything in my chest what I have not inserted in Abu Bakr's chest." (ii) "Abu Bakr has not become obtainer of benefits on account of the abundance of his prayers (*kasrat-i-namaz*) and excess of fasting (*kasrat-i-suyum*), but he has received this position (of superiority over other companions) because of the things that penetrated his heart.
38. Shaikh Ahmad Sirhindi, *Radd-i-Rawafiz*, pp. 41-48.
39. Ibid., pp. 49-55.
40. Ibid., pp. 60-67.
41. The only manuscript of the work is reported to be in the possession of Muhammad Hashim Jan Mujaddidi of Tandu Sain Dad in Pakistan. It was published by Matba Ansari of Delhi in 1889 and Munshi Nawal Kishore of Kanpur in 1891. A version edited by Maulana Nur Ahmad was brought out by Matba Mujaddidi of Amritsar in 1912. It was published under the supervision of Hakim Abdul Majid Saifi from Lahore in 1956. A version edited by Maulana Mahbub Ilahi was published by Idarah-i-Mujaddidiyah Saidiyah in 1965. Another edition appeared from Karachi in 1968. Saiyyid Zawwar Husain Shah brought out an edited version with introduction, annotation and translation which was published by Idarah-i-Mujaddidiyah of Karachi in 1984. This edition has been utilized by the present writer in the preparation of this article.
42. Yohanan Friedmann, op. cit., pp. 5-6.
43. For details on the different ranks in the spiritual hierarchy of mystics, see A.J. Arberry, *Sufism: An Account of the Mystics of Islam*, London, 1950.
44. Shaikh Ahmad Sirhindi, *Mabda o Maad*, Ed., Saiyyid Zawwar Hasan Shah, Idarah-i-Mujaddidiyah, Karachi, 1984, p. 9.
45. During the later years of his life, Sirhindi claimed the position of Qaiyyum for himself and his successors. In his opinion, the Qaiyyum was an exalted person on whom the whole order of existence depended. All spirits, angels and human beings and every other object looked towards him for assistance. He served as an intermediary between man and God for all spiritual and worldly benefits. The gnostic (*arif*) on whom the dignity of Qaiyyum was bestowed, acted like a minister to a king. All business of

created beings was conducted through him. Saiyid Athar Abbas Rizvi, *Muslim Revivalist Movements in India in the Sixteenth and Seventeenth Centuries*, p. 266.

46. For details regarding Khwaja Bahauddin Naqshband and Khwaja Alauddin Attar, see Ali bin Husain al-waiz Kashifi, *Rashahat Ain-ul-Hayat*, Munshi Nawal Kishore, Lucknow, 1890.
47. Shaikh Ahmad Sirhindi, *Mabda o Maad*, pp. 9-11.
48. A saint of the Qadiri order, Shah Kamal flourished during the sixteenth century and lived in Kaithal near Ambala (modern Haryana). Having died in 1573, he was buried in the same place. For details see Khwaja Muhammad Hashim Kishmi, *Zubdat-ul-Maqamat*, pp. 305-308.
49. Shaikh Khizar was treated as a prophet. Several passages in the Quran are associated with him e.g. Surah XVIII, Verse 66-68 with reference to Prophet Moses. Shaikh Khizar has been a popular imaginary spiritual guide of the mystics. He was regarded as a protector of people in distress, particularly the travellers on land and sea.
50. Shaikh Ahmad Sirhindi, *Mabda o Maad*, pp. 12-14.
51. Ibid., pp. 21-22.
52. Ibid., pp. 56-57.
53. Ibid., p. 81.
54. Ibid., pp. 76-77.
55. Ibid., pp. 23-26.
56. Ibid., pp. 44-48.
57. Ibid., pp. 51-52.
58. Ibid., pp. 53-56.
59. Ibid., p. 87.
60. A manuscript of this work is available in the personal collection of Hafiz Muhammad Hashim Jan Mujaddidi of Tandu Sain Dad in Sind (Pakistan). Another manuscript is found in the collection of brochures at Rabat-i-Mazhariyah in Madina (Saudi Arabia). A critically edited text, with an introduction and Urdu translation, has been prepared in 1914 by Ghulam Mastafa Khan and published by Idarah-i-Mujaddidiyah, Karachi (Pakistan) in 1964.
61. Shaikh Ahmad Sirhindi, *Mukashifat-i-Ainiyah*, Ed., Ghulam Mustafa Khan, Idarah-i-Mujaddidiyah, Karachi, 1964, pp. 7-8.
62. Ibid., pp. 8-15.
63. Ibid., pp. 16-23.
64. Ibid., pp. 23-24.
65. Ibid., pp. 25-26.
66. Ibid., pp. 35-36.
67. This is a collection of the sermons of Shaikh Abdul Qadir Jilani in Arabic. It was translated into Persian by Abdul Haq Muhaddis Dehalvi during the reign of Akbar. It has been published several times from different places in the Indian subcontinent.
68. Shaikh Ahmad Sirhindi, *Mukashifat-i-Ainiyah*, pp. 41-43.
69. The concept of *tauhid-i-wujudi* was propounded and developed by the great mystic thinker of Islam, Shaikh Muhiuddin Ibn-i-Arabi, who is regarded

as Shaikh-i-Akbar by his admirers. His monumental works, *Fusus al-Hikam* and *Futuhat-i-Makkiya*, have been the magnum opus for the sufis of different orders throughout the centuries. For details, see A.E. Affifi, *The Mystical Philosophy of Muhyuddin Ibnul Arabi*, Cambridge, 1939; William C. Chittick, *The Sufi Path of Knowledge: Ibn al-Arabi's Metaphysics of Imagination*, State University of New York, Albany, 1989; *Encyclopaedia of Islam*, Vol. III, E.J. Brill, Leiden, 1971, pp. 707-11.

70. Shaikh Ahmad Sirhindi, *Mukashifat-i-Ainiyah*, pp. 43-44.
71. Ibid., pp. 44-45.
72. A manuscript of this brochure, which was transcribed in 1241 AH/1825-26 AD, is reported to be available in Khanqah-i-Sirajiyah in Pakistan. It was first published by Majlis-i-Ilmi from Dabhol, District Surat, but the date of publication is not mentioned. It was published in 1376 AH/1956 AD by Hakim Saifi. In 1965 Mahbub Ilahi edited a text which was published by Idarah-i-Saidiyah Mujaddidiyah, Lahore (Pakistan). In fact, this text is a part of *Rasail-i-Mujaddidiyah* which has been brought out by the same editor and publisher.
73. Yohanan Friedmann, op. cit., p. 5.
74. Shaikh Ahmad Sirhindi, *Rasail-i-Mujaddidiyah*, Ed., Mahbub Ilahi, Idarah-i-Saidiyah Mujaddidiyah, Lahore, 1965, pp. 145-46.
75. Zawwar Hasan, *Hazrat Mujaddid Alf-i-Sani*, p. 680; also see, *Hayat-i-Mujaddid*, Lahore, 1958, p. 253.
76. Shaikh Ahmad Sirhindi, *Rasail-i-Mujaddidiyah*, pp. 151-153.
77. Ibid., pp. 181-186.
78. Ibid., pp. 186-192.
79. Ibid., pp. 207-214.
80. It appears from the text of the work that it was written by Sirhindi after the death of his father because, at one place, he uses the term 'May God make him pious and exalted (*Qaddas Allah-i-Sirrahu*)' which is only written after the names of saintly people who are no more. (Shaikh Ahmad Sirhindi, *Rasail-i-Tahliliyah*, Ed., Mahbub Ilahi, Idarah-i-Saidiyah Mujaddidiyah, Lahore, 1965, p. 9). Another source indicates that this work was produced before Sirhindi joined the Naqshbandi order as a disciple of Khwaja Baqi Billah. Therefore, it is safe to suggest that the work was written around 1007-08 AH/1598-99 AD. Khwaja Muhammad Hashim Kishmi, *Zubdat-ul-Maqamat*, p. 131.
81. For detailed discussions on Akbar's act, see Abdul Qadir Badauni, *Muntakhab-ut-Tawarikh*, Vol. II, p. 273; V.A. Smith, *Akbar: The Great Mogul*, pp. 154-159; Muhammad Aslam, *Din-i-Ilahi Aur Us Ka Pasmanzar*, pp. 182-184.
82. Shaikh Ahmad Sirhindi, *Rasail-i-Mujaddidiyah*, pp. 4-15.
83. Apart from being an eminent mystic, Khwaja Baqi Billah was a poet. Most of his poetry is in the form of *masnavis* and *rubaiyat*. For details, see Zaid Abul Hasan Faruqi, *Kulliyat-i-Khwaja Baqi Billah*, Lahore, 1969.
84. Shaikh Ahmad Sirhindi, *Rasail-i-Mujaddidiyah*, pp. 221-248.

13

Some Prominent Strands in the Poetry of Sultan Bahu

Tahir Kamran

The eminence that Sultan Bahu (1630-1691) holds as a sufi poet is firmly established, despite the fact that very little has been written about him. The information about his life is patchy. It is largely based on guesswork that has been collected mostly by his disciples after his demise. Even his poetry has yet to be tangibly and analytically commented upon by literary experts. Therefore, any attempt to delve deep into the spiritual recesses of Sultan Bahu's sufi thought and its existential underpinnings, as articulated through his poetry, seeks no less than a Herculean venture by some one, not only initiated in sufism but also having travelled some distance into the amorphous and esoteric realm of mysticism. Conscious of his somewhat limited expertise in the area that he intends to tread, this writer recognises the importance of sufi thought in the present era of religious extremism and suicide bombings in the name of religion. In these extenuating circumstances, the sufi thoughts of Sultan Bahu have the potential of finding new relevance, since his primary message was love (*ishq*). In the following pages, an attempt is being made to build a perspective in which sufism acquired salience (particularly in the context of Muslims), to underline the antithetical disposition of the theologians towards the mystics and to reconstruct the historical conditions in the Indian subcontinent during the seventeenth century. Against this background, we seek to analyse Sultan Bahu's sufic insights that are implicit in his Punjabi poetry. However, this exercise would not preclude a brief account of his life without which the evolution of his esoteric experiences in the domain of spirituality can hardly be spelt out.

Theology and Mysticism

Sufism is believed to be a seminal agency in the dissemination of Islam in multi-lingual, multi-cultural and multi-religious South Asia. Initially the practitioners of sufism lived an ascetic life, renouncing the very materiality of the physical world, leaving the institutions of the state and society to the discretion of the theologians (*ulema*). However, the sufis gradually evolved a corporate system, particularly in the social sense of the word, synthesizing variegated strands of thought, including Christian and Buddhist monasticism, philosophy of Neo-Platonism and Upanishadic concepts. Subsequently, these diverse strands were syncretised with the influences from the framework of Islam, thus giving the Islamic persuasion a distinct character. On the other hand, the *ulema* represented the other streak and systematized themselves into a body of religious scholars in the wake of Nizam-ul-Mulk Tusi's (c.1018-1092) initiative of setting up the educational system generally known as Dars-i-Nizami.[1] As a consequences, the institution of seminary (*madrasah*) sprang up with the express design to provide the instruction of Islam, prioritizing singularly the injunctions and edicts of *shariah* along with the rational sciences (*maqulat*). However, the study of Quranic exegesis (*tafsir*), Prophetic traditions (*hadis*) and Muslim jurisprudence (*fiqh*) became the mainstay of *madrasah* education.[2] This form of Islamic knowledge, as disseminated at the *madrasah* by the *alim*, was formal. On the other hand, mystical knowledge centered around the doctrine of the unity of being (*wahdat-ul-wujud*) or ontological monism and was propounded initially by Muhiuddin Ibn-i-Arabi (d.1240).[3] His argument that all phenomena are manifestation of a single being, which was encapsulated in the dictum 'All is God', had made it possible for Muslims not only to tolerate Hindus but also to search for common ground they might share."[4] Hence Arberry's description of sufism as 'the attempt of the individual Muslims to realize in their personal experience the living presence of Allah' seems valid if seen in the perspective of Ibn-i-Arabi's thought.[5]

The stress of *shariah* on the immutability of laws and regulations, as prescribed in the Quran and traditions of the Prophet (*sunnah*) and which were professed and exhorted upon as the ultimate truth for all the people and for all the times to come, left little space for those belonging to different religious persuasions. The beholders of other faiths either had to submit to the call of Islam or to accept the suzerainty of the Muslim overlords and pay *jaziya* (religious tax levied on the non-Muslims by a Muslim state). The general belief among a substantial section of the Muslim literati considered *ulema* as the representatives of the view whereby *shariah* held primacy. The Dars-i-Nizami *ab initio* determined the epistemic parameters for the *madrasahs* by laying out syllabi in order to "produce scholars of the Ash'ari School qualified to run the government in accordance with orthodox Sunni ideas." Moreover, the *madrasahs* and the *ulema*, who taught there, eked out their subsistence from state grants and stipends. *Ulema* were dependent on the state or the nobility, despite their religious prestige. Therefore, the knowledge of jurisprudence mostly sided with those already ensconced in ruling position, acting willingly as a counterpoise against military adventurers or recalcitrants. In case of medieval India, they drew their importance mostly as state functionaries.[6] Even in freakish circumstances, they could not muster any support for themselves from the general masses. They used to issue legal opinions (*fatwas*) forbidding any opposition to the ruler's authority and enunciating such an act as heinous sin for the true believers in Islam. However, the instances reaching us through S.A.A. Rizvi, reveal that the open opposition of the *ulema* also forms a part of history.[7] That probably was the reason why most sultans and emperors in medieval India aspired to draw a substantial measure of support from the sufis who, in spite of having a huge following among the populace, generally abstained from engaging in political intrigue, though they deployed a different technology of control. Richard M. Eaton sheds exhaustive light on the evolution of the sufi orders:

> There also emerged various schools of mysticism oriented around particular modes of spiritual discipline. Named after their founders, these schools soon coalesced into stable organizations, or orders, whose networks criss-crossed the Muslim world and beyond, knitting together widely scattered communities with shared literatures and spiritual genealogies.[8]

According to the general perception emanating from any major text on medieval Indian thought, sufis and hospices (*dargahs*) are depicted as the binary opposite to the *alim* and *madrasah*. The former are inscribed as practitioners in syncretic cultural ethos, preachers of universal love and adherents of the unitarian (*wujudi*) ideals. In contrast, the latter are portrayed as believers in religious exclusivity and puritanical traditional thoughts and rituals. Nevertheless, the *ulema* could not attain all that importance or clout in medieval India before the advent of Shah Waliullah (1703-1762) and his legacy of political Islam that eventually culminated in the establishment of Deoband and Wahabi movement. During the colonial dispensation, the Weltanschauung prevalent in the medieval period, whereby sufis and their esoteric methods of reaching the Ultimate had acquired the role of a kingpin, was totally displaced. Western rationality and exoteric (sensory) way of determining the truth transposed to a great extent the centrality that sufis had been enjoying for centuries. The onset of colonialism and the corresponding discourses that it generated in the course of eighteenth and nineteenth centuries left a lot of space open for the *ulema* to organize themselves into a distinct body. Essentially the *ulema* emphasized on reverting to Islamic tradition and treated the *shariah* as the sole identity marker for the Muslims. In the process, they drew intellectual support from the rationality emanating essentially from the West. The seminary of Deoband exemplifies this trend in a conspicuous way. Evangelical missionaries and their penchant for disseminating the Christian message proved to be the most important catalyst in bringing to the fore the zeal for religious exclusivity that offered a fertile ground for the *ulema* to flourish.

In the medieval times the sufis did not face much confrontation from the *ulema*. In fact, the sufis themselves condemned sufis of other orders. In more explicit terms, sufis hailing from the Suhrawardi and Naqshbandi orders showed a strict adherence to the *shariah*. Therefore, for them, the sufis of Chishti and Qadiri orders, who were proponents of syncretic social and cultural values, were nothing but a band of heretics. Shaikh Ahmad Sirhindi and subsequently Shah Waliullah Dehlvi were established sufis, yet their uncompromising espousal of the *shariah* as the only way leading to the ultimate truth transformed them into personalities, deemed worth emulating by puritanical *ulema* of the later centuries. Ascendancy in the power and prestige of the *ulema*, as mediating force between the Ultimate and mortal beings (humans), became an unequivocal fact of the history of the modern South Asia. Yet the role of sufis and reverence enjoyed by them for many centuries could hardly be overlooked. One such example is Sultan Bahu who is an important link in the long chain of sufi saints. He propagated and promoted mutual love, peace and equanimity among the Punjabi folks irrespective of religion, caste or creed. Thereby he lent sustenance to the legacy of Ali bin Usman Hujwiri (d.1072) and particularly that of Shaikh Farid Ganj-i-Shakar (d.1265) and Shah Husain Lahori (1539-1599). Although all of them represented different sufi orders, yet many similarities punctuated their respective thoughts. It is significant that sufis from the same order could adhere and project divergent views. At the same time, sufis from different orders demonstrated deference and accommodation for each other. There has hardly been any instance of one sufi denouncing the other as infidel (*kafir*) or renegade.

Life and Times of the Sufi Poet

Before dwelling on the sufi thoughts of Sultan Bahu, as articulated in his poetry, it seems necessary to examine the context in which he gave expression to his intuitive self i.e. the political and social conditions in the Indian subcontinent during the seventeenth century. During this period, the Mughal empire reached the zenith of its power and prestige.

Its territorial limits touched the Himalayas in the north and the coastline in peninsular India. The occupation of Kangra and the subjugation of Mewar confirmed the military might of the Mughal state. Though Malik Ambar blocked the Mughal advance in the Deccan, yet the Mughals managed to subjugate Bijapur and Golconda in 1636 and to annex these kingdoms in 1686. In spite of the failure to recover Qandhar from the Persians, the Mughals held Afghanistan firmly in their control and even penetrated as far as Balkh. The Mughal rulers, assisted by an ethnically heterogeneous nobility, established a uniform administration in all the provinces of the empire. In this gigantic task, they received valuable support from the landed elites and middle classes. The Mughal success was manifested in the expansion of trade and towns as well as the patronage of arts. We must hasten to point out that the picture was not entirely rosy. We encounter the emergence of factors, which led to political instability and social tensions, particularly during the second half of the seventeenth century. The Mughal empire found it increasingly difficult to run two institutions – the *mansabdari* and *jagirdari* – in a satisfactory manner. The Afghan tribes which inhabited the trans-Indus tract, were up in arms against the Mughals. In parts of northern India, several social groups – Sikhs, Jats and Satnamis – posed a challenge that was as serious as the Marathas in the Deccan.[9] In the early seventeenth century, Shaikh Ahmad Sirhindi (1564-1624) made a vigorous attempt to bring the Mughal state under the Naqshbandi influence. It was, however, the Qadiri order that acquired a considerable prominence under Miyan Mir (1550-1635) of Lahore. Prince Dara Shukoh, who was a strong adherent of this sufi fraternity, produced several works on Islamic mysticism and comparative religion. Though the Qadiris professed unflinching adherence to the *shariah*, yet they came up with a different exegesis of Islam, whereby the single source of origin for everything formed the cardinal theme. Such an interpretation virtually wiped out the differences between Islam and other religions of Perso-Indian roots. It may be suggested that these historical developments must have shaped, to a certain extent, the ideas and outlook of Sultan Bahu.

Sultan Bahu was born in 1630 in village Awan, which was located not very far from Garh Maharaja, a town in tehsil Shorkot of district Jhang.[10] According to Sultan Hamid, the author of *Manaqib-i-Sultani*, Sultan Bahu's forebears migrated to India after Hasan and Husain, the grandsons of the Prophet, were martyred. They initially settled in the outskirts of Pind Dadan Khan (presently in the Jhelum district of Pakistani Punjab) and Ahmadabad where they defeated the local Hindus, which eventually led to the massive conversion of Hindus to Islam. Afterwards a part of Sultan Bahu's clan moved to Jhang.

Shahjahan accorded tremendous respect and honour to the clan. Sultan Bahu's father Bazaid Muhammad was bestowed a military rank (*mansab*) with an appropriate revenue assignment (*jagir*).[11] In this manner, he was elevated to the position of an important person of the area, which was indicative of his high status and sound economic background. Sahibzada Sultan Ahmed Ali reveals that there was the fort Kahergan in a close proximity to Multan, which was considered impregnable and the Mughal army could not capture it despite many attempts. However, Bazaid Muhammad managed to conquer that fort. Therefore Shahjahan bestowed a *jagir* on him that included the fort of Shorkot and a big chunk of land in the outskirts of the city.[12] Besides Bazaid Muhammad was well versed in the Quran and other Islamic sciences and followed the edicts prescribed by the *shariah* in letter and spirit. Unfortunately he died when he was hardly in his adolescence. As a result the sole responsibility of Sultan Bahu's brought-up fell on the shoulders of his mother Rasti Bibi, a lady with a tranquil temperament. She fulfilled her responsibility with all earnestness. For this Sultan Bahu always felt beholden to his mother and declared:

Bliss of God for Rasti be,
For with truth is gifted she.[13]

His mother gave him the name Bahu. *Ba* means 'with' and *Hu* means 'God'. The name therefore denotes 'united with God'. Sultan Hamid, the author of *Manaqib-i-Sultani,* while drawing on Sultan Bahu's own book in Persian *Ain-ul-Fuqara,* alludes to the indebtedness which Sultan Bahu felt towards his mother for giving him that name "which, with the addition of one dot under Ba, becomes Yahu. Yahu means 'O' and is an invocation through which sufis ask god for his mercy and grace." The name Bahu meant so much for him because it resonated to the full eventual merger between the mortal and the Lord that is reflected in his *abyat*:

> Then in an ecstasy of love, you will repeat the name of Hu constantly / Devoting every breath of your life in contemplation of Him / Only when your soul merges in the essence of the Lord, will you deserve the name 'Bahu'.[14]

The prefix Sultan was a later addition to his name, probably because of his impressive personality and saintly traits. He usually referred to himself as Bahu Awan because he hailed from the Awan tribe. Many anecdotes defying reason or commonsense have been in circulation and, in spite of all the fabrications that lend incredulity to those 'tales', have a strong mythological reflection and impact, so that Sultan Bahu has been cast in the image of some Hindu god. According to his biographer Sultan Hamid, since Sultan Bahu was a born saint (*madarzad wali*), as a child there used to be a halo of light around his face, which impressed the Hindus so much that a large number of them embraced Islam as a result.[15] Another reference pointing to the freakish acts and ideas Sultan Bahu fell for was his bid to adopt his mother as his mentor (*murshid*). Since the lady was aware of the edicts prohibiting women to act as *murshid*, she sent him to a sufi Syed Habibullah Shah Qadiri who lived in a village by the name of Baghdad, on the bank of the Ravi and south of Shorkot. Habibullah Shah was a Gilani Syed who was born in Baghdad (Iraq) and migrated to Punjab on the instructions of Shaikh Abdul Qadir Gilani, the founder of the Qadiri order. He came and laid the foundation of a village which was named as Baghdad (his original place of birth). Widely held view subscribes that Sultan Bahu proved to be too perceptive for Syed Habibullah Shah's relatively limited esoteric expertise. Not only did he learn whatever his teacher was capable of teaching, but soon he had overtaken Syed Habibullah Shah himself. Such a quick progress of his pupil led him to refer Sultan Bahu to Syed Abdul Rahman in Delhi.[16] Sultan Bahu's stay with Syed Habibullah Shah was ephemerally short, yet his impact on the discple's spiritual explorations was quite indelible. He must have initiated Sultan Bahu in the Qadiri order. The new teacher of Sultan Bahu was apparently a worldly person, who lived a comfortable and luxuriant life, with no abstemious pretensions. He served as a Mughal officer (*mansabdar*) too. But he was a genuinely accomplished sufi, having graduated to a higher level of spiritual consciousness. He was said to have been a descendant of Abdul Qadir Gilani.

Those were the times of Aurangzeb's reign (1658-1708) and Qadiri sufis were being persecuted because of the simple reason of Dara Shukoh's adherence to that particular sufi order. Needless to mention that Dara Shukoh and his younger brother Aurangzeb fought for the throne and the latter had the last laugh. Dara Shukoh was executed ostensibly because of his 'heretical' views. In these circumstances, Sultan Bahu landed in Delhi and the emperor made all the necessary arrangements to monitor his movement and activities.[17] Although the modern writer Sultan Bakhsh Qadiri states that Aurangzeb held Sultan Bahu in high esteem,[18] yet Sultan Hamid and Lajwanti Rama Krishna hold the opposite view. Both of them concur on the raging contradiction between the emperor and Sultan Bahu. That probably was the reason for Sultan Bahu's return to his native place in Punjab. After coming back to his village, he devoted his life for the attainment of higher levels of spiritual sublimity. Having said that, one must not be led to believe that his life was devoid of worldly comforts and privileges that were absent in the lives of sufis like Shaikh Farid Ganj-i-Shakar, Miyan Mir, Mulla Shah Badakhshi and Shah Abdul Latif Bhittai. Our saint married four times and one of his wives was a Hindu by faith. Besides his four wives he had seventeen concubines. He was blessed with eight children. Following his death in 1691, he was buried at Qila Kahergan, which was located very close to the Chenab. With the ascendancy of the Sikh confederacies in the mid-eighteenth century, the chieftains of Bhangi *misl* Ganda Singh and Jhanda Singh ravaged Shorkot. Impending fear of wide scale destruction and bloodshed forced the relatives and disciples of Sultan Bahu to flee away, leaving the mausoleum absolutely deserted. But one disciple held the fort to save the mausoleum from the feared onslaught. Luckily the marauders did not cause any harm to the mausoleum nor to the disciple living there. In 1775 the river Chenab changed its course towards the mausoleum, but the coffin was removed from there well in time and entombed under a *peepal* tree, not far from the town of Garh Maharaja. Sultan Bahu did not initiate any sufi order of his own. Even then, an order in his name, Qadiriya Masrooria, was established by his disciples after his death.

We do not have evidence regarding the nature of formal education acquired by Sultan Bahu. Yet he was thoroughly conversant with Arabic and Persian apart from his native Punjabi. Owing to his esoteric experiences and absence of formal education, he used to relate himself with pride to the Prophet of Islam. Our saint, who was not educated in the exoteric system of knowledge but with the wealth of revelational (esoteric) experience, evolved himself into a unique historical personality. Despite this handicap, he is said to have written 140 books.[19] Two dozen of his works are available in Urdu. If the fact regarding the number of his books is accepted, even then his writings in prose fail to leave any lasting impression on the reader. These writings are wanting in profundity of thought. Even any coherence in the style is glaringly missing. In these books and pamphlets, he emerges as a hard core Qadiri sufi who disdainfully dismisses other sufi orders, calling them heretics or at times even non-believers.[20] However, his poetry in his mother tongue, *lehndi*, a dialect of Punjabi, has given him the wider acclaim instead of his books in Persian. He used to compose verses in both Persian and Punjabi. Like Asadullah Khan Ghalib, the famous Urdu/ Persian poet of the nineteenth century, Sultan Bahu too had the penchant for composing verses in Persian. He was not very proud of his Punjabi poetry, which was put together posthumously by his disciples. Ironically, it was his Punjabi poetry that brought him everlasting fame. It also constitutes the major source of learning about his sufi thoughts, which are radically different from what is articulated in his prose.

Features of Mystic Poetry

The seeds of sufi poetry in the regional languages of India, which were sown by Shaikh Farid Ganj-i-Shakar and Shaikh Hamiduddin Nagauri, continued to flourish and showed extraordinary resonance.[21] Sufi poets not only wrote *ghazals* and *masnawis* in regional languages and dialects, but also composed *dohas* and *sakhis*. Sultan Bahu exercised a slight deviation from other sufis, as he deployed a different medium of articulating his existential experience. His Punjabi poetry comprises approximately two hundred *abyat* and has been composed in the form of *siharfi*. In Persian *see* means thirty and *harf* stands for word. Literary critics find no traces of *siharfi* in Persian poetry, confirming its local origin. Sultan Bahu pioneered in deploying this genre in the Punjabi poetry.[22] In case of the Indian subcontinent, it signifies the convergence of the 'content' whereby the streams of *wahdat-ul-wujud* and *vedanta* seemed to be entwined inextricably and the same happened also in the 'form'. Inference that can easily be drawn here is the thorough acquaintance of Sultan Bahu with local forms of expression. *Siharfi* is a tri-literal technique of literary articulation, which he mastered like no one before him or after, particularly in the Punjabi language. Another important feature of his poetry that accorded it a peculiarity of its own is the usage of an alphabetical letter at the very beginning of every verse or *bait*. It may be mentioned that *abyat* is the plural of *bait* which is in fact an Arabic word, adopted into Urdu and Punjabi by the Muslim poets. The very first *bait* can be put forward as illustration:[23]

> *Alif Allah chambe di bootee murshid man wich laaee hoo / Naffee asbat daa pani milias, har rage har jaee hoo / Andar bootee mushk machaaiaa jaan phullan te aaee hoo / Jeeve murshid kaamil Bahu jain eh bootee laaee hoo*
>
> My master has planted in my heart the jasmine of God's name. Both my denial that the creation is real and my embracing God the only reality, have nourished the seedling down to its core. When the buds of mystery unfolded into the blossoms of revelation, my entire being was filled with God's fragrance. May the perfect master, who planted this jasmine in my heart, be ever blessed, O Bahu.

Another distinctive feature of Sultan Bahu's poetry is the expression *Hoo* that comes at the end of every line. As alluded to earlier, *Hoo* is Allah's attribute and its repetitive usage gives his poetry a very strong mystic colour. Muhammad Yunas Hasrat interprets *Hoo* as the Creator (Allah as transcendent entity).[24] However, analyzing *Hoo* in the broader context, Hasrat's verdict seems out of tune with the overall thought content that Sultan Bahu ventures to propound through his poetry. The metaphor of *chambe dee bootee* for *Hoo* (God) stands in absolute contrast to Hasrat's assertion. This writer describes God as creator, the exclusivity and transcendentalism being His chief attributes, rather than the source of origin for every thing that exists, a thought implicit in the philosophy of immanence culminating subsequently in the typically *wujudi* concept of unity in diversity.

Alif aihad jad dittee wikhaalee, az khud hoiaa faanee hoo / Qurb wisaal maqaam nah manzil, nah uth jism nah aanee hoo / Nah uth ishq muhabbat kaaee, nah uth kaun makaanee hoo / Ain o ain theeose Bahu, sir wahdat subhanee hoo

When the one lord revealed himself to me, I lost myself in him. Now there is neither nearness nor union. There is no longer a journey to undertake, no longer a destination to reach. Love, attachment, my body and soul and the very limits of time and space have dropped from my consciousness. My separate self has merged in the whole. In that, O Bahu, lies the secret of the unity that is God.[25]

Inadequacy of Knowledge

Sultan Bahu was deeply concerned with the nature and purpose of knowledge (*ilm*) in the domain of mysticism. Most often, he perceives *ilm* as synonymous with two similar words viz. reason (*aql*) and intellect (*fikr*). While examining the nature of *ilm*, *aql* and *fikr*, he juxtaposes them against love (*ishq*). He has serious doubts about the utility of *ilm* and the classes (*mulla, pandit* and *jotshi*) who are associated with the dissemination of *ilm*. Some people acquire a huge amount of knowledge by studying thousands of books and, in the process, spend a considerable amount of time and energy. It is quite possible that they earn some social recognition for their learning. But this kind of *ilm* leads to negative consequences. To understand the real nature of *ilm*, we must pay our attention to the uses to which this *ilm* is put and the consequences it leads to. Firstly, it must be understood that *ilm* does not lead to spiritual betterment but, instead, it generates satanic pride (*takabbur*) in the minds of the learned.[26] This arrogance over one's scholarship is worst among all sins. Secondly, the scholars use their erudition to curry favour of the contemporary rulers. They were found ever willing to act as tools in the hands of kings and nobles and, in return for compromising their position, they get material gains in the form of land grants and cash stipends. By this objectionable conduct, they make their position untenable and exposed themselves to scathing criticism of sufis like Sultan Bahu.

Parh parh ilm mulook rijhaavan kia hoiaa is parhiaan hoo / Hargiz makkhan mool nah aave phitte dudh de karhiaan hoo / Aakh chandooraa hath keeh aaiaa es angooree phariaan hoo / Hik dil khastaa raazee rakkheen laieen ibadat varahian hoo

Priests and scholars parade their learning to please the kings. Of what avail is such erudition? Reading scripture is like boiling curdled milk in the false hope of obtaining butter. No more profitable to them is their chanting than is chirping to the mimicking *chandoor*. If you bring inner comfort to a heart in distress, you will earn the merit of years of worship.[27]

Sultan Bahu nurtures a poor opinion regarding the religious pursuits of the worldly scholars. They believed in recitation of the scriptures in a purely mechanical manner. Such exercises raised false hopes of spiritual benefit but, in the end, they turned out to be futile because they were devoid of genuine feeling of one's love for the Supreme Being. The discerning individuals began to criticize the orthodox clerics, owing to their excessive occupation with the formal mode of worship and for having reduced spirituality into specific acts of formal behaviour, with the result that the duality of God-man relationship continued to persist for ever.[28] In other words, the over-engagement of theologians with the outward forms of devotion led to a situation where they lost their ability of introspection and bound themselves with terrestrial gains, thus becoming the slaves of the world. Not only this, they were found suffering from greed. Their services were indispensable for performing religious ceremonies but, even on these occasions, they behaved in an avaricious manner. They called themselves Shaikhs, but performed only outward worship (*ibadat dohree*), so that temptation entered their heart like a thief.[29] Many a times, the clerics (particularly the *hafiz* who is invited for reciting the Quran on special occasions) were seen rushing through streets, carrying books under their armpits, just like hawkers who went through the residential areas selling their wares. Wherever they found a prosperous household, they recited the scripture in a loud voice with the object of securing a lucrative payment. In the eyes of Sultan Bahu, such people were guilty of putting God's name on sale just to make a living and, therefore, they became spiritually bankrupt in this world and lost their honour in the next world.[30] In other words, they wasted the opportuni-ties of doing good deeds on earth and, as a consequence, faced humiliation while explaining their conduct after death. That is why, in spite of their knowledge, they feared the impending torments of hell.[31]

The knowledge as acquired and propagated by the theologians, suffered from serious limitations.[32] It does not pay attention to the oneness of God, which is symbolized by the letter *alif*. Similarly, they do not aspire for union (*wisal*) with the Supreme Being which can light up the fourteen spiritual realms (*chaudan tabaq*). Without these two elements – oneness of God and the union with Him – the entire stock of knowledge is like a fable that disappears in smoke.[33] However, the greatest limitation of scholars lies in their reluctance to understand the significance of love (*ishq*). Knowledge and lve stood poles apart, with no scope for any common ground. Those who subscribe to knowledge were incapable of leading others on the spiritual path. On the other hand, the followers of the creed of love can guide others to salvation with ease. Let us take a closer look at this proposition.

Parh parh ilm hazaar kitaaban, aalim hoe bhaare hoo / Harf ik ishq daa parh naa jaanan, bhulle phiran vichare hoo / Ik nigaah je aashiq vekhe, lakkh hazaaraan taare hoo / Lakkh nigaah je aalim vekhe, kise nah kaddhee chaarhe hoo / Ishq aqal vich manzil bharee, saiaan kohaan de pare hoo / Jihnaan ishq khareed nah keetaa, doheen jahaaneen mare hoo

They have read a thousand books. They have come to be known as great scholars. But they cannot grasp the one word 'love'. So they helplessly wander in delusion. A lover, with just one glance, can carry millions to their deliverance. But a million glances cast by a scholar will not ferry a soul across to salvation. There is a vast gulf between love and knowledge. In the market of love, O Bahu, they will always be losers in this world and the next.[34]

Primacy of Love

Love forms the most significant theme of Sultan Bahu's sufi poetry. This is understandable as it constitutes the core of his theoretical stance. It is the most recurrent phrase, appearing in no less than 61 of the 182 stanzas (*abyat*).[35] Love (*ishq*) is an inalienable part of the sufi thought that refuses to accept the Lord as the fearsome controlling authority. To the sufis belonging to the *wujudi* school of thought, the Lord is a beloved and the seeker wants to be a part of the Beloved and, thus, achieves a state of merger (*wasl*) into an eternal being that is so passionately loved by the sufis. This state of merger, the ultimate goal of a sufi, is achieved only through love. It is only through love that the state of separation (*firaq*) and the melancholy emanating from it can be overcome. Shuja Alhaq contends, "In reality there is none but He, but man worships so many other things besides Him that affirmation of His reality demands a continual process of realization and negation of all that is not-He."[36] Hence, the affirmation of Him is the only reality, to see Him all around and not to find one's own finite self in this realm of infinity. This, in fact, forms the essence of Sultan Bahu's conception of unity. Man's being is of cardinal importance so far this conception is concerned. For Sultan Bahu, his (man's) own being must become the centre of truth. As long as the truth resides outside him, he will continue to be an idol worshipper. Truth, that is He, has to coalesce in the being of man. That is how union can be achieved through the agency of love.

In the understanding of Sultan Bahu, lovers were a unique class of people. They remain completely intoxicated in the ecstasy of their love for the beloved. They have sacrificed their lives to the Beloved while still living on this earth and, by doing so, have immortalized themselves in both the worlds.[37] A person who is afflicted by love perceives love wherever he looks. In fact, he can find no place that is bereft of love. He is able to experience this feeling ever since his perfect master (*murshid kamil*) opened the sealed window of his heart and, therefore, he is willing to sacrifice his life for his mentor who revealed the divine secrets.

Enriched by this experience, the lover is elevated from the earth to the sky and is inspired by love to explore the heavens. In the process, he develops a strong aversion to the world in which he was living till then. Sometimes, the lover feels that love has forced its way into his heart in an act of daring trespass. When he looked into his heart, he was amazed to find that the Beloved was already present therein.[38] But things are not so easy for the lover. Though his heart is as soft as wax, the response of the Beloved is slow. He becomes as vigilant as the hawk in his anxiety to seek out the Beloved. Since he is tied down with the earthly strings, he cannot undertake an uninhibited flight in the sky like the hunting bird.[39] When his heart is saturated with the love of God, he keeps his lips sealed and does not share his joyful experience with anyone. Though every pore of his body has a million tongues to sing the praise of the Beloved, yet it is his silence which expresses his true feelings. He experiences this particular spiritual state when he is bathed in the ocean of oneness (*dariya wahdat nahaate hoo*).[40] But this experience cannot be the monopoly of one person. In fact, this experience of love can touch all human beings from the mighty kings to the lowly beggars. Sultan Bahu elucidates this point in the following manner:

> *Ishq dee baazee har ja khedee, shah gadaa sultaanan hoo / Aalim faazil aaqil daanaa, karda chaa hairanaan hoo / Tamboo thok lattha vich dil de, laaeos khilwat khaanaan hoo / Ishq ameer faqeer manende, keeh jaane begaanaan hoo*
>
> Every one from king to beggar has played the game of love. It equally astounds the intellectual, the scholar and the wise. Love has firmly entrenched itself within me, establishing its private chamber in my heart. Love has touched the heart of the rich and the poor alike. How can an outsider, who has never tasted love, realize its bliss and splendour.[41]

Sultan Bahu discovers that the path of the lovers is beset with innumerable hazards. They are required to undergo a long period of suffering before they can enjoy the bliss of union with the Beloved.[42] They warm themselves on the fire of love, but this fire is fed with the fuel of their bones. They carve out the flesh of their hearts and roast it on the fire of love. Distraught in love, they wander listlessly and quench their thirst with their own blood.[43] They are constrained to bow their head at every doorstep. Since they are constantly engaged in contemplation of the Beloved, they deny themselves the comfort of sleep. They remain restless during the day and do not get a wink of sleep at night. They also cry in the pain of their separation from the Beloved.[44] While travelling on the spiritual path, they come across fierce waves, deadly whirlpools and dense forests and deserted wastelands. They experience the waves of the stormy ocean of love rising to the sky, where even the large and sturdy ships cannot survive.[45] They can not foresee that love would make impossible demands, like craving fruit of summer in the cold winter months (*poh magh kharbooze mange*).[46] Sometimes, they face opposition at the hands of people who hurl abuse at them and brand them as infidels (*kafir*). But they learn to take these things in their stride, because they are aware that even Mansur, who knew all the divine secrets, was sent to the gallows.

> *Aashiq ho te ishq kamaa, dil rakheen vaang pahaaraan hoo / Sai sai badeean lakh ulaame, janeen baagh bahaaraan hoo / Chaa soolee Mansur dittaa jo, waaqif kul asraaraan hoo / Sajdion sir nah chaaee-e Bahu, kaafir kehan hazaaraan hoo*
>
> Become a lover and let your heart be as tough as mountains. People will hurl hundreds of abuses on you, but you must accept them as a blessing. Even Mansur, who knew all the secrets of God, was sent to the gallows. Once you have bowed your head in prayer, do not lift it again, O Bahu, although the multitude may brand you an infidel.[47]

Every religious system was characterized by a set of beliefs and corresponding rituals. Love, as seen in this light, has come to possess its own beliefs and practices. Not only this, the followers of this path have given a new meaning to traditional customs, which does not conform to the orthodox view of religion. According to Sultan Bahu, when the *muazzin* of love gives the call for prayer (*namaz*), the lovers undertake ablutions (*wuzu*) with the blood of their heart.[48] On some occasions, the lovers did so with the tears of their eyes and, at other times, with the exalted name of God (*karde wuzu ism azam da*). We know that ordinarily Muslim purify themselves with ablutions (*wuzu*) prior to every prayer (*namaz*) i.e. five times a day. But lovers could purify themselves with only a single ablution, so that its impact lasted till the day of judgement.[49] The prayer (*namaz*) offered by the lovers is different from that of other devout persons, because this is the prayer of love (*namaz piram di*) which is offered in an unspoken language and no words are spoken. This kind of prayer is not known to everyone. It is known only to the lover whose heart aches for the beloved. It is only a rare lover who is intimately familiar with this prayer, for which the tongue does not move and the lips do not flutter. Whereas the ordinary devotees offer five prayers a day, the lovers are constantly engaged in prayer. Day and night, they prostrate themselves and keep their heads in supplication. This is so because their real destination is located a thousand regions beyond the paradise.

> *Aashiq hiq wuzoo jo keeta, roz qiyamat taeen hoo / Wich namaaz raku sajoode, raihande sanjh sabaaheen hoo / Ethe othe doheen jahaaneen, san faqar deeaan jaaeen hoo / Arshaan ton sai manzil agge, paindaa kam tihnaaeen hoo*
>
> A lover purifies himself just once. This single ablution would hold till the day of judgement. Day and night he prostrates himself and keeps his head

> bowed in supplication. The faqirs are at home in this world and the next. But their real home lies a thousand regions beyond paradise.[50]

Sultan Bahu believed that religious devotions, which are performed outside the human body are futile, because the mystics realized God within their inner self. He argues that the human body is the abode of the True Lord (*eh tan rab sachhe da hujra*). A seeker should peep inside to feel the presence of the water of life (*aab hayati*). Without seeking the help of Khwaja Khizar,[51] he should light the lamp of love in his heart, so that the darkness is dispelled and the long-lost treasure is discovered. Since the human body is a divine abode, it is a fragrant garden with eternally fresh blossoms. It also possesses prayer mats, places for prostration and means of ritual ablution. Therefore, a seeker/lover feels the presence of Kaaba inside his heart.[52] He transforms his body into a city for his Beloved (*tan main yaar da shaihar banaya*), where he constructs a special quarter for this purpose. When the Beloved starts residing in this place, the seeker is blessed with profound happiness.[53] He strikes the bargain of love inside the heart. But if he does not do so, then his heart ought to be treated as a stone which is mired in apathy (*ghaflat*). If he does not feel the pangs of separation, then he will be labelled as spiritually impotent and compared with dumb driven cattle.[54] The mystics believe that the heart is deeper than the ocean (*dil dariya samundron doonge*), so that it is impossible to fathom its mysteries. Though violent storms appear on its surface, yet the seeker sails through it like a skilled sailor. He also knows that the fourteen spiritual realms (*chaudaan tabaq*), each with its own tent, are also located inside the heart.[55] A seeker, who learns the secrets of the heart, succeeds in experiencing the supreme reality. As he advances in his contemplation, he realizes that the heart is the symbol of perfection in form and beauty. He also feels that the unity of being (*wahdat*) is written on the tablet of his heart. By focusing attention on the name of God, he enshrines Him in his heart (*dil da daftar wahdat wala*) and, as a result, begins to command both the worlds.[56]

Role of the Murshid

We are quite aware that one of the most important aspects of Islamic mysticism was the institution of discipleship (*piri muridi*). The spiritual teachers (*murshid* or *pir*) lived in convents (*khanqahs*) and imparted training to their disciples both in the basic and advanced elements of the spiritual discipline. With the passage of time, the mutual relation between the mentor and seeker/novice (*murid*) came to be governed by certain universally acceptable principles. The mystic-teachers came to occupy an extraordinarily exalted position in their respective orders in general and in the life of their disciples in particular.[57] It is, therefore, understandable that Sultan Bahu nurtures a high opinion regarding the role of the spiritual preceptor in the spiritual growth of the novice. Time and again, he underlines the indispensability of the spiritual preceptor and avails of every opportunity to highlight the benefits that flowed from him to his disciples. Sultan Bahu perceives a strong emotional bond between the *murshid* and *murid*. The latter always wishes to be in the physical presence of his *murshid*. He gazes at his *murshid* with untiring zeal. So strong is his desire to see him that even if every pore of his body turns into a million eyes, his urge remains unsatisfied. He regards a single glance of the *murshid* as meritorious as millions of pilgrimages to Mecca.[58] He feels that his *murshid* is his very life, as he had permeated every pore of his being. Even if the two are separated by a distance of thousands of miles, the disciple can feel the physical presence of the *murshid*. In fact, the *murshid* is himself compared with Mecca, the reverence for him to the shrine of Kaaba and the disciple as the pilgrim (*haji*).[59] The following *bait* expresses the sentiments of the disciple in a most accurate manner.

> *Murshid mainoon hajj makke daa, raihmat daa darwaza hoo / Karaan tawaaf davaale qible, hajj hove nit taaza hoo / Kun faikoon jadokaa suniaa, dittha oh darwaza hoo / Murshid sadaa hayatee waalaa, oho Khizar te Khwaja hoo*
>
> A visit to my master is, for me, like a pilgrimage to Mecca. My master is indeed the gateway to God's mercy. My life revolves around my master, just like a pilgrim circambulates the shrine of Kaaba. By meeting him, my pilgrimage is renewed everyday. Ever since God ordained the creation, I saw the door leading to my master. My master has been living for ever like Khizar who has conquered death and like the creator who lives in the human form.[60]

Since the *murshid* virtually acts as the architect of the spiritual growth of the *murid*, the latter is advised to choose him with great circumspection. The *murshid* should be a person who can bestow the blessings of both the worlds on the *murid*. At the outset,[61] he drives away all kinds of fear from the *murid's* heart and then reveals the path of God. The *murshid* transforms the barren land of the *murid's* heart into fertile soil, so that the seed of God's name is planted on it. The *murshid* is compared to the royal falcon (*shahbaaz*), a bird of paradise which flies with its own kind. But such a *murshid* is found only with divine favour (*taqdeer ilahee*) and good fortune (*naseebaan*). Such a *murshid* cures lepers of their leprosy and removes deformities of the spiritually crippled. He possesses the panacea for all the ills and, therefore, the *murid* would not like to be left to the care of physicians. In spite of the innumerable qualities of the *murshid*, the *murid* cannot take him for granted and should be willing to assess his own spiritual progress under his tutelage. If the *murid* finds that the *murshid* has failed to guide him in a satisfactory manner, then he should realize that he (*murshid*) has been feeding him on false promises (*korrey laarey*).[62] A perfect mentor (*kamil murshid*) is one who scrubs his *murid* just as a washerman who needs washing soda and soap (*sajjee saaban*). But the *murshid* purifies merely with his glance (*naal nigaah de paak kare*).[63] Let us consider the following *bait* in which our saint poet compares the role of the *murshid* with the work of a goldsmith (*suniara*) in a most vivid manner.

> *Murshid vaang suniaare hove, ghat kuthaalee gale hoo / Paa kuthaalee baahar kaddhe, bunde gharhe yaa vale hoo / Kanneen khoobaan tadon suhaavan, jad khatte paa ujaale hoo / Naam faqeer tise daa jerhaa, dam dam dost sambhale hoo*
>
> The master should be like that goldsmith who melts and purifies gold in his crucible. Then he takes this purified metal out of the crucible and moulds it into beautiful ornaments, be they studs or earrings. Only after they have been sculpted and polished are they considered fit to adorn the Beloved's ears. Only such a mentor deserves to be called an ascetic (*faqir*), who takes care of his friend (disciple) every moment.[64]

Sultan Bahu was convinced that the *murshid* was indispensable for a seeker/novice. It was not possible to undertake the spiritual journey without the guidance of the *murshid*. If a seeker, out of ignorance or arrogance, embarks on the spiritual path (*faqr*) without the guidance of the *murshid*, he is likely to stray away from his chosen destination.[65] He may drown himself in the mire of infidelity (*kufr*). He may establish himself as a Shaikh (sufi) and, residing in a cell (*hujra*), assume such saintly titles as Ghaus and Qutb. Such a person can be seen sitting in a mosque, with a rosary in his hand. His state is like that of a mouse, who lives in the darkness of his hole, but sticks out his head in an attempt to observe the happenings of the world outside. On the other hand, a directionless seeker fails to understand that the night is dark and the path is steep, while the entire journey was plagued with untold pitfalls.[66] Thus we see that a seeker, who fails to enroll himself under a suitable mentor, renders himself incapable of any spiritual attainment.

All *murshids* were not worthy of respect. Many of them did not possess spiritual knowledge and piety. They managed to acquire acceptability through clever postures. Sultan Bahu appears to have been familiar with such false *murshids* and issues a clear warning to his contemporaries regarding the dangers of enrolling under them. The false *murshids* do not acquire any spiritual training themselves, but contrive to make disciples of others as an act of favour. They befool their disciples without any fear of God. Crooked in their ways, they loose their footing in the slippery game of love. A false *murshid* is not capable of meeting the needs of his disciple and therefore is not worthy of being called a spiritual guide (*pir*). There is no need for a *murshid* who is unable to provide proper instructions, which are required by the seekers of the spiritual path. If the *murshid* does not initiate the novice in the divine mysteries, then keeping awake to pray all through the night will be of no use. In fact, the company of a seductress is less corrupting than that of a false *murshid*, who deceives others by his garb of piety.[67]

From the point of mystic ideology (and not chronology), the position of Sultan Bahu as a Punjabi sufi poet is peculiar in the sense that he stands between Shaikh Farid, on the one hand, and Shah Husain and Bulleh Shah, on the other. It is possible to comprehend the 'middle' position of Sultan Bahu when we construct the critical discourse – drawing from the mystical poetry of four prominent sufi poets – which has been directed against the hegemonic socio-religious and political powers of medieval Punjab. Sultan Bahu is neither a 'moderate' sufi poet-critic like Shaikh Farid, nor is his poetic rhetoric as romantic and rebellious as that of Shah Husain and Bulleh Shah. Shaikh Farid composed his verses at a time when there was political instability and violent warfare in the region. That is the reason we find in his poetry the notes of pains and pangs, which are communicated in a female voice. This voice which was, in fact, the cry of the suppressed and subalterns, was not as loud and vocal as it was to be in poetry of his successors, Shah Husain and Bulleh Shah. The kind of boldness, which we encounter in Shah Husain's poetry, alludes to the non-conformist nature of the Qalandari order to which he belonged. Besides this, one may also discern in Shah Husain's stance the rebellious mood of the age in which Dulla Bhatti rose against the Mughal centralization which was unleashed by Akbar. Similarly, Bulleh Shah's insurgent sufic voice was in consonance with widespread peasant uprising during the first half of the eighteenth century. In contrast, we find in Sultan Bahu's poetry a didactic tone, philosophical compactness and sociological rhetoric. He does not speak in a female voice. He is clear and straightforward. He speaks more like a teacher than as a saint. When we study his concept of love and reverence for the spiritual preceptor, we discover in him a vociferous critic of religious fanaticism and pedantry, of abstract logic and of shallow reasoning. His sharply chiseled verses retain their freshness as well as relevance even as we have entered the twenty first century.

NOTES AND REFERENCES

1. Nizamul Mulk Tusi was the celebrated minister of the Saljuqid rulers Alp Arslan and Malik Shah. He served the Ghaznavids in the beginning of his career and shifted to the Saljuqids in 1040. As *wazir* he took part in the military campaigns of Alp Arslan. When Malik Shah ascended the throne on 1072, Nizamul Mulk became the real ruler for the next 20 years. Not an innovator, he organized Saljuqid polity on the lines of the Ghaznavids.

His famous work *Siyasat Nama* comprises advice on the art of government, which was illustrated by historical anecdotes. M.T. Houtsma and et. al, (Eds.), *The Encyclopaedia of Islam*, Vol. III, E.J. Brill, Leiden, 1936, pp. 932-934.

2. S.A.A.Rizvi, "Islam in Medieval India," in *A Cultural History of India*, Ed., A.L. Basham, Oxford University Press, Delhi, 1983. p. 287.
3. Aziz Ahmad and G.E. Von Grunebaum, *Muslim Self-Statement in India and Pakistan-1857-1968*, Suhail Academy, Lahore, 2004, p. 1.
4. S.A.A.Rizvi, "Islam in Medieval India," in *A Cultural History of India*, pp. 286-287.
5. Ibid., p. 283.
6. Ever since the establishment of the Delhi sultanate in the early thirteenth century, the *ulema* were appointed to posts in the judicial and ecclesiastical departments. Apart from teachers in the schools run by the state, the *ulema* were appointed as *sadr-i-jahan, Shaikh-ul-Islam, qazi, mufti, muhtasib, imam* and *khatib*. Khaliq Ahmad Nizami, *Religion and Politics in India during the Thirteenth Century*, Oxford University Press, Delhi, New Edition, 2002, pp. 169-170.
7. Rizvi, op. cit., pp. 283-293.
8. Richard M. Eaton, *Essays on Islam and Indian History*, Oxford University Press, Delhi, 2000, p. 31.
9. For detailed discussions on the factors leading to the decline of the Mughal empire, see Satish Chandra, *Medieval India: Society, Jagirdari Crisis and the Village*, Macmillan, New Delhi, 1982, pp. 46-75; Irfan Habib, *The Agrarian System of Mughal India*, Oxford University Press, Delhi, Second Revised Edition, 1999, pp. 364-405.
10. Presently Garh Maharaja is not the part of tahsil Shorkot of district Jhang. In 2006, a tahsil Ahmedpur Sial was created and Sultan Bahu's mausoleum falls in its jurisdiction. For the location of Shorkot and Ahmedpur Sial see, *Gazetteer of the Jhang District, 1883-84*, Sang-e-Meel, Lahore, 2000, Reprint, pp. 170-71.
11. Qazi Javed, *Punjab Key Sufi Danishwar,* Fiction House, Lahore, 2005, p. 144.
12. Sahibzada Sultan Ahmed Ali, 'Afkar-i-Hazrat Sultan Bahu' *Nawa-i-Waqt*, Milli Edition, 13 June 2008.
13. Sultan Bahu quoted in J.R. Puri and Kirpal Singh Khak, *Abyat of Hazrat Sultan Bahu*, Ed., Maqsood Saqib, Suchet Kitab Ghar, Lahore, 2004, p. 26.
14. Ibid.
15. Bilal Zubairi, *Tazkira-i-Auliya-i-Jhang,* Jhang Adabi Academy, Jhang, 2000, p. 117.
16. Saiyyid Athar Abbas Rizvi, *A History of Sufism in India,* Vol. II, Suhail Academy, Lahore, 2004, p. 440.
17. Qazi Javed, *Punjab Key Sufi Danishwar*, p. 147.
18. J.R. Puri and Kirpal Singh Khak, *Abyat of Hazrat Sultan Bahu*, p. 29.
19. Qazi Javed, *Punjab Key Sufi Danishwar,* p. 148.
20. Ibid., p. 173.
21. Rizvi, *A History of Sufism in India*,Vol. II, p. 433.

22. Sultan Bahu, *Chambey di Buty,* Translated and edited by Muhammad Yunas Hasrat, Book Home, Lahore, 2005, p. 21.
23. Puri and Khak, *Abyat of Hazrat Sultan Bahu,* Bait No. 1, p. 31.
24. Sultan Bahu, *Chambey di Buty,* p. 22.
25. Puri and Khak, *Abyat of Hazrat Sultan Bahu,* Bait No. 3, p. 33.
26. Ibid., Bait Nos. 29, 31; pp. 59, 61.
27. Puri and Khak, *Abyat of Hazrat Sultan Bahu,* Bait No.30, p. 60.
28. Shuja Alhaq, *A Forgotten Vision: A Study of Human Spirituality in the Light of the Islamic Tradition,* Vanguard Books, Lahore, 1996, p. 714.
29. Puri and Khak, *Abyat of Hazrat Sultan Bahu,* Bait No. 32, p. 62.
30. Ibid., Bait No. 31, p. 61.
31. Ibid., Bait No. 29, p. 59.
32. Similar views have been expressed by Bulleh Shah, who believes that worldly knowledge can be a hindrance to the realization of God. He argues that reading a large number of books, including scriptures, was futile. Knowledge generates pride in scholars, because they are devoid of spiritual wealth. The preachers exploit the ignorant masses in the name of religion. There is lack of correspondence between what they preach and what they practice. Their motivating force is personal gain and self-aggrandizement. What is required is the knowledge of the unity of God (*alif*) and practice of the written word under the guidance of a master. J.R. Puri and T.R. Shangari, *Bulleh Shah: The Love Intoxicated Iconoclast,* Radha Soami Satsang, Beas, Amritsar, 1986, pp. 219-21.
33. Puri and Khak, *Abyat of Hazrat Sultan Bahu,* Bait No. 28, p. 58.
34. Ibid., Bait No. 33, p. 63.
35. Shuja Alhaq, *A Forgotten Vision,* p. 708.
36. Ibid., p. 710.
37. Puri and Khak, Bait No. 124, p. 155.
38. Ibid., Bait Nos. 137 & 138, pp. 168-169.
39. Ibid., Bait No. 125, p. 158.
40. Ibid., Bait No. 130, p. 161.
41. Ibid., Bait No. 127, p. 158.
42. As early as the eleventh century, the sufi theorists have debated whether or not the relation of love (*ishq*) exists between man and God. Some sufis held that excessive love was permitted from man to God, but not from God to man. Others believed that God cannot be the object of man's excessive love, because such love involves a passing beyond limits, while God is not limited. The moderns assert that excessive love in this world and next, properly applied only to the desire of attaining the essence of God. They feel that instead of excessive love (*ishq*), we should use the words love (*muhabbat*) and pure love (*safwat*). This is so because excessive love (*ishq*) requires actual vision of God, who is unseen in this world. Ali bin Usman Hujwiri, *Kashf-ul-Mahjub,* English Translation, Reynold A. Nicholson, Darul Ishat, Karachi, 1990, p. 310.
43. Puri and Khak, *Abyat of Hazrat Sultan Bahu,* Bait No.133, p.164.
44. Ibid., Bait No. 123, p. 154.
45. Ibid., Bait No. 132, p. 163.

46. Ibid., Bait No. 129, p. 160.
47. Ibid., Bait No. 122, p. 153.
48. Ibid., Bait No. 120, p. 151.
49. Ibid., Bait No. 126, p. 157.
50. Ibid.
51. Khwaja Khizar was honoured as the god of water, who was also confided with the care of travellers. He was visualized as standing on fish, wearing green robes and supporting a flowing white beard. He presided over the well of immortality and acted as the giver of its water. A learned person, he was a known patron of learning. He was worshipped by both Hindus and Muslims, particularly by Jhinwars, Mallahs and all whose occupations were connected with water in any form. He was propitiated by people travelling by river or sea or descending into a well. H.A. Rose, *A Glossary of the Tribes and Castes of the Punjab and North West Frontier Province*, Vol. I, Languages Department of Punjab, Patiala, Reprint, 1970, pp. 562-564.
52. Puri and Khak, *Abyat of Hazrat Sultan Bahu*, Bait Nos.15-16, pp. 45-46.
53. Ibid., Bait No. 41, p. 72.
54. Ibid., Bait Nos. 53-54, pp. 84-85.
55. The phenomenon of sufism, subjectively speaking, may be defined as heart-wakefulness. The Quranic perspective agrees with that of the whole ancient world, both of East and of West, in attributing vision to the heart and in using the word to indicate not only the bodily organ of that name, but also what this corporeal centre gives access to, namely the centre of the soul, which itself is the gateway to a higher 'heart', namely the spirit. Thus 'heart' is often found as a synonym of intellect, in the sense of the Latin word intellectus, that is the faculty which perceives the transcendent. Martin Lings, *What is Sufism*, George Allen & Unwin, London, 1975, p. 48.
56. Puri and Khak, *Abyat of Hazrat Sultan Bahu*, Bait Nos. 74-79, pp. 105-110.
57. Even among sufis who insisted on the observance of the *shariat*, the spiritual status and authority of the *murshid* had (for the genuine *murid*) an overriding character, though it was not proclaimed as a doctrine and was not too openly expressed in practice. In the opinion of Shaikh Nizamuddin Auliya, a *murid* who offered his prayers five times a day and repeated some litany (*wazifah*) for a while, but had absolute faith in his *murshid* and was intensely devoted to him, was better than a *murid* who spent his time in prayer, fasting, litanies and performance of Hajj, but was wanting in faith and devotion to his *murshid*. M. Mujeeb, *The Indian Muslims*, George Allen & Unwin, London, 1967, p. 126.
58. Puri and Khak, *Abyat of Hazrat Sultan Bahu*, Bait No. 11, p. 41.
59. Ibid., Bait No. 168, p. 200.
60. Ibid., Bait No. 165, p. 197.
61. A study of the Chishti and Suhrawardi order, which enjoyed a strong position in Punjab during the sultanate period, indicates that the *murid* was required to completely abdicate his judgement, to surrender his will and to obey blindly each and every command of his master. The control of the *murshid* over the *murid* was two-fold – by the *murid* surrendering his will and in influencing the *murid's* actions and affairs. Riazul Islam, *Sufism*

in South Asia: Impact on Fourteenth Century Muslim Society, Oxford University Press, Karachi, 2002, pp. 387-390.

62. Puri and Khak, *Abyat of Hazrat Sultan Bahu*, Bait Nos.166-167, pp. 198-199.
63. Ibid., Bait No. 152, p. 183.
64. Ibid., Bait No. 164, p. 196.
65. Speaking in the same vein, Bulleh Shah pays rich tributes to his *murshid* Shah Inayat Qadiri, for whom he has intense love. He expresses his sorrow at not being able to see his *murshid* often enough. He begs of him not to deprive him of the boon of seeing him. Smitten by his love, the poet searches for him in the wilderness and runs to the river in pitch dark. Puri and Shangari, op cit., p. 332.
66. Puri and Khak, *Abyat of Hazrat Sultan Bahu*, Bait No. 171, p. 203.
67. Ibid., Bait Nos. 18, 36, 65, 75; pp. 48, 67, 96, 106.

PART III

SUFI SHRINES

14

Early Sufi Tombs in South-Western Punjab

Understanding the Architectural Features

Subhash Parihar

South western Punjab figures prominently in the annals of the Indian subcontinent. Geographical location of the area played a crucial role in shaping the course of its history. Its hot and dusty plains were penetrated by the perennial rivers of the Indus basin, the Satluj and Ravi. A major trans-continental trade route, which linked Delhi and Qandhar, passed through it. It was closely associated with the regions of Rajputana and Sind, while it enjoyed a variety of contacts with the trans-Indus lands of Afghanistan and Persia. It became a part of the Ummayyad caliphate when it was annexed by Muhammad bin Qasim to a newly created kingdom in Sind. Subsequently it was ruled by the Qarmathians for long periods till it was conquered (1175) by Sultan Muizzuddin of Ghur. With the establishment of the Delhi sultanate, Multan and Uch were grouped together in one governorship (*iqta*), which was often engaged in the subjugation of the Sumras.[1] During the thirteenth century, the area experienced internal political strife and foreign invasions. Many of its governors – Nasiruddin Qubacha, Kabir Khan Ayaz and Izzuddin Balban Kishlu Khan – ruled independently of the Delhi sultanate. The area bore the brunt of recurrent attacks by such invaders as the Mongols, Khwarizmians and Qarlughs.[2] Sultan Muhammad, the son of Ghiasuddin Balban, lost his life in a battle (1285) against the Mongols. It was only with the appointment of Ghazi Malik as the governor of Dipalpur in the reign of Alauddin Khalji that the Mongol invasions were effectively checked and normal economic activities were revived. In the middle of the fourteenth century, Ainul Mulk Mahru, the governor of Multan, created a network of canals in the region and paved the way for agrarian expansion with the help of land grants.[3] It may be added that the long distance merchants, who were engaged in the commerce of non-agricultural goods, were popularly known as Multanis. This indicated the role of Multan and its merchants in the economic life of the Indian subcontinent.[4]

South western Punjab appears to have come under the cultural influence of Islam since the Arab conquest of Sind in the early eighth century. Later on, a large number of Muslim migrants, who had been uprooted from their native places in Central Asia and Persia by the Mongols inroads, poured into north-western India and settled in its towns along with the new Turkish rulers of the Delhi sultanate. During the course of the thirteenth century, several religious institutions of Islam (including mosques and seminaries) had begun to receive financial assistance from the Delhi sultanate and the patronage was continued well into the fourteenth century.[5] This historical phenomenon underlines the strong presence of Islam in south-western Punjab. It was in these circumstances that a native of Multan, Shaikh Bahauddin Zakariya (1182-1262) laid the foundation of the Suhrawardi order in the region. A profound scholar who had travelled extensively in the Islamic lands, he laid emphasis on a strict observance of Islamic religious practices. Some important features of the Suhrawardi order included an extensive hospice (*khanqah*) in Multan, accumulation of wealth, intimate relations with the contemporary rulers and hereditary succession to spiritual authority. In due course, Shaikh Bahauddin Zakariya was succeeded by his son Shaikh Sadruddin Arif (d.1286) and grandson Shaikh Ruknuddin Abul Fateh (d.1335) who carried on the mystical traditions of the Suhrawardi order. Another branch of the Suhrawardi order was established by Syed Jalaluddin Surkh Bukhari (d.1291) at the town of Uch which was situated to the south of Multan and on the confluence of the Satluj and Chenab. It was under the headship of his grandson Syed Jalaluddin Bukhari Makhdum-i-Jahaniyan Jahangasht (1308-1383) that the Suhrawardi order began to play a significant role in the socio-cultural life of north-western India.[6] Scholars are familiar with his mystical discourses (*malfuzat*) which are available in several compilations. But the Suhrawardi order has left behind an equally important legacy in the form of tombs of the mystic masters. Some of these memorials have been transformed, in due course, into shrines that became centres of pilgrimage for the common people.[7] These tombs mark a significant stage in the evolution of Indo-Muslim architecture in the Indian subcontinent. In the present paper, an attempt is being made to focus on the architectural features of the sufi tombs that are located at Multan and Uch.

It may be remembered that the whole of west Punjab (which lies in the modern Pakistan), is studded with sufi tombs of varying popularity. Some of these, like the tomb of Data Ganj Bakhsh at Lahore or the tomb of Shah Rukn-i-Alam at Multan, enjoy the status of the presiding shrines of the city, whereas the others are venerated just by local populace. From a survey of these tombs in the west Punjab, six major centres of sufism emerge – namely Multan, Uch, Pakpattan, Qasur, Lahore and Gujarat – which are situated at the angles of an irregular hexagon, completely covering the region in between the rivers Chenab and Sutlej. Any architectural study of the sufi tombs is destined to suffer from a dearth of source material. Most of them have been considerably renovated to preserve any architectural originality. Hardly any of them bears a historical inscription recording the date of its erection. As stated, this paper is limited to the study of the sufi tombs of Multan and Uch, two of the earliest centres of sufism in the Indian subcontinent. The tombs at these centres – some of these being in their original form – are the earliest specimens of Indo-Muslim architecture which influenced the course of Islamic architecture of the rest of the subcontinent. The tombs of Multan are better preserved probably because the city has been an administrative headquarters throughout the medieval period. Its importance did not wane even during the British and the modern periods.

The bulk of the tombs in Multan, Uch and their neighbourhood belong to sufis of the Suhrawardi order.[8] The second largest group of mausoleums belong to the Qadiri order. However, the Multan sufis belonged to a larger variety of orders as compared to those from Uch. The shrines at both the places were constructed almost during the same time span. It is strange that the architectural remains of the Sultanate period at Lahore are few. This paucity is probably indicative of the lesser significance of Lahore, particularly as a centre of sufism, during this period.

Sufi Tombs of Multan

The geographical location of Multan, just opposite the Bolan Pass, assigned it a decisive role in history of the Indian subcontinent. The trade route connecting the subcontinent with Qandhar and the world beyond, passed through it. And as long as the Bolan served as the main Pass, the town formed a gateway to India. The Chinese pilgrim Hwen-Tsang who visited it in 641, gives its name as MU-LO-SAN-P'U-LU or Mulasthanapura.[9] He saw the Buddhist monasteries (*sangharamas*) of the town in ruins. By this time, Buddhism had been replaced by Hinduism as attested by the existence of eight temples of the Brahmanical gods, including the "very magnificent and profusely decorated" temple dedicated to the Sun-god, Aditya. Along with Sind, Multan was the earliest part of the subcontinent to have been conquered by the army of Muhammad bin Qasim, as early as 714. Since then up to its conquest by Maharaja Ranjit Singh in 1818, it has almost continuously been under the Muslim rule. These eleven centuries of Muslim rule have left their mark on the socio-cultural life, most prominently in the form of sufi tombs. The following are the major sufi tombs in the town:

1. Tomb of Shah Yusuf Gardezi (c. 1150)
2. Tomb of Shah Baha al-Haq or Shaikh Bahauddin Zakariya (d. 1262)
3. Tomb of Sadna Shaheed or Shahid Shaheed or Shah Dana Shaheed (d.1270)
4. Tomb of Shah Shams Sabzwari (wrongly identified by Cunningham with the renowned saint Shamsuddin Tabrezi)[10] (d.1276)
5. Tomb of Shaikh Ruknuddin Abul Fateh, popularly known as Shah Rukn-i-Alam (d. 1334-35)

These tombs are prominent examples of the provincial style of Punjab that flourished between 1150 and 1325. This style grew independent of the imperial Sultanate style that developed in Delhi and its surrounding region, before the advent of the Mughals.[11] Its characteristic features were determined by the geological formation of its land. No building stone is available in the plains of Punjab, but its alluvial soil can be easily moulded into fine bricks. Hence brick has been the chief building material in Punjab since earliest times as indicated even at the Harappan sites. To strengthen the brick walls, these were given a slight camber and occasionally timbers were embedded in them. Another method of providing stability to the structures was by appending buttresses and towers to their corners. But plain brick structures would have given a very monotonous look. To add colour to their monuments, the Punjab builders made use of coloured glazed tiles. It may be noted here that although the technique of glazing was known in ancient India, but the use of glazed tiles for architectural decoration was imported from Persia. The region of Multan and Sind, due to its proximity to Persia, was the earliest to use this mode of decoration. Gradually the rest of Punjab became as great a centre of this craft as Sind and Multan. And from this region, the use of glazed tiles spread to the rest of the Indian subcontinent.

The earliest of the Multan memorials, the tomb of Shah Yusuf Gardizi (c.1150), is a cubical structure covered with a flat roof. The entrance to the interior is provided through an archway placed in a projected bay in the southern wall. The whole of the exterior of this simple structure has a veneer of painted square encaustic tiles. But only the tile work in the rectangular panel above the entrance, in the form of low-relief decoration, appears to be original, the rest dating from some later period.

The next in chronological order is the tomb of Shaikh Bahauddin Zakariya (1182-1262), considered to be one of the greatest saints of the Suhrawardi order. Unfortunately, the building was considerably damaged in the siege of Multan by the British in 1848.[12] Many alterations must be dating from this period of renovation. Moreover, repeated application of plaster and whitewash obscures much of the details of external surfaces. But not much seems to have been changed in its broad features which are a square tomb chamber, surmounted by a high octagonal drum and the whole crowned with a hemi-spherical dome, all having excellent proportions. The towers at corners of the building and its octagonal drum give the feeling of some lightness to the structure. Kamil Khan Mumtaz considers it "the most elegant of the Multan shrines".[13] Percy Brown also praises that "this tomb has an appearance of purposeful strength combined with a simple elegance which is noteworthy."[14] Undoubtedly, the tomb of Shaikh Bahauddin Zakariya established a tomb-type to be followed for many centuries to come. It has been brought to our notice that, at the door of the tomb, Pakistani musicians sing Fakhruddin Iraqi's (d.1289) Persian verses which are imbued with love.[15]

The tombs of Sadna Shaheed (d.1270) and Shah Shams Sabzwari (d.1276) were built within fifteen years after the tomb of Shaikh Bahauddin Zakariya. The tomb of Sadna Shaheed is quite austere in its treatment whereas the tomb of Shah Shams Sabzwari is a highly ornate version of the same. Anyway both of these carry the style forward.

The provincial style of Punjab reached its apex in the tomb of Shaikh Ruknuddin Abul Fateh (popularly known as Shah Rukn-i-Alam),[16] the grandson of Shaikh Bahauddin Zakariya.[17] This magnificent tomb is believed to have been erected by Sultan Ghiyasuddin Tughluq (r.1320-25) for himself, during the period of his governorship of Multan, under the title of Ghazi Malik.[18] But later he is said to have donated the structure for the burial of the saint, building for himself a new tomb at Tughluqabad (Delhi). In many respects, this tomb which Sir John Marshall considers 'one of the most splendid memorials ever erected in honour of the dead' is a landmark structure.[19]

Here it is for the first time that we come across an octagonal plan for a Sultanate building which appeared some fifty years later at Delhi in the tomb of Khan-i Jahan Tilangani.[20] From the point of view of size, it is a monumental structure rising from an octagonal base, 90 feet [27.4 m] in diameter and the whole soaring to a height of 115 feet [35 m]. The effect of height becomes more pronounced as the tomb stands on the fort mound which itself rises some 50 feet [about 15 m] higher than the surrounding country. The tapering walls of its octagonal first storey, having a domed and pinnacled buttress appended to each corner, impart the structure an appearance of great solidity and mark a major advance in architectural style. The first storey is externally decorated with a dado of carved bricks and tiles. Above the arched recesses of openings on each side of the octagon, there is a decorative frieze. After thirty courses of bricks above the frieze lies the parapet of the first storey. The lowest part of the parapet consists of an arabesque design, which is composed of chain mouldings of bricks. The first storey rises to a height of 12.40 metres.[21]

The second storey of the tomb is also octagonal in form. Each side corresponds to the first storey and has an arched opening, which is provided with an architrave decorated with cut bricks. We also come across eight merlons which, seen as a façade, are filled with intricate geometrical patterns. While the frieze consists of inverted merlons, the parapet is composed of blind merlons. Each side of the storey is provided with a small turret, which is almost similar to those seen at the top of the circular buttresses of the first storey. The second storey is topped by a hemispherical dome which rises to a height of 8.98 metres. At its base, the dome possesses decorative mouldings that consist of alternate rosettes and merlon designs. The main structure of the dome is devoid of decoration as it is covered with thick plaster which, in turn, is coated with accumulated layers of whitewash.[22]

A prominent feature of the monument is its consummate adornment in a variety of mediums. The interior of the tomb originally bore painted decoration, but only a few of its traces were extant when Cunningham visited the place in 1872-73. Throughout the interior elevations are seen exposed horizontal beams, some of which are carved with geometrical motifs and arabesque designs. In the corners, there are wooden brackets with carved motifs, though somewhat crude in execution. There is elaborate decoration with cut brickwork forming geometrical and calligraphic designs, in relief, giving a rich play of light and shade. However, the richest in effect are the raised patterns that are formed with unglazed bricks, having its interstices inlaid with glazed tiles. Cunningham realises the difficulty of this mode of decoration, but praises its increased effect as it united all the beauty of variety of colour with light and shade of a raised pattern.[23] It is strange that this type of glazed tile work was not used in the rest of Punjab before the seventeenth century.

It has been observed that the finest decorative work is present around the mihrab, which is entirely encased in wood (*shisham*). Same is the case with the curve of the niche, which is carved with ocatagonal and other polygonal designs. The mihrab is enclosed on three sides by a band of calligraphy, while the text is punctuated by geometric and floral designs.[24] Thus, in so far as the decorative motifs are concerned, the tomb of Shah Rukn-i-Alam forms a veritable art gallery. In most cases, the designs are geometrical and calligraphic in nature. One motif of particular interest is the swastika, usually regarded as a Hindu motif.[25] But in fact, the swastika motif "was used in the Mediterranean countries and the Near East from c. the 3rd millennium B.C. and remained one of the commonest decorative devices except possibly in Egypt, Babylon and Assyria."[26] This motif also appears in the cut brick decoration of the tomb of Shaikh Bahauddin Zakariya. [27]

The architectural features observed in the Multan tombs persisted in the monuments of the Punjab even during the Mughal period when the whole of the empire was following a single imperial style. Even then the Mughal monuments of the region were able to preserve their distinctive character.

Sufi Tombs of Uch

The town of Uch, situated 100 kilometres to the south-south-west of Multan and 60 kilometres to the south-east of Bahawalpur, is a place of great historical and archaeological significance. It was situated on the southern bank of the Satluj and opposite to its confluence with the Chenab.[28] In the twelfth century, according to a traditional account, Uch was known as Deogarh (the stronghold of gods). Its ruler Deo Singh fled to Marwar when Syed Jalaluddin Surkh Bukhari arrived here to lay the foundation of a branch of the Suhrawardi order. He is said to have converted Sundarpuri, the daughter of Deo Singh, to Islam and directed her to build a fort called Uch (high). Since then it came to be known as Uch Sharif (Uch the Sacred). Raverty identified Uch with the town of Bhatiah near Multan, which was annexed by Sultan Mahmud of Ghazni. After its occupation by Sultan Muizzuddin of Ghur, it became the chief town of Upper Sind under Nasiruddin Qubacha. In 1223 it was ravaged by Jalaluddin Mangbarni, the fugitive prince of Khwarizm. At this time, it was already known as a centre of Islamic learning, as the historian Minhaj us-Siraj Juzjani served as the chief of the Firuzi college (*madrasah*). In the early twentieth century, Uch was seen as a group of three villages, built on as many mounds which represented the debris of successive urban settlements. However, throughout the medieval period, Uch retained its fame as a place of great religious sanctity in the eyes of the Muslims, as the town contained several sufi shrines in charge of Bukhari and Gilani Makhdums, who have descended from the original founders (belonging to the Suhrawardi order).[29] The town was even associated with the Sikh tradition. It is believed that after the battle of Chamkaur (1705), Guru Gobind Singh was escorted to the safety of Malwa region by two Pathan brothers of Machhiwara, Nabi Khan and Ghani Khan. On this occasion, it was given out that Guru Gobind Singh was, in fact, a saint of Uch (*Uch Da Pir*).

As already seen at Multan, at Uch too, two types of tombs are seen: one type having flat-roofs and the other type domed. The tombs of Abu Hanifa, Syed Safiuddin Haqani (d.1007), Jalaluddin Surkh Bukhari (d. 1291)[30], Raju Qattal, Syed Jalaluddin Bukhari Makhdum-i-Jahanian Jahangasht (died 1383; tomb built in 1453)[31], are the prominent specimens of the first type. Each flat-roofed tomb consists of a rectangular hall, sometimes provided with a wooden entrance porch as seen in the tombs of Raju Qattal and Makhdum-i-Jahanian Jahangasht. The timbered roofs of this type of tombs are supported on slender square, circular or octagonal wooden columns surmounted by carved capitals. Wooden beams are also embedded in the walls. Windows are usually screened with carved wooden lattices. The wooden columns and ceilings are richly adorned with painted or lacquered floral designs. Yellow, green, red and orange colours have been used in the tomb of Raju Qattal.[32] But the details of woodwork are characteristic of the domestic architecture of the region during nineteenth and twentieth centuries. Moreover, these tombs bear inscriptions of restorations in the nineteenth and twentieth centuries. So it is difficult to discern how much of their fabric is original, i.e. belonging to the thirteenth or fourteenth centuries. Describing the tomb of Syed Safiuddin Haqani, Abdul Rehman writes that 'the walls and beams are original whereas the roof and wooden posts have been repaired with time.'[33] Similar may be the case with some other tombs. The tomb of Abu Hanifa is considered to be more or less original.

The tombs of Baha al-Halim, also called Bahauddin Uchi (built c. 1349-78), Bibi Javindi (built 1499), Ustad Ladla (designer and builder of the tomb of Bibi Javindi), Bibi Aisha and Musa Pak Shaheed belong to the category of the domed type. All the tombs of the domed type are damaged. However, the buildings still preserve their distinctive character. Each tomb of this type consists of a square or octagonal structure, strengthened with turrets at corners, surmounted by an octagonal drum supporting a slightly pointed hemispherical dome. One can trace the development of this domed type of tomb structure from the anonymous tombs at Mithri and Sibri (both near Karachi) built in eleventh-twelfth centuries.[34] The anonymous tombs at Lal Mehra Sharif (District Dera Ismail Khan), dated by Taj Ali in the eleventh and early half of the twelfth centuries, also stylistically stand very close to the domed tombs at Uch.[35]

The most distinctive feature of the Uch tombs of both types is their revetment with white, ultramarine and turquoise coloured glazed tiles, so much so that hardly any part of their brick fabric is visible. In some cases, not only the exterior but the interior is also ornamented in a similar fashion. The tilework usually takes the shape of horizontal diaper patterns consisting of geometrical designs, sometimes taking the shapes of stars or stylised flowers. This type of tilework, also seen on some anonymous tombs of Lal Mehra Sharif in Gomal Valley, is not found in the rest of Punjab where it followed a different course. In the rest of Punjab, up to the first half of the sixteenth century, only square tiles of ultramarine and turquoise blue colours were used. During the later half of the sixteenth century, tiles of green and yellow colours were also introduced. But the first quarter of the seventeenth century witnessed a different development. Now, first a design, usually geometrical, was formed with raised brickwork or unglazed tiles and then the sunken spaces in the design were inlaid with cut tiles of various colours. This type of work is seen in the tomb of Shah Rukn-i-Alam. But it is strange that this style of tilework took about two and three quarters of a century to spread in the rest of Punjab. Here it developed still further and took the form of tile-mosaics of very intricate designs, the type of work never seen at Multan or Uch.

Usually scholars regard the architectural style of the monuments at Uch as an extension or derivation of Multan style, but art-historian Kamil Khan Mumtaz thinks that "the characteristics of Uch monuments are sufficiently distinct to be identified as a related but independent building tradition.[36] He adds that "while the brick-domed structures might well have been inspired by Multan precedents, the reverse might equally be true of the flat-roofed timbered forms".

[Sources for figures and plates: Abdul Rehman, *Historic Towns of Punjab: Ancient and Medieval Period* (Rawalpindi, 1997); Ahmad Nabi Khan, *Uchchh: History and Architecture* (Islamabad, 1980); idem, *Multan: History & Architecture* (Islamabad, 1983); idem, *Islamic Architecture of Pakistan: An Analytical Exposition* (Islamabad, 1990); Kamil Khan Mumtaz, *Architecture in Pakistan* (Singapore, 1985). However, I have redrawn some plans afresh on the basis of those published in the above books and reworked most of the plates in Adobe Photoshop.]

List of Figures

1. Multan: Tomb of Shah Yusuf Gardezi, plan
2. Multan: Tomb of Bahauddin Zakariya, plan and section
3. Multan: Tomb of Shah Dana Shaheed, plan and section
4. Multan: Tomb of Shams Sabzwari, plan and section
5. Multan: Tomb of Shah Rukn-i-Alam, plan
6. Multan: Tomb of Shah Rukn-i-Alam, section
7. Uch: Tomb of Abu Hanifa, plan
8. Uch: Tomb of Jalaluddin Surkh Bukhari complex, plan
9. Uch: Tomb of Jahanian Jahanghasht, plan
10. Uch: Tomb of Baha al-Halim, plan
11. Uch: Tomb of Bibi Javindi, plan, elevation and section

List of Plates

1. Multan: Tomb of Shah Yusuf Gardezi
2. Multan: Tomb of Bahauddin Zakariya
3. Multan: Tomb of Shah Dana Shaheed (an old view)
4. Multan: Tomb of Shams Sabzwari
5. Multan: Tomb of Rukn-i-Alam
6. Multan: Tomb of Rukn-i-Alam, various decorative patterns
7. Swastika motif on (A) the tomb of Bahauddin Zakariya and (B) the tomb of Rukn-i-Alam
8. Uch: Tomb of Abu Hanifa
9. Uch: Tomb of Raju Qattal
10. Uch: Tomb of Makhdum-i-Jahaniyan Jahangasht, painted ceiling
11. Uch: Tomb of Baha al-Halim, exterior view
12. Uch: Tomb of Baha al-Halim, view from inner side
13. Uch: Tomb of Bibi Javindi

NOTES AND REFERENCES

1. Andre Wink, *Al-Hind: The Making of the Indo-Islamic World*, Vol. II, Oxford University Press, Reprint, 1997, pp. 242-245.
2. For details of these developments, see A.B.M. Habibullah, *The Foundation of Muslim Rule in India*, Central Book Depot, Allahabad, Third Revised Edition, 1976, pp. 96-119, 169-191.
3. Surinder Singh, 'The Making of Medieval Punjab: Politics, Society and Economy, c.1200-c.1400,' Presidential Address (Medieval Section), Punjab History Conference, 40th Session, Punjabi University, Patiala, 14-16 March 2008, pp. 38-41.
4. The Multanis, who have been mentioned in conjunction with the Sahs, had acquired abundant wealth by undertaking commerce and advancing loans to the ruling class of the Delhi sultanate. Tapan Raychaudhury and Irfan Habib, *The Cambridge Economic History of India,* Vol. I, c.1200-c.1750, Orient Longman, New Delhi, Reprint, 2004, pp. 85-86.
5. Surinder Singh, 'Dynamics of Statecraft in the Delhi Sultanate: A Reconstruction from the Letters of Ainul Mulk Mahru,' *Proceedings of the Indian History Congress*, 61st. Session, Kolkata, 2001, p. 287.
6. Khaliq Ahmad Nizami, *Religion and Politics in India during the Thirteenth Century*, Oxford University Press, Delhi, Reprint, 2002, pp. 238-245.
7. In the eyes of the devotees, the sufis were saints who possessed spiritual power (*baraka*) to intercede with God on their behalf. After the death of a prominent sufi, the spiritual power adhered to his burial place which, after a complex process involving customary rituals and role of the custodians, evolved as a busy centre of pilgrimage. The devotees visited the shrine to seek divine aid in their personal and business affairs. This role of the shrine has turned out to be resilient in spite of the opposition of reformist and fundamentalist elements among the Muslims. Richard M. Eaton, 'The Political and Religious Authority of the Shrine of Baba Farid,' in *Essays on*

Islam and Indian History, Oxford University Press, Delhi, 2000, p.204; Marc Gaborieau, 'Introduction to the New Edition,' in *Muslim Shrines in India: Their Character, History and Significance*, Ed., Christian W. Troll, Oxford University Press, Delhi, 1989, p. xv.

8. Khurram Qadir, "Architectural Remains of the Sultanate of Delhi at Uchchh and Multan: Indicators of Political History" in Sultanate Period Architecture (Proceedings of the Seminar on the Sultanate Period Architecture in Pakistan held in Lahore, November 1990), eds. Siddiq-a-Akbar, Abdul Rehman & Mumtaz Ali Tirmizi, Anjuman-i Mimaran, Lahore, 1991, pp. 62-63.
9. Hiuen Tsiang, *Buddhist Records of the Western World*, Trans., Samuel Beal, 1884; Reprint, Munshiram Manoharlal, New Delhi, 2004, p. 274. For the ancient history of Multan, see, Alexander Cunningham, *The Ancient Geography of India*,1871; Reprint, Low Price Publications, New Delhi,1990, p. 194-203; idem, *Archaeological Survey of India Report for the Year 1872-73*, Vol. V, 1875; Indological Book House, Varanasi, Reprint 1966, pp. 114-36.
10. *ASI Report 1872-73*, pp. 134-35.
11. The provincial style of Punjab was the earliest of the eight provincial styles, the other seven being those that developed in Bengal, Gujrat, Jaunpur, Malwa, Deccan, Bijapur & Khandesh, and Kashmir. For details of these styles, see Percy Brown, *Indian Architecture (Islamic Period)* 1956; Taraporevala Sons, Bombay, Reprint 1975, pp. 31-83.
12. *ASI Report 1872-73*, p. 131. The changes of details can also be seen by comparing its pictures in various books, e.g, Percy Brown, pl. XXIII, fig. 2; Ahmad Nabi Khan, *Multan: History and Architecture*, Institute of Islamic History, Culture and Civilization, Islamabad, 1983, pls. 12, 14; Abdul Rehman, *Historic Towns of Punjab: Ancient and Medieval Period*, Ferozsons, Rawalpindi, 1997, fig. 5.1.8
13. Kamil Khan Mumtaz, *Architecture in Pakistan*, Concept Media, Singapore, 1985, p. 44
14. Percy Brown, p. 33.
15. Fakhruddin Iraqi (1213-1289), who was born in Hamadan, arrived in India along with a group of Qalandars. He became attached to Shaikh Bahauddin Zakariya and stayed in Multan for twenty five years. He composed mystical verses in Persian which were dominated by the theme of passionate love. They became extremely popular in Multan, where they were sung in the markets and taverns to the accompaniment of musical instruments. Shaikh Bahauddin Zakariya had a favourable opinion of the mystic inclinations of Iraqi and even married his daughter to him. The popularity of Shaikh Bahauddin Zakariya as a mystic is attributed, to an extent, to the presence of Iraqi in his hospice. Annemarie Schimmel, *Mystical Dimensions of Islam*, Sang-e-Meel Publications, Lahore, Reprint, 2003, pp. 352-253.
16. Ruknuddin Abul Fateh (d.1335) maintained cordial relations with the Khalji and Tughluq rulers. He was on friendly terms with Shaikh Nizamuddin Auliya, the most eminent Chishti saint of the period. During his frequent visits to Delhi, he presented the petitions of the people before the Delhi sultans and secured a positive response from them. His intervention saved

the people of Multan from punishment at the hands of Muhammad bin Tughluq (r.1325-51), who had crushed the rebellion of the local governor Bahram Aiba Kishlu Khan. He received a grant of 100 villages from the victorious sultan. He has figured frequently in the account of Ibn Battuta. Saiyid Athar Abbas Rizvi, *A History of Sufism in India*, Vol. I, Munshiram Manoharlal, New Delhi, 1978, pp. 210-214.

17. The fourteenth century Moroccan traveller Ibn Battuta, during his travels in India, was recommended by the pious Shaikh Burhanuddin al-Araj at Alexandria to meet Shaikh Ruknuddin Abul Fateh at Multan. Ibn Battuta sojourned at Multan from 5 November 1333 to 27 January 1334. *The Rehla of Ibn Battuta*, Eng. Tr., Mahdi Husain, Oriental Institute, Baroda, 1976, p. 6. For a brief biographical account of Shah Rukn-i Alam, see N.K. Singh, *Sufis of India, Pakistan and Bangladesh*, Vol. III, Kitab Bhavan, Delhi, 2002, pp. 1-5.
18. The closeness between Shah Rukn-i-Alam and Sultan Ghiyasuddin Tughluq is attested by the fact that the saint was with the Sultan at the time of the death of the latter. *Rehla of Ibn Battuta*, p. 55. But nowhere the construction of the Multan tomb by Ghiyasuddin Tughluq is mentioned.
19. J. Burton Page, "Tomb of Rukn-i Alam" in *Splendours of the East*, ed. Mortimer Wheeler, Spring Books, London, Reprint 1970, p. 75. The article is illustrated by very beautiful plates of the tomb.
20. Recently, Shaikh Khursheed Hasan has brought to light an anonymous octagonal tomb at Mithri (District Karachi), dated by M. Usman Hasan as back as 11th-12th century. Shaikh Khursheed Hasan, *The Islamic Architectural Heritage of Pakistan: Funerary Memorial Architecture*, Royal Book Company, Karachi, 2001, p. 33, pl. IIIa; M. Usman Hasan, "Influence of Central and West Asian Religions and Culture since 7th Century on Construction and Decoration of Tombs and Graves in Baluchistan and the Sub-continent", *Journal of Central Asia*, 16(1-2), Islamabad, July & December 1993, pp. 251-52; interestingly, the very first Islamic monument, the Dome of the Rock (completed in 691) at Jerusalem (Israel) has an octagonal plan. For the plan, section and some excellent plates of the monument see, Richard Ettinghausen, Oleg Grabar & Marilyn Jenkins-Madina, *Islamic Art and Architecture 650-1250*, Mapin, Ahmedabad, Reprint 2002, figs. 4-11; Page attributes the octagonal plan to the local genius. J. Burton Page, op. cit., p. 75.
21. Syed Abdul Quddus, *Punjab: The Land of Beauty, Love and Mysticism*, Royal Book Company, Karachi, 1972, pp. 368-369.
22. Ibid., p. 369-370.
23. *ASI Report 1872-73*, p. 133.
24. Syed Abdul Quddus, op. cit., pp. 370-371.
25. Khurram Qadir (p. 70) also considers it an essentially Aryan motif, associated with Hinduism. But his own hypothesis regarding other geometrical motifs "that the shapes have no definite religious implication" but are derived directly from the geometric innovation, also holds true about this motif. p. 69.
26. Harold Osborne, ed., *The Oxford Companion to the Decorative Arts* (Oxford, 1975), p. 753. See also, Thomas Wilson, *The Swastika (The earliest known Symbol, and its migrations with observations on the Migration of certain Industries*

in Pre-Historic times) Oriental Publishers, Delhi, Reprint 1973.

27. Ahmad Nabi Khan, *Islamic Architecture of Pakistan: An Analytical Exposition*, National Hijra Council, Islamabad, 1990, p. 59, fig. 18.
28. Cunningham identifies Uch with the place *Askaland-usah*, mentioned by Rashiduddin (1247-1318) the author of the Islamic history *Jami-ut-Tawarikh*, which according to him was a corruption of *Alexandria Uchha*. He also believes that Uch must also be the Iskandar or Alexandria of the Chachnamah, which was captured by Chach during his expedition against Multan. Alexander Cunningham, *Ancient Geography*, p. 205.
29. Imperial Gazetteer of India, *Provincial Series: Punjab*, Vol. II, Superintendent of Governmen Printing, Calcutta, 1908, pp. 354-355.
30. It is believed that he was buried at his hospice in Rasulpur, which was situated at a distance of six *kos* from the Chenab. Owing to recurrent floods of the river, his body was shifted four times to safer places. The present building of his tomb was constructed in 1845 by a famous landlord named Nawab Bahadur Khan. He also constructed a well and water reservoir in the precincts of the shrine. In 1883 Nawab Sadiq Muhammad Khan IV, the ruler of Bahawalpur, undertook the extension and renovation of the building. Shaikh Parwaiz Amin Naqshbandy, *The Saints of Punjab*, Umar Publications, Lahore, 1998, p. 778.
31. Syed Jalaluddin Bukhari Makhdum-i-Jahanian Jahangasht (1308-83) was an interesting personality. A grandson of Syed Jalaluddin Surkh Bukhari, he was appointed as Shaikhul-Islam and granted several villages along with a hospice at Siwistan by Muhammad bin Tughluq (r.1325-51). Discarding this patronage, he undertook wide travels in the Islamic lands. He appears to have returned to Uch during the reign of Firuz Shah Tughluq (r.1351-88). He enjoyed intimate relations with the Sultan, whom he met during several visits to Delhi. His intercession enabled the Sultan to establish peace in Sind. His mystical discourses indicate that he gave an orthodox Sunni interpretation to sufism. He is credited with rejuvenating the Suhrawardi order in Uch, when it had declined in Multan after the death of Shaikh Ruknuddin Abul Fateh. Saiyid Athar Abbas Rizvi, *A History of Sufism in India*, Vol. I, Munshiram Manoharlal, New Delhi, 1978, pp. 277-279.
32. Raju Qattal was the grandson of Syed Jalaluddin Surkh Bukhari and brother of Makhdum-i-Jahanian Jahangasht. Though his original name was Syed Sadruddin, he acquired fame under the nickname of Raju and Qattal (slayer) on account of his militant evangelism. This attitude was illustrated by an incident recorded in Maulana Jamali's *Siyar-ul-Arifin*, according to which Raju Qattal's intolerance led to the execution of Nawahun, the Hindu darogha of Uch. Rizvi, op. cit., pp. 279-281.
33. Abdul Rehman, p. 115.
34. Khursheed Hasan, pp. 33, 34, pls. IIIa and IIIb.
35. Taj Ali, *Anonymous Tombs in the Gomal Valley, and the Beginning of Tomb Architecture in Pakistan*, Universitat Bonn, Bonn, 1987, p. 94, pls. 3, 5, 9, 10a, 13, 14, 15a, 19.
36. Kamil Khan Mumtaz, *Architecture in Pakistan*, p. 46.

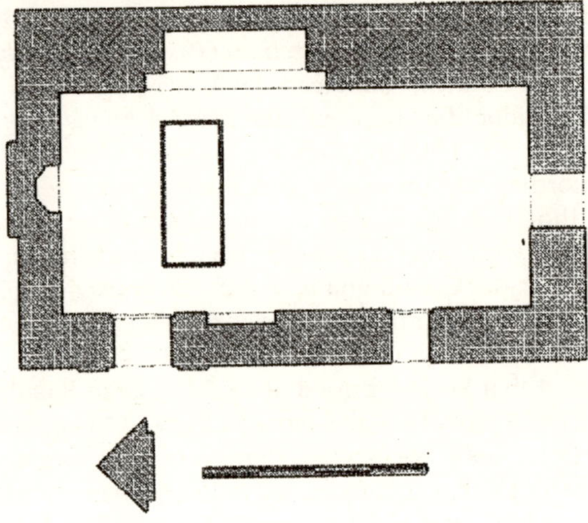

Fig. 1: Multan: Tomb of Shah Yusuf Gardezi, plan

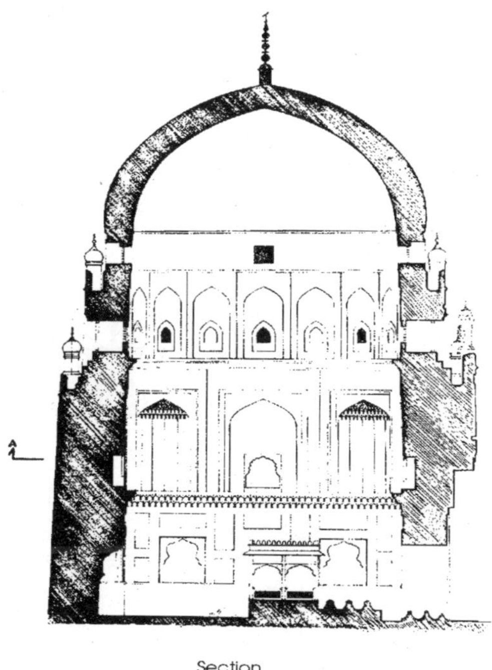

Section

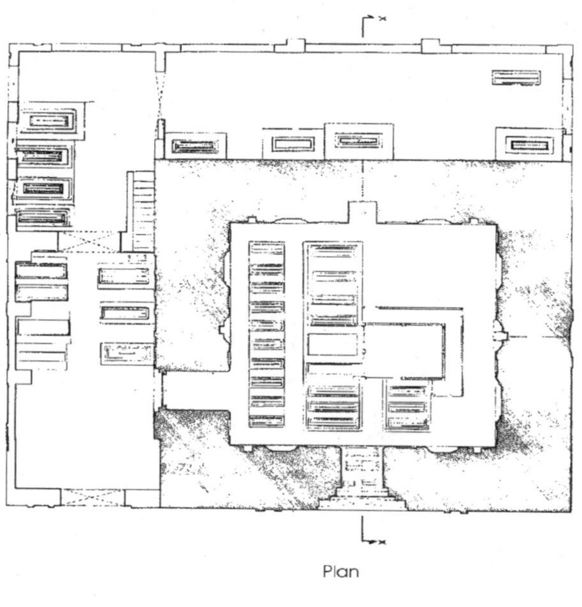

Plan

Fig. 2: Multan: Tomb of Shaikh Bahauddin Zakariya, plan and section

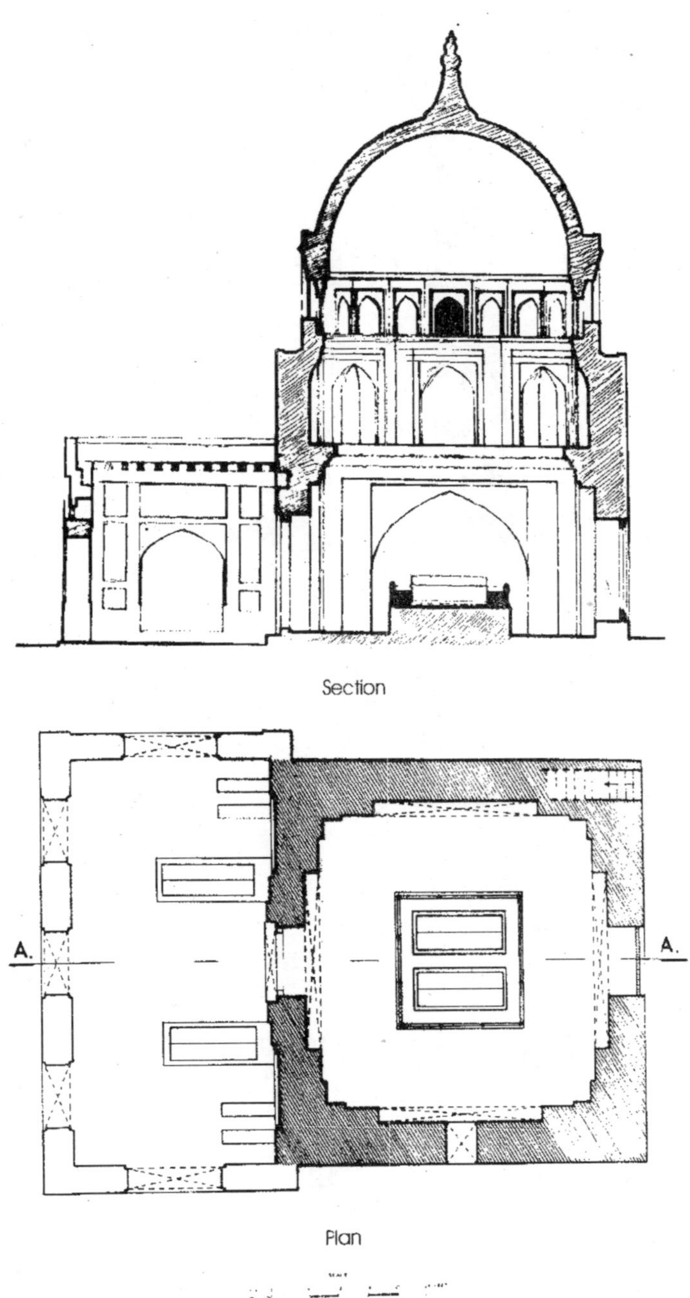

Fig. 3: Multan: Tomb of Shah Dana Shaheed, plan and section

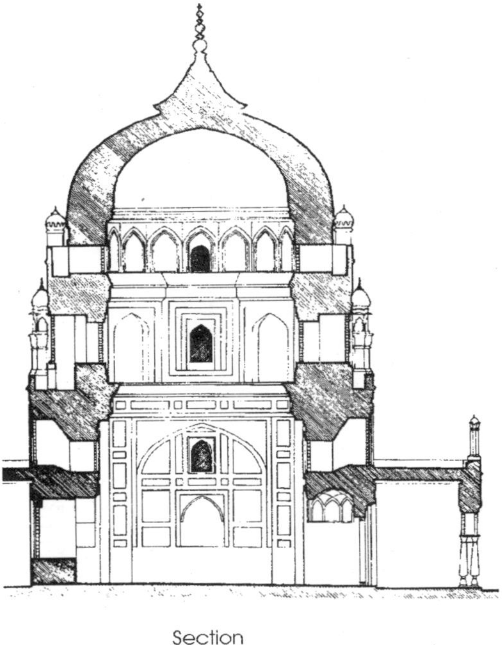

Section

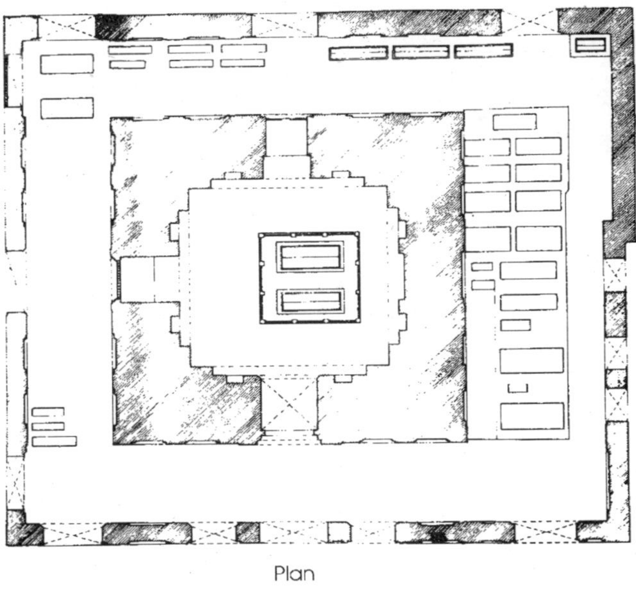

Plan

Fig. 4: Multan: Tomb of Shams Sabzwari, plan and section

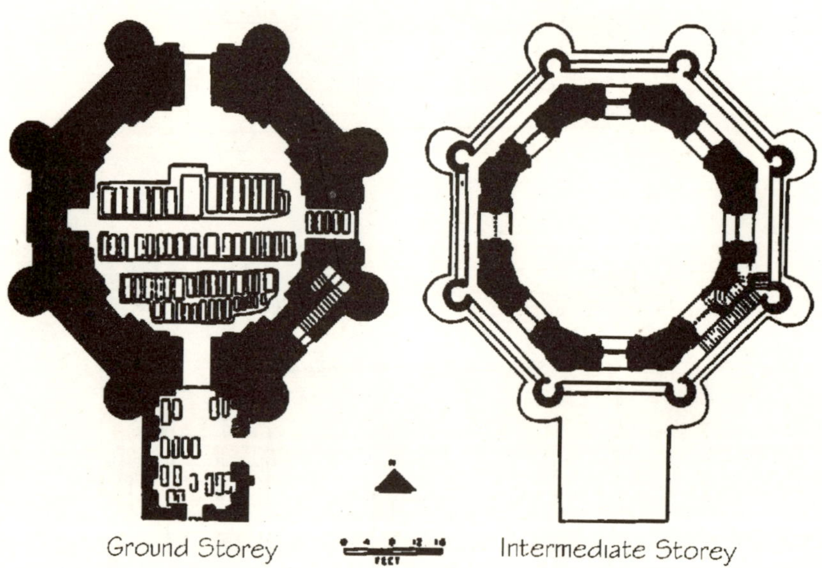

Fig. 5: Multan: Tomb of Shah Rukn-i Alam, plan

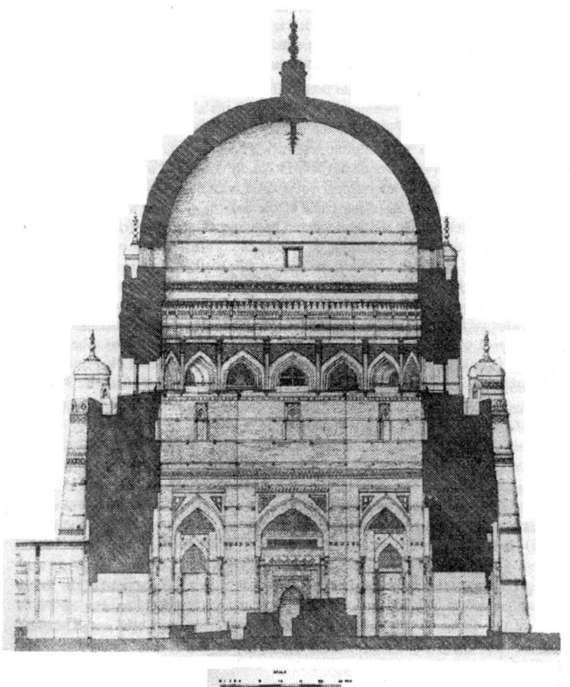

Fig. 6: Multan: Tomb of Shah Rukn-i Alam, section

Fig. 7: Uch: Tomb of Abu Hanifa, plan

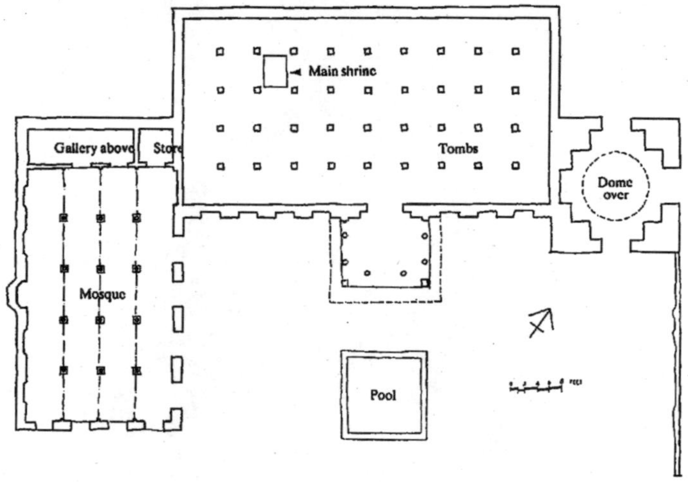

Fig. 8: Uch: Tomb of Jalaluddin Surkh Bukhari complex, plan

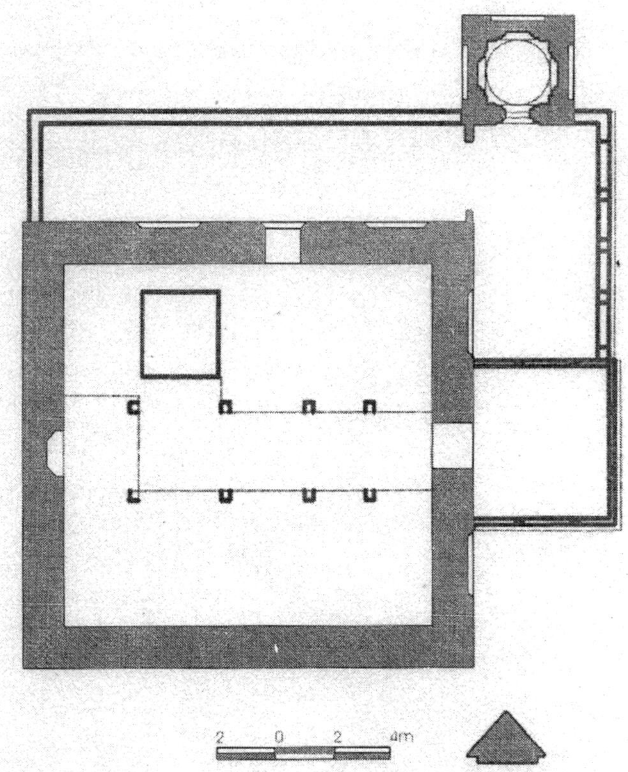

Fig. 9: Uch: Tomb of Makhdum-i-Jahanian Jahanghasht, plan

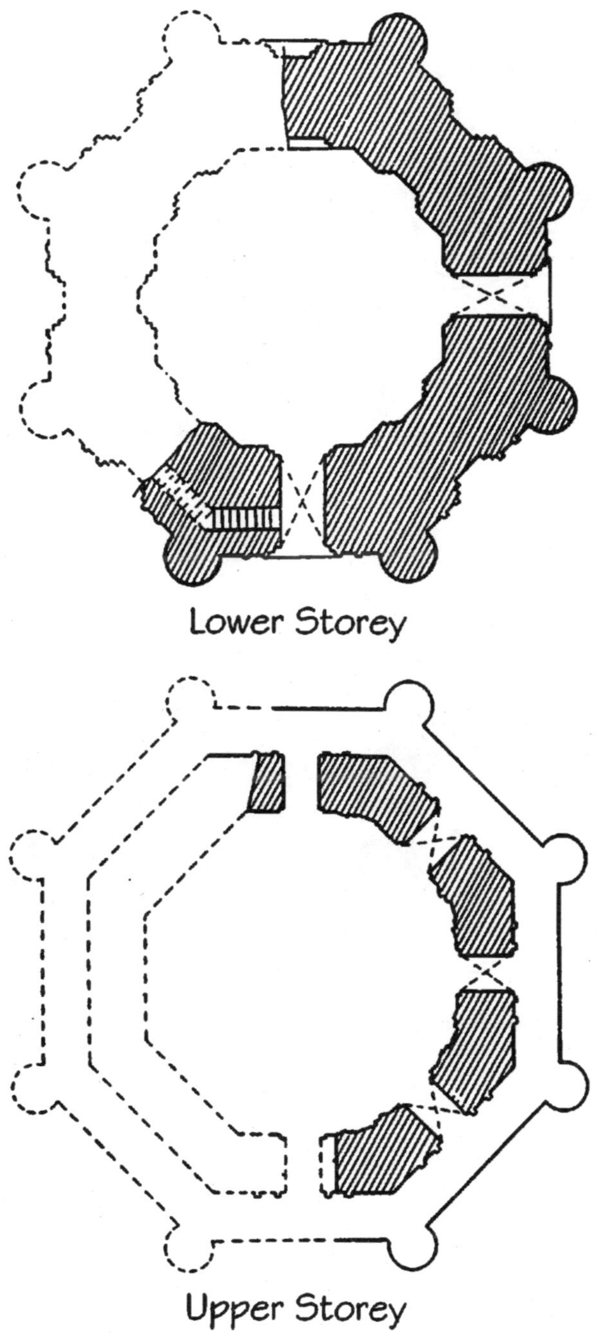

Fig. 10: Uch: Tomb of Baha al-Halim, plan

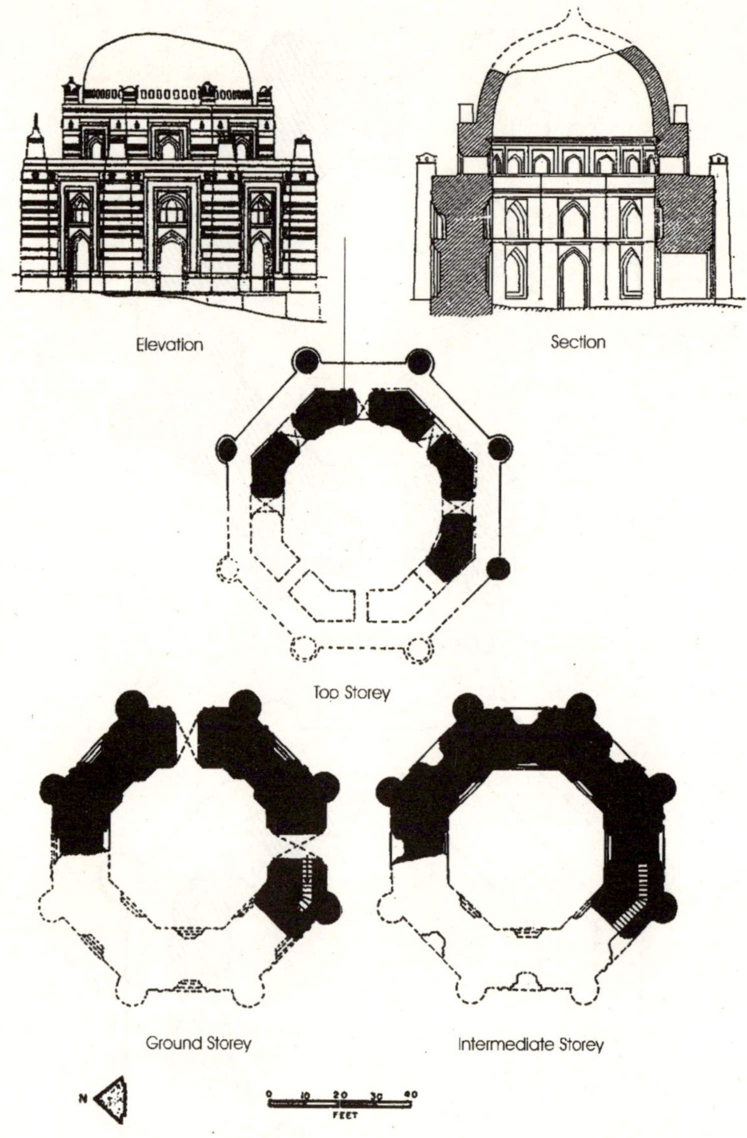

Fig. 11: Uch: Tomb of Bibi Javindi, plan, elevation and section

Plate 1. Multan: Tomb of Shah Yusuf Gardezi

Plate 2. Multan: Tomb of Shaikh Bahauddin Zakariya

Plate 3. Multan: Tomb of Shah Dana Shaheed (an old view)

Plate 4. Multan: Tomb of Shams Sabzwari

Plate 5. Multan: Tomb of Shah Rukn-i Alam

Plate 6. Multan: Tomb of Shah Rukn-i Alam, various decorative patterns

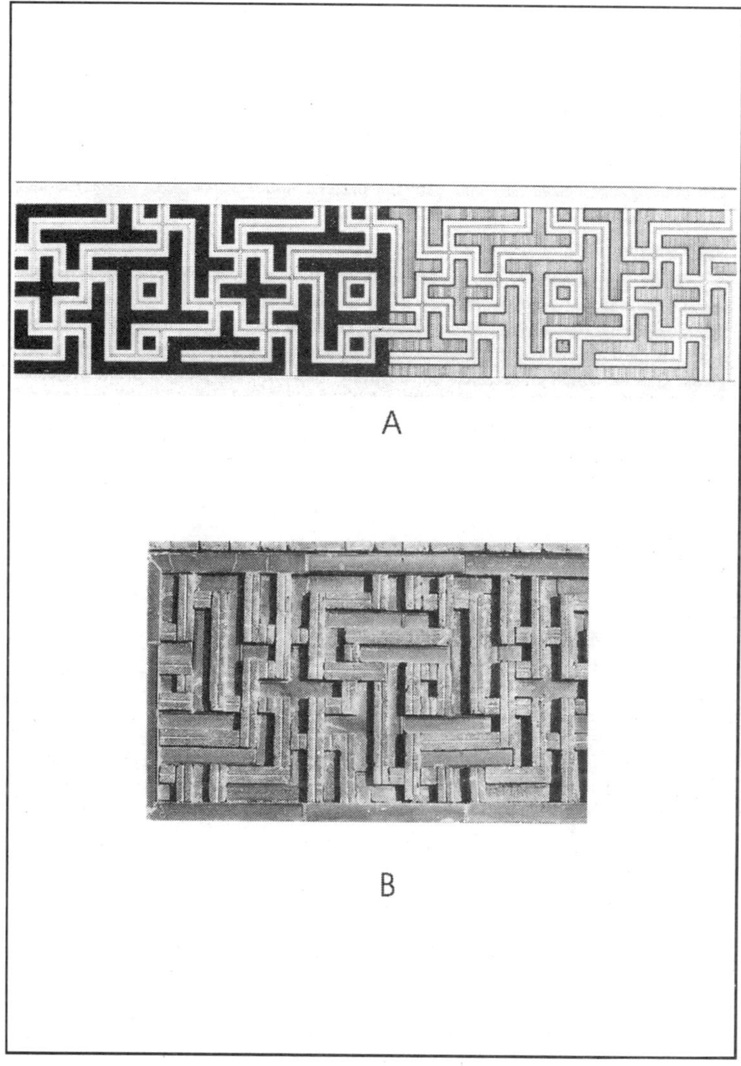

Plate 7. Swastika motif on (A) the tomb of Shaikh Bahauddin Zakariya and (B) the tomb of Shah Rukn-i Alam

Plate 8. Uch: Tomb of Abu Hanifa

Plate 9. Uch: Tomb of Rajan Qattal

Plate 10. Uch: Tomb of Makhdum-i-Jahaniyan Jahangasht, painted ceiling

Plate 11. Uch: Tomb of Baha al-Halim, exterior view

Plate 12. Uch: Tomb of Baha al-Halim, view from inner side

Plate 13. Uch: Tomb of Bibi Javindi

15

Some Prominent Sufi Shrines of South-Eastern Punjab

A Study of their History and Form

Hitender Kumar

Archaeology, which is generally perceived as a science related to excavation, has broadened its area and concerns in recent times. It is no longer limited to excavation only. Rather, it takes into account those monuments and sites that are standing on the surface. Medieval archaeology, being an offshoot of historical archaeology, is concerned with the study of relics of the medieval period.[1] It is particularly associated with the location, material and nature of these relics. "The manner in which some of the well documented public buildings of the medieval period continue to be neglected expresses our sense of history and how we view the past."[2] It is our common experience that major archaeological remains, which have become places of tourist attraction, have been often spoiled by the visitors themselves. The neglect is more visible in the scattered rural hamlets, where small structures are vulnerable to vandalism by local elements, who lack the consciousness regarding the preservation of our common heritage. The wave of commercialization of agricultural land and the relentless expansion of urbanization, which have assumed a fast pace in the last two decades, have posed new challenges to this heritage. In many cases, the governmental agencies have failed to protect medieval monuments from damage, owing to natural and human factors. In these circumstances, a study of structures and sites that have survived the uncertainties of time assumes considerable importance. In this paper, an attempt is being made to examine the architectural features of some prominent sufi shrines of south-east Punjab (present state ofHaryana) in the context of their historicity.

Sufism (*tasawwuf*) is a term that has been applied to the mystical dimension of Islam. It is a mode of thinking and feeling in the religio-spiritual sphere. The original source of sufism must be traced to the Quran, the life of Prophet Muhammad and the practices of his companions. In its early phase, the nature of sufism was basically ascetic and quietist. This attitude was a reaction against wealth and luxury that had destroyed Islam's primitive simplicity and other-worldliness. This ascetic movement gradually spread from Madina to Kufa, Basra, Damascus, Baghdad, north-east Persia and Sind. The transition from this simple asceticism to a complex theory of mystical discipline, and therefore to a highly developed theosophy, took place during the ninth century.[3] It has been rightly observed that sufism had become a movement by the thirteenth century and that, as a result of its powerful influence, it brought Islam to the masses and masses towards Islam.[4] So far as medieval India was concerned, Abul Fazl has provided a list of fourteen sufi orders.[5] But four of them were more prominent than the others. These were Chishti, Suhrawardi, Qadiri and Naqshbandi. In north-western India, the Chishti and Suhrawardi orders acquired unprecedented popularity during the thirteenth and fourteenth centuries.

This brings us to our specific area of study. South-eastern Punjab was enclosed between two major rivers, the Satluj and Yamuna. The area between these two rivers was traversed by two seasonal streams, the Ghaggar and Sarsuti, both of which flowed down from the chain of hills in the north-east. During the medieval times, south-east Punjab acquired considerable importance both from the political and social angles. During the late twelfth and early thirteenth century, the region became an arena of struggle for supremacy between the Turkish invaders and Rajput rulers. After the establishment of the Delhi sultanate, the region was divided into a number of revenue assignments (*iqtas*) which were assigned to the members of the military bureaucracy. The region was a witness to several Mongol invasions as well as internal revolts. During the fourteenth century, the Tughluq rulers established alliances with rural intermediaries of the region, with a view to increase the central control. In the middle of this century, Firuz Shah Tughluq (r.1351-1388) created a large network of canals in the region and, thus, brought about a major agrarian expansion and economic development.[6] It is another matter that the region experienced widespread destruction and dislocation during the course of Timur's invasion. When these political developments were taking place, a number of places were acquiring fresh importance as sufi centres. We find that sufis, some belonging to known sufi orders and others entirely independent of the institutional orders, constructed their hospices (*khanqahs*) at these places and began to disseminate the teachings of their spiritual discipline among the people. Sometime in the fourteenth century, a traveller informed Shihabuddin Umari at Damascus that there were about two thousand sufi hospices in Delhi and the surrounding areas.[7] It may be suggested that the reporter included the sufi establishments of south-eastern Punjab in this number.[8] In the prsent study, we would focus our attention on the major sufi shrines that were located at Hani, Panipat and Thanesar.

Chahar Qutb at Hansi

During the early phase ofthe history of the Delhi sultanate, Hansi emerged as an important centre of the Chishti order. Situated on the trade route liking Delhi with Multan,it was regarded by the ruling elite as a strategic military base and by the sufi fraternity as a frontier between the Chishti and Suhrawardi spiritual domains. Shaikh Farid spent a considerable part of his life in this town before ultimately shifting to Ajodhan.[9] Subsequently, four successive saintsrose to grat digity andacquired mch populaity. They were Shaikh amaluddin, Shaikh Burhanuddin, Shaikh Qutbuddin Munawwar and Shaikh Nuruddin. Shaikh Jamaluddin, who stood at the top of this spiritual lineage, was one of the most senior disciples of Shaikh Farid. He began his career as a sermonizer (*khatib*), but relinquished the job on the occasion of his enrolment under Shaikh Farid, because state service was regarded as incompatible with the basic princiles of the Chishti mytic discipline.[10] Shaikh Farid lived in Hansi for twelve years owing to his deep attachment to Shaikh Jamaluddin. He ofte used to eclare that amal was th beauty (*jamal*)of his spiritual disciplie. We are inormed that Shaikh Bahauddin Zakariya offered to exchange all his disciples for Shaikh Jamaluddin. Shaikh Farid declined the offer on the grounds tat this kind of deal was possible concerning property (*mal*), ut not in te case of beauty (*jamal*). When Shaikh Farid granted the certificate of succession (*khlafatnama*) o any disciple, the latter was required to go to Shaikh Jamaluddin for securing his approval, without which the certificate did not take effect. In case, Shaikh Jamaluddin refused to give his approval, even Shaikh Farid became helpless in the matter.[11] Shaikh Jamaluddin was a man of learning, as is indicated by two srviving works – an Arbic treatise on mysticism entitled *Mulhamat* ana Persian collection of poetry. In the wake of Shaikh Jamaluddin's death (1260, his tender aged son Burhanuddin was enrolled by Shaikh Farid as a disciple. After a short period of tutelge, he was granted the certificate of succession and advised to complete his traiing at Delhi under Shaikh Nizamuddin Auliya. On his part, Shaikh Burhanuddin did not enroll any disciple, because he did not deem it appropriate to do so,while Shaikh Nizamuddin Auliya was there.[12]

Shaikh Qutbuddin Munawwar stood next in the line of Chishti saints of Hansi. As a son of Shaikh Burhanuddin and a grandson of Shaikh Jamaluddin, he was brought up in an atmosphere imbued with piety. He was a disciple of Shaih Nizamuddin Auliya and after receiving his certificate of succession (*khilafatnama*), he was allowed to settle in Hansi. He was a man of simple living and kept away from the ruling elite. He acquired a lot of popularity among the masses. This fame roused the jealousy of his opponents, who poisoned the ears of the Delhi sultan, Muhammad bin Tughluq. We come across two episodes which indicate serious differences between the Sultan and the Shaikh. The Sultan sent a royal order conferring two villages on the Shaikh through Qazi Kamaluddin. The Sultan's offer was motivated by the desire to test the Shailkh's asceticism. The Shaikh refused to accept the offer and expressed his commitment to the high ideals laid down by Shaikh Farid. On another occasion, the Sultan passed through Hansi and learnt that the Shaikh did not pay homage to the rulers in the customary manner. The Sultan summoned the Shaikh to his presence at Delhi. The Shaikh went to meet the Sultan, because he was convinced that he was doing so under duress. In any case, the Sultan was impressed by the Shaikh's honesty and, admitting that he had been wrongly informed, offered a gift of cash (2000 *tankahs*) which, however, was distributed in charity.[13]

It appears from contemporary documentation that the Chishti saints of Hansi continued to attract the attention of the Delhi sultans. After assuming power, Firuz Shah Tughluq marched from Thatta to Delhi and, while travelling through Hansi, he paid his respects to Shaikh Qutbuddin Munawwar on the advice of the famous Chishti saint of Delhi, Shaikh Nasiruddin Chiragh-i-Delhi. On this occasion, Shaikh Qutbuddin Munawwar advised the Sultan to give up two bad habits, drinking wine and hunting animals.[14] After his death, the Shaikh was succeeded by his son Shaikh Nuruddin to the spiritual seat of Hansi. A spiritual preceptor of the historian Shams Siraj Afif, Shaikh Nuruddin commanded tremendous respect for his spiritual qualities. When Firuz Shah Tughluq founded the city of Hissar-Firuza, he invited Shaikh Nuruddin to settle in the new urban centre and even offered to build a new hospice (*khanqah*) for his residence. Shaikh Nuruddin declined the offer, because he remained committed to the spiritual domain of Hansi, which had been granted to his forefathers by such eminent Chishti saints as Shaikh Farid and Shaikh Nizamuddin Auliya. The contemporaries believed that when Timur plundered (1398-99) the capital city of Delhi, the people of Hansi and Hissar-Firuza remained safe on account of the blessings of Shaikh Nuruddin.[15]

The above four Chishti saints lie buried in a mausoleum at Hansi, which is popularly known as the Chahar Qutb. The structure (**Plate A**) reflects the characteristics of early Indo-Muslim architecture. It is one of the most authentic architectural specimens of the transitional period, which falls before the arches and domes gained currency. The main enclosure measures 47′x 22′.3″ and almost the entire is made of bricks and plaster. The main inner part is a simple pavilion of plain pillar series, while the rest of the room is characterized by a surrounding corridor of corner parts. The ground plan of the Chahar Qutb becomes a unique construction, owing to the rectangular middle parts in simple

domed and gable vault roofs. The four circular pillars provide an additional reinforcement for the pillars and beams by supplementing them on cardinal points. At the corner of the square, the three interior pillars – two pentagonal side pillars and one square sectioned corner pillar – form a triangular unit. The central dome of the roof has an octagonal drum and low hemispherical domes, whereas the peripheral domes and vaults are fixed within the parapets. "The corridored arrangement of the dargah with pillared inner main compartment was a persuasive example of a direct use of the Hindu type pavilion for an Islamic dargah."[16] Here the pillars of trabeate style are used in giving

the shape of an arcuate style. Today, we find that the three pillars have been closed by a brick screen wall (**Plate B**).

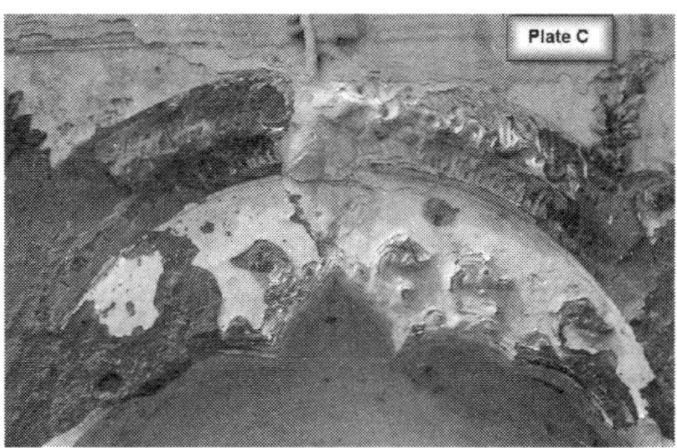

It also appears that the Chahar Qutb has been repaired and modified from time to time (**Plate C**), particularly during the reign of Firuz Shah Tughluq (1351-1388). In this context, Afif observes:

> To earn the merit and blessing of God, the Sultan, during his reign, undertook the task of restoration and renovation of the tombs of the previous sultans, saints and shaikhs. The tombs of all the previous sultans were repaired de novo and renovated. It is evident that such an act on the part of the Sultan was to earn the grace of God and was the result of the Sultan's good and honest disposition, otherwise the kings, on account of their majesty and awe, seldom remember the dead kings, what to talk of the repair of their tombs. As a result, the graves of the past kings remain dilapidated. This sorry state of affairs harmed those attached to the tombs. In the edicts of kingship, it is customary that every ruler, on his accession, grants villages and territories for the maintenance of religious persons attached to the tombs and hospices. The revenue of such lands is entrusted to these persons for the maintenance of tombs, so that after their demise, the expenses of the tombs and madrasahs attached therewith may be met from such grants.[17]

The large mosque, which stood near the above mausoleum, contains four inscriptions. A perusal of this record indicates that the tomb of Shaikh Jamaluddin was constructed by one Raza Ali in 903 AH/1497 AD. Shaikh Jamaluddin was the son of Sultan Hamiduddin who had accompanied Sultan Shihabuddin (Muizzuddin) from Ghazni and participated in the occupation of Hansi. Shaikh Jamaluddin, the son of Sultan Hamiduddin, was placed in charge of Hansi. Sometime after this, Shaikh Jamaluddin withdrew from state service and, having turned a recluse, became a disciple of Shaikh Farid, the Chishti saint of Pakpattan. Shaikh Jamaluddin died in 670 AH/1271 AD. The inscription reads, "His shrine (*hazira*) is pure, handsome and in contiguity with a mosque." According to another inscription on the mosque which was written by Raza Quli, a resident of Muhalla Zuhdjan at Hansi in Muharram 877 AH/1472 AD, the mosque was built by Shaikh Abdul Fateh who was a disciple of Shaikh Jamaluddin. The mosque, with several excellent inscriptions, measures 60'.6" from its northern to its southern ends and 33'.1" from east to west. The walls of this imposing edifice, which acquire a height of nearly 50 feet, are 4'.6" in thickness.[18] However, the most beautiful tomb in the shrine complex is that of a merchant called Alam, who is said to have been a disciple of Shaikh Jamaluddin. This structure measures 137' in total circuit, allowing 34'.3" for each face, as the building is quadrangular, and 46'.9" high. The walls of this handsome mausoleum are 6'.3" thick. Hence the inside area is 22'.10" clear each way, while the lower vault contains nine tombs. The façade has an intricate and impressive design, which has been wrought in stained glass. Its glazed tile work is marked by freshness and harmony of its colouring. Its vault was one of the very first to undergo the process of embellishment, when the art of burning the tiles was in its early stages. Undoubtedly, this structure is the most beautiful of all the tombs in the complex.[19]

Shrine of Bu Ali Qalandar at Panipat

The town of Panipat which was situated on the Delhi-Lahore highway, has acquired importance as a historic battlefield where the supremacy over northern India was contested by rival political formations. The place also earned fame as the abode of Shaikh Sharafuddin (d.1324), who was popularly known as Bu Ali Qalandar. It is difficult to reconstruct a sober account of his life. He appears to have been a native of Iraq and migrated to India in the middle of the thirteenth century. He is said to have been a disciple of Shaikh Khizar Rumi or Syed Najmuddin and, therefore, linked with Khwaja Qutbuddin Bakhtiar Kaki (d.1235) who was a prominent Chishti saint of Delhi. But Shaikh Abdul Haq Muhaddis Dehalvi, the author of *Akhbar-ul-Akhyar*, rejects the claim of Bu Ali Qalandar as a disciple of Khwaja Qutbuddin Bakhtiar Kaki or Shaikh Nizamuddin Auliya.[20] An attempt has been made by Abul Fazl to piece together the information regarding Bu Ali Qalandar that was available in the later half of the sixteenth century, including one of the writings of the saint himself. We learn that Bu Ali Qalandar arrived in Delhi at the age of forty and received instructions from Khwaja Qutbuddin. He was also associated with several other learned men of the day – Maulana Wajihuddin Paili, Maulana Sadruddin, Maulana Fakhruddin Nafilah, Maulana Nasiruddin, Maulana Muinuddin Daultabadi, Maulana Najibuddin Samarqandi, Maulana Qutbuddin of Mecca, Maulana Ahmad Khansari and others – who authorized him to teach and pronounce legal decisions. He held this office for twenty long years. Thereafter, he received a sudden call from God, threw his books into the Jamuna and set out on travel in the western Islamic lands. During the course of his sojourn at Roumelia, he met two eminent mystics, Shamsuddin Tabrezi and Jalaluddin Rumi. From them he received three presents – a robe, a turban and many books – which he threw into a river in their presence. Subsequently, he returned to Panipat and settled as a recluse.[21] Having renounced the world, he became engaged in self-mortification and contemplation. Since he had adopted the path of the Qalandars, he did not observe the rules of the canonical law (*shariat*).[22] He had a scholarly bent of mind and several works are attributed to him. It appears that the *Hukmnama* and *Hikmatnama* are spurious, but his *masnavi* and *maktubat* (letters) bear the signs of authenticity. An examination of the latter two works indicates that, as a mystic, he was fresh, outrageous and uncompromis-ing. In one of his letters, he recognizes beauty as a step leading to an understanding of the beloved, which made the lover and beloved identical. He treated heaven as a stage of union and hell as a station of separation.[23]

Like most other mystics, Bu Ali Qalandar is remembered in several legends which are punctuated with miraculous elements. They provide interesting insights into his image in the eyes of his contemporary followers and later admirers. According to one of them, Prophet Muhammad conferred on him the status of 'Fragrance of Ali' (Bu Ali) for having performed the ordeal of standing in water for thirty six years at Karnal. After achieving this status, he was visited by many sufi saints. There is another legend which explains his name. According to it, Prophet Muhammad appeared to him in a dream and asked him to express a wish. The Qalandar asked for the prophethood, but he was told that all such positions had been occupied and that of Muhammad was the last one. When he asked for the position of Ali, he received the same answer. At last, he asked for at least the 'Fragrance of Ali' which was granted. It is believed that Bu Ali is simply another form of Kuniyyat Abu Ali. Another legend would have us believe that a disciple of Shamsuddin Turk went to the city on an errand and saw Bu Ali Qalandar riding on a lion. On hearing the experience from his disciple, Shamsuddin Turk said, "Go to the house of the Qalandar and if you see him riding the lion, tell him that the lion should live in the jungle." The disciple went to the house of the Qalandar and, on seeing him in that condition, conveyed the message of his master. The Qalandar immediately rose from his place and went to the jungle. After many years of devotion, it is believed, that he disappeared into the sky in the presence of his disciples. Another legend says that a few days before his death, the Qalandar directed his disciples to bury him at Panipat.

Later, he did not feel well and left for Karnal, where he went into a state of ecstasy (*jazb*) while holding a branch of tree to stand. He stood there like a statue and died in that posture. The people of Karnal buried him there. The same night, Prophet Muhammad appeared to Hazrat Sirajuddin Makki (the teacher of Bu Ali Qalandar in the *shariat*) and directed him to take the body of the deceased to Panipat for burial. In the morning, Makki went to Karnal for the purpose, but the local people prevented him from doing the needful. He made a coffin and, putting some bricks in it, carried it to Panipat. He thought that the Qalandar, if a true saint (*wali*), would come into the coffin on his own. When Makki reached near Panipat, he met the ruler of the place. The ruler asked Makki about the identity of the person whose body was in the coffin. Makki replied that the body was that of Bu Ali Qalandar. The ruler desired to see the face of the deceased. When Makki removed the sheet, he was amazed to see that the body was really that of Bu Ali Qalandar. Thereafter, Makki carried the coffin to Panipat and buried it there.

The shrine of Bu Ali Qalandar, which is presently located in a congested commercial cum residential area of Panipat, commands considerable historical and architectural significance. It is a fine specimen (**Plate D**) of architectural skills of medieval north India. The

Plate D

whole structure is quite large in size. The main enclosure measures 155′x 143′, whereas the northern one measures 138′ x 146′ and the southern one measures 60′ x 51′.The tomb itself is located in the northern enclosure. The entrance is from the middle one, which measures 42′x 42′ on the outside and 25′ x 25′ on the inside. The tomb is a single dome structure, mostly made of red sandstone and decorated with beautiful sculpture. The beauty of the structure is enhanced by the use of white marble. The Khurasani arch is used between the main enclosure and verandah. Brackets represent the trabeate style. The cenotaph is made of marble and is decorated with impressive sculpture. It has a verandah on its southern side, the outer one having eight pillars of Kasauti stone (**Plate E**).[24] A perforated stone screen, which separates the tomb from the enclosure, displays fine workmanship and echoes the Mughal style *jalis* present in the buildings at Delhi and Agra. On the western side of

Plate E

the enclosure, we come across the mosque of Bu Ali Qalandar. It is nothing more than a corridor converted into a mosque, with its dimensions measuring 47′ x 13′ from inside. Its distinctive features are five arches of equal span on the eastern elevation (**Plate F**), several pillars and an arched recess in the western wall. The buds on the voussoirs of the arches give an impressive look. The building is made of red

Plate F

sandstone. Though small in size, it was found striking in appearance and in perfect condition,[25] at least during the late nineteenth century.

It is believed that the tomb of Bu Ali Qalandar was built by Khizar Khan and Shadi Khan, the sons of Sultan Alauddin Khalji who ruled from 1296 to 1316. It appears that the monument has undergone additions and alterations at different points of time. For example, Muqarrab Khan, a physician in the service of Emperor Akbar, built a tomb for himself in 1643-44. His son, Rizqullah Khan, added the Kasauti pillared verandah in 1660 AD. In the southern enclosure was constructed the tomb of Nawab Sadiq Ali Khan who served as the prime minister (*wazir*) under the three Mughal emperors – Bahadur Shah, Farrukh Siyar and Muhammad Shah. He also built a Naqqar Khana on the other side of the bazar opposite to the main gateway.[26] Another notable addition to the enclosure is the tomb of the famous Urdu poet Altaf Husain Hali (1837-1914). With the passage of time, a noticeable change has taken place in the structure of the complex. The plaster has been replaced. Stone tiles have been fixed on the walls of the room just below the main dome. The calligraphy decorating the walls of the verandah has lost its grace. Except the verandah, every part of the monument has been repainted many times.

Shrines at Thanesar

The town of Thanesar was situated between Karnal and Ambala on the Delhi-Lahore highway. During the early medieval period, it was the scene of military conflict between Sultan Muizzuddin of Ghazni and the Rajput rulers of northern India. It had a special place in the minds of the people, as it was located near a famous centre of pilgrimage (Kurukshetra). During the sixteenth century, it emerged as a major Chishti centre in the whole of the Indian subcontinent, owing to the efforts of Shaikh Jalaluddin (d.1582).[27] His ancestors had migrated from Balkh at some unknown point of time. He acquired traditional education and began his career as a teacher and jurist (*mufti*) who delivered legal opinions (*fatwas*) on the basis of Quranic verses. Thereafter, he renounced his profession and enrolled himself under Shaikh Abdul Quddus Gangohi, who had shifted (1491) from Rudauli to Shahabad near Ambala. Both Abul Fazl and Abdul Qadir Badauni have spoken highly of Shaikh Jalaluddin. The latter had attained a considerable exoteric and esoteric learning and employed himself in imparting instructions on subjects related to divinity and mysticism. Often seen in a state of trance, he was obsessively fond of musical sessions (*sama*) and even made vigorous physical movements during the performance. Like his Chishti predecessors, he based his mystical practices on the rememberance of God's name (*zikr*) and various forms of breath control (*pas-i-anfas*).[28] He had received a land grant (*aimma*) from the Mughal state, as is indicated by his visit (1561) to Agra which was undertaken to settle its affairs. During his last years, he abandoned the pursuit of secular knowledge and, adopting privacy instead of publicity, devoted himself to the reading of Quran, the works of supererogation and prayer. Even though he became feeble due to old age, he performed ablutions and offered prayers without any assistance.[29] A year before his death (1582), Emperor Akbar and Abul Fazl paid a visit to his hospice (*khanqah*) at Thanesar and had an illuminating discussion on philosophical matters.[30] The saint has left behind two works. The first one, *Irshad-ul-Talibin*, discusses aspects of the spiritual path. The second one, *Risala Tahqiqat-i-Arazi-i-Hind*, dealt with the various categories of land rights.[31] The illustrious tradition of Shaikh Jalaluddin was ably carried forward by his son-in-law and spiritual successor (*khalifa*) Shaikh Nizamuddin bin Abdul Shukur, who was an erudite scholar and author of several books on religious subjects.

The mausoleum of Shaikh Jalaluddin Thanesari is situated on the north western side of the town of Thanesar. It is a square building measuring 18′.5″ x 18′.5″ and is mostly made of red sandstone. Originally the structure was supported by twelve sandstone pillars but, later on, the interstices have been filled with fine lattice work in brick. (**Plate G**). Pillars and brackets represent the trabeate style. The dome is plastered and hemispherical in shape, with an inverted lotus at the top.

Plate G

In each of the 21 marlons of the two sides and back the word Allah is inscribed. In front, there is a geometric design on each marlon. Beneath the structure, we come across the remains of a mosque, as some of its portions are still visible (**Plate H**). In front of the mosque there are remains of a well which have been covered with bricks by the local inhabitants. Along with the well, there was a provision for warm water which was used for ablutions during the cold months of winter. The site is maintained by the Punjab Wakf Board. This institution provides a meager assistance of Rs. 300 per month to a caretaker, which covers his salary as well as the cost of the maintenance of the structure. Apart from this, it also provides an annual assistance of Rs.4000 for observing

the death anniversary (*urs*) which falls in the month of Zilhijja i.e. fifteen days after Id-ul-Zuha. In spite of the control and responsibility of the Punjab Waqf Board, the site is in a state of neglect and no attempt has ever been made for its restoration.[32]

Besides the mausoleum of Shaikh Jalaluddin, the tomb of Shaikh Chilli is also located in the town of Thanesar. In the present state of our knowledge, it is not possible to confirm the identity of Shaikh Chilli. Rodgers suggests that Chilli was not his real name; rather, it was only a title which was conferred on someone who frequently performed the forty-day spiritual penance (*chilla*).[33] Furthermore, there are differences regarding the name of the saint. Some called him Abdul Rahim, some knew him as Abdul Karim and still others identified him as Abdul Razzaq. But the more familiar names are Shaikh Chilli and Shaikh Tilli. He is said to have been the author of a book on Muslim saints. He is also believed to have been the writer of some popular moral tales, allegories and ballads. But Cunningham failed to trace his name in any of the books to which he had access. The popular belief strongly held that Shaikh Chilli was the spiritual advisor of Dara Shukoh, who was deeply inclined towards mysticism. It is quite possible that the tomb was built at the instance of the prince.[34] After all, the construction and maintenance of such a lavish structure could not have been possible without financial assistance from the ruling family. However, it is not possible to agree with the suggestion that Dara Shukoh established this vast institution to promote the Qadiri order in a region which was a centre of the Chishtis.[35] We need more concrete evidence to reach any definite conclusion regarding the spiritual affiliation of the saint who is interred at the shrine.

The tomb of Shaikh Chilli (**Plate I**) is the most picturesque mausoleum in north India and David Ross has rightly ranked it second only to the grand Taj Mahal at Agra. The tomb is an octagonal building of white marble, 18 feet on each side and 44 feet in diameter. It is crowned by a white marble dome and surrounded by a courtyard which has an area of 174 square feet and is paved with marble.[36] The structure

Plate I

commands a lofty position, because the courtyard rises 41 feet above the ground and measures 164′.7″ from north to south and 169′.5″ from east to west. The walls of the enclosure are adorned with 12 cupolas (**Plate J**), which are dressed in glazed tiles with *kangura* arch and are surrounded by small *jalis* of red sandstone (**Plate K**). The traces of blue,

Plate J

purple and green tiles are still extant on some of them (**Plate L**). In the words of a modern specialist, "Façade opened by a deep, multi-lobed, arched niche in which there are two windows, one on top of the other:

Plate K

the lower one is rectangular, the other is pointed arch in shape and is filled with *jali* (**Plate I**). A wide *chajja* runs all around the top of the solidity and terminates with a frieze of crenellations decorated at corners by slender domed terminals. It is surrounded by a fine, slightly pear-shaped dome resting on a high cylindrical drum. Inside, the dome is decorated with pleasant paintings."[37] At one time, the tomb was surrounded by open work balustrades. But at present all of them have crumbled, except one. In the centre of the chamber, there is a cenotaph of Shaikh Chilli, while the actual grave is located in the lower apartment to which a narrow gallery leads from the *madrasah*. The mausoleum is said to have been turned into a *gurdwara* by the Sikhs, who carried away portions of its marble lattice work to Kaithal. This might have happened in the late eighteenth century. In 1839 William Barr found the building in a state of ruins. Still he inferred that in its pristine condition, it was deficient neither in beauty nor elegance. Later on, the edifice was restored by the Archaeological Survey of India.[38]

Adjoining the tomb stands a monument which has been identified by Cunningham as a seminary (*madrasah*). Made of stone, the edifice is 174 square feet from outside, forming an interior courtyard of 120 feet on each face. The main entrance is on the eastern side and is reached by a steep flight of steps from the main road between the city and the fort. There is a smaller doorway in the south-west corner towards the Pathriya Masjid. It is not possible to ascertain the date of the structure. But owing to its evident connection with the tomb, Cunningham suggests, the seminary must have been built at the same time as a part of the religious establishment of the saint's shrine.[39] Associated with the tomb is a garden of Charbagh style. In the midst of the garden is a reservoir in which stands a fountain. There is a deep well, known as Otwala Kuan, at the southern edge of the *madrasah*. The well is 12 feet broad and 54 feet deep. It was apparently employed to supply water to the reservoir as well as the fountain. Even at present, it is possible to see a set of channels on the roof of the *madrasah*. The lime coating on the channels proves that they were used for carrying water, as lime prevents the seepage of moisture. Both the monuments, the tomb and the *madrasah*, are under the protection and maintenance of the Archaeological Survey of India. During the course of its renovation, the department has made some changes in the entrance to the buildings. At present, we encounter at the entrance a blind flight of steps which lead to the *madrasah*. This, however, does not conform to the pattern of Mughal architecture. This contention is based on the fact that the arch after the entrance has been filled and closed with bricks.[40]

The religious life of Islam is intimately connected with sufi saints and their veneration. Its history is so intertwined with them that it is impossible to conceive one without the other. During the medieval period, the sufi saints played a multifarious role in the society. Their generous and tolerant attitude towards the common masses paved the way for interaction between adherents of diverse religious traditions. During their lifetime as well as after their death, they have been looked upon as examples of piety and spiritual excellence. The contemporary historians – like Ziauddin Barani, Shams Siraj Afif, Abul Fazl and Abdul Qadir Badauni – have noted the lives and deeds of these men. In addition to this, we have the sufi memoirs (*tazkiras*) and mystical discourse (*malfuzat*) which provide adequate information about them. Even the rulers gave heed to their teachings, spent much time in their company, built elaborate tombs over their graves and undertook pilgrimages to their shrines. The worship of sufi saints, however, is not peculiar to the subcontinent. In fact, the practice came readymade to India. These places are known as the common place of devotion, where people belonging to different religious persuasions assembled during ceremonial occasions and, thus, came close to one another. The popularity of a shrine depended on several factors – the spiritual excellence and noble qualities deemed to have been possessed by the saint in his lifetime, the spiritual greatness of his immediate successors, manner of expansion of the sufi order and the legends that have developed about the supernatural powers of the shrine. The sheer size of the shrine complex indicated the popularity of a sufi saint. Usually there are special days during every week on which the shrines are visited. The great day of the year for each saint is the time of the death anniversary (*urs*) which often lasts for several days. Such occasions provided opportunities for great rejoicing, meeting of friends and feasting, besides the observance of religious exercises in the memory of the sufi saint.

Leaving aside a few specialists, the common people do not know much about the historicity of the sufi saints. Whatever little is known must be attributed to their shrines. With the shrine are associated a large corpus of folklore and legends. Unfortunately, at present most shrines are not found in a satisfactory condition. The above study indicates that, except the shrines of Bu Ali Qalandar and Shaikh Chilli, such monuments have been reduced to ruins on account of neglect. The structures and traditions of these old sites, which are an integral part of our cultural heritage, are being destroyed under the pressure of rapid urbanization. They are not merely structures of bricks and stones, but they have specific architectural characteristics and historical importance. If we wish to preserve our cultural heritage, the shrines of sufi saints – including those located in south-eastern Punjab – cannot be left in the hands of their custodians. Very often, well meaning individuals are ignorant of the shrine's true architectural significance and allow important parts to crumble, while subjecting the rest to over-restoration and modernization. If they are properly conserved, they can become treasure houses of the past and a mirror to the posterity. If they are developed, they can serve as centres of tourist interest for all those who wish to enquire into the past. It has rightly been pointed out that a close association between archaeological study and tourism industry can prove to be the best method of bringing history close to the people.[41] It is common experience that tourists belonging to different regions and religions flock to such places to appreciate the artistic creativity and engineering skills of pre-modern times and seek divine pleasure. "In recent years archaeology has often been utilized to justify issues that are essentially non-archaeological. Politicization of archaeology has caused serious tensions in our social life and cultural ethos. The foundation of our plural society has received a serious jolt."[42] Hence, there is an urgent need to comprehend the significance of sufi shrines in their diverse contexts – historical, archaeological and cultural.

NOTES AND REFERENCES

1. R.N. Mehta, *Medieval Archaeology*, Ajanta Publications, Delhi, 1979, p. 24.
2. Sanjay Subodh and Amit Chaudhary, "Material Remains and Historical Sense: A Study of Medieval Archaeology," *Proceedings of the Indian History Congress*, 61st. Session, 2001, p. 527.
3. A.J. Arberry, 'Mysticism', *The Cambridge History of Islam*, Vol.II, Ed., P.M. Holt, Ann K.S. Lambton and Bernard Lewis, Cambridge University Press, Cambridge, 1970, pp. 604-606.
4. M. Mujeeb, *The Indian Muslims*, Munshiram Manoharlal, Reprint, New Delhi, 1995, p. 116.
5. Abul Fazl Allami, *Ain-i-Akbari*, Vol. III, Eng. Tr., H.S. Jarrett and Jadunath Sarkar, Munshiram Manoharlal, New Delhi, Reprint., 1978, p. 393. Compare with a detailed account of the early sufi orders existing before the eleventh century. Ali bin Usman Hujwiri, *Kashf-ul-Mahjub*, Eng. Tr., Reynold A Nicholson, Taj Company, New Delhi, Reprint, 1982, pp. 176-266.
6. The Tughluq rulers developed intimate political relations with the diverse

local elements of Punjab viz. the tribal chiefs, rural intermediaries and sufi shrines. This enabled them to lay a network of canals in south-east Punjab, which led to important social-economic consequences. Surinder Singh, 'The Making of Medieval Punjab: Politics, Society and Economy c.1200-c.1400,' Presidential Address, (Medieval Section), Punjab History Conference, 40th. Session, Punjabi University, Patiala, 14-16 March 2008, pp. 19-38.

7. Shihabuddin Umari, *Masalik-ul-Absar fi Mamalik-ul-Amsar*, Eng. Tr., M. Zaki, *Arab Accounts of India (During the Fourteenth Century)*, Idarah-i-Adabiyat-i-Delli, Delhi, 1981, p. 19.
8. In the Islamic world, the place of grave is known as *maqbara* in Arabic and *qabrgah* in Persian. Paradaman K. Sharma, *Mughal Architecture of Delhi: A Study of Mosques and Tombs*, Sundeep Publications, New Delhi, 2000, p. 47. It may be noted that from the religio-legal point of view the construction of monumental tombs (*maqbaras*) is un-Islamic. The Prophet prohibited building with mortar on graves and placing inscriptions on them. For details, see R. Nath, *Indigenous Characteristics of Mughal Architecture*, D.K. Printworld, New Delhi, 2004, p. 25.
9. Khaliq Ahmad Nizami, *The Life and Times of Shaikh Fariduddin Ganj-i-Shakar*, Idarah-i-Adabiyat-i-Delli, Delhi, Reprint, 1973, pp. 31-32.
10. Abul Fazl Allami, Ain-i-Akbari, Vol. III, p. 411.
11. Khaliq Ahmad Nizami, *The Life and Times of Shaikh Fariduddin Ganj-i-Shakar*, pp. 68-70. It is said that Shaikh Farid sent Makhdum Ali Sabir to Shaikh Jamaluddin Hansavi to get such an *ijazatnama* before settling at Delhi. Shaikh Jamaluddin received him cordially, but when he was reading the charter of succession (*khilafatnama*) the lamp was suddenly extinguished. Makhdum Ali Sabir lighted it miraculously by his breath. At this, Shaikh Jamaluddin said that the people of Delhi would not be able to stand the severity of his breath and tore the document to pieces. Makhdum Ali Sabir got annoyed and, telling Shaikh Jamaluddin that he had cut the chain of his *silsilah*, went to Shaikh Farid. The latter however said that he could not stitch what had been torn by Shaikh Jamaluddin. S. Moinul Haq, 'Rise and Expansion of the Chishtis in the Subcontinent II, *Journal of Pakistan Historical Society*, Vol. 22, Part IV, Karachi, 1974, p. 220.
12. Khaliq Ahmad Nizami, *Religion and Politics in India during the Thirteenth Century*, Oxford University Press, Delhi, Reprint, 2002, pp. 207-208.
13. Amir Khurd, *Siyar-ul-Auliya*, pp. 250-255, cited in Saiyid Athar Abbas Rizvi, *Tughluq Kalin Bharat*, Part I, Aligarh Muslim University, Aligarh, 1956, pp. 145-147.
14. Shams Siraj Afif, *Tarikh-i-Firuz Shahi*, Eng. Tr., R.C. Jauhri, Medieval India in Transition: A First Hand Account, Sundeep Prakashan, New Delhi, 2001, pp. 57, 65-66.
15. Ibid., pp. 95-96.
16. K.V. Sondararajan, *Islam Builds in India: Cultural Study of Islamic Architecture*, Agam Kala Prakashan, Delhi, 1983, pp. 84-85.
17. Shams Siraj Afif, *Tarikh-i-Firuz Shahi*, p. 188.
18. H.B.W. Garrick, 'Report of A Tour in the Punjab and Rajputana in 1883-84,' *Report of the Archaeological Survey of India*, Vol. XXIII, Indological Book

House, Varanasi, Reprint, 1972, pp. 14-16.
19. Ibid., p. 17.
20. Saiyid Athar Abbas Rizvi, *A History of Sufism in India*, Vol. I, p. 305.
21. Abul Fazl Allami, *Ain-i-Akbari*, Vol. III, p. 410.
22. Qalandars were an antinomian sufi sect, which was not organized strictly as a sufi order.The word Qalandar conjures up the image of a renouncer, totally indifferent to the external world and its normative order, who was always in an ecstatic mood which could be further intensified by uninterrupted consumption of barbiturates. Having rejected the authority of the Muslim law, the Qalandars showed similarities with the Tantric cults that thrived in the womb of Hinduism. Kumkum Srivastava, 'The Qalandars and the Qalandriyya Tariqa,' in Anup Taneja, *Sufi Cults and the Evolution of Medieval Indian Culture*, Indian Council of Historical Research and Northern Book Centre, New Delhi, 2003, pp. 247-248.
23. Bruce B. Lawrence, *Notes from A Distant Flute: Sufi Literature in Pre-Mughal India*, Imperial Iranian Academy of Philosophy, Tehran, 1978, pp. 79-82.
24. Sanjay Subodh and Amit Chaudhary, 'Material Remains and Historical Sense: A Study in Medieval Archaeology,' *Proceedings of the Indian History Congress*, 61st. Session, 2001, p. 529.
25. Charles Rodgers, *Report of the Punjab Circle of the Archaeological Survey for 1888-89*, Calcutta, 1891, p. 44.
26. Ibid., p. 44.
27. Saiyid Athar Abbas Rizvi, *A History of Sufism in India*, Vol. II, Munshiram Manoharlal, New Delhi, 1983, p. 264.
28. Ibid., pp. 264-265.
29. Abdul Qadir Badauni, *Muntakhab-ut-Tawarikh*, Vol. III, Eng. Tr., Wolseley Haig and B.P. Ambashthya, Academica Asiatica, Patna, 1973, p. 5.
30. Abul Fazl, *Akbar Nama*, Vol. III, Eng. Tr., Henry Beveridge, Ess Ess Publications, New Delhi, Reprint, 1975, p. 500.
31. Irfan Habib, *The Agrarian System of Mughal India*, Oxford University Press, Delhi, Second Revised Edition, 1999, pp. 349-350, n. 41.
32. Sanjay Subodh, 'Medieval Remains in Thanesar: An Exploration in Medieval Archaeology,' *Proceedings of the Indian History Congress*, 59th. Session, 1998, p. 1990.
33. Charles Rodgers, *Report of the Punjab Circle of the Archaeological Survey of India for 1888-89*, Calcutta, 1891, p. 10.
34. Alexander Cunningham, *Four Reports Made During the Years 1862-65*, Vol. II, Archaeological Survey of India, New Delhi, Reprint, p. 223.
35. Subhash Parihar, *Some Aspects of Indo-Islamic Architecture*, Abhinav Publications, New Delhi, 1999, p. 171.
36. Alexander Cunningham, *Report of the Archaeological Survey of India 1863-64*, Varanasi, Reprint, 1972, p. 223.
37. Biyanka Maria Alfiri, *Islamic Architecture of the Indian Subcontinent*, Laurence King Publications, London, 2000, p. 259.
38. Subhash Parihar, *Mughal Monuments in the Punjab and Haryana*, Inter-India Publications, New Delhi, 1985, pp. 35-36.
39. Alexander Cuningham, *Report of he Archaeological Survey of India 1863-64*,

Indological Book House, Varanasi, Reprint, 1972, p. 222.

40. Sanjay Subodh, 'Medieval Remains of Thanesar: An Exploration in Medieval Archaeology, *Proceedings of the Indian History Congress*, 59th. Session, 1998, pp. 989-990.
41. Sanjay Subodh and Amit Chaudhary, op. cit., p. 527.
42. Gautam Sengupta, 'Archaeology in India: Some Urgent Issues,' Presidential Address, Section V, (Historical Archaeology, Epigraphy, Numismatics and Archives), *Proceedings of the Indian History Congress*, 56th. Session, Calcutta, 1995, p. 924.

16

Shrine of Shaikh Sadruddin at Malerkotla

History, Politics and Culture

Salim Mohammed

Shaikh Sadruddin, an Afghan, was a sufi ascetic as well as the founder-ruler of the Malerkotla state in medieval Punjab. In the entire history of the sufis of the Indian subcontinent, he was perhaps the only one who combined a recluse and a ruler. To present an account of this unique sufi celebrity, popularly known as Haidar Shaikh, it seems necessary to situate him in the historical context of the Malwa region of Punjab in general and in that of Afghan political power in particular, because the Afghan rulers of Malerkotla trace the history of their family to the period of the Lodis. Since the demise of Shaikh Sadruddin in 1508, the glory and grandeur of his 'spiritual court' or shrine (*dargah*) still remains intact than that of his successors' royal court, which came to an end in 1956.

The Malwa Region of Punjab

In medieval Punjab, broadly speaking, Multan, Dipalpur, Uch, Lahore and Pakpattan had been the centres of sufism, while Amritsar, Taran Taran, Jandiala and Goindwal were the cradle/hub-towns of Sikhism. The third important belt of Punjab, known as Malwa, lies between the river Satluj in the north and the river Ghaggar in the south. In the eighteenth century the Malwa Sikhs "richly contributed in men, resources and legendary bravery to the ascendant Sikh movement."[1] Malwa was the heartland of Pepsu (Patiala and East Punjab States Union that came into existence in July 1948) which comprised the princely states of Patiala, Nabha, Jind (Sangrur), Malerkotla, Nalagarh, Faridkot, Kapurthala and Kalsia. Nalagarh belonged to a Hindu Rajput chieftain, Malerkotla to a Muslim Afghan and the rest were ruled by Sikh chiefs. Known for its secular and non-conformist character, Malwa in late 1940s was in the grip of a powerful peasant movement and in 1960s it was a hot spot of left politics and ultra left (Naxalite) movement. The medieval Malwa had four important towns – Anandpur Sahib, Bhatinda, Sirhind and Malerkotla – reminding a student of Punjab history of the important events like the creation of the Khalsa, the piety of Pir Haji Rattan, the rise of Afghans and the popularity of Haidar Shaikh.

Anandpur Sahib has acquired great historical importance as being the birth place of the Khalsa. Now situated on the left bank of the river Satluj, it is situated at a distance of about forty-one kilometers from Ropar on the Chandigarh-Nangal road. The ninth Guru of the Sikhs, Teg Bahadur, founded it. Guru Gobind Singh, the son of Guru Teg Bahadur, spent nearly two-third of his life at this place. It was here that in 1699 Guru Gobind Singh baptized the first five Sikhs called 'Panj Payaras' and raised the saint-soldier fraternity of the 'Singhs' which he named as the 'Khalsa'.

Bhatinda is one of the oldest towns of the Malwa belt of the east Punjab. It is now a railway junction for Patiala, Chandigarh, Delhi, Ferozepur, Bikaner, Rewari and Abhoar. There is an ancient fort which is said to have been in existence for the last about 1800 years. It was in this fort that Sultan Raziya (r.1236-1240), the daughter and successor of Sultan Shamsuddin Iltutmish (r.1210-1236), was first incarcerated on her defeat and dethronement. Here in Bathinda, the shrine of Pir Haji Rattan attracts devotees from all faiths. Tradition makes Haji Rattan himself a Hindu, by name Rattan Pal, who assumed the title of Haji Rattan on conversion. In the last quarter of the nineteenth century H.A. Rose recorded the legend of Pir Haji Rattan: "Born a Chauhan Rajput, like Gugga, his knowledge of astrology told him that a prophet called Muhammad would be born in Arabia who would spread the religion of Islam. In order to be able to see the Prophet he practiced restraining his breath, and after the Prophet had performed the miracle of splitting the moon into two, he [Pir Ratan Haji] set out to Mecca in order to meet him. There he embraced Islam and lived with the Prophet thirty years, so that he was numbered among the companions (*ashab*) of the Prophet. After that period, he returned to India by the order of the Prophet and stayed at the place where [Bhatinda] his shrine is now and where he continued the practice of restraining his breath." Legends tell us that he lived for two centuries. It is also said that he breathed his last in 1277 AD. Baba Rattan was also considered by the gardeners of Constantinople to be their patron saint.[2] Before the partition of Punjab in 1947, a massive fair used to be held at the mausoleum (*mazar*) of Pir Haji Rattan. A number of sufi saints participated in it. In the premises of the shrine, the qawwals sang the *kafis* of Shah Husain and Bulleh Shah, while outside the shrine balladeers (*kavishers*) entertained the folk with popular songs of devotion. Babu Rajab Ali, the celebrated *kavisher* of

Malwa, was passionately attached with the fair held in the sacred memory of Pir Haji Rattan.[3]

Sirhind, which is situated in the vicinity of Patiala, is an ancient town of Punjab. It came into prominence as a hub of Afghan power during the middle of the fifteenth century. The Sirhind division (*sarkar*) of the Mughal province of Delhi commanded a position of immense strategic significance. It was surrounded on the eastern side by the Yamuna and Sirmur hills, on the west by the Satluj and the state of Bahawalpur, by mountains on the north and by the desert of Bikaner on the south. The invader, after crossing the Satluj, could straightway march to Delhi. That is why the Sirhind plain has served as the battlefield of India from time immemorial. It was studded with strong forts, such as Delhi, Hissar, Bhatner, Kaithal, Sirhind, Ludhiana and Machhiwara.[4] Sirhind was the strongest Afghan fortification between Lahore and Delhi. Well aware of the significance of Sirhind as a strategic place, Babur marched against the last Lodi ruler, Ibrahim, via Sirhind in 1525. Before he proceeded to Panipat for his trial of strength with the sultan of Delhi, he encamped at Sirhind and completed his military preparations.[5] The town of Sirhind treasures the history of the martyrdom of the two younger sons (*sahibzadas*) of Guru Gobind Singh, Zorawar Singh and Fateh Singh. They were bricked alive in 1704 by the Mughal governor (*faujdar*) of Sirhind, Wazir Khan. Banda Bahadur plundered the town during the course of his anti-Mughal revolt. Shaikh Ahmad Sirhindi (1564-1624) consolidated the Naqshbandi order and undertook revivalist activities from this town.

Malerkotla, one of the oldest towns of Punjab, came into existence more than five centuries ago. It has layers and layers of history beneath its present structures. It has been the headquarters of a Muslim state for a long period. Malerkotla has been a part of the cis-Satluj group of the erstwhile princely states of east Punjab. After independence, it was the only Muslim majority town in the east Punjab with a cultural identity of its own. It has a sprinkling of Hindu and Sikh population as well. The three communities, living in peace and communal harmony, present a true picture of unity in diversity. With its liberal ethos, the town has preserved its unique non-sectarian and secular character. It is noteworthy that when the Indian subcontinent was engulfed in communal frenzy in 1947, the town presented an excellent example of peaceful co-existence, brotherhood and harmony. Muslim subjects of all the princely states and those living in the east Punjab migrated to Pakistan, but Malerkotla did not witness any such exodus. The town was absolutely free from bloodshed, loot and plunder. People of Malwa remembered and still remember the noble gesture of Nawab Sher Muhammad Khan of Malerkotla, who lodged a strong protest against the execution of the two younger sons (*sahibzadas*) of Guru Gobind Singh. Most people in the town speak a mixture of Punjabi, Urdu and Hindi. Apart from this peculiar accent, the people of the town share a common life style and breathe in a common socio-cultural milieu, which has been evolved over the years.

Surrounded by a cluster of about three hundred villages, Malerkotla is a tahsil as well as sub-division of Sangrur district of the east Punjab. It is the only town to have Muslims in majority. Of the total populace, seventy percent are Muslims; and among the Muslims the Sunnis are in majority. After the partition, many well off Muslim families migrated to Pakistan. The Sunni Muslims have numerous ethnic and professional service castes: Kambojs, Pathans, Rajputs, Mughals, Sayyids, *teli* (oilmen), *lohar* (ironsmiths), *julahas* (weavers), *mochis* (tanners), *kasais* (butchers), *nais* (barbers), *dhobis* (washer men) etc.[6] The Muslim, Hindu and Sikh segments of the town celebrate the festivals and fairs of every religious community with fervour and enthusiasm. The town is situated on the Ludhiana-Sangrur road at a distance of 44 kilometers from the former and 32 kilometers from the latter. It was bounded on the north by the district of Ludhiana and in the east by the territories of the Phulkian princely states of Nabha and Patiala.

Malerkotla derives its name from two revenue settlements, named Maler and Kotla. According to the popular version, the genesis of Maler is linked with Raja Maler Singh, who constructed a fort near the village Bhumsi and named it Malergarh. The new settlement, which emerged in the vicinity assumed the name of the fort and came to be called Maler.[7] As per another version, recorded in Rose's *A Glossary of the Tribes and Castes of the Punjab and North-West Frontier Province*, an aged Muslim woman, named Mali, became the first follower of Shaikh Sadruddin (Haidar Shaikh) and from her Maler takes its name.[8] It is also said that Shaikh Sadruddin founded Maler in 1466 AD. About two hundred years later in 1656 AD, the Kotla segment of Malerkotla town was founded by Bayazid Khan (1606-1659 AD), who was a great grandson and descendent of Shaikh Sadruddin. The word Kotla derives its origin from Kot, which means a walled area. Kotla was a walled town with seven gates: Mandi Darwaza, Maleri Darwaza, Sarhandi Darwaza, Dehli Darwaza, Sunami Darwaza, Dhabi Darwaza and Sherwani Darwaza. In earlier times, it has been learnt, the gates were closed with the fall of night. Nawab Ahmed Ali, who became the ruler in 1911 AD, constructed the Moti Bazar and linked Maler and Kotla, so that the two settlements were combined into the nomenclature of Kotlamaler, which was later changed to Malerkotla.

Founder of the Malerkotla State: Political Context

Hazrat Shaikh Sadruddin Sadar-i-Jahan, popularly known as Haidar

Shaikh or Baba Hazrat Shaikh, was born in Darban (Afghanistan) in 1434 AD. During the course of his upbringing in this town, he received education from Maulana Jamaluddin Khurasani.[9] The rise of Afghans as political power in the Punjab might have encouraged Shaikh Sadruddin to migrate to Punjab and to join his Afghan ethnic fraternity. It has also been mentioned that his father and uncle held high offices with the sultan at Delhi. There is ample evidence which testifies that the towns of Chhat and Banur (now near Zirakpur and Chandigarh) were granted to his father. In these towns are located the graves of Shaikh Ahmad Zinda Pir and Shaikh Ghulam Dana, the father and uncle respectively of Shaikh Sadruddin. This might have motivated Shaikh Sadruddin to shift to Hindustan.[10]

Since Shaikh Sadruddin was a man of spiritual predilection, he first reached Multan in 1449. This city was famous for spiritual pursuits and was the centre of Suhrawardi order. Shaikh Bahauddin Zakariya (1182-1262) had already established an extensive hospice (*khanqah*) at Multan in the thirteenth century. Thus Shaikh Sadruddin's arrival at Multan alludes to his connections with Suhrawardi order. But that his spiritual mentor was Shaikh Ruknuddin Abul Fateh, who is said to have directed him to propagate the Suhrawardi discipline, is not consistent with latter's life's span. Shaikh Ruknuddin Abul Fateh died in 1335, whereas Sadruddin was born a century later. It may be premised that after having received his spiritual training at Multan, he might have decided to move to the vicinity of Sirhind, which had emerged as a centre of Afghan power under the emerging leadership of Bahlul Lodi. Shaikh Sadruddin might have moved to Bhumsi after having spent a couple of years at Multan. It has been observed that arriving "a few years before the Lodi conquest of Delhi, the Shaikh might easily have been part of the rising tide of Pathan Afghan power in the region."[11]

However, the rise of Shaikh Sadruddin as the ruler of Malerkotla can be best understood in the context of the political turmoil in Punjab in the wake of Timur's invasion and the emergence of Bahlul Lodi as the governor of Sirhind. After the departure of Timur in the winter of 1398-99, two power centres appeared in north-western India, viz. Delhi and Multan.[12] As the last Tughluq ruler Sultan Nasiruddin Mahmud had taken refuge at Dhar, it was Mallu Iqbal Khan who called the shots at Delhi till his death in 1405. On the other hand, Khizar Khan had been placed in control of Multan and Dipalpur by Timur. The local officers, who were posted in different parts of Punjab, frequently shifted their allegiance from Delhi to Multan and vice versa. Khizar Khan crushed Mallu Iqbal Khan in a fierce battle (12 November 1405) and began to extend his sway over the cis-Satluj territories, as a prelude to the final assault on Delhi. After the death of Sultan Nasiruddin Mahmud

(October 1412) and the short reign of Daulat Khan Lodi,[13] Khizar Khan established the Saiyyid dynasty on 6 June 1414. The period of Saiyyid rule was marked by a large number of military campaigns in all directions – Punjab, Mewat, Katehar and Gwalior – with the limited object of extracting tributes from local elements.[14] The new sultan expended his resources in suppressing rebellious elements and regaining control of a troubled area comprising Samana, Sirhind and Ferozepur. However, the most serious challenge to the Delhi sultanate was posed by the rebellion of Jasrath Khokhar. During a period of over two decades (1420-1441), he carried out regular plundering raids on different places in northern and central Punjab viz. Jammu, Lahore, Dipalpur, Kalanaur, Gurdaspur, Jalandhar, Ludhiana, Sirhind and Ropar.[15] The situation was further complicated when the ruler of Kabul, Shaikh Ali, invaded Punjab three times (1430-1433) at the invitation of Faulad Turkbacha, who was a slave of the former governor of Bathinda. Shaikh Ali's incursions affected the areas of Shorkot, Multan, Montgomery Diplapur, Lahore and Bathinda.[16] In spite of the military expeditions of the Delhi sultan and the support of some local officers, peace and stability could not be restored in Punjab.

And this brings us to the growing presence of the Afghans in the north-western India. In the middle of the thirteenth century, the Afghans served the Delhi sultanate as ordinary soldiers. Gradually, they began to acquire higher positions, so that by the reign of Muhammad bin Tughluq (r.1325-1351) they formed an important element among the centurion nobles (*sadah amirs*). The position enjoyed by the Afghans as *sadah amirs* enabled them to transform themselves into *zamindars* in the late fourteenth century, taking advantage of the hereditary principle in public appointments as implemented by Firuz Shah Tughluq.[17] We also find that the governors posted in the frontier provinces often employed Afghans who continuously migrated from their ancestral lands. Malik Bahram Lodi (the grandfather of Bahlul Lodi), an Afghan merchant, entered the service of Malik Mardan Daulat, the governor of Multan. Some time later, Malik Sultan Shah, the son of Malik Bahram Lodi, was employed by Khizar Khan during the latter's tenure as the governor of Multan. Malik Sultan Shah, in view of his exemplary services for Khizar Khan, was given the title of Islam Khan and the governorship of Sirhind.[18] The military resources of Islam Khan comprised 12,000 Afghans, most of whom were his clansmen. He nominated his nephew Bahlul Lodi as his successor in Sirhind. In spite of the opposition of his kinsmen and pro-Delhi elements, Bahlul Lodi established his sway in the area extending from Sirhind to Panipat and went on to occupy Lahore, Dipalpur, Sunam and other places, without the permission of the Saiyyid ruler Sultan Muhammad Shah.[19] After assuming sovereign power at Delhi in 1451, Bahlul Lodi undertook several steps to consolidate his position. He sent a general invitation to the Afghan tribesmen of Roh,[20] who were asked to serve in India and to improve their economic condition. He also began to weave alliances with influential local elements. He gave one of his daughters in marriage to the son of Shaikh Yusuf Qureshi, who was a spiritual descendant of the famous Suhrawardi saint Shaikh Bahauddin Zakariya. Shaikh Yusuf Qureshi had ruled over Multan for almost two years with the support of the inhabitants of Multan, before he was removed by the Langahs.[21] In 1454 Bahlul Lodi gave another daughter, Taj Murassa Begum, in marriage to Shaikh Sadruddin of Malerkotla and also conferred on him a grant of 69 villages.[22] Twelve of these were big villages (*mauzas*), namely Firozpur Kothala, Sandaur, Butha, Daholiar, Luchhabadi, Mohammed, Madevi, Bhural, Darahoon, Bari, Jhuner and Bhudan. Fifty seven villages (asamees) were small namely Thoaa, Ranwan, Rawal Dalow, Jaitwal, Daryapur, Shaikhpur Chuk, Dhadewara, Man Muzra, Cheema Chohan, Damam Mohli, Badshahpur Mandyala, Rasulpur, Manakwal, Natho Heri, Husainpur, Dhadewari, Borano, Qasimpur, Manki Kalan, Katra Hakimpur, Sheikhupura (Bos-Harawan), Panjgraiyan, Bapla, Hatiwal, Shakopura, Manak Mazra, Naundharani, Bagri, Bhopa, Fatehpur, Khaiwan, Mohamedpur, Bharota, Baryamoon (Kalan), Sudanpur, Faridpur, Shahidwari, Eisapur Ladda, Mono Dolo, Manki Khurd, Choturkoy, Malikpur, Bapli, Sangala, Akbarpur (Sangali), Runtool, Madevi, Mukhdoompur, Rurka, Takhar, Badhacha, Bahmanian, Purtabpur, Baryamoon (Khurd), Alipur, Adanwall and Mohamed Alipur.[23] The Shaikh was also awarded a cash grant of rupees three lakhs per year.

In the light of the two matrimonial alliances made by Bahlul Lodi, one with the son of a spiritual descendant of the Suhrawardi saint, Shaikh Bahauddin Zakariya, and the second with Shaikh Sadruddin, a follower of the same Suhrawardi order, it is possible to suggest that Bahlul Lodi himself owed spiritual allegiance to the said order. It may be recalled that his grandfather and father had lived for a long time at Multan, the chief centre of the Suhrawardi order in north-western India. Moreover, the Suhrawardis themselves were always keen to associate themselves with the contemporary rulers.

Assessing the position and status of Shaikh Sadruddin, the big and small chiefs of Punjab began to seek his friendship and favour. The ruler of Kapurthala, Rai Behram Bhatti, gave his daughter in marriage to the Shaik in the year 1458. The Shaikh and his Afghan wife (daughter f Bahlul Loi) bore two children, a daughter named Bibi Mangi and a son named Hasan. Two sons were born from te Shaikh's marriage to th Kapurthala Rajput princess. They were Isa and Musa. Musa died in the lifetime of the Shaikh. The descendants of his second son Hasan became the aretakers (*mujawirs*) of th shrine f Shaikh Sadruddin. Isa became the subsequent *jagirdar*. 'As *jagirdars*, the family was always dependent upon th goodwill of the ruler of Delhi. Not until 1657, under the Mughal rulr Aurangzeb, did the region become a quasi-independent principality (*riasat-i-Malerkotla*) when Bayazid Khan was granted te title of Nwab.'[24] Thus the family of the erstwhile ruler, the Nawab of Malerotla traces its lineage fro Shaikh Sadruddin's son, Isa. One can uggest that the spiritual domain of Shaikh Sadruddin remained and remains in the hands of Afghan blood, whereas, the *nawabship* was partly Afghan and partly Rajput.

Face and Features of the Shrine

The origin of the shrine ofhaikh Sadruddin is obscure nd cannot be ascertained through conventional historical methods. According to a popular belief, the tomb was built by genii (*jins*) in one night. Be that as it may, the present structure of the shrine (except the graves and the outer boundary wall) is relatively modern. This is somewhat surprising in view of the saint's spiritual eminence and his elevation as the ruler of Malerkotla. It has been learnt that, before the partition of the Indian subcontinent, the grave of the saint was placed under a tent. Afer 1947, a simple pillared structure was erected which gave the appearance of a canopy. This small building was dismantled in 2007 when the present edifice was raised. As mentioned above, the outer boundary wall is one of the few structures that have survived from the pre-modern times. Believed to have been built five centuries ago, it has been constructed with boulders without using any mortar or cement. On three sides

Outer boudary wall of the shrine

The outer gate

beyond this wall, we observe the residential quarters of the local inhabitants. The main gateway to the shrine is located on the northern side. This structure, which is made of small bricks, was built nearly a century ago. At its base, we encounter as many as fifteen steps. The gateway is topped by a lintel which joins the roof of adjoining room on two sides. On passing through the gateway, one enters a courtyard which surrounds the shrine on all the four sides. The tomb is located at a distance of 200 yards from the main gateway.

Inner Gate

The second gateway, which stands on the southern side, is an impressive modern structure. The arched entrance bears a marble slab on which the name of the saint is inscribed, while the upper portion is provided with a ornamental central canopy and flanking towers on two corners. The passage leading to the tomb is bifurcated by an iron railing, so as to regulate the entry and exit of the devotees. The tomb itself is a six-pillared octagonal structure, which is covered by an onion-shaped dome. The inner side of the dome is ornamented with multi-coloured glass work, which has been executed by craftsmen from Delhi.

Sanctum Sanctorum

The grave of Shaikh Sadruddin is raised on a three feet high platform. It is made of marble, while the sides are gilded with granite stone. It remains clad in thick and embroidered sheets of cloth. It is surrounded by an iron grill for the purpose of safety. The place is lighted by a large chandelier which hangs down from the roof. The western courtyard has two features. There is a single room (*ibadatgah*) where Shaikh Sadruddin used to sit for meditation. It has three graves of the saint's sons – Shaikh Musa, Shaikh Isa and Shaikh Hasan. The eastern courtyard has the graves of the saint's wife Taj Murassa Begum, grandson Shaikh Sulaiman and three other relatives. A few rooms and a verandah are located along the northern wall, somewhat towards the west of the enclosure. Beyond the shrine complex, we encounter two edifices which have been built in more recent times – a mosque for offering prayers (*namaz*) and a pillared hall which accommodates pilgrims coming from different places during the festivities.

Festivities, Rituals and Pilgrims

In the following section we seek to explore the manner in which Shaikh Sadruddin is remembered. His lore i.e. story and tradition is mediated by various factors such as (i) the *dargah* and festivities, (ii) devotees,

Glasswork inside the pillared dome structure

(iii) *khalifas*, (iv) pamphlets and (v) audio-video cassettes. Our narrative of the *dargah* may open with the general socio-cultural significance of a sufi shrine as understood by Richard M. Eaton, "If a living sufi had only minimal influence in the religious life of non-Muslim Indians, a deceased sufi, especially one blessed with sainthood by the local population, could literally work miracles. This was because the charisma or *baraka* of a spiritually saturated sufi saint became, with time, transformed to his tomb. And since brick and mortar shrines have much greater longevity than sufism in flesh and blood, self-sustaining centres of religious power were able in this way to grow and span many centuries."[25] Pilgrimage made by the devotees to the *dargah* of Shaikh Sadruddin may be divided into two categories: ordinary and festive. The ordinary pilgrimage (*ziyarat*) is made on one day of the week, customarily on the eve of Friday i.e. on Thursday evening which is called *jumeraat*. On this day the devotees made obeisance at the *dargah* of the Shaikh, deposit an offering and pray for a favour. The annual festive pilgrimage takes place in the month of May-June (*Jeth*) on the eve of *Nirjila Ikadeshi* of *Jeth Sudi*. It is known as the *Mela of Haidar Shaikh*. On this occasion thousands of people, irrespective of their community, caste and creed affiliations, arrive as pilgrims from all parts of Malwa, in addition to Haryana, Himachal Pardesh, Calcutta and Bombay.

Before we proceed to explain the communal harmony and the shared cultural space, which the pilgrimage at the *dargah* of Shaikh Sadruddin symbolizes, let us know about *Nirjila Ikadeshi Jeth Sudi*. *Sudi* refers to a fortnight part of the lunar month. The new moon (*masya*) divides the lunar month into two fortnights: a dark fortnight (*Krishan pakh* or *badi*) when the moon is waning and light fortnight (*chanan pakh* or *sudi*). The *sudi pakh* or light fortnight is believed to be ominous for performing festive ceremonies.[26] According to Vishnu Purana, Chandara or Chandrama (the Moon planet) takes Nectar from the Sun and supplies it to the angels as well as to flora and fauna on the earth. A mythical legend is popular in Punjab about the Moon. Before the appearance/birth of Chandrama, there was no pleasure and flavour on the earth. Neither human relations had any attraction, nor were eatables flavoursome. Then the Almighty in order to create flavour and pleasure created Chandrama by taking light from the Sun, coolness from breezes, fertility from the earth and love was given by the Almighty.[27]

Jeth is a month of the Indian samvat calendar. It is a month of extreme summer season. The eleventh day of the light fortnight of the lunar month is called *Sudi Ikadeshi*. So the eleventh day of the light fortnight of *Jeth* is called *Jeth Sudi Ikadeshi*. *Ikadeshi* was a splendid Goddess-Virgin who emerged from the *soma* of Lord Vishnu in order to destroy demons.[28] On this day (i.e. *Jeth Sudi Ikadeshi*) Hindus observe the fast of *Nirjal Ikadeshi*. Even drinking of water is prohibited during the fast, which lasts for twenty-four hours. The festive pilgrimage made to the *dargah* of Shaikh Sadruddin coincides with *Jeth Sudi Ikadeshi* / *Nirjal Ikadeshi*. On this occasion, two festivals – *Nirjal Ikadeshi* and the fair held in the revered memory of Shaikh Sadruddin – fuse together. *Chhabils* (spots where sweetened water is distributed gratuitously) serving the pilgrims mark both the observance of the *Nirjal Ikadeshi* and commemoration of Shaikh Sadruddin.

The concomitant celebration of the two festivals, one Muslim and the other Hindu, in the month of May-June alludes to the rhythm of seasons in medieval or pre-industrial Punjab, "marked at regular intervals by calendrical festivals, partly manifesting or anticipating the state of the agricultural cycle, partly incorporating religious observances and rites."[29] The annual festivals and fairs, in conjunction with the unfolding of the seasons are classified into four groups: summer (April-June), monsoon (July-September), winter (October-January, and spring (February to March).[30] With regard to the two festivals/fairs under our discussion, which are celebrated in May-June, it needs to be understood that after harvesting in the month of April, the peasants wait for pre-monsoon rain so that paddy could be sown. In order to appease the sufi, Shaikh Sadruddin, who rests in his *dargah* and who, when alive, was not only the chief (*jagirdar*) but also the founder of the agricultural society, a number of rituals are performed.[31]

On Thursday evening there is hustle and bustle of devotees around the area of the shrine (*dargah*). An important element in the socio-religious and cultural fusion is the 'sacred geography' of the *dargah*, which ensures solidarity among the devotees who gather from all points of the compass, also from very great distances by taxis, buses, trains and other modes of transportation. "The festivals restores, Richard Lannoy writes, "the sense of unity which specialization endangers; this is generally accomplished by a reversal of the customary regulation of daily social interplay and work...excessive inter-caste rivalry or sense of exclusivism is countered by festivals in which the entire community co-operates"[32] The devotees perform the ceremony called *Hazrat Shaikh ki Chauki* by keeping awake the whole night i.e. a vigil. After taking bath, a symbol of renewal, the devotees, beating drums and dancing, proceed to the *dargah* and make obeisance. It becomes a spectacle of collective ecstasy, 'a possession syndrome.' The sound of beating drum is vital in building up the atmosphere of festive pilgrimage and is particularly impressive in a culture based on oral traditions and not on written texts. It is said that the drums are a magical form of speech "which by their rhythm lock themselves together with the rhythm of movement, of heartbeat, of breathing, of measured development within a framework of regularity, transcending biology and individuality, giving validity and outward form to the moral dimension of life."[33] Various offerings are made, such as money, clothes, gold, silver, rice, goats, fowls etc. Of these offerings, the *rot* (a big sweet loaf cooked in a heap of dried cakes of cow-dung) is ritually the prominent one. Since the *dargah* and its adjacent area are considered a spiritually elevated abode of the Shaikh, the devotees sleep on the bare ground, a symbol of submission. . It is believed that whosoever sleeps on a cot, offends the Shaikh and hence is subject to his wrath.[34] The entire 'territory' of the *dargah* is illumined with the earthen lamps. Devotees get together in groups, beat drums and dance. Many of them go into trance, saying that the sacred soul (*ruh*) of Babaji (Shaikh Sadruddin) has possessed them. Recognizing the healing and miraculous power of the Shaikh, the devotees communicate their demands and wishes to be fulfilled and enquiries about their future. H.A. Rose narrates the scene of the state of ecstasy and trance of a woman devotee:

> "Women believe that all worldly desires are fulfilled by the Shaikh. To gain any wish they vow to make a special offering to the shrine in case it is realized. They often perform the ceremony called 'Hazrat Shaikh *ki chauki*'. [They] employ a *mirasan* who sings, especially eulogies of the Shaikh, and sometimes play the *chauki* in the daytime. The woman who is to do this, bathes, puts on the best new clothes she can get and sits on the bare ground with other women round her. The *mirasan* beats her drum and sings the Shaikh's praise. At first the woman sits silent with her head lowered and then begins to roll her head with hair disheveled. Then the *mirasan* sings

> more vigorously, generally repeating over and over again the part of the song at which the woman showed the first sign of having fallen under the Shaikh's influence. In a few moments the Shaikh expresses through the woman what he wants of her and what she must do for him and where. After this all the women round her question her and receive her response. She then attends the shrine and offers something according to her promise."[35]

The devotees visit the Shaikh /*dargah* to be blessed with a son and to ward off the evil spirits who have possessed a person. No marriage is considered blessed unless the newly wedded couple visits the *dargah*. Thus the locale, structure and spiritual power of the shrine combine to transform its character from a *mazar* to a *dargah*, which is a nobler term (in contrast to *mazar*), "meaning palace or royal court."[36] This 'spiritual' court where petitioners, afflicted ones (suffering from mental disorders and physical deformities, chickenpox, typhoid and other such ailments) and aspirants come with all humility in the form of devotees and seek favour of Shaikh Sadruddin. In other words, they seek the blessings and 'aid' of the Shaikh when their own predicament seems to have become untenable. The devotees also get the privilege to have a sight of the relics of the Shaikh: his silken robe and shoes. They enter the spiritual court with offerings (*nazrana*) of numerous kinds.[37] They prostrate and make their appeals. Islam means surrender. A Muslim is a man or a woman who has made this submission of his/her entire being to Allah. Prostrations counter the hard arrogance. They re-educate a Muslim or a devotee to lay aside his/her pride.[38] The devotee wears a green headgear decorated with golden ruffles or frills on his/her head when he/she makes an appeal to the court of Sadar-i-Jahan. It is a dress code that is observed by a devotee. Many a devotee approach the entrance of the *dargah* while crawling on his elbows and knees, called *dandaut*.

A number of shops supply the green headgears to the devotees. Special stall are set up for the sale of sweetmeats like *ladoos, jalebis, elaichi dana* and *makhana*. There are vendors selling toys, bangles and posters. A brisk business is done by those who sell audio-cassettes and CDs, which contain devotional songs relating to the spectacular deeds of Shaikh Sadruddin. These stalls blare loud music in order to attract the customers. Brochures and booklets narrating the history of the saint and the town, which have been written by local writers like Sufi Muhammad Ismail and Muhammad Khalid Zubairi and which are available in Urdu, Punjabi and Hindi, are also available for sale. The nearby Lal Bazar, Sadar Bazar, Talab Bazar and Telian Bazar meet the multifarious needs of the devotee-customers by supplying them the locally manufactured articles, particularly the utensils made of iron and steel. Our description of the festivities will be incomplete without referring to the popular concerts of the Qawwals. Some groups of singers, who use the single-stringed folk instrument and are known as the Toomba Parties, narrate such tales (in addition to the spiritual eminence of Baba Haidar Shaikh) as Yusuf Zulaikha, Daud Badshah and Tota Maina.

Transmitting the Lore of the Shaikh

The Hindus, Sikhs and Muslims constitute the entire gamut of the devotees of the Shaikh. Their lore about the Shaikh, which is also mingled with their respective religious milieus, histories and legends, facilitates inter-religious dialogue, strengthens communal harmony, enriches the shared cultural space and, hence, counters the communal ideology and its advocates. Many factors such as longstanding family traditions, group solidarity and personal devotion and faith as well as historical legends inspire the devotees to visit the *dargah*. Among these devotees, the local populace of the Hindus of Malerkotla believes Shaikh Sadruddin and Baba Atma Ram to be contemporary saints who were intimate friends. But the latter is said to have lived in the eighteenth century. Similarly, the non-resident devotees displace the Shaikh from the fifteenth century to the eighteenth century by attributing to him the 'Slogan of Protest' (*ha da nara*), which was actually raised by Nawab Sher Muhammad Khan against the execution of the two younger sons of Guru Gobind Singh.[39] Such type of stories, as narrated by the devotees of Shaikh Sadruddin, transcending the boundaries of 'historical' time and chronology, underscore the phenomenon of religio-cultural fusion in oral history from below. Such folk stories, borrowing R.C. Temple's phrase, 'run in cycles.' In connection with the legends of the Punjab, he states, "The tendency of bards is to make their stories run in cycles. They love to connect all their heroes in some way or the other...it must not be presumed that hero and story, or story and incident, have any real historical connection, until it is demonstrated that such is the case...many a purely mythical genealogy may well have arisen from no other cause than a desire to rouse interest in the actors in a tale by connecting them with a great national movement or recognized national heroes...In the *Janam Sakhi*, or orthodox *life* of Baba Nanak, the founder of the Sikh Religion, are long purely mythical chapters, containing his adventures in lands he could never have seen and his dealings with such personages as Shekh Farid and Bahau'L-haqq, who were not his contemporaries at all and did not even live in the same century as he did."[40] Thus what we wish to suggest is that the 'imagined' association of Shaikh Sadruddin with the Hindu ascetic Baba Atma Ram and with the Sikh history of the eighteenth century refers to the ecumenical character of the devotees' lore woven round the persona of Shaikh

Sadruddin. The Shaikh has gone deep into the folk memory. He occupies his own place in the folk religion of Punjab. The Malwa folk remember and revere him thus in their folksong:

Devi di mein karan karahi, pir fakir dhiavan
Haidar Shaikh da devan bakra, nangen pairin javan
Hanuman di devan manin, ratii fark nan pavan
Ni mata bhagvatey, mein tere jas gavan.

I offer a cauldron of sweet pudding to goddess Devi, and remember pirs and faqirs. /With bare feet I go to the dargah of Haidar Shaikh and offer a goat. /Without any discrimination, I offer a thick sweet loaf to Hanuman. O Mother Goddess, I sing your praises.

Next to the devotees, the *khalifas* and attendants are the transmitters of the lore of Shaikh Sadruddin. They recount the miracles of the Shaikh, his encounters with Bahlul Lodi, his disinterestedness in worldly affairs, his superiority of spiritual power over worldly authority, and the significance and sanctity of his shrine. The *khalifas* narrate these attributes of Shaikh Sadruddin with reference to (i) his blessings bestowed on Bahlul Lodi when the latter requested the Shaikh to pray for his success in the war, (ii) his miraculous power to produce a thousand horses just like the one which Bahlul Lodi had presented to the Shaikh and which was given by him (the Shaikh) to someone else, because he was a saint who had nothing to do with the gift of a horse presented by a sultan, and (iii) his character as a saint-warrior. Anna Bigelow cites a story as narrated by a *khalifa* to her during an interview with him. "Baba Hazrat Shaikh Sadruddin was a general in the army, but he was a fakir also. Once the king asked him to go somewhere because at that place a revolt was going on. But when the command came to him he took it and threw it on one side, because he was doing *zikr* at that time in the Lord's name. So his followers, who were *jinn*, picked it up. They understood that they were given this command and they went to that place and they conquered it. And they got the booty from the people there and the king asked, "My army didn't go there how were they conquered?" And he inquired [of Haidar Shaikh], "If my general was here and my army was also here, who went to conquer that place?" He answered, "Your command came but I was praying and threw it to one side and my followers thought the command was for them so they went there and conquered." So the king ordered that he [Shaikh Sadruddin] should not be given any work, he should only rest. But he left [the king's service]. Because his secret was laid open in front of every one, which is not good. So his *pir* ordered him to go to Malerkotla and spread Islam there and pray to God.'[41]

The lore of the Shaikh is also mediated through devotional songs (*qawwalis*) recorded in audio-video-cassettes and popular variety of printed booklets written in the vernacular – Punjabi, Hindi and Urdu. Both these media narrate the brief life history of the Shaikh, his charisma, his miraculous powers and his encounter with Bahlul Lodi. Owing to the paucity of space, we will confine ourselves to only of one audiocassette, titled *Darshan Pauan Sangatan*. It is the *qissa* of *Kotley da Pir* (a poetic-narrative of the *pir* of Malerkotla) in which the life story of Shaikh Sadruddin has been told in the genre of a *qawwali* sung by the lead qawwal, Muhammad Anis Nazir and his accompanists. In the present times, on the level of popular culture, *qawwali* music has created its own clientele through the recording industry. The *qawwali* performers or *qawwals*, known or lesser known, provide the service of a public nature, namely to articulate a valued cultural tradition. The said cassette has been released by Hazrat Shaikh Music Centre, Malerkotla.

The town of Malerkotla is known for its rich tradition of *qawwali*, though no substantial research has been conducted so far on this musical tradition. In the month of May-June when the festive pilgrimage to the *dargah* of Shaikh Sadruddin takes place at Malerkotla, a number of sufi-concerts are held in the shrine. In the *qawwali*-parties, renowned *qawwals* like Salim Qawwal, Shauqat Qawwal, Karamat Qawwal, Anis Qawwal and Sharif Qawwal sing their respective poetry (*qalam*) to commemorate the eminence of Shaikh Sadruddin. Among them Salim Qawwal is a son of Rahmat Khan, the famous Qawwal of Malerkotla, who is said to have composed a popular *nat* in the praise of Prophet Muhammad. *Qawwali* is an Arabic word meaning recited. "This name, writes Carl W. Ernst, "preserves an old terminology, since Arabic sufi texts from nine centuries ago refer to the reciter (*qawwal*) of poetry as a central figure in musical rituals."[42] *Qawwali* is a method of worship and a means of spiritual advancement. It underlines the power of the human voice to bring out powerful emotion. It is also a food for the soul. To the performer, it is mainly a musical genre with its distinct character for worship. To the observer, it is above all music performed very obviously with continual reference to its context (as Shaikh Sadruddin is the context of the *qawwali* under reference). Thus *qawwali* is music in context. The context is the primary message as opposed to the music. This stands in contrast to the classical musical tradition which confers primacy to music over text/context. For centuries, the sufi communities of the Indian subcontinent have sustained this *qawwali* musical tradition in the *mahfil-i-sama*, the assembly for listening, and it remains the central ritual of sufism to this day.[43] The said ritual is performed in numerous vernacular forms.

The *qawwali* under reference, *Darshan Pauan Sangatan*, narrates in the Punjabi vernacular the story of Shaikh Sadruddin, his miracles and his meetings, at different point of times, with Bahlul Lodi. The entire episode, repeatedly interrupted by a brief commentary made by the *qawwal*, has eight segments. These segments can be condensed broadly into three parts. The first two parts narrate the life story of Shaikh Sadruddin: his coming to Multan, his permanent settlement at Malerkotla, his meetings with Bahlul Lodi, his marriage with the daughter of the sultan and with the daughter of the ruler of Kapurthala, his miraculous power to divert the current of the Satluj, to make a violent storm ineffectual so as to protect his hut and to produce a thousand horses like the one gifted by Bahlul Lodi. All these accounts told by the *qawwal* are well known at the level of popular memory and are available in sources dating from the early seventeenth century to the present day, such as Khwaja Niamatullah Harvi's *Tarikh-i-Khan Jahani wa Makhzani-i-Afghani*, H.A. Rose's *A Glossary of the Tribes and Castes of the Punjab and North-West Frontier Province, the Gazetteer of Malerkotla State* and the popular printed pamphlets written in vernacular.

So far as the above aspects of the life and miracles of Shaikh Sadruddin are concerned, we will focus on one episode pertaining to the early life of Shaikh Sadruddin. The *qawwal* apprises us that the Shaikh was born in Kabul-Qandhar. His father was Hazrat Ahmed Shaikh. After a brief introduction, the *qawwal* begins the *qissa* with the miraculous power of the Shaikh, when he was a child of merely five years. At this age, he went to a jungle and returned with a lion while holding the wild savage by an ear. Seeing such a strange sight, the mother of the Shaikh became transfixed with surprise. She approached her husband and revealed the incident. The latter asked her not to be petrified. Recognizing an ascetic (*fakkar*) in the person of his son, the father told his wife that the Almighty (*rab*) had bestowed a tremendous power on him (*fakkar di zat nu rab ne bari taaqat bakhshi hai*). The lion episode, associated with the child (Shaikh Sadruddin) alludes to the motif of (i) tamed lions who are shown sitting before a sufi in an Indian painting of seventeenth century[44] and (ii) the guard-lion standing on a hill, as shown in a poster depicting the shrine of Abdul Rahman Baba in Bombay.[45]

The third part of the *qawwali* under study is associated with the praise of Shaikh Sadruddin. The *qawwal*, Muhammad Anis Nazir, besides bringing himself and his accompanists into the arena of eulogizing the Shaikh, also presents Shaikh's father and Bahlul Lodi as *qawwals* who sing the glories of the Shaikh. The *qawwal* transports the listener to Kabul-Qandhar and makes him/her listen what the father sings in the praise of a *fakkar* and recounts his spiritual power:

> *Sadka fakkar da jagg vasey / fakkar ayee bala nu rokdey ne / Bulleh Shah da kaul nishan sacha/ fakkar rekh ch mekh nu thokdey ne.*

May the world of a *saint* exist long and flourish/ *The saints* prevent calamities from happening. / Bulleh Shah has rightly said that the *saint* diverts the currents of destiny.

After this, the *qawwal* himself sings in the praise of Shaikh Sadruddin:

Jag te naubat vajdi ae Baba Sadrodin di / than than charchey hon paiey murshid merey dian shanan di / asin hor kisey dar kion jaiaey sada pir lasani hai / aithey sab nu mildi ae dault sidik yakin di / aithey aa key jhukdey sarey dubdey berey is ne tarey / aeh hai maula Ali da piara / baba ji da mukhra piara / surat hai Yasin di.

The sounds of a kettle-drum praising Baba Sadrodin [Shaikh Sadruddin] are widespread. / The glory of my mentor is talked about in each place. / Our *pir* [spiritual guide] is unique, perfect and peerless, why should we wander from door to door? / Here [at the *dargah*] all are blessed with the wealth of patience and faith; here every one prostrates. He has relieved all of us of distress and difficulty. He is a beloved of Ali [son-in-law of Prophet Muhammad, titular head of all sufi lineages]. The countenance of Babaji is charming and kind; his visage resembles with Ya-Sin [Ya-Sin is usually treated as a title of the holy Prophet].

The *qawwal* also makes Bahlul Lodi sing and dance, which in sufi terminology is called *sama* and *raqs*. The vernacular and Indic character of the said *qawwali* may be discerned, when a listener finds in it a genre of folk songs, called *tappe*, and a singer assumes the voice of a female-devotee. For instance, the Sultan Bahlul Lodi sings:

Ki karna jagiran nu / seeney nal lai firdi terian tasviran nu / painda hijar da muk javey / baba tera naun sun key / dil sijde ch jhuk jandan / pani chhapri chon kan peeta / terey vichon rab disda / tainu sijda hi tan keeta.

The *jagirs* are of what use! / I wander with the your [Shaikh Sadruddin] pictures or images close to my heart. / The distance of disunion is covered the moment your name is remembered. / A crow drinks water from a pit / God mirrors in you / Thus I bow in adoration.

The female voice is a symbol of humility and elegance. The focus of the audio cassette, *Darshan Pauan Sangatan*, is on the spiritual power and glory of Shaikh Sadruddin in contrast to that of Bahlul Lodi, the sultan, who is shown to be a disciple (*murid*) of the Shaikh. We also find Islamic and Quranic allusions in the *qawwali* under study. By narrating the life story of the Shaikh and singing his praise, the *qawwal* develops a rapport with his own 'vernacular' community. His motive is to satisfy the emotional, psychological and devotional needs of his listeners, the devotees of Shaikh Sadruddin. Thus a communicative channel is created. Outside the spiritual territory of the *dargah* of the Shaikh, a singer and his songs as recorded in an audio cassette, assume the role of a mediator between the Shaikh and his devotees.

A pageant of devotion, ritual, colour, entertainment and commerce get fused together in the festive pilgrimage made to the *dargah* of Shaikh Sadruddin.

NOTES AND REFERENCES

1. Harjot Oberoi, *The Construction of Religious Boundaries: Culture, Identity and Diversity in the Sikh Tradition*, Oxford University Press, Delhi, 1997, p. 44.
2. H.A. Rose, *A Glossary of the Tribes and Castes of the Punjab and North-West Frontier Province*, Language Department Punjab, Patiala, Second Reprint,1990, (first edition 1883), Vol. I, p. 552.
3. Karam Singh, *Bathinda*, Bhasha Vibhag, Patiala, 1996, pp. 12-18.
4. Hari Ram Gupta, *History of the Sikhs: The Sikh Gurus, 1469-1708*, Vol. I, New Delhi, Munshiram Manoharlal, New Delhi, Revised Edition 1984, p. 10.
5. Fauja Singh, Sirhind During the Sultanat Period' in Fauja Singh, Ed., *Sirhind Through the Ages*, Punjabi University, Patiala,1972, p. 19.
6. Muhammad Khalid Zubairy, *Malerkotla: Itihas ke Darpan Mein* (Hindi), Tarkash Publications, Malerkotla, 2000, p. 48.
7. Nawab Iftikhar Ali Khan, *History of the Ruling Family of Sheikh Sadruddin: Sadar-i-Jahan of Malerkotla (1449 AD to 1948 AD)*, Ed., R.K. Ghai, Punjabi University, Patiala, 2000, p. 6.
8. H.A. Rose, *op. cit.*, Vol. I, p. 644.
9. Mohammed Khalid Zubairy, *op. cit.*, p. 9.
10. Nawab Iftikhar Ali Khan, *op. cit.*, p.3.
11. Anna Bigelow, *Sharing Saints, Shrines and Stories: Preaching Pluralism in North India*, Doctoral Dissertation, Department of Religious Studies, University of California, Santa Barbara, 2004, pp. 145.
12. Sri Ram Sharma, 'The Punjab under Sayyids and Lodhis,' in Fauja Singh, (Ed.), *History of the Punjab (AD 1000-1526)*, Vol.III, Punjabi University, Patiala, 1972, p. 183.
13. Yahya bin Ahmad bin Abdullah Sirhindi, *Tarikh-i-Mubarak Shahi*, English Translation, Henry Beveridge, Low Price Publications, New Delhi, 1990, pp.180-186; Khwaja Nizamuddin Ahmad, *Tabqat-i-Akbari*, Vol.I, English Translation, B. De, The Asiatic Society, Calcutta, 1973, pp.190-192; Muhammad Qasim Farishta, *Tarikh-i-Farishta*, English Translation, John Briggs, Low Price Publications, New Delhi, 1990, Vol. I, pp. 290-294.
14. Mohammad Habib and Khaliq Ahmad Nizami, (Ed.), *A Comprehensive History of India*, Vol. V, (Delhi Sultanate AD 1206-1526), People's Publishing House, New Delhi, 1970, p. 630.
15. Yahya bin Ahmad bin Abdullah Sirhindi, *Tarikh-i-Mubarak Shahi*, pp. 200-205, 220, 231; Khwaja Nizamuddin Ahmad, *Tabqat-i-Akbari*, Vol. I, pp. 300-305, 315-316,328.
16. Yahya bin Ahmad bin Abdullah Sirhindi, *Tarikh-i-Mubarak Shahi*, pp. 225-238; Khwaja Nizamuddin Ahmad, *Tabqat-i-Akbari*, Vol. I, pp. 312-320; Muhammad Qasim Farishta, *Tarikh-i-Farishta*, Vol. I, 305-308.
17. Habib and Nizami, op. cit., pp. 667-668.
18. Kishori Saran Lal, *Twilight of the Sultanate*, Munshiram Manoharlal, New Delhi, Revised Edition,1980, p. 131.
19. Khwaja Nizamuddin Ahmad, *Tabqat-i-Akbari*, Vol. I, p. 334; Muhammad Qasim Farishta, *Tarikh-i-Farishta*, Vol. I, pp. 317-319.
20. The Afghan state, as developed by Bahlul Lodi, was different from the

Turkish state of the thirteenth and fourteenth centuries. It was largely based on the support of Afghan tribesmen. The ruler was merely one among the peers, in keeping with the tribal sentiments of the Afghans. The idea was to establish a confederation of Afghan tribes. The power and prestige of nobles was raised at the expense of the sultan. Though the experiment awakened a spirit of loyalty among the different tribal leaders, yet it led to rebellious tendencies in the long run. R.P. Tripathi, *Some Aspects of Muslim Administration*, Central Book Depot, Allahabad, 1974, Reprint, pp. 83-84.

21. Habib and Nizami, op. cit, p. 679.
22. The land grants were termed as *milk, inam* and *idrar* though these terms were interchangeable. They represented the grant of revenue of villages or lands to the grantees for lifetime or in perpetuity. Such forms of revenue transfer went largely to maintain the religious intelligentsia and other dependents of the ruling class. Tapan Raychaudhuri and Irfan Habib, Eds., *The Cambridge Economic History of India, Vol. I: c.1200-c.1750*, Orient Longman, New Delhi, Reprint, 2004, p. 75.
23. Nawab Iftikhar Ali Khan, *op. cit.*, pp. 9-10.
24. Anna Bigelow, *op. cit.*, p. 126.
25. Richard M. Eaton, 'Approaches to the Study of Conversion to Islam in India' in David N. Lorenzen, ed., *Religious Movements in South Asia 600-1800*, Oxford University Press, Delhi, Second Impression 2006, p. 117.
26. Sohinder Singh Wanjara Bedi, *Panjabi Lokedhara Vishav Kosh*, Vol. III, Lok Prakashan, New Delhi, 1979, p. 729.
27. Sohinder Singh Wanjara Bedi, *Panjabi Lokedhara Vishav Kosh*, Vol. VI, National Book Shop, New Delhi, 1992, p. 1304.
28. Sohinder Singh Wanjara Bedi, *Panjabi Lokedhara Vishav Kosh*, Vol.II, Lok Prakashan, New Delhi, 1978, p. 339.
29. Harjot Oberoi, *op. cit.*, p. 182.
30. Ibid.
31. It reminds us of Ghazi Miyan who is considered as the master of the harvest. See Marc Gaborieau, 'The Ghazi Miyan Cult in Western Nepal and North India' in M. Waseem, Tr. and Ed., *On Becoming an Indian Muslim: French Essays on Aspects of Syncretism*, Oxford University Press, Delhi, 2003, pp. 238-263.
32. Richard Lannoy, *The Speaking Tree: A Study of Indian Culture and Society*, Oxford University Press, London, 1971, p. 193.
33. Pierre Verger, 'Trance and Convention in Nago-Yoruba Spirit Membership' in John Beattie and John Middleton, Eds., *Spirit Membership and Society in African*, African Publishing, New York, 1969, p. 59.
34. Sohinder Singh Wanjara Bedi, *Panjabi Lokedhara Vishav Kosh*, Vol. VI, National Book Shop, New Delhi, 1992, p. 927.
35. H.A. Rose, *A Glossary of the Tribes and Castes of the Punjab and North-West Frontier Province*, Vol. I, p. 644.
36. A.R. Saiyed, 'Saints and Dargahs in the Indian Subcontinent: A Review' in Christian W. Troll, Ed., *Muslim Shrines in India: Their Character, History and Significance*, Oxford University Press, Delhi, New Hardback Edition, 2003, p. 242.

37. In the nineteenth century these offerings comprised horses, donkeys, cows, buffaloes, goats, fowls, clothes, money, grain of all kinds and food. Of these offerings the *khalifas* took elephants, horses, donkeys, complete suits of clothes and rupees, while all other offerings were taken as of right by the caretakers (*mujawars*). H.A. Rose, *A Glossary of the Tribes and Castes of the Punjab and North-West Frontier Province*, Vol. I, p. 644.
38. Karen Armstrong, *Islam: A Short History*, The Orion Publishing Group, 2006, London, p. 5.
39. Anna Bigelow, *op. cit.*, pp. 131-139.
40. R.C. Temple, *The Legends of the Panjab*, Vol.II, Department of Languages, Punjab, Patiala, Reprint, 1963, pp. ix-xi.
41. Anna Bigelow, *op. cit.*, pp. 141- 142.
42. Carl W. Ernst, *The Shambhala Guide to Sufism*, Shambhala South Asia Editions, Massachusetts, p. 186
43. For detail see Regula Burckhardt Qureshi, *Sufi Music of India and Pakistan: Sound, Context and* Meaning *in Qawwali*, Cambridge University Press, Cambridge1986, pp. 1-65.
44. Annemarie Schimmel, *Mystical Dimension of Islam*, Sange-e-Meel Publications, Lahore, Reprint, 2003, p. 349.
45. Carl W. Ernst, *The Shambhala Guide to Sufism*, p. 76.

17

Devotional Linkages of Punjab with the Chishti Shrine at Ajmer

Gleanings from the Vikalatnamas

Syed Liyaqat Hussain Moini

Sufism, or more correctly *tasawwuf*, is the essence of Islamic thought and philosophy. It is based on high ethical values, purity of living and spiritual emotions par excellence. It originated and developed in Arabia (Hijaz), flourished in Iran (Persia) and Central Asia (Transoxiana) and lastly reached its zenith in the Indian subcontinent, now known as South Asia. Right from the twelfth century onwards, when the various sufi orders had been organized on a firm basis, India became an abode of hundreds of sufis who had thousands of followers. They made a deep and everlasting impact on the day-to-day life of the people, with regard to their social norms, religious practices and personal etiquettes. Among the many sufi orders which penetrated the Indian subcontinent, the Chishtis were the earliest and the most popular. They outclassed the other sufi orders in attracting the people to their fold, owing to their modest approach and liberal outlook which was manifested in humaneness, piety, universal brotherhood, harmony and tolerance.

Up to the fourteenth century, the illustrious line of Chishti stalwarts and their distinguished successors – Khwaja Muinuddin Chishti, Khwaja Qutbuddin Bakhtiyar Kaki, Shaikh Fariduddin Ganj-i-Shakar, Shaikh Nizamuddin Auliya and Shaikh Nasiruddin Mahmud Chiragh-i-Dehli – directed the affairs of the order and deputed trained disciples to the different parts of India. As a result, a number of cities and towns – Ajmer, Nagaur, Delhi, Hansi, Pakpattan, Kaliyar, Narnaul, Nandurbar, Gulbarga, Pindwa and Pattan – emerged as important centres of Chishti mystical activities. At the same time, an atmosphere of communal harmony and mutual understanding was created among the various sections of the Indian society and that too in a period of political turmoil.

With the disintegration of the Delhi sultanate and the decentralization of the Chishti order after the death of Shaikh Nasiruddin Mahmud, the provincial successors (*khalifas*) assumed the task of organizing the affairs of their respective areas of spiritual influence (*wilayat*) in Malwa, Gujarat, Deccan, Jaunpur, Bengal and several other parts of northern India. Owing to the propagation of the lofty Chishti ideals and philosophy, these areas became the nucleus from where the universal message of the Chishti order flowed like a stream of spirituality and,[1] in the process, influenced even the saints of the bhakti movement during the fifteenth and sixteenth centuries.

By the advent of the Mughals, the Chishtis had influenced every section of the Indian society. It was due to their vigorous efforts that a peaceful revolution had taken place in the Indian subcontinent. The Mughal rulers largely benefited from this scenario, as they took full advantage of it. In particular, Akbar and his successors utilized the new situation to introduce the principle of peace with all (*sulh-i-kul*) and regarded it as an effective device to secure the emotional integration of the Indian people, irrespective of the differences of caste and creed. In this manner, the concepts of universal brotherhood, communal harmony and composite culture began to take shape under the royal patronage.[2] We may, however, recall that there was no towering personality and central figure at the head of the Chishti order between the fourteenth and seventeenth centuries. It was at this time that the shrines (*dargahs*) of prominent Chishti saints – Khwaja Muinuddin Chishti at Ajmer, Shaikh Nizamuddin Auliya at Delhi, Shaikh Fariduddin Ganj-i-Shakar at Pakpattan – filled the vacuum and came to occupy a crucial position among the followers of the spiritual path. In fact, the shrine of Ajmer became a great symbol of spirituality and universalism, so that large crowds of people were always found performing pilgrimage (*ziyarat*) and observing other rituals.[3]

Chishti Revival in Punjab

The north-western region of Punjab had the distinction of receiving the earliest sufis of the Indian subcontinent at Lahore viz. Shaikh Husain Zinjani and Shaikh Ali bin Usman Hujwiri. We come across the traditions regarding Baba Rattan and the tomb of a prophet at Bathinda. But it was due to the extraordinary efforts of Shaikh Fariduddin Ganj-i-Shakar, the most prominent Chishti saint of Punjab, that the Chishti order was firmly established in a region where a strong presence was registered by the Suhrawardis, Qadiris, Qalandaris and Naqshbandis. Later on, several other saints – Bu Ali Qalandar, Shamsuddin Turk, Jalaluddin Kabir-ul-Auliya of Panipat and Shaikh Jalaluddin of Thanesar – contributed to the popularization and expansion of the Chishti order in Punjab.[4] With the decline of the Mughal empire in the early eighteenth century, the Chishti renaissance was brought about by the spiritual successors (*khalifas*) of Shah Kalimullah Jahanabadi, viz. Nizamuddin Aurangabadi and his able pupil Khwaja Fakhruddin Dehalvi. Their disciples led the revival of the Chishti order in an area which was passing through political turmoil and chaotic conditions, because the Mughals, Sikhs and Afghans were bitterly contesting the political control, whereas the Marathas were leading predatory raids for ransom money.

Khwaja Fakhruddin Dehalvi (1714-1785) employed the same methods which the senior Chishti examplers, particularly Khwaja Muinuddin Chishti, had followed. He was a firm believer in the philosophy of Unity of Being (*wahdat-ul-wujud*) and regarded the doctrine as indispensable to the mystical discipline.[5] He held regular sessions of devotional music (*sama*) and nurtured a liberal attitude towards the non-Muslims. Once, during the course of a visit to Ajmer, he met a Hindu Jogi along with his 314 disciples and organized an audition (*sama*) in which musical instruments (*sama-bil-mazamir*) were played. He had enrolled several Hindus as his disciples and, as a typical Chishti master, made a distinct contribution to the Chishti renaissance of the eighteenth century. He had even challenged Shah Waliullah's theory regarding the Chishti spiritual pedigree (*shajrah*) which disputed the name of Hassan Basri as a successor of Hazrat Ali on the grounds that the former had never met the latter. In his masterly work, *Fakhr-ul-Hassan*, Khwaja Fakhruddin Dehalvi refuted Shah Waliullah's claim by proving that Hassan Basri had duly met Hazrat Ali and had received his blessings.[6] He was a staunch devotee of Khwaja Muinuddin Chishti. It is claimed that the Khwaja or the custodians (*khuddam*) of his mausoleum had bestowed upon him the title of Mohibb-i-Nabi in a dream. In return for this honour, Khwaja Fakhruddin Dehalvi addressed the custodians as Sahibzadas. It may be added that he regularly visited the Chishti shrine at Ajmer.

The spiritual successors (*khalifas*) of Khwaja Fakhruddin Dehalvi established several Chishti centres in Punjab during a period of socio-political unrest. Khwaja Nur Muhammad Muharvi (1730-1791) was the first and most popular Chishti saint of the area. He stationed himself at Muhar (Bahawalpur), a rural tract where the population was dominated by the Afghan tribes and Jat clans, while non-Chishti orders – Suhrawardis and Qadiris – had flourished since long. It is interesting to note that another spiritual successor of Khwaja Fakhruddin Dehalvi, Shah Niyaz Ahmad, founded a hospice at Bareilly in the Rohilkhand region, where the Rohilla Afghans were making efforts to establish their political power when the Mughal empire was on the verge of disintegration. Khwaja Nur Muhammad Muharvi originally belonged to a Jat family of Chautala (near Muhar, Bahawalpur). His original name was Bhabbal. It was his spiritual preceptor who had given him the name of Nur Muhammad. After completing his initial education in religion,[7] he became a disciple of the leading Chishti saint of the times, Khwaja Fakhruddin Dehalvi, who soon bestowed upon him all his spiritual blessings along with the honour of succession. When some other disciples objected to this, the astute mentor exclaimed:

Tan matki man jharna surat maluan haar
Makhan Punjabi ley gaya chhachh piyo sansar

Khwaja Nur Muhammad Muharvi propagated Chishti mysticism in the rural areas of Bahawalpur, Dera Ismail Khan, Dera Ghazi Khan, Multan and even Sind. He asked the people to follow moral values and ethical norms in their living. He believed that one should not loose one's temper, that one should not declare someone guilty on a simple complaint and that one should not discuss worldly matters.[8] These teachings turned out to be extremely effective in a society that was based on tribal instincts and caste consciousness. Since he was personally fond of devotional music (*sama*), he exerted himself to popularize the same. Some of his leading disciples – Khwaja Nur Muhammad at Naruwala (Sind), Hafiz Muhammad Jamal at Multan, Qazi Aqil Muhammad at Kot Mithan (Dera Ghazi Khan)[9] – worked zealously for the propagation of the ideology and practices of the Chishti order, including audition (*sama*), in areas where the puritanical mystic orders like Suhrawardis and Naqshbandis were dominant and the local population was somewhat harsh.

However, the most successful and famous spiritual successor (*khalifa*) of Khwaja Nur Muhammad Muharvi was Khwaja Sulaiman of Taunsa (Dera Ghazi Khan). Since he was an Afghan who belonged to the Jafari tribe, he was also known as the Pir-i-Pathan. He established a hospice (*khanqah*) at Taunsa which, for the next one hundred years and even at present, occupied an important position among the Chishti centres of north-western India. Following the footsteps of his mentor, he was a distinguished scholar, an ardent follower of the philosophy of Unity of Being (*wahdat-ul-wujud*) and a keen practitioner of audition (*sama*). He was liberal and tolerant in his attitude towards the non-Muslims.[10] As the most prominent leader of a distinct branch of the Chishtis, he attracted hundreds of disciples who belonged to south-western Punjab,[11] distant parts of India and even Central Asia. Some of his leading disciples were Hafiz Muhammad Ali Khairabadi (who in turn was the mentor of Maulana Fazle Haq Khairabadi, the great mystic and scholar who emerged as a prominent leader of the revolt of 1857), Shamsuddin of Siyal and his own grandson Khwaja Allah Bakhsh who took charge of the Chishti seat at Taunsa and carried on the mission of his grandfather. Haji Najmuddin of Jhunjhunu (Shekhawati), a descendant of Sufi Hamiduddin Nagauri, was a favourite disciple who revived the Chishti order in a remote part of Rajputana, particularly among the warlike Qiyamkhanis and, thus, followed in the footsteps of his grand mentor (*pir-i-uzzam*).[12]

Role of the Khuddam and Vikalatnamas

One of the interesting aspects of these Chishtis of Punjab was their intimate devotional link with Khwaja Muinuddin Chishti, his shrine, the spiritual head (*sajjadah nishin*) and custodians (*khadims*) of the holy place. We have already referred to the attachment of Khwaja Fakhruddin Dehalvi to the Khwaja Ajmeri, his descendants and custodians of the shrine. Khwaja Nur Muhammad Muharvi adopted the same attitude and even enrolled a number of custodians (*khadims*) as his disciples. This tradition was followed by Khwaja Sulaiman Taunsavi and his successors. Even at present, we find that the people associated with the shrine of Ajmer, particularly the custodians (*khadims*), continue to secure initiation (*bait*) in his distinct branch of the Chishti order. This phenomenon assumes importance because, as mentioned above, the community of custodians (*khadims*) played a vital role in the development of rituals and practices of the shrine, propagated the Chishti philosophy among the people and provided a variety of services to the pilgrims (*zairin*). In their capacity as the representatives (*vakil*) of the pilgrims, they offered prayers and observed rituals on behalf of their clients. They took care of their worldly and spiritual needs, offered instructions (*adab-o-ziarat*) in the performance of the pilgrimage and provided guidance in the matters of religion (*rushd-o-hidayat*). It was on account of their nearness to the shrine and their religious duties that they have always been held in high esteem by the pilgrims, who gave them a variety of offerings (*nazr-o-niyaz*). With the increase of interference from the managers of endowments, the community of custodians (*khadims*) took a number of steps to safeguard their interests and, for this purpose, they developed many systems to ensure their continued linkage with Khwaja Muinuddin Chishti, his shrine and of course the devotees. One of these was the practice of procuring bonds of acceptance (*vikalatnamas*) authorizing them, as representatives of the pilgrims, to perform the required rituals on their behalf.[13] Their clients included ruling elites, saints of various sufi orders, spiritual heads (*sajjadah nishins*) of prominent shrines, government officials, common people and even non-Muslims. Recently, the present author unearthed hundreds of *vikalatnamas* from the private custody of custodians. He has also published some of these documents pertaining to prominent Hindu chieftains (Rajputs, Marathas and others) covering a period of 150 years from 1658 to 1808.[14]

The people of Punjab had a long standing devotional link with the

Chishti shrine at Ajmer. It is traditionally claimed that Guru Nanak paid a visit to this sacred place. Moreover, when Emperor Bahadur Shah was passing through Ajmer on his way to the Deccan, Guru Gobind Singh was in the imperial army and,[15] therefore, there is every possibility that the Guru had performed pilgrimage (*ziarat*) at the shrine. Regarding the Chishti saints of Punjab, we have already mentioned the devotion of Khwaja Fakhruddin Dehalvi to Khwaja Muinuddin Chishti and his shrine. In one of his letters to his representatives (*vakil/khadim*) at the shrine, he addresses him with honorific titles including *sahib-i-meharban* (one who always blesses). In another letter, he gave the assurance that, in accordance with his wishes, he had asked the officials at Delhi to release his relatives (Syed Umar and Syed Hayat) who were held in custody.[16] His principal successor in Punjab, Khwaja Nur Muhammad Muharvi, followed the same attitude towards the people associated with the shrine at Ajmer. In his letters, he addressed his representative (*vakil/ khadim*) as *khwaja sahib meharban, siyadat-wa-sharafat panah, dudman-i-tasawwuf* and *kulasa-i-khandan-i-nabvi*. Thereafter, he humbly requested the representative to regularly remember him in his prayers (*dua*), as these would assist him in both the worlds. It is quite possible that these letters might have been written, out of respect, in his own hand. He expressed his gratitude for several items – turban (*dastar*), rosary (*tasbih*) and other sacred gifts (*tabarruk*) – which he had received and which made him happy. The letters are usually concluded with expressions of respect.

In another letter to Syed Masud (*khadim*), which is addressed with the same honorific titles, Khwaja Nur Muhammad Muharvi expressed kissing of feet (*qadambosi*) and made the usual request for prayer (*dua*). He also gave the assurance that he had asked Khudadad Khan (the son of Khudayar Khan of Thatta) who was then at Delhi, to send the offerings (*nazar*) for the addressee (Appendix A). Several relatives and disciples of the saint – Muhammad Maqsood, Murad Khan Kunja, Ghulam Shah Abbassi, the son of Khudayar Khan – dispatched similar letters, costly cloth for the ceremonial covering of the sacred tomb (*ghilaf/ chadar*) and robes (*khilat*) for the *khadim* with the seal 'Due to the blessings of Nur Muhammad' (*Zi lutf-i-nur Muhammad*). Many other custodians (*khadims*) of the shrine adopted similar insignia on their seals, indicating that the people associated with the shrine had entered the saint's circle of influence.[17] In this regard, Khwaja Sulaiman Taunsavi appears to have been the most influential spiritual master (*pir*). He nurtured immense devotion for Khwaja Ajmeri and regularly visited the shrine, sometimes via Sind, Bikaner and Shekhawati region. On the way, he enrolled hundreds of people in the Chishti fold. Many prominent custodians (*khadims*) of the shrine at Ajmer became his close disciples and this tradition continues till today. The descendants of Khwaja

Sulaiman Taunsavi make regular visits to the shrine, so as to pay homage to Khwaja Muinuddin Chishti, to secure the blessings of his holiness and to enroll the caretakers as disciples. In recent times, Ghulam Allah Bakhsh, a direct descendant of Khwaja Sulaiman Taunsavi, visited the shrine at Ajmer and intiated many young members of the community of custodians (*khadims*) into the Sulaimania branch of the Chishti order.[18] It is interesting to note that the portraits of Ghulam Allah Bakhsh are found in many houses at Ajmer.

Devotees from Punjab

Besides this branch of the Punjabi Chishtis, several prominent people – religious dignitaries, heads of famous sufi shrines (*sajjadah nishins*), high ranking nobles and officials – cultivated devotional links with the shrine at Ajmer through their respective representatives (*vakils/khadims*) who, in most cases, were Syed Murad or his son Syed Masud.[19] Shaikh Rustam Shah Farooqi, who succeeded as the spiritual head (*sajjadah nishin*) of the shrine of Shaikh Fariduddin Ganj-i-Shakar at Pakpattan,[20] addressed his representative Syed Murad with the same reverential tone and honorific titles, informed the addressee about the death of his spiritual mentor and his own succession to the spiritual seat (*gaddi*) occupied by his predecessor. The writer also requested the representative to pray for him so that he was able to perform his new duties in a proper and honest manner, besides promising to send the offerings (*nazr-o-niyaz*) soon. Another head (*sajjadah nishin*) of the same shrine, Shaikh Muhammad Saeed, has referred to Syed Murad as holder of guidance (*hidayat dast gah*) and knower of secrets (*haqaiq o maarif agah*), while considering himself merely as a servant of the mendicants (*khadimul fuqara*). He also thanked the representative (*khadim*) for several items – six turbans, six rosaries of sandalwood, jasmine oil and other sacred gifts (*tabarrukat*) – which he had received from him. He also sent an offering (*nazr*) to the representative, with a request to perform the prayers (*fatiha*) at the shrine on his behalf and to remember him in his prayers.[21] (Appendix B).

We come across an interesting letter from Syed Dargahi Qadiri, the head priest of the shrine of Shah Daula at Sadhura, which was written to Syed Murad in response to a communication and sacred gifts (*tabarrukat*). The writer addresses Syed Murad as holder of virtues and unity (*khusasiat wa ittehad dastgah*). He states that, as per the traditions and practices (*dastur-ul-amal*) of this shrine, the spiritual heads did not send offerings (*nazr-o-niyaz*) to any other place (or perhaps do not offer the same in person) and, therefore, he should be exempted from the task. But he requests that the addressee should keep in touch, because it was through letters that half the meeting became possible. It is one the best written letters as the style is unique and it is transcribed on the finest quality paper bearing gold petals.[22] Syed Ahmad Gilani, who was most probably related to the Uch branch of the Qadiri order, has also referred to the representative of the shrine as holder of unity (*yagangat dastgah*), thanked him for the sacred relics, expressed a passionate desire to visit the shrine for circumambulation (*tawaf*) and requested him to regularly pray for him.[23] Muhammad Bhadan Shah (or Bhawan Shah), a descendant of Shaikh Bahauddin Zakariya of Multan, thanked Syed Masud for sending the sacred gifts (*tabarrukat*) and dispatched the stipulated offerings (*nazr*) through a bill of exchange (*hundi*).[24] It may be noted that during the seventeenth regnal year of Muhammad Shah, the officials of the grain house (*bulghur khana*) of the Ajmer shrine, acting on the recommendation of the *Qazi-ul-Quzat* and the orders of Muazzam Khan, assigned 20 measures (*asar*) of grain and a daily allowance (*yomia*) of one rupee from the endowment (*waqf*) for Muhammad Baqar and eleven women from the family of Shaikh Bahauddin Zakariya, who were on a pilgrimage to Ajmer and stayed there for a long time. This attitude of the people associated with the Ajmer shrine indicates the mutual respect between the adherents of the different sufi orders and shrines. This relation had developed owing to the efforts of Syed Murad, the representative (*khadim/vakil*) of Muhammad Bhadan Shah, as is evident from the latter's expression of gratitude for the valuable assistance.[25]

In another letter, Malik Bahadur Ghulam Qadir belonging to the Afghan tribe of Kakars (an old resident of Hissar, but then residing at Thanesar as well as a slave (*ghulam*) of Shah Qamis Azam Qadiri, a descendant of Ghaus Pak of Shikarpur) expressed his devotion to Khwaja Muinuddin Chishti and thanked his representative (*khadim*) for bestowing the sacred gifts (*tabarrukat*) on him.[26] During the seventeenth regnal year of Muhammad Shah, Syed Muhammad Yusuf, son of Syed Mahmud Qadiri from the Banori shrine, and Fateh Muhammad Qadiri, the son of Hasan Mahmud Qadiri of Karnal, sent similar letters to their representative at the Ajmer shrine.[27] It may be added that the high ranking Mughal officers, who were serving in Punjab during the first half of the eighteenth century, treated themselves as the devotees of the Ajmer shrine. Two famous governors of the province – Abdul Samad Khan and Zakariya Khan[28] – sent letters expressing gratitude to their representative in reverential tone and also dispatched offerings (*nazar*) through bills of exchange (*hundi*). One of the governors of Punjab was a disciple of Shaikh Muhammad Salim Shah Chishti. Following the example of the governors, their non-Muslim *diwans* viz. Kadumal (Kaura Mal) and Lakhpat Rai,[29] have shown the same veneration towards the Ajmer shrine.[30] (Appendix C)

Devotees from Multan and Sind

The influence of Khwaja Nur Muhammad Muharvi extended beyond Punjab to the neighbouring areas of Baluchistan, Sind, Multan and the North West Frontier Province. It is necessary to mention some prominent local figures who were linked with the Muharvi Chishti branch and, as a result, had established devotional contacts with the Ajmer shrine. Foremost among them was the prominent Abbasi family of Sind. Nur Muhammad Khudayar Khan Salabat Jang Abbasi (who was given the title of Shah Quli Khan by Nadir Shah) held the governorship of Thatta.[31] Although his ancestors were the followers of Shaikh Muhammad Mahdi of Jaunpur, his father had become a disciple of Khwaja Nur Muhammad Muharvi and most probably named his son Nur Muhammad after his spiritual mentor. The seal of Khudayar Khan Abbasi bore the phrase *Zi-lutfi Nur Muhammad* (due to the blessings of Nur Muhammad). He used to send Rs.1000 annually as offerings (*nazr-o-niyaz*) out of which Rs.500 was exclusively meant for the cooking of cauldron (*deg*) and the remaining amount was treated as offering (*nazr*) for the representative (*khadim/vakil*). His son Khudadad Khan and other relatives – Ghulam Hussain Abbasi, Fazil Khan Abbasi, Athar Khan Abbasi, Muradyar Khan Abbasi, Ahmadyar Khan Abbasi and officials named Lutfullah Hussaini, Diwan Muhammad Maqsood, Shaikh Azizullah, Chankamal and Qasim Kotwal – followed the example of their elders and masters in cultivating relations with the Ajmer shrine. All of them addressed Syed Murad and his son Syed Masud as *vakil-i-dargah*, *pir*, *sajjadah nishin*, centre of promotion of mysticism (*farogh kashnai-i-tasawwuf*), holder of unity etc. On one occasion, the women belonging to the family of the ruler of Sind desired that they be remembered in prayers and letters.[32] (Appendix D)

The letter written by Sultan Khan of Dera Haji Khan is interesting and beautifully written. Addressing Syed Murad as *vakil-i-dargah* and *sajjadah nishin*, it informs him that a copy of the Quran (perhaps written by Sultan Khan himself, as the writing of the Quran had become a practice among the nobles of the period) kept in a box and placed on an elephant, along with a *hundi* of Rs.5000, had been dispatched under the custody of Shaikh Hidayatullah (*sawar*), along with the details in a separate written statement (*fard*). The letter instructs that the Quran be kept in the shrine and three reciters (*qaris*) be employed to recite ten chapters (*parahs*) on a payment of Rs.5 each. After offering the prayer (*fatiha*), the Quran was to be offered to the soul of the Holy Prophet and in the name of Khwaja Muinuddin Chishti and his own presence (*hazri*) was to be registered at the shrine. An officer named Fateh Chand and one Hafiz Shihabuddin were sent as escorts, with instructions to take care of their charge. Syed Murad was requested to keep a vigil over his affairs, to pray regularly for him and to send some dust of the shrine along with sacred gifts (*tabarrukat*).[33] No doubt, the entire act was a unique expression of devotion (*aqidat*). (Appendix E)

We come across another letter (*arzdasht*) that is written on a costly paper bearing golden petals. It was sent by Haji Khan Baloch of Dudai tribe who was a landed magnate (*zamindar*) of Multan.[34] He has addressed Syed Murad as the possessor of miraculous and spiritual powers (*karamat-o-vilayat imbatah*). He thanked his representative (*vakil*) for the gifts (*tabarruk*), requested him to remember him in regular prayers and assured him of sending offerings in the near future through a trusted person so that they were delivered safely. Sultan Ali Khan, son of Ishaq Ali Khan, the *diwan* of Multan, and two of his non-Muslim officers Megh Nath and Karam Chand sent offerings (*niyaz*) and expected prayers for their welfare. After the death of Haji Khan Baloch, his son and successor Ghazi Khan Baloch, continued to keep in touch with their representatives (*vakils/khadims*) at the Ajmer shrine. Interestingly, his seal bore the phrase regarding four companions of Prophet Muhammad (Chaharyar-i-Muhammad), perhaps to counter the growing influence of Shias in that area.[35] A letter of Bhaikhan Muhammad Shafi, the son of Syedul Khan of Khudabad (Thatta), also bore the same seal. This letter of gratitude mentions Birbal as the name of the bearer (*qasid*) of the sacred gifts (*tabarrukat*).[36]

We come across letters from the prominent and influential families of the area. One such letter (*arzdasht*) has been sent by Sanjar Khan, the head of Daudpotra family. It is addressed to Syed Murad to whom he expresses his devotion towards Khwaja Muinuddin Chishti. In another letter, his son Sadiq Khan informed his representative (*vakil*) from Shikarpur about the change of his address and desired that the future correspondence be directed to the new place of residence. A letter of authorization (*vikalatnama*) bearing the seals of several persons – Sanjar Khan, Muhammad Sadiq, Muhammad Fazil, Muhammad Ikhtiyar Khan, Mubarak Khan, Maroof Khan and Murad Khan – accepted Syed Murad as their representative (*vakil*) at the Ajmer shrine. This indicates that the entire family of Daudpotras was ardent follower of Khwaja Muinuddin Chishti and had signed the above document during one of its visits to Ajmer. Later on, when Fazil Khan received a robe of honour (*khilat*) from Syed Murad, he dispatched two bundles (*than*) of Karbalai (a costly and famous cloth of the time) to the said representative (*vakil*) whom he considered as a blesser of virtues (*faizrasan*). On one occasion, Khan Muhammad Daudpotra, a member of the same family, presented a tent (*shamiana*) with four silver maces (*chob*) for the Ajmer shrine. This was done through the representative (*vakil*) Syed Masud, who was addressed with the usual honorific titles. During the twentieth regnal year of Muhammad Shah (1738-39), Bazullah Khan (the son of Fazil Khan) was thrilled on receiving sacred gifts (*tabarrukat*) from the Ajmer shrine.[37] Letters from Ikhlas Khan (eighth regnal year of Aurangzeb) and Mahmud Khan (forty sixth regnal year of Aurangzeb), of Qasur – both of whom were the relatives of Abdullah Khan Khweshgi, the author of *Marij-ul-Vilayat* – were addressed to Syed Jafar, the father of Syed Murad. These were perhaps the earliest documents under reference. They reveal that the letters of authorization (*vikalatnamas*) of princes and grandees were procured through petty officials.[38]

Devotees: Elite and Ordinary

The rulers of the principality of Malerkotla, who were the descendents of Shaikh Sadr-i-Jahan Suhrawardi,[39] showed devotion towards the Ajmer shrine. In their letters, Nawab Sher Muhammad Khan nd Nawab Muhammad Umar Khan ddressed Syed Murad as the Kaaba o both the worlds (*Kaaba har do jahan*). They used to send regular offerings (*nazr-o-niyaz*) which ranged from Rs.500 to Rs.5000.[40] According to tradition, Nawab Sher Muhammad Khan had reservations, and even opposed, the brutal killing of the sons of Guru Gobind Singh.[41] Leters of other prominent persons of Punjab and those who servd the Mughal government include Hadi Ali Khan and Hidayaullah Khan, both o whom were the sons of Amir Khan. Initially theyaccepted Syed Hasan, the brother o Syed Murad, as their reprsentative (*vakil*), but later shiftedin favour of Syed Murad. Referring to the Ajmer shrine as the placeof prostration for angels, they desired to bow and offer their respects (*kornish* and *taslim*) to the representative (*khadim/vakil*). In 1130 AH/ 1717 AD Mir Muhammad Hadi, a natie of Lalpur (Rohtak), had signed a leter of authorization (*vikalatnama*). Ibrahim Khn and Kamal Kan, the sons of amal Muhammad Khan and hs brothers (all of whom belonged to Kamalgarh) had signed their letters of authorization (*vikalatnamas*) during thei visit to Ajmer. A similar documentwith regard to Syed Fateh, the servant o Izzuddaulah Khan Alam, beongs to the seventh regnal year (1725) of Muhammad Shah. Letters fm Din Muhammad Barua and Saikh Azizullah of Samaa were written in grtitude after receiving the sacred gifts (*tabarrukat*) from their reresentative (*vakil*).[42]

It is interestig to note that, quite often, the residents of a village acted in a collective manner while establishing their relation with the Ajmer shrine. The letter f authorization (*vikalatnama*), which was pepared by the people of village Kohna (*sarkar* Hissar) bore the seals ofMuhammad Ujali Khan Farruhshahi, Malik Khattab Khan of theAfghan Kakar tribe and Ialdarmir, a non-Muslim wose seal bor the phrase 'dust of the foot of the Prophet (*khak pai Musafa*). Other signatories included several members of the Afghan Kakar tribe and local officials such as *chaudharis*, *qanungos*, *mqaddams* and easants (*mzarian*), indicating that the message of equality emanated from the sufi shrines. We come across a similar document from the residents of village Shahabad (*chakla* Sirhind). It bears the sel of Shaikh Achhu along with tenty other signatories including Syeds, *qazis, khwajas, zamindas* and pofessiona groups like blacksmiths (*ahangar*) and *noorbaf*. The document also contains the signature of one Ugar Sahani. Documents ofthe same category have come from several places in Punjab, viz. Bajwara (Hshiarpur), Jlandhar Dab, Dipalpur Abohar, Fazila, Jhajja and Sisa. Anothr document, hough in the name of two representatives (*khadims/ vakils*) and belonging to a later period, has come from the people of Dadri.[43] (Appendix F) Thse documents show that the Chishti order was deeply ooted in Punjab and the neighbourig areas.

When we consider the social composition of the devotees of the Ajmer shrine, we encounte a cosmopolitan situation. On the one hand, we see the upper classes (*ashraf*) among the Muslim who included Syes, Shaikhs, governmet functonaries and indigenous landed gentry. On the other hand, we also find the members of the lower social strata including artisans of various kinds. All these people, irrespective of the social rank and religious affiliation, displayed unbounded respect for Khwaja Muinuddin Chishti nd deep attachment to the Ajmer shrine. They did no hesitate to avail of the services of the caretakers (*khuddam*) during the course of their pilgrimage to Ajmer and even when they ere confined to their homes in different parts of north India. Hindus, particularly those serving under high-ranking Muslim ruling elite, displayed a considerable enthusiasm in their devotion to the Ajmer shrine, as is indicated by their regular offerings and requests for blessings of both the worlds (*din-o-duniya*). We have already examined the presence of a fair number of Hindus in the correspondence (*vikalatnamas*) of the caretakers (*khuddam/vakils*). These Hindu officers were Raja Sabha Chand 'Nadar' (*diwan* of Zulfiqar Khan, who held the *wizarat* of the Mughal empire in the early eighteenth century)[44] who was also the disciple of Bahlol Barki Chishti (a spiritual successor of Miran Shah Bhikh of Jalandhar), Lakhpat Rai (the *diwan* of Abdul Samad Khan, the governor of Punjab), Izaldarmir who was associated by Ujali Khan, Karam Chand and Megh Nath (who were the *diwans* of Ghazi Khan and Haji Khan), Kadumal and Shambhu Prasad (the *diwan* of Khudayar Khan Abbasi and Khudadad Khan Abbasi, the governors of Thatta), Gulab Rai Allahyar Khani and Bhawani Ram of Sodhra-Ibrahimabad.[45] (Appendix G)

In addition to their belief in God, the people of Punjab were devoted to mystics belonging to different sufi orders and the cult of shrines. It is therefore not surprising that they had deep reverence for Khwaja Muinuddin Chishti and equally strong devotion to the Ajmer shrine.

In the process, they developed intimate relations with the spiritual heads (*sajjadah nishin*) and the caretakers (*khuddam*) of the shrine. This relation was based on two pillars, attachment (*nisbat*) and respect (*adab*), which paved the way for spiritual progress. They believed that it was only due to the intercession and prayers of their representatives (*khuddam*) that they could earn the blessings of Khwaja Muinuddin Chishti and ensure the fulfillment of their vows. They accepted the services of the caretakers (*khuddam*) in providing guidance during their pilgrimage (*ziarat*) to the Ajmer shrine. Even when devotees were unable to travel all the way to Ajmer from their native places, they could depend on their representatives (*khadim/vakil*) for performing all the rituals on their behalf, for remembering them regularly in their prayers and for dispatching the sacred relics (*tabarruk*) through messengers. In return, the representatives were entitled to the payment of remuneration (*nazr-o-niyaz*) which was remitted with respect and devotion. Irrespective of all social and cultural divisions, the people of Punjab signed bonds (*vikalatnamas*) – individually and collectively – particularly during the eighteenth century. They had been inspired by the Chishti examplers of Punjab to develop intimate devotional links with the shrine of Khawaja Muinuddin Chishti at Ajmer, which had emerged as a centre of spiritualism and communal harmony.

NOTES AND REFERENCES

1. For details, see Saiyid Athar Abbas Rizvi, *A History of Sufism in India*, 2 Vols., Munshiram Manoharlal, New Delhi, 1978-1983; Khaliq Ahmad Nizami, *Tarikh-i-Mashaikh Chisht*, Nudwat-ul-Musannifin, Delhi, 1953; Khaliq Ahmad Nizami, *Some Aspects of Religion and Politics in India during the Thirteenth Century*, Idarah-i-Adabiyat-i-Delli, Delhi, Reprint, 1974; Carl W. Ernst, *Sufi Martyrs of Love: The Chishti Order in South Asia and Beyond*, Palgrave Macmillan, New York, 2002; Syed Liyaqat Hussain Moini, *The Chishti Shrine of Ajmer: Pirs, Pilgrims and Practices*, Publication Scheme, Jaipur, 2004.
2. Syed Liyaqat Hussain Moini, 'Akbar and Ajmer Shrine,' *Islam and Modern Age*, (Zakir Husain Institute of Islamic Studies, Jamia Millia Islamia, New Delhi), Vol.XXXV, No.1, February 2005, pp. 121-136.
3. Syed Liyaqat Hussain Moini, *The Chishti Shrine of Ajmer*, pp. 1-35.
4. Khaliq Ahmad Nizami, *The Life and Times of Shaikh Fariduddin Ganj-i-Shakar*, Idarah-i-Adabiyat-i-Delli, Delhi, Reprint, 1973, pp.67-78; Saiyid Athar Abbas Rizvi, *A History of Sufism in India*, Vol. I, pp. 114-189; Carl W. Ernst and Bruce B. Lawrence, *Sufi Martyrs of Love: The Chishti Order in South Asia and Beyond*, pp. 64-83.
5. Haji Najmuddin Nagauri, *Manaqib-i-Mahbubin*, Rampur, 1389 AH, p. 52.
6. Khaliq Ahmad Nizami, *Tarikh-i-Mashaikh-i-Chisht*, p. 479.
7. Haji Najmuddin Nagauri, *Manaqib-i-Mahbubin*, pp. 53-54.
8. Gul Muhammad Marufi Karkhi, *Takmila-i-Siyar-ul-Auliya*, Delhi, 1312 AH/

1894 AD, p. 137.

9. Haji Najmuddin Nagauri, *Manaqib-i-Mahbubin*, pp. 105-127.
10. Ibid., p. 227; Maulana Imamuddin, *Nafais-ul-Salikin*, Lahore, 1868, p. 176.
11. The erudition and eloquence of Khwja Sulaiman Taunsawi attracted even the non-Muslims, including the Sikhs, who sought to discuss spiritual matters with him. Though he fell into ecstasy on recalling the Punjabi romance of Hir and Ranjha, yet he asserted that the *shariat* was superior to mysticism and that union with God could be achieved by divine grace which was superior to asceticism. Haji Najmuddin Nagauri, *Manaqib-i-Mahbubin*, pp. 288-289.
12. Ibid., pp. 369-375.
13. These documents are found in the Syed Murad-Syed Masud Collection. The present writer has consulted these documents through the courtesy of his brother-in-law (who is a direct descendant of Syed Murad) and some other custodians. These documents are bound in volumes called registers. Each register has been provided with a number. So is the case with every document in a register. In the references given below, the first number pertains to the register and the second one applies to the document.
14. Syed Liyaqat Hussain Moini,'The Hindus and the Dargah of Ajmer AD 1658-1737,' in *Art and Culture*, Vol. I, Ed., A.J. Qaisar and S.P. Verma, Publication Scheme, Jaipur, 1993, pp. 155-163; Syed Liyaqat Hussain Moini, 'The Hindus and the Dargah of Ajmer AD 1737-1857,' in *Art and Culture*, Vol. II, Ed., A.J. Qaisar and S.P. Verma, New Delhi, 1996; these articles have been combined and revised by the present writer in his book, *The Chishti Shrine of Ajmer*, pp. 53-95.
15. It seems certain that Guru Gobind Singh joined Bahadur Shah at some point when the prince was marching from Lahore to Agra in order to contest the throne with his brother, Azam Shah. The Guru might have received an official rank and might have been present when the battle was fought (18 June 1707) at Jajau, between Agra and Dholpur. William Irvine, *Later Mughals*, Vol. II, Ed., Jadunath Sarkar, Munshiram Manoharlal, New Delhi, Reprint, 1971, pp.89-90; also see, Zahiruddin Malik, *The Reign of Muhammad Shah 1719-1748*, Asia Publishing House, Bombay, 1977, p. 51.
16. Register No. 11, Document No. 11.
17. Register No. 5, Document Nos. 2, 3, 3b, 6b, 39; even a noble Zaman Khan of Jaunpur employed the same lines on his seal. Register No. 5, Document No. 47.
18. *Oriental College Magazine*, Vol. 14, 1965, pp. 246-247.
19. Syed Muhammad Murad (1638-1737) belonged to the community of custodians, which was attached to the Ajmer shrine since its inception. His great grandfather Shaikh Chandan was a man of influence as he had received 140 *bighas* as land grant (*madad-i-maash*) from Akbar. His father Syed Jafar was a well known *khadim* and was held in high esteem by the ruling elite. Syed Murad appears to have held a *mansab* and served as newswriter (*swanih nigar*) of Ajmer for sometime during the reign of Muhammad Shah. Owing to his influence, he procured *vikalatnamas* from

prominent Mughal nobles, both Hindus and Muslims. Syed Liyaqat Hussain Moini, *The Chishti Shrine of Ajmer*, p. 55.

20. After the death (1265) of Shaikh Farid, his tomb at Pakpattan began to develop gradually as a popular shrine. His direct descendants held the spiritual headship (*sajjadah nishin*) during the subsequent centuries. The Tughluq rulers not only constructed a magnificent building, but also bestowed land grants for its maintenance. The spiritual head (*sajjadah nishin*) became instrumental in agrarian expansion among the neighbouring pastoral tribes and, in this role, came to be known as the *diwan*. The shrine performed the historical role of connecting the rustic clans politically with the Delhi-based state and religiously with Islam. Richard M. Eaton, 'The Political and Relgious Authority of the Shrine of Baba Farid,' in *Essays in Islam and Indian History*, Ed., Richard M. Eaton, Oxford University Press, Delhi, 2000, pp. 203-224.
21. Register No. 5, Document Nos. 4, 5; it appears that the spiritual heads (*sajjadah nishins*) of prominent shrines sought the approval for their succession from the custodians (*khadims*) at the Ajmer shrine. The spiritual head (*diwan*) of the Ajmer shrine himself sought such approval from the custodians. Syed Liyaqat Hussain Moini, *The Chishti Shrine of Ajmer*, pp. 18, 126.
22. Register No. 5, Document No. 6a.
23. Register No. 5, Document No. 1.
24. The most characteristic credit institution in India was the bill of exchange (*hundi*), which promised payment after a specified period, normally two months or less at a particular place. It also allowed a discount which included interest, insurance charges and cost of transmission of money. Bills of exchange, rather than cash, increasingly became the standard form of payment in major commercial transactions. In long distance trade, this form of payment not only met the requirements of an expanding demand for credit, but reduced the risks involved in the transmission of cash to distant places. Tapan Raychaudhuri and Irfan Habib, *The Cambridge Economic History of India*, Vol. I, *c.1200-c.1750*, Orient Longman, Reprint, 2004, p. 346.
25. Register No. 5, Document no. 7; Register No. 13, Document Nos. 81, 83.
26. Register No. 5, Document No. 24.
27. Register No. 5, Document No. 6b, 9.
28. Abdus Samad Khan, who was related to Nizamul Mulk and Itimad-ud-Daula I, served as the governor of the Mughal province of Punjab from 1713 to 1726. His son Zakariya Khan held this governorship from 1726 to 1745, while Multan was added to his charge in 1739. During their administration, the Sikh rebellion was ruthlessly suppressed. But the region suffered from widespread unrest among *zamindars*, economic dislocation and breakdown of the *jagirdari* arrangements. For detailed discussions, see Jadunath Sarkar, *Fall of the Mughal Empire*, Vol. I, Orient Longman, Reprint, 1971, pp. 116-119; Muzaffar Alam, *The Crisis of Empire in Mughal North India: Awadh and the Punjab 1707-1748*, Oxford University Press, Delhi, 1986, pp. 134-203.

29. Lakhpat Rai, who served as the *diwan* of Punjab during the governorship of Zakariya Khan, led repressive measures against the Sikhs. On the other hand, Kaura Mal, who served as the *diwan* of the province during the governorship of Muinul Mulk, adopted a friendly posture towards the Sikhs and rose to be the governor of Multan. Hari Ram Gupta, *History of the Sikhs*, Vol. II, Munshiram Manoharlal, New Delhi, Third Revised Edition, 1978, pp. 74-82, 98-110.
30. Register No. 5, Document Nos. 13, 14.
31. The ancestors of Khudayar Khan Abbasi had risen from the position of holders of land grants (*madad-i-maash*) to that of *zamindars* and chieftains. During the reign of Farrukh Siyar, Khudayar Khan received a *mansab*, title and honours. Owing to his victory over the ruler of Kalat, he received the title of Khan Bahadur Salabat Jang and a *mansab* of 5000. In 1736, he was made the governor of Thatta and was conferred with the *sarkar* of Bhakkar. He refused passage to Nadir Shah for invading India via Kabul. On returning to Kabul after the sack of Delhi, Nadir Shah attacked the territories of Khudayar Khan and reached Dera Ghazi Khan. Though Khudayar Khan took shelter in the fort of Amarkot, yet he surrendered to the invader. Nadir Shah returned one-third of Khudayar Khan's territory to him and distributed the remaining to the Daudpotras and *zamindars* of Bhakkar. Towards the end of the eighteenth century, the place was still held by the descendants of Khudayar Khan Abbasi. Shahnawaz Khan and Abdul Hayy, *Maasir-ul-Umara*,Vol. I, English Translation, H. Beveridge and Baini Prashad, Second Edition, Janaki Prakashan, Patna, 1979, pp. 817-819.
32. Register No. 5, Document Nos. 15a-b, 16, 17, 18a-b, 19, 20, 21, 31, 32, 38, 41, 45, 60; Register No. 11, Document No. 41; Register No. 12, Document Nos. 26, 27, 28, 29, 45.
33. Register No. 5, Document No. 28; Register No. 12, Document No. 25.
34. The class of *zamindars* formed the upper crust of rural society in Mughal India. Owing to possession of military power, they enjoyed several social and economic privileges on a hereditary basis. They also competed with the Mughal state in the appropriation of agricultural surplus. They have been classified into three categories viz. chieftains, intermediary and primary *zamindars*. S. Nurul Hasan, 'Zamindars Under the Mughals,' in *The Mughal State 1526-1750*, ed., Muzaffar Alam and Sanjay Subrahmanyam, Oxford University Press, New Delhi, 1998, pp. 284-298.
35. Register No. 5, Document Nos. 22, 23, 29, 30, 64.
36. Register No. 5, Document No. 42.
37. Register No. 5, Document Nos. 47, 48, 58, 62.
38. Register No. 5, Document Nos. 26, 27.
39. Shaikh Sadruddin, popular as Sadr-i-Jahan and Haidar Shaikh, was a native of Afghanistan. On migrating to Punjab, he enrolled himself as a disciple of a prominent Suhrawardi saint of Multan. He established himself as a saint at Malerkotla. He married the daughter of Bahlol Lodi and, having received nearly seventy villages in dowry, founded the principality of Malerkotla in the middle of the fifteenth century. His shrine has emerged

as an important place of pilgrimage. For details, see the article by Salim Muhammad in the present volume.

40. Register No. 5, Document Nos. 66, 67, 69, 70.
41. Nawab Sher Muhammad Khan (1672-1712) ruled Malerkotla as a feudatory chief of Aurangzeb and performed military services for the Mughal state. As a reward for his victory against the Rohillas, he was appointed the deputy *chakladar* of Sirhind and granted several villages as revenue assignment (*jagir*). He lodged a strong protest in the presence of Wazir Khan, the *chakladar* of Sirhind, against the draconian punishment to the younger sons of Guru Gobind Singh, Fateh Singh and Zorawar Singh. Nawab Iftikhar Ali Khan, *History of the Ruling Family of Shaikh Sadruddin Sadr-i-Jahan of Malerkotla 1449-1948*, Ed., R.K. Ghai, Punjabi University, Patiala, 2000, pp. 28-34.
42. Register No. 5, Document Nos.12, 13, 27, 42, 43, 49, 53, 33, 34, 35, 37.
43. Register No. 5, Document Nos. 8b, 10, 27, 51, 52, 55; Register No. 7, Document No. 398.
44. After the death of Bahadur Shah, the Mughal state made a conscious attempt to patronize the Khatris. Under Jahandar Shah and Farrukh Siyar, the Khatris obtained high positions. Sabha Chand, a mere letter writer (*munshi*) of the *wazir* Zulfiqar Khan, rose to the office of *diwan-i-khalisa*. However, he was dismissed and imprisoned when Farrukh Siyar began to punish the adherents of Zulfiqar Khan. Muzaffar Alam, op. cit., p. 170.
45. Register No. 3, Document No.34; Register No.5, Document Nos. 8, 22, 30, 33, 35, 37, 50, 53b, 57a-b, 65.

APPENDIX A

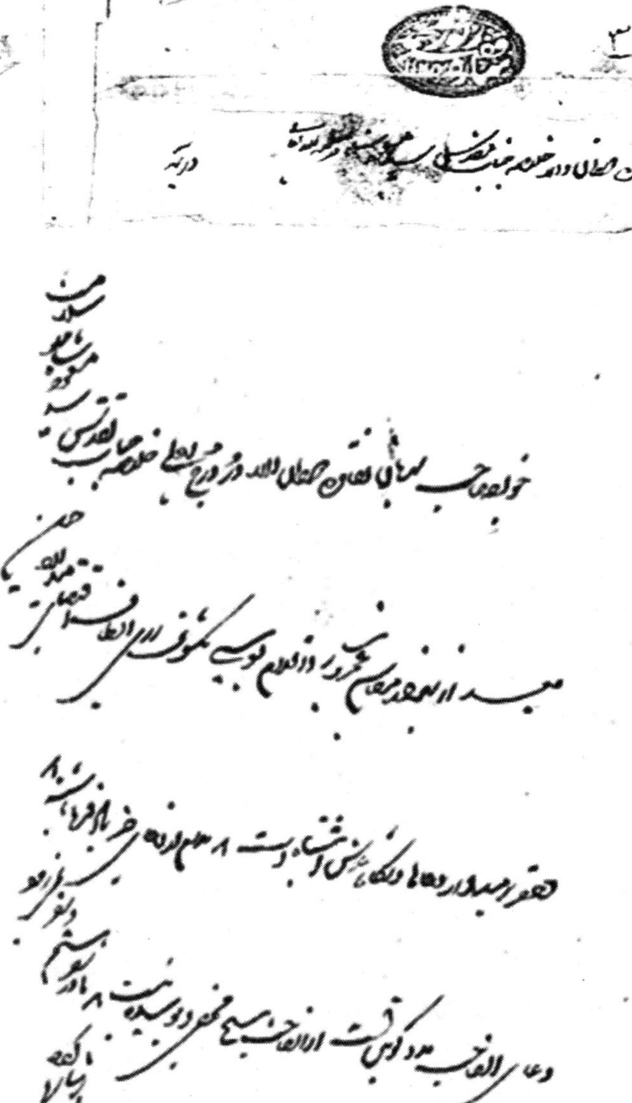

APPENDIX B

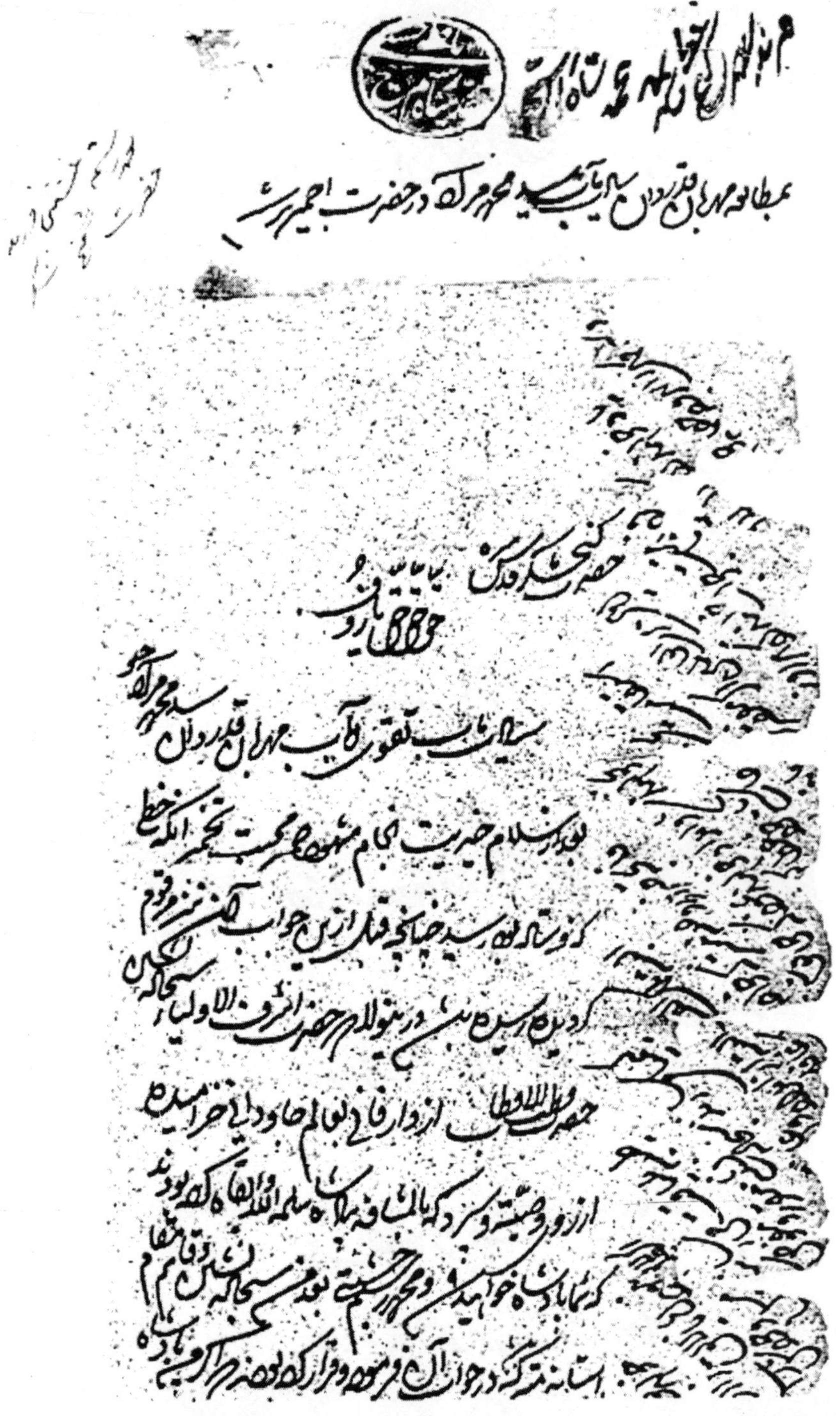

APPENDIX C

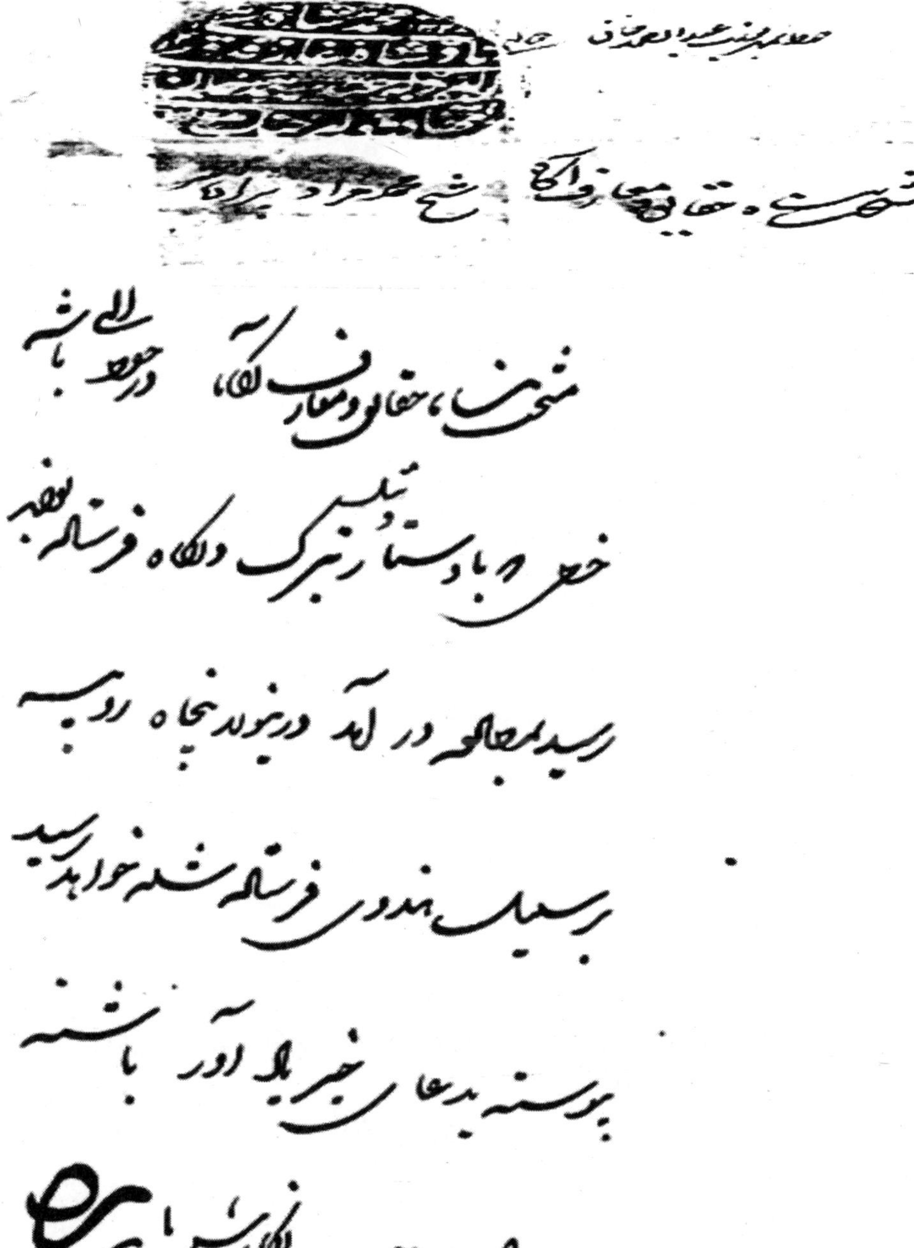

APPENDIX D

سید محمد برادر سید محمد جعفر سجاده نشین درگاه

حقایق و معارف آگاه سیادت و شرافت پناه

APPENDIX E

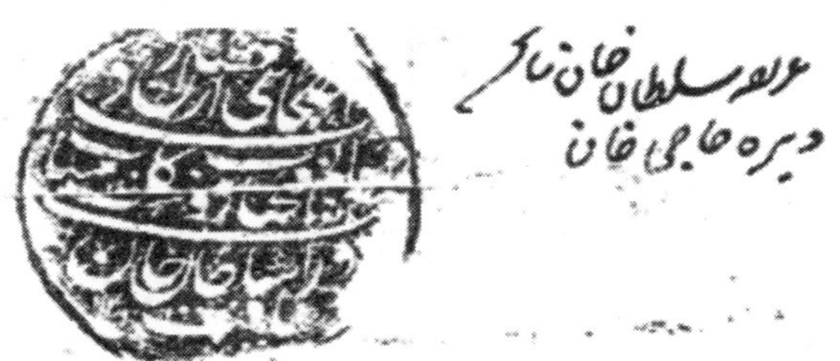

APPENDIX F

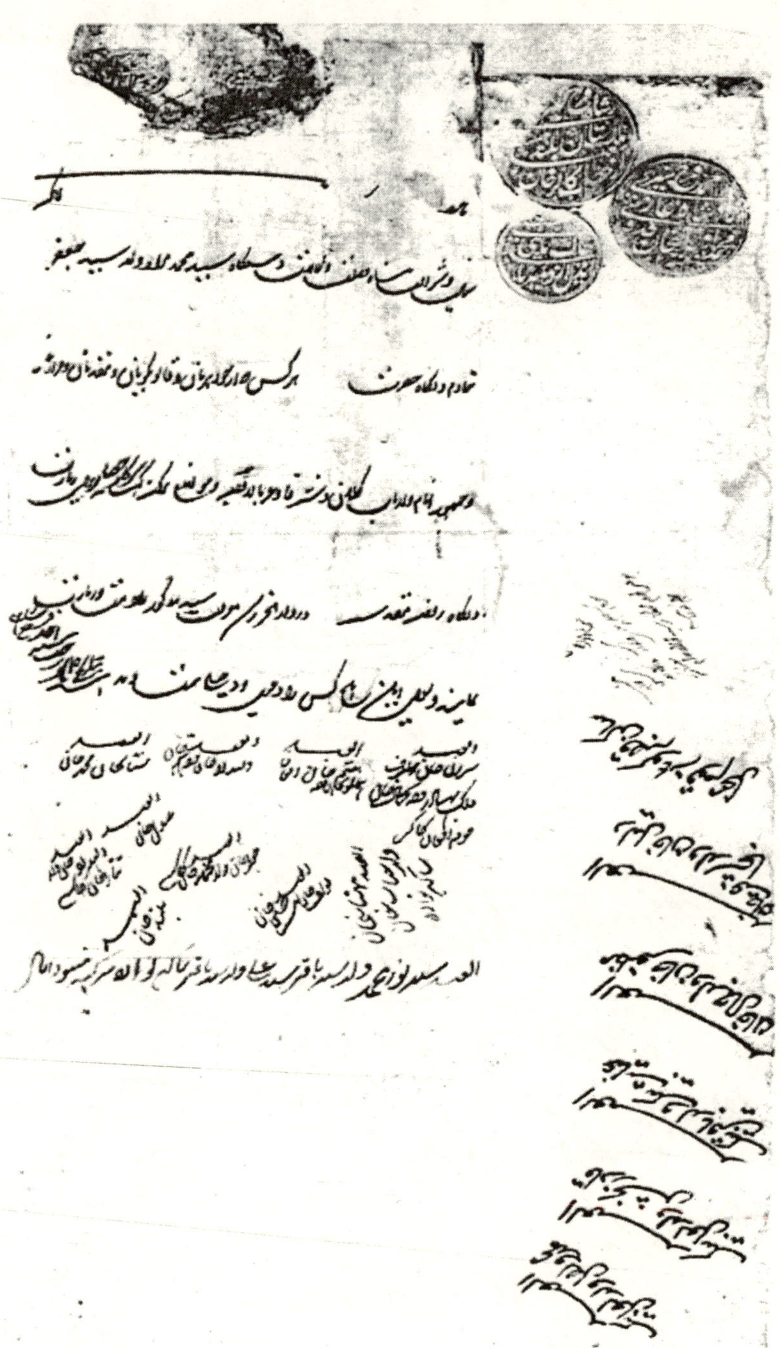

APPENDIX G

18

Historicity, Orality and the 'Lesser Shrines'

Popular Culture and Change at the Dargah of Panj Pir at Abohar

Yogesh Snehi

Punjab has had the precedence over other regions of India in receiving the influence of early sufi masters. Since eleventh century, this region has been a recipient of sufis from Shaikh Husain Zinjani to Shaikh Ali Hujwiri. Their presence not only popularised sufism but also gave rise to the dargah cult in this region. Among the sufis who had a long-term influence on the social milieu of the region were Shaikh Bahauddin Zakariya (Multan) and Shaikh Fariduddin Ganj-i-Shakar (Pakpattan). Besides these, the shrines of Shaikh Muinuddin Chishti (Ajmer), Shaikh Qutubuddin Bakhtiyar Kaki (Delhi), Shaikh Nizamuddin Auliya (Delhi), Lal Shahbaz Qalandar (Sehwan) and Syed Jalaluddin Bukhari (Uch) were equally popular. Many Punjab tribes have traced their conversion to Islam to the sufis of Punjab.[1]

In the centuries before the British arrived, networks of shrines loosely linked within the sufi orders spread through much of the province, as the descendants and successors (*khalifas*) of many prominent saints established their own hospices (*khanqahs*),[2] which in turn developed into new sufi shrines. Besides these imposing sufi shrines, there was an emergence of 'lesser shrines' dedicated to one or many, major or minor, sufi centres of medieval Punjab. While the shrines, like those of Shaikh Bahauddin Zakariya and Baba Farid had wide renown, those of many lesser saints had only the most localized significance, being associated with particular villages or tribes or, with particular instrumental needs, such as curing snake bite or driving away spirits (*jinn*) from possessed women. Such shrines varied widely not only in importance, but in religious rituals as well.[3] The networks became particularly dense in parts of the Indus valley; in south-western Punjab the shrines of the descendants of Syed Jalaluddin Bukhari of Uch dotted the countryside when the British arrived. Though loosely linked, each of these shrines maintained its distinctive identity.[4] They played a crucial role in the Islamization of the locality. To the Muslim rulers, they represented the local outposts of Islam. To the people, at large, they represented sources of power to all in need of superhuman intervention. They were open to people from all religious persuasions. This all-inclusive approach was the local face of Islam.[5] There was yet another practice of constructing 'memorial shrines' which gradually developed into distinctive centres of cultural practice, often denoting local as well as long-term geographical influences.

With regard to western Punjab, Gilmartin observes that its Islamic institutions reflected an interaction between the often 'tribal' organization of the localities and the Islamic tradition embodied in the culture of an imperial state. The religious devotions and the historical development at these institutions varied widely, but nearly all the major shrines that emerged in the centuries after the arrival of Islam served in some degree, as links in the larger 'cultural system' of Punjabi Islam or as hinges that flexed in two directions. In one sense, the shrines served as symbols of the distant, yet transcendent, cultural authority of the Muslim state. In another sense, the shrines embodied diverse local cultural identities, whose variety reflected both the diversity of ecological, social and kinship organization in Punjab and the diversity in the spiritual needs of the people.[6] The ubiquitousness of sufis in rural Punjab dramatised the centrality of 'sufi idioms' in rural religious life. If the saints served as mediators, they also embodied a pervasive ideal of religious authority. The saints buried at the shrines were not just mediators but exemplars as well, their lives dramatised in the innumerable hagiographic stories and tales that inhabited the world of rural Punjabi folklore. As exemplary patrons and intermediaries, they helped to shape a distinctive style of 'rural Islam'.[7] The folk writers had very little concern with Islamic theology, liturgy, mysticism, ontology, cosmology and even with the historical-mythical characters of Islamic tradition. The Muslim folk literature in Bengal (for example) became almost exclusively focused on the most popular object of their veneration and supplication during the trials and tribulations of their everyday life, namely the spiritual preceptor (*pir*).[8]

Eaton shows that during the reign of Tughluqs small memorial shrines dedicated to Baba Farid began appearing, scattered throughout the countryside of central Punjab. Significantly, he adds, these memorial shrines were built not by Tughluq sultans as were the main structures of the Ajodhan complex, but by the common people themselves.[9] The appearance of these shrines shows that a certain tract of the Punjab became identified with Baba Farid's spiritual kingdom (*wilayat*) which to his devotees was perceived as having specific geographic boundaries that bordered such domains of other saints.[10]

'Rural Islam' had another significant aspect which was much more pervasive and penetrated deep into Punjab. While west Punjab (Pakistan) became a major centre of emergence and dissemination of sufism in the medieval period, it was east Punjab (India) which was the recipient of the vast influence of sacred shrines in Sind, Multan, Bahawalpur and Montgomery districts of the colonial India. Among the frontier districts of east Punjab was the district of Ferozepur which experienced the direct influence of the shrines of Shaikh Bahauddin Zakariya, Baba Farid and others. Towns like Abohar, Fazilka and Jalalabad became active recipients of this influence. Abohar would form a common ground for the influence of sufism from Sind, Bahawalpur, Multan and Montgomery districts (now in Pakistan).[11] But the form in which sufism came and was disseminated in these regions was different from the major centres.

These traditions emerged in a localised framework, often adapting itself to an older tradition of the medieval period. Asim Roy categorises some of these as 'fictitious pirs' who emerged out of some old popular beliefs and practices associated with a particular locality or a site and sought to be Islamized through the protean process of pirification.[12] Often these processes would assimilate themselves into an earlier tradition like that of Khwaja Khizar. This saint is believed to ride upon a fish, which was adopted as a crest by the rulers of Oudh and appears on their coins. Possibly in this case there is also a survival of the fish-avatar of Vishnu.[13] Conversely, they would reinterpret themselves as in the case of *Panj Pir*. From the Hindu perspective, the cult of 'Panch Pirs' (five pirs) may have been inspired by the worship of the five Pandavas. Its Islamic source of inspiration is, interestingly enough, a Shia one: the reverence for the *panj tan i pâk* or 'five sacred bodies'viz. the Prophet Muhammad, his son-in-law Ali, their two sons Hasan and Husain, and Ali's spouse Fatima.[14] Such traditions have a mythical component and emerge through complex historical processes. Their complex framework renders the task of historicising these traditions difficult, as most of the information is derived from oral sources.

Keeping in view the above debates, the present study focuses on the 'lesser shrine' of Panj Pir at Abohar and its development in a specific social milieu. This shrine can more appropriately be categorised as a 'memorial shrine'. It offers a fascinating perspective on the emergence of such shrines throughout India. It will be our endeavour to trace the emergence and theorise the role of this shrine through textual and oral traditions and explore the continuity of tradition associated with it. We shall try to look into the complexities faced by a researcher when one tries to draw a trajectory of this *dargah* through historical and oral sources. It will also be pertinent to look at how sufi institutions survived in a part of the country in which the Muslim community was severely affected by the population movements following the partition (1947).[15]

Complexities of Partition

Partition of Punjab in 1947 into eastern and west Punjab led to the emergence of immense social complexities. We saw an unprecedented migration of millions of people across the Radcliffe Line. It gave rise to the exodus of the non-Muslims from west Punjab and Muslims from east Punjab.[16] A large number of refugees from Bahawalpur State and from Montgomery and Lahore districts entered India through the border along the Ferozepur district.[17] Among all the districts in Punjab, Ferozepur district accommodated the largest number of the refugees from Pakistan. Refugees from the Bahawalpur State entered from Fazilka and Abohar side, whereas those from the Montgomery District, mostly belonging to rural areas, entered from the Fazilka side. Those from the rural areas of Lahore district, entered from the Ferozepur and Jalalabad side. According to the 1951 Census, 3,49,767 refugees from Pakistan settled in the Ferozepur district (including the Moga and Muktsar tahsils that were transferred to Faridkot district in 1972).[18]

Displaced persons from Pakistan (selected districts) who settled in the Ferozepur (including Moga and Muktsar tahsils, transferred to Faridkot District in 1972)

District of Origin in Pakistan	*Persons*	*Males*	*Females*
Lahore	1,22,224	66,207	56,017
Sheikhupura	11,090	5,986	5,104
Montgomery	1,44,022	76,779	67,243
Lyallpur	17,960	9,576	8,381
Bahawalpur	34,030	19,315	14,715

Source: *Census of India, 1951, Punjab District Census Hand Book, Volume II,* Firozpur District, D-V, p. clxvi.

This migration not only affected the demographic, economic and political configurations but also led to a serious break in that social fabric of Punjab which had been woven through centuries of social and political changes. It led to the creation of boundaries in a social milieu which developed out of a long tradition of exchange between cultures and communities. While colonial Punjab was characterised by multi-faceted identities from different socio-religious groups, partition almost dissolved these identities. But the shared cultural past continues to live in the memories of Punjabi psyche and folklore.

Colonial Punjab was entirely different from the communal perspective presented for the partition of Punjab. For instance, *Hir*, which was versified by Waris Shah in the eighteenth century, exemplifies a cultural scenario where a sufi-poet draws characters from Punjabi folk tradition and continues to have an indelible imprint on the social psyche of Punjab.[19] Sufi shrines were centre of attraction for Hindus, Muslims and Sikhs alike. It was this social context which was badly shaken with the partition of Punjab. A local shrine of Panj Pir at Abohar was witness to one such social void. Partition led to the migration of the entire population of Muslims from this region, including the ones who were caretakers of this shrine. This shrine remained desolate for several years until 1950, when it was taken over by Ghela Ram Kamboj[20] who migrated to Abohar from Montgomery district of west Punjab. Today it is an important centre of pilgrimage for people throughout Punjab, Rajasthan and Haryana.[21] It would be important to understand why in the aftermath of partition, when Muslims en masse migrated to Pakistan, this shrine continues to attract people. In a majority of studies the survival of such shrines is seen in terms of its continued relevance to their followers' lives.[22] This relation and the adaptation of the shrine to bureaucratisation and systematisation in the post-partition scenario shall be crucial to our understanding of the dargah culture in Punjab.

Dargah of Panj Pir: Oral Traditions

Tradition of constructing dargahs of Panj Pir (five pirs) has been widespread across the Indian subcontinent. There is a 'Panj Pir Wali Mazar' in Jalandhar, besides the Panj Pir dargahs in Gurdaspur and Abohar in Punjab. Panj Pir are also venerated in Rajouri (Jammu). There are several dargahs of Panj Pir in Burdwan, Midnapore and Sonargaon in West Bengal. Besides these, there are Panj Pir graveyards in Shikarpur (Karachi) and Lahore in Pakistan. Several places like a village Panj Pir in Swabti (North-West Frontier Province) in Pakistan and Pir Panjal in Kashmir (India) owe their name to this common tradition. Panj Pir are also venerated across North-Western India through a network of 'memorial shrines' which often get coalesced with Hindu gods and goddesses. Interestingly at some places Panj Pir (*panchopirs*) represent a terminal synonym for five Hindu 'clan deities'.[23] But the names of Panj Pir differ from place to place.

> In some parts of the country the Hindus are fond of representing themselves as followers of the Panj Pirs or Five Saints. Who these five saints are is a matter which each worshipper decides according to his taste. Sometimes they are the five Pandavas; sometimes they are the five holy personages of Shiaism, viz. Muhammad, Fatima, Ali, Hasan and Husain; sometimes they are a selection of Musalman saints, as Khwaja Qutb ud-Din, Khwaja Muain-

> ud-Din Chishti, Shaikh Nizam-ud-Din Aulia, Nasir-ud-Din Abul Khair, and Sultan Nasir-ud-Din Mahmud or as Khwaja Khizr, Said Jalal, Zakaria, Lal Shahbaz and Farid Shakarganj.[24]

In fact, all the places across Punjab have different names associated with these five pirs. Even at places where all the pirs are associated with Muslim saints, large number of non-Muslims flock to their shrines for veneration. According to Blunt, the five are worshipped by some 53 castes in North India, of which some 44 are wholly or partly Hindus.[25] Most of them, however, do not identify all the Panj Pir. The Panj Pir dargah at Abohar has special significance in terms of understanding this tradition, because of the availability of oral traditions which relate and at times mythicise Panj Pir. Interestingly, Panj Pir have been a significant part of folk traditions in colonial Punjab (we will discuss it in the latter part of the discussion). Some colonial ethnographers like H.A. Rose (1911), R.C. Temple (1884) and W. Crooke (1896) have also documented this tradition. Thus, we have substantial oral information to relate it with documentary evidences and see the underlying contradictions within it. The earliest substantiated version of the tradition associated with 'Panj Pir dargah at Abohar' was recorded in the *Final Report on the Revision of Settlement of the Sirsa District, 1879-83*, reproduced in the *Gazetteer of Ferozepur District, 1915*.[26] This version narrates the event of arrival of the Panj Pir.

> ...the villagers have a tradition that many centuries ago it (Abohar) was held by a Rajput Raja Abramchand. They tell that his horses were one day carried off in a raid (*dhar*) made by the Saiyads of Uchan (Uch) towards Multan, and as he (the Raja) had no son, his daughter dressed like a man, went after the raiders armed with sword and spear and gun and bow and arrow, and after various exploits brought back the spoil of Uchan (Uch) which consisted chiefly of horses. The Saiyads of Uchan (Uch), being holy men, endeavoured to get back their property by threatening to curse the spoilers, and forming a *mela* or cursing committee, they came and sat (on a) *dharna*, as it were, on the sand-ridge east of Abohar. But the Raja held out so long that the women of the Saiyads at Uchan (Uch) got tired of waiting for the return of their lords, and came in a body to look for them. When the Saiyads on the ridge saw their wives approaching they called down curses on all around, and they themselves and their wives and the inhabitants of the town all died on the spot. The *pakka* tomb of the women in the cemetery, and that of the holy men (*pir*) on the sand-ridge exist unto this day.[27]

Another colonial documentation of the tradition, though with slight modification, is found in Rose's Glossary (1911).

> Abohar was ruled by Raja Aya Chand who had an only daughter. On his death bed he expressed deep regret that he had no son to go to the Panj Piran at Uch in Bahawalpur and mount the horses there. His daughter

> courageously assured him that she would go and fetch the horses from Uch. So accompanied by a small band she went there and carried off the horses of the Panj Pir. They came after her and begged her to return them, but she refused and so they had to wait in patience for their return. The Pir's wives being tired of waiting followed their husbands to Abohar where with their beloved spouses they breathed their last, cursing the lady and the place.... The five Pirs were interred at a place in the village and near them the remains of their wives. The shrine contains the tombs of the five Pirs and those of their five wives which are surrounded by a brick wall, but have no roof. The administration of the Khanqah is carried on by two Musalman *faqirs* caste Lad (?). They keep it clean and light a lamp in the evening.[28]

Though both the versions give an almost similar narration, Rose names the Raja of Abohar as Aya Chand where as Revision Settlement of the Sirsa District names him as Raja Abramchand. The pirs supposedly belonged to Uch in Bahawalpur and arrived at Abohar to take back the horses recovered by the daughter of the Raja. Additionally, SFSR mentions the Panj Pir as Syeds. As regards the caretaker of the dargah is concerned, Rose's version says that its administration was undertaken by two Muslim *faqirs*. We shall discuss some other aspects of these versions in a subsequent part of the paper.

Another version narrated by the *sevadar* gives an alternate account of the reasons for which the Raja wished to obtain the horses of Panj Pir and their interlude with Ranjha and Baba Ramdev.[29] Raja Chander suffered from leprosy. On the recommendation of an astrologer he sent his soldiers to Pirepur (Multan) where the Panj Pir resided. They stole the horses of Panj Pir and took them to Abha Nagri. Raja bathed in the blood of these five horses and was cured of leprosy. When these Qadiri Panj Pir came to know about the theft of their horses, they began a journey to Abha Nagri. After crossing Bahawalnagar, they reached near river Chenab (?) where they met Ranjha. Impressed by the deep devotion of Ranjah, Panj Pir bestowed (*baksh*) him Hir. Panj Pirs then reached Pokharan in Rajasthan and rested at Baba Ramdev's residence...[30] This version weaves the narrative of two significant popular cultures of this region, one associated with the shrine complex of Baba Ramdev at Ramdevra (Rajasthan) and another associated with the literary tradition of Waris Shah. Dominique-Sila Khan has recently documented the Punjabi oral tradition of Panj Pir. Regarding the route taken by Panj Pir to reach Abohar, he narrates the following account which is also corroborated by the *sevadar* of the dargah.

> Characteristically, this tour starts in Multan, the abode of the Pirs.... From there the five saints intend to go to Abohar, the ruler of which has stolen their five horses. On their way they stop near Pokaran, where they meet Ramdev. They perform miracles in front of him by throwing on the ground

A poster on sale outside the Dargah of Panj Pir at Abohar

> their five tooth-brushes out of which grow five Pipal trees.[31] ...from Pokaran they go to Jalandhar, then to Ferozepur, and finally reach Abohar, where they try to get back their horse. However, the king does not behave well and the Pirs curse his city which immediately falls into ruins. Later on, a grave was built at this place to commemorate the five Pirs.[32]

Interestingly, the author himself questions the authenticity of the route.[33] But this account is important since it relates to the meeting of Panj Pir and Baba Ramdev and can be useful in determining the antiquity of the tradition. We shall delve on this issue in the latter part of our discussion.

The *sevadar* of the dargah at Abohar names Panj Pir as Baba Khwaja Khizar, Baba Shakar Ganj, Baba Zakariya Pir, Baba Syed Jalal Bukhari and Baba Lal Shah. In fact, the *sevadar* also relates these names with those mentioned by Waris Shah in his *Hir*.[34] These have been identified by Rizvi as Khwaja Khizar (the lord of all the waters), Baba Farid Shakarganj of Ajodhan/Pakpattan, Shaikh Bahauddin Zakariya of Multan, Makdum Jahaniyan Jalal Bukhari (Saiyyid Jalaluddin Bukhari of Uch) and Lal Shahbaz Qalandar of Sehwan (Sind). The version of Rizvi is a reiteration of Panj Pir mentioned by Waris Shah.[35] There are many other versions of Panj Pir in different parts of India which are, at times, related with mythical characters. In the small district of Benares, Crooke discovered five different lists of Panj Pir with eleven names.[36] The following table narrates some of these versions prevalent in Punjab.

Names of Panj Pir

R.C.Temple[37]	*Shangari and Puri*[38]	*Anonymous dictionary*[39]	*H.A. Rose*
Khwaja Qutbuddin Bakhtiar Kaki of Delhi	Ghazi Mian (Salar Masud)	Hazrat Baba Farid Shakarganj	Muham-mad
Khwaja Muainuddin Chishti of Ajmer	Zinda Ghazi	Hazrat Nizamuddin Auliya	Fatima
Shekh Nizamuddin Aulia of Delhi	Shaikh Farid	Hazrat Ali-ul- Hiwari (Shaikh Ali Hujwiri)	Ali
Nasiruddin Abul-khair Abdullah Ibn Umar Al-Baizavi	Khwaja Khizar	Shaikh Muinuddin Chishti, Ajmer	Hasan
Sultan Nasiruddin Mahmud	Pir Badar	Hazrat Shamas Tabrezi	Hussain

Rose mentions that the Bhattis of the Gujranwala District narrate their five saints as Shaikh Samail, Shah Daulat, Shaikh Fateh Ali, Pir Fateh Khan and Shah Murad, all patrons of the Bhatti race. In Ludhiana Khwaja Khizar, Durga Devi, Vishnu, Sakhi Sarwar and Guru Gobind Singh and in Shimla Guga Pir, Balaknath, Thakur, Sakhi Sarwar, and Shiv are worshipped as Panj Pir. 'Panjpirias' are found all over the province from Muzaffargarh to Delhi and there is a place in the Shahpur District, 10 miles south of Sahiwal (Montgomery), where a large fair is held every year in the honour of the Panj Pir. Some persons, wishing to be more specific, declare themselves to be followers of the *Chahar* Pir or Four Saints; by this is generally implied the four friends of the Prophet, whose admirers are found both among Musalmans and Hindus'.[40] The tradition of Panj Pir at Abohar shows close relation with the narration of Waris Shah. Interestingly Malkahans[41] (now in Montgomery/Sahiwal district of Pakistan) the village where Waris Shah had supposedly composed *Hir*[42] has geographical proximity with Abohar (see Map).[43] The map also reflects on the route supposedly taken by Panj Pir, which possibly formed the *wilayat* of this tradition.

Historicity and the Contradictions with Orality

Till now we have tried to comprehend the nature of the Panj Pir tradition, dargah at Abohar, its origin as reflected in the folklore, the break and continuity after partition and the emergence of a new scenario in which the dargah attains popularity in the realms of the society. In the following discussion we shall try to correlate these oral accounts with documentary evidence and try to see the contradictions and complexities which emerge out of it.

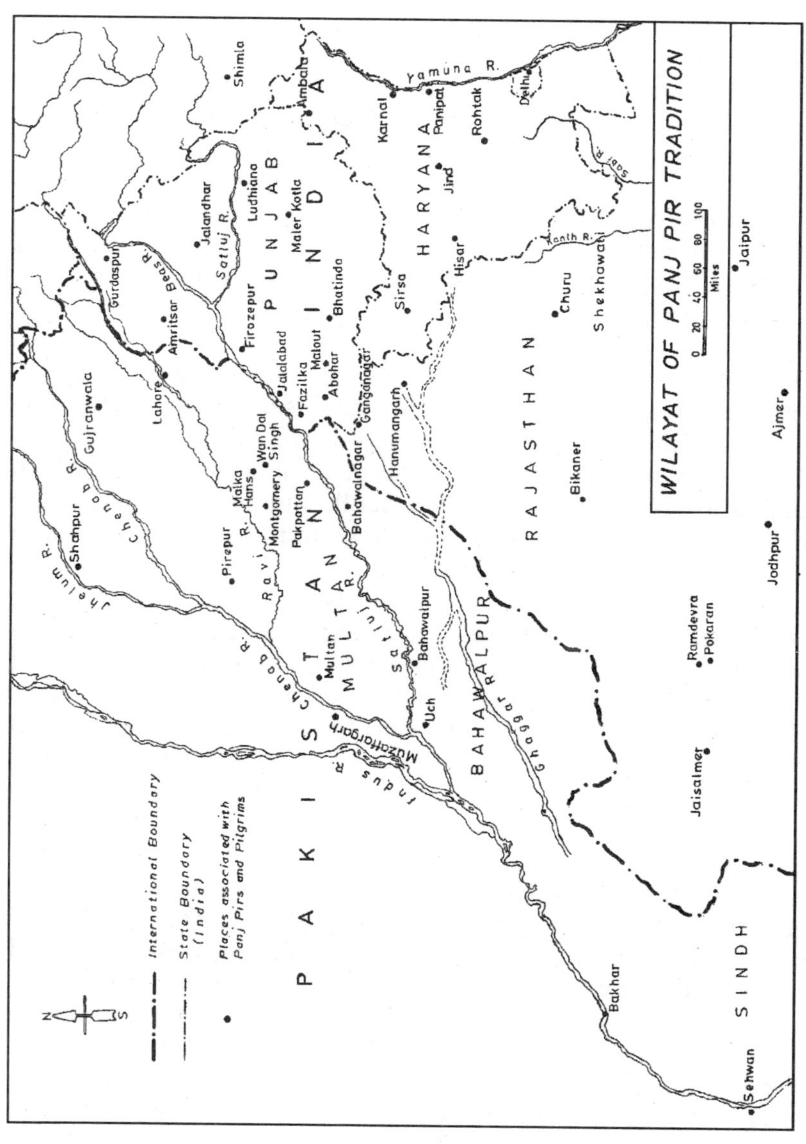
WILAYAT OF PANJ PIR TRADITION
International Boundary
State Boundary (India)
Places associated with Panj Pirs and Pilgrims
Miles
0 20 40 60 80 100
PAKISTAN
INDIA
PUNJAB
HARYANA
RAJASTHAN
MULTAN
BAHAWALPUR
SINDH
Shekhawati
Shimla
Ambala
Karnal
Panipat
Rohtak
Delhi
Jind
Hisar
Sirsa
Ludhiana
Jalandhar
Maler Kotla
Bhatinda
Firozepur
Gurdaspur
Amritsar
Lahore
Gujranwala
Jalalabad
Fazilka
Malout
Abohar
Ganganagar
Hanumangarh
Wan Dal Singh
Malka Hans
Montgomery
Pakpattan
Bahawalnagar
Pirepur
Shahpur
Multan
Bahawalpur
Uch
Muzaffargarh
Bakhar
Sehwan
Churu
Jaipur
Ajmer
Bikaner
Jodhpur
Ramdevra
Pokaran
Jaisalmer
Yamuna R.
Satluj R.
Beas R.
Ravi R.
Chenab R.
Jhelum R.
Indus R.
Ghaggar R.
Kanth R.
Sabi R.

The structure of the dargah as it exists today has no architectural significance in terms of its association with one or other forms of architecture. Rose gives the description of the dargah as it existed in the nineteenth century. 'The shrine contains the tombs of the five Pirs and those of their five wives which are surrounded by a brick wall, but have no roof.'[44] According to this description the graves of five Pirs and their wives are (apparently) contained within the main structure which is surrounded by a brick wall. But this account is not supported by the structure, as it exists today. The main structure merely contains the graves of five pirs and the graves of their wives are not part of this structure. Latter's graves are situated at a distance of about fifty metres from the main complex.[45] Possibly, the area under the main structure might have been larger earlier. But the graves of the pirs and their wives were never enclosed together inside a common walled structure.

The structure of dargah seems to be a reconstruction of an earlier structure which predates the colonial period. An examination of the walls and bricks used in the dargah present an interesting complexity.[46] There were three different types of bricks used in constructing the present structure. On the exterior-most side were the 'modern bricks' and there were two other types of bricks on the inner side, one of which belonged to the medieval period.[47] Another important aspect of the finding was the distinct type of bricks found outside the main compound.[48] Thus it becomes difficult to reach any conclusive argument to date the structure. The only thing which can be said with regard to the structure is that it was reconstructed out of an older structure. This argument is supported by analysis of the wall around the graves of pirs, which correlates to the medieval period, keeping in mind its thickness.[49] There is also an impression of a *mihrab* on the western wall of the dargah, which is prominently visible on the exterior side of boundary wall. Adjoining one wall around the graves is an old tree locally known as *van* (*Salvadora oleoides*). According to the *sevadar* of the dargah, the tree is more than 500 years old, which would mean that it was planted somewhere around fifteenth century.[50] The origin of the dargah in the fifteenth century is supported by another tradition of Baba Ramdev. As discussed earlier, Panj Pir supposedly stayed overnight with Baba Ramdev near Pokharan on their way to Abohar. The date associated with Panj Pir dargah can thus be worked on the basis of its linkages with the tradition of Baba Ramdev, which has been situated in this period. It is said that Mokal Singh (r.1419-1433), the ruler of Chittorgarh, the former capital of Mewar, was childless. Since Ramdev Pir had the reputation of a miracle-maker, he thought of inviting him to his kingdom and asking him for the boon of a son. However, instead of coming himself, the 'Pir of Runicha' delegated his uncle, whom he invested with supernatural powers.[51]

Dependence on the traditional accounts associated with Panj Pir and Baba Ramdev is, however, problematic. According to Rose's account Raja Aya Chand (Abram Chand according to Sirsa Settlement Report) ruled 'nearly nine hundred years ago'.[52] Further, the Patwari records present a complex picture as far as the existence of the dargah is concerned. Significantly, until 1965-66 the dargah was not entered as associated with Panj Pir. In 1922-23, a major part associated with Panj Pir today was entered as *shamlat patti bakhshian-makbuza ahl-i-Islam*,[53] while two others were under private ownership. In 1943-44, this entire area was entered as *shamlat*. But existence of the dargah is corroborated by Rose's account which predates the accounts of Patwari and of Nazar Masih.[54]

Position of Panj Pir as per the records of Patwari of Abohar

Item Number	*Area*	*Comments*
		1922-23
2173	01 bigha 17 biswa	Hakim, Haider and Ali s/o Wahib
2174	29 bigha	*shamlat patti bakhshian- makbuza ahl-i-Islam* (common land divided into separate strips, assigned to and occupied by people who practise Islam)
2474	24 bigha 13 biswa	-do-
2475	01 bigha	Sarâb, Nawab and Kamir s/o Shâmu
Total	**55 bigha 30 biswa**	
		1943-44
2173	01 bigha 17 biswa	*shamlat patti bakhshian- makbuza ahl-i-Islam*
2174	29 bigha	-do-
2413	07 biswa	-do-
2474	24 bigha 13 biswa	-do-
2475	01 bigha	-do-
Total	**56 bigha 37 biswa**	
		1965-66
499	**17 kanal 07 marla**	*ghair mumkin kabristan panj pir* (barren graveyard of Panj Pir)

Source: Land records of the Patwari at Abohar for the relevant years and for translation of terms H.H. Wilson, *Glossary of Judicial and Revenue Terms and of Useful Words Occurring in Official Documents Relating to the Administration of the Government of British India*, Munshiram Manoharlal, New Delhi, 1855 (reprint 1968).

Although the origin of Panj Pir tradition may be situated in fifteenth century, the actual existence of five saints is crucial towards our understanding of this tradition. As we have discussed earlier, the account of Waris Shah provides a clue on the names of Panj Pir. Following table gives details the names associated with Panj Pir at Abohar.

Panj Pir at Abohar

Names	*Birth*	*Death*
Khwaja Khizar	–	–
Shaikh Fariduddin Ganj-i Shakar (Baba Farid)	1172	1265
Shaikh Bahauddin Zakariya	1170	1267
Syed Jalaluddin Bukhari	1199	1291
Lal Shahbaz Qalandar	1177	1274

Khwaja Khizar is identified with river-god or spirits of wells and streams. On the Indus the saint is often identified with the river and he is sometimes represented as an old man clothed in green. His principal shrine is on an island of the Indus near Bhakkar in Sind.[55] Baba Farid, one of the most revered Chishti saints of medieval Punjab, was the successor of Khwaja Qutbuddin Bakhtiyar Kaki, settled in Pakpattan (Montgomery, now Sahiwal). Shaikh Bahauddin Zakariya was a Suhrawardi saint and disciple of Shaikh Shihabuddin Suhrawardi of Baghdad. Zakariya later settled in Multan. Syed Jalaluddin Bukhari was a Suhrawardi and a disciple of Shaikh Bahauddin Zakariya. He settled in Uch in Bahawalpur.[56] Lal Shahbaz Qalandar was born in Marwand now Afghanistan. He was also a disciple of Shaikh Bahauddin Zakariya. He migrated to Sind and settled in Sehwan.

The above table apparently contradicts with both – the account of Rose and the association of Panj Pir with Baba Ramdev. While Rose's account ascribes nine hundred years to the tradition, i.e. somewhere in tenth century, the association with Baba Ram Dev locates Panj Pir in the fifteenth century. The map on the *wilayat* of Panj Pir tradition offers a more plausible explanation of the growth and development of this tradition. All the principal shrines of sufi saints associated with Panj Pir from Lal Shahbaz Qalandar of Sehwan, Khwaja Khizar of Bhakkar, Syed Jalaluddin Bukhari of Uch, Shaikh Bahauddin Zakariya of Multan to Shaikh Farid of Pakpattan are situated either on the banks of river Indus or on its tributaries (Chenab and Satluj). Significantly, the location of these shrines also coincides with the medieval trade routes linking Sind with Multan and Multan with Delhi.[57]

Abohar was situated on this important trade route linking Sind (through Sehwan, Bhakar and Uch) and Multan (through Pakpattan and Abohar) with Delhi.[58] The tradition of Panj Pir at Abohar, thus, gradually developed with the growth of trade and military activities along this route and traders, possibly Arabs and locals, played a significant role in this regard in the period after thirteenth century. The oral narratives on Panj Pir lay primary emphasis on the 'horses'- pir's association with horses, raid for horses, etc. The myth associated with Panj Pir could have thus emerged out of early medieval influence of Turks and their association and tussle with local rulers. The places associated with Panj Pir tradition at Abohar i.e. Sehwan, Bhakkar, Uch, Multan and Pakpattan emerged as major centres of pilgrimage and veneration. Impressive shrines were constructed on the graves of Shaikh Fariduddin Ganj-i-Shakar (d. 1265), Shaikh Bahauddin Zakariya (d. 1267), Syed Jalaluddin Bukhari (d. 1291) and Lal Shahbaz Qalandar (d. 1274) after 13th century AD. The shrine associated with Khwaja Khizar could have emerged much earlier due to its association with seafaring Arabs. [59] These five shrines were centres of pilgrimage in the pre-partition times also and Panj Pir dargah could have been a dedication, as a memorial shrine, for these saints.

Tradition, Continuity and Pilgrimage

After the partition of India, the shrine complex remained desolate until 1950 when the dargah was taken over by Gehla Ram Kamboj, father of the present *sevadar* Bool Chand. He was caretaker of the dargah until his death in 1960 at the age of 90 years. Since then Bool Chand has been taking care of the dargah. He was officially granted the license of the dargah in 1989-90 by the Punjab Wakf Board. A *chiragh* (an oil lamp with five wicks) keeps burning at the dargah, a tradition which is common at all dargahs in India.[60] It 1965, Bool Chand started *langar* at the dargah and a *langar-khana* was constructed for this purpose. Since then *langar* has become a regular feature of the dargah and is held every week on Thursdays.[61] Besides this, a continuous *langar* is organised during the annual *urs* (locally known as *mela*) held during fifteenth of Sawan (July-August) each year for three days.

During these three days, people from far-flung areas of Punjab come on a pilgrimage and pay their obeisance at the dargah. Devotees – Hindus, Muslims and Sikhs – come from as far as Delhi and West Bengal. Since the shrine is also associated with Baba Ramdev, it attracts people from Hanumangarh and Sri Ganganagar districts of Rajasthan. Occasionally, few Muslims from Lahore and Pakpattan (Montgomery) regions of Pakistan also flock to the shrine during *urs*. Qawwals from different places, who are private individuals, also visit the dargah. Offerings at the *urs* range from green embroidered *chadars*, sweets, oil, ghee to hens. Women bring pots containing water (*ghadolian*) and offer them to the pirs. The devotees pray and tie a knot for fulfilment of their wish (*sukhna/mannat*). The *langar-khana* works overtime during these days and pilgrims are offered *dal-roti, kheer, halwa, jalebi, poori,* rice, milk,

People visiting the dargah at anuual *urs*

etc. Besides this annual celebration, Muslims offer the *namaz* of Id-ul Fitar at the dargah. The ritual tradition at the dargah evolved out of multiple factors of isolation, continuity and initiation. Partition created a socio-cultural vacuum which was substituted through regularisation of such centres and institutions associated with dargahs such as *langar*.

On 30 July 2006, the last day of *urs*, a survey was conducted on the nature of ritual practices and pilgrims at the annual *urs* (fair in the memory of *pirs*) at Panj Pir. This survey aimed at gathering socio-anthropological data on pilgrims who visit this shrine during annual *urs*. Panj Pir dargah at Abohar has the largest following among Kambojs, Bagri Jats, menial castes (Dhanuk, Kumhar, Chamar, Regar, etc.), Rais and Mazhabi Sikhs, Sidhu, Sekhon and Mehra Sikhs, Aroras and Mahajans, Khatris, Rajputs and even Brahmins, Kabirpanthis and Udasis. Besides, few Saifi, Ansari and Pathan Muslims also frequent the dargah.

For most of the pilgrims, dargah of Panj Pir is a wish-fulfilling shrine and catered to their material needs rather than spiritual ones. Pilgrims bring all kinds of offerings like *chadar,* oil, broom (especially for treatment of boils), essence and *mauli* (sacred thread to tie around the *van* tree) for fulfilment of their wishes (*mannat*) viz. business undertakings and boy/ child bearing. Pilgrims from Ferozepur and places as far as Ludhiana and Amritsar arrive at the shrine during *urs*. Villages adjoining Abohar, Fazilka and Malout attract the largest gathering during the annual *urs*. Most of the Bagri Jats visit the shrine due to its association with Baba Ramdev, who is worshipped as a primary deity in their families. Many pilgrims who visit this dargah associate themselves with other popular pirs also. Pilgrims mentioned the presence of dargahs dedicated to Baba Ali Mohammad, Lalan Wala Pir, Baba Bulleh Shah, Baba Bhoman Shah, Baba Pir Khumber, Baba Lakhdata, Baba Khetarpal, Baba Ahmed Shah, Dipalpur Pir and Baba Nahre Shah, etc. as objects of veneration in their villages.[62] One of the most significant aspects of this pilgrimage is the affinity of pilgrims with pre-partition times. Many amongst them narrated their association with areas like Arif Mandi in Montgomery (Pakistan) and with villages which had memorial shrines related to numerous local pirs. Census of India 1961 gives a vivid description of such fairs which recreate the lived past in the form of popular memories through popular experiences. Dominique-Sila Khan mentions that the shrines dedicated to Panch Pir (in Rajasthan) ...can be regarded as Hindu or Muslim places of worship, but in all cases devotees of both communities gather at the same place without wondering about its 'religious identity'.[63]

The shrine at Abohar also attracts folk artists who sing popular ballads narrating, often, recreated memories of the legend of Panj Pir and at times, relating it along with some other tradition. The most fascinating aspect of these shrines is the way in which pilgrims emulate sufi and Islamic symbols by wearing green clothes and Muslim caps (primarily by Mazhabi and Rai Sikhs and bazigars). It possibly explains the process of Islamization through popular culture in pre-colonial and colonial Punjab. Dargah in the present context represents an admixture of traditional practices and modern influence. The present day fair looks like a typical fair in rural Punjab associated with market and business activity of the poor, besides the usual means of recreation (swings, merry-go-rounds, etc). One also experiences the presence of pilgrims wearing green clothes and headgears, imitating as *murids* (*qalandars*?), and exhibiting transcendental experiences and at times crawling towards the dargah.

Conclusion

The dargah of Panj Pir reflects upon the larger 'culture of pirs' in this region. The development of Panj Pir tradition has been a part of socio-historical process of acculturation and assimilation and had also

Another poster on sale at the Panj Pir dargah

complemented the process of Islamisation in the medieval and modern times. According to the Census of India 1961, in Ferozepur district alone, there were some 26 annual fairs organised in the memory of one or the other pir.[64] Significantly, just three among them shared a common saint. This 'pirification' of the social milieu has had significant growth after the partition of India. Pirification refutes some of the conventional theories of Islamisation in India, viz., military force and official patronage, while at the same time substantiating other theories like social liberation and immigration.[65] Pirification of Punjabi society cannot be concluded with either of these theories. Significantly, the 'dargah' has been a common place for veneration for different religious groups – Hindus, Muslims and Sikhs.[66]

The experience of Panj Pir also raises certain conceptual questions for the practice of historiography and its influence on the understanding of 'popular Islam' in South Asia. Asim Roy argues that the focus of Islamicist explanation on the historical development of Islamic society, in terms of long, slow and gradual process of Islamisation which eventually brings about a heterodox-heteroprax to orthodox-orthoprax religious orientation, gives a narrow understanding of popular Islam as it reduces it as 'festers' that could be 'cured'.[67] While proposing a complementarity between historical and sociological understanding of Islam, he argues that syncretistic traditions in Bengal have rather been a necessary stage of its historical development. The case of Panj Pir amply illustrates that while earlier tradition like Panch Pandavas of Mahabharata or Shia version of 'five sacred bodies' did play a significant role in the later development of the Panj Pir tradition, the local socio-cultural context and geographical influence played an important role in transforming it into a shared cultural complex.

Socio-anthropological understanding further strengthens the argument that post-partition scenario of continued popularity of such dargahs is an expression of pre-partition milieu of shared cultural sites. These dargahs could have played an important role in Islamization, yet they existed as 'cult centres' and 'principal deities' for Sikhs and Hindus alike. Significantly, these shrines have earlier existed independent of state-control i.e. in the popular domains of the society. The *wilayat* of such shrines extended beyond the political boundaries of either medieval or modern states and provided an alternative expression of social space. In the Patwari records from 1922-23 to 1965-66, the area associated with Panj Pir has generally been entered as 'common land'. Thus it remained outside the domains of bureaucratisation and systematisation which was typical to the advent of colonialism in India, possibly because it remained functional in the popular domain.[68] It was only after the formation of Central Wakf Council in 1964 that such 'lesser shrines' also came under the control of Punjab Wakf Board and it started exercising control over its income.[69]

The continuous popularity and increasing income from these centres has exposed them to greater intervention of the State. In 1989-90 Punjab Wakf Board had fixed an amount of Rs.5000 as license fee for the control of the dargah. It was increased to Rs.1,70,000 in the year 2006-07.[70] In June 2007, Punjab Wakf Board came up with the scheme of entrusting the maintenance of Panj Pir at Abohar to the highest bidder. *The Tribune* reported that the board had issued license in favour of Mohinder Singh for one year, supposedly against the payment of Rs.2.10 lakh. The latter claimed to have paid a donation of Rs.50,000 in addition to the license fee. Bool Chand, the existing *sevadar* of the dargah, said that he too was ready to increase the annual licence fee from Rs.1.70 lakh to Rs.2.10 lakh at par with Mohinder Singh, who had otherwise no association with the place of worship.[71] Bool Chand was finally entrusted the management of the dargah for 2007-08 against a license fee of Rs.3,00,000.[72] The association of *sevadars* with the sacred centres in pre-partition times has recently found significant weight in claims to control over such shrines. Recently the entrance to the shrine was adorned with a semi-circular board mentioning the name of the dargah as 'Panj Pir Khanqah (dargah)' and name of the sevadar as 'Bool Chand Kamboj (Pakpattan *wale*)' along with the Islamic symbol of a crescent moon and a star. Significantly, despite the growing following and income, the shrine complex has structurally remained intact in its pre-partition form.

In the aftermath of partition, popular dargahs in Punjab have undergone another significant changeover. Many existing dargahs have non-Muslim *sevadars* and it is pertinent to note their role in the affairs of these dargahs. As has been said earlier, technically *sevadars* are mere custodians authorised by the Wakf Board for the upkeep of the dargah on the payment of license fee, yet his position has significant bearing on his relation with pilgrims who flock to this centre. In the colonial Punjab, the position of *gaddi* played an important role in determining succession and running the day-to-day affairs of a sufi shrine, which usually followed the customary practices.[73] Adjoining the graves of five pirs at Abohar, there is a *gaddi*, where the *sevadar* sits and offers his blessing and *prasad* to the devotees. Significantly this is the same place where his father Gehla Ram Kamboj sat, emulated and performed the duties of a *gaddi-nishin*. Thus, even in the aftermath of partition, we see continuity in the practices and symbols associated with dargahs which were co-opted in the post-partition scenario.

Gradual increase in popularity of the dargah has led to the development of certain myths and associations with other centres like Baba Ramdev in Ramdevra (Rajasthan). The dargah, however, might have had experienced different phases of popularity. Rose's work on tribes and castes of Punjab and NWFP, which was compiled in 1911, mentions that 'few people attend it, mostly Madari, Naushahi, etc.'[74] But the manner in which Panj Pir tradition gets associated with the tradition of Baba Ramdev suggests that the dargah was quite popular in the late medieval times. Nevertheless, the Panj Pir dargah at Abohar continues to attract pilgrims of different faiths from a number of Indian states. Besides, such lesser shrines have left an indelible mark on the folk literature of Punjab, influencing writers like Damodar and Waris Shah and continue to inspire folklore and folk-culture. Dargahs also provided a vital link between Muslims and non-Muslims of Punjab. Significant numbers of mostly rural pilgrims attracted to the dargah are low-caste non-Muslims. Pilgrims from the urban centres primarily belong to trading classes.

Contemporary research on sufism in Punjab has failed to give a satisfactory explanation of the manner in which essentially esoteric mystical traditions might have filtered down to commoners in some sort of comprehensible and appealing form.[75] Eaton argues that one likely reason for the failure to explain the attraction of Hindu non-elites to sufis has been the tendency among scholars of sufism to concentrate almost exclusively to the mystical literature as opposed to folk literature, as representing the sum and substance of the sufi movement. In the context of Deccan villages, he suggests that until the twentieth century, when radio and cinema took its place, folk poetry of sufi origin had occupied a dominant position in the folk culture and became a link

Gaddi of *sevadar* kept adjoining the five graves

between the religious philosophy and popular religion of Islam.[76] However, Eaton cautions, this process should not be construed as 'conversion' to Islam, nor should the sufis themselves be considered as Muslim 'missionaries'.[77] During the annual *urs* at Panj Pir dargah in Abohar, folk artists[78] flock the shrine and narrate folk verses on the life of Baba Farid and at times give an alternative identity to Panj Pir by relating them to Baba Lakhdata.[79]

Dargahs and folk literature have to be understood as a gradual and on-going process of Islamic acculturation through adaptation of symbols of dress, food, speech, etc. It is in this context that the role of Punjabi folk culture needs to be understood. The process of establishment of such centres is an ongoing process and reference should be made to the establishment of a *gaddi* (seat) associated with Ajmer Sharif by Firoz Khan (28 years) at Indira Nagri (Abohar) in 1998. He is a disciple *(murid)* of Sabir Pak (Shaikh Alauddin Ali bin Ahmad Sabir), founder of Silsilah Chishtia Sabiria and is a *shagird* of Ghulam Jilani, *khadim* and *gaddi-nishin* at Kaliyar Sharif (near Roorkee). He has been administering the wishes of his pir at Abohar.[80] Firoz Sabiri Chishti (Firoz Khan) regularly visits Ajmer Sharif and Kaliyar Sharif. He plays the role of a mediator between the Shaikh and people who come from places as far as Amritsar and Chandigarh to meet him. Present research compels us to rethink the effects of the partition on sufi centres of Punjab. Significantly, these centres have continuously been reorienting the socio-cultural milieu of Punjab. It is this continuity which is significant to the growth and evolution of sufism in modern Punjab.

NOTES AND REFERENCES

1. David Gilmartin, *Empire and Islam: Punjab and the Making of Pakistan*, Oxford University Press, Delhi, 1989, p. 40 (hereafter cited as Gilmartin). Underlining significant factor for the rise of rural Islam, Eaton argues that the pattern of conversion in rural Punjab was a product of simultaneous ecological and political change, as pastoralists in western Punjab adapted both to a spreading agricultural way of life and to the political and cultural hegemony of imperial Muslim states. In this context the great medieval sufis were symbolically important. Ibid., p. 41.
2. The construction of sufi hospices (*khanqahs*) and later sufi tombs, produced symbolic cultural outposts of the power of Islam and of the Muslims in a world where local, tribal identities continued to be of vital importance. Imposing sufi tombs, constructed by Muslim sultans, underscored the importance of Islamic shrines as sites of access to transcendent spiritual authority. Ibid., pp. 41-42.
3. Ibid., pp. 41-42.
4. Ibid., pp. 43-45.
5. Claudia Liebeskind, *Piety on Its Knees: Three Sufi Traditions in South Asia in Modern Times*, Oxford University Press, Delhi, 1998, p. 2.
6. Gilmartin, op. cit. pp. 41-42.
7. Ibid., pp. 45-46.
8. Asim Roy, *The Islamic Syncretistic Tradition in Bengal*, Princeton University Press, Princeton, 1983, pp. 207-208.
9. Richard M. Eaton, *Essays in Islam and Indian History*, Oxford University Press, New Delhi, 2000, p. 210.
10. Ibid., p. 210.
11. Abohar is situated in the southwest corner of eastern Punjab. It is situated at a distance of less than 60 kiolometres from Pakpattan and was a major town along the Multan-Delhi trade route, which linked the costal areas of Sind with Delhi. Its geographical location makes it closer to the influences of the major centres of sufism in medieval and colonial Punjab.
12. For a useful discussion on 'pirification' in Bengal see Roy, op. cit., pp. 207-248.
13. Muslims offer prayers to Khwaja Khizar at the first shaving of a boy, and a little boat is launched at the same time; also at the close of the rainy season. H.A.R. Gibb and J.H. Kramers, *Shorter Encyclopaedia of Islam*, E.J. Brill, Leiden, 1953, p. 235 (hereafter cited as Gibb and Kramers).
14. Dominique-Sila Khan, *Conversions and Shifting Identities: Ramdev Pir and the Ismailis in Rajasthan*, Manohar, New Delhi, 2003, p. 90.
15. For some useful studies on colonial and post-colonial experience of sufi shrines in Lucknow, Rai Bareli and Bara Banki see Leibeskind. This study tries to address both the problem of how sufi institutions namely Takiya Sharif, Kakori, of the Khanqah Karimiya, Salon, and of Haji Waris Ali Shah, Dewa responded to processes of systematization and rationalization in society as well as to the spread of post-enlightenment thought and movements of Islamic reform in a context in which their support had been threatened and eroded. Leibeskind, op. cit., p. 4.

16. Soon after the announcement of the boundary award in mid-August 1947, the trickle of uprooted persons developed into a spate and they started pouring in and going out in an unending stream. *Punjab District Gazetteer, Firozpur District*, Revenue Department, Punjab, Chandigarh, 1983, p. 57.
17. Of these, about four-fifths are settled in the rural areas and the rest in the urban areas of the District. Ibid., p. 66.
18. Ibid., p. 57.
19. Waris Shah was born in the village Jandiala Sher Khan near Gujranwala and studied at Qasur under Hafiz Ghulam Murtaza. In his youth he fell in love with a village girl of Pakpattan. Scandalised by a Saiyyid stooping to such depths, the villagers drove him out of their village and Waris Shah was forced to retire to a village in the Sahiwal district. There he found spiritual comfort by versifying the romance of Hir-Ranjha. Although several other reversifications exists- one of them by the sixteenth century poet Damodar (1556-1605) - it is the artistry of Waris Shah which has made his Hir-Ranjha immortal. Saiyyid Athar Abbas Rizvi, *A History of Sufism in India*, Vol. II, Munshiram Manoharlal, New Delhi, 1983, p. 447.
20. Kamboj's association with the dargah at Abohar adds significance to the tradition of Panj Pir. The Kambos (Kambojs) belonged to one of the Hindu castes of Punjab and were either peasants or daily wage earners. They emerged as a new social formation owing to their association with the Suhrawardis of Multan. Their children were educated in the madrasah founded by Shaikh Bahauddin Zakariya. Siddiqui, 2005, pp. 10-23.
21. The present *sevadar* Bool Chand (76 years, a resident of Anand Nagri, Abohar) says that during the annual *urs* people from as far as West Bengal and Pakistan come to pay obeisance at this dargah (interviewed on 01 March 2006).
22. Leibeskind, op. cit., p. 4.
23. Crooke mentions that Patwas who are generally Viashnavas of eastern Uttar Pradesh districts include Mahabir, the Panchonpir and Harditha among their clan deities. W. Crooke, *Popular Religion and Folklore of Northern India*, Archibald Constable and Company, Westminster, 1896, pp. 172-173.
24. H.A.Rose, *A Glossary of Tribes and Castes of the Punjab and North-West Frontier Province*, Vol. I, Department of Languages, Patiala, 1911, Reprint, 1970, pp. 572-573.
25. E.A.H. Blunt, *The Caste System of Northern India*, Oxford University Press, Madras, 1931, cited in Gibb and Kramers, p. 457.
26. *Punjab District Gazetteers, Ferozepur District*, 1915, Revenue Department, Punjab, Chandigarh, (Reprint), 1991.
27. J. Wilson, *Final Report on the Revision of Settlement of the Sirsa District in the Punjab, 1879-83*, Calcutta Central Press Company, Calcutta, 1884, pp. 194-95.
28. Rose, op. cit., p. 573.
29. This account was recorded by Muhammad Ishrat Khan as 'Panch Pir Sufion ka Dharmik Sthal' based on an interview with Bool Chand. Muhammad Ishrat Khan, 'Panch Pir Sufion ka Dharmik Sthal', in *Swagat*, Indian Airlines, New Delhi, December 1993, pp. 72-74.

30. Ibid., p. 72.
31. This particular episode is common to the Ramdev folklore, with the difference that the Pir of Runicha (place where Baba Ramdev supposedly resided, known as Ramdevra today) eventually proves his superiority by performing a still more difficult 'trick': he brings instantaneously in front of them their five bowls which had remained inside a locked room in Mecca. We need to specify that in the older devotional tradition, for instance in a *bhajan* by Likhmoji Mali (eighteenth-nineteenth century), these five Pirs are said to have come from Multan: *mahimâ sun multân mulk râ âyâ pîr milân tâhi* . . . ('hearing of his glory, from the country of Multan the Pirs came to meet him'). In Ramdev's hagiography, it is said that one of the Pirs who had acknowledged his superiority and given him the title *hinduô kâ pîr,* decided to remain in the kingdom of Pokaran. Dominique-Sila Khan, op. cit., p. 91.
32. Ibid., p. 91.
33. He says that 'a look at the map will immediately reveal that the five Pirs' itinerary is not at all logical: the choice of Pokaran as a halting place when going from Multan to Abohar is not exactly what one would call a short-cut and much more than a simple detour'. Ibid., p. 92.
34. These names have been put up in a photo-frame on the wall in the room adjoining the graves of Panj Pirs at Abohar. Besides the photo-frames of Mecca, Baba Ramdev and six holy saints and their respective dargahs are also kept in and around the dargah at Abohar. These six holy saints are portrayed sitting together and facing each other. They include Hazrat Ghaus Pak (Abdul Qadir Gilani, Baghdad), Hazrat Bu Ali Sharaf (Bu Ali Qalandar, Panipat), Hazrat Mahbub-i-Ilahi (Nizamuddin Auliya, Delhi), Hazrat Khwaja Gharib Nawaz (Muinuddin Chishti, Ajmer), Hazrat Khwaja Qutbuddin (Qutbuddin Bakhtiyar Kaki, Delhi) and Hazrat Baba Farid Shakar Ganj (Shaikh Fariduddin Ganj-i-Shakar, Pakpattan).
35. Waris Shah has mentioned the names of Panj Pir in *Hir* as 'Khawaja Khizr, Shakarganj, Zikriya of Multan, Syed Jalal Bukhariya and Lal Shahbaz'. Sant Singh Sekhon, *Heer Waris Shah* (Punjabi), Sahitya Akademi, New Delhi, 1969, p. 59.
36. Cited in Gibb and Kramers, p. 457.
37. The *Panj Pir*(*s*) are really any five saints the author may remember or worship. The Nawab (Alauddin Ahmad Khan) of Loharu, nephew of Nawab Shamsuddin Khan, who had sent a manuscript in the Persian character to Mr. Delmerick in 1872 narrates his version of Panj Pir in 'The Ballad of Sarwan and Pharijan'. R.C. Temple, *The Legends of the Punjab*, Vol-II, Department of Languages, Patiala, 1884 (reprint 1963), f.n.*, p. 372. Besides the reference of Waris Shah, Panj Pir are also mentioned in the folk version of Hir Ranjha ('The Marriage of Hir and Ranjha' as related by Jats from the Patiala State, recorded by Temple. Ibid., p. 525). Interestingly while Waris Shah mention Khwaja Khizr among the Five Pirs, this folk version lists Panj Pir similar to 'The Ballad of Sarwan and Pharijan' as recorded by Temple. Ibid., f.n.*, p. 372.
38. Panj Pir are also referred to as *hawas-i-bâtani*. The text quotes Waris Shah

saying *'panch pir ne panch hawas tere'*. T.R. Shangari and J.R. Puri, *Sain Bulle Shah* (Urdu), Sartaj Printing Press, Jalandhar, 1987, f.n., pp. 77-78.

39. Quoted in ibid., p. 78.
40. Rose, op. cit., p. 572.
41. Malkahans lies on the road from Pakpattan to Montgomery.
42. Onkar Nath (77 years, presently a resident of Jain Nagri, Abohar), was a resident of Malkahans (named as such because majority of population was that of Hansis), Montgomery, Pakistan before the partition of Punjab (interviewed on 26 March 2006). For a discussion on Waris Shah, see Sekhon, pp. 9-27.
43. Bool Chand adds that before partition people from his village Wan Dal Singh (neighbouring Malkahans) and community (Kambojs) used to come to the market of Abohar (Abohar *ki maal mandi*) to purchase bullocks and thus had knowledge of the dargah and its relation with Waris Shah's *Hir* which was then a popular text. He narrated that he was born with the blessing of Shaikh Farid. Before the partition of Punjab he had spent three years in Pakpattan and his school was situated just below the dargah of Shaikh Farid. He used to offer his services at this dargah. His family primarily had a following with Baba Bhumman Shah, an Udasi saint of medieval Punjab. Baba Bhumman Shah was born on 14 April 1687 at Behlolpur village, Montgomery District in Pakistan, in a family of Kamboj lineage. Significantly, Bool Chand had never been to the dargah at Abohar before migrating from Pakistan in 1947, but has read about them in *Hir*. He was 17 years old then. His father used to light a lamp every morning and return in the evening. He also narrated certain myths associated with Shaikh Farid. For instance he never walked, but used to fly 100 *kos* a day. He also recited some lines from *Hir* (interviewed on 4 April 2006).
44. Rose, p. 573.
45. Interestingly, men are not allowed in the courtyard where the wives of five pirs are buried. There is a popular myth that if a man enters this area he shall go blind.
46. I came across this exposed wall which was put up for repairs on 25 March 2006.
47. The bricks were used in the wall along the surface of raised platform where the graves of Panj Pir are located. One of the inner bricks was 4 cms thick and 11 cms long suggesting a medieval association, while the other one was 5 cms thick and 20 cms long which is the size of modern brick tiles used in flooring.
48. One brick was found on the backside and another on the opposite side of the dargah. These bricks were of unusual dimensions- 4.5- 5.0 cms thick and 20 cms broad.
49. The wall measured 49 inches in thickness (including the much recent plastering). There were three niches in the surrounding wall which were around 31-32 inches deep (including plaster).
50. According to the *sevadar,* the exact date of the trees is written on the wall of a temple in village Patrewala in Fazilka. The circumference of the tree measures around 22 feet.

51. Dominique-Sila Khan, op. cit., p. 81. Incidentally Mokal's reign coincides with the dates traditionally ascribed to Ramdev Pir by the *bhajniks*- Samadhi in 1458. Ibid., pp. 81-82.
52. Rose, op. cit., p. 573.
53. Gazetteer of the Multan District mentions one proverbial characteristic of Multan city, i.e. the prevalence of graveyards; and in the district at large the graveyards are a marked feature in the landscape. 'They are generally on ground too high for irrigation or cultivation, often on ruined *bhirs*, and are entered somewhat pathetically in the revenue records as *makbuza ahl-i-Islam*. It is common to bury in the neighbourhood of some saint's grave, and in such cases the wood round the grave is allowed to grow, it being considered profanity to lay hands upon it. Though most of the graveyards are bare unlovely spots, there is a tendency, where possible, to find a shady place for graves.' *Gazetteer of the Multan District*, Civil and Military Gazette Press, Lahore, 1901-02, p. 81.
54. Rose, op. cit., p. 573. Nazar Masih (80 years, a resident of Jammu Basti, near Kabristan) was interviewed on 28 March 2006.
55. Rose identifies Khwaja Khizar as Sultan Naisruddin Mahmud (1246-1265). Ibid., p. 573. The long list of religious virtues attributed to the Sultan by tradition was first put forth by Isami. The Sultan took nothing from the public revenue but earned his livelihood by making copies of the Quran and selling them secretly. 'He was one of the chosen people of God, always absorbed in thoughts of Allah... Some people say he was a saint, while others put him among the prophets...' Cited in Mohammab Habib and Khaliq Ahmed Nizami, (eds.), *A Comprehensive History of India*, Vol. 5, The Delhi Sultanat AD 1206-1526, People's Publishing House, New Delhi, 1996, f.n. 5, pp. 257-258.
56. Rizvi identifies Waris Shah's Syed Jalal Bukhariya as Jahaniyan Jalal Bukhari who is also known as Makhdum Jahaniyan Jahangasht (1308-1385). Rizvi, op. cit., p. 447. He does not mention why the latter couldn't be Syed Jalaluddin Surkh Bukhari (1199-1291), who was latter's grandfather. In fact when Baba Farid, Shaikh Bahauddin Zakariya and Lal Shahbaz Qalandar are contemporaries, Waris Shah's Syed Jalal Bukhariya ought to be Syed Jalaluddin Surkh Bukhari (1199-1291). The principal shrines of both the pirs are located at Uch in Bahawalpur.
57. Siddiqui adds that since Ajodhan was situated on the merchant caravan route linking Multan, the border city, with Delhi and other parts of Delhi Sultanate, the merchants, nobles and soldiers travelling from and to Delhi paid visits to the dargah and invoked the saint's help and blessing for success as well as safety from dacoits, illness and wild animals. Iqtidar Husain Siddiqui, 'The Early Chishti Dargahs', in Christian W. Troll (ed), *Muslim Shrines in India: Their Character, History and Significance*, Oxford University Press, New Delhi, 2003, pp. 14-15.
58. Ibn Battuta says that the first town reached after leaving Multan was Abohar, which was the first town in India. Ibn Batuta, *Travels in Aisa and Africa 1325-1354*, English Translation, H.A.R. Gibb, Routledge, London, 2004, p. 190.

59. Significantly, travelling in the fourteenth century Ibn Battuta reached Abohar through Sehwan, Uch and Multan. Zulfiqar Ahmad, *Punjab: Selections from Journal of the Punjab Historical Society,* Vol. II, Sang-E-Meel Publications, Lahore, 1982, p. 89.
60. Rose mentions that a lamp is lighted at the dargah in the evening. Rose, op. cit., 573.
61. Bool Chand proudly narrates a three-month long *langar* during the Indo-Pak war of 1971 and the army was stationed near the *dargah.*
62. A survey on the nature of pilgrims on the occasion of the annual fair at Panj Pir Dargah, Abohar, was conducted by the present writer on 30 July 2006.
63. Dominique-Sila Khan, op. cit., p. 90.
64. *Census of India 1961,* Punjab District Census Handbook, No. 12, Ferozepur District, Superintendent of Census Operations, Government of Punjab, Chandigarh, pp. 105-123.
65. For a useful discussion on the theories of Islamisation see Richard M. Eaton, *The Rise of Islam and the Bengal Frontier, 1204-1706,* Oxford University Press, New Delhi, 2000, pp. 113-134.
66. Siddiqui says that unconverted Hindus also often remained sincerely attached to the dargah, paid visits there, and made offerings in cash or kind. Their descendents followed this tradition. It is worth recalling that in medieval period, Hindus and Muslims often vowed offerings to a patron saint or deity if their prayers were answered. Sometimes faced with serious problems such as illness of only son or the desire for a male child, Hindus seem to have vowed that they would accept Islam. For Hindus, and often for new converts to Islam whose conversion was partial, the dargah was a substitute for the idol. Siddiqui, 'The Early Chishti Dargahs', p. 7.
67. Asim Roy, 'Thinking Over 'Popular Islam' in South Asia: Search for a Paradigm', in Mushirul Hasan and Asim Roy (eds), *Living Together Separately: Cultural India in History and Politics,* Oxford University Press, New Delhi, 2005, p. 39.
68. However, the impact of nineteenth and twentieth century movement of revival and reform in Punjab on the following of this shrine needs to be studied in further detail.
69. Significantly, in the year 2001, Punjab Wakf Board (a composite Board managing thirty six thousand properties in three states of Punjab, Haryana and Himachal Pradesh and the union territory of Chandigarh) was entrusted as the richest Board in India with 'a record revenue income of Rs.15.09 crore during the financial year 2000-01'. Press Information Bureau Release, Government of India, 21 December 2001.
70. A letter no. Eo/PWB/FZR/2007/3110 dated 03-09-07 from Estate Officer, Punjab Wakf Board, Ferozepur to Yogesh Snehi, Abohar, in response to latter's query on lease status of Panj Pir dargah at Abohar under Right to Information Act 2005.
71. 'Panjpeer Mazaar Complex: Wakf Board in Dock for Changing Lease' in The Tribune, 10 June 2007.
72. A letter no. Eo/PWB/FZR/07/3281 dated 27-12-07 from Estate Officer,

Punjab Wakf Board, Ferozepur to Yogesh Snehi, Abohar, in response to latter's query on Wakf property in Abohar under Right to Information Act 2005.

73. *Gaddi* occupied a significant place in the debates on succession to sufi sacred centres in colonial Punjab; whether the shrine was to be understood fundamentally as a local institution, which governed its affairs according to its own customs, or as an Islamic institution, governing its affairs according to Islamic law. Eaton narrates one such case before Lahore High Court on the question of succession to the shrine of Baba Farid. Often the defendant's lawyers vigorously argued that because the *shariat* was not generally interpreted as sanctioning primogeniture and thus the *gaddi* followed custom and and not Mohammadan Law. Richard M. Eaton, *Essays on Islam and Indian History*, pp. 232-33.
74. Rose, op. cit., 573. One possibility of Rose's observation could be that the surveyor visited the shrine on weekdays other than Thursday and annual *urs*. This day is considered auspicious for visit to shrine. Besides, in the late nineteenth century the place was indeed situated atop a desolate sand ridge, at a distance from the main city.
75. Eaton raises this pertinent question in the case of studies on sufism in India. He tries to suffice this gap through a discussion on the role of sufi folk literature in the expansion of Islam in Deccan. Richard M. Eaton, *Essays on Islam and Indian History*, pp. 189-99.
76. Ibid., pp. 190-91.
77. The main problem is that both terms 'conversion' and 'missionaries' carry connotations of a nineteenth and twentieth-century Christian movement in India, a context in which 'missionary' denoted a self-conscious propagator of the Christian faith and 'conversion' a self-conscious turning around in religious conviction. Ibid., p. 199.
78. Two such folk renderings on Baba Lakhdata and Baba Farid were recorded at the annual *urs* on 30 July 2006 at Dargah Panj Pir, Abohar.
79. The name *lakhdata* literally means the giver of hundreds of thousands. It signifies this Pir's status as a giver of sufi wisdom. The life of Pir Lakhdata is shrouded in mystery. In one tradition, he is associated with Shaikh Ali Hujwiri of Lahore. In another tradition he is said to have been a close associate of Guru Nanak, the first guru of the Sikhs. The cult of Pir Lakhdata is particularly popular among the agriculturist castes of Punjab and Rajasthan, both Hindu as well as Muslim. This tradition is linked with the cult of Guga Pir, said to be a Rajput chieftain who converted to Islam. In some versions of the account of Guga Pir's life, he and Pir Lakhdata are presented as one and the same person. Yoginder Sikand, 'The Sufi Shrines of Jammu', *ISIM Newsletter*, www.isim.nl, June 2000, pp. 19-20.
80. He narrated that once he had a revelation (*kaifiyat*) which revealed to him the existence of the grave of Zameel Shah Chishti several feet below the surface in the backyard of Rajindra Theatre at Abohar. He got the grave dug in 1997-98 and since then the site has been a popular place of veneration. His father Muhammad Qamruddin (60 years) had earlier established a Madina Masjid at Abohar. His grandfather Muhammad

Salabuddin was primarily a native of Dibai (district Bulandshahr, Uttar Pradesh) and was a resident of Abohar in pre-partition times and was associated with the dargah of Shaikh Shamsuddin Turk Panipatti at Panipat (Interviewed on 20 June 2008).

Appendix

Shrine of Miyan Mir at Lahore

A Note from the Tahqiqat-i-Chishti

Surinder Singh

[Nur Ahmad Chishti (d.1867), who served as a teacher in the government seminary (*madrasah*) at Lahore, was a reputed scholar and writer. He taught languages – Urdu, Persian and Punjabi – to a large number of senior British officers. He was a witness to the socio-cultural scenario of the city during the reign of Ranjit Singh and his successors, who were followed by the British in 1849. One of his works, *Tahqiqat-i-Chishti*, was published in 1859 by the Wattan Agency, Lahore.[1] It is a virtual encyclopaedia of historical places and important persons associated with the city. In addition to the residential bungalows and gardens, the author has paid particular attention to the tombs of sufi saints and sacred places associated with Hindus and Sikhs. His account, which is detailed and vivid, is based on personal observation and official documents which are not available to us. This is applicable in the truest sense to his description of the shrine of Miyan Mir, the famous Qadiri saint of Lahore. The narrative provides information – which is significant, interesting and authentic – regarding the management of the shrine over a long period of two hundred years from the death of Miyan Mir to the early nineteenth century. Of particular interest are the customs and practices regarding the succession to spiritual headship (*sajjadah nishin*) and distribution of the income of the shrine among the claimants, as adjudicated by a judicial commission established by Ranjit Singh. The author also describes the changes experienced by this particular locality (Miyan Mir) of the city where the shrine was located. In the following pages, we provide the said account.[2]]

At the outset, Dara Shikoh summoned from Sehwan Muhammad Sharif, the son of Miyan Mir's sister, who appears to have been the nearest descendant of the saint, to Lahore and appointed him as the first *sajjadah nishin* of the sacred place (*rauza munawwara*). The entire complex – consisting of the tomb, associated structures and *jagirs* – were placed under his charge (*tafwiz*). A royal order (*farman badshahi*) regarding this arrangement was in the possession of Muhammad Sharif and his descendants.

On his death, Muhammad Sharif left behind two sons, Shaikh Nur Ali and Mahdi Shah. The latter became *sajjadah nishin* in 1052 AH/1642 AD. He was very fond of horses. On one occasion, some of his mares (*aspan madi*) were grazing in Hashimpur, where they were captured by the local *zamindars*. Mahdi Shah sent a message to the *zamindars*, asking them to release the mares. When they refused to meet the demand, he complained to the governor (*nazim*) of Lahore. Ultimately the mares were released in response to the official orders. The *zamindars* continued to nurse a grievance. When, in the evening, mendicants attached to the shrine (*faqiran rauza*) went to Hashimpur for begging, the Dhodhi people (on account of their anger) closed the gates of the village and did not permit them to enter. The mendicants returned to the shrine and complained to Mahdi Shah. The news also reached Dara Shikoh who issued an order to the governor (*nazim*) of Lahore for destroying Hashimpur. As a result, the inhabitants of the village were scattered and were forced to settle at different places viz. Kot Khwaja Saeed, Jeo and Lahore. Some relatives of Mahdi Shah, who had their houses in village (*mauza*) Hashimpur, were also forced to shift. Mahdi Shah permitted his son Jaafar Shah to construct a bungalow (*haveli*) adjacent to the southern wall of the shrine (*rauza*), where the graveyard of Qasai Chaudhary Khuda Bakhsh is located at present and close to it are found the tombs of Jamiat Shah, Bahar Shah and Darbar Shah Naqib-ul-Majlis. As such, Jaafar Shah built a bungalow (*haveli*) at this place and lived there for some time.

After the death of Jaafar Shah, his son Masum Shah constructed a residence in Bagh Mulla Shah and came to reside in it. After the death of Masum Shah, there was anarchy in Lahore owing to the decline of the Mughal empire (*sultanat Chaghtai*). At one one time, there were three rulers (*hakims*) at Lahore. People living in the neighbouring localities, owing to the fear of loot and plunder, used to take shelter in the garden. As soon as the threat was over, they would return to their homes. Since the place was surrounded by a pucca boundary wall (*chardiwari pukhta*), it was regarded as a safe refuge. During the time of Arif Zaman Shah, the garden became famous as a fort and this situation continued for a long time. During this period, the Gujjars came to the Maidan Miyan Mir to graze their cattle. Masum Shah had permitted a few persons – two Gujjars named Dusu and Ladha, a Rajput named Jorha and a Jat named Fazil (whose son Pir Bakhsh is still alive) – to establiblish themselves here. Following in their footsteps, several other people arrived and settled here, so that a village came into being. Masum Shah had two children, a son named Hanif Shah and a daughter named Bibi Zohra. This daughter was married to Qadir Bakhsh bin Murad Bakhsh who was a descendant of Muhammad Sharif. Hanif Shah had four daughters. He gave one of them, Fazl-ul-Nissa, in marriage to Khuda Bakhsh, the son of his sister Bibi Zohra. This alliance produced three sons viz. Muhammad Shah, Amir Shah and Karam Shah. At present (last quarter of the nineteenth century) Muhammad Shah is serving as the *sajjadah nishin* of the shrine of Miyan Mir.

Now we come to the division of shares of the income (*zar amdani*) of this newly established village (*mauza nau-abadi*). Hanif Shah was appointed as the headman (*nambardar*). Hanif Shah did not have any son, but he had four daughters. One of them Mai Fazl-ul-Nissa was married to Khuda Bakhsh bin Qadir Bakhsh bin Murad Bakhsh bin Shaikh Azizullah bin Shaikh Muradullah bin Shaikh Nur Ali bin Muhammad Sharif. The second daughter Mai Mehar-un-Nissa was married to Isa Shah and gave birth to a number of sons, of whom four have survived viz. Nathey Shah, Karam Shah, Muhammad Shah and Akbar Shah. These four persons, in turn, have been blessed with children (*sahib-i-aulad*) and they receive one fourth of the income of the shrine of Miyan Mir from the *sajjadah nishin* Mahbub Shah and also meet one-fourth of the expenditure. The third daughter Karam-ul-Nissa was married to Syed Akbar Shah of Sharaqpur. Her son Ahmad Shah is presently living in Sharaqpur. This son does not voluntarily claim his share. But he can take it, should he so desire. The fourth daughter Khair-ul-Nissa was married to Mulla Imam Gamon, who is the *imam* of Masjid Wazir Khan. Their tombs are located to the south of the mosque, adjacent to its well. Two daughters were born to them. The elder one Bibi Sakina, who is married to Akbar Shah, the *imam* of Masjid Muhalla Haveli Miyan Khan, is still living these days. The second daughter Bibi Aisha is married to Syed Amir Ahmad of Lahore, who is a resident of Mochi Darwaza. Their children are also alive at present. These descendants of the fourth daughter of Hanif Shah can claim their respective shares from the income of the shrine of Miyan Mir, if they so desire.

It has become known that the income and expenditure of the shrine of Miyan Mir was shared equally between the sons of the first *sajjadah nishin* Muhammad Sharif viz. Mahdi Shah and Shaikh Nur Ali. In accordance with the provisions of the Muslim law (*hukm-i-shariah*), Bibi Zohra, the great grand daughter of Mahdi Shah, was receiving one third of the share (which is half of what her brother Hanif Shah enjoyed) as well as half the income from the position of headship (*sajjadgi*) of the shrine. According to this arrangement, her husband Qadir Bakhsh became a claimant (*malik*) of four shares. This calculation was made in the following manner. If the income from headship (*sajjadgi*) was divided into six parts, Qadir Bakhsh and Hanif Shah received three parts each. Out of these three parts belonging to Hanif Shah, his sister Bibi Zohra (wife of Qadir Bakhsh) was entitled to one part which, according to the provisions of the canonical law (*shariat*), belonged to the daughter. Therefore, her husband Qadir Bakhsh became a claimant (*malik*) of four parts, while her brother Hanif Shah actually received only two of the three parts which, in fact, constituted half of the income from headship (*sajjadgi*) of the shrine.

When Hanif Shah died, one of his four daughters Fazl-ul-Nissa claimed one-fourth of the above mentioned two parts which remained with her father. In Samvat 1885 during the rule (*amaldari*) of Maharaja Ranjit Singh, there was a legal dispute (*muqaddima*) between the grandsons (*nawasa-ha*) of Hanif Shah and the offspring (*aulad*) of Fazl-ul-nissa. When the case reached the government (*sarkar*), it constituted the following five member judicial commission (*munsifan sarkari*) to adjudicate:

1. *Sajjadah nishin* of the tomb of Hazrat Madho Lal Husain
2. Karam Husain and Hasan Din custodians (*mujawirs*) Hazrat Miran Badshah
3. Miyan Shadi and Miyan Budha attendants of the tomb of Hazrat Pir Ali Ganj Bakhsh Hujwiri
4. Karam Ali Shah *sajjadah nishin* Sadar Diwan
5. Azam Shah custodian (*mujawir*) Khanqah Ali Jah Hazrat Bibi Pakdamanan

The above judicial commission after proper investigation and in accordance with the official orders and canonical law (*shariat-i-Muhammadi*), ruled that the income (*zar amdani sajjadgi*) from the shrine of Miyan Mir be divided into four parts. Out of these, three parts were allocated to Karam Shah, the son of Khuda Bakhsh. The fourth part was granted to Mai Waziran, the wife of Hanif Shah, and this was duly handed over to their son-in-law (*damad*) Miyan Isa Shah, who was the husband of Mehar-ul-Nissa. The order of the judges is being given below.

At the time of the judgement, the shares of income from the shrine (*amdani darbar*) were divided according to the following recommendations. Karam Shah, the son of Khuda Bakhsh, will be the claimant (*malik*) of three parts, while Isa Shah, the son-in-law of Hanif Shah, will be entitled to one part. The three offspring (*aulad*) of Khuda Bakhsh – Mahbub Shah, the son of Muhammad Shah, the son of Khuda Bakhsh; Alif Shah, the son of Karam Shah, the son of Khuda Bakhsh; and Mehar Shah, the son of Qutb Shah, the son of Amir Shah, the son of

Khuda Bakhsh – live at one place and there is unity (*itfaq*) among them. Mahbub Shah is providing (*parvarish*) for every one and the latter are also satisfied. If any one of them wishes to separate, he can surely claim his share without any hesitation. If he does separate, he can claim one of the three parts and, corresponding to this share, contribute to the expenditure on the death anniversary of Miyan Mir (*urs*).

The third part of the income, which has been granted to Isa Shah, will be allocated in the following manner. His four sons – Natha Shah, Muhammad Shah, Karam Shah and Akbar Shah – who are presently alive, will share one-fourth of this one part. These four sons of Isa Shah also receive the share of their mother Mehar-ul-Nissa, the daughter of Hanif Shah. Hanif Shah had three daughters. One of them Fazl-ul-Nissa enjoyed her patrimonial share (*hissa pidri*) and gave it to her husband Khuda Bakhsh. The other two daughters of Hanif Shah viz. Karam-ul-Nissa and Khair-ul-Nissa as well as their offspring (grandchildren of Hanif Shah) are alive at present, but they are not claiming any share. If they so desire, they can do so in accordance with the rules of the sacred law (*shariat*) regarding the division of property, provided they bear the expenditure also.

When Hanif Shah, the *sajjadah nishin* and *nambardar*, died in 1221 AH/1806 AD, Khuda Bakhsh (son-in-law and sister's son of Hanif Shah) persuaded Ladha Gujjar to perform the duties associated with *nambardari*, on the plea that he had been brought there by their elders. As such, Ladha Gujjar performed this service till his death which occurred in 1233 AH/1817 AD. When Khuda Bakhsh, the actual occupant (*asl qabiz*), and Dargahi Gujjar (the son of Ladha Gujjar) died, then Muhammad Shah (the son of Khuda Bakhsh) became the *nambardar* in the forty-fourth year. Thereafter Amir Shah (the brother of Muhammad Shah) and regent (*sarprast*) of Mahbub Shah (the present *sajjadah nishin*) said to Mahi Gujjar, the son of Ladha Gujjar, "Since I am a recluse (*mard-i-faqir*) and inhabitant of the desert (*badiya nishin*), you should assume the responsibility of *nambardari*." After the death of Amir Shah, Karam Shah became the regent (*sarprast*) of Mahbub Shah and appointed Arurha Jat as *nambardar* in succession to Mahi Gujjar. The incumbent has continued in this position under the British government. The *sajjadah nishin* Mahbub Shah has appointed Gama Rajput, a resident of village Shergarh (which has become desolate after its inclusion in the cantonement of Miyan Mir), as the *nambardar* along with Arurha Jat. Gama Rajput died without any issue. Arurha Jat also was no more. After these deaths, the son of Arurha Jat was appointed as *nambardar* of Miyan Mir. This situation was prevailing when the research for the present volume (*Tahqiqat-i-Chishti*) was being carried out.

NOTES AND REFERENCES

1. Ganda Singh, *A Bibliography of Punjab*, Punjabi University, Patiala, 1966, p. 185.
2. Nur Ahmad Chishti, *Tahqiqat-i-Chishti*, Al-Faisal Nashiran wa Tajiran Kutb, Lahore, Reprint, 2001, pp. 288-293.

Contributors

Surinder Singh is Professor and (former) Chairperson at the Department of History, Panjab University, Chandigarh. His major area of interest is the socio-cultural history of north-western medieval India. On this subject, he has published over two dozen research papers which have appeared in such journals as the *Islamic Culture, Proceedings of the Indian History Conference, Panjab Past and Present* and *Proceedings of the Punjab History Conference*. He has three books to his credit viz. *A History of Medieval India 1000-1526* (1997), *The Political Memoirs of an Indian Revolutionary: Naina Singh Dhoot 1904-1989* (2005) and (co-edited with Ishwar Dayal Gaur) *Popular Literature and Pre-modern Societies in South Asia* (2008). He has served as the President, Medieval Section, Punjab History Conference, 40th Session, 14-16 March 2008. As his presidential address, he has brought out a monograph entitled, *The Making of Medieval Punjab: Politics, Society and Economy c.1200-c1400* (2008).

Ishwar Dayal Gaur is Reader in History at the Department of Evening Studies, Panjab University, Chandigarh. His research pertains to culture, folklore and literature. He has versified the cultural mosaic of Punjab in two collections of poetry. In addition he has authored four books viz. *Essays on History and Historiography* (1998), *Martyr as Bridegroom: A Folk Representation of Bhagat Singh* (2008), (co-edited with Surinder Singh) *Popular Literature and Pre-modern Societies in South Asia* (2008), *Society, Religion and Patriarchy: Exploring Medieval Punjab through Hir Waris* (2009). In collaboration with Surinder Singh, he has organized three national seminars at the Panjab University, Chandigarh, during 2005-07.

Iqtidar Husain Siddiqui has served as Professor and Chairperson at the Centre of Advanced Study in Medieval Indian History, Aligarh Muslim University, Aligarh. A prolific writer, his area of interest is the political and social history of the Delhi sultanate and the Afghans. His major publications are *Some Aspects of Afghan Despotism in India* (1969), *History of Sher Shah Sur* (1971), *Mughal Relations with the Indian Ruling Elite* (1983), *Islam and Muslims in South Asia: Historical Perspectives* (1987),

Tarikh-i-Sadr-i-Jahan (1988), *Perso-Arabic Sources of Information on the Life and Conditions in the Sultanate of Delhi* (1992), *Medieval India: Essays in Intellectual Thought and Culture, Vol. I,* (2003), *An Eighteenth Century History of North India: An Account of the Rise and Fall of the Rohilla Chiefs in Jan Bhasha by Rustam Ali Bijnori* (2005), *Authority and Kingship under the Sultans of Delhi: Thirteenth-Fourteenth Centuries* (2006). He was elected as the President, Medieval Section, Indian History Congress, 54th Session, Mysore, 1993. He has made scholarly contributions to the *Encyclopaedia of Islam* and *Encyclopaedia Iranica*.

Tanvir Anjum is Assistant Professor at the Department of History, Quaid-i-Azam University, Islamabad (Pakistan). Her areas of interest are sufism, medieval state and intellectual history of the Muslims of South Asia. She has contributed more than a dozen articles to research journals and international conferences. She was awarded the Charles Wallace Fellowship (2001) at the School of Oriental and African Studies, University of London (UK) and Kodikara Research Award (2000) by the Regional Centre for Strategic Studies, Sri Lanka. She has presented papers at the seminars organized by the Aligarh Muslim University, Aligarh and Panjab University, Chandigarh. Currently she is working under a Post Doctoral Fellowship at the University of North Carolina, Chapel Hill, USA.

Humaira Arif Dasti is Professor and Chairperson at the Department of History, Bahauddin Zakariya University, Multan (Pakistan). Her chief areas of interest are regional studies, mystical movements and medieval culture. She is the author of *Multan: A Province of the Mughal Empire*, (1993). Having attended nearly thirty national and international conferences, she has travelled extensively in England, Italy, Germany, France, Spain, Egypt, India and middle eastern countries. She was awarded the British Council Fellowship in 1995 and Charles Wallace Fellowship in 2001. Apart from guiding fifteen dissertations and theses, she has undertaken research projects on endowments attached to the Gardezi shrines at Multan and Qadiri shrines at Uch.

Aneesa Iqbal Sabir is a Research Scholar at the Centre of Advanced Study in Medieval Indian History, Aligarh Muslim University, Aligarh. She is a product of the Bombay University from where she obtained her post-graduate degree in History (1996). She completed her M.Phil (2001) with a dissertation on *Muslim Education and Learning under the Mughals*. She taught for two years, as Lecturer in History, at the Pendharkar College, Mumbai. Recently she has submitted her Ph.D. thesis on the topic *Muslim Education and Learning under the Delhi Sultans (1206-1398)* under the supervision of Dr. Azra Alavi. Her research papers, which are devoted to the education of women in medieval India, have been published in the issues of the *Indica* during 2007 and 2008. She has also contributed to the *Dr. K.N. Chitnis Felicitation Volume: Some Aspects of Medieval India*, Ed., G.S. Gaekwad, (2006).

Jigar Mohammed is Professor and (former) Chairperson at the Department of History, University of Jammu, Jammu. Apart from a book entitled *Revenue-Free Grants in Mughal India: Awadh Region in the Seventeenth and Eighteenth Centuries* (2002), he has published nearly thirty articles on the socio-economic history of Jammu, Kashmir and Ladakh. He has served at the University of Jammu as the editor of the *Journal of Social Sciences* and convener of the Heritage Cell. He has also served as the President of the Medieval Section, Punjab History Conference, Punjabi University, Patiala (1989-99).

Zahir Uddin Malik retired as Professor from the Centre of Advanced Study in Medieval Indian History, Aligarh Muslim University, Aligarh. An authority on the history of the eighteenth century, he has written extensively on the political, social and economic aspects of the period. He was also interested in the nature of contemporary Persian records, chronicles and documents. His major publications are *A Mughal Statesman of the Eighteenth Century: Khan-i-Dauran, Mir Bakhshi of Muhammad Shah* (1973), *The Reign of Muhammad Shah 1719-1748* (1977) and *Agrarian System of Medieval India: Land Revenue Assignments in Sarkar Shahabad (Bihar), 1734-1790* (2001). He has also written over three dozen articles which have been published in such journals as *Medieval India: A Miscellany, Indian Economic and Social History Review, Proceedings of the Indian History Congress, Indo-Iranica* and *Studies in Islam*. He has also contributed twenty entries on the Muslim leaders of modern India to the *Urdu Encyclopaedia*, Hyderabad. He served as the President of the Medieval Section, Indian Histcry Congress, 51st Session, Kolkata, 1990 and contributed a presidential address entitled 'The Core and Periphery: A Contribution to the Debate on the Eighteenth Century.'

Mohammad Tazeem is a product of the Department of History and Culture, Jamia Millia Islamia, New Delhi. He earned his doctoral degree for a thesis entitled *Ahd-i-Aurangzeb Key Muwarikheen aur unki Tarikh Nigari* (Historians and Historiography during the Reign of Aurangzeb). He possesses proficiency in such languages as Persian, Arabic, Urdu, English and Hindi. This has enabled him to pursue research in the fields of medieval chronicles, political history and religious developments. He has over two dozen research papers to his credit, which have been presented in national seminars and conferences. He has translated a few history books of the NCERT into Urdu. Presently he teaches History at the Senior Secondary School, Jamia Millia Islamia, New Delhi.

Saeed Ahmad is Associate Professor at the Government Commerce College, Rawalpindi (Pakistan). For several decades, he is engaged in two missions which are intimately connected with each other: firstly, to propagate the teachings of the Punjabi sufi poets and, secondly, to secure a rightful place in the society for the mother tongue Punjabi. As a linguist, he has prepared dictionaries of Urdu-Esparanto. Under a series entitled *Great Sufi Wisdom*, he has published nearly a dozen volumes on the poetry of Baba Farid Ganj-i-Shakar, Shah Husain, Sultan Bahu, Bulle Shah, Khwaja Ghulam Farid, Waris Shah and Miyan Muhammad Bakhsh. For wide circulation, these works have been transliterated into several scripts – Shahmukhi, Gurmukhi and Roman – besides explanations in Punjabi, English, French and Esparanto. Over 2 lakh copies of these books have been published during the last eight years. He has contributed over a hundred columns to the Punjabi newspaper *Khabran* (Lahore) and www.apnaorg.com. He nurtures a personal website www.sufiwisdom.org to popularize his ideas.

S.M. Azizuddin Husain is Professor at the Department of History and Culture, Jamia Millia Islamia, New Delhi. His areas of interest are political and social history of medieval India, historical records and collections of letters in Persian, besides medieval archaeology. A prolific writer both in English and Urdu, he has written nearly fourteen books and fifty research papers. His major publications are *Kalimat-i-Taiyibat: Collection of Aurangzeb's Orders* (1982), *Kalimat-i-Aurangzeb* (1983), *Tazkirat-ul-Umara of Kewal Ram* (1985), *Raqaim-i-Karaim: Epistles of Aurangzeb* (1990), *Medieval Towns: A Case Study of Amroha and Jalali* (1995), *Qazi Saiyyid Nurullah Shustari: Biography of an Eminent Scholar* (2001), *Structure of Politics under Aurangzeb* (2002), *Ahd-i-Wusta Ka Hindustan* (2003), *Tarikh-i-Ahd-i-Wusta* (2004), *Calendar of M.A. Ansari's Correspondence* (2005) and *Madrasah Education in India from 11th to 21st Century* (2005). At present, he is pursuing research projects on Mir Syed Ali Hamadani, development of Unani medicine in India, and Persian and Urdu documents relating to the revolt of 1857.

Iqbal Sabir is a Senior Lecturer at the Centre of Adanced Study in Medieval Indian History, Aligarh Muslim University, Aligarh. A product of the Lucknow University, he undertook his research at Aligarh under the supervision of Prof. Khaliq Ahmad Nizami. His area of specialization is religious movements in medieval India, with particular reference to the Naqshbandi order. His M.Phil dissertation (1985) pertained to the hagiographical literature of the Naqshbandis, while his Ph.D. (1991) thesis was devoted to the life and thought of Shaikh Ahmad Sirhindi. Besides these themes, his research is focused on the relations of the Mughals rulers with the religious intelligentsia and the role of Sir Syed Ahmad Khan. His research papers have been published in the volumes edited by such distinguished scholars like Iqtidar Husain Siddiqui, Mansura Haidar, Abdul Ali, Zafarul Islam, G.S. Gaekwad, Shihabuddin Iraqi and Shah Muhammad Waseem.

Tahir Kamran is Associate Professor and Chairman at the Department of History, Government College University, Lahore (Pakistan). Specialising in the history of Punjab, he has written extensively on issues of culture, religion and identity. He holds a Ph.D. on the legislative politics of Punjab and has authored two books entitled *Idea of History through the Ages* and *Tarikh-i-Pakistan*. He has also translated half a dozen important works into Urdu. He is the founder editor of a bi-annual journal *The Historian*. He organized an international conference on *Punjab and the Raj* (5-7 January 2006) and published the proceedings in the *Journal of Punjab Studies* (Spring 2007). He has been associated as fellow with the universities of Bradford and Southampton (UK). He has made scholarly presentations at the School of Oriental and African Studies, University of Coventry, University of Karachi and Jawaharlal Nehru University (New Delhi). Currently he is putting together a volume on colonial Punjab, besides working on sectarian militancy in Pakistan.

Subhash Parihar is an internationally known art historian. He holds post-graduate degrees in History and History of Art, besides M.Phil and Ph.D. He serves as a senior teacher at the Government Brajindra College, Faridkot. A profilic writer, he has written several scholarly works on the architectural heritage of north-western India. His important books are *Mughal Monuments in the Punjab and Haryana* (1985), *Muslim Inscriptions in the Punjab, Haryana and Himachal Pardesh* (1985), *Some Aspects of Indo-Islamic Architecture* (1999), *History and Architectural Remains of Sirhind* (2006), *Land Transport in Mughal India: Agra-Lahore Mughal Highway and its Architectural Remains* (2008), *Architectural Heritage of A Sikh State: Faridkot* (in press). He has published more than three dozen research papers in such journals as *Oriental Art* (London), *Journal of the Royal Asiatic Society* (London), *East and West* (Rome), *Muqarnas* (Leiden), *Journal of the Pakistan Historical Society* (Karachi), *Islamic Studies* (Islamabad) and *Marg* (Mumbai). He was awarded the Homi Bhabha Fallowship in 1994-96. He undertook a photographic survey of the Architectural Heritage of Haryana under a senior fellowship of the Ministry of Culture, Government of India in 2001-03. His project on the Agra-Lahore highway was partially financed by the Barakat Trust (London).

Hitender Kumar is a research scholar at the Department of History, University of Hyderabad, Hyderabad. He is engaged in research for his Ph.D. on the topic 'Hydrology and Technology of Building Construction in the Subah of Delhi.' Earlier he had earned his M.Phil from the Kurukshetra University for his dissertation on *Sufi Shrines of Medieval Haryana: A Study in Medieval Archaeology*. He was also associated with the UGC Major Research Project on 'Material Remains and Historical Reconstruction: A Case Study of Haryana,' which was undertaken by the Department of History, Kurukshetra University,

Kurukshetra during 2003-05. He has also submitted a dissertation entitled 'Role of G.D. Birla in the National Movement' during his post-graduate diploma course at the National Archives of India, New Delhi.

Salim Mohammed, a native of Malerkotla, is deeply involved in education and research. He holds post-graduate degrees in History, Persian, Punjabi, English and Economics. His M.Phil. dissertation pertained to the development of architecture during the reign of Shahjahan, while his Ph.D. thesis was devoted to Sultan Zainul Abidin of Kashmir (1420-1470). Two of his books have appered under the title of *Loyal Rulers of the Patiala State* (1997) and *Shahidan Dey Sartaj: Sri Guru Tegh Bahadur* (1995). He has produced nearly a score of articles which have been published in the *Panjab Past and Present*, *Proceedings of the Punjab History Conference*, *Journal of the Folklore Society and Cultural Heritage of India*. Presently he is engaged in research on the history of the Nawabi State of Malerkotla as well as the soldiers (Sappers and Miners) who served in the Second World War. He serves as a teacher at the Government Senior Secondary School at Siahar, near Ludhiana.

Syed Liyaqat Hussain Moini is Associate Professor at the Centre of Advanced Study in Medieval Indian History, Aligarh Muslim University, Aligarh. His areas of interest are medieval Rajasthan, the city of Ajmer and sufism. His first book was entitled *The Chishti Shrine of Ajmer: Pirs, Practices and Pilgrims* (2004), while the second one *The City of Ajmer under the Mughals* is in the press. He has produced over two dozen research papers on the various historical aspects of the shrine of Khwaja Moinuddin Chishti at Ajmer. These have been presented at the sessions of the Indian History Congress and national seminars on sufism. Some of these have been published in the volumes edited by A.J. Qaisar, S.P. Verma, Christial W. Troll and Neeru Misra. Being a scion of a distinguished family of the custodians (*khuddam*) of the Ajmer shrine, he is the first scholar to have studied rare documents of the Mughal period, which illumine the little known aspects of the history of the sacred place.

Yogesh Snehi is teaching in the Post-graduate Department of History, DAV College, Amritsar. His area of interest is the social history of north-western India. He has earned his doctorate for a thesis on gender relations, with reference to literacy and empowerment. He is also contributing to the debates on popular syncretism and sufi shrines (*dargahs*), besides undertaking extensive field work on medieval monuments which have been documented on digital modes. During his days as a research scholar at the Panjab University, Chandigarh, he organized several academic activities on behalf of the *Critique*, a students' discussion forum. His publications have appeared in such journals as the *Indian Economic and Social History Review* and *Economic and Political Weekly*.

Index

aab hayati 292
Abdul Haq Muhaddis Dehalvi 6, 16, 99, 144, 224
Abdul Karim 348
Abdul Qadir Badauni 60, 346, 351
Abdul Qadir Gilani 125, 137, 140, 270, 284
Abdul Qaiyum Rafiqi 119
Abdul Rahim 348
Abdul Rahman Baba 373
Abdul Rahman Chishti 14
Abdul Rahman Mirza Madari 147
Abdul Rahman Zaffari 114
Abdul Razzaq 348
Abdul Rehman 168, 310
Abdul Rehman Zaffari 113
Abdul Samad Khan 385, 389
Abdullah Ansari Harawi 270
Abdullah Khan Khweshgi 388
Abdullah Khan Uzbek 261, 263
Abdur Rahim Khan-i-Khanan 259
Abha Nagri 408
Abhoar 357
Abida Parveen 23
Abohar 37, 389, 404, 405, 406, 407, 408, 409, 410, 412, 413, 414, 415, 416, 417, 419, 420, 421
Abrahamic 235
Abram Chand 413
Abu Abdul Rahman al-Sulami 191
Abu Bakr 182, 226, 264, 266, 268, 269
Abu Bakr Tusi 59
Abu Hanifa 310, 311, 312
Abu Huraira 138
Abu Ishaq Shami 15
Abu Najib Abdul Qahir 84, 92
Abu Saeed al-Hujwiri 180
Abu Said 27, 28
Abu Said bin Abi al-Khair 233
Abu Yazid Bistami 3
Abul Abbas Ahmad bin Muhammad Ashqani 179
Abul Fazl 25, 258, 338, 342, 346, 347, 351
Abul Fazl Muhammad bin Hasan Khattali 179
Abul Hasan Fushanja 181
Abul Maali 148
Abul Qasim Gurgani 179
abyat 286, 289
Adanwall 362
Aden 99, 109
Adi Granth 32, 33, 198
Adil Shahi 11
Aditya 305
Afghan 198, 356, 358, 360, 362, 363, 380, 381, 385
Afghan empire 136
Afghan tribes 136, 282, 388
Afghanistan 81, 88, 158, 166, 257, 282, 303, 360, 414
Afghans 51, 158, 357, 360, 361, 380
Afif 341
Africa 59
Afzal-ul-Fawaid 5, 219
Agra 145, 258, 259, 345, 346, 348
Agra-Lahore highway 258
Ahadis 266

ahimsa 25
Ahirs 15
Ahkam-i-Alamgiri 220
ahl-i-bait 264, 267
ahl-i-daawat 144
ahl-i-hawas 146
ahl-i-hirfat 142
ahl-i-sunnat wa jamaat 263, 266
Ahmad Barani 110
Ahmad Beg Khan 139
Ahmad Gujjar 236
Ahmad Shah 158
Ahmad Shah Abdali 123
Ahmadabad 58, 282
Ahmadpur 165, 167
Ahmadyar Khan Abbasi 386
Ahsa 100
aimma 346
Ain-i-Akbari 122
Ain-ul-Fuqara 283
Ainul Mulk Mahru 303
Aisha 258, 264
Ajam 7
Ajami 49
Ajami tradition 50
ajlaf 66
Ajmer 13, 14, 37, 55, 56, 58, 65, 69, 70, 81, 120, 153, 162, 208, 214, 378, 379, 380, 382, 383, 384, 385, 386, 387, 388, 389, 390, 402
Ajmer Sharif 421
Ajmer shrine 387, 388, 389, 390
Ajodhan 29, 56, 57, 64, 70, 71, 72, 73, 74, 120, 126, 179, 197, 204, 207, 208, 214, 215, 216, 217, 220, 225, 229, 338, 403, 409
Akbar 8, 14, 24, 60, 136, 137, 145, 153, 208, 257, 258, 259, 260, 272, 295, 379
Akbarpur 362
Akhbar-ul-Akhyar 6, 69, 100, 223, 342
akhirat 112
Akhnur 124
Alam 342
Alam Ganj 139
Alam-i-Alavi 227
alam-i-arwah 270
alam-i-ghaib 142
alam-i-malkut 140, 148
Alam-i-Safli 227
Alauddin Jahansoz 81
Alauddin Khalji 83, 303
Alfred von Kremer 2
Ali 226, 263, 265, 268, 269, 343, 374, 380, 404, 406, 410, 413
Ali bin Usman Hujwiri 1, 2, 3, 97, 122, 179, 281
Ali Haider 25
Ali Khokhar Darvesh 85
Ali Muhammad Khan 168
Aligarh 110
Alipur 362
Alla Pir 125
Allah Diya Chishti 69
Altaf Husain Hali 346
Amal wa Asghal 115
Amal-i-Saleh 135
Amar Singh 130
Ambala 209, 346
Amir Hasan Ala Sijzi 4, 214, 219, 220
Amir Khan 388
Amir Khurd 55, 68, 69, 70, 220, 221, 225, 228
Amir Khusro 5, 120, 234, 262
Amir Muawiya 264
Amir Timur 123
Amritsar 32, 164, 356, 421
Amroha 214
anahat shabd 169
Anand Sahib 128
Anandpur Sahib 357
Aneesa Iqbal Sabir 34
Angithi 244
Anglo-Sikh 33
Anis Qawwal 372
Anis-ul-Arwah 5, 218, 228
Anna Bigelow 371
Annemarie Schimmel 26, 30, 86, 243
Annie Leclerc 248
Ansari 416
Antonio Gramsci 205
Aqaid-i-Nafsi 113
aql 29, 261, 287
Aqtab-i-Muhammadiyyah 265
Arab 28

Arab Emirates 100
Arabia 16, 24, 125, 257, 357, 378
Arabian Sea 82
Arabic 199, 259, 272, 286, 338, 372
Arabs 414
Arafat 190
Arains 168
Arbain Sufiya 114
Arif Mandi 417
Aroras 416
Arthur J. Arberry 3
Asadullah Khan Ghalib 285
ashab 103, 107, 357
ashab-i-suffa 181
Ash'ari School 280
ashiq 22, 146, 233
ashraf 66, 389
Ashraf Ali Thanvi 17
Ashraf Jahangir Simnani 18
Asiatic Society of Bengal 230
Asim Roy 404, 418
Asin Palacios 2, 3
Asl-i-Khalis 265
Asrar-ul-Auliya 5, 216, 219, 228, 229
Asrar-ul-Dawat 113, 114
Assyria 309
Athar Khan Abbasi 386
audition 190, 191, 192
Auliya 225
aurad 5, 6, 219
Aurangzeb 8, 25, 220, 284, 363, 388
Aush 197
avidya 28
Awan 282, 283
Awarif-ul-Maarif 3, 99, 113, 114, 115, 215, 229, 270
ayan-i-sabilah 269
Ayaz 81
Azarbaijan 179
Aziz Ahmad 29

Baba 124
Baba Ahmed Shah 417
Baba Ali Mohammad 417
Baba Atma Ram 370
Baba Barkat Ali Shah 124, 125
Baba Bhoman Shah 417
Baba Buddhan Ali Shah 124, 125, 128
Baba Bulleh Shah 417
Baba Farid 25, 55, 63, 64, 65, 67, 68, 69, 70, 71, 72, 74, 164, 197, 198, 199, 200, 202, 203, 205, 206, 207, 403, 404, 409, 414, 421
Baba Haidar Shaikh 370
Baba Hazrat Shaikh 360
Baba Jiwan Shah 123, 125, 126, 130
Baba Karam Shah 123
Baba Khetarpal 417
Baba Khwaja Khizar 409
Baba Lakhdata 417, 421
Baba Lal Shah 409
Baba Latifuddin Rishi 123, 125
Baba Nahre Shah 417
Baba Nanak 370
Baba Pir Khumber 417
Baba Pir Tode Shah 125
Baba Rah 123, 125
Baba Ramdev 408, 412, 414, 415, 417, 420
Baba Rattan 357, 379
Baba Sain Lal Din 125
Baba Shah Ghulam Badshah 131
Baba Shakar Ganj 409
Baba Sher Khan Pathan 124
Baba Syed Jalal Bukhari 409
Baba Zakariya Pir 409
Babu Rajab Ali 357
Babur 24, 208, 358
Babur Bani 24
Babylon 309
Badakhshan 145, 147, 217
Badaun 204
Badhacha 362
Badhrawah 125
Badruddin Ghaznavi 218, 229
Badruddin Ishaq 5, 216, 227, 228, 229
Badruddin Sirhindi 264
Badshah Nama 135
Badshahpur Mandyala 362
Bagh Abdul Rahim Khan-i-Khanan 139
Bagh Anarkali 138
Bagh Baddu 139
Bagh Faizi 139

Bagh Hoshiar Khan 139
Bagh Jawahar Khan 139
Bagh Khan Azam 139
Bagh Khatun 139
Bagh Mirza Kamran 138
Bagh Mirza Momin 139
Bagh Mulk Ali Kotwal 139
Bagh Murtaza Khan 139
Bagh Qaleech Khan 138
Bagh Qasim Khan 139
Bagh Raju 139
Bagh Sultan Parvez 138
Bagh Swami Jal 138
Bagh Wazir Khan 139
Baghbanpura 150
Baghdad 7, 49, 51, 59, 80, 97, 109, 125, 179, 217, 228, 229, 284, 338, 414
Baghdad-Khurasan-Bukhara 18
Baghicha Naulakha 138
Bagri 362
Bagri Jats 416, 417
Baha al-Halim 310, 311, 312
Bahadur Shah 346, 383
Bahauddin Sam 81
Bahawalnagar 408
Bahawalpur 12, 166, 309, 358, 380, 381, 404, 405, 407, 414
bahishti darwaza 12, 207
Bahlol Barki Chishti 389
Bahlul Lodi 360, 361, 362, 371, 372, 373
Bahmani 18
Bahmanian 362
Bahraich 14
Bahrain 100
Bahu Awan 283
Bairagis 168
Bajwara 389
Balaknath 410
Balkh 99, 282, 346
Balnath jogi 236
Baluchistan 136, 386
Banda Bahadur 33, 202, 358
bani 20, 243
Banni 125
Banur 360
baolis 129
Bapla 362
Bapli 362
baraka 12, 208, 366
baramah 20, 22, 237, 247
Bargad Ali Shah 124
Bari 362
Bareilly 380
Baryamoon 362
Basal Qutb 99
basant mela 15
Basoli 125
Basra 338
Batala 136
Bathinda 81, 82, 361
Bauli Daulat Khan 139
Bayaniyah 263
Bayazid Bistami 27, 28, 180, 201, 244
Bayazid Khan 359, 363
Bazaid Muhammad 283
Bazdawi 98
Bazullah Khan 387
be-shara 29
Beas 82, 92
Benares 81
Bengal 81, 171, 379, 403, 418
Bhadrawahi 122
Bhai Gurdas 23
Bhaikhan Muhammad Shafi 387
Bhakkar 82, 137, 414, 415
bhaktas 19, 21, 32, 159, 167, 197, 200
bhakti 34, 236, 245, 249
Bhambar 244
Bhangi 285
Bharota 362
Bharuch 115
Bhatiah 309
Bhatinda 357
Bhatner 358
Bhattis 410
Bhawani Ram 389
Bhera 147, 148
Bhogiwal 138, 139
Bhopa 362
Bhudan 362
Bhumsi 359, 360
Bhural 362

Bibi Aisha 310
Bibi Fatima 226
Bibi Haj Taj 139
Bibi Javindi 310, 311, 312
Bibi Mangi 362
Bibi Sharifa 71
Bihar 81, 147
Bijapur 11, 119, 120, 249, 282
Bikaner 13, 357, 358, 383
Birbhan 170, 171
Bismillah 204
Bistam 179
Blunt 407
Bokhara 240
Bolan Pass 305
Bombay 366
Bool Chand 415, 419
Borano 362
Brahman 201
Brahmins 172, 416
Brajbhasa 20
bridal mysticism 21, 241
bridal symbolism 21
British 13, 16, 23, 31, 305, 307, 402, 403, 413
British East India Company 2
Bruce B. Lawrence 15, 16, 17, 218
Bu Ali Qalandar 1, 59, 97, 342, 343, 344, 345, 352, 379
Buddhism 24, 305
Buddhist 279
Buddhist monasteries 305
Bukhara 54, 80, 90, 99, 144
Bulbul Shah 123
Bulleh Shah 2, 19, 21, 22, 25, 26, 29, 152, 169, 197, 202, 234, 235, 237, 238, 239, 240, 241, 243, 244, 245, 247, 248, 249, 250, 295, 357, 374
Bundelkhand 172
Burdwan 406
Burhanpur 151
Burhanuddin 338
Burhanuddin Gharib 222, 223, 224
Butha 362

C.M. Wades 207
Cairo 2
Calcutta 111, 170, 366
Cambridge University 115
Canada 17
Captain Wahid Bakhsh Sial 17
Carl W. Ernst 15, 16, 17, 20, 201, 218, 222, 223, 224, 372
Caspian Sea 179
Central Asia 1, 35, 50, 51, 52, 54, 56, 123, 136, 179, 229, 257, 269, 304, 378, 381
central Punjab 208, 361
Central Turkistan 168
Ceylon 100
Chachran 165, 167
Chahar Gulshan 168
Chahar Pir 410
Chahar Qutb 338, 340, 341
chakki 120
chakki-nama 120, 249
Chamar 416
Chamkaur 309
chanan pakh 367
Chandara 367
Chandavan 170
Chandigarh 32, 357, 360, 421
Chandigarh-Nangal road 357
Chandrama 367
Changi 139
Chankamal 386
Charbagh 350
charkha 120, 249
charkha-nama 120, 249
chaudharis 388
Chauhan Rajput 357
Chautala 380
Cheema Chohan 362
Chenab 82, 285, 304, 305, 309, 408, 414
Chengiz Khan 56, 88, 89, 242
Chhabils 367
Chhaj 244
Chhajli 244
Chhat 360
Chhatrasal Bundela 172
chilla 104, 107, 187, 348
China 88, 100, 257
Chiragh-i-Dehli 222
Chisht 15, 70, 203

Chishti/Chisti order 1, 4, 5, 6, 7, 8, 11, 13, 14, 15, 16, 17, 18, 28, 29, 34, 36, 50, 53, 55, 56, 58, 64, 65, 68, 72, 74, 80, 91, 93, 97, 100, 104, 108, 122, 124, 158, 159, 162, 164, 165, 167, 198, 203, 204, 206, 208, 214, 215, 216, 218, 219, 220, 221, 222, 224, 225, 230, 268, 281, 338, 339, 341, 346, 348, 378, 379, 380, 381, 382, 384, 389
Chishti saints 7, 216, 379, 380, 381, 383
Chishti shrine 380, 383
Chishtia Sabiria 421
Chittorgarh 412
Chotala 164
Choturkoy 362
Christian 201, 279, 281
Christianity 2, 3, 202
Christians 262, 267
Chuchak Siyal 237
cis-Satluj 358, 360
Cunningham 204, 308, 348, 350

Dadri 389
Dadu 171
Dafalis 14
Daholiar 362
Dai Dilaram 139
Dakhani 11, 120
Dal Khalsa 33
Dalil-ul-Arifin 5, 218, 228
Dalpatian Mohallah 127
Damam Mohli 362
Damascus 86, 99, 179, 228, 338
Damodar 420
Damra dynasty 122
Dar-ul-Aman 123
Dara Shukoh 1, 8, 9, 135, 136, 138, 144, 146, 147, 148, 149, 150, 151, 152, 282, 284, 348
Darahoon 362
Darban 360
dargah 13, 14, 37, 50, 51, 55, 56, 60, 207, 208, 280, 340, 356, 365, 366, 367, 369, 370, 374, 379, 402, 405, 407, 408, 409, 410, 412, 415, 416, 417, 418, 419, 420, 421
Dargah of Panj Pir 406
Dars-i-Nizami 279
Darwesh Muhammad 126
Daryapur 362
dastar 100, 142
dastar bandi 12, 70
Dastur-ul-Amal 168
Data Ganj Bakhsh 179, 304
Daud Badshah 370
Daudpotras 387
Daulatabad 5, 139
David Ross 348
Deccan 222, 282, 379, 383, 420
Deccanis 11
Dedhraj 171
Dehli Darwaza 359
Delhi 1, 4, 5, 7, 15, 36, 52, 55, 56, 58, 67, 69, 70, 71, 72, 73, 81, 82, 88, 91, 97, 100, 101, 102, 104, 120, 143, 147, 158, 164, 170, 197, 204, 207, 208, 209, 214, 217, 220, 222, 225, 229, 284, 303, 306, 338, 339, 342, 345, 346, 357, 358, 360, 362, 363, 365, 378, 379, 383, 402, 410, 414, 415
Delhi Sultanate 1, 12, 67, 81, 82, 83, 92, 101, 206, 207, 214, 242, 303, 304, 338, 361, 379
Delhi sultans 52, 54
Deo Singh 309
Deoband 280, 281
Deogarh 309
Dera Ghazi Khan 164, 381
Dera Haji Khan 386
Dera Ismail Khan 310, 381
Dera Mehta 125
dervishes 130, 201
Deva Chandra 172
Devnagari 32
Dhabi Darwaza 359
Dhadewara 362
Dhadewari 362
Dhanuk 416
Dhar 360
Dharsu 171
Dhido Ranjha 237, 240, 245, 246
dhobis 359
Din Muhammad Barua 388

Din-i-Ilahi 24
Dipalpur 82, 208, 303, 356, 360, 361, 389
Diwan Kirpa Ram 122
Diwan Muhammad Maqsood 386
diwans 6, 12, 13, 70
Doda 124, 125
Dogri 122
dohas 20, 26, 170, 197, 242, 248, 286
Dominique-Sila Khan 408, 417
Doms 15
Dulla Bhatti 136, 295
Durga Devi 410
Durr-ul-Maarifat 259

E.H. Palmer 2
east Punjab 32, 200, 357, 358, 359, 404, 405
Edward G. Browne 2
Egypt 59, 99, 309
Egyptian 241
Eisapur Ladda 362
Emperor Akbar 346, 347
English 168
Europe 17, 168, 239

F.R.D. Tholuck 2
Faizi 25, 258
Fakhruddin Iraqi 85, 93, 307
fakkar 373
fana 17, 244, 272
faqih 109
faqir 29, 183, 294, 371, 408
Faqir Baba Faiz Bakhsh Shah Bukhari 124, 125
faqiri 29
faqr 112, 183, 294
Fard Faqir 2, 25, 240
Farid Sani 25, 32
Fariddudin Attar 2
Faridkot 356, 405
Faridpur 362
Fariduddin Qadiri 131
Farrukh Siyar 346
Fasus-ul-Hikam 85, 138
Fateh Chand 386
Fateh Muhammad Qadiri 385
Fateh Singh 358
Fatehpur 362
Fatehpur Sikri 14, 208
fatiha 384, 386
Fatima 226, 264, 404, 406, 410
fatwas 346
faujdar 358
Faulad Turkbacha 361
Fawaid-ul-Fuad 56, 67, 69, 218, 219, 220, 221, 228, 229
Fawaid-ul-Salikin 219
Fazal Shah 124
Fazil Khan 387
Fazil Khan Abbasi 386
Fazilka 389, 404, 405, 417
Fazlullah bin Ziaul Abbasi 109
Fazlullah Jamali 6
Ferozepur 139, 357, 361, 404, 405, 409, 418
Fidak 264
fikr 287
fiqh 93, 103, 105, 110, 113, 279
firaq 289
Firoz Khan 421
Firoz Sabiri Chishti 421
Firozpur Kothala 362
Firuz Shah Tughluq 54, 72, 74, 101, 102, 105, 110, 111, 208, 258, 338, 339, 341, 361
Firuzabad 101
Fredrick Drew 122
French 168
futuh 6, 12, 18, 52, 56, 71, 72, 128, 166, 206, 215
Futuh-ul-Ghaib 270
Futuhat-i-Makkiya 137
Fuwaid-ul-Fuad 4, 5, 6, 16, 88, 91, 103, 214, 216, 217
Fuwaid-ul-Mukhlisin 111
Fuwaid-ul-Salikin 5

gaddi 384, 420
gaddi-nishin 129, 420, 421
Galen 261
galim 203
Ganda Singh 285
Ganeshdas Badehra 122, 126

Ganges 262
Gangetic plain 1, 136, 179
Garh Maharaja 282, 285
Gazrun 51, 99
geet 20
Gehla Ram Kamboj 415, 420
German 30, 168
Gesudaraz 18
Ghaggar 338, 356
ghani 142
Ghani Khan 309
Ghar-i-Hira 107, 144
Ghaus 294
Ghazi Khan 389
Ghazi Khan Baloch 387
Ghazi Malik 303, 307
Ghazi Mian 410
Ghazipur 170
Ghaziuddin Khan 164
Ghaznavids 1, 81, 179, 198
Ghaznavid empire 179
Ghazni 14, 50, 66, 81, 88, 179, 228, 262, 309, 341, 346
Ghazzali 3, 167, 180, 260
Ghela Ram Kamboj 406
Ghiasuddin Balban 53, 57, 71, 228, 303
Ghiasuddin Tughluq 208
Ghiyaspur 72, 225
Ghulam Allah Bakhsh 384
Ghulam Farid 197
Ghulam Hussain Abbasi 386
Ghulam Jilani 421
Ghulam Shah Abbassi 383
Ghund 244
ghungat 245, 246
Ghur 88, 303, 309
Ghurabiyah 263
Ghurids 81
Ghuzz 7, 81, 198
Gilani Makhdums 309
Gilani Syed 284
Gilmartin 403
Gita 160
gnosis 112, 161, 181
goddess Devi 371
Goddess Kali 171
Goil 244
Goindwal 356
Gojri 122
Golarah 165
Golconda 8, 282
Golden Temple 164
Gomal Valley 311
Greek Neo-Platonic 25
Gugga Pir 15, 357
Gujarat 1, 58, 98, 102, 111, 115, 136, 240, 249, 305, 379
Gujjars 130, 147, 236
Gujranwala 410
Gulab Rai Allahyar Khani 389
Gulabnama 122
Gulbarga 120, 378
Gulshan-i-Raz 86
Gulzar-i-Abrar 69
Gummat 131
Gurbachan Singh Talib 199
Gurdaspur 361, 406
gurdwara 350
Gurgaon 171
gurmat-kav 21
Gurmukhi 20, 32
guru 33, 198
Guru Amar Das 198
Guru Arjun Dev 9, 33, 135, 164, 198, 202
Guru Gobind Singh 23, 309, 357, 358, 359, 370, 383, 388, 410
Guru Granth Sahib 59, 198
Guru Hargobind 135, 164
Guru Nanak 24, 128, 198, 199, 200, 202, 243, 383
Guru Nanak Dev University 32
Guru Ram Das 198
Guru Teg Bahadur 202
guru-gaddi 198
gurus 19, 21, 32, 200

H.A. Rose 209, 357, 359, 368, 373, 407, 408, 410, 412, 413, 414
H.H. Wilson 413
ha da nara 370
Habibullah Shah 284
habs-i-dam 197
Hadi Ali Khan 388

hadis 80, 83, 90, 93, 103, 110, 113, 140, 167, 247, 263, 268, 279
Hafiz Muhammad Ali Khairabadi 381
Hafiz Muhammad Jamal 381
Hafiz Shihabuddin 386
Hafiz Ziauddin 126
Haft Tamasha 168
Haidar Shaikh 356, 357, 359, 371
Haidari Qalandars 59
Haj 54, 99, 154, 162, 189, 205, 206
haji 293
Haji Imdad Allah 17
Haji Khan 389
Haji Khan Baloch 387
Haji Muhammad Banyani 147
Haji Mustapha 147
Haji Najmuddin 381
Haji Niamatullah Sirhindi 138
Haji Sharif Zandani 65
Hakim 413
Hakimis 180
Halaku 82
Hamid bin Mahmud 113
Hamid Qalandar 4, 215
Hamiduddin 83
Hamiduddin Khan 220
Hamiduddin Nagauri Suwali 91
Hanabalite schools 262
Hanafite school 262, 265, 267
Hansi 1, 36, 56, 58, 73, 81, 197, 214, 338, 339, 341, 342, 378
Hanuman 371
Hanumangarh 415
haqiqat 105, 106, 107, 140, 143, 271
Haqiqat-i-Muhammadiyyah 265, 271
Harmandir Sahib 33, 135
Haryana 31, 197, 336, 366, 406
Hasan 282, 363, 404, 406, 410
Hasan Mahmud Qadiri 385
Hashim 236
Hasht Bahisht 69
Hassan Basri 380
Hatiwal 362
Hazarat Nazar Ali Shah 125
hazira 341
Hazrat Ahmed Shaikh 373
Hazrat Ali 226
Hazrat Baba Latifuddin 126
Hazrat Haji Muhammad Akram 125
Hazrat Inayat Khan 17
Hazrat Jiwan Shah 123
Hazrat Kasim Shah 125
Hazrat Khizar 84
Hazrat Miskin Shah Kishtwari 125
Hazrat Muahmmad Akhyaruddin 124
Hazrat Muhammad Asraruddin 124
Hazrat Nadir Ali Shah Baghdadi 125
Hazrat Sayyid Abu Sikandar Ali 125
Hazrat Shah Muhammad Ghazi 125
Hazrat Shaikh ki Chauki 368
Hazrat Shaikh Sadruddin Sadar-i-Jahan 359
Hazrat Shaikh Zainuddin 126
Hazrat Shawan Sarkoti 125
Hazrat Sirajuddin Makki 344
Hazrat Zainuddin Rishi 123
Hazrat-i-Khwajgan 268
Hazrat-ul-Quds 264
Hejaz 98
Herat 53
Hidaya 98, 113
Hidayat-ul-Qawanin 16
Hidayatullah Khan 388
Hijri calendar 226
Hikmatnama 343
Himachal Pardesh 31, 366
Himalayas 282
Hindi 56, 60, 170, 359, 369, 372
Hindko 20
Hindu/Hindus 9, 25, 28, 31, 36, 37, 55, 58, 59, 82, 120, 122, 159, 168, 170, 172, 200, 204, 262, 279, 282, 284, 285, 309, 340, 357, 358, 359, 367, 370, 380, 382, 389, 404, 406, 407, 410, 415, 417, 418, 419
Hindu ascetics 159
Hindu bhaktas 35
Hindu bhakti 158, 159
Hindu Law 169
Hindu religion 159
Hindu yogis 56

Hinduism 24, 25, 26, 32, 60, 129, 168, 171, 202, 305
Hindustan 24, 89, 127, 206, 208, 238, 360
Hindustani 32
Hindvi 120
Hir 22, 23, 136, 203, 237, 239, 243, 244, 246, 249, 406, 409, 410
Hir Siyal 235
Hir-Ranjha 20, 22, 26, 234, 249, 251
Hira 161
Hissar 197, 358, 385, 388
Hissar-Firuza 339
Hitender Kumar 36
Hoshiarpur 389
hujra 106, 110, 141, 294
Hukmnama 343
Hulegu 59
Hululis 180
Humaira Arif Dasti 34
human spirituality 30
Humayun 136, 208
hundi 385, 386
Husain 282, 404, 406
Husainpur 362
husan 21, 22
Hussain 410
huzur-i-qalb 140
Hwen-Tsang 305

ibadatgah 365
Ibn Arabi 27
Ibn Hazam 3
Ibn-i-Arabi 2, 3, 9, 36, 85, 86, 137, 152, 167, 235, 279
Ibrahim 10, 358
Ibrahim Khan 388
Ichhra 139
Id-ul Fitar 416
Id-ul-Zuha 348
Ikadeshi 367
Ikhlas Khan 388
ilm 22, 241, 287
ilm-i-aqwal 105
ilm-i-batin 137, 267
ilm-i-kalam 271
ilm-i-zahir 267
Imam Abu Hanifa 267
Imam Husain 226
Imam Rafiuddin 258
imam-i-adil 258
Imamiyah 263
iman 182, 183
inamdars 11
Inayat Shah 238, 246
Inayatullah Khan 220
India 25, 28, 49, 51, 54, 55, 56, 59, 64, 69, 72, 88, 98, 100, 110, 122, 123, 136, 168, 201, 205, 242, 247, 262, 282, 285, 338, 342, 357, 362, 378, 379, 389, 402, 404, 405, 406, 409, 418
Indian National Movement 24
Indian subcontinent 9, 15, 19, 23, 50, 56, 119, 121, 124, 257, 263, 281, 286, 303, 304, 305, 346, 358, 363, 372, 378, 379, 406
Indian Unitary thought 28
Indian Vedanta 2
Indic 20
Indira Nagri 421
Indo-Muslim architecture 304, 305, 340
Indo-Pak subcontinent 26, 233
Indonesia 257
Indus 414
Indus valley 402
Iqbal Sabir 36
iqta 303, 338
Iqtidar Husain Siddiqui 34
Iran 50, 82, 99, 125, 150, 244, 378
Iranis (Shias) 8
Iraq 99, 109, 179, 284, 342
Iraqi 85, 86
Iraqian school of mysticism 247
Irshad-ul-Talibin 169, 347
Irtida Ali Khan 16
Isa 363
Isami 234
Isbat-un-Nubuwwah 258, 259
ishq 21, 22, 29, 36, 121, 146, 186, 278, 287, 288, 289
Ishtiaq Husain Qureshi 8, 29
Ishwar Dayal Gaur 35
Islah-ul-Amal 169

Islam 2, 17, 19, 24, 49, 60, 94, 129, 140, 153, 160, 161, 168, 171, 179, 180, 197, 202, 204, 227, 233, 235, 245, 259, 260, 262, 263, 272, 279, 280, 282, 285, 304, 309, 338, 351, 357, 369, 371, 402, 403, 413, 418, 421
Islam Khan 361
Islamic architecture 305
Islamic mysticism 1, 2, 159, 161, 214, 292
Islamicate 20
Ismailiyah 263
Israruddin 126
Izaldarmir 388, 389
Izzat Beg Mirza 240
Izzuddaulah Khan Alam 388
Izzuddin Balban Kishlu Khan 81, 88, 92, 303
Izzuddin Husain 81

J.G. Herder 30
Jadunath Sarkar 29
Jafar Badr Alam bin Jalaluddin Maqsud Alam 115
Jahandar Shah 168
Jahangir 9, 135, 144, 149, 150, 153, 164, 208, 257
Jahud tribe 130
Jai Singh 130
Jaipur 124
Jaitwal 362
Jalal 241
Jalalabad 404, 405
Jalali 214
Jalalpur 165
Jalaluddin Kabir-ul-Auliya 379
Jalaluddin Khwarizm Shah 52
Jalaluddin Mangbarni 88, 309
Jalaluddin Rumi 2, 36, 86, 148, 235, 238, 343
Jalaluddin Surkh Bukhari 310, 311
Jalaluddin Tabrezi 91, 218, 228, 229
Jalandhar 179, 209, 361, 389, 406, 409
Jalandhar Doab 389
jama-i-suf 181
jamaat khanah 29, 65, 66, 71, 72, 204, 206, 215
Jamal 241, 338
Jamal Muhammad Khan 388
Jamaluddin 197
James William Graham 2
Jami 167
Jami Saghir-i-Suyuti 258
Jami-ul-Saghir 113
Jami-ul-Ulum 85, 102, 103, 104, 105, 107, 109, 113, 114, 215
Jammu 35, 119, 123, 124, 127, 128, 129, 130, 132, 361, 406
Jammu hills 119, 121, 122, 124, 125, 127, 128, 130, 131
Jamuna 343
Janam Sakhi 370
Jandiala 356
jangnamas 14
Jasrath Khokhar 361
Jats 12, 13, 158, 282, 380
Jaunpur 100, 147, 379, 386
Jawahir Khamsa 169
Jawaliqs 58, 59, 87
Jawami-ul-Kilam 103
jawanmardi 233
jazbah 140, 268, 269
jaziya 8, 262, 279
Jehlam 148
jesht mela 15
Jesus Christ 262, 267
Jeth 366
Jeth Sudi 366
Jeth Sudi Ikadeshi 367
Jews 262
Jhajjar 389
Jhajpur 171
Jhanda Singh 285
Jhang 235, 237, 282
Jharu or baukar 244
Jhelum 282
Jheni 60
Jhuner 362
Jhunjhunu 381
Jibreel 104
Jigar Mohammed 35
Jind 356
Jiwan Shah 130
Jiwan Shah Muhallah 125

Jogi 22, 158, 168, 205, 227, 236, 246, 380
John F. Richards 14
John Malcolm 2
John P. Brown 2
jotshi 287
journal 32
Julahas 15, 359
jumeraat 366
Junaid Baghdadi 3, 50, 247
Junaidis 180

Kaaba 84, 190, 292, 293
Kabir 170, 171, 246
Kabir Khan Ayaz 81, 88, 92, 303
Kabirpanthis 416
Kabul 144, 196, 361, 373
Kadumal 389
kafi 20, 22, 26, 197, 238
kafir 104, 281, 291
kafis 197, 243, 244, 248, 249, 357
Kahergan 283, 285
Kahtwal 56, 197, 229
Kaithal 350, 358
Kalal 147
Kalanaur 361
kalima 107
Kaliyar 58, 378, 421
Kalsia 356
Kamal Khan 388
Kambojs 359, 416
Kambos 51
Kamil Khan Mumtaz 307, 311
Kangra 9, 145, 282
Kanpur 163
Kanz-ul-Rumuz 86
Kapurthala 356, 362, 373
Karachi 310, 406
Karam Chand 387, 389
Karamat Qawwal 372
Karbala 15, 226
Karl Marx 27
Karma 169, 172
Karnal 209, 344, 346, 385
Kasabnama Bafindgan 240
kasais 359
kasb 18
Kashani 222
Kashf-ul-Mahjub 34, 35, 50, 115, 179, 180
Kashmir 35, 119, 120, 121, 122, 123, 125, 136, 147, 163, 406
Katehar 361
Kathua 124, 125
Katra 130
Katra Hakimpur 362
Kaura Mal 385
kavisher 357
Kazakistan 125
Kerala 119
Kewal Ram 221, 222
khadim 382, 383, 384, 385, 386, 421
Khafipura 138
Khair-ul-Majalis 4, 5, 6, 103, 215, 216, 217, 218
Khaiwan 362
Khaki Shah 124
khalifas 54, 55, 56, 66, 67, 68, 70, 73, 80, 97, 98, 99, 100, 124, 165, 167, 169, 268, 347, 366, 371, 379, 380, 381, 402
Khalifis 180
Khaliq Ahmad Nizami 6, 7, 17, 32, 70, 110, 119, 120, 204, 215, 218, 224
Khalji 208
Khalsa 357
Khan Muhammad Daudpotra 387
Khan-i Jahan Tilangani 307
Khan-i-Azam 259
Khan-i-Azam Zafar Khan 110
Khan-i-Jahan 102, 105, 259
khanqahs 1, 7, 11, 23, 51, 52, 54, 59, 60, 72, 73, 74, 87, 91, 93, 97, 100, 106, 113, 120, 124, 126, 129, 130, 131, 159, 162, 165, 166, 167, 204, 205, 214, 217, 226, 227, 228, 292, 304, 337, 339, 347, 360, 381, 402, 408
kharaj 262
Khari Boli 20
Kharijites 182, 262
Kharraz 3
Kharrazis 180
khatib 338
khatra 141, 145
Khatris 416

Khazana-i-Jalali 215
Khazana-i-Jawahar-i-Jalaliya 109
Kheras 248
khilafat 34, 51, 56, 64, 67, 68, 70, 100, 165, 266
khilafatnama 7, 99, 217, 225, 338, 339
khirqa 51, 68, 100, 226
khirqa-i-mairaj 227
khirqa-i-muraqqa 142
Khitabiyah 263
Khizar Khan 345, 360
Khudadad Khan Abbasi 383, 386, 389
Khudayar Khan Abbasi 383, 386, 389
khuddam 13, 37, 64, 380, 390
Khulasat-ut-Tawarikh 122
Khurasan 51, 56, 80, 82, 99, 144, 201, 263
Khusrau Malik 198
Khwaja Abdul Haiy 259
Khwaja Abdul Khaliq Ghujdawani 269
Khwaja Abu Ahmad 65
Khwaja Abu Dinawari 65
Khwaja Abu Ishaq Shami 65
Khwaja Abu Muhammad Chishti 65
Khwaja Abu Yusuf Chishti 65
Khwaja Alauddin Attar 265, 269
Khwaja Allah Bakhsh 381
Khwaja Bahauddin Naqshband 265, 267
Khwaja Baqi Billah 10, 122, 258, 265, 267, 269, 271, 272
Khwaja Fakhruddin Dehalvi 380, 381, 382, 383
Khwaja Ghaur 70
Khwaja Ghulam Farid 2, 19, 223
Khwaja Hasan Basri 218
Khwaja Hasan Nizami 17
Khwaja Kamaluddin 223
Khwaja Khizar 137, 266, 292, 404, 407, 409, 410, 414, 415
Khwaja Maudud Chishti 65
Khwaja Muhammad Aqil 167
Khwaja Muhammad Hashim Kishmi 259
Khwaja Muhammad Naqshband 266, 269
Khwaja Muhammad Parsa 269
Khwaja Muinuddin Chishti 5, 6, 13, 14, 15, 37, 55, 56, 65, 66, 67, 68, 162, 197, 199, 205, 378, 379, 380, 382, 383, 384, 385, 386, 387, 389, 390, 402, 406
Khwaja Muzaffar 179
Khwaja Niamatullah Harvi 373
Khwaja Nizamuddin 71
Khwaja Nur Muhammad Muharvi 124, 164, 165, 167, 380, 381, 382, 383, 386
Khwaja Qutbuddin Bakhtiyar Kaki 5, 6, 55, 56, 197, 218, 342, 378, 402, 414
Khwaja Sulaiman Taunsawi 165, 166, 381, 382, 383, 384
Khwaja Ubaidullah Ahrar 269
Khwaja Usman Harwani 65
Khwaja Zoar 70
Khwarizm 88, 309
Khwarizmians 92, 303
Kirman 204
Kish 179
Kishtwar 124, 125, 130, 131
Kitab-i-Muttafiq 113
Kitab-i-Sama 191
Koh-i-Labnan 99
Kokaltash Khan 168
Kol 214
Konya 86
Kot Aror 51
Kot Karor 80
Kot Mithan 381
Kotla 359
Kotlamaler 359
Kotley da Pir 372
Kotmattan 167
Krishan pakh 367
Krishna 25
Kubrawi 123
Kufa 338
kullah 68, 70
Kulzum Sarup 172
Kumhar 416
Kuniyyat Abu Ali 343
Kunjwani 124
Kurukshetra 346

Lahore 1, 34, 50, 53, 81, 82, 88, 97, 110, 111, 122, 130, 136, 137, 138, 139, 141, 143, 144, 145, 147, 148, 149, 150, 151, 164, 168, 169, 179, 197, 209, 242, 304, 305, 346, 356, 358, 361, 379, 405, 406, 415
Laila 108
Lailat-ul-Qadr 152
Lajwanti Rama Krishna 24, 25, 28, 30, 32, 169, 284
Lakhdata Bazar 130, 131
Lakhpat Rai 385, 389
Lal Bazar 369
Lal Begis 15
Lal Mehra Sharif 310, 311
Lal Shahbaz Qalandar 59, 402, 407, 409, 414, 415
Lalan Wala Pir 417
Lamaat 86
Langahs 362
langar 12, 50, 60, 72, 73, 128, 159, 163, 166, 167, 199, 415
langar khana 207, 415
Lataif Ghaibia 169
Latifuddin 125
Lehandi 35, 199
Lodis 356, 358, 360
Lord Krishna 22, 169, 236
Lord Vishnu 367
lori-nama 120, 249
loris and pahelis 120
Luchhabadi 362
Lucknow 2
Ludhiana 358, 361
Ludhiana-Sangrur 359
Lutfullah Hussaini 386
Lyallpur 12, 405

M. Louis Massignon 2
Maarif-i-Ladunniyah 271
Maarifat-i-Haqaiq 259
Maasir-ul-Umara 222
Mabda o Maad 264, 265, 271
Machhiwara 309, 358
Madain 99
Madari 420
Madevi 362
Madina 80, 98, 99, 109, 114, 338
madrasah 53, 90, 93, 106, 159, 164, 165, 197, 279, 280, 309, 341, 350
Mafuziyah 263
Maghrabi tradition 49
Mahabharata 418
Mahajans 416
Mahar 164, 165
Maharaja Gulab Singh 123, 129
Maharaja Pratap Singh 130, 131
Maharaja Ranbir Singh 122, 130
Maharaja Ranjit Singh 122, 123, 129, 180, 306
Maharan 197
mahfil-i-sama 372
mahinwals 240
Mahmud Khan 388
Mahmud Shabistari 86
Mahmud Sherani 111
mahzar-i-sama 225
Maihana 179
Majma-ul-Akhbar 83
majzubs 11
Makhdum Sharif 167
Makhzan-ul-Aras 16
Maktubat-i-Imam Rabbani 258, 264, 267
Malamati 148, 184
Maler 359
Malergarh 359
Maleri Darwaza 359
Malerkotla 1, 36, 356, 357, 358, 359, 362, 363, 370, 371, 373, 388
malfuzat 4, 5, 6, 35, 55, 67, 69, 100, 109, 214, 215, 218, 219, 221, 222, 223, 224, 230, 304, 351
Malik Ambar 282
Malik Bahadur Ghulam Qadir 385
Malik Bahram Lodi 361
Malik Khattab Khan 388
Malik Mardan Daulat 361
Malik Shamsuddin 89
Malik Sultan Shah 361
Malikite 262
Malikpur 362
Malkahans 410
Mallu Iqbal Khan 360

Malout 417
Malwa 36, 309, 356, 357, 358, 366, 371, 379
Man Muzra 362
Manak Mazra 362
Manakwal 362
Manaqib-i-Makhdum-i-Jahaniyan 111
Manaqib-i-Sultani 282, 283
Manazil-i-Sairin 270
Mandi Darwaza 359
Mangal Shah 124
Mangu Khan 82
Manki Kalan 362
Manki Khurd 362
Mansur al-Hallaj 3, 27, 28, 107, 108, 109, 180, 233, 291
Maqabis-i-Majalis 223
Marathas 158, 282, 380, 382
Mardana 128
Maroof Khan 387
Maruf Karkhi 2
Marvi 23
Marwa 190
Marwand 414
Marwar 309
Marxists 31
Mashar-ul-Haram 190
Mashariq-ul-Anwar 113, 225
Mashhad 261, 263
masnawis 286, 343
Massignon 3
masya 367
Matlub-ul-Talibeen 223
Maudud 203
Maulana Ahmad Khansari 342
Maulana Ali bin Ahmad Ghuri 85
Maulana Badruddin Ishaq 204
Maulana Burhanuddin Sufi 73
Maulana Fakhruddin Dehalvi 35, 162, 164
Maulana Fakhruddin Nafilah 342
Maulana Fakhruddin Safahani 74
Maulana Fazal Rehman Ganj Muradabadi 163
Maulana Fazle Haq Khairabadi 381
Maulana Husamuddin Tirmizi 80
Maulana Jamal Hanswi 204
Maulana Jamaluddin Khurasani 360
Maulana Kamal Kashmiri 258
Maulana Minhajuddin Tirmizi 197
Maulana Muhammad Mujeer Wajih 223
Maulana Muinuddin Daultabadi 342
Maulana Najibuddin Samarqandi 342
Maulana Nasiruddin 342
Maulana Niamatullah 137
Maulana Qutbuddin of Mecca 342
Maulana Saadullah 137
Maulana Sadruddin 342
Maulana Wajihuddin Paili 342
Maulana Yaqub Charkhi 266, 269
Maulvi Ghulam Murtaza 169
Mawra-ul-Nahr 143
Max Arthur Macaullife 32
Mazhabi Sikhs 416, 417
Mazhar-i-Jalali 111
Mecca 54, 80, 84, 98, 99, 100, 109, 113, 114, 123, 125, 144, 189, 190, 206, 293, 357
Medieval Punjab 19
Medina 113
Mediterranean 309
Megh Nath 387, 389
Mehra Sikhs 416
Mela of Haidar Shaikh 366
Merv 179
Mewat 147, 361
Mian Muhammad Ibrahim 131
Midnapore 406
Mifati-ul-Jinan 223
Miftah-ul-Ashiqin 5
Mina 190
Minhaj us-Siraj Juzjani 309
Mir Muhammad 137
Mir Muhammad Hadi 388
Mir Muhammad Numan 268
Mir Syed Ali Hamadani 123, 125
Mir Waliullah 168
Mira Bai 23
Miran Shah Bhikh 389
Mirasis 15
Mirat-i-Aftab Numa 168

Mirat-i-Ahmadi 168
Mirat-i-Masudi 14
Mirat-i-Sikandari 102
Mirdad 138
Mirza Darab 259
Mirza Fakhruddin 168
Mirza Hakim 136
Mirza Hasan Qatil 168
Mirza Kamran 138
Mirza-Sahiban 245
misals 33, 285
Mishkat-i-Tabrizi 258
Mishkat-ul-Masabih 99, 113, 258
Miskin Shah Sahib 124
Mithri 310
Miyan Abul Maali 147, 148
Miyan Haji Muhammad Banyani 152
Miyan Mir 1, 9, 24, 29, 33, 35, 60, 97, 135, 136, 137, 139, 140, 141, 142, 143, 144, 145, 147, 148, 149, 150, 151, 152, 163, 164, 284
Miyan Muhammad 142
Miyan Muhammad Murad 147
Miyan Natha 144, 147, 148
Moga 405
Mohammed Alipur 362
Mohammad Habib 3, 4, 5, 6, 216, 217, 218, 220, 221, 222, 228, 229, 230
Mohammad Tazeem 35
Mohan Singh 169
Mohan Singh (Diwana) 23
Mohinder Singh 419
mojizat 258, 261
Mokal Singh 412
Mongolia 100
Mongols 1, 7, 52, 53, 80, 82, 88, 89, 92, 123, 198, 217, 229, 242, 303, 304, 338
Mono Dolo 362
Montgomery 12, 361, 404, 405, 406, 410, 414, 415, 417
Moses 187
Moti Bazar 359
Muazzam Afzaluddin Fuzail 71
Muazzam Khan 385
Mubarak Khan 387
Mufti Ghulam Sarwar Lahori 1
Mughal empire 1, 8, 14, 16, 136, 158, 198, 257, 258, 259, 281, 379, 380, 389
Mughal state 8, 9, 35, 136, 153, 257, 282, 346
Mughals 282, 306, 359, 379, 380
Muhalla Baghbanan 138
Muhalla Zuhdjan 342
Muhammad 30, 357, 406
Muhammad Anis Nazir 372, 373
Muhammad Ayub Qadri 115
Muhammad Baqar 385
Muhammad Bhadan Shah 385
Muhammad Bihamad Khani 55
Muhammad bin Fazlul Balkhi 181
Muhammad bin Qasim 303, 305
Muhammad bin Tughluq 5, 54, 73, 100, 208, 339, 361
Muhammad Fazil 387
Muhammad Ghori 242
Muhammad Hashim Kishmi 264, 267, 268
Muhammad Ikhtiyar Khan 387
Muhammad Iqbal Mujaddidi 110
Muhammad Jafar Tumasi 111
Muhammad Khalid Zubairi 369
Muhammad Maqsood 383
Muhammad Najib Qadiri 16
Muhammad Sadiq 387
Muhammad Shah 170, 346, 385, 387, 388
Muhammad Siddiq Kishmi 264, 265
Muhammad Taqi 139
Muhammad Ujali Khan Farrukhshahi 388
Muhammad Yunas Hasrat 286
Muhammad Zaffari 114
Muhar 380
Muharram 207, 226
Muhibullah 5
Muhibullah Allahabadi 9
Muizzuddin Muhammad bin Sam 242
mujaddid alf-i-sani 8, 9, 257, 265
mujahida 137, 140, 190, 227
mujawirs 363
mujtahid 51, 267
Mukashifat-i-Ainiyah 267
mukat 245

Mukbal 236
Mukhdoompur 362
Muktsar 405
Mulasthanapura 305
Mulhamàt 338
Mulla Abdul Ghafur 147
Mulla Abdul Hakim Sialkoti 140
Mulla Hamid Gujjar 141, 147
Mulla Khwaja Kalan 138
Mulla Saeed Khan 145
Mulla Saleh 152
Mulla Sangin Sufi 145
Mulla Shah Badakhshi 9, 60, 136, 142, 143, 148, 151, 163, 164, 284
Multan 1, 7, 34, 36, 51, 52, 53, 54, 55, 56, 57, 65, 73, 80, 81, 82, 85, 86, 87, 88, 89, 90, 91, 92, 93, 94, 97, 98, 122, 128, 164, 179, 197, 204, 207, 214, 228, 242, 283, 303, 304, 305, 306, 307, 309, 310, 311, 338, 356, 360, 361, 362, 373, 381, 385, 386, 387, 402, 404, 407, 408, 409, 414, 415
Multanis 82, 83, 304
Muqarrab Khan 346
Muqarrir Nama 111, 112
Murad Khan 387
Murad Khan Kunja 383
Muradabad 115
Muradyar Khan Abbasi 386
muraqaba 148
muraqqa-i-khiraq 184
murid 214, 251, 292, 293, 374, 417, 421
Murray T. Titus 121
murshid 36, 198, 199, 214, 284, 289, 293, 294, 295
Murtaza Husain 172
Musa 363
Musa Pak Shaheed 310
Muslim Asia 242
Muslim jurisprudence 110, 113
Muslim law 110, 111, 259
Muslim/Muslims 9, 31, 49, 52, 55, 58, 59, 83, 159, 161, 166, 170, 172, 226, 257, 260, 262, 263, 278, 279, 281, 309, 359, 370, 389, 405, 406, 415, 418, 420, 421
Mustafa 123, 125
Mustafa Baba 125
Mutazilite 113, 182, 262
Muzaffar Khan 102
Muzaffargarh 410
Muzdalifa 190

Nabha 356, 359
Nabi Khan 309
nafs 140, 267
Nagaur 57, 214, 378
naghma-i-Hindi 143
Nahrwala 242
nais 359
Najibuddin Mutawakkil 229
Najm Hosain Syed 240
Nalagarh 356
Nam Dev 59
namaz 107, 138, 140, 185, 291, 365, 416
namaz-i-jamaat 140
namaz-i-maghrib 141
Nanak 23, 171
Nand Rishi 120
Nandurbar 378
Naqqar Khana 346
Naqshbandi/Naqshbandi order 1, 8, 36, 97, 122, 123, 124, 257, 258, 265, 268, 271, 272, 281, 282, 338, 358
Naqshbandi saints 268, 269
Naqshbandis 35, 153, 267, 268, 379, 381
Narnaul 170, 171, 214, 378
Naruwala 381
Nasir-ud-Din Abul Khair 407
Nasiruddin Mahmud Chiragh-i-Dehli 4, 5, 6, 18, 81, 82, 216, 222, 223, 224
Nasiruddin Qubacha 52, 81, 87, 88, 303, 309
nat 372
Nath Panthi Yogis 59
Natho Heri 362
Nats 15
Nau Gaza Pir 123, 125, 131
Naundharani 362
Naushahi 420
Nawab Ahmed Ali 359
Nawab Muhammad Umar Khan 388

Nawab Sadiq Ali Khan 346
Nawab Sher Muhammad Khan 358, 370, 388
Naxalite 357
Nazar Masih 413
nazr 384, 385, 386
nazr-o-niyaz 382, 384, 386, 390
nazrana 12, 369
Neo-Platonism 2, 279
Niffari 3
nikah 22
nimaz 199
nirguna 32, 197, 245
nirguna bhakti 200
Nirjila Ikadeshi 366, 367
Nishapur 179
Nizam-ul-Mulk Tusi 279
Nizam-ul-Qulub 16
Nizami Dahlavi 205
Nizamuddin Aurangabadi 16, 380
Noah 268
non-Muslims 380, 381, 382, 385, 387, 388
North India 344, 407
north-east Persia 338
North-West Frontier Province 386, 406, 420
north-western India 24, 52, 58, 214, 216, 304, 338, 361, 362, 406
northern India 36, 198
Nua Baba 125
Nur-ul-Khalaiq 259
Nuris 180
Nuruddin Rishi 121
Nusrat Fateh Ali Khan 17, 23
Nuzhat-ul-Arwah 86

orientalists 2, 17
Otwala Kuan 350
Oudh 404

P.M. Currie 13, 69
Pabuji 15
Pakistan 34, 197, 304, 358, 359, 404, 405, 406, 410, 415, 417
Pakistani Punjab 282
Pakpattan 1, 7, 12, 13, 29, 80, 82, 97, 165, 197, 203, 204, 207, 209, 215, 224, 227, 305, 341, 356, 378, 379, 384, 402, 409, 414, 415, 419
Palestine 80
Panch 125
Panch Pandavas 418
Pandava 406
Pandavas 404
pandit 287
Pandoke 169
Panipat 1, 36, 59, 97, 209, 214, 338, 342, 343, 344, 358, 361, 379
Panj Payaras 357
Panj Pir 15, 37, 124, 203, 236, 404, 406, 408, 409, 410, 412, 413, 414, 416, 417, 418, 419, 420, 421
Panj Pir Khanqah 419
Panj Pir Wali Mazar 406
Panjab Past and Present 32
Panjab University 32
Panjabi 26
Panjgraiyan 362
Panjnad 98
Panna 172
partition of India 415, 418
Partition of Punjab 405, 406
pas-i-anfas 197, 346
Pashto 26
patched coat (khirqa)/patched frock 184, 185, 226
Pathan Afghan 360
Pathan Muslims 416
Pathaney Khan 23
Pathans 359
Pathriya Masjid 350
Patiala 32, 356, 357, 358, 359
Pattan 378
Pepsu 356
Percy Brown 307
Persia 64, 65, 123, 130, 168, 179, 257, 303, 304, 306
Persian 24, 25, 26, 28, 35, 50, 168, 199, 204, 230, 235, 261, 282, 285, 286, 338
Persian poetry 2
Persian wheel 12
Peshawar 81, 242
Peshrau Khan 139

Phulkian 359
pilgrimage 189, 190
Pilu 245
Pind Dadan Khan 282
Pindwa 378
pir 50, 55, 56, 57, 58, 124, 140, 165, 198, 200, 236, 266, 294, 371, 374, 407
Pir Ali Shah 124
Pir Baba Karam Shah 125
Pir Baba Tode Shah 125
Pir Badar 410
Pir Buddhan Ali Shah 123
Pir Fateh Khan 410
Pir Ghulam Badshah 125
Pir Haji Rattan 357, 358
Pir Koh 127
Pir Lakhdata 123, 124, 125, 129, 131
Pir Mitha 123, 124, 125, 127, 128, 130
Pir Muhabbat Ali Shah 124, 125
Pir of Runicha 412
Pir Panjal 406
Pir Roshan Ali Shah 124, 125
Pir Roshan Shah Wali 124, 126
Pir Roshan Wali Shah 123, 131
Pir Sayyid Ghulam Shah Badshah 125
Pir Shahan Shah Wali 124
Pir Wali Shah 125, 130
Pir Zahir Wali Shah 123, 124
Pirepur 408
piri-muridi 18, 35, 105, 146, 230, 292
pirs 214, 371, 404, 415
Pokharan 408, 412
Poland 242
prabhu 199, 241
Pran Nath 171, 172
Pranami Sampradaya 172
Pre-Nanak 32
Prince Fateh Khan 101
Princeton University 115
pritam 199, 241
Prophet Muhammad 21, 25, 52, 66, 67, 80, 84, 103, 104, 107, 114, 126, 137, 138, 145, 160, 161, 169, 172, 184, 187, 190, 191, 199, 226, 227, 238, 259, 260, 261, 262, 263, 265, 266, 268, 272, 282, 285, 338, 343, 344, 357, 372, 374, 386, 387, 388, 404, 410
Punch 124, 125
Punjab 1, 7, 12, 13, 14, 19, 21, 25, 26, 27, 28, 29, 31, 32, 33, 34, 35, 36, 37, 49, 50, 51, 52, 54, 55, 56, 58, 60, 72, 74, 80, 81, 82, 88, 92, 97, 98, 101, 111, 119, 122, 123, 124, 125, 127, 128, 132, 135, 136, 153, 158, 159, 163, 164, 165, 166, 169, 179, 196, 199, 200, 203, 207, 216, 238, 284, 295, 306, 307, 309, 311, 356, 357, 358, 360, 361, 362, 367, 370, 371, 379, 380, 382, 383, 385, 386, 388, 389, 390, 402, 403, 405, 406, 407, 409, 414, 417, 419, 420, 421
Punjab hill states 122, 136
Punjab History Conference 33
Punjab Wakf Board 347, 415, 419
Punjabi 20, 56, 58, 60, 216, 285, 286, 359, 369, 372
Punjabi poetry 278, 286
Punjabi sufi poetry 19, 20, 21, 22, 23, 25
Punjabi University 32
Punjabi verses (qafis) 136
Punjabis 169
Punjabization of Islam 19
Puranas 172
Purdah 171
Purmandal 125
Purtabpur 362

Qadiri/ Qadiri order 1, 11, 29, 35, 59, 60, 97, 122, 123, 124, 125, 126, 136, 137, 138, 148, 152, 153, 163, 268, 281, 282, 284, 285, 305, 338, 348, 379, 380, 385, 408
Qadiriya Masrooria 285
Qaiyyumiat 265
Qalandars 50, 58, 59, 87, 124, 295, 343, 379
Qandhar 82, 150, 282, 303, 305
qanungos 388
Qarlughs 92, 303
Qarmathians 303
Qarsum Bibi 197
Qasida-i-Lamiya 113
Qasidah-i-Burdah 258

qasidahs 85
Qasim Kotwal 386
Qasim Shah 124
Qasimpur 362
Qassaris 180
Qasur 168, 169, 305, 388
qawwali 12, 23, 36, 371, 372, 373, 374
Qawwals 105, 143, 370, 372, 373, 415
qayyum 9
qazi 87, 98, 99, 104, 196, 237, 239
Qazi Abu Yusuf 108
Qazi Aqil Muhammad 381
Qazi Bahlul Badakhshani 258
Qazi Hamiduddin Nagauri 57, 217, 218
Qazi Javed 92
Qazi Kamaluddin 339
Qazi Qadin 137
Qazi Qutbuddin Kashani 90
Qazi Sayin Ditta bin Qazi Qalandar Faruqi 137
Qazi Shuaib 197, 198
qazis 237, 389
qissa 20, 22, 235, 240, 243, 245, 246, 250, 372, 373
qissa Hir 203
qissa-kars 22, 236, 237, 238, 250, 251
Qiyamkhanis 382
Qubacha 89
Qulich Khan 259
Quran 21, 27, 28, 49, 80, 83, 106, 110, 112, 113, 115, 160, 161, 169, 172, 185, 186, 190, 202, 204, 238, 247, 261, 262, 263, 265, 266, 267, 269, 279, 283, 288, 338, 347, 374, 386
Quranic Unitarian thought 25, 30
Qutb 294
Qutbuddin Aibak 81
Qutlugh Khan 82
Qutub Alam 130
Qutub Zaman Hazrat Baba Jiwan Shah 123, 124

R.C. Temple 370, 407
Rabia Basri 36, 137, 245
Rachel Bowlby 234
Rachna Doab 136
Radcliffe Line 31, 405
Rah Baba 124, 131
Rahat-ul-Qulub 5, 35, 216, 217, 218, 219, 220, 221, 222, 223, 225, 227, 228, 230
Rahmat Khan 372
Rai Behram Bhatti 362
Rai Chaturman 168
Rai Pithora 55
Rai Raju 179
Rai Sikhs 416, 417
Raja Abramchand 408
Raja Aya Chand 407, 413
Raja Biram Dev 130
Raja Chander 408
Raja Maler Singh 359
Raja Sabha Chand 'Nadar' 389
Raja Sarab-li-Dhar 126
Raja Sohar Dev 15
Rajasthan 1, 13, 14, 406, 408, 415, 417, 420
Rajasthani 20
Rajdarshani 122, 126, 130, 131
Rajouri 124, 125, 129, 131, 406
Rajput 8, 13, 15, 338, 346, 356, 359, 363, 382, 416
Rajput Raja Abramchand 407
Rajputana 119, 303, 382
Raju Qattal 73, 310, 312
Ram Nagar 125
Ram Prasad Sen 171
Ramban 124
Ramdev 408
Ramdevra 408, 420
Ramla 179
Ramnagar 125
Ramzan Qalandar 59
Ranjha 22, 136, 203, 244, 248, 249, 408
Ranjit Dev 123
Ranjit Singh 23, 33
Ranwan 362
raqs 109, 143, 192, 374
Rasti Bibi 283
Rasulpur 362
Rattan Pal 357
Rauzat-ul-Arifin 126
Ravi 82, 136, 139, 284, 303

Rawal Dalow 362
Raza Ali 341
Raza Quli 342
Regar 416
Rewari 357
Reynolds A. Nicholson 2, 3
Riasi 124
Riazul Islam 18
ribats 52
Richard Lannoy 368
Richard M. Eaton 11, 13, 119, 120, 208, 280, 366, 403, 420
Rihari 124
Risala Radd-i-Rawafiz 258
Risala Tahqiqat-i-Arazi-i-Hind 347
Risala-i-Makkiya 114, 115
Risala-i-Qushairiya 115
Risala-i-Tahliliyah 272
Risalah Radd-i-Rawafiz 261
Rishi 123, 124, 125, 126
riyazat 106, 137, 140
Rizqullah Khan 346
Roh 362
Rohilkhand 380
Rohri 104
Rohtak 388
Roorkee 421
Ropar 357, 361
Roumelia 343
Roz-i-Ashura 226
Rudauli 346
Ruhulla 172
Rukn-i-Alam 312
Ruknuddin Dabir Kashani 6, 222, 223, 224
Ruknuddin Firuz Shah 81
Ruknuddin Ruhela 139
Rum 191
Runtool 362
Rurka 362

S.M. Azizuddin Husain 35
S.R. Sharda 25, 28, 169
Saba Sanabil 66
Sabaiyah 263
Sabir Pak 421
Sabzwar 130
sadah amirs 361
Sadar Bazar 369
Sadar-i-Jahan 369
Sadhs 29, 170
Sadhura 384
Sadiq Khan 387
Sadna Shaheed 306, 307
Sadr-i-Jahan 259
Sadruddin Ahmad bin Najmuddin Saiyyid Husaini 93
Sadruddin Qunvi 85, 86
Saeed Ahmad 35
Safinat-ul-Auliya 135
sahib 241
sahiban-i-sukr 233
Sahibzada Sultan Ahmed Ali 283
sahibzadas 358, 359
Sahih Muslim 113
Sahih-ul-Bukhari 113, 258
Sahiwal 410, 414
Sahl bin Abdullah 182
Sahl bin Tustari 145
Sahlis 180
Sahs 82
Said Jalal 407
Saifi 416
Saifuddin Hasan Qarlugh 82
sain 241
Sain Lal Din 125
Saiyid Athar Abbas Rizvi 8, 119, 218, 280, 409
Saiyyid dynasty 361
Saiyyid Husaini 86
sajan 241
sajjadah nishin 12, 13, 34, 63, 64, 67, 68, 69, 70, 72, 73, 74, 98, 99, 111, 112, 114, 121, 126, 129, 382, 384, 386, 390
sajjadah-i tariqat 68
sajjadah 67, 68, 69, 70, 74
Sakhad 165
Sakhi Sarwar 410
sakhis 286
Sakinat-ul-Auliya 135, 136, 147, 148
Salar Masud Ghazi 14
Sali Nuyin 89
Salim Mohammad 36
Salim Qawwal 372

Saljuqs 81
saloka 7, 33, 35, 198, 201
sama 16, 17, 105, 109, 143, 190, 197, 204, 346, 374, 380, 381
Samana 111, 136, 361, 388
Samarqand 99, 179
Samba 124
Samma chiefs 101, 110
Sandaur 362
Sangala 362
Sangrur 356, 359
Sanjar Khan 387
Sanjha Pir 123, 124
sannyasis 158, 168
Sant Singh Sekhon 23, 416
Sarai Khushal Khan 139
Sarhandi Darwaza 359
Sarraj 2
Sarsuti 338
Sarwar 69
Sassi 23
Sassi-Punnun 20, 22, 26, 234
Satluj 82, 136, 303, 304, 309, 338, 356, 357, 358, 373, 414
Satnamis 282
Satwari 124
Saudi Arabia 100
Sayeen 124
Sayyaris 180
Sayyid Bahauddin Samani 126
Sayyid Fariduddin 126
Sayyid Fariduddin Qadiri 130
Sayyid Shah Ghulam Badshah 124
Sehwan 59, 100, 402, 409, 414, 415
Seljuqs 179
sevadar 408, 409, 412, 419
Shab-i-Ashura 226
Shab-i-Barat 111
shab-i-mairaj 226
Shadi Khan 345
shadi-nama 120, 249
Shafite 262, 267
shah 241
Shah Abdal 126
Shah Abdul Latif Bhittai 26, 284
Shah Abul Maali 136
Shah Alam Suhrawardi 58
Shah Dana Shaheed 311, 312
Shah Daula 1, 384
Shah Daulat 410
Shah Fazlullah 151
Shah Ghulam Badshah 129
Shah Husain 2, 19, 26, 29, 136, 152, 197, 235, 237, 238, 239, 240, 241, 243, 244, 247, 248, 249, 250, 251, 281, 295, 357
Shah Inayat Qadiri 169
Shah Kalimullah Jahanabadi 380
Shah Kamal Qadiri 266
Shah Mina 16
Shah Muhammad Bulaq 223
Shah Murad 139, 410
Shah Niamatullah Qadiri 163
Shah Niyaz Ahmad 124, 380
Shah Qamis Azam Qadiri 385
Shah Rukn-i-Alam 305, 306, 307, 309, 311
Shah Shams Sabzwari 306, 307
Shah Waliullah 234, 280, 281, 380
Shah Yusuf Gardezi 306, 311, 312
Shah-i-Hamadan 123
Shahabad 346
shahadat 269, 272
shahadat-i-uzma 269
Shahdara 139
Shahidwari 362
Shahjahan 8, 150, 151, 153, 283
Shahmukhi 20, 32
Shahpur 11, 410
Shaikh Abdul Ahad Faruqi 258, 266
Shaikh Abdul Fateh 342
Shaikh Abdul Haq Muhaddis Dehalvi 100, 223, 342
Shaikh Abdul Qadir Gilani 59, 60, 265, 268
Shaikh Abdul Qadir Sani 60
Shaikh Abdul Quddus Gangohi 266, 346
Shaikh Abdul Rahman 139
Shaikh Abdullah Matri 98, 114
Shaikh Abdullah Yafai 98, 100
Shaikh Abdus Subhan 75
Shaikh Abu Ishaq 136
Shaikh Abu Ishaq Gazruni 99

Shaikh Achhu 389
Shaikh Ahmad Sirhindi/Sirhindi 1, 8, 10, 34, 36, 97, 120, 138, 147, 153, 164, 179, 257, 258, 259, 260, 261, 262, 263, 264, 265, 266, 267, 268, 269, 270, 271, 272, 281, 282, 357, 358, 360, 361, 389
Shaikh Ahmad Zinda Pir 360
Shaikh Alauddin 75
Shaikh Alauddin Ali bin Ahmad Sabir 421
Shaikh Alauddin Ali Sabir 58, 74
Shaikh Alauddin Mauj Darya 208
Shaikh Ali 361
Shaikh Ali bin Usman Hujwiri 50, 180, 181, 182, 183, 184, 185, 186, 187, 188, 189, 190, 191, 192, 379, 402
Shaikh Allah Jawaya 75
Shaikh Aminuddin Gazruni 99
Shaikh Arif 74
Shaikh Ataullah 75
Shaikh Azizullah 386, 388
Shaikh Badruddin Ghaznavi 217, 225
Shaikh Badruddin Ishaq 58, 72, 74
Shaikh Badruddin Sulaiman 69, 72, 75
Shaikh Bahauddin Zakariya 1, 7, 34, 51, 52, 53, 54, 65, 68, 73, 80, 83, 84, 85, 86, 87, 88, 89, 90, 91, 92, 93, 94, 97, 143, 163, 197, 217, 228, 229, 304, 306, 307, 309, 311, 312, 338, 360, 362, 385, 402, 404, 409, 414, 415
Shaikh Bayazid Bistami 50
Shaikh Bilawal 138
Shaikh Burhanuddin 58, 226, 338
Shaikh Chilli 348, 350, 352
Shaikh Chuhar 139
Shaikh Daud 60, 136
Shaikh Daud Bhervi 141
Shaikh Ehsanul Haq 115
Shaikh Faizullah 75
Shaikh Fakhruddin 69
Shaikh Farid 1, 2, 4, 5, 6, 7, 12, 19, 21, 23, 29, 32, 33, 34, 35, 55, 56, 57, 58, 68, 80, 97, 126, 128, 163, 197, 198, 204, 215, 217, 218, 219, 220, 221, 222, 224, 225, 226, 227, 228, 229, 235, 237, 239, 240, 241, 242, 244, 247, 248, 250, 281, 284, 285, 295, 338, 339, 341, 378, 379, 384, 402, 407, 410, 414, 415
Shaikh Farid Bhakkari 222
Shaikh Farid Bukhari 259
Shaikh Fariduddin Qadiri 124
Shaikh Fateh Ali 410
Shaikh Fazl 75
Shaikh Ghulam Dana 360
Shaikh Ghulam Rasul 75
Shaikh Haidar 1
Shaikh Hamid Bengali 268
Shaikh Hamid Qadiri 60
Shaikh Hamiduddin Nagauri 55, 121, 285
Shaikh Hamiduddin Sufi Nagauri 53
Shaikh Hasan 365
Shaikh Hidayatullah 386
Shaikh Hindi 179
Shaikh Hud 138
Shaikh Husain Zinjani 50, 379, 402
Shaikh Hussamuddin 69
Shaikh Ibrahim 32, 75, 198
Shaikh Ibrahim Farid 24
Shaikh Ibrahim Muradabadi 115
Shaikh Imamuddin 99
Shaikh Isa 365
Shaikh Jalaluddin 346, 347, 348, 379
Shaikh Jalaluddin Surkh Bukhari 54
Shaikh Jalaluddin Tabrezi 53, 85, 88
Shaikh Jalaluddin Thanesari 347
Shaikh Jamal Khandan Ru 98
Shaikh Jamali Kambo 99
Shaikh Jamaluddin 58, 338, 339, 341
Shaikh Jamaluddin Hansavi 73, 74, 225
Shaikh Junaid Baghdadi 3, 49, 83, 92, 139, 218
Shaikh Kamal 268
Shaikh Khizar 137
Shaikh Khizar Rumi 342
Shaikh Mirak 137
Shaikh Mirak Mir 123
Shaikh Muhammad 75
Shaikh Muhammad al-Hussaini 59, 136
Shaikh Muhammad Ashraf 75

Shaikh Muhammad bin Hasan al-Khattali 50
Shaikh Muhammad bin Tahir 268
Shaikh Muhammad Inayatullah 168, 169
Shaikh Muhammad Lahori 142, 147
Shaikh Muhammad Mahdi 386
Shaikh Muhammad Saeed 75, 384
Shaikh Muhammad Salim Shah Chishti 385
Shaikh Muhammad Yar 75
Shaikh Muhammad Yunus Jamaluddin 59
Shaikh Muhammad Yusuf 75
Shaikh Muizzuddin 70, 75
Shaikh Munawwar 75
Shaikh Musa 365
Shaikh Najibuddin Mutawakkil 74, 229
Shaikh Nasiruddin Mahmud Chiragh-i-Dehli 4, 5, 65, 100, 101, 108, 215, 378, 379
Shaikh Niamatullah Qadiri 123
Shaikh Nizamuddin Auliya 4, 5, 6, 15, 18, 53, 56, 57, 58, 63, 64, 65, 66, 68, 71, 72, 73, 74, 84, 87, 91, 197, 204, 206, 208, 214, 215, 216, 219, 220, 222, 223, 225, 227, 228, 229, 251, 338, 339, 342, 378, 379, 402, 407
Shaikh Nizamuddin Aurangabadi 162
Shaikh Nizamuddin bin Abdul Shukur 347
Shaikh Nuruddin 73, 75, 120, 338, 339
Shaikh Nuruddin Muhammad 69
Shaikh Nuruddin Rishi 125
Shaikh Qutb 142
Shaikh Qutbuddin Damishqi 114, 115
Shaikh Qutbuddin Munawwar 73, 338, 339
Shaikh Rafiuddin Bayazid 69
Shaikh Rizqullah Mushtaqi 58
Shaikh Ruknuddin Abul Fateh 53, 65, 68, 82, 92, 94, 98, 105, 108, 304, 306, 307, 360
Shaikh Rustam Shah Farooqi 384
Shaikh Saaduddin Hamviya 229
Shaikh Sadruddin 36, 356, 359, 362, 365, 366, 367, 369, 370, 371, 372, 373, 374, 388
Shaikh Sadruddin Arif 53, 54, 65, 73, 87, 94, 98, 304
Shaikh Safiuddin Gazruni 51
Shaikh Saifuddin Bakharzi 217
Shaikh Salim Chishti 14, 208
Shaikh Samail 410
Shaikh Shamsuddin Turk 58
Shaikh Sharafuddin 342
Shaikh Sharafuddin Mahmud Tustari 99
Shaikh Shihabuddin 114
Shaikh Shihabuddin Suhrawardi 3, 7, 51, 80, 83, 84, 85, 87, 92, 97, 99, 114, 217, 228, 266, 270, 414
Shaikh Sulaiman 17, 365
Shaikh Tajuddin Mahmud 75
Shaikh Tilli 348
Shaikh Usman Haruni 5, 216
Shaikh Wajihuddin 80
Shaikh Yaqub Sarafi Kashmiri 258
Shaikh Yar Muhammad Jadid Badakhshi 259
Shaikh Yusuf Qureshi 362
Shaikh Zain Alla Din 124
Shaikh Ziauddin Abu Sa'id 69
Shaikh Zu ul-Nun Misri 218
Shaikh-ul-Islam 52, 54, 100, 228, 265
Shaikhpur Chuk 362
Shaikhzada Fakhruddin Gazruni 113
Shaikhzada Muazzam Afzaluddin Fuzail 70
Shakopura 362
Sham 236
Shamail-i-Tirmizi 258
Shamail-ul-Atqiya 222, 224
Shambhu Prasad 389
Shams Sabzwari 311, 312
Shams Siraj Afif 68, 339, 351
Shams Tabrez 197
Shamsuddin Iltutmish 81, 87, 89, 92
Shamsuddin Kurt 53
Shamsuddin Tabrezi 306, 343
Shamsuddin Turk 343, 379
Sharafuddin Yahya Maneri 18

Sharfuddin Yahya Maneri 108
Sharh Kabir Chahl Ism 113
shariat 9, 10, 35, 50, 51, 83, 92, 93, 103, 104, 105, 106, 107, 109, 112, 139, 140, 143, 148, 160, 166, 181, 257, 262, 266, 267, 271, 279, 281, 282, 283, 343, 344
Sharif Qawwal 372
Shattari 11
Shauqat Qawwal 372
Sheikhupura 362, 405
Shekhawati 381, 383
Shemeem Burney Abbas 233
Sher Khan 81, 82, 217
Sher Shah Sur 60
Shergarh 60
Sherwani Darwaza 359
Shia/Shias 9, 15, 100, 258, 261, 262, 263, 266, 404, 418
Shiaism 406
Shihabuddin Umari 338
Shikarpur 385, 387, 406
Shimla Guga Pir 410
Shiraz 99, 109
Shiv 410
Shokarah 99
Shorkot 282, 283, 284, 285, 361
Shuja Alhaq 10, 27, 28, 30, 31, 205, 289
Sialkot 81, 136, 147, 258
Sidhu 416
siharfi 26, 286
Sikh 7, 34, 36, 128, 153, 200, 358, 359, 370
Sikh confederacies 285
Sikh gurus 135, 136, 164, 197, 198, 202
Sikh kingdom 33
'Sikh' mysticism 23
Sikh tradition 135
Sikhism 24, 32, 33, 202, 356
Sikhs 31, 33, 135, 158, 165, 198, 200, 282, 350, 356, 357, 370, 380, 406, 415, 418, 419
Simon Digby 66
Sind 7, 26, 52, 54, 59, 81, 98, 101, 136, 303, 304, 305, 306, 338, 381, 383, 386, 404, 409, 414
Sind Sagar Doab 82
Sindi 20, 26
Sir John Marshall 307
Siraiki 20, 32
Siraj-ul-Hidaya 110, 215
sirguna 32, 197, 245
Sirhind 1, 97, 120, 138, 147, 164, 179, 258, 357, 358, 360, 361, 389
Sirmur hills 358
Sirsa 389, 408, 413
Siva Narayanis 170
Sivanarayan 170
Siwistan 54, 137, 228
Siyal 165, 203, 237, 381
Siyaq Nama 16
Siyar-ul-Aqtab 69
Siyar-ul-Arifin 86, 102
Siyar-ul-Auliya 4, 6, 16, 55, 68, 69, 70, 218, 220, 221, 228, 229
Sobayah 261
Sohni 23, 240
Sohni-Mahiwal 20, 22, 26, 234
soma 367
Somnath 168
Sonargaon 406
South Asia 11, 14, 18, 279, 281, 378, 418
South Asian societies 18, 31
south-eastern Punjab 36, 337, 338, 352
south-western Punjab 35, 303, 304, 381, 402
Southeast Asian languages 20
Sri Ganganagar 415
Subhash Parihar 36
Sudanpur 362
sudi 367
Sudi Ikadeshi 367
Sufi Hamiduddin Nagauri 382
Sufi Muhammad Ismail 369
Sufi Nasir 145
sufi-kav 21
Suhadeva 122
suhag 22, 241
suhagan-nama 120, 249
suhaila 120
Suhrawardi/Suhrawardis 1, 6, 7, 28, 34, 36, 55, 56, 65, 73, 74, 80, 91, 92, 97, 100, 104, 214, 122, 281, 338, 360, 362, 379, 380, 381, 414

Suhrawardi order 51, 54, 58, 94, 98, 163, 304, 305, 309
sukr 3, 92, 108, 147
Sulaiman 90
sulh-i-kul 379
Sultan Alauddin Khalji 207, 345
Sultan Ali Khan 387
Sultan Bahu 2, 19, 21, 22, 26, 29, 36, 197, 236, 237, 239, 278, 281, 282, 283, 284, 285, 286, 287, 289, 290, 291, 292, 293, 294, 295
Sultan Bakhsh Qadiri 284
Sultan Ghiyasuddin Tughluq 307
Sultan Hamid 282, 283, 284
Sultan Hamiduddin 341
Sultan Ibrahim 179
Sultan Khan 386
Sultan Mahmud 14, 309
Sultan Muhammad 303
Sultan Muhammad Shah 361
Sultan Muizzuddin 81, 303, 309, 341, 346
Sultan Nasiruddin Mahmud 57, 228, 360, 407
Sultan Raziya 81, 357
Sultan Shamsuddin Iltutmish 52, 55, 56, 357
Sultan-ul-Azkar 152
Sumras 303
Sunam 81, 147, 361
Sunami Darwaza 359
Sunan-i-Abu Daud 113
Sundarpuri 309
sunnah 3, 49, 185, 189
Sunni/Sunnis 100, 182, 190, 261, 263, 280, 359
surah-i-fatiha 110, 265, 267
Surat-ul-Nisa 115
Surinder Singh 35
Sutlej 305
Swabti 406
Syed Abdul Rahman 284
Syed Ahmad Gilani 385
Syed Ahmad Kabir 73, 98
Syed Alauddin Ali bin Syed Husaini 102, 114
Syed Ali Hamadani 123
Syed Bahauddin 73
Syed Dargahi Qadiri 384
Syed Fateh 388
Syed Habibullah Shah Qadiri 284
Syed Hamid Kabir 74
Syed Hasan 388
Syed Hilal 123
Syed Jafar 388
Syed Jalaluddin Bukhari Makhdum-i-Jahaniyan 1, 18, 34, 54, 73, 85, 92, 94, 98, 99, 100, 101, 102, 103, 104, 105, 106, 107, 108, 109, 110, 111, 112, 113, 115, 215, 258, 304, 310, 311, 312, 402, 403, 409, 414, 415
Syed Jalaluddin Surkh Bukhari 73, 94, 98, 304, 309
Syed Liyaqat Hussain Moini 13, 37
Syed Mahmud Kirmani 204
Syed Mahmud Nasiruddin 74
Syed Mahmud Qadiri 385
Syed Masud 383, 384, 385, 386, 387
Syed Muhammad 73
Syed Muhammad Gesudaraz 18, 66, 85, 225, 229
Syed Muhammad Kirmani 71
Syed Muhammad Yusuf 385
Syed Mulla Hamid 147
Syed Murad 384, 385, 386, 387, 388
Syed Najmuddin 342
Syed Qutub Alam 130
Syed Safiuddin Haqani 310
Syed Sharfuddin 122, 123
Syeds 67, 124, 130, 359, 361, 389, 407, 408
Syria 99, 109, 179, 228, 242

tabarrukat 63, 68, 383, 384, 385, 387, 388, 390
Tabrez 99
tafsir 93, 114, 279
Tafsir-i-Baizawi 258
Tafsir-i-Kashshaf 113
Tafsir-i-Madark 113
Tafsir-i-Wahidi 258
Taha Husain 161
Tahir Kamran 36
Taifuris 180

Taj Ali 310
Taj Mahal 348
Taj Murassa Begum 362, 365
Tajuddin Abu Bakr Ayaz 81
Tajuddin bin Muin Siyahposh 111
Tajuddin Yalduz 81
Takht Hazara 240, 245
Talab Ananta 139
Talab Bazar 369
Taliqat bar Sharh-i-Rubaiyat 272
Tanvir Anjum 34
tappe 374
Taran Taran 356
Tarb-i-Majalis 86
Tarbai Toqshin 88
Tarikh-i- Farrukhabad 168
Tarikh-i-Faridi 205
Tarikh-i-Firuz Shahi 68
Tarikh-i-Khan Jahani wa Makhzani-i- Afghani 373
Tarikh-i-Muhammadi 55
tariqat 83, 93, 103, 105, 106, 107, 140, 181, 267, 271
tasawwuf 113, 160, 197, 214, 338, 378
tasbih 142
tashahhud 90
Tasmiya Khwani 114
tauba 3, 109, 183, 266
tauhid 148, 160, 182, 270, 272
Taunsa 17, 165, 381
tawakkul 18, 56, 141
tawiz 7, 12, 204
tawiz-futuh 12
Tazkira-ul-Umara 221
Teg Bahadur 357
Telian Bazar 369
Thanesar 36, 209, 338, 346, 347, 348, 379, 385
Thar Desert 82
Thatta 110, 111, 137, 339, 383, 387, 389
Timur 339, 360
Torah 262
Tota Maina 370
trans-Indus sufism 25
Transoxiana 88, 261, 263, 378
trikuti 169
Trimingham 15
trinjan 20
Tughluqabad (Delhi) 307
Tughluqs 12, 69, 360, 403
Tuhfat-ul-Hind 168
Tuhfat-ul-Majalis 103
Tulamba 82
Tulla 240
Turkey 257
Turkic 20
Turkish 26, 197, 199, 338
Turkistan 82, 122, 179
Turks 242, 415
Tus 179
Tuzuk-i-Jahangiri 135

Uch 1, 7, 35, 36, 51, 54, 55, 59, 73, 81, 82, 87, 88, 90, 94, 98, 101, 104, 109, 111, 113, 114, 242, 258, 303, 304, 305, 309, 310, 311, 356, 385, 402, 403, 407, 409, 414, 415
Udasis 416
Udhampur 124, 125, 130
Udhaya Das 170
Ugar Sahani 389
Ujali Khan 389
ulema 26, 28, 164, 172, 259, 279, 280, 281
Ulugh Khan 57, 82
Umar Faruq 137, 226, 258, 263, 264, 265
Ummayyad caliphate 303
Unitarian doctrine 27, 28, 29
Unitarian philosophy 170
Unitarian sufis 28
Unity of Being 161
Upanishads 172
Urdu 25, 32, 60, 120, 230, 285, 286, 359, 369, 372
urs 12, 15, 129, 131, 222, 348, 351, 415, 416, 421
USA 17
Usman 104, 226
Usman Haruni 5, 15
Ustad Ladla 310
Uttar Pradesh 100
Uwaisi 137, 152, 265
Uzbegs 144

Uzkand 179

Vaishanavas 169
Vaishnava Vedantic Bhakti 25, 169
vakil 382, 387, 388
vedanta 286
Vedanta philosophy 25
Vedantic 25, 27, 28, 30
Vedantic unitary thought 28
vernacular sufism 19
vernacularization 19
vernacularization of Islam 19
vernacularization of sufism 26
vidya 28
vikalatnamas 13, 37, 382, 388, 389, 390
virah 246, 247
virahini 246
Vishnu 404, 410
Vishnu Purana 367
vuzu 199

W. Crooke 407
Wahabi 16, 17
Wahabi movement 280
wahdat 270, 292
wahdat-ul-shuhud 9, 10, 257
wahdat-ul-wujud 3, 8, 9, 10, 24, 158, 162, 279, 257, 258, 286, 380, 381
wajh-i-halal 142
Wakf Board 420
Waris Shah 22, 197, 203, 236, 237, 238, 243, 245, 246, 251, 406, 408, 409, 410, 414, 420
Wazaif-i-Shahi 111
Wazir Khan 358
Wazirabad 136
Weltanschauung 162
West Asia 7, 18, 87, 93
West Bengal 406, 415
west Punjab 200, 235, 237, 240, 304, 305, 404, 405, 406
wilayat 6, 13, 63, 64, 103, 214, 267, 269, 270, 272, 379, 404, 410, 419
wilayat-i-Ibrahimi 10
wilayat-i-Muhammadi 10
William Barr 350
William Jones 2

Yamuna 338, 358
Yar Muhammad 126
Yazid 226
Yemen 99, 109
Yogesh Snehi 37
Yohannan Friedmann 9, 10, 265
Yunusiyah 263
Yusuf Zulaikha 370

Zad-ul-Musafirin 86
Zahir Uddin Malik 35
Zahira Bibi 15
Zainuddin Rishi 125
Zakariya Khan 385
zakat 186, 205
Zakhirat-ul-Khwanin 222
Zaman Shah 158
zamindars 166, 361, 389
zanbil gardani 204
Zauqi Shah 17
Ziauddin Barani 53, 68, 82, 351
zikr 16, 17, 83, 84, 85, 107, 161, 186, 197, 243, 250, 346, 371
Zinda Ghazi 410
Zirakpur 360
Ziya-ul-Qulub 17
Zorawar Singh 358
Zu ul-Nun Misri 3, 181, 191, 241, 217
Zubdat-ul-Maqamat 264, 267
Zulfiqar Khan 389